the Unofficial Guide® to

Cruises

8th Edition

the Unofficial Guide® to Cruises

8th Edition

Kay Showker
with Bob Sehlinger

WILEY

Please note that prices fluctuate in the course of time, and travel information changes under the impact of many factors that influence the travel industry. We therefore suggest that you write or call ahead for confirmation when making your travel plans. Every effort has been made to ensure the accuracy of information throughout this book, and the contents of this publication are believed correct at the time of printing. Nevertheless, the publishers cannot accept responsibility for errors or omissions or for changes in details given in this guide or for the consequences of any reliance on the information provided by the same. Assessments of attractions and so forth are based upon the author's own experience, and therefore, descriptions given in this guide necessarily contain an element of subjective opinion, which may not reflect the publisher's opinion or dictate a reader's own experience on another occasion. Readers are invited to write the publisher with ideas, comments, and suggestions for future editions.

Published by:

John Wiley & Sons, Inc.

111 River Street

Hoboken, NJ 07030

Produced by Menasha Ridge Press
Cover design by Michael J. Freeland
Interior design by Michele Laseau

For information on our other products and services or to obtain technical support please contact our Customer Care Department within the U.S. at (800) 762-2974, outside the U.S. at (317) 572-3993 or fax (317) 572-4002.

John Wiley & Sons, Inc. also publishes its books in a variety of electronic formats. Some content that appears in print may not be available in electronic formats.

ISBN 0 7645-3979-5

Manufactured in the United States of America

5 4 3 2

Contents

List of Maps and Illustrations

Acknowledgments

Laurels for the Laborers

It goes almost without saying that a book of this scope—covering more than 100 cruise lines with upwards of 400 ships sailing to destinations from the North Pole to the South Pole and around the world—is the work of many people. It requires extensive research, interviews with passengers, seemingly endless discussions with specialized travel agents and other knowledgeable people about cruises, not to mention the incredible amount of follow-up due to the constantly changing nature of the cruise industry.

So many people were tireless in their effort to help that it would take another book to name them all, but we would be remiss not to mention some.

Steve Gordan, publisher and managing editor of *Star Service*, which issues reports and evaluations on hotels and cruise ships worldwide for its travel agency subscribers, generously allowed us access and use of the publication's material.

Lloyd Cole of Valerie Wilson Travel, Dr. Bradley Feuer of Pace Travel, and Lisa Haber of Cruise Professionals gave us plentiful insights and never seemed to tire of our endless questions.

We are grateful to all our public-relations friends at the cruise lines who helped us check the nitty-gritty details and who have been our hosts over the years without any obligation. Rich Steck, formerly of Royal Caribbean Cruise Lines, and Julie Benson, Princess Cruise Lines, went above and beyond the call of duty and have our everlasting gratitude.

Text Contributions

Time constraints in writing a book such as this make it impossible for two people to visit and revisit every ship prior to our deadlines, as we would want to do. We called on colleagues for help, particularly on writers who specialize in cruising and are as qualified as we to write this book.

Some folks contributed material written specifically for the book, others shared their knowledge from recent cruises or allowed us to use material from recent research published elsewhere, while still others reviewed or helped with the updating of information we had written. Specifically for Part One, Tim Dubacky (of American Express Travel Services); in Part Two, sections were written by Matt Hannafin ("Glacier Bay Cruises"); Dave Houser ("Cruise West"); and Ted Scull ("American Safari Cruises"); for Part Three, Ted Scull ("Norwegian Coastal Cruises and European Cruise Ferries") and Dave Houser ("Freighter Cruises"), who not only wrote parts of this book but also generously contributed their insights and information to many of the cruise lines and ships profiled in Part Two; Ann Kalosh ("Abercrombine & Kent International") and Shann Davies ("Yangtze River Cruises in China"), both in Part Three, and Susan Milne, who prepared the itineraries.

Many other writing colleagues shared their firsthand experience with us, too. We particularly want to thank Arlene and Sam Blecker, Ernest Blum, Deborah Boyd, Jerry Brown, Michael Brown, Anne Campbell, Lisa Chickering, Georgina Cruz, George Devol, Michael Driscoll, Marilyn Green, Francis Kay Harris, Elizabeth Harryman, Mary Ann Hemphill, Michael Iachetta, Paul Lasley, Marcia Levin, Henry Magenheim, Susan Pierres, Jeannie Porterfield, and Molly Staub.

Many, many friends, friends of friends, travel agents, and cruise passengers along the way willingly gave us their time for interviews, helped with ship ratings, and phoned and sent us letters about their latest cruise, and to them we express our heartfelt thanks.

Last but not least, we thank the staff of Menasha Ridge Press, who worked tirelessly on the manuscript, researching, and checking facts.

Kay Showker
Bob Sehlinger

Introduction

About This Guide

How Come "Unofficial"?

The material in this guide has not been edited or in any way reviewed by the cruise lines profiled. In this "unofficial" guide we represent and serve you, the consumer. If a ship serves mediocre food, has cramped cabins, or offers poor shore excursions, we will say so. Through our independence, we hope we can make selecting a cruise efficient and economical and your cruise experience on-target and fun.

Making It Easy

In the nearly two years it took to write the first edition of this book, Kay had pinned on a wall in front of her a note that read: "This book has one purpose: To help readers select the right cruise—i.e., the cruise that's right for them." She kept it there to make sure we never lost sight of that goal.

Most guides to cruising approach their subject on a ship-by-ship basis, giving only the briefest attention to the cruise line and emphasizing ships—the hardware. But people don't buy ships, they buy cruises, and those cruises—the software—have been designed according to cruise lines' business plans, which define the types of cruises they offer. The cruise lines are challenged daily by their competitors and all the other leisure products vying for your attention—from the latest car and computer to a Disney vacation—to make their cruises irresistible. Yet they freely admit that although there's a cruise for everyone, not every cruise is for everyone. What it boils down to is that you can listen to Beethoven's Ninth Symphony played by an amateur band, or you can hear it played by the New York Philharmonic. It's the same music, but it's going to come out differently.

This book is designed to help you recognize the differences. By understanding the cruise lines and the experiences they offer, you will be able to recognize the different types of cruises available and identify the ones likely to appeal to you. Each line offers cruises with features that distinguish them from the others. It is these features—or "style" as we call it—that are the essence of the cruise experience.

A Carnival cruise is a Carnival cruise, for example. Each Carnival ship offers a "Fun Ship" vacation, and, except for the cruise's length and destinations, the experience varies little among ships. Carnival has designed it that way.

The same is true of Royal Caribbean Cruise Line, Holland America, Seabourn, and every other line that has built ships of a class or style from the same mold. However, a Carnival cruise is as different from a Princess, Holland America, Crystal, or Seabourn cruise as night is from day.

As cruise lines continue to standardize their operations to keep costs down and distinguish themselves from their competition, it becomes more important for you (or your travel agent), as you select a cruise, to understand the line and the type of cruises it offers. With that goal in mind, this guidebook is organized in three parts:

Part One, Planning Your Cruise Vacation, covers basic information on what cruises contain, tips on finding the best values, and preparing for your cruise.

Part Two, Cruise Lines and Their Ships, profiles all major "mainstream" cruise lines that sell primarily to U.S. and Canadian travelers. At the end of Part Two are ships also in the mainstream but not necessarily on this side of the Atlantic. Most are based in Europe, cruise less-traveled routes, and cater mainly to Europeans.

Part Three, Cruising Alternatives, describes other options, such as river, adventure, and expedition cruises, plus freighters, coastal ships, cruise ferries, and sailing ships.

Letters, Comments, and Questions from Readers

Many who use the *Unofficial Guides* write to us with questions, comments, or their own strategies for planning and enjoying travel. We appreciate all such input, both positive and critical. Readers' comments are frequently incorporated into revised editions of the *Unofficial Guides* and have contributed immeasurably to their improvement. Please write to:

Kay and Bob
The Unofficial Guide to Cruises
P.O. Box 43673
Birmingham, AL 35243

Please put your return address on both your letter and envelope; the two sometimes become separated. Also, include your phone number if you are available for a possible interview. And remember, our work often requires that we be out of the office for long periods, so forgive us if our response is slow. If you'd like a faster response, you can also try e-mailing us at unofficialguides@menasharidge.com.

A Reader Survey is included at the end of the book. We urge you to copy or clip it out, add your impressions, and send it in.

Cruising: A Look Back, A Look Ahead

Modern cruising in 2004 marks its 38th anniversary. December 19, 1966, is recognized as a landmark because on that date a series of cruises was launched that, for the first time, was created and packaged as a mass-market product and sold on a year-round basis. The ship, the *Sunward* of the Norwegian Caribbean Line (later renamed the Norwegian Cruise Line), sailed from Miami to Nassau with 540 passengers on the first three- and four-day cruises to be offered year-round between Miami and the Bahamas. No one, including the creators, imagined where that small step would lead. Indeed, many in the steamship business dismissed the idea as crazy, declaring there was not enough of a market to support such cruises.

Cruising, of course, did not actually start in 1966; it evolved over a time span of 150 years. But it's true that until the 1960s the closest most people got to a big ship was on the big screen, either in movies about glamorous people living romantic lives, or in newsreels of the duke and duchess of Windsor arriving on the *Queen Mary,* or F. Scott and Zelda, the Astors, the Vanderbilts, and other celebrities sailing stylishly to Europe aboard an elegant oceanliner.

From the start of the first regular transatlantic steamship service by Samuel Cunard in 1840, a voyage on a great liner became the ultimate dream shared by people worldwide. In the early days, a sea voyage was more of an expedition, requiring passengers to endure hardships with few amenities on-board ship or at ports. Passenger comfort, even in first class, was not a priority, but as competition developed and steamship travel gained popularity, each generation of ships brought enhanced comfort.

Then, too, throughout the late 19th century and up to World War I, ships carrying passengers had other purposes. Among them was transporting thousands of immigrants to the New World and a new life. To meet the demand—and reap large profits—many steamship companies were born and ships built, and, except for the war years when the vessels transported troops, oceanliners paraded across the Atlantic and Pacific in an endless stream, with the world's elite in their top decks and the huddled masses below.

Then in 1921, passage of the Immigration Act, intended to slow the torrent of new arrivals, forced steamship companies to change course. To make up for lost revenue from steerage, companies created cabin or tourist class in the several decks below first class and unwittingly took the next step toward modern cruising. Although a voyage remained a means of getting from one continent to another, it was no longer a pastime only for the privileged. Cabin class did not have the elegance and panache of first class, but it wasn't bad. It found a ready market in the GIs who had fought in Europe and wanted to return with their families, immigrants who had made good and wanted to visit relatives in their homelands, and America's growing middle class, who wanted to emulate the celebrities and aristocrats in first class.

The Golden Age

The Roaring Twenties was a golden age for steamship travel. It was a time of new prosperity, blithe spirits—and Prohibition in America. With alcoholic beverages legal at sea, ship companies offered a new type of short cruise—the party, or booze cruise—that made getting there half the fun.

In the dining room, passengers sat at long tables on chairs bolted to the floor (ships did not have stabilizers). In 1910, Ritz restaurants, replicating the setting of their shore-side operations, introduced round tables and carpeted floors in first class on ships of Hapag-Lloyd of Germany. The style soon became the standard for other ships. Private bathrooms were available in first class on the grandest liners, but in cabin class, passengers shared bath facilities until the 1950s. Air-conditioning was introduced by P&O Lines in the 1930s but did not become common until the 1950s.

The first indoor swimming pool appeared in 1910 on the *Olympic* of White Star Line. (It was the first of the line's three superliners; the others were the *Titanic* and the *Gigantic,* later renamed *Britannic.*) Known as a plunge bath, it had a balcony where others could watch the bathers. The first permanent outdoor pool was introduced in 1926 on the *Roma* of Italian Lines. Until the late 1950s, the top deck was fitted with machinery and was off-limits to passengers. Today, it's usually a sports deck.

A New Era

After weathering the Great Depression and another war, oceanliners resumed their traditional role, and by the 1950s were conveying hordes of students to Europe and masses of refugees to U.S. shores. The glamour returned with the comings and goings of a young Liz Taylor and the sailing of Grace Kelly to her fairyland prince. After World War II, the addition of radar and improved navigational equipment made passenger ships safer and more accurate in regard to arrival times, enabling operators to plan reliable itineraries. By the mid-1950s, most oceanliners had stabilizers. Radios were added in staterooms. The tradition to separate first class and tourist class on transatlantic service continued, but in 1958, Holland America launched the *Rotterdam,* which could be converted to one class. However, by decade's end, most elite passengers had taken flight—literally.

The final blow came in 1958, when the first commercial jets streaked across the Atlantic, cutting travel time from five days to just over five hours. Instead of dying out, however, the ships changed course and became part of the revolution that took place on the sea as well as in the sky.ª

The Cruise Revolution

The turnaround of the 1960s brought radical changes. New cruise lines, untethered to the past, exchanged formality for fun and brought a new atmosphere to shipboard life. The barriers of separate classes were removed, and the space was used for sports, recreation, and entertainment, turning the ships into floating resorts. Getting there was no longer half the fun—it *was* the fun. Passengers no longer bundled under blankets in deck chairs. Instead, they bounced in aerobics classes, swung at golf and tennis balls, plunged into the sea with masks and fins, soaked in hot tubs, and luxuriated in shipboard spas. Bingo survived, but it now competed with jazzy casinos, Broadway shows and discos, wine and piano bars, comics and cabarets. New and younger passengers were attracted by the activity and informality. Families with children, too, were finding cruises to be ideal vacations.

But change came wrapped in skepticism. For example, the hot news in 1968 was the new, mod look of the *S.S. Independence*. With a red, orange, and yellow sunburst splashed across the length of its sides and a riot of interior color, it was quickly dubbed the psychedelic ship. A magazine called the shakedown cruise a "floating water pad for the turned on generation" and suggested that "dancing until the wee hours . . . the informal atmosphere of the one-class ship, and ever-changing program of *top-talent* entertainment may prove a real drawing card."

The 1970s began with Royal Caribbean Cruise Lines making its debut with a fleet of ships built specifically for Caribbean cruising. It was followed two years later by Carnival Cruise Lines, which developed the "Fun Ship" concept to scuttle the elitist traditions of oceanliners and appeal to a mass market of younger, first-time passengers from all walks of life.

As the revolution's final irony, the spectacular growth in cruise vacations really took off in the 1970s, when cruise lines joined forces with airlines, which had almost put the steamship companies out of business. The union created air/sea programs that combined air transportation and ground transfers with a cruise in one package at one price. The programs enhanced the value of cruise vacations, simplified their purchase, and eliminated hassles for travelers. With the packages, cruise lines virtually brought their ships to people's doorsteps, regardless of where they lived. The marriage enabled cruise lines to base their ships in warm-weather ports from where they could cruise year-round and to fly passengers from faraway places to begin their cruises. A relaxed, informal holiday in the sun —and available year-round—became the essence of modern cruising. Flying passengers to their ships saved time and enabled cruise lines to offer shorter, less expensive cruises that fit into the national trend toward shorter vacations. It also allowed cruise lines to open new parts of the world to cruising; itineraries multiplied. No matter how many cruises a person took, new ones remained. Or so it seemed, until the oil crisis of the early 1970s, when dark clouds again threatened the future of vacations at sea.

Then, in 1978, despite skyrocketing fuel prices and predictions that cruising was doomed, Carnival Cruise Lines ordered a large, technologically advanced passenger ship. It became the forerunner of the 1980s superliners. Two years later, Norwegian Cruise Line shocked the cruise world by buying the fabulous *France* and transforming her into the *Norway.* The floating resort set cruise trends for the decade, introducing innovations, including a variety of entertainment lounges, a theater for Broadway-scale productions, a shopping plaza, and a "sidewalk" cafe. Holland America followed with *Nieuw Amsterdam* and *Noordam,* twin ships with square sterns that allowed over 20% more deck space for recreation, including two swimming pools. The ships also introduced computer keys to open cabin doors and other innovations.

Princess Cruises' stylish *Royal Princess,* which debuted in 1984, set new standards of comfort with all outside cabins fitted with minibars, television, and baths with tubs in every category. About the same time, the *QE2* introduced the first Golden Door spa at sea, the first computer learning center, and the first satellite-delivered newspaper.

Among the most interesting entries was the *Windstar* in 1986, a cruise ship with computerized sails. *Windstar* married the romance of sailing under canvas with the comforts of a cruise ship and the electronic age. At the same time, Carnival's superliners, *Holiday, Jubilee,* and *Celebration,* were introduced. Their madcap design totally changed the look of ship interiors and the use of public space.

Yet nothing since the *Norway* caused as much excitement as the 1988 debut of Royal Caribbean Cruise Line's *Sovereign of the Seas.* The world's largest cruise ship at the time, she became the pacesetter for the 1990s. Among her features was the first shipboard atrium, rising through five decks and creating a new environment. The ship offered such numerous and varied entertainment and recreation options that passengers needed several cruises to experience them all. As the decade closed, some old lines disappeared in mergers, and new lines popped up. Health and fitness facilities were integrated into cruising. Healthful foods were readily available. Well equipped gyms, elaborate spas, VCRs, cable television, and worldwide direct-dial telephones were rapidly becoming standard amenities. Small boutique ships, including those of the Seabourn and Silversea lines, brought new levels of luxury to cruising. Special-interest lines were finding their niche. Increased interest in adventure and nature cruises caused some traditional cruise lines to add them. Environmental concerns had a major impact on cruise ship technology. The late 1960s and early 1970s saw the conversion of oceanliners to cruise ships and the first ships built specifically for cruising, but the 1980s became the decade of innovation, particularly aboard ships designed to sail in warm climates. People who might never have considered taking a cruise booked them.

In the New Millennium

Well into its fourth decade, the cruise boom shows no signs of letting up. In that time, the number of passengers has swelled from under 500,000 annually to almost 8 million. Fourteen of the twenty-three members of the Cruise Lines International Association, the major cruise trade association, did not exist 20 years ago.

The 1990s were a blockbuster decade, with more than three dozen new ships costing an estimated $12 billion in the water. Now, another $15 billion will result in at least five dozen more ships by 2005. Most of the ships are bigger, with more dazzle, and travel specialists were asking, "Where's the sky?"

The ships over 80,000 tons—and particularly those over 100,000 tons—represent a new generation of megaliners. Most have new design features and facilities—such as the highly publicized 18-hole miniature golf course on *Legend of the Seas,* the virtual-reality theater on Princess Cruises' *Grand Princess,* and the interactive computers on Celebrity's *Century* and *Galaxy.*

But the capper was *Voyager of the Seas,* the first of the three 142,000-ton ships built by Royal Caribbean, which debuted in November 1999 with cruising's first rock-climbing wall and ice rink. The rock-climbing wall proved to be so popular that RCL is installing them fleetwide.

Cunards's *Queen Mary 2,* scheduled to debut in December 2003, is the biggest, widest, longest and most expensive ship ever built, and at 150,000 tons will dwarf all predecessors. The much-anticipated *QM2* comes with the first and only spa at sea operated by the world-famous Canyon Ranch health resorts; the world's first and only planetarium at sea; the largest ballroom at sea; the largest library at sea; the largest wine cellar at sea; ten different dining venues, including the first and only shipboard restaurant by popular American chef Todd English; and a learning center with guest lecturers from Oxford University.

Along with innovations, the new ships are enhancing the cruise experience. Passengers will find larger standard cabins on most new ships and more verandas in the midprice range. More dining options are becoming standard, as are more entertainment choices, more sports opportunities, greatly expanded childrens' facilities, larger, more elaborate spas, Internet cafés; and on the newest ships, in-cabin Internet access.

Other ways the cruise experience is being enhanced are through innovation enrichment programs, such as Crystal Cruises' Creative Learning Center, offering courses in cooking, art, business, technology, and health, and on the line's new *Crystal Serenity*, even learning to play the piano in an arrangement with Yamaha that provides instructors. Passengers can also take classes in fine art, drawing, sculpture, painting, floral design, and interior design by faculty from the Parsons School of Design in New York. Another such program is Princess Cruises' ScholarShip@Sea (which Princess calls "edu-tainment"), introduced on the *Coral Princess* with topics ranging from cooking taught in a demonstration kitchen like those seen on television, to pottery classes with the first shipboard kiln.

There has also been a vast improvement in the variety and number of shore excursions (although not an improvement in price)—particularly in the Caribbean—for active passengers to enjoy hiking, biking, kayaking, golf, swimming with dolphins, and more. Cruise lines faced with intense competition—again, particularly in the Caribbean—have looked for new and more varied itineraries, but the biggest shift has come with a new emphasis on "homeland" cruising. That has resulted in more ships based in new U.S. ports and many more itineraries along the East and West coasts of the U.S., Mexico, and Central America. In addition to attracting travelers who do not want to stray far from home, this has stimulated a market of drivers who do not want to fly out of fear or who prefer not to deal with the security hassles and delays at airports.

Although innovation and product refinement is common throughout the cruise industry, Princess Cruises and Norwegian Cruise Lines have led the way. Most of the innovations address longstanding complaints of cruise passengers (they really do read all those survey forms). For cruisers who disliked being relegated to a specific seating for dinner, or for that matter, eating in the same restaurant each night, many vessels, particularly the newest ones, now offer multiple dining venues that operate like shoreside restaurants. Make a reservation or just show up at the restaurant of your choice.

Specialties at these standalone eateries cover a wide variety of cuisines, from Japanese to Mexican and Italian to Chinese. Princess, for example, has installed a steakhouse on each of its Sun-class ships. The Princess Personal Choice Dining program also includes an Italian trattoria, a Southwestern restaurant, and a 24-hour buffet and bistro. Norwegian Cruise Line's Freestyle Cruising offers as many as ten different restaurants on a single ship, each with its own identity and area of specialization. On the Disney Cruise Line, passengers rotate to a different restaurant each night. The line also features a reservations- and adults-only Italian restaurant on each ship.

Carnival introduced "Total Choice" dining, enabling passengers to choose from four seating times in the main dining room instead of the usual two. The four seatings stagger the arrival of diners, preventing the galley from being inundated and allowing the waitstaff to concentrate on a smaller number of passengers at any given time.

Although more choice in dining sounds like a definite perk, there's a downside. A great number of singles and couples depend on meeting new friends at their assigned table in the main dining room. For many, their assigned dinner companions become their social circle for the duration of the cruise. Each night, they meet over dinner and discuss the day's activities. Some coordinate shore tours or enjoy each other's company outside the dining room, and it is a common occurrence for tablemates to become close friends and to keep in touch once they return home. Needless to say, it's much harder to get acquainted and form friendships when your assigned dinner companions are off trying the alternative dining venues each night.

Among other notable initiatives is the Princess FlightChoice program that confirms air itineraries purchased through Princess 60 days prior to the cruise date, allowing passengers ample time to make changes if desired. In a related program, Princess has also established an express check-in, where passengers can avoid the hassle of dockside check-in by completing boarding documents and mailing them to Princess in advance.

Norwegian Cruise Line has taken a much-welcomed and long-overdue crack at easing the discomfort of disembarkation. On most larger vessels, you are run off the ship by 8 a.m. to make way for passengers going on the next cruise. Norwegian's new program allows passengers to occupy their stateroom until midmorning and enjoy a leisurely breakfast before disembarking. Along similar lines, the Disney Cruise Line allows passengers to disembark whenever they please as soon as the ship has been cleared by customs. If ever there were initiatives that we'd like to see emulated industry-wide, it's these.

More and more cruise lines enable passengers to "stay connected" by providing Internet access, including wireless connection. A few offer it free, but most charge per usage, and some have a plan for unlimited Internet access during a cruise for a single rate, which is a better deal for frequent users. Crystal Cruises enables passengers to have their own shipboard e-mail address. Crystal, as well as several other lines, have computer schools at sea.

For those who believe it is better to receive than send, there has been a proliferation of live, real-time television available on your stateroom. In addition to CNN, the Discovery Channel, ESPN, TNT, and CNBC are now available on many cruise liners, depending on their location.

The Big Three

Although not many cruisers know it, three companies control the lion's share of the American cruise market. These companies set the pace and establish norms for the mass-market cruise industry. Then, too, when there's a depressed travel market as there has been since 9/11, their discounts impact even the luxury end of the market.

First of the three is Carnival Corporation, which owns Carnival, Holland American, Cunard, Seabourn, Windstar, Costa Cruises, and its most recent acquistion, P&O/Princess Cruises (which in turn includes P&O Australia, AIDA, Swan Hellenic Cruise Lines, and several small lines created to serve specific markets, such as Germany). Next is Royal Caribbean International (RCI), which operates Royal Caribbean Cruise Line and Celebrity Cruises. RCI made a bid to merge with Princess, but lost out to Carnival Cruises.

Number three, Star Cruises, is Asia's largest cruise line and owns Norwegian Cruise Line; together, they have as many ships as Carnival Cruises or RCI. The deep pockets of Star Cruises have enabled NCL to grow with new ships that are among the most innovative and put NCL once again in its role as the trendsetter of the cruise industry. In 2003, to the envy of its rivals, NCL launched Project America, which gives it a near monopoly in the Hawaii market (see the NCL profile in Part Two for details).

Cruise lines big and small got off to a rough start in 2001. First, there was the soaring price of fuel, followed by a serious dip in the economy. These hit at a time when the big three, as well as several other lines, were awash with new ships with thousands of extra berths to fill. By the time the first quarter of calendar year 2001 ended, ships were sailing with empty cabins, and the fight for available passengers was running at full tilt.

Then came the events of September 11, 2001, as cruising, along with most travel in general, came to a screeching halt. By the 2001 Christmas season, cruising had begun its slow comeback, and the winter season, particularly in the Caribbean, was better than anticipated. Nonetheless, three cruise lines went out of business, and a fourth declared bankruptcy.

Among the casualties were American Classic Voyages, parent company of American Hawaii and Delta Queen Steamboat Compary, and Renaissance. Just the year before, two other smaller cruise lines, Premier and Commodore, went belly-up, while several others struggled and remained vulnerable. By 2003, two more—Regal Cruises and World Explorer Cruises—had departed. The loss of these lines is especially sad because they were small, moderately priced operators serving areas that the big lines had ignored or could not serve with their huge ships.

On the bright side, Delta Queen Steamboat Company was bought by a financially strong company and restarted; and a new cruise line, Oceania Cruise Lines, was launched in summer 2003, using two of Renaissance Cruises' former vessels and modeling itself, more or less, after that now-defunct line. Despite the soft travel market, it has managed to do well. Other former Renaissance ships have found their way to exploration and cultural cruise lines, such as Abercrombe & Kent and Swan Hellenic Cruises, and as a result, have set a new deluxe standard for these types of cruises.

The Future

Ask a cruise-line executive where growth in cruising is coming from, and she'll tell you that cruising is chipping away at the "land" vacation market. True enough, but for the moment, passengers stolen from land vacations plus the population of prior cruisers are not sufficient to fill all the ships. This reality and the overall climate for travel will create some great bargains for years to come.

But there's a downside. The big three have staying power. They don't like compromising yields, but they'll do it to fill cabins and build their customer base. As we have already seen, the cruise lines that have really felt the pinch are the smaller and medium-sized ones—lines that don't have the advertising dollars or market clout to compete head-to-head with the big guys and that cannot afford to offer comparable discounts.

The loss of each small or medium cruise line is important because it diminishes competition and concentrates more power in the larger lines, especially in the American market. And while cruise passengers might enjoy bargain prices for now, that will likely not be the case in the future if consolidation and diminution of competition continue.

Despite the setbacks and uncertainties, cruising as a vacation choice continues to attract new travelers by the thousands and has devotees returning year after year. That's because the fundamental attraction of cruising—value for money—has not and is not likely to change.

Part One

Planning Your Cruise Vacation

Understanding Cruises

The Cruise Package

Although it's possible (and sometimes desirable) to buy the components of a cruise vacation à la carte, most cruises are sold as complete packages. The basic package includes:

1. Shipboard accommodations.

2. Three full-service dining room meals daily (breakfast, lunch, and dinner), plus alternative breakfast, lunch, and late-night buffets. On most ships, room service meals do not cost extra. Many ships also offer options, such as early-bird breakfast, morning bouillon, and afternoon events, including tea, pizza snacks, ice cream parties, wine and cheese tastings, and poolside cookouts.

3. All shipboard entertainment, including music, dancing and shows in the lounges, discos, live bands, Las Vegas–style productions, nightclubs, karaoke, and movies.

4. All shipboard sports and recreational facilities, including swimming pools, health club or exercise room, promenade or jogging track, Jacuzzi, sauna, library, game room, and child-care facilities. (Spa and beauty treatments and some specialized sports equipment often cost extra.)

5. All shipboard activities, including the casino, on-board games and contests, lectures, demonstrations, and children's program (where applicable, baby-sitting services are extra).

6. Stops at ports of call on the itinerary.

7. Round-trip airfare* to and from the port city.

8. Transfers (ground transportation) from airport to ship and from ship to airport (see "What Happened to 'Free' Air?").

Port charges (about $120 per person on a seven-day Caribbean cruise) are usually included in the advertised cruise price. If not, the line's brochures will show the cost for each cruise.

Taxes, optional shore excursions, alcoholic beverages and soft drinks, casino play, onboard shopping, and tips are not included in most cases. On a few very upscale lines, tipping and wine and alcoholic beverages are included in the cruise price. On some, tips are pooled (you are asked to contribute a suggested amount per day to be divided among all staff except officers and senior staff). We include a section on tipping in Part Two.

Cruising's Unfortunate Stereotypes

You have probably heard that "cruising is not for everyone." But that's like saying travel is not for everyone. If you like to travel, you will almost certainly enjoy cruising. It's that simple. Cruising, however, has accumulated unfortunate stereotypes, which continue to recycle.

Myth No. 1: I'll Be Bored   Many people, particularly men and younger, active folks, believe cruising is dull and sedentary. They picture bulk loaders crowding buffets while active folks sit bored and unstimulated. Sorry, not so.

Today, most cruises offer around-the-clock activities. Ships have workout rooms with quality equipment, jogging tracks, pools, and daily exercise classes. Some larger ships have volleyball, basketball courts, and even climbing walls and ice rinks. At ports of call, a variety of sports—from golf to cycling, snorkeling to kayaking—are offered. There are far more opportunities for sports and athletics than most of us have at home. If you go on a cruise and sit on your butt, that's your decision.

For the active but less athletic, most ships offer swimming, shuffleboard, table tennis, walking areas, and spa amenities, including hot tubs and saunas. Many ships offer yoga or stretching classes. At night, for the energetic, there's dancing in many forms, from ballroom to reggae to line dancing to salsa.

A range of organized activities targets gregarious and fun-loving people. Versions of television game shows are popular, as are more traditional events, such as bridge tournaments, arts and crafts classes, and dancing lessons. Most cruise ships have casinos, and almost all have bingo.

If learning is your goal, dozens of cruises specialize in providing educational experiences and exploration of a region accompanied by experts. Like floating graduate schools, these cruises may focus on political and natural history or may even offer lectures on topics unrelated to the ship's destinations.

Finally, there is no place better than a cruise ship to relax. The favorite cruise activity for many people is curling up in a comfortable deck chaise with a good book. Even a big ship with constant activity offers quiet spots for meditation, reading, or just enjoying the beauty of the sea.

Myth No. 2: Cruising Is for Rich People; I Can't Afford a Cruise   If you take a vacation of three or more days during which you stay in hotels and eat in restaurants, you can afford a cruise.

Let's compare cruising to a modest vacation: Vic and Edna's one-week trip to Gatlinburg, Tennessee, and the Smoky Mountains. Driving from their home near Cleveland, Ohio, Vic and Edna spent about $300 on gas for the Chevy. They averaged $65 a night plus tax for motels, or $498 for the week. For breakfast and lunch, it was Shoney's- or Denny's-type restaurants. They'd go more upscale for dinner, and they liked beer or wine with their meal. Total for seven days' food: $388. In the mountains, they mostly hiked and drove around. One day, however, they played golf; on another they visited a museum and a theme park. On the Friday before heading home, they rented horses for half a day. Golf, admissions, and horses came to approximately $190. Recapping:

VIC AND EDNA'S SPLENDID VACATION

Lodging	$498
Gas	$300
Meals	$388
Admissions	$190
TOTAL	$1,376

During the same period, Norwegian Cruise Line, a good middle-of-the-market line (not super-budget or super-luxury), offered a seven-night southern Caribbean cruise on *Norwegian Sky* for $671 per person, including round-trip airfare. The cruise visited San Juan, St. Thomas, Martinique, Tortola, the British Virgin Islands, Antigua, and St. Maarten. Even better values can be had with Celebrity and Holland America's promotional fares, which can go as low as $599 for nicer cabins on even newer ships.

These were promotional rates, not the "rack" rates listed in the brochures. The point is, on the seven-night cruise, Vic and Edna could have enjoyed the amenities of a full resort, dined in grand style, danced to live music, visited six beautiful tropical islands, and soaked in a whirlpool under the Caribbean moon for about the same amount they spent on their road trip. We are not suggesting Vic and Edna should swap the Smokies for the Caribbean, only that they could afford to do so if they are inclined.

Myth No. 3: Cruises Are Stuffy, Elitist, and Formal   Most cruises are none of the above, though the description might fit some passengers. A few cruises resemble floating debutante balls, but these are easily avoided. Cruises cover a broad range of dress and social protocols. You can choose a cruise at whatever level of formality or casualness feels right for you. Overall, cruises have become very casual and informal. Even on "formal" nights—such as the captain's welcome-aboard party and/or farewell party—half of the men wear business suits, and women don cocktail or party dresses. Newer ships offering alternative (to the main dining room) dining options make it possible to avoid formal events entirely. On the most informal ships, like Carnival, where you can wear anything short of a burlap bag, people dress to the nines—and it's often the men more so than the women. And they love it.

Myth No. 4: Cruises Are Too Regimented for Me   Granted, it takes organization to get everyone on board a cruise ship. It takes similar regimentation to get everyone off at the end of the cruise. At ports, you need only get back on board before the ship sails.

Some folks lump cruises into the same category as whirlwind bus tours—eight countries in five days and that sort of thing. A cruise might visit eight countries in five days, but you will have to check in and unpack only once. That's the beauty of cruising—you can hang out on the ship and just enjoy the ride, or you can get off at each port and pursue your own agenda.

Myth No. 5: I'm Afraid I'll Get Seasick   Well, you might, but the vast majority of people don't, particularly on a Caribbean cruise, where the ocean is usually as smooth as bathwater. Even those who get queasy in a car can usually handle a cruise. Over-the-counter antinausea medications like **Bonine** (doesn't make you drowsy) or **Dramamine** get most folks over the acclimatization period of the first few hours at sea. Bring some; you may never need it, but having it is comforting. Usually, Dramamine or Bonine is available from the purser's desk or your cabin steward.

If you are really worried, buy **Sea Bands**—a pair of elasticized wristbands (similar to tennis bands), each with a small plastic disk that applies pressure to the inside wrist, according to acupressure principles. They are particularly useful for people who have difficulty taking medication. Sea Bands are sold in drug, toiletry, and health-care stores and can be ordered from **On the Go Travel Accessories** (5603 NW 159th Street, Miami, FL 33014; (888) 303-3039; **www.onthegoaccessories.com**). If you take precautions and become seasick anyway, the ship's doctor can administer more powerful medication.

In regard to seasickness, remember: Don't dwell on your fear, and if you become queasy, take medicine immediately. When you deal with symptoms quickly, relief is quick.

Minimize the probability of getting seasick by choosing an itinerary in calmer waters: Alaska's Inside Passage, the Caribbean, the Mediterranean, and the Gulf of Mexico. Less smooth are voyages on the Atlantic, Pacific, or Indian Oceans or the South China Sea.

Myth No. 6: I'm Apprehensive about Walking on a Moving Ship   If you are not agile or fit on land, you might envision tortuous trips down narrow gangways or climbing ladders through tiny hatches while the ship rolls and pitches. But generally, if you can handle a hotel, you can handle a cruise ship. Large vessels have wide, carpeted halls and slip-resistant outside decks. Elevators serve all passenger decks, so using the stairs may not even be necessary. Passengers use no tricky ladders or tiny hatches.

Modern cruise ships have stabilizers, and even in bad weather and heavy seas they are amazingly stable. Small ships, depending on their draft and build, may be more subject to the motion of the ocean and are a little more challenging to get around. Being smaller, however, there's less territory to cover. Most ships launched in the last ten years were built with consideration for healthy passengers as well as those with ambulatory disabilities. Many modern ships offer wheelchair-accessible cabins and ramps.

A Typical Day on a Cruise

Let's say we're cruising the Caribbean. You can start your morning with an early-bird breakfast or a walk or jog around deck, or you can have breakfast from the menu in the dining room. Late sleepers can order breakfast from room service or catch the breakfast buffet, which stays open later than the dining room. It usually is served on the "lido" deck— a casual indoor/outdoor dining facility on the same deck as the swimming pool or sports facilities. The lido buffet has longer and more flexible hours, enabling you to come and go at will.

Days at sea are the most relaxing of the cruise itinerary. The casino, shopping arcade, spa, exercise room, and shore-excursion desk are open. Programs and activities are virtually nonstop on large ships; most folks, however, hang out by the pool or on deck to enjoy the beauty of the sea and the relaxing movement of being underway. The captain may update passengers over the public-address system on the ship's progress toward the next port. The captain or cruise director may also point out interesting sights.

Lunch works much like breakfast: You can eat in the dining room and order from the menu, or you can stay in your swimsuit and eat burgers or pizza by the pool, where there is likely to be a music combo playing upbeat rhythms. You can join the pool games—always a good way to meet people—or just watch or ignore them. You then might work out, read, nap, play bridge, learn the latest dance steps, or attend orientation lectures about the next port. Recently released movies are shown in the ship's movie theater or on cabin television in the afternoon. On some ships, afternoon tea is a big deal—white gloves and all. At cocktail hour, there is usually live music by the pool, often with special drinks or appetizers, or happy hour in one of the bars.

As dinner approaches, it's time to dress for the evening. The dress code generally is specified on the daily agenda slipped under your door every evening. It is also spelled out in the cruise line's brochure, so you can pack accordingly. (More information on dress codes is available under "Preparing for Your Cruise.")

Some passengers stroll the deck before dinner, particularly at sunset, a beautiful time at sea. Others have a drink in one of the lounges. Dinner in the dining room is a social culmination of the day's activity. Spirits are always high.

After lingering over several well-prepared courses, it's off to the show-room, where live entertainment, ranging from Las Vegas–style variety shows to Broadway musicals, is offered nightly. After the show, early risers and those who had a long day of touring retire to their cabins. The more nocturnal or party-minded guests head for the casino, disco, or a lounge with entertainment. By now, it's time for the midnight buffet, often the chefs' most creative venue. Each night may have a theme—pasta, salads, desserts, barbecue, and so on. But at least one night will be the Grand Buffet. Bring your camera; every platter is a work of art. Before turning in, stretch out in a chaise lounge on deck with a glass of wine. Breathe in the balmy salt-sea air and be caressed by the warm breeze. Lose yourself among the million stars of the Caribbean night.

Usually, cruise ships sail through the night and arrive at the next port early in the morning. If you have been smart and risen in time to enjoy the early morning—the most beautiful time at sea—you can watch your ship dock. It's interesting and fun. After breakfast, the captain announces that the ship has been cleared by local officials and that passengers may disem-bark. Those signed up for shore excursions are given last-minute instruc-tions about when and where to meet and are normally first to go ashore.

Although port calls range from three hours to two days (with an overnight at dock), most are five to ten hours—hardly enough time to sample an island or city. As you disembark, crew members remind you of the sailing time and make sure you are carrying your cruise identifica-tion, which you must present to reboard. Once ashore, some people explore on foot, taking walking tours, shopping, and perhaps trying a shoreside restaurant. Others hire a cab for a driving tour, and still others take shore excursions purchased aboard ship.

Shore excursions take many forms. Some are passive (bus tour), but others are active (snorkeling, sailing, hiking, biking, or fishing). Surpris-ingly, many folks, particularly experienced cruisers, stay aboard ship. It's quiet—almost empty of passengers—but it's in full operation, except for casinos and shops. Lunch is served on schedule in the dining room.

At least 30 minutes before sailing, you reboard the ship. Just before castoff, go topside to watch the crew prepare for departure. Leaving port is always interesting, and a ship's higher decks offer a great viewing plat-form. Once at sea, the ship settles into its normal nighttime routine, and so do you.

So Many Cruises to Choose From

To the first-time cruiser and many veterans, the number of cruise lines, ships, and itineraries is staggering. Travel agencies that sell only cruises ease their customers into the array of choices by comparing cruise lines with well-known hotel chains, and such a comparison is useful. They might see Carnival, for example, as the Holiday Inn of cruises. Holland America and Celebrity Cruise Line are up a notch, perhaps at the Hyatt level.

Ritz-Carlton cruises might appeal to the most discriminating cruisers and are at the upper end of price, service, and amenities. Ships in this class include Crystal Cruises' *Crystal Harmony* and Seabourn's *Sun*. Boutique cruises overlap the deluxe category and include the smaller, all-suite ships of Radisson Seven Seas, Silversea, Seabourn, as well as the cruise/sail ships of Windstar.

Be aware that none of the hotel chains mentioned (except Radisson and Hyatt) have anything to do with cruising, and these are only a handful of the lines available. Though the foregoing comparison may help you see where you fit into the general scheme, you must dig much deeper to find your perfect cruise.

Getting Your Act Together

Cruises vary widely. To pinpoint your requirements and preferences in a cruise, you need to ask yourself dozens of questions. Once you settle on what you want, it's easier to match your demands and budget with the appropriate line and ship.

What Is My Vacation Budget?

Unless price is no object, start your planning with your budget. How much can you afford, and what are you willing to spend for your cruise? Consider what you must or may add to the cruise price: port charges and taxes, shore excursions, shopping, drinks and dinner wine (on most ships), gambling in the casino, spa services, laundry, and tips for crew members. Once you figure your uppermost limit for all costs, you can begin to explore what kind of cruise you can buy.

Although we will revisit this issue in "How to Get the Best Deal on a Cruise," let's say three-day cruises start at about $280 a person, assuming two people to a cabin. Seven-day cruises begin at about $550, and ten-day cruises are about $800 and up. These prices are deeply discounted and represent the least you would expect to pay, usually for a cabin without windows.

How Many Days Do I Want to Cruise?

Your available vacation time and budget are factors in your answer. Generally, the larger your budget, the more cruise days you can buy. That is, the longer the cruise, the more it will cost. If your budget isn't up to the number of days you have your heart set on, you still have options. First, trade luxury for cruise days; consider a cruise on a less-luxurious ship. The fee for a week on an upscale ship will easily buy two weeks on a midrange vessel. However, don't veer too far from your lifestyle or expectations, or you will be disappointed with your cruise. Second, cruise during the off-season, when prices are lowest. Third, settle for the least expensive cabin. Once aboard, all passengers have the same privileges, eat the same meals, and enjoy the same entertainment. Unless you plan to spend an extraordinary amount of time in your cabin, you probably can tolerate less expensive accommodations. We're not talking about special suites, just the difference between the highest deck outside cabin (with a window) and the lowest deck inside cabin (no window). For example, on a seven-day Celebrity Cruise Line itinerary to Bermuda, the upper-deck outside cabin costs more than twice as much as the lower-deck inside cabin.

In the Caribbean and Mexico, a seven-day cruise is about right for your first trip, but if you can't afford the time or money, a three- or four-night cruise will give you a good enough overview of ship life that you can determine whether cruising is something you'll enjoy again in the future.

Where Do I Want to Go?

You can cruise just about anywhere there is enough water to float a ship. This includes all of the world's oceans and seas and many rivers. Where you want to cruise depends primarily on your own "wild goose." It also hinges on your preferred style of cruising and whether you enjoy the destinations or the ship more.

Some destinations, including Alaska and Europe, are seasonal. Others, including the Caribbean and Mexico, are year-round. Almost all cruises worldwide are tailored to the market and the weather. Many to the Caribbean and Mexico, for example, are festive and high-spirited, emphasizing activity and fun. Mild temperatures allow time outdoors, and passengers tend to be younger. By contrast, Alaskan, Canadian, North Atlantic, Scandinavian, and Baltic Sea cruises are more passive, focusing on the beauty of the forests, islands, fjords, and glaciers. For these northerly venues, longer cruises and colder temperatures contribute to a more sedate experience and attract families or older passengers. Mediterranean itineraries generally revolve around antiquities and port cities of southern Europe, northern Africa, and the Middle East. Most ships visit a port each day, and sight-seeing is the backbone of the vacation. On ships where English is spoken and the majority aboard are Americans, the clientele are age 50 years and older and affluent. On cruise ships where Europeans predominate, passengers are younger, and sun and fun are emphasized, like in the Caribbean.

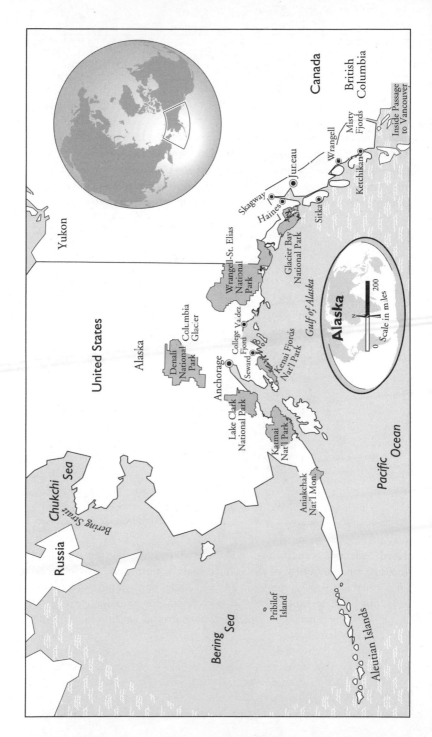

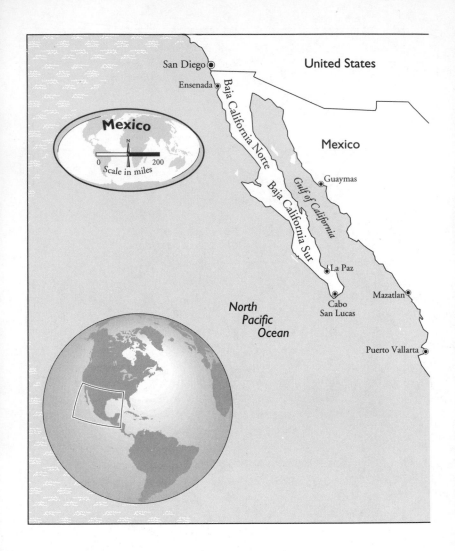

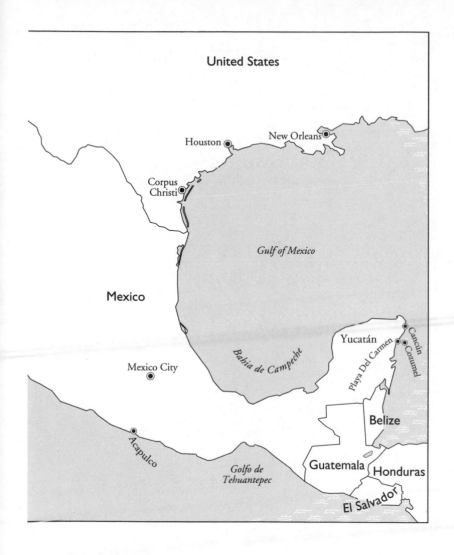

United States

Houston

New Orleans

Corpus
Christi

Gulf of Mexico

Mexico

Yucatán

Cancún

Bahía de Campeche

Cozumel

Playa Del Carmen

Mexico City

Belize

Acapulco

*Golfo de
Tehuantepec*

Guatemala

Honduras

El Salvador

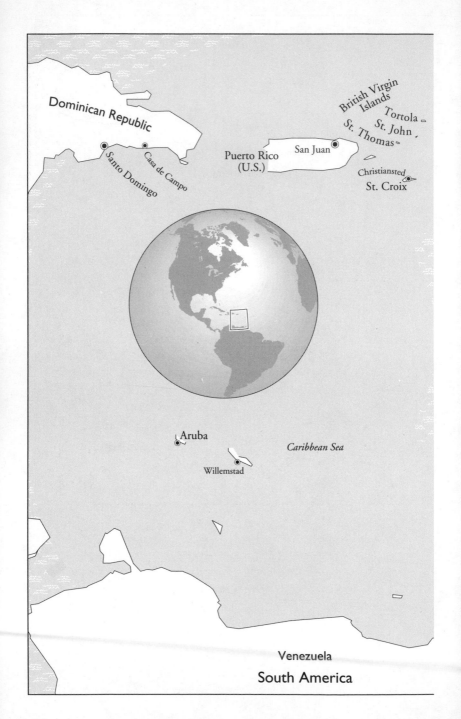

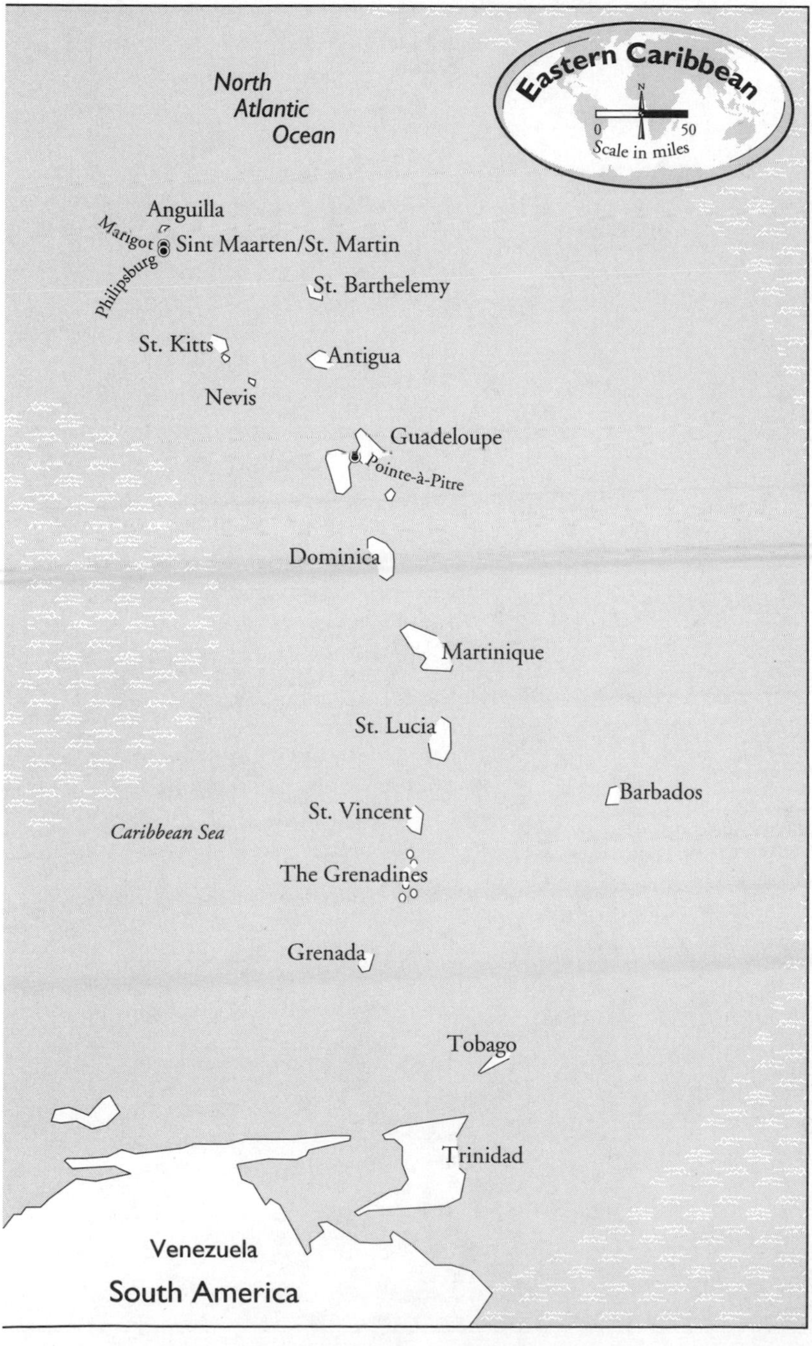

North
Atlantic
Ocean

Eastern Caribbean

N

0   50
Scale in miles

Marigot
Anguilla
Philipsburg
Sint Maarten/St. Martin

St. Barthelemy

St. Kitts
Antigua

Nevis

Guadeloupe
Pointe-à-Pitre

Dominica

Martinique

St. Lucia

Caribbean Sea
St. Vincent
Barbados

The Grenadines

Grenada

Tobago

Trinidad

Venezuela
South America

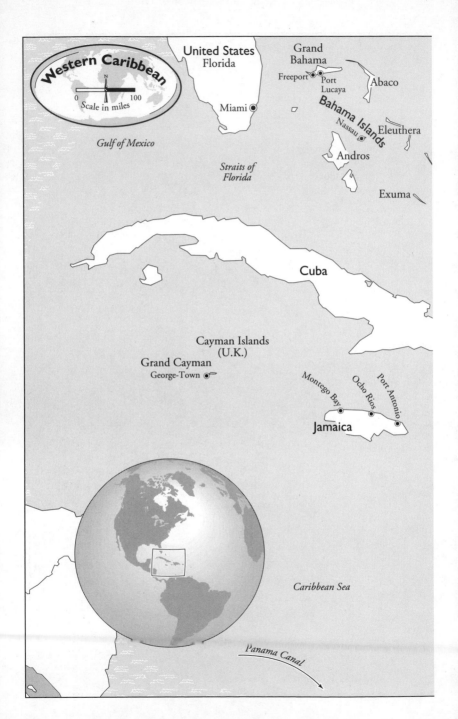

Western Caribbean

N

0   100
Scale in miles

United States
Florida

Gulf of Mexico

Miami

Straits of
Florida

Grand
Bahama

Freeport   Port
Lucaya

Abaco

Bahama Islands

Nassau

Eleuthera

Andros

Exuma

Cuba

Cayman Islands
(U.K.)

Grand Cayman
George-Town

Montego Bay

Ocho Ríos

Port Antonio

Jamaica

Caribbean Sea

Panama Canal

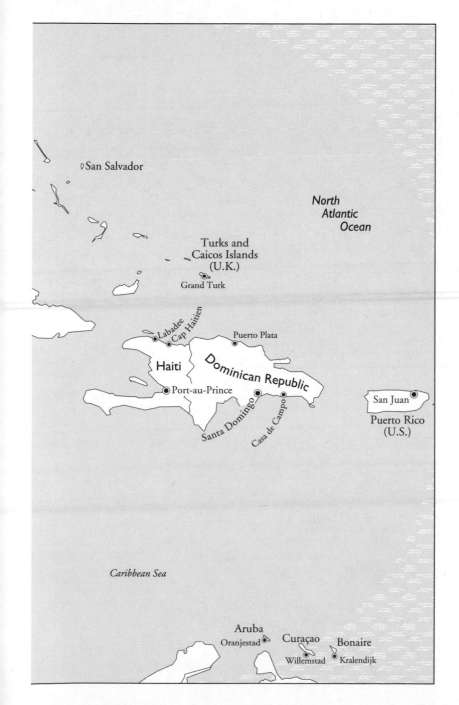

San Salvador

North
Atlantic
Ocean

Turks and
Caicos Islands
(U.K.)
Grand Turk

Labadee
Cap Haïtien
Puerto Plata

Haiti

Dominican Republic

Port-au-Prince

Santa Domingo

Casa de Campo

San Juan

Puerto Rico
(U.S.)

Caribbean Sea

Aruba
Oranjestad
Curaçao
Bonaire
Willemstad
Kralendijk

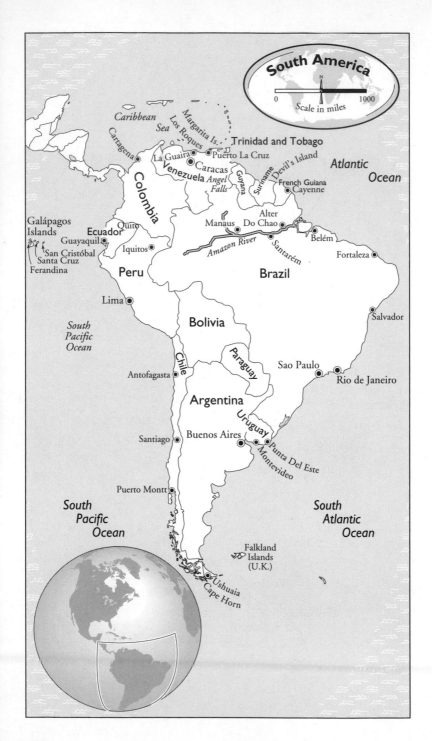

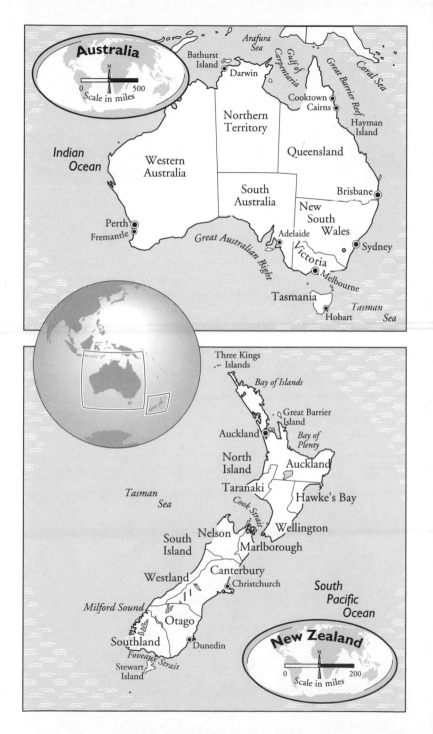

Australia

Scale in miles
0   500

Arafura Sea

Bathurst Island

Darwin

Gulf of Carpentaria

Great Barrier Reef

Coral Sea

Cooktown

Cairns

Hayman Island

Northern Territory

Queensland

Indian Ocean

Western Australia

South Australia

Brisbane

New South Wales

Perth

Fremantle

Great Australian Bight

Adelaide

Victoria

Melbourne

Sydney

Tasmania

Hobart

Tasman Sea

Three Kings Islands

Bay of Islands

Great Barrier Island

Auckland

Bay of Plenty

North Island

Auckland

Taranaki

Hawke's Bay

Tasman Sea

Cook Strait

Nelson

Wellington

South Island

Marlborough

Westland

Canterbury

Christchurch

South Pacific Ocean

Milford Sound

Otago

Southland

Dunedin

Foveaux Strait

Stewart Island

New Zealand

Scale in miles
0   200

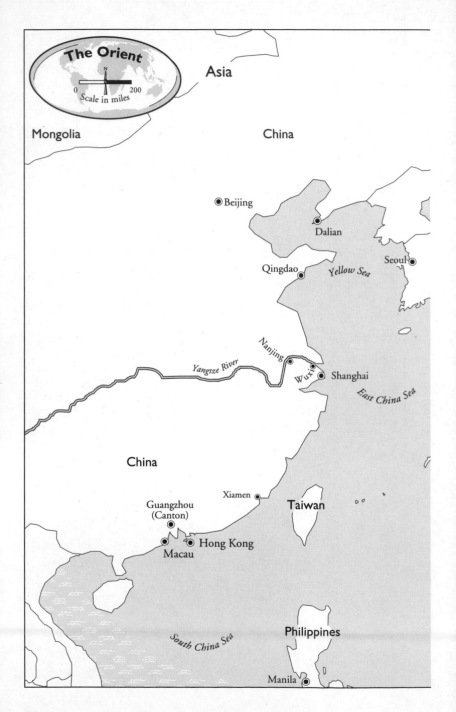

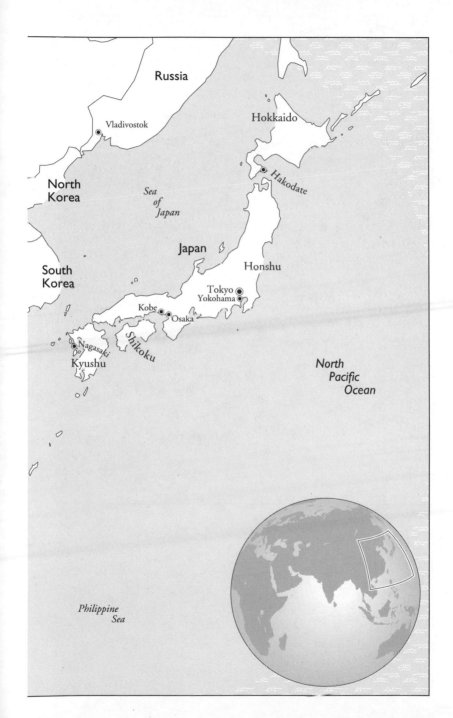

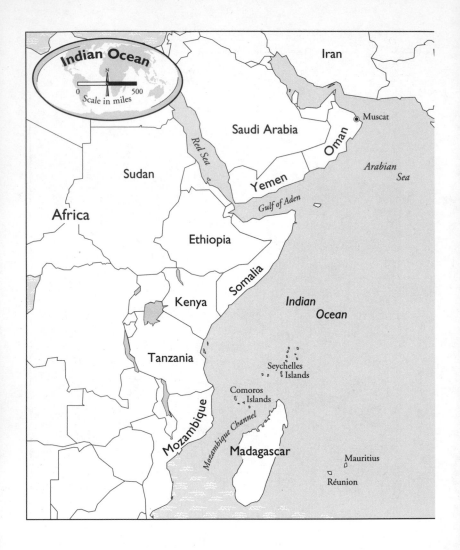

Indian Ocean

N

0   500
Scale in miles

Iran

Saudi Arabia

Muscat

Oman

Red Sea

Sudan

Yemen

Arabian Sea

Gulf of Aden

Africa

Ethiopia

Somalia

Kenya

Indian Ocean

Tanzania

Seychelles Islands

Comoros Islands

Mozambique

Mozambique Channel

Madagascar

Mauritius

Réunion

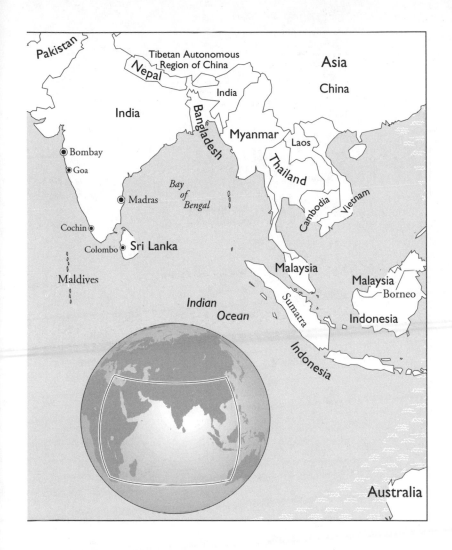

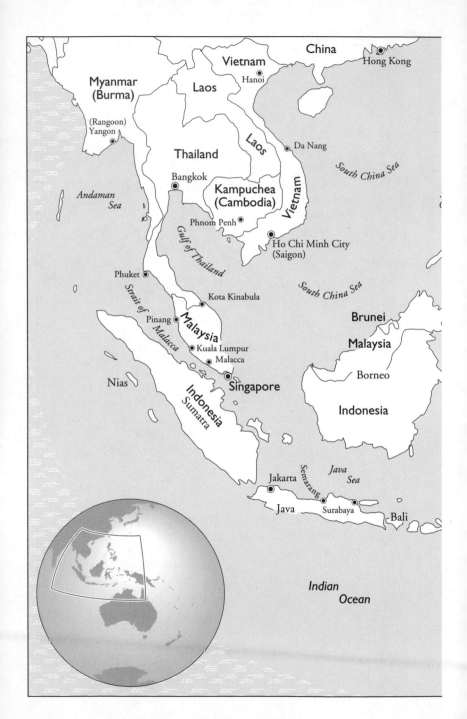

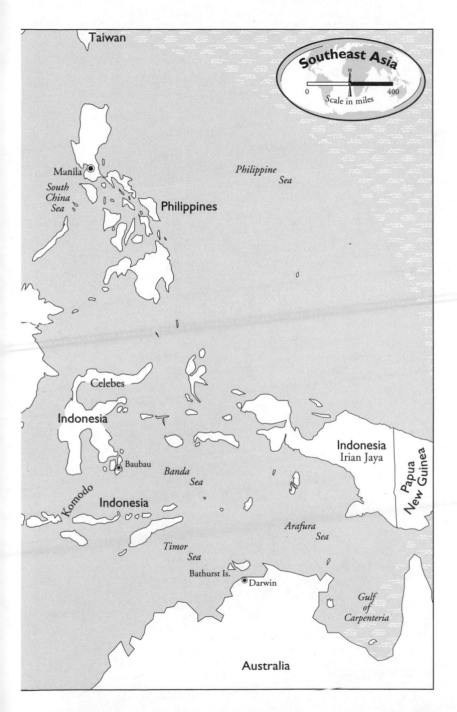

Taiwan

Southeast Asia

N

0   400
Scale in miles

Manila

Philippine Sea

South China Sea

Philippines

Celebes

Indonesia

Indonesia
Irian Jaya

Papua New Guinea

Baubau

Banda Sea

Komodo

Indonesia

Arafura Sea

Timor Sea

Bathurst Is.

Darwin

Gulf of Carpenteria

Australia

Moldova

Ukraine

Odessa

Yalta

Georgia

Constanta

Black
Sea

Black
Sea

rna

Istanbul

Bosporus

Eastern Mediterranean

N

0   100
Scale in miles

Turkey

Izmir
Ephesus
Kusadasi
Bodrum

Antalya   Alanya

Latakia

Syria

Rhodes

Cyprus

Limassol

Beirut
Lebanon

Haifa

Tel Aviv
Ashdod   Jerusalem

Port Said

Israel   Jordan

Alexandria

Egypt

Cairo

Elat   Al Aqabah

Saudi
Arabia

Egypt

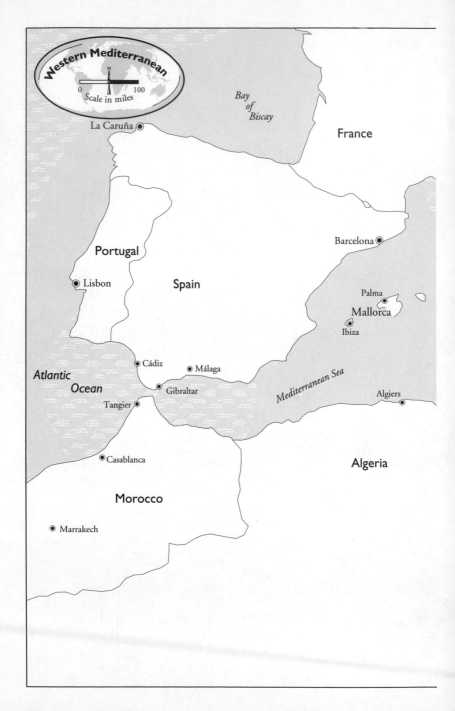

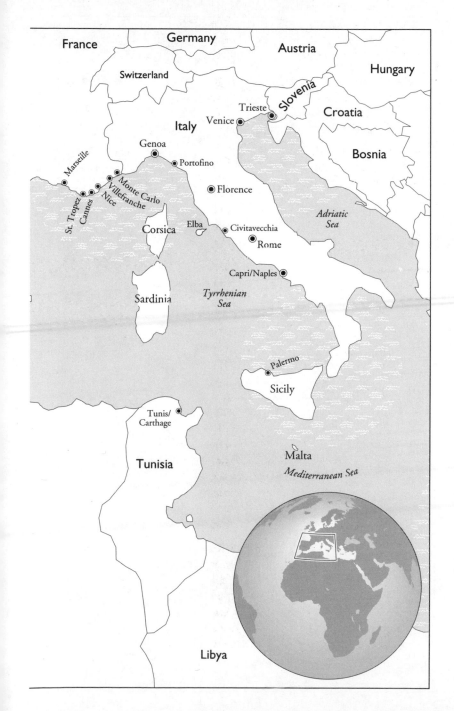

France

Germany

Austria

Hungary

Switzerland

Slovenia

Trieste

Croatia

Italy

Venice

Bosnia

Genoa

Marseille

Portofino

Monte Carlo

Villefranche

Florence

Adriatic
Sea

St. Tropez

Cannes

Nice

Corsica

Elba

Civitavecchia

Rome

Capri/Naples

Sardinia

Tyrrhenian
Sea

Palermo

Sicily

Tunis/
Carthage

Tunisia

Malta

Mediterranean Sea

Libya

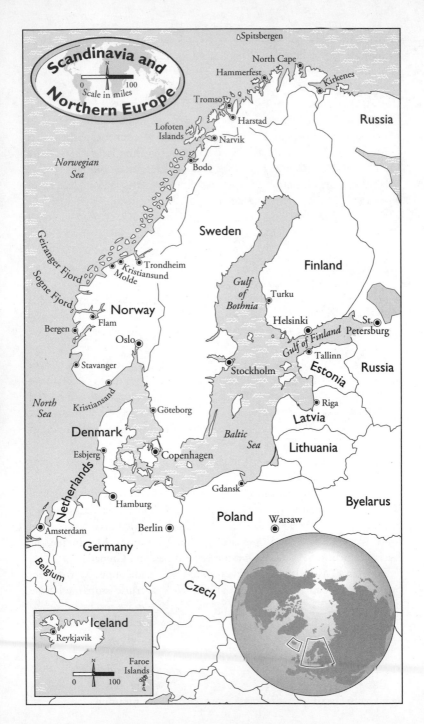

Scandinavia and Northern Europe

0   100
Scale in miles

Spitsbergen

North Cape
Hammerfest
Kirkenes
Tromso
Harstad
Lofoten Islands
Narvik
Bodo

Russia

Norwegian Sea

Sweden

Finland

Geiranger Fjord
Trondheim
Kristiansund
Molde

Sogne Fjord

Norway
Flam
Bergen

Oslo

Stavanger

Gulf of Bothnia

Turku

Helsinki

Gulf of Finland

St. Petersburg

Tallinn

Estonia

Russia

North Sea

Kristiansand

Göteborg

Stockholm

Riga

Latvia

Denmark

Baltic Sea

Lithuania

Esbjerg

Copenhagen

Gdansk

Byelarus

Netherlands

Hamburg

Poland

Warsaw

Amsterdam

Berlin

Belgium

Germany

Czech

Iceland
Reykjavik

Faroe Islands

0   100

Hawaiian cruises occupy the middle, emphasizing both festivity and scenery, though passengers are older on average than those in the Caribbean. For other North Pacific, South Pacific, Indian Ocean, and South China Sea settings, the distance of the cruise areas and home ports from the United States ensures an older, wealthier market. Like Mediterranean cruises, sight-seeing and cultural attractions are the focus.

Though a great way to see exotic places without shuffling among hotels, cruises allow only a cursory glimpse of the countries visited. Ten hours in Venice on a cruise is no substitute for visiting Italy. Even in the Caribbean, short stopovers on small islands leave much undiscovered.

Some travelers use cruising to sample cities and countries to determine whether they might want to return later for a more prolonged visit. If you are interested in further exploring a destination, consider the add-ons most lines offer at the beginning and end of cruises. Two- or three-night packages include a hotel and some sight-seeing. They are usually well-priced and can be booked at the time you buy your cruise.

Defining the Caribbean   On a map with the arm of the compass pointing north, the islands closest to the United States are the Greater Antilles; they include Cuba, the Caymans, Jamaica, Haiti, the Dominican Republic, and Puerto Rico. All but Cuba are visited by ships from U.S. ports and have daily, direct air service from major U.S. cities.

The Bahamas and the British colony of the Turks and Caicos lie north of the Greater Antilles and southeast of Florida. They are entirely in the Atlantic Ocean, but because their tropical environment is similar to that of the Caribbean, they are viewed as part of the region. The Bahamas, not the Turks and Caicos, are cruise stops; both have air service from the United States.

In the eastern Caribbean are the Lesser Antilles, starting with the Virgin Islands in the north and curving south to Grenada. The northern of these many small islands are called the Leewards and comprise the U.S. and British Virgin Islands, Anguilla, St. Maarten, St. Barts, Saba, St. Eustatius, St. Kitts, Nevis, Antigua, Barbuda, Montserrat, and Guadeloupe. The south islands, called the Windwards, include Dominica, Martinique, St. Lucia, Barbados, St. Vincent and the Grenadines, and Grenada.

The Virgin Islands, St. Maarten, Antigua, Guadeloupe, Martinique, St. Lucia, Barbados, and Grenada are frequent cruise stops and have direct air service from the United States. The others are reached through local airlines, and most are stops for small ships, particularly during winter cruise season. In the south are Aruba, Bonaire, Curaçao, and Trinidad and Tobago, which lie off Venezuela. In the western Caribbean off the Yucatán Peninsula are the Mexican islands of Cancún and Cozumel.

Along the 2,000-mile Caribbean chain, nature has been extravagant with its color, variety, and beauty. Verdant mountains rise from sun-bleached shores. Between towering peaks and the sea, rivers and streams cascade over rocks and hillsides and disappear into mangrove swamps and deserts. Fields of flowers, trees with brilliant blossoms, and a multitude of birds and butterflies fill the landscape. The air, refreshed by tropical showers, is scented with spices and fruit.

Yet what makes the Caribbean islands unique is their combination of exotic scenery and the kaleidoscope of diverse cultures. The people and their cultures have evolved from traditions, music, dance, art, architecture, and religions from around the world.

To be fair, we should warn you that the exponential growth of cruising in the Caribbean has had a tremendous, and many would say negative, impact on some islands. Cruise ships disgorging thousands of passengers a day on a tiny island disrupt the normal rhythms, changing a quaint, sleepy, laid-back port into a frenetic, artificial tourist attraction. Sprawling malls have sprung up like ragweed around the docks, and whole native populations have abandoned their lifelong vocations to cater to tourists. Real Caribbean countries have become just like the private islands owned by several cruise lines: plastic, idealized versions more familiar to fans of *Gilligan's Island* than to veteran Caribbean travelers.

When Do I Want to Go?

Cruises follow the sun, visiting destinations during their best weather. Hence, for some exotic destinations and such seasonal cruise areas as Alaska, the British Isles, Canada, and Antarctica, you have only a two- to five-month window of opportunity. For the Caribbean, Mexico, Hawaii, and the Orient, among others, cruises are available all year.

Following is a sampling of popular destinations and cruising seasons.

Africa	Year-round, but mostly May–October for north Africa; November–April for eastern and southern Africa
Alaska	May–September
Asia and the Orient	Mainly October–March
Baltic	May–October
Bermuda	May–October
Black Sea	April–October
Canada	May–October
Caribbean	Year-round
Hawaii	Year-round
India and Southeast Asia	Year-round; mostly November–April
Mediterranean	March–November
Mexico	Year-round
New England	May–October
Panama Canal	September–May

| **South America** | North coast, year-round; other areas, September–April |
| **South Pacific** | Year-round; mainly November–April |

For every area, periods of peak demand are called high season; moderate demand, shoulder season; and low demand, low season or value season. Usually high season occurs when good weather in the cruise area coincides with times when people want to take vacations. In the Caribbean, that's between Christmas and the middle of April, and from June 15 to August 15. Yet within high season are often valleys when prices are likely to be their lowest for the year, offering you an opportunity to save a bundle. In the Caribbean, for example, immediately after the Christmas–New Year holiday demand drops, the first two weeks in January offer value season rates. If you can be flexible, shifting cruise dates a week or two may offer big savings. Always check the period immediately before or after your selected dates to find out your options.

The January–April market targets seniors and Northerners seeking a respite from the winter. Although weather in summer is not as good as between January and April, families create high demand during midsummer when school is out. When demand tapers off, shoulder season follows, giving way to low season as cruise demand continues to decline.

During high season, ships generally are full (more crowded) and cruises are more expensive (because demand is high). If your plans are flexible, it is usually possible to identify several times in the year when your destination's weather is predictably good but cruise demand is moderate or low. Cruising during these periods provides lower prices, less-crowded ships, and good weather. Caribbean cruises in November and early December before Christmas are good examples. Hurricane season is over, prices are low, and ships are significantly less crowded. Early May for Alaska is another excellent time.

If your travel schedule is not flexible, shoulder seasons (early June or late August) may be your best bet.

What Sort of Lifestyle or Activity Level Am I Seeking?

As baby boomers enter middle age and relative affluence and as younger couples and families discover the economy of cruise vacations, cruising's demographics are changing. On most midmarket cruises of two weeks or less, passengers are amazingly diverse. Responding to a widening range of energy and interests among these passengers, lines have developed activities that offer something for almost everyone.

Even so, lines continue to fine-tune their product for their primary markets. Thus, although Celebrity Cruise Lines might develop programs and activities for younger clients, these cruisers continue to be a secondary market. The line's real focus is the 45–65 age group. That means a younger person will have a good time on Celebrity, but an over-40 person will probably have a better time because the cruise is built around the latter's preferences.

How cruise lines serve their primary, secondary, and even tertiary markets makes relevant the question, "What sort of lifestyle or activity level am I seeking?" In each of our cruise line and ship profiles, we pinpoint the style, tenor, and activity level of the cruises offered. Look for an activity and social mix that seems right for you, but don't get bogged down in demographics. Many older people are active, athletic, and like to party, and many young people appreciate a sedate cruise and may spend their days doing nothing more than reading in a lounge chair.

The choice to participate in activities or party all night is entirely yours. Do, however, pay attention to the ship's size. A small ship carrying 250 or fewer passengers may have only one or two lounges and limited deck space. If you don't care for a full day or evening of shipboard activity, you'll enjoy its low-key ambience. Large ships have the resources to offer considerable variety. Carnival Cruise Line, for example, pretty much wrote the book on party cruising, but even on a Carnival ship it is possible to relax. Ships carrying 1,000 or more passengers have plenty of places to escape the festivities.

Most ships offer a variety of dance music. Many even have separate nightclubs offering different types of music, dancing, and entertainment.

Cruise lines design their promotional brochures to appeal to their target markets. If you identify with the people and activities depicted in the brochure, you probably will feel at home on one of that line's ships. Lines that do not cater to families, for instance, do not feature them in their literature. Study the brochures from your travel agent. Are the passengers pictured your age or of varied ages? Is the emphasis on shipboard activities or ports and scenery? Does shipboard life look like a 24-hour party, or do photos show a more laid-back experience? On-board facilities need no interpretation. They're spelled out.

What Level of Formality Do I Prefer?

Most cruises give passengers an opportunity to play dress-up. On certain evenings in the main dining room, men wear jackets, tuxedos, or dark suits, and women wear cocktail dresses or gowns. Most ships have a dress protocol that passengers are expected to observe. (See "Dress Codes" under "Preparing for Your Cruise.")

Formality (or lack thereof) is a way cruise lines set themselves apart. A luxury line targeting highly affluent passengers almost always will be more formal than a midmarket line. Family and budget lines are less formal, and adventure cruises are usually the most informal.

The bottom line is how much formality you want. The great majority of cruises vary attire from night to night and won't punish someone who breaks the dress code. If, for example, a man wears a dark suit instead of a tuxedo for the captain's party, no one will turn him away. On the other hand, even an informal ship might ask passengers not to wear shorts and tank tops in the dining room and be strict about it. Most passengers don't spend a lot of time worrying about formality, but if it's important to you, check the ship's dress code before you book.

What Standards Do I Require for Dining and Food Quality?

Food—its quality and the overall dining experience—is cited by most passengers as a critical element of their cruise. The fare on cruise ships is generally very good—impressive considering that shipboard meals represent the ultimate extension of catered banquet dining.

Feeding 300 to 1,400 persons at a sitting is challenging under any circumstances. Doing it at sea with attention to detail, quality ingredients and preparation, and beautiful presentation is one of cruising's miracles. Ships have made an art of serving palatable food to crowds of diners. Hotel food and beverage managers could learn a lot from cruise ship chefs.

However, you can't expect the same excellence from a galley serving hundreds of dinners as you can from an upscale restaurant cooking to order for a small number of guests. A few small ships do rival better restaurants, but they are the exception.

The quality of meals and sophistication of the dining experience vary considerably among ships. Although luxury ships serving fewer passengers in single seatings have the greatest potential for serving memorable meals, midmarket lines like Celebrity have shown they can approach similar standards of excellence serving larger numbers.

If you have a refined palate and eat exclusively in the finest restaurants, you may meet your dining requirements only in the high-end group of cruise ships. If, however, you dine regularly in restaurants of varying quality, are acquainted with the world's major cuisines, and understand the limitations of cruise food service, you will find numerous ships capable of meeting or exceeding your expectations.

For those not hung up on gourmet food, suitable cruises are many, and even better, among the most affordable. You can use your cruise dining experience to broaden your culinary horizons, or you can save bucks aboard a ship specializing in good but less expensive American fare.

Many people pay for food much fancier than their taste requires. Meat-and-potatoes people get a better deal putting their dollars into a cabin upgrade on a midmarket line rather than paying for fancy food on a luxury line.

Cruise lines have tended to offer good dining room meals or good buffets, but seldom both. Almost all lines have cut back on the midnight buffet, except for one extravaganza when chefs go all out to show off their culinary skills.

Under Norwegian Cruise Line's "Freestyle Cruising" program, you can eat in one of two main dining rooms, at whatever time you choose during normal hours of operation, or you can make reservations at any of six alternative restaurants. On the *Norwegian Sun,* for example, there are Le Bistro serving French cuisine; East Meets West with Pacific Rim and Asian Fusion fare; Las Ramblas, a tapas bar; Il Adagio for Italian cuisine; Pacific Heights, specializing in healthy, light California cuisine; and Ginza, offering sushi, sashimi, and teppanyaki dining. If none of that works for you, the Garden Café operates a buffet around the clock, or alternatively there's 24-hour room service. The reservations-only alternative restaurants impose a surcharge of $10 per person, but it's worth it. The restaurants are elegant, quiet, and intimate, and the food rivals that of good onshore restaurants— or perhaps more relevant, the fare served on ships in the luxury market. Aside from the surcharge, the main downside is that you don't have the opportunity to meet people and form friendships like you would in a conventional dining arrangement where you eat in the same place, at the same assigned table, and with the same people, every night.

Among other cruise dining innovators, Princess's Personal Choice Dining program offers multiple restaurants and no assigned seating, or alternatively, passengers can opt for the traditional dining arrangement. The Disney Cruise Line also features several dining venues, but on the Disney ships, passengers rotate among three different themed restaurants according to a prearranged schedule. And, in a concession to those passengers who develop a fondness for their wait staff, their waiter and his assistant rotate right along with them. Carnival, with yet another approach, offers "total choice" dining, where passengers can choose from four seating times in the main dining room instead of the usual two. The four seatings stagger the arrival of diners, preventing the galley from being inundated and allowing both chefs and wait staff to concentrate on a smaller number of diners at a given time.

Weather and lifestyle have clearly affected cruise dining. Because most ships spend all or part of the year in the Caribbean and Mexico, where passengers remain in their bathing suits most of the day, the lines found that it makes sense and saves money to expand the lido breakfast and lunch. Lido dining also gives passengers relief from the regimentation of dining room hours.

A recent trend in onboard dining is the availability of stand-alone specialty restaurants in addition to the main dining room and buffet. Found almost exclusively on ships carrying 1,000 or more passengers and operating like a restaurant on shore, these specialized eateries offer an intimacy and ambience impossible to match in the ship's grand dining room. Like most upscale restaurants, the sea-going versions accept reservations, or alternatively, you can just show up during operating hours and hope to get a table. Cuisines and specialties available run the gamut from steak to sushi, Cantonese to California nouvelle cuisine.

How Gregarious Am I (Are We)?

Generally, it's easier to meet folks on a small ship. There are fewer passengers, and you see the same people more often. Conversely, on a large ship, the only folks you see regularly are your dinner table companions (hope you like them!). On larger ships, if you meet somebody you would like to see again, get their name and cabin number. We once met a nice woman checking in on the 2,300-passenger *Monarch of the Seas*. In a week aboard, we never again saw her.

Large ships offer many social settings. It's possible to meet people in bars, lounges, and nightclubs; on shore excursions; in the health club; around the pool; and in the casino. But the easiest time to meet them is at planned activities. Whether it's aerobics and line dancing or bridge and wine tasting, such activities help people with similar interests come together.

The style of a cruise is important. If you are gregarious, you might prefer a ship that promotes a party atmosphere. If you are more solitary or are taking a romantic cruise with your significant other, you may prefer a less frenetic social agenda.

Most cruisers solve the problem of companionship by taking significant others, friends, relatives, or all of the above with them. As on Noah's ark, the majority of passengers arrive already paired up. This is attributable in part to the double-occupancy norm for cabins. Solo passengers pay a hefty "singles supplement" for the privilege of having a cabin to themselves. Ships schedule gatherings where singles can meet, and some try to seat singles at the same dining tables, but singles generally have to scout around to find other people who are flying solo.

The Other Passengers:
What Kind of People Am I Most Comfortable With?

The less expensive the cruise, the more varied the passengers. Aboard a recent, affordable four-day cruise were retired seniors, middle-aged professionals, 20-something newlyweds, a bowling team from Pennsylvania, families with young children, a group of pipe fitters, and college students on spring break.

On upscale cruises of two weeks or longer, the cost ensures that passengers are somewhat more affluent and perhaps less diverse. On a seven-day Caribbean or Mexico cruise with midmarket lines, such as Royal

Caribbean, Princess, Celebrity, and Holland America, you will find more seniors, more professionals, fewer tradespeople, fewer families with children (except during summer), and fewer people younger than age 25. Passengers are even less varied on the same lines' seven-day or longer cruises to the more expensive destinations of Alaska and the Mediterranean.

On the most upscale lines, including Seabourn, Radisson Seven Seas, and Silversea, the average passenger is older than age 55 and affluent. Passengers younger than age 20 are likely traveling with parents or grandparents. Some lines don't take children or discourage their presence because they do not have the facilities or atmosphere for them. Couples account for 80% of those on board. Singles are likely to be widows, widowers, or mature singles able to afford the lifestyle.

For our profiles of cruise lines and ships, we carefully scrutinized their passengers so you'll know what to expect. We believe the inclusion of this information is one element that makes this book different from other guidebooks on cruises. If you have strong feelings about who your fellow passengers will be, pay close attention to these descriptions.

What Kind of Itinerary Do I Prefer?

Among itineraries, there's a world to choose from. You can have mostly days at sea, mostly days in port, or a balance of the two. Your cruise can be educational or just fun. There are theme cruises where entertainment or education is the focus, such as a jazz festival, and cruises where specific activities are emphasized, such as scuba diving, golf, sailing, or viewing wildlife.

Start by deciding how much time at sea versus time in port you prefer. If you are more interested in visiting ports, seek an itinerary with many of them. (Be aware that when a ship visits more than five ports on a seven-day cruise, some stops will be half-day.) Port-intensive itineraries are most plentiful on Mediterranean and eastern Caribbean cruises. Compare itineraries for different lines listing the same ports. When figuring your time in each port, remember that your ship must clear Customs on arrival before passengers are allowed to disembark. A ship making port at 8 a.m. may not put passengers ashore before 9 or 9:30 a.m. Most ships require passengers to be aboard 30 minutes or more before leaving port. Thus your time in port could be trimmed by an hour or more coming and going.

Another important consideration, if you want to maximize your time in port, is whether your ship ties up at the dock or anchors offshore. Having to use a tender (a small commuting boat) to reach shore can take a big bite out of your port time. The larger the ship, the more likely the need to use a tender. The published itinerary or your travel agent will provide information on tendering.

Many passengers—usually experienced cruisers—relish the serenity of being at sea. In recent years, they have been very vocal in opposing cruise lines' cramming ports into their itineraries to attract first-time cruisers who commonly perceive value in the number of ports visited. It's more difficult to find itineraries featuring days spent at sea than to uncover itineraries with daily port calls. Most three-, four-, and seven-day cruises spend more daylight hours in port than at sea. Longer cruises typically feature more time at sea. Itineraries list days spent under way as "cruising" or "at sea."

A map highlighting ports of call in the world's cruise areas shows the hundreds of ports ships can add to their itineraries. With the possible exception of the Atlantic coast of Africa, most ports are close enough to one another to allow a port visit every day. Fortunately, most itineraries of seven or more days strike a balance. A typical seven-day itinerary includes two days at sea. Three or four days of cruising is typical of 10-day itineraries; 4–5 days on 12- to 14-day itineraries.

Repositioning cruises are the best buys for those who crave more days at sea. They are also the best bargains. They occur at the end of the season in a cruise area when lines reposition their ship(s) by dispatching them to other areas where new seasons are beginning. Thus, Princess repositions some of its Caribbean fleet in April (the end of Caribbean high season) to the Pacific Northwest for summer cruises to Alaska. Royal Caribbean at the same time might dispatch ships from the Caribbean to Europe or the Mediterranean. Repositioning cruises stop at some ports, but there usually is a high ratio of sea days to days in port. Because such voyages occur only twice a year, they are difficult for lines to promote, and passage usually is discounted significantly.

Specialized Itineraries and Specialized Ships

Passengers aboard most large ships determine for themselves how they will use their time. Specialty cruises, by contrast, focus on a specific activity or pursuit. Some may specialize in whale-watching, others in exploring ancient ruins. Sometimes the vessel sets the focus. Smaller, 20- to 150-passenger ships can dock in small ports and anchor in secluded coves. This facilitates fishing, swimming, snorkeling, scuba diving, and water skiing (participants carry their own sports equipment) and makes a difference in the way passengers use their time.

Traditional ships sometimes offer theme cruises. For example, professional football players may be aboard and reruns of famous games are shown. Passengers should inquire about themes and book the cruise only if they're interested. A cruise ship can be the medium for countless activities and themes. For additional information on specialty cruises, see Part Three, Cruising Alternatives.

Big Ships versus Small Ships

Hardly a week passes that some cruise line doesn't announce plans for another ship—bigger and, of course, better than the last. But bigger isn't necessarily better for a cruise.

New words have crept into the cruise lexicon. Not everyone agrees on their definitions, but these are the currently accepted parameters:

Megaliner   A cruise ship with a basic capacity (i.e., 2 people per cabin) of more than 2,000 passengers.

Superliner   A cruise ship with a basic capacity of about 1,000 to 2,000.

Midsize   A cruise ship with a basic capacity of 400 to 900.

Small Ship   A cruise ship with a basic capacity of under 400.

Boutique Ship   A luxury cruise or expedition ship with a basic capacity of under 300.

Oceanliner   Generally, any oceangoing passenger vessel, but tends to be used for former steamships that provided transatlantic and worldwide service and have since been converted into cruise ships.

Until you sail on small ships, you may not realize their special pleasures. Small ships are fewer but more diverse in style than larger ones. They range from traditional sailing ships, such as Star Clipper's tall ships, to computer-driven ones like Windstar Cruises', and in the degree of comfort and service from the modest vessels of American Canadian Caribbean Lines to Seabourn's ultraluxurious Sea Goddess twins. Prices likewise vary from the moderate Windjammer Barefoot Cruises to très cher Seabourn Cruises.

It's difficult to generalize, but all small ships are cozy, imparting warmth never felt on a superliner. The smallest ones, such as American Safari's 12–21-passenger ships, are like private yachts—yet surprisingly affordable.

Small ships are people-sized. It's easy to learn the layout on the first day. Life aboard is casual, even on the most luxurious ships. Informality and friendliness go hand in hand. Passengers are fewer, and making friends is easy—an advantage for singles. The congenial atmosphere also enhances interaction between passengers and crew, who are likely to call you by name from the first day.

Small ships with their shallow drafts, turn-on-a-dime maneuverability, and fewer passengers can gain access and acceptability in places where large ships simply cannot go. Their size makes them welcome at private islands and exclusive resorts and allows them to nudge into shallow bays and hidden coves. Their ports tend to be offbeat and uncommercialized.

Some small cruisers have bow or stern ramps, enabling them to disembark passengers directly onto beaches or into remote villages. Others carry Zodiacs and/or sea kayaks to transport passengers into wilderness. Some have retractable marinas, enabling passengers to water ski or swim from the ship.

A small ship offers exclusivity, even if it is unintended. Seating is unassigned at single seatings for meals. On deluxe ships, dining is even at the time of your choosing. There are no crowds, no long lines, almost no regimentation. Best of all, on shore, you don't feel like part of a herd.

Today's superliners and megaliners are self-contained floating resorts with facilities that operate almost around the clock. The bigger the vessel, the more the ship becomes the focus and ports matter less.

For small ships, destinations are key, and sight-seeing is the main activity. They offer more varied and unusual itineraries than larger ships can and often carry experts to discuss destinations and accompany passengers on shore excursions.

Small ships draw experienced, discriminating, and independent travelers who enjoy low-key ambience and appreciate what is not available as much as what is. They neither want nor need nonstop activities. A few small vessels have tiny casinos and small-scale entertainment, but most substitute conversation and companionship, or lectures by various experts for chorus lines and cabarets.

The smaller size attracts all age groups. Sailing ships, particularly schooners, draw the young and adventuresome, attracted by the lower price and the opportunity to work alongside the crew. Deluxe ships and those with longer itineraries attract older travelers, many of whom are young in spirit and intellectually curious. They appreciate an island's culture and are eager to interact with the locals.

Sound appealing? Then consider one of the three basic types of minisships: Ultraluxurious liners offer privacy and pampering, exclusivity and elegance, tastefully opulent suites, gourmet dining, and often formal evenings. In sharp contrast are adventure-oriented ships, whose destinations are chosen for their natural beauty, wildlife, or cultural interest. Activities include hiking, kayaking, and birding. Cabins usually are modest, service minimal, and cooking down-home. They appeal to people who spurn luxury but are keenly interested in participatory travel. A third type strikes a middle ground, offering comfortable (but not lavish) accommodations, good food, and attentive service. There is some adventure, some history and wildlife, and some time for sports. Evening entertainment includes games, movies, local talent, and guest speakers.

Even with these choices, small-ship cruising is not for everyone. Some would find it boring or confining. But if you abhor lines or regimentation, operate on your own juices, yearn for a more intimate environment, or want to try trimming the sails or floating in luxury, small ships might be right for you.

Old Ships versus New Ships

Poets praise the beauty of sailing ships. But observers of classic cruise ships like the *QE2* have been equally captivated by noble grace that is both massive and subtle. Examine the *Norway* closely and discover there is scarcely a straight line in her. Alas, such ships will never be built again.

Are old or new vessels better? The debate rages. Classic ships still in service, as opposed to those merely old, offer ambience that no newer ship can duplicate. But the newest cruise vessels have advantages only dreamed of in 1960. Because there are well-maintained and up-to-date older ships in service, you have a choice between the old and the new afloat. Find your preference by surveying what each type of ship has to offer.

Notice first the appearance of any vessel, old or new. The newest ships are designed from the inside out to provide more and better public rooms and the most amount of usable deck space. These vessels spend most of their days in calm seas. None will cut through the North Atlantic at full speed to maintain a schedule, so the fine lines and razor-sharp bow of the *QE2* aren't needed. Instead, new ships have squared sterns and chunky superstructures that provide many benefits internally but none externally.

As with some prima donnas, most new ships have one or two good angles. Publicity materials show profile shots and aerials of raked stems and funnels and broad decks for recreation. But approach the ship in person, and you see what she really looks like: a full-figured lady from bow to stern.

Once inside your cabin, however, you may forget your ship's outward appearance. The space available to modern designers has generally made possible standard, usually larger cabins for everyone. Some older ships offer comfortable space in every cabin, but they can't match the improved bathrooms and lighting of newer ships.

Luxury versus Midprice and Economy Cruises

Spending more on a cruise does not necessarily get you more or better facilities. Some of the most extraordinary spas, gyms, pools, lounges, and showrooms are found on the megaships of affordable midmarket lines such as Carnival, Princess, and Royal Caribbean Cruise Lines. Likewise, dropping big bucks will not ensure that your ship is newer, nicer, or more competently and courteously staffed. (Check the ratio of passengers to crew. The lower the ratio, the more service you should get.) Booking a luxury cruise may get you a larger cabin (suites aboard Silversea or Seabourn Cruise Line) and almost certainly buys a roomier bath with tub and shower.

Regarding food, luxury lines have the edge. Usually they feed fewer passengers at a single seating spanning a couple of hours. Passengers arrive at the dining room a few at a time, like at a restaurant ashore. The staggered arrivals allow the galley the flexibility to provide more choice and cook dishes to order.

Most midmarket and economy cruises have two seatings for each meal. When their seating is called, passengers stampede into the dining room like marines hitting the beach. Surprisingly, however, the quality of meals on some luxury ships is only marginally better than that of better midmarket lines. Midmarket Princess Cruises makes dining a top priority and serves meals comparable to those on cruises costing much more. Generally, the extra dollars for a luxury cruise buy exclusivity. For those who can afford it, that's saying a lot.

Special People with Special Needs

Some passengers require special services or accommodations. If you are a honeymooner, single, disabled, require a special diet, or plan to travel with young children or teens, read on.

Singles

Safety and security, comfort, convenience, companionship, fun, and freedom—all are reasons that cruises are among the fastest-growing options available to travelers who want to go it alone.

A cruise ship is about the safest, most secure environment you can find. A woman might hesitate to talk with someone in a hotel bar, dine alone in a fancy restaurant, or walk alone into a nightclub, but such barriers don't exist on a ship.

Furthermore, the fun is at your fingertips. The nightclub, disco, casino, and theater are walking distance from your cabin. Relieved of the need for an escort and with ready-made companions for dinner or activities, single people—men and women—vacation on their own terms.

Cruise prices are based on two people sharing a cabin. For one person to occupy a cabin alone, cruise lines impose an extra charge over the per-person double-occupancy rate. This "single supplement" varies from 10% to 100% (expressed as 110–200%), depending on the line, ship, itinerary, season, and cabin category. The most frequent charge is 150% for all except suites, which usually go for 200%. Brochures always publish the rate. Your choices are to pay it, bring a friend, or take one of these options:

Guaranteed Single Rate   You pay a set price published in the brochure, which is comparable to the low end of a per-person double-occupancy rate. The line assigns your cabin at embarkation. You don't have a choice, but you do have a guarantee of price and privacy.

You are likely to be assigned an inside cabin. If you select low season (October in the Caribbean), the start of a new season (May in Alaska), or a repositioning cruise when the ship is unlikely to be full, you might get a nice outside cabin. Royal Caribbean Cruise Line and Norwegian Cruise Lines offer a guaranteed single fare, which includes air transportation. Some lines do not show a guaranteed single rate in their brochure but will accept a reservation when bookings are light. Be sure to ask.

Low Single Supplement   Some lines have single supplements of 115% or less. Seabourn offers 110% on some cruises; Silversea has a few at 125%, though most are at 150%. In all cases, you pay slightly more than the per-person double rate, but you get privacy, and in the case of Seabourn and Silversea, all accommodations are deluxe suites.

Flat Rate   Clipper Cruises, Star Clipper, and some other lines charge a flat rate for single occupancy. You pay more but are ensured privacy and choice.

Guaranteed Share   The line plays travel matchmaker. You pay the per-person double-occupancy price, and the line matches you with a cabin mate (same gender and smoking preference). If the line does not find a suitable mate, you get the cabin to yourself at no extra charge. The savings—and drawbacks—are obvious. It's a bit of Russian roulette. You stand a better chance of having a cabin to yourself during low season or on a repositioning cruise. Some lines don't publicize a guaranteed share program but will accept a reservation. Be sure to ask.

Single Cabin   Some older ships have single cabins. The price is set but not necessarily comparable to a per-person double rate. More likely, a surcharge has been built into the price.

Find single cabins on Cunard—136 on *QE2* and 73 on *Caronia*—and on many Maine Windjammer vessels.

Also, some lines charge singles minimal or no surcharge for less desirable cabins, such as inside rooms with upper/lower berths.

CRUISING FOR SINGLES

S = Single cabins available
GSP = Guaranteed share program available
Single Supplement = Percentage of fare based on per-person double occupancy rate

	S	GSP	Single Supplement
Alaska's Glacier Bay/Voyager	No	No	175%
American Canadian Caribbean	Yes	Yes	175%
Carnival Cruise Lines	Yes	Yes	150–200%
Celebrity Cruises	Yes	No	150–200%
Clipper Cruise Line	No	Yes	150%
Costa Cruise Lines	Yes	No	150–200%
Cruise West	Yes	No	175%
Crystal Cruises	No	No	125–150%
Cunard Line	Yes	No	140–200%
Delta Queen	Yes	Yes	150–200%
Disney Cruise Line	No	No	175–200%
Holland America Line	Yes	Yes	135–200%
Norwegian Cruise Line	No	Yes	150–200%
Orient Lines	No	Yes	125–200%

			Single
Cruise Line	**S**	**GSP**	**Supplement**
Princess Cruises	No	No	160–200%
Radisson Seven Seas	No	No	Varies by cruise
Royal Caribbean	No	Yes	150–200%
Royal Olympia Cruises	No	Yes	150–200%
Seabourn Cruise Line	Yes	No	110–200%
Silversea Cruises	No	No	110–175%
Star Clippers	No	Yes	150–200%
Windstar Cruises	No	No	175%

CRUISING FOR SINGLES *(continued)*

Helpful Hands

Golden Age Travellers (Pier 27, The Embarcadero, San Francisco, CA 94111; (800) 258-8880) or (415) 296-0151; **www.gatclub.com**), offers about 300 cruises a year and provides a cabin-mate matching service and lower supplements based on bargaining clout. Limited to those age 50 and up. Annual fee is $10 per person; $15 per couple.

Travel Companion Exchange (P.O. Box 833, Amityville, NY 11701; (800) 392-1256 or (631) 454-0880; **www.whytravelalone.com**), offers membership, a matching service, and bimonthly issues of a 20-page newsletter for $159 (first-time enrollment; regular annual rate is $298).

Finally, watch for specials and find a knowledgeable travel agent to help you. A smart, experienced agent knows which, when, and how cruise lines make special deals for singles, and they can often unearth ways that advance purchase and special promotional fares, even though based on double occupancy, can be applied to single travelers.

Other Tips for Sailing Solo The cruise industry has a long way to go in handling the singles market. The probability of finding love at sea varies according to age group. Twenty-somethings should look to the Caribbean on cruise lines that target a younger market, though the average passenger age remains above age 35.

Singles wanting to meet people should participate in activities, shore excursions, and sports. Small ships generally are preferable to large ones because it is easier to mix and the staff works harder to involve you in the ship's social life. Among small ships, adventure and educational cruises are singles' best choices; camaraderie quickly develops among passengers. Also, the number of unattached men is likely to be higher than on traditional cruises.

If you're 40-something or an older single woman who loves to dance, book a ship with gentlemen hosts—single males, age 50 or older, who dine and dance with all unattached women—no favoritism or hanky panky allowed. Crystal, Cunard, Delta Queen, Holland America, and Royal Olympic Cruises have them.

On singles cruises offered four times annually, Windjammer Barefoot Cruises all but guarantees a 50–50 ratio of males and females. Ages vary widely. You get no break on price—the single supplement is 150%—unless you are willing to share.

A common complaint we hear from singles concerns table assignment for dining. Some singles are unhappy because they're seated with married folks. Others are annoyed because they're seated with other singles and resent the cruise line playing matchmaker. Response varies, but your best bet is to submit a written request in advance outlining your preference in dining companionship. Aboard, if you are disenchanted with your table mates, ask the maître d'hôtel to move you.

Honeymooners

If there is a better honeymoon option than a cruise, we can't think of it. There is nothing more romantic than balmy nights and sunny days under a Caribbean or Mediterranean sky. Your cabin is your honeymoon suite; room service usually is complimentary, so you never have to leave unless you want to. Forget the car, unpack only once, and still visit exotic places. Many lines (with advance notice) will provide a cozy table for two in the dining room. Regardless, tell the cruise line you are newlyweds. You will probably get preferential treatment, a bottle of champagne, flowers in the room, a souvenir photo, or even a cabin upgrade.

If you are contemplating a cruise honeymoon, consider: If you marry on Saturday, then Sunday or Monday departures are most convenient. Check on the availability of bathtubs versus showers if that is important to you. Ask whether room service is available at all three meals and whether you can choose from the regular menu (room service menus are often limited).

Nonambulatory Disabled Passengers

Many people who use a wheelchair or other mobility aids have discovered the pleasures of cruising firsthand. However, you need to be very direct and specific when exploring your options. Dining rooms, showrooms, or public rest rooms are not wheelchair-accessible on many ships. A few small ships have no elevators; on others, particularly older ships, elevators do not serve every deck. Most ships require that you bring your own wheelchair, often one that is collapsible or narrow-gauge. Do not count on a lot of wheelchair-accessible facilities or cabins. On the most wheelchair-accessible ships, no more than two dozen cabins will have wheelchair-accessible bathrooms, and there usually is no way to get a wheelchair into a regular cabin's bathroom. If you need an accessible cabin, book well in advance. We list the number of wheelchair-accessible cabins available under each line's Standard Features and each ship's Cabin Specifications. Look for a ship with a lot of elevators relative to its complement of passengers. Divide the number of passengers by the number of elevators. Generally, the lower the calculated number, the less time you will spend waiting for elevators.

It is important that you book your cruise through an agency specializing or experienced in travel for the handicapped.

If you power your own wheelchair, unaided by a companion, bring something to extend your reach. A rubber-tipped teacher's pointer is good, a collapsible one is ideal. You need the pointer to reach elevator buttons, some light switches, and the closet rod and higher storage space in your cabin, even in some wheelchair-accessible rooms.

Make sure that dining rooms, rest rooms, showrooms, lounges, promenade decks, and the pool areas are wheelchair accessible. Determine whether gangways are accessible at ports. If tenders are used, will you be able to board in a wheelchair? In the dining room, will your table accommodate your wheelchair, or must you shift to a regular chair? If you cannot shift yourself, will you need a companion to help or are crew members allowed to assist? Can crew members help in your cabin and elsewhere aboard ship? Must you sign a medical waiver or produce documentation from your physician to obtain a wheelchair-accessible cabin? No matter how dependable your travel agent is, call the cruise line and double-check all important arrangements yourself.

Partially Ambulatory Disabled

If you use a wheelchair sometimes but can walk a little way, you will do fine on most ships large enough to have elevators. You will be able to get around your cabin and into the bathroom on foot. A collapsible wheelchair will enable you to cover longer distances. Crutches are iffy on ships, walkers better, but the safest way for the partially ambulatory to get around is in a wheelchair.

Larger ships have wide passageways, spacious public areas, and, most likely, an adequate number of elevators. Smaller ships often have tight passageways, steep stairs, and no elevators. Older vessels may have bulkhead doors with raised thresholds, blocked passageways with steps to the next level, and no elevator access to some decks.

Choose a cabin near the elevators. Book one with a shower (with metal chair or stool); many ships' bathtubs are higher and/or deeper than yours at home. Ask whether the cabin's bath has sturdy hand grips.

Consider booking an itinerary on calmer water, such as Alaska's Inside Passage or the Mississippi River. If you cruise on the open sea, choose a cabin on a lower deck in the vessel's center; this area is least susceptible to motion.

Passengers with Sight and/or Hearing Impairments

Most people with sight or hearing impairments travel with a nondisabled companion. Regardless, be sure to inform your cabin steward of your disability. In the event of an emergency, he should know to check your cabin immediately to make sure your companion is with you and to assist you if the aide isn't. If you are hearing-impaired, your steward should be given permission to enter your cabin in an emergency if there is no response to a knock.

Passengers with Diet Restrictions

Diet restrictions usually pose no problem on cruise ships. The galley will prepare meals to your specification and serve them at regular seatings in the dining room. Orthodox religious practitioners who must verify that a meal is prepared in a certain way should ask whether such verification will be possible. All lines request advance notice—two to three weeks—for specific needs. We provide this information under cruise lines' Standard Features. Also, cruise line brochures detail procedures for diet requests.

Families with Younger Children

Although some lines are equipped to handle younger children, we do not recommend cruising for kids younger than age five. Lines that really want family business advertise that fact. If you have young children and want them to enjoy the cruise, but do not necessarily want to tend to them 24 hours a day yourself, book with a line specializing in family cruises. Its ships will have play areas and supervised activities and sometimes a separate swimming pool for children. Best of all, the chaperoned children's program provides a respite from constant parenting. If, however, your rich Aunt Hattie wants to treat you and your little nippers to a luxury cruise, don't decline because the ship's brochure doesn't picture kids. Little ones on essentially adult cruises fare reasonably well. Although planned activities may be few or none for them, your children will revel in the adventure of being at sea.

Usually, the children's center will be a sort of seagoing day care or in-cabin baby-sitting. If both in-cabin baby-sitting and all-meal room service are available, you've got it made. Sign up for second seating in the dining room, or go late if there is only one. Let the kids enjoy room service in the cabin, or take them to the buffet or informal dining area. Then turn the fed-and-scrubbed munchkins over to the sitter and head for the dining room. Of course, you can take your children to the dining room, but if they are age six or younger, once may be enough.

If your ship has a children's program, your kids will be on the go all the time. However, we've seen children who scarcely countenance their parents at home refuse to leave them and go to the children's center aboard ship. To

avoid this issue, before you leave home explain how things work and negotiate what time you will spend together and apart. If your children are too
young to negotiate such deals, save the family cruise for another year or put
the kids into the children's center and deal with any fallout.

CRUISING FOR CHILDREN

This chart includes only those cruise lines with facilities for children; for details, see
the line's profile in Part Two. Many lines not included on this chart accept children
and offer cruises appropriate for them, but have no special facilities for children.
Also, note that age limits vary from "no age restriction" to "no children younger
than age 18 permitted." Always check with the cruise line before making plans.

(R) Reduced third or fourth berth rate, regardless of age
(S) Seasonally

CRUISE LINE	Age Limit for Child Discount	Air/Sea Rate	Baby-sitting Available	Special Shore Excursions	Teen Center/Disco	Playroom/Youth Center	Youth Counselors
American Canadian Caribbean Line	No	Yes	No	Some	No	No	Some
Carnival	(R)	Yes	Yes	Some	Yes	Yes	Yes
Celebrity	(R)	Yes	Yes	Yes	Some	Yes	Yes
Costa	17	Yes	Yes	Some	Yes	Some	Yes
Crystal	12	Yes	Yes	No	Yes	Yes	Yes
Cunard	(R)	Yes	Yes	(S)	Some	Some	Some
Delta Queen	16	Yes	No	No	No	No	No
Disney	17	Yes	Yes	Yes	Yes	Yes	Yes
Holland America	18	Yes	Yes	Some	Yes	Some	Yes
Norwegian	(R)	Yes	Yes	Some	Yes	Yes	Yes
Princess	(R)	No	Yes	Some	Yes	Yes	Yes
Royal Caribbean	11	Yes	Yes	(S)	Most	Most	Yes
Royal Olympic	12	Yes	Yes	No	(S)	(S)	(S)

Consider accommodations: Cabins are much more confining than
children's homes or bedrooms. Your kids will size up your cabin in about
ten seconds and figure there is not much to do there. From that point,
they will be obsessed with running loose around the ship. Anticipate this
response. Set limits in advance about bedtime, naps, meals, and parental

private time, and plan for each day. Television, when available, is usually limited to a news channel, movies, and information about the ship and shore excursions. Therefore, bring games, books, and toys to keep the children reasonably content in the cabin. If you can afford it, putting the children in an adjoining cabin is best. If you buy kids their own cabin, the cruise line will usually include airfare in the deal. If you bunk the young ones in your cabin, you have to buy their airfare as an add-on. A few cruise lines offer a discount on a connecting cabin, where available, especially during low seasons.

Families with Teens

Teens do pretty well on cruises. They are old enough not to need constant supervision, will definitely eat their money's worth of food, and collect new experiences they can talk about back home. Teens are allowed to enjoy everything aboard except the casino and some lounges. On some ships, teens accompanied by parents are allowed in the disco and other adult areas. Family and midmarket ships often have clubs where teens can dance and arcades with Ping-Pong, pool, or electronic games.

A cruise is a totally new environment for children—some embrace it with gusto, eager to learn, to find every nook and cranny, but others are intimidated and need help. For the right kids, it's a fabulous, fun learning experience. With teens, as with younger kids, negotiate and set your limits before you leave home. Because teens can be messy and monopolize the bathroom, we double our recommendation that you get them an adjoining cabin. Finally, though we believe teens on their own are safe aboard ship, we suggest you keep them under tight rein ashore. If this is your first cruise and you have qualms about taking children, go without them and size up the situation. All of you might enjoy it more if you know the territory.

Additional Information

In both the cruise lines' Standard Features and the cruise ship profiles, we include a section on children's facilities. These references are a start. Also consult **Family Travel Times** (40 Fifth Avenue, New York, NY 10011; phone (888) 822-4FTT, **www.familytraveltimes.com**), an online publication of TWYCH (Travel With Your Children) that frequently reports on family cruises, down to the last playpen and high chair. Annual subscriptions are $39, which buys you access to six online issues.

A Word of Warning

One person's darling can be another person's pain in the neck. We have received a surprising number of complaints from readers about children on their cruises. However, most referred to cruises during holidays, spring break, and summer, when there can be 300 or more children aboard a ship. In such cases, even people who adore children might find their patience wearing thin if the children are rowdy and ill-behaved or if the cruise lines fail to supervise them adequately. As cruise popularity and family travel increase, the two converge with greater frequency. The simple fact is that cruising can be a wonderful family vacation.

If you do not want to cruise with children, avoid holiday periods, particularly on mass-market lines that promote family travel and cruise to the most popular Caribbean, Mexican, and Alaskan destinations. If, however, these are the only times you can travel (if you are a teacher, for example), search for ships that sail off the beaten track or focus on enrichment rather than entertainment. Finally, an experienced travel agent should be able to help you find the right ship—or the ones to avoid.

Shopping for and Booking Your Cruise

Gathering Information

Now that you have outlined your requirements and preferences, compare them against the profiles of the cruise lines and ships described in this book. After you identify several lines that seem to meet your needs, obtain their promotional brochures through a travel agent or by contacting the lines directly using phone numbers and addresses in the profiles.

A travel agent specializing in cruises or selling them routinely can be a good source of information. Many agents can provide firsthand information about ships and lines. Also, many will put you in touch with clients willing to share thoughts and opinions. However, always understand from a self-interest perspective that cruise lines pay the agent a commission on every cruise the agent sells.

In addition to obtaining promotional materials, buy several Sunday newspapers: (1) one in a primary geographic market for the cruise industry, including New York, Chicago, Dallas, or Los Angeles; (2) your local paper; and (3) the paper of the largest city within 200 miles of your home. The travel sections in these papers indicate where the deals are. If you live in a medium-sized city like Charlotte, North Carolina, for example, you may uncover cruise deals in the Atlanta paper that beat anything in your local paper.

Finally, here are some helpful magazines, periodicals, and Internet sites: **Cruise Critic** on America Online (access with keyword: Cruise Critic); **www.cruisemates.com**, written and hosted by Anne Campbell, former author of *Fielding's Guide to Worldwide Cruises* and a veteran cruise writer; and **www.cruise411.com.** Their candid ship reviews are based on firsthand experience. They also have cruise line information, news updates, information on promotions, and best deals. AOL's Cruise Critic also has a "Caribbean Ports of Call" feature by one of this book's authors, Kay Showker. Another website, at **www.cruiseopinion.com**, offers lots of detailed ship evaluations written by passengers who submit monthly reviews.

Two other websites worth checking out are found at **mytravelco.com** and **www.i-cruise.com**. Mytravelco.com offers virtual tours of many ships, while i-cruise.com has a "beat your best price" feature. All of the sites listed sell cruises in addition to providing comparative information.

Cruise Week (Lehman Publishing, 910 Deer Spring Lane, Wilmington, NC 28409; (800) 593-8252; fax: (910) 790-3976; cruiseweek@ aol.com; **www.cruise-week.com**), a two-page weekly industry newsletter available by fax or e-mail, is produced by an editor who has reported on the industry for many years. It's directed to the travel industry, but consumers interested in tracking news about cruising will find it a timely resource. Annual subscription: $125.

Cruise Reports (5 Washington Street, Morristown, NJ 07960, call (973) 605-2442, fax (973) 605-2722); cruises@cruise-report.com; **www.cruise-report.com**) offers evaluations and firsthand comments by travel agents. Annual subscriptions of 12 e-mailed issues cost $50.

Cruise Travel magazine (P.O. Box 342, Mt. Morris, IL 61054; (800) 877-5893) is unabashedly rah-rah cruising and contains no critical content, but it's a good source of information. Its six issues a year contain ads from dozens of cruise discounters, consolidators, and cruise specialty travel agents. Subscriptions run about $18 a year in the United States, $40 in Canada.

Ocean & Cruise News (P.O. Box 92, Stamford, CT 06904; (203) 329-2787; **www.oceancruises.com**) reports on the industry and reviews a different ship in each issue. A much-publicized annual evaluation of lines and ships in the February issue is based on subscribers' votes, which tend to reflect seasoned cruisers' preferences for established lines. Subscriptions are $30 annually for 12 issues for U.S. readers ($36 elsewhere).

Porthole (P.O. Box 469066, Escondido, CA 92046; (800) 776-PORT; **www.porthole.com**) is by far the most attractive and lively magazine on cruises. It offers a range of interesting articles by knowledgeable writers. Annual subscription: $19.95.

TravLtips magazine (P.O. Box 580188, Flushing, New York, 11358-0218; (718) 939-2400; info@travltips.com; **travltips.com**) is a good bet if you are interested in freighter cruising, expedition cruising, or bargain around-the-world cruising on conventional cruise ships; it's published bimonthly. Subscriptions are $20 per year.

In addition, you can check out the previously mentioned websites found at **i-cruise.com, mytravelco.com,** and **cruise.com.** All three provide reviews, deck plans, tips for singles, and, of course, hot deals.

How to Read a Cruise Line Brochure

Cruise brochures are very elaborate. Because they contain so much information, we offer a systematic approach to evaluating and understanding their contents.

Look at the Pictures

All photos in the brochures have been carefully chosen to excite the people for whom the cruise line tailors its product. If you identify with the activities depicted, this may be a good cruise line for you. Pay attention to ages of the people shown.

Sizing up the Ships

Look at the ships. Are they too big, too small, about right, or you don't care as long as they float? Most brochures also contain a deck-by-deck schematic of the ship. Concentrate first on the ship's layout, looking for features important to you. If you work out, look at the relative size of the exercise room and try to find a photo of it so you can check the equipment. If you have mobility problems, look for elevators. Because upper decks offer the best views at sea, note inside and outdoor public areas, particularly on the top two and promenade decks.

Itineraries

Read the itineraries, making preliminary selections on where and how long you want to cruise. On what days and at what times does the cruise begin and end? Do these work for you? Focus on a couple of cruises. Read the itineraries, observing how much time the ship spends at sea and in port, how much cruising is during waking hours, and whether the number of ports and the time allowed to see them suits you.

For practice, let's look at a ten-day itinerary from Copenhagen to London/Tilbury.

Day	Date	Port	Arrive	Depart
Sunday	June 4	Copenhagen		6 p.m.
Monday	June 5	Cruising		
Tuesday	June 6	Helsinki	8 a.m.	6 p.m.
Wednesday	June 7	St. Petersburg	8 a.m.	
Thursday	June 8	St. Petersburg	6 p.m.	
Friday	June 9	Stockholm	4 p.m.	
Saturday	June 10	Stockholm	3 p.m.	
Sunday	June 11	Cruising		
Monday	June 12	Oslo	8 a.m.	5 p.m.
Tuesday	June 13	Cruising		
Wednesday	June 14	London/Tilbury	7 a.m.	

The cruise sails at 6 p.m. Sunday, allowing several options. Because most flights from the United States to Europe depart in the late afternoon and evening, a person living in the eastern United States could work most or all of Friday and catch an evening flight to Copenhagen, arriving Saturday morning. They would have until about 3:30 p.m. Sunday to rest and see Copenhagen. Alternately, they could fly out Saturday evening and arrive in Copenhagen on Sunday morning with four or five hours at their disposal before boarding. A third possibility, of course, would be to arrive before Saturday and enjoy a leisurely weekend. The first day at sea is a wonderful start, providing a chance to catch up on jet lag and explore the ship.

This cruise calls on four ports, not counting ports of origination and termination. This is fewer than average for a ten-day cruise, but all are major cities. The itinerary gives lots of time in each port. In St. Petersburg and Stockholm, the ship anchors overnight. If you're interested in St. Petersburg and Stockholm, this works well. If not, it's a long time in port. Full days (8 a.m. to 5 or 6 p.m.) are planned in Helsinki and Oslo. In total, the cruise is 229 hours, of which 153 hours (67%) are at sea and 76 hours (33%) are in port. However, only 71 hours of the 153 hours at sea are during waking hours (7 a.m. to 10 p.m.).

Rates

Flip to the rate charts to determine whether the cruises you like fall roughly within your budget. We do mean roughly: Almost nobody pays the brochure rates. Brochure rates are helpful only in providing a base for calculating discounts. You should anticipate paying 25% to 50% less depending on the line, ship, itinerary, season, and market condition. We describe available discounts in "How to Get the Best Deal on a Cruise."

Most lines present their fares in a chart like the one below for Royal Caribbean International Cruise Line's *Rhapsody of the Seas'* Western Caribbean seven-night itinerary.

The fares are per-person, based on two persons sharing a cabin (double occupancy). If the per-person fare for a cabin on Main Deck, Category F, in fall is $1,949, you and your spouse or companion would pay $3,898 ($1,949/2) for the cabin. For singles supplement, see "Singles" in this chapter for a rate explanation.

As many as five persons may share a cabin, depending on its configuration. Rates for the third, fourth, and fifth persons are deeply discounted, sometimes as much as 66% off the double-occupancy fare. Let's say Tom, Ed, John, and Earl are willing to share a "B" Deck, Category I cabin that goes for $1,799 per person double occupancy. The line charges the double-occupancy price ($1,799) for two of the four men, and the third/fourth person rate of $999 for the remaining two. Thus, the tab for all four:

Person 1	$1,799	Cruise Only
Person 2	$1,799	Cruise Only
Person 3	$999	Cruise Only
Person 4	$999	Cruise Only
Total	$5,596	

Usually, for cruise lines that bundle airfare to the port into the total price of the cruise, the airfare is normally included only for the two persons paying the double-occupany rate. The cruise line will arrange airfare, often at a discounted rate, for the third and fourth persons.

If Tom, Ed, John, and Earl want to split the cost of their Royal Caribbean cruise equally, here's the way the finances average out:

| Cruise fare for all four guys | $5,596 |
| Final cost per person | $1,399 |

Because most cabins are small with tiny bathrooms and little storage, we do not recommend cruising with more than two persons in a cabin unless your budget dictates it. If you do elect to cruise with extra people in your cabin, select your roommates with care. Make sure everyone is compatible regarding smoking, snoring, and sleeping hours. Most of all, be tolerant and bring your sense of humor. Start with a cruise in a warm clime, when you can spend more time on deck than in your cabin. One reason a cabin on a Caribbean or Mexico cruise is much less significant than one on a chillier itinerary relates to the amount of time you are likely to spend in your cabin. In the Caribbean, you do little more than sleep and change clothes there. Finally, pack light.

RHAPSODY OF THE SEAS RATE CHART

Holiday cruises—add $250 to special holiday cruises.
Single Guarantee Program guests add $500.

Stateroom Categories		List Price Per Person	Book Early and Save Prices Starting From
Balcony Staterooms/Suites	R	$7,349	$4,049
	A	$5,099	$2,549
	AA	$5,099	$2,549
	B	$3,599	$1,749
	C	$2,699	$1,449
	D	$2,399	$1,249
Ocean View	FF	$2,249	$1,199
	F	$1,949	$979
	H	$1,879	$929
	I	$1,799	$899

RHAPSODY OF THE SEAS **RATE CHART** *(continued)*			
Interior	J	$1,729	$859
	K	$1,649	$809
	L	$1,629	$799
	M	$1,599	$789
	N	$1,569	$779
	O	$1,549	$769
	P	$1,519	$759
	Q	$1,499	$749
3rd / 4th Guests		**$999**	**$499**

Accommodations in categories R–D have a private bathroom, vanity area, closed-circuit TV, radio, and phone.

Accommodations in categories FF–Q have two twin beds that convert to a queen size, private bathroom, vanity area, closed-circuit TV, radio, and phone.

Rates include port charges. Air transportation and certain taxes and fees are additional.

All rates quoted in U.S. dollars, per person, double occupancy.

Sailing Dates

Check the sailing dates of cruises that interest you, looking for those compatible with your schedule. Check dates around these to see if a slight shift puts you into a lower-priced season.

Cabin Category and Ship Deck Plans

Now look at the types of cabins available. Many brochures include floor plans for several types of cabins showing their size, configuration, and placement of furniture and fixtures. Some brochures include color photographs of cabins.

Although some upscale lines offer only suites, most ships provide a choice of cabins. The top of the line—usually on the top decks—are the palatial owner's suite or royal suite, comparable to the presidential suite in a good hotel. Next are a small number of one- or two-bedroom suites, followed by a larger number of mini- or demisuites. Suites, particularly on newer ships, often have verandas. After these deluxe accommodations come standard cabins, which account for about 85% of accommodations on most ships. Now, on more of the new, large ships, even some standard cabins have verandas. Outside standard cabins with a window are generally preferred to inside standard cabins without windows, but they are more expensive. Usually, the higher the deck, the higher the cabin's price.

Standard cabins on ships built since 1988 generally are the same throughout the ship. Windows may decrease in size as you descend from deck to deck. Although the Royal Caribbean International chart does not specify whether the window view is obstructed, this information is provided on most rate charts.

Cabins toward the middle of the ship are considered more desirable than cabins on either end, because center cabins are closer to stairs and elevators and are less affected by the ship's back-and-forward motion (pitching). The side-to-side motion (rolling) is more pronounced the higher you go and is felt least on lower decks. The most stable cabins are at the water line near the center of the lower passenger decks—the best cabins for travelers prone to motion sickness. But the fact is, on large cruise ships, you will feel very little motion of the sea, except perhaps on the highest decks.

Before selecting a cabin category, study the ship's deck plan. Normally, the schematic is near scale and is color-coded for cabin category. Checking the Royal Caribbean rate chart with the ship schematic for *Rhapsody of the Seas,* you see the most expensive accommodations are on the Bridge Deck, the fourth-highest of ten decks. They are centrally located mini-suites with verandas, and the Bridge Deck is removed from noise of the galley, engines, lounges, pool area, and showroom.

Check the drawing for decks where passengers walk or jog. Avoid cabins beneath jogging tracks or promenades. Similarly, avoid cabins where the window overlooks a track or walkway. Pinpoint lounges, showrooms, the casino, discos, and other potentially noisy, late-night areas. Avoid cabins directly above or below them. Engine noise may be audible in lower-deck cabins toward the stern.

Though private verandas, or balconies, have become increasingly popular and affordable, not all balconies are created equal. Some are barely large enough for a chair, while others can accommodate a chaise lounge, a couple of chairs, and a table. Some balconies are covered, providing both shade and privacy, but others are open to the weather, not to mention the nosy gaze of passengers on higher decks. Balconies on the bow face forward and are often subject to a great deal of wind when the ship is under way. Stern balconies on the other hand offer more protection and additionally provide sweeping views to either side of the ship.

Even veteran cruisers have difficulty gleaning this information from a deck plan, but a knowledgeable travel agent knows how to check out these details when you ask. Analyze what you get for a few dollars more or less. In the chart above, for example, an outside cabin on "B" Deck is only $50 more than an inside cabin on the higher Bridge Deck.

A Preliminary Look at Discounts and Incentives

You should now know whether you are interested in a cruise offered in the brochure you are reading. If you are, the next step is to check the line's price incentives and discounts.

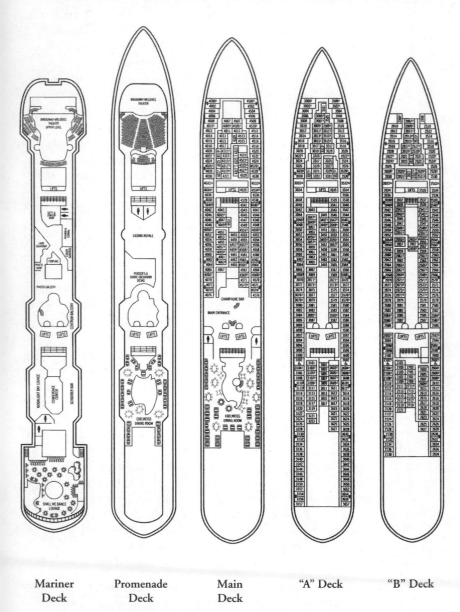

Mariner Deck   Promenade Deck   Main Deck   "A" Deck   "B" Deck

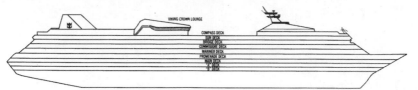

Length: 915'• Beam: 105.6'• Draft: 25'• Gross tonnage: 75,000 tons • Passenger capacity: 2,000 double occupancy • Total staff: 765 • Cruising speed: 22 knots

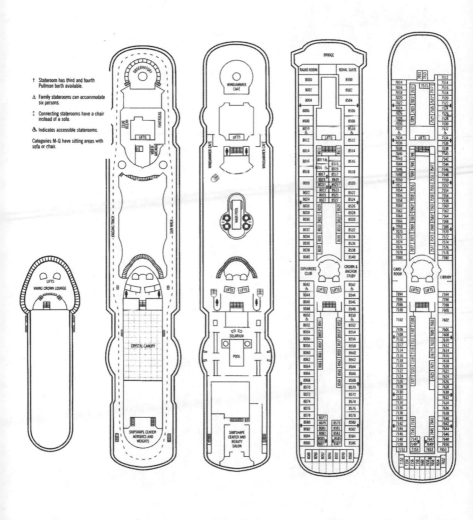

† Stateroom has third and fourth
Pullman berth available.

Δ Family staterooms can accommodate
six persons.

‡ Connecting staterooms have a chair
instead of a sofa.

♿ Indicates accessible staterooms.

Categories M-Q have sitting areas with
sofa or chair.

Viking
Crown Deck

Compass
Deck

Sun
Deck

Bridge
Deck

Commodore
Deck

PRINCESS CRUISES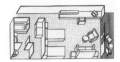

MINISUITE WITH
PRIVATE BALCONY

(Category A)

Large bedroom with twin beds, which make up into a comfortable queen-size bed. Sitting room area and private balcony for entertaining. TV. Spacious closets. Refrigerator. Bath with tub and shower.

OUTSIDE DOUBLE WITH
PRIVATE BALCONY

(Category BA, BB, and BD)

Two lower beds, which make up into a comfortable queen-size bed. TV. Spacious closet. Refrigerator.

OUTSIDE OR
INSIDE DOUBLE

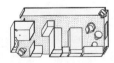

(Category CC, C, D, EE, E, FF, F,
GG, G, H, I, J, K, L, and M)

Outside staterooms have a picture window. Two lower beds, which make up into a comfortable queen-size bed. Many staterooms with two upper berths. Television. Spacious closet. Refrigerator. GG has a queen-size bed. G has one lower bed, one upper berth, and portholes.

Although the cruise market continues to grow, supply (the number of ships and cabins) has historically run several years ahead of demand, with more cabins to fill than people to fill them. With dozens of new ships coming on-line in the recent past and near future, competition will put pressure on cruise lines to cut deals to keep their ships filled, and a buyer's market will prevail.

Incentives and discounts offered in the lines' brochures are varied. First, the line prices according to times of greatest demand. High season is most expensive, followed by shoulder season, then low season. Savings may not be spectacular, judging from the brochure prices.

Remember: Fares in the brochure are base prices to which discounts are applied. Also, ships are less crowded and cabin upgrades more readily available during low and shoulder seasons.

After studying seasonal discounts, check early-booking discounts. Lines offer fairly substantial discounts to travelers who are willing to book six months to a year ahead. The line has use of your money in advance and gets critical information on whether a particular cruise is filling. Early-booking discounts commonly are 15–45% off the seasonal rate or a two-for-one deal. Either way, early-booking incentives are generally the largest discounts given directly by the lines. You get other benefits, too: your choice of cabin, the most direct air routing, and your dining-room seating preference (if the line bases seating on first-come, first-served). That's the kind of information available in fine print or from an experienced travel agent.

Cruise lines also may offer cabin upgrades, credit for shipboard purchases, receptions with the captain, or a couple of nights at a hotel at the originating or terminating port. In addition to early-booking discount, almost all lines offer other discounts (often up to 50%) to repeat passengers. Many discounts from cruise lines, travel agents, wholesalers, and consolidators never appear in the cruise lines' basic brochures. For help in finding them, read the section "How to Get the Best Deal on a Cruise."

Round-trip Airfare

Unless you live within driving distance of your cruise's originating port, you will require transportation to it. Until recently, most lines included air transportation in the cruise cost and promoted it as "free air." But times are changing.

What Happened to "Free" Air?

First, check the cruise brochure to determine whether prices include air transportation. When lines include air transportation in their packages, they agree to fly you round-trip from specific "gateway" cities. These gateway cities vary among cruise lines but usually include all major U.S.

and Canadian cities and many smaller cities. If air transportation is part of the cruise package but your gateway city is especially far from the port, an air supplement—extra charge—may be levied.

Until recently, air/sea packages were touted as all-inclusive, with "free" airfare. Nothing, of course, was ever free. Cruise lines built air transportation into the cruise cost and called it "free." By buying in advance and in large volume, lines could negotiate big discounts on airfares. These discounts enabled the cruise lines to offer complete vacation packages—the cruise with airfare—for a good price. Since 1997, however, cruise lines have increasingly published their rates as "cruise-only" fares and sell the air transportation as an add-on. The reason for the change is that demand for air travel has increased and airlines have radically reduced the availability and size of discounts for cruise lines. Even in a post-9/11 world, airlines can fill their planes without offering reduced fares for weekend flights to major ports. Today, cruise lines can obtain the discounts required for a good air/sea package only by buying airlines' least desirable flights, including late-night flights, circuitous routes, and multiple stops. Luxury cruise lines are the exceptions, as they continue to offer air-inclusive packages to ensure that their customers get the most direct and convenient flights.

At the same time, passengers often are discovering they can get better airfares and routing on their own. Plus, they receive their tickets well in advance. Often with air/sea packages, airlines issue tickets only at the last minute (to distribute passengers equally among available flights). The practice panics cruise passengers near departure who wonder where their tickets are. As it happens, cruise lines accumulate reservations for several months before contacting the airlines and nailing down flight itineraries and seats. Standard practice is to advise you of your air itinerary 30–45 days prior to sailing (Princess has a program called Flight Choice where flight notification is made 60 days in advance). Understand, however, that we're only talking about flight *information*. Actual ticketing does not begin until about 30 days from your sailing date, and your tickets might not arrive until a week or two before you walk out of the door. The process affords the cruise line maximum flexibility but vastly increases the probability of you receiving an inconvenient itinerary with little time left to make changes. As a kicker, you may be surprised to discover that making your reservations well in advance doesn't mean that you'll get one of the better flight itineraries. A few lines give priority to early bookers, with flight itineraries based on the "seniority" of cruise reservations that are paid in full. With many other lines, it matters not whether you booked eight months or eight weeks ahead—you'll get what's available at the time the cruise line finally books the air travel.

If the air itinerary provided by the cruise line is not acceptable, you can request a change or particular routing through your travel agent. Many cruise lines maintain "Air Deviation" desks to handle requests from passengers who want to change their assigned routing. Changes can cost $35–$100 (as if you changed a ticket directly with an airline), and an additional air supplement may be charged if no seats are available in your designated airfare category. So you ask, how bad can flight itineraries arranged by the cruise line be? A California couple was ushered off their ship and shuttled to the San Juan, Puerto Rico airport at 9:30 a.m. for a flight home that departed at 6 p.m. Following a cruise, a family of six were split up with four of the party scheduled for an early flight and the other two reserved for a flight that arrived eight hours later.

If you purchase an air-inclusive cruise but elect to arrange (and pay for) your own air transportation, the cruise fare will be decreased because you are not using the air-travel part of the package. The amount to be lopped off your package price is shown at the bottom of the rate sheet as "Cruise-Only Travel Allowance." The allowance, for example, is about $250 on one-week Caribbean air/sea packages.

Passengers also are irritated because flights arranged by the cruise lines are often not eligible for frequent-flier mileage, and when they are, passengers or their travel agents must call the airline and provide frequent-flier numbers after the tickets have been issued.

Price and itineraries, however, are not the only considerations in buying air from the cruise line. When you buy the line's air add-on or an air-inclusive cruise, transfers are included. The cruise line will meet you at the airport and transfer you to the ship. Likewise, at the end of the cruise, the line will return you to the airport.

When you purchase your air transportation independently or if you use frequent-flier awards, you can usually buy airport transfers from the cruise lines. Carnival, for example, offers one-way and round-trip transfers, which must be booked 14 days in advance; price varies with location. Without such an arrangement, you must set up your own transfers. This seems complicated, but a travel agent can handle such details for you—and we advise you to let them. Be aware that at cruise's end only, some lines provide this transportation service regardless whether you bought your air through them.

When a line arranges your air transportation, it also arranges for your luggage to go directly to the ship. Once you check your luggage at the departure airport, you usually won't see it again until it's delivered to your cabin. If the airline booked by the cruise line loses your luggage, the cruise line will get it to you (once it's recovered) even if the ship has sailed.

During busier times, cruise lines may fly you to the port city a day in advance and provide hotel accommodations. If you live in the western United States and are sailing from an eastern port, the cruise line may fly you to the port city on a late-night flight with arrival between midnight and 9 a.m. More considerate lines arrange hotel day rooms where you can rest before boarding your ship later in the day. Similar arrangements are sometimes made for Eastern passengers embarking on the West Coast and passengers on European or Asian cruises.

The line, when it puts you in a hotel, assumes responsibility for transporting you to the pier. If you are to be accommodated in a hotel before embarkation, pack an overnight bag; you may not have access to your luggage until you're aboard ship.

Most air transportation purchased through cruise lines is coach class. Your travel agent can arrange seat assignments, boarding passes, and upgrades (when available).

If you are cruising during autumn (excluding holiday periods) or when airfares are discounted in your city, or if you can reach the port on a discount airline (like Southwest), you may want to book your own air travel to save money. If you can book your flights at or near the cruise line's air allowance, you will be able to choose your airline, ensure a good flight itinerary, accrue frequent-flier miles, and receive your tickets well before your departure date.

If you choose the air-inclusive package or buy air transportation as an add-on, take these precautions:

1. Do your homework.   Ask the cruise line if preferred air itineraries are allocated according to reservations seniority (i.e., those who book earliest get the best itineraries). Also ask when your booked flight itinerary will be available. If the cruise line does not give priority to those who book early or does not provide flight information far enough in advance to make changes, book your own air.

2. Call early to reserve.   Remember that cruise lines contract for a specific number of seats for every cruise—when they're filled, the line has to scramble for additional ones. That's when you're likely to get a circuitous routing. But, to put this in perspective: The airline crunch comes at holiday times—Labor Day, Thanksgiving, Christmas, spring break through Easter—and can be exacerbated by bad weather. So, if you plan a cruise during a holiday period, arrange it early and save yourself a pile of headaches. As a veteran travel agent advised, "Passengers should seriously consider taking the air/sea package from the cruise line during the winter months, especially if they are flying from a cold-weather gateway. If there are weather- or equipment-related delays, the cruise line will help air/sea passengers get to the ship. If passengers have booked their own air, they are on their own if they miss the ship. Passengers who do their own air would also be well advised to purchase third-party travel insurance that covers trip interruption, delay, or cancellation due to weather- or equipment-related problems."

The travel agent's advice is valid, but only up to a point. The cruise line sees itself as merely an airline ticketing agent. As a matter of customer relations, many cruise lines will step in and assist a passenger who is delayed or misses the boat because of problems with flights that the cruise line booked. The salient point, however, is that the cruise line is under no obligation to help. If you read the terms and conditions of your Passage Contract, you'll almost immediately bump into language like the following: "Under no circumstances does [X Cruise Line's] responsibility extend beyond the ship. All arrangements made for the guests with independent contractors [such as airlines] are made soley for the convenience of the guest and are at the guest's risk." We'll explore the ramifications of this and related issues later under "When Things Go Wrong." For now, let us add that we recommend third party travel insurance whether you book air through the cruise line or not.

3. Ask your travel agent when you can expect your tickets. Most cruise brochures tell this in the fine print. If not, your travel agent will know from experience or can ask the cruise line. Normally, they arrive two to three weeks before departure. Smaller cruise lines generally deliver earlier than the big guys do.

4. Plan your route. If you have a specific route you want to fly to your departure port, tell your travel agent when you book or as soon as possible so that your plane tickets can be issued properly. If you receive tickets requiring layovers and a change of planes, have your agent contact the cruise line's Air Deviation desk.

How to Get the Best Deal on a Cruise

To get a good deal on a cruise, know the players and how the game is played. In the case of cruising, game rules pivot on the unalterable reality that a cruise is a time-sensitive product. If a cabin is not sold by sailing time, it loses all of its value. This makes selling cruises like playing "Beat the Clock." From the time a cruise is announced, the line is on a countdown to sell all the cabins. The immense expense of operating a cruise ship makes the selling a high-pressure, big-stakes endeavor.

For consumers, the time sensitivity is a major plus. Any time a dealer must make a sale or write off the inventory (empty cabins, in this case), wheeling and dealing are likely, and it almost always benefits the buyer. However, we emphasize that there's more to buying a cruise than its price. If you allow yourself to be influenced only by "getting the best deal," you are likely to end up on the wrong cruise.

Note that in American ports, it is no longer possible to show up at the dock, suitcase in hand, and negotiate a last-minute fare with the purser. For security reasons, cruise ships must submit passenger manifests to the FBI several days prior to departure.

The Players: Cruise Lines

Lines have sales offices and can sell cruises directly to consumers. But as many as 95% of all cruises are sold through travel agents or other players, and you usually get a better price by buying from them. To their credit, cruise lines are loyal to those who sell their product and won't usually undercut the prices available to them. Practically, the lines don't want the bother, plus it wouldn't be cost-effective. It costs cruise lines far more to maintain sales offices to serve the general public than it does to maintain a sales network through travel agencies and Internet sellers. Some sell directly to consumers on the Internet—not necessarily at a discount.

There's a lot confusion and acrimony in the cruise marketplace at the moment. Cruise lines offer lower prices to key accounts such as large, cruise-specialty mega-agencies, and major Internet giants such as Expedia, Travelocity, Orbitz, and Cruise411.com, to mention a few. The only way smaller, general-service travel agencies can compete is to lower prices to customers by sacrificing their commission. Carnival Cruise Line, saying that it "would rather have 35,000 people selling Carnival than 10," closed ranks with the little guys by offering the same prices to all of its accounts. Most other lines, however, continue to offer large operators preferential pricing. To gain an even greater advantage, the big sellers use their extensive resources to gobble up blocks of cabins at group rates and then resell the cabins one at a time to individual travelers. The smaller agencies are smacked a third time by the way the cruise lines handle "distressed inventory," i.e., cabins yet unsold as the sailing date for a cruise approaches. Once again, not unexpectedly, these bargain basement goodies are handed over to the line's big-volume accounts to move. Though most of us like to root for the underdog, it's tough to walk away from the great prices offered by larger sellers. It's worth remembering, however, that the big guys usually can't compete with a good hometown brick-and-mortar agent when it comes to service, accessibility, and peace of mind.

The Players: Wholesalers and Mega-Sellers
Wal-Mart founder Sam Walton taught Americans that the more of something you buy, the lower the price should be. Businesspeople call it buying in quantity or volume discounting. In cruising, travel wholesalers and mega-sellers are volume buyers. Booking well in advance, they buy large numbers of cabins on specific cruises with the intention of reselling the cabins at a profit. Advance purchasing and volume discounts, coupled with the fact that the cruise lines do not have to pay commissions, allows them to buy at prices substantially below what an individual could obtain. Some cabins that go unsold can be returned to the cruise company by a certain date; others are bought on a nonreturnable basis. In the latter case, the wholesaler or mega-seller absorbs the costs of any cabins that aren't sold. The biggest cruise discounts available to any player go to those who buy cabins in bulk on a nonreturnable basis. Wholesalers sell to travel agents and, often, like mega-sellers, directly to consumers. If the wholesaler sells a cruise through a travel agency, then the wholesaler pays the agent a commission.

Note that these players generally deal with lines having large ships, or they offer the best deals on a limited number of ships and lines. If they spread themselves too thinly over the spectrum of cruises, they diminish their clout with specific lines. Remember: It's in the wholesaler's or mega-seller's interest to steer you to ships where they get the best deal. That may or may not be in your best interest.

The Players: Travel Agents

Travel agents act as sales representatives of the cruise lines. Unlike wholesalers and consolidators, they don't buy cabins. Instead, they sell from the line's inventory on commission. Like cruise lines and wholesalers, however, agents earn the most when they sell in volume.

Some full-service travel agencies specialize in cruises, whereas others are cruise-only agencies, selling nothing but cruises and cruise-related travel. The latter sell so many cabins for certain lines that they earn "override commissions"—a commission on a commission. There is usually a volume threshold where the override kicks in. Some general travel agencies and independent agencies cash in on override commissions by joining a consortium—a group of agencies that pool their sales to receive the overrides.

To make the most in commissions and overrides, agents push selected cruise lines, known in the industry as preferred suppliers. If the line that interests you is among your agent's preferred vendors, great. If not, your agent will probably try to interest you in a line with which the agency has such an arrangement.

Because most cruises are sold by travel agents, it is critically important for cruise lines to develop extensive systems of loyal travel agents. Competition among cruise lines to influence agents is so heated that consumers sometimes become pawns in a marketing chess game.

Over the years, for example, Holland America has awarded its agencies bonus points redeemable for chocolate, picnic lunches, dinners in local restaurants, or any number of other choice perks Such incentives may influence agents' recommendations and narrow consumers' choices. These are all reputable cruise lines, but they are not necessarily a good fit for all of an agent's customers. Good agents place their client's needs and preferences first, but some agents go for the largest commissions and the most goodies.

Some agents sacrifice part of their commission or override to make a cruise more affordable to a good customer. Some agencies selling cruises in volume take lower commissions to underprice other agencies. In many locations, competition among agencies for cruise business is as keen as it is among cruise lines, partiularly with the proliferation of cruise-only agencies and large Internet sellers. And now with airlines decreasing agents' commissions, the competition for cruise business has grown even hotter.

In the final analysis, buyer beware. Protect yourself best by developing a long-term relationship with a knowledgeable travel agent who works to put you on the cruise that's right for you.

Helping Your Travel Agent Help You   When you call a travel agent, ask whether he or she has cruised. Firsthand experience is invaluable. If the answer is no, find another agent or be prepared to give your agent copious direction. Ask who your agent's preferred vendors are. Just asking that question will tell the agent you are a savvy buyer. Compare the agent's recommendations with information in this guide. Request permission to contact other clients who have been on the cruise line recommended, and ask your friends. Someone you know may have sailed on the line. Also check the independent cruise websites listed earlier under "Gathering Information." These sites feature cruise reviews from both travel writers and the general public.

To help your travel agent obtain the best possible deal, do the following things:

1. Determine from brochures, friends' recommendations, the Internet, and this book where and when you want to cruise, which lines offer the kind of cruise that most appeals to you, and how much you can spend.

2. Check cruise ads in the Sunday travel section of your local newspaper and compare them to ads in the newspapers of a key cruising market (New York, Philadelphia, Los Angeles, Phoenix, Dallas, Chicago, Boston, Washington, or Atlanta) near you. Look for deals that fit your plans and that include a line you like. Also, read ads in specialty magazines, such as *Cruise Travel,* and check out Internet sites selling discounted cruises.

3. Call consolidators or retailers (including Internet sites) whose ads you have collected. Ask about their offers, but do not book your trip with them directly.

4. Tell your agent about cruises you find, and ask if he or she can match or beat the price. The newspapers' deals will probably be a good benchmark against which to compare alternatives proposed by your agent. Be aware that promotional ads are often bait to get your attention. The "lead" price probably applies to a limited number of cabins on a specific sailing. This element is probably the trickiest part of obtaining the best deal. Every ship has 6–20 categories of cabins. Often, unless you can pinpoint the date, itinerary, and cabin category being advertised, it may be hard to know whether you are getting a good deal. Nobody said this was easy.

5. Choose among options uncovered by you and your travel agent. Whatever option you elect, have your agent book it. It may be

commissionable (at no additional cost to you) and will provide the agent some return on the time invested on your behalf. Also, your agent should be able to help you verify the quality and integrity of the deal.

How the Game Is Played: The Sales Countdown

Cruise lines work well in advance to schedule cruises and develop promotional brochures. It is essential to roll out marketing campaigns quickly to avoid panic sales as sailing dates near.

Most itineraries and dates are announced 10–14 months in advance. Particularly attractive dates on popular ships and itineraries sell out quickly. Likewise, cruises to seasonal destinations like Alaska fill fast. The highest- and lowest-priced cabins sell out first. Usually the last cruises to fill are low- and shoulder-season cruises to year-round areas. Many consumers used to wait for last-minute discounts available when cruise lines hit the panic button. The lines finally wised up, reasoning that early-booking discounts could generate cash flow and indicate sales prospects for each cruise. Although some distress selling continues, cruise lines are learning to control the inventory more efficiently. Now, natural disasters, political crises, and other sudden events beyond the cruise lines' control (such as the terrorist attacks of 9/11) are likely to cause fire sales.

Escalating Base Rate Model

To see how this works, let's examine a pricing model adopted by several prominent cruise lines. When the cruise is announced, the line advertises a base fare, discounted from the brochure figure by, say, 40%. The line warrants that the discounted base fare may increase as the countdown progresses, but will never be lower. Therefore, a consumer who books a November cruise in the preceding April would pay less than a passenger who books in June. That passenger, in turn, would pay less than someone booking in August, and so on.

This strategy allows the line and the travel agent to tell the customer that "this cruise will never be cheaper than today." The customer knows that the rate may rise, but will never be lower. The line can maintain the discounted rate if the ship is filling slowly, or raise it incrementally as the cruise approaches being sold out. We call this the escalating base rate model.

Identifying the pricing model is useful because then it's easier to understand what the cruise line does to nudge the ship to capacity. Pay attention: What the cruise line tells the customer is that the base rate will never be cheaper than today. That's very different from telling the customer the base rate is the deepest discount available.

In practice, cruise lines operate two pricing systems. Primary is the escalating base rate system. If the cruise sells to near capacity, only that system will be employed. If sales lag behind expectations, however, the line goes to its separate and collateral model: the special situations system.

Special Situations System

Special situations initiatives—usually time-limited and tightly targeted efforts for boosting sales—run concurrently with and independently of the escalating base rate system. Examples of such initiatives include a deeply discounted senior citizen's rate, a direct mailing to previous customers offering a big discount, a regional campaign, advertising last-minute bargains on the Internet, or a heavily discounted group sales overture to a large company for their executives or employees.

Each special situation initiative targets a carefully selected market segment. Initiatives may run sequentially or concurrently but usually are short-lived and end when the cruise sells out. What is really important about special situation initiatives is that the discount offered might be much greater than the base rate discount. If you can locate such an initiative, you may have found the lowest possible fare. If the special is advertised in Atlanta and you live in Buffalo, the package's air component will be useless to you. However, if you can buy the cruise-only part of the special and arrange affordable airfare from Atlanta, you've got a deal.

A common special situations approach is for the cruise line to join forces with specific travel agents or Internet sellers. Like travel agents who have preferred suppliers, cruise lines have preferred retailers. When a cruise is not selling to expectations, the line will enlist its favorite big-volume agencies to help move the remaining cabins. Because the line is anxious to sell the cabins, it develops promotions with these agents featuring extra-deep discounts and special incentives, such as cabin upgrades or discounted air add-ons. Many preferred agencies and websites sell cruises only and field hundreds of calls daily. If they have an especially juicy deal to offer, they can sell lots of cabins fast. Big-volume, cruise-only agencies advertise in magazines, including *Cruise Travel, Travel & Leisure,* and *Condé Nast Traveler,* and in large-market newspapers.

The Dump Zone

In the cruise marketplace, anything can happen. Some lines are either unequipped to nudge sales effectively or just aren't very good at it. Sometimes, lines expert in special situations campaigns don't fill their cruises. The upshot is that a goodly number of empty cabins may be sold at distress prices during the final eight weeks before sailing, especially in the off-season.

When time is short, agents and cruise lines know it is much easier and less complicated to sell a cruise to someone who doesn't require air transportation to the port. Florida is a huge market for late-breaking deals because of its large population of retirees and its proximity to ports. Major ports on the Pacific Coast and northeast likewise enjoy distress sales. If you live within easy driving distance of a major cruise ship port, you live in a dump zone. You are well situated to benefit from last-minute discounts, but you probably will have no choice in cabin selection or dining room seatings.

Discount Alphabet Soup

Before you shop for discounts, pick the cruise type that appeals to you. Once you start looking, don't get sidetracked by price. Instead, stay doggedly on the trail of the cruise that meets your needs. Never equate cheapest with best, but don't equate it with worst, either.

More than a dozen types of cruise discounts are commonly offered, other than seasonal discounts. As you encounter them, be aware that catchy marketing come-ons, like "two-for-one" or "sail three days free," aren't always what they seem. For example, a promotion advertising 50% off on the second person in the cabin (a frequent gimmick) is nothing more than 25% off for both (you probably could have done better with an early-booking discount). The best method for comparing rates, with or without discounts, is to calculate the per diem (per day) cost of your cruise vacation. Add the cruise cost and the airfare cost if it isn't included, plus taxes, port charges, and other applicable fees (transfers, etc.). Divide the total by the number of nights you will stay on the ship or in hotels included in the package.

Always compare apples to apples. Some cruising areas are more expensive. For example, Caribbean cruises should be compared to Caribbean cruises, not to Alaskan or Mediterranean cruises. Remember also that cruise lines are not created equal. Comparing a seven-day Carnival (Holiday Inn) cruise with a seven-day Silversea (Ritz-Carlton) cruise is meaningless. The cruise line profiles in Part Two will describe the differences.

Early-Booking Discounts

The more common of two kinds of early-booking discounts, the escalating base rate model, was described earlier. Each line has a different name for it. Escalating base rates are capacity-controlled and can be withdrawn or escalated without notice. Most of the major lines employ capacity-control pricing. The second type of early-booking discount is the flat cut-off date. If you book before the specified date, you get the discount. This, too, is common practice on selected itineraries. Passengers who pay in full by a specified date (as much as six to nine months before the cruise) receive a 10% to 20% discount. This discount is popular with Crystal, Silversea, and others in the luxury market.

Free Days

Passengers are offered 7 days' cruising for the price of 6, or 12 for the price of 10. Variations include complimentary days (with hotel) in the port city before and/or after the cruise, or "book a seven-day cruise and receive a free two- or three-day land package." Divide the double occupancy price by the number of days in the package to get a per diem cost for comparative purposes.

Two-for-One and Second Passenger Cruises Free

The deal is that two passengers cruise for the price of one, but some tricky math is involved. Pick your cruise and cabin category and find the double-occupancy price per person, air included, on the brochure's rate chart. The two-for-one price is this rate less the cruise line's air cost for one person from your gateway city.

Let's say the brochure's air-inclusive double-occupancy rate is $2,000. Have your travel agent call the cruise line to learn the round-trip airfare cost from your gateway city. This amount is subtracted from $2,000, and the remainder is your cruise-only cost for two persons. You must then make your own air arrangements or buy airfare from the cruise line as an add-on. Celebrity, Princess, Costa, and Holland America frequently offer two-for-one promotional fares. They work well if you can travel to and from the port on frequent-flier miles or by car. If you have to pay for air, however, comparative math might demonstrate that a discounted air/sea package is a better deal.

Two-for-one offers come and go with supply and demand. It's difficult to keep up with them. Normally, two-for-one fares are offered far in advance with a cut-off date to secure early bookings. They also might pop up on short notice. Such fire-sale fares aim to boost short-term sales and can be withdrawn at any time.

Flat Rates

This is an early-booking program in which every cabin in the ship, except probably the luxury accommodations, is sold for the same flat rates (one for inside cabins and one for outside cabins) on a first-come, first-served basis. The earlier you book, the nicer your cabin. Flat rates are usually cruise only, but airfare may be purchased as an add-on. Flat rates are frequently offered by Princess, Crystal, and Norwegian Cruise Lines.

X% Off Second Passenger in a Cabin

In this very common discount offered by many cruise lines, the first passenger pays the double-occupancy brochure rate and the second passenger gets 40% to 70% off. Some simple averaging demonstrates that this works out to a discount of 20% to 35% per passenger.

Reduced Rate Air Add-ons

If you purchase airfare from the cruise line separately (as opposed to included in the cruise price), that is an air add-on. Sometimes cruise lines will couple a discounted cruise-only rate (no airfare) with a very attractive air add-on. This usually occurs when the cruise line is able to negotiate an exceptionally good bulk airfare purchase with an airline from a specific gateway city. In essence, the cruise line is passing some of their savings along to the consumer. Typically, this kind of deal applies only to specific cities and is offered only for a short time. It often results from an airline's slow sales and its need to stimulate air travel from a particular area, as opposed to being a cruise line initiative.

Senior Citizen Discounts

Because seniors have traditionally been the backbone of the cruise market, they are often one of the first groups targeted for a discount program if a line is having difficulty filling a cruise. Usually the discount requires that one person sharing the cabin must be at least 55 years old. The size of discount varies, as does the inclusion of airfare.

Kids or Third/Fourth Passengers Go Free or at Reduced Rate

This discount is a fairly common for lines like Carnival, Disney, and Celebrity that target families and younger cruisers. Third and fourth persons or children sharing a cabin cruise free or at a substantial discount. Airfare for the third/fourth person or children is usually not included. Third/fourth person rates are generally part of a cruise line's basic rate structure (rather than promotional fares). They normally appear in the cruise line's brochure and are applicable year-round. Their promotional use might come into play seasonally by being reduced or waived altogether, perhaps in summer to stimulate family travel or in the shoulder season to stimulate first-timers to buy a cruise when three or four friends can share the cost.

Back-to-Back or Contiguous Segments Discounts

The seven-day cruise is the most popular product offered by any cruise line, as it suits the vast majority of people in terms of time and cost. However, there are people who have both the time and means for longer cruises. To satisfy both groups, the cruise lines have several choices. They may break longer cruises into seven-day segments, enabling a passenger to board in one port and depart from another. Or, they may offer two 7-day segments with different itineraries as one 14-day cruise, offering the second week at a greatly reduced price. For example, a ship departing from Miami that sails one week to the eastern Caribbean and the next week to the western Caribbean. In combining the two, the only port repeated in 14 days is Miami, the departure port. Throughout our cruise line profiles, we highlight ships whose itineraries lend themselves to this sort of coupling and who offer attractive discounts for the second segment.

Repositioning Cruises

When a cruise line moves a ship from one cruise area to another, this is called a repositioning cruise—and it represents one of the year's biggest bargains. Rather than dispatch a ship empty, lines sell their repositioning cruises; to attract as many passengers as possible, they offer them at cut-rate prices. The majority of repositioning cruises are in spring and fall when the great "migration" of ships occurs—mostly when ships that have spent the winter on Caribbean, Panama Canal, and Mexico cruises are dispatched to Alaska or to New England/Canada and/or Europe for the summer; and again in autumn, when these ships return.

Repositioning cruises with interesting and unusual itineraries, such as from the Caribbean to New England via the Eastern Seaboard, are unlikely to have as much of a discount as those with few ports of call, such as transatlantic crossings. Those with more days at sea, however, appeal to folks who really love to cruise and cherish having uninterrupted days or weeks at sea.

Group Discounts

Persons traveling together can almost always negotiate a group rate. The larger the group, the better the rate. For a big group, at least one free berth or cabin is customarily provided for the organizer. What constitutes a group varies among cruise lines, but eight or more persons traveling together and occupying at least four cabins generally can obtain a discount, extra amenities, or a cabin upgrade.

Standby Rates

Lines may offer deeply discounted standby rates for specific itineraries and sailing dates. Normally, you rank your ship, departure, and cabin preferences and submit them to the line with a deposit. If your preferred date is available, the line notifies your travel agent at least 30 days in advance. If you are offered your first choice, the deposit is nonrefundable. Airfare is additional.

Cabin Upgrades

Four basic ways to get a cabin upgrade are:

1. **Advertised or Unadvertised Specials** Usually publicized only to travel agents, upgrade programs give them a powerful selling tool. Upgrades apply to specific sailings and can be guaranteed by the agent and line at time of booking. Such specials allow consumers to buy the cheapest fare and be upgraded from one to five cabin levels.

2. **Soft Sailing Upgrades** A soft sailing refers to a cruise that is likely to depart at substantially less than full capacity. Booking the least expensive cabin category on a low- or shoulder-season cruise offers the best opportunity for receiving an upgrade. Early booking an inside cabin on a ship with few inside cabins (study the ship's deck plans) might result in upgrading to an outside cabin.

3. **Guarantees** If a cruise is sold out of the cabin category you request when booking, the line will offer a guarantee, promising a cabin in your preferred category or better. You pay the same rate as for the cabin you requested, including early-booking or other applicable discounts. Because guarantees are offered only when a cruise is sold out or oversold in a requested category, chances of getting the upgrade are good. Cabin location is up to the cruise line.

4. **Paid Upgrades** A number of lines, particularly on soft sailings, sell upgrades. Sometimes the upgrades are as little as $15 per person per cabin category.

Confusion among passengers regarding cabin-upgrade availability often leads to frustration and disappointment. A travel agent wrote us:

PLEASE, PLEASE tell your readers that cabin upgrades are a privilege and not a right....With most ships sailing at [near] 100% capacity, most people have a slim-to-none chance of getting upgraded —and almost certainly not from an inside cabin to an outside cabin. Many cabin upgrades are given at the time of booking, but "guaranteed cabin categories" do not mean guaranteed upgrades—these are based solely on availability. The only thing that is guaranteed is that they will get a cabin in at least the category they are booked in! Former passengers and people who book the earliest are the most likely to get upgrades, if they become available. If a certain cabin category is that important to someone, they should book it and pay for it, and not hope to be upgraded to it.... Plus, any travel agent that tells [clients] to take a "guaranteed" or "run of ship" rate to increase their chances of being upgraded, is setting up their clients for disaster. The agent may say one thing, but the client hears the word "upgrade" and thinks this is a given. Then when it doesn't happen, the client gets angry with the travel agent and the cruise line.

Free Stuff

Cruise lines might offer cameras, binoculars, and other goods as booking incentives. Or, freebies may be tied to a theme cruise; for example, a photography cruise sponsored by a camera manufacturer.

Organizational Discounts

Cruise lines commonly develop relationships with organizations like the American Automobile Association or AARP. Check for discounts available through organizations to which you belong.

Credit Card Programs

Some cruise lines have credit card programs. Whenever you use the credit card, you accrue points or "cruise dollars." These can be applied toward a cruise or taken as a credit to spend aboard. Cardholders receive mailings promoting discounts, and charging a cruise on the card may result in cabin upgrades. Similarly, miles accrued on the American Express program offering one mile for every dollar charged are redeemable for cruises.

Travel Agents' Discounts

We have found that agents selling the same discount program for a cruise often quote different prices. Usually the difference is small, 2% to 5%. What's going on is that some retailers are sacrificing part of their override commissions to lowball the competition. Big-volume, cruise-only agencies routinely do this, but local agents frequently will knock a few dollars off their commission to retain a good customer. Ads that claim "We will beat or match your best offer" usually mean an agent is rebating some commission to his or her clients. But beware of this practice. Commissions represent an agent's costs and profit. As any businessperson knows, if you give away your profit, you will end up with red ink.

Cruise Loan Programs

Pioneered by Princess, cruise loan programs are seen by the lines and travel agents as "a tool for taking away one of the clients' biggest stumbling blocks: paying in full for a cruise before sailing." Loans may also help sellers trade the customer up. Basically, you borrow your cruise's cost on a revolving line of credit (like most credit cards) and pay off the loan in 24, 36, or 48 installments, like a mortgage or car loan. The main difference between a mortgage or car loan and a cruise loan is that the former are secured by pledging your home or car as collateral. Because there is nothing to pledge as collateral on a cruise loan, interest rates are much higher. In 2003, the lowest annual percentage rate for a cruise loan was 8.5%; the highest, 28%. Loans are administered by participating banks that are unaffiliated with the cruise lines. If you obtain the lowest interest rate on a 36-installment loan, the monthly payment for a seven-day cruise costing $5,000 per couple is $161 per month. Multiply the $161 by 36 months to see you'll actually be paying $5,796 for your cruise. Most people would do better taking out a loan on their own.

Lost in the Information Haze

Deals come and go so rapidly that a travel agency has to be knowledgeable, well staffed, and computerized to keep on top of the action. Though big cruise-only agencies are the best equipped to handle the information flood, even they occasionally lag.

The National Association of Cruise-Only Agencies can provide a list of member agencies in your area. Discount agencies usually advertise widely. Always check the reliability of any agency with whom you do business.

Cruising the Internet for Cruises

Cruise information on the Internet has increased 1,000% in the past two years. There are thousands of websites to investigate. Even if you're a wiz at searches, you'll still need a great deal of time and infinite patience to find the facts you need. Cyberspace is chaotic. We can't organize it for you, but here are facts that can help you navigate your own way on the ocean of information.

Essentially, cruise-related information on the Internet is precisely that—information. You can ask questions and order brochures, but only a few cruise lines have taken the next step enabling you to buy a cruise directly from them on the Internet.

The Internet has, however, become a handy tool for advertising last-minute specials. There are a number of sites which, after you sign up, will automatically send you a weekly e-mail advertising deeply discounted cruises. Several sites specialize in cruises, while others offer air, hotels, rental cars, and a range of other travel products. Many sites will provide a form for you to complete listing the kind of deals (cruises, air, hotels, etc.) that you're interested in. When they send out their weekly e-mail, they limit the message to those products. Some of the best deals we've seen are on these websites, but buyer beware. Some websites have sold cruises without advising the customer of required passport and visa requirements or other pertinent information.

The best way to find out if a particular cruise line is selling online is to check out its website. The web addresses for all major cruise lines and many small, specialized ones are included in this book.

Information is also available from these sources:

- **Cruise Associations**   Trade organizations, including Cruise Lines International Association, that have their own websites (**www.cruising.org**).

- **Travel Agencies**   Hundreds of agencies have web pages, and others participate through their trade organizations. Most take bookings online or via e-mail.

- **Travel Publications**   Major travel magazines, such as *Travel & Leisure and Travel Weekly,* and book publishers, including John Wiley & Sons (which publishes this book), have websites.

- **Individuals**   Recognized travel experts and some people who consider themselves cruise experts or are interested in cruises have created their own sites.

- **Subscriber Services**   Many, such as AOL, have programs on cruises.

The typical cruise line website offers about the same information available in a cruise brochure. However, fares are likely to be sample prices only. Cabin sizes or configurations aren't specific. You usually can request a brochure by e-mail or on the web (you may be required to give a phone number or e-mail address), but such sites are most useful when you know where and when you plan to cruise. Information, of course, covers the host cruise line only.

Some sites are well done, fun, clever, and even amusing, and they are getting better. Others are basic and slow to load—you would learn more by reading the line's brochure. The best sites have special features, such as itineraries with links to maps and port information or the facility to search by ZIP code for travel agencies near you. Often, the site is linked to other cruise-related information.

The range of information is as broad as it is voluminous—Princess Cruises' website is huge! There is no uniformity in presentation, style, or amount of detail between cruise lines. On Windstar Cruises' website, you can go through a typical day on board, see a sample dinner menu, review itineraries with sailing dates, and read about special fares and onboard credits for Internet users. Carnival Cruises, with one of the most extensive sites, offers pictures and descriptions of each cabin category, including drawings and pictures of cabin layouts—a rare feature.

For news, guidance, and evaluations, AOL's "Cruise Critic" is maintained by a team of cruise specialists and knowledgeable persons. Included are candid, continuously updated ship reviews and evaluations on more than 100 ships, with descriptions on facilities, activities, amenities, itineraries, and fellow passengers; news on industry developments; and features ranging from seasickness to bargains. The Cruise Critic library contains AOL members' trip reports and travel tips.

Similar information is available from **www.cruisemates.com,** a site by veteran cruise writer Anne Campbell and a group of established writers who specialize in cruises. When Campbell cruises, she sometimes offers daily reports with video. In addition to constantly updated information on special deals, Cruisemates promotes several specially priced cruises throughout the year. Campbell and others host message boards where people can ask questions or post their opinions on cruises, ports, and related matters.

Cruise Opinion (**www.cruiseopinion.com**) claims to have the largest database of cruise ship reviews on the web. All are recently written and based on personal experiences. Each reviewer evaluates the ship in 42 categories using a rating of 0 to 100 and describes the cruise experience. Most reviews were provided within the last year. A recent check showed nearly 4,500 reviews on file, with more added daily.

CruiseReviews (**www.cruisereviews.com**) is limited but more current. The site lists about 20 major cruise lines and all their ships. About a third had been reviewed recently. Those we checked were short, but pointed. Other sites you might want to check out include:

- **Expedia.com, orbitz.com, and travelocity.com.** The three big boys in Internet travel sales. Besides offering copious content, both post weekly discounts on a broad range of travel products.

- **Lastminutetravel.com** offers a full range of travel products, including cruises and air.

- **Lowestfare.com** sells all travel products but limits its emails to a small number or particularly hot deals.

- **Trip.com** posts a weekly newsletter advertising mostly air and hotel deals.

- **Bestfares.com** is a good all-purpose travel discount site.

Additional websites specializing in cruise information and discounts include **seasavers.com, cruise.com, i-cruise.com, mytravelco.com, cruise411.com,** and **cruisecritic.com.**

These websites offer deck plans; ship descriptions and reviews; tips on insurance; advice for couples, singles, seniors, and the disabled; and of course, hot deals. Cruisecritic.com is our choice for the most dependable and informative content. Last-minute specials and bargain rates can be found on all of the sites.

Buying on the Internet

If you want to purchase a cruise from an Internet company, first try to run the transaction through your travel agent. If the deal is only available through the Internet direct to the consumer, make sure before you buy that the site provides a phone number so that you can get a real person on the line if something goes amiss. If possible, make the booking through the site's phone number as opposed to purchasing electronically. Even if you handle the entire transaction electronically, verify by calling the seller's phone number that competent help in the form of a live person is available if you need it. Because many online sites specialize in last-minute deals, you probably won't have much time to resolve a problem should one occur. Before you book, ask the seller when your reservation will be recorded as fully paid in the cruise line's system. Repeat the process with the airline if you buy air from the cruise line. On the date provided by the seller, call the cruise line and airline directly to confirm that everything is order. If time is short when you make your reservations, you can request to pick up your cruise documents at the pier. Otherwise, fork over the bucks for overnight delivery. Regarding air travel purchased through the cruise line, ask for electronic ticketing. That way you won't have to worry about paper tickets being delivered on time.

Online Auctions

The latest twist in discounting is auctioning cruises online at such sites as **www.onsale.com, www.ubid.com,** and **www.allcruiseauction.com.** If ever there were a need for "buyer beware," it is here. We know that some people have scored true bargains, but we also hear of people bidding more for a cruise than they would have paid through their travel agent.

The bottom line: If you want information, cruising the Internet can be useful and fun. It can also be frustrating and time-consuming. You will learn quickly which sites are worthwhile. Be cautious about comments on message boards, forums, and chat rooms from unidentified sources whose reliability you can't check.

We believe that this book—we say in all modesty—together with cruise lines' compendiums and a knowledgeable travel agent (particularly for first-timers), remains the most efficient and effective way to help you select the right cruise—that is, the cruise right for you.

Price Protection

The airlines and cruise lines encourage you to book early to obtain the lowest fares. But what if you plunk down $1,200 for a cruise and discover a few months later that the same class of cabin on the same cruise is selling for $800? Getting a refund for the difference or being able to cancel and rebook at the lower rate is known as price protection. The cruise lines claim to be flexible and cooperative in this regard, but when it comes to giving back money already in their pocket, things usually get sticky. Sometimes customers must "qualify" for deals offered at lower prices. These qualifications sometimes make sense, as when a deal is offered to persons over 65 years of age, or to a promotional fare offered on a strictly regional basis, for example to residents of Dade Country, Florida. Often, however, the qualifications for obtaining the lower rate are specious in the extreme. A common practice among cruise lines is to reject requests to rebook after the passenger has made his final payment. If you have been a good little passenger and paid on time, you're rewarded for your punctuality by being prohibited from taking advantage of lower fares available to most everyone else. Another way cruise lines accomplish the same thing is to limit the lower fare to "new bookings only." In other words, if the right fist doesn't get you, the left will.

Almost all cruise lines assess penalties for canceling within a certain number of days from the sailing date. If you cancel before the applicable penalty date, you're free to rebook at the lower promotional fare. Problem is, cruise lines time the announcement of cut-rate deals to fall well inside the penalty period.

The most straightforward and consumer-friendly policy we were able to uncover is offered by Royal Caribbean and Celebrity. These lines will allow a passenger to rebook at any lower rate for which they qualify until the "sailing closes" (usually one or two days prior to departure). If you're 50 and try to take advantage of a senior deal, you won't qualify, but for deals offered to the broader market, you'll be allowed to rebook without penalty.

Finally, the best price protector you'll ever have is a good travel agent. A good agent can often use her influence and clout to beat some of the silly arbitrariness out of the cruise lines. If the agent can't arrange an actual rebate, she frequently can get you compensated through other concessions such as cabin upgrades, shipboard credit, and the like.

Remember that your agent will probably have dozens, if not hundreds, of clients booked on various cruises at any one time. Thus, it's unrealistic to expect her to monitor discount deals circulated by the cruise lines. It's your job to check for lower prices periodically, and if you find something, bring it to her attention.

Pulling It All Together

You know the players and how the game is played. Now it's time to put your knowledge into action.

Step 1. To Agent or Not to Agent

Your first big decision is whether to use a travel agent. This guide, cruise lines' brochures, Sunday newspaper travel sections, cruise specialty magazines, and the Internet will enable you to narrow your choices. Even so, a reliable travel agent can contribute immeasurably in offering advice and facilitating the process. If you have a travel agent who has served you well, particularly if you're a volume customer, you should use him or her. If you don't have a regular agent, ask your friends for recommendations. Try to select a travel agent near your age or one who shares your interests and lifestyle. Make sure the agency has a good reputation and that the agent with whom you are dealing is experienced in selling cruises. Using a travel agent will not cost you more, since the cruise line pays any commissions.

Step 2. Narrow Down

Using this book and the other material, make a priority list of four lines, ships, and cruises. Be flexible. Also be alert to the possibility of travel agents pushing their preferred suppliers, who may not be on your list.

Step 3. Scout the Discounts

Using information collected from newspaper travel sections, Internet, and other sources, ask your agent if he or she can meet or top any special deals you have found. Call a few high-volume cruise-only agencies on your own. Ask about cruises on your priority list, then ask what's the best deal the agency is selling. Always ask for the bottom-line cost in dollars rather than the percentage discount. Repeat the quote to the agent and verify what is included (airfare, accommodations, transfers, and so on). Take notes.

Never fall into the trap of buying a cruise simply because it sounds like a great deal—especially if you are buying your first cruise. Your top priority is to determine which cruise is right for you. Only then is it time to scout deals. The best way to ruin your cruise vacation is to book the wrong ship in an effort to save a few dollars.

Step 4. Buy Early or Buy Late

As we said, the biggest discounts are usually given for buying early (four to eight months before sailing) or late (during the last month). First-time cruisers have greater choice and peace of mind taking the early-bird route. Experienced cruisers are in a better position to play the best-deal game. But any time you hold out for a deal, you decrease your options on getting the cabin, dining room seating, and airline routing you prefer. In the long run, these factors are much more important to the quality of your cruise than saving $50 or $100.

Step 5. Give the Seller a Price to Beat

When you've narrowed the field to one or two cruises and you're ready to buy, call the four or so retailers who quoted the best prices in your first round of inquiries. Say, "I've been quoted a price of $X for this particular cruise; can you beat it?" Give your travel agent a chance to match it. If he can't, he may be able to verify the deal's integrity or uncover hidden problems. If the deal is commissionable, have your agent book it, or if the agent has invested a lot of time on your behalf, offer a $50 or $100 consultation fee. You will probably find the agent more receptive to working with you in the future.

Step 6. Check It Out

If you decide to buy from an agency outside your city or state, try to determine whether it's bonded and a member of its local Better Business Bureau and/or Chamber of Commerce. Also check whether it's a member of the American Society of Travel Agents (ASTA), the National Association of Cruise Only Agencies (NACOA), or Cruise Line International Association (CLIA). Membership isn't a guarantee of ethical business practices, but the organizations have a vested interest in maintaining the good reputation of cruising and try to attract only upstanding members.

American Society of Travel Agents	(703) 739-2782	**astanet.com**
Cruise Line International Association	(212) 921-0066	**cruising.org**
National Association of Cruise-Only Agencies	(305) 663-5626	**nacoaonline.com**

To find out how consolidators and wholesalers respond to questions about their affiliations and accreditations, we called all of the cruise discounters advertising in *Cruise Travel* and *Condé Nast Traveler* magazines. Some agencies were gracious and seemed to understand that customers have a right to check their credentials. An amazing number, however, were surly and uninformative. "Who are you?" and "What do you need to know that for?" were typical responses. Representatives from four agencies said they didn't know the answers to our questions but would call us back. Of course, we never heard from them. When you call to check an agency, accept nothing less than complete courtesy, openness, and cooperation. Life's too short, and your cruise is too important to deal with rude salespeople. Remember to show the same respect. Good travel agents will work hard for you, but they can spot someone on a fishing expedition.

Step 7. Protect Yourself

When you pay for your cruise, use a credit card and insist that the charge be run through the cruise line's account, not the agency's account. This precaution is important. Financially shaky agencies sometimes use their customers' payments to settle agency debts instead of securing the customer's booking. If these agencies fold, the customer is often left with no cruise and no refund. Paying with a credit card allows you to cancel payment if the cruise is not provided as promised. Reputable travel agents and other sellers are more than happy to run the charge through the cruise line's account and will absolutely not be offended by your request. Financially sound sellers make a practice of running credit card charges through the cruise line's account anyway. This is done so that the cruise line will have to pay the credit card merchant fees. If you purchase your cruise from any seller other than your usual travel agent, ask the seller when the paid reservation will be posted in the cruise line's system. On the date provided, call the cruise line directly to confirm the reservation.

Protect your cruise investment with travel insurance. Most comes with lots of bells and whistles, but three things should concern you: (1) loss of your paid fare if you must cancel or if your cruise is interrupted, (2) the potentially huge costs of emergency medical evacuation, and (3) major medical expenses while traveling that your primary health insurance doesn't cover.

Though overpriced at about $5–$8 per every $100 of coverage, travel insurance nevertheless is a prudent expenditure. You never know when you might become ill, have a death in the family, or miss your sailing because of a flight cancellation or delay.

Although travel insurance coverages can be purchased separately, they are usually "bundled." We recommend you purchase good coverage for trip cancellation/interruption and emergency medical evacuation. Trip cancellation/interruption insurance covers the insured traveler and traveling companion(s) against losses caused by illness, injury, or death. Most policies cover losses resulting from the interruption of your trip by the death, serious injury, or serious illness of a close family member back home. **Access America** (**www.accessamerica.com**) and **Travel Guard** (**www.travel-guard.com**) offer coverage for the illness, injury, or death of a business partner.

If you must cancel your cruise before departure, your cancellation/interruption insurance will reimburse you for the cruise's full cost less any refund you receive from the cruise line. Though cancellation and refund policies vary, most lines provide a full refund if you cancel 61 or more days before your departure date. Remember that these policies cover only the extent of your investment. If you are buying a $1,500 cruise, you don't need $10,000 in insurance.

Ideally, insurance will allow you to cancel your trip for any reason. Most policies, however, stipulate situations that qualify for coverage. At a minimum, insist on being covered for death, injury, illness, jury duty, court appearances, accidents en route to the airport or pier, and disasters at home, including fire or flood. The same coverage applies to your traveling companion(s). If you buy a cruise at the double-occupancy rate and your companion must cancel, your policy should cover the single supplement if you want to continue alone.

Policies usually cover airline or shipworker strikes but not earthquakes, or other disasters at scheduled ports of call. Cruise lines reserve the right to alter the itinerary once under way to avoid bad weather or other problems.

The fine print in many policies can be tricky, and seemingly innocuous loopholes limit the carrier's obligation. One essential question regarding cancellation/interruption insurance is whether it covers pre-existing conditions: any for which you were treated by a physician in the 60 days (90 days in Maryland) before the policy was purchased. In better policies, if the pre-existing condition is controlled by medication, it is covered. In insurance company language, however, "controlled" is very different from "treated." If you have high blood pressure and medication maintains it at normal, safe levels, your condition is controlled. If you have a tumor and are receiving radiation, carriers would say you are being treated, but that your condition is not controlled. If your tumor caused you to cancel your cruise, the policy would not reimburse you. The same stipulations regarding pre-existing conditions apply to your family back home. If, for example, your mother dies while you're traveling, your trip interruption coverage would be void if her death was related to a pre-existing condition. We recommend that you question the insurance carrier directly about any health problems, obtaining written confirmation if necessary.

Pregnancy is covered by most policies if you cruise during your first two trimesters. If a complication arises, the policy will pay. Amazingly, if you deliver your baby normally while on a cruise, you are not covered. Many cruise lines won't accept a pregnant passenger in her third trimester.

Another potential land mine in cancellation/interruption insurance is operator failure. What if your travel agent, airline, or cruise line goes belly up? Although brochures and most policies say they will pay in the event of operator failure or default, fine print sometimes defines *failure* and *default* as bankruptcy. Because many businesses fail without declaring bankruptcy, this is an important distinction. Note that most policies exclude the failure of the company that sold the cruise (usually a travel agent) or the company that sold the insurance. If you buy insurance from a travel agency, you're covered if the cruise line or airline fails, but not if the agency fails. This is yet another reason you should pay for your cruise with a credit card and insist that the charge be run directly through the cruise line's account, not the travel agent's. It's also a good reason to buy travel insurance directly from the insurance company, something easily done on the Internet. If all of this sounds far fetched, think again. Four established cruise lines—Commodore, Premier, Renaissance, and American Hawaii—went under within the past few years.

Trip interruption coverage, sold with trip cancellation policies, supplements what you recover from the cruise line if something goes wrong during your trip. If a family member dies, for example, and you must fly home from a port mid-cruise, the interruption coverage will pay for your plane ticket home plus reimburse you for the unused portion of your cruise (less any refund you receive from the cruise line). The policy also would pay the single supplement of your cabin companion if he or she remains on the cruise.

Trip interruption insurance covers fire, flood, vandalism, burglary, and natural disaster as it affects your home, but does not cover similar catastrophic events if they occur at your place of business. In our estimation this is a huge gap in travel insurance coverage. As it turns out, it's also a gap in standard business casualty insurance. If your office building burns down while you're cruising in Alaska, chances are about 99 to 1 that your business insurance will decline to reimburse you for the cost of returning home or for the unused portion of your cruise.

Something much less likely than a fire at your office, however, is now covered. As a consequence of the September 11, 2001 terrorist attacks, most travel insurance policies offer coverage for cancellation or interruption occasioned by an act of terrorism. Coverage varies from policy to policy.

A common but very important coverage exclusion, relates to "travel arrangements canceled or changed by an airline, cruise line, or tour operator, unless the cancellation is the result of bad weather or financial default." What this means is that your trip cancellation/interruption insurance doesn't cover you if, say, your flight is cancelled for reasons other than weather, and you miss the boat. Logically, one would think, this is exactly the sort of circumstance for which you need travel insurance. When we asked the insurance companies why such events are excluded, their response, to quote one company representative, was, "Oh, we couldn't cover that. It happens too often." Isn't that reassuring?

Bundled with trip cancellation/interruption is emergency medical evacuation insurance. This pays to transport you to a place where you can obtain quality medical care. In the Caribbean and more remote cruise areas, you might prefer not to entrust your care to local doctors. The insurer in conjunction with a qualified physician usually must verify your condition and authorize the evacuation. Once authorized, the insurer usually selects the means of transportation.

As a rule, evacuation insurance does not cover hospital stays, doctors, diagnostic procedures, treatments, or medications, though medical coverage sometimes is bundled with a comprehensive policy covering trip cancellation/interruption. Ask your primary health insurance, Medicare, or HMO whether you are covered for medical attention required when traveling abroad. If you are not covered, buy supplemental insurance.

If you book an upscale cruise and pack Rolex watches, gems, and other valuables, check your homeowners policy to determine what's covered when you travel. If you aren't covered, take out a rider. When you travel, carry your valuables on your person, not in checked luggage. Even better, leave them at home.

Cruise lines and travel agencies, as a rule, do not self-insure. In other words, the policy they sell is an off-the-shelf or customized product of an independent travel insurance company. This is true even when the policy has the cruise line's name in the title, for example, "Happy Sea Cruise Line Total Protection." As mentioned earlier, any third party selling a policy is automatically excluded from "supplier default" coverage. Thus, if you buy that Happy Sea travel insurance and Happy Sea Cruise Line goes belly up, you could get caught holding the bag. Because of many cruise lines, wholesalers, and travel agencies defaulting (going out of business) in the wake of 9/11, most travel insurance companies now maintain a list of travel suppliers, including cruise lines and cruise retailers, that they will not cover. Most of the failed cruise lines were on those lists prior to their ultimate collapse.

Finally, most travel insurance companies post their policies, as well as their list of excluded travel suppliers, on the Internet. Read the policies before you buy, make sure you don't purchase coverage you don't need, and call the company's customer service representative if you have any questions. Here are several major insurers and their phone numbers and Internet sites:

Access America Service Corporation	(866) 807-3982	**www.accessamerica.com**
CSA Travel Protection	(800) 234-0375	**www.travelsecure.com**
Travelex	(888) 457-4062	**www.travelex-insurance.com**
Travel Guard	(800) 826-4919	**www.travelguard.com**
Travel Insured	(800) 243-3174	**www.travelinsured.com**

When shopping for travel insurance, remember that language in the brochure is marketing language. The language in the policy legally defines the carrier's obligations.

If your cruise line underwrites its own policy, compare it with one or more of the policies listed above. If the cruise policy is comparable and the line's in good shape financially, consider it. The line has a greater interest in your satisfaction than an insurance company does and may be more helpful in a crisis. Be aware, however, that there is some risk involved with buying your insurance from the cruise line. If the line goes out of business, as Commodore, Renaissance, American Hawaii, and Premier did, your claim will be thrown in with claims of all of the cruise line's creditors waiting to be reimbursed.

When you buy travel insurance, make sure the policy covers you *from the date of purchase until the day you arrive home from your vacation.* This is extremely important: You can't imagine the problems some folks have had with policies that did not take effect until departure time or that didn't cover the travelers' whole time away from home. In one example, a couple from Texas bought travel insurance from a cruise company. On their own, they scheduled a two-night hotel stay at their originating port and another two-night stay at their port of disembarkation. When the husband became ill on the second day after the cruise, they tried to invoke the medical coverage on their travel insurance. Much to their chagrin, they were told that their policy only covered the days of the cruise, not the extra precruise and postcruise days the couple had arranged themselves. This is yet another example of why it's usually preferable to purchase your policy directly from the travel insurance company.

Finally, be aware before you leave home that if you need to make a claim, the travel insurance companies will hold you to an exacting standard of documentation. From the time you book your cruise, hang onto every correspondence, invoice, statement, canceled check, and receipt. For trip cancellation/interruption, travel delay, and/or medical claims you will need some or all of the following:

1. Proof of complete trip payment.
2. Proof of insurance payment.
3. Invoice from your travel agent or tour operator showing complete trip costs and cancellation penalties.
4. If your situation involves illness, accident, or death, you'll need to produce doctor's medical records, hospital records, and/or a death certificate.
5. Paid receipts for all expenses incurred.
6. Original travel documents

When Things Go Wrong

As you've ascertained from the discussion of travel insurance above, there are number of things that can go wrong between the time you book your cruise and the day when you arrive back home. Long-range planning minimizes bad surprises and generally allows sufficient time to work out any snags. Last-minute deals can sometimes save a ton of money, but cramming all of your planning and arrangements into a few short weeks or days before departure increases the probability of a problem arising with little or no time to resolve it.

Eliminating problems should be an integral part of your long-term planning. Begin by analyzing your risks. Take a look at your health and the health of your family and business associates. There may be foreseeable risks which suggest that it's not really the best time to take a cruise. Before you book your cruise, get a handle on the financial stabilty of your intended cruise line. Make sure you pay with a credit card and have the charge run through the cruise line's account as opposed to the travel agent's or other third-party seller. Buy travel insurance that takes effect on the date of purchase and provides coverage until you get home. Buy it directly from the insurance company. If you are traveling to a part of the world where you'd prefer not to be treated by the local health care industry, make sure emergency medical evacuation coverage is included in your policy. Go over all pre-existing medical conditions with the insurance carrier before you buy. Make sure you have already acquired trip cancellation/interruption coverage. If you have special concerns, such as the possible death of an aging parent or business partner, make sure those situations are covered by the policy. Realize that there are a number of circumstances besides death that may require your unexpected return home. We have readers whose cruises were interrupted by a fire at their place of business, a tree falling on their home, a burglary, and an unexpected lawsuit to name a few. In short, the broader and more inclusive your trip cancellation/interruption coverage, the better.

Problem 1 — Missing Flight Information

If you purchased your air from the cruise line or if air was included in the price of your cruise, you should receive your flight itinerary 30-45 days prior to departure. If less than 30 days remain prior to departure and you haven't received your information, call your travel agent and have her find out what's going on. If you bought your cruise through the Internet or from a nonlocal seller, call the cruise line first to make sure your reservation is in their system and that full payment has been received. If everything checks out, phone the seller. Work your way from reservationist to supervisor to manager to owner as required until you get a satisfactory explanation. Take the same approach with the seller if the cruise line has no record of your reservation.

Problem 2 — Missing Cruise Documents or Airline Tickets

Your date of departure is looming, but you haven't received your airline tickets and/or cruise documents. If you have a good travel agent, you are virtually assured that everything will get sorted out in plenty of time. If you purchased on your own through a print ad, the Internet, or from a seller with whom you do not ordinarily do business, the situation is iffier. In that case, start by calling the cruise line directly and making sure that your reservation is in order and *that payment has been received.* If you purchased air with your cruise, and you know your flight itinerary, go through the same process with the airline. If everything is properly recorded, next call the seller. You'll probably be told that late delivery of documents, especially airline tickets, is standard practice (unfortunately true) and not to worry. Most of the time this will be valid advice, but if something is actually screwed up (documents lost in mail, misplaced, etc.), you won't have much time, once the seller acknowledges a problem, to resolve it. The one thing you can count on is that the cruise line and airline are going to refer you back to the seller for resolution. The only exception to this is when your cruise reservation is paid in full and the cruise line knows that the seller has gone belly-up. In this case, the cruise line will usually arrange for you to pick up your cruise documents at the pier. Regarding the airline, if your reservation is in the system and fully paid, and if you have an electronic ticket, you're home free. Just go to the airport and produce your photo ID and confirmation. If paper tickets are lost, you're back to dealing with the seller. If it's a weekend or holiday and you can't contact the seller, call the airline and ask for a customer service representative. All airlines have different policies, but the representative will usually try to help if the reservation is in his system and fully paid.

If your reservations, either air or cruise, are not in the cruise line's or airline's system, you've got a big problem. It could be a simple as a transmission error between the seller and the cruise line, or it could mean that the seller lost your reservations; failed to record your payments; erroneously cancelled your reservations; or is about to, or has, gone out of business. Assuming the seller is still in business, call the seller, explain your situation, and then start working your way up the chain of command until you get someone on the phone with the knowledge and authority to address your problem.

Most of these situations can be avoided, of course, by doing business with a brick-and-mortar travel agent in your hometown and by arranging your air itinerary through the travel agent (or on your own) rather than through the cruise line. Buying your own air, unfortunately, puts you at some risk for a couple of other unpleasant eventualities having to do with missing the boat and losing your luggage, but we'll deal with those problems later. Finally, on the topic of arranging your own flight itinerary, we don't want to overstate the case. While working on this section of the guide, we received a direct mail promo from an excellent European cruise line offering outside cabins at half price with air to Europe included. Would we hesitate to buy because the cruise line is providing air? Not for a second.

Problem 3 — Bad Weather or Traffic Delays on Departure Day

When you book your air, either on your own, or through the cruise line, give some thought to what weather and air-traffic conditions are likely to be on your day of departure. If you're traveling over a holiday period or at a time of year when bad weather is likely, you might want to take some precautions. Begin analyzing your airport choices. In the New York area, for example, be aware that Newark and Kennedy have longer runways, more de-icing equipment, and electronic/traffic control systems that allow them to function when La Guardia is shut down. New Yorkers can also take a train directly to the Baltimore/Washington Airport (BWI) from Penn Station in under three hours. BWI has a better track record than any of the three New York airports for on-time departures.

During holiday periods or bad weather, the chance of a serious snafu increases exponentially with every flight connection you have to make. If, with a little inconvenience, you can eliminate a connection, it's usually worthwhile to do so. Let's say you live in Louisville, Kentucky; Columbus, Ohio; or Charleston, West Virgina, and you're flying to Fort Lauderdale for a cruise out of Port Everglades. If there's no direct flight, you might be better off driving to the Cincinnati Airport (located in northern Kentucky) and taking a direct flight from there to Fort Lauderdale, thereby eliminating the connecting flight.

Always, always, always book the earliest flight of the day on an airline that offers a number of flights throughout the day to your destination. Early morning flights have a much better on-time record than do flights later in the day. Plus, if there's an equipment problem or a cancellation, the airline can put you on a later flight. For maximum peace of mind, travel to the port of departure one or two days prior to your sailing date. If things go awry on your travel day, you've still got sufficient time to make alternative arrangements.

You've probably heard the ongoing debate regarding electronic versus paper airline tickets. Generally speaking, we prefer electronic tickets with the proviso that you double-check with the airline to insure that your correct itinerary is in their system and that your reservations are shown as fully paid. The one situation where paper tickets are preferable is when your flight is cancelled and your airline cannot book you on another flight. In this case, you'll want to make arrangements with an alternative carrier. Most carriers will honor the tickets of another airline in the event of cancellations or labor actions, but they will require paper tickets as documentation.

Problem 4 — Missing the Boat

This is the nightmare scenario that haunts all cruisers. If you're savvy in your travel planning, and especially if you plan to arrive at your departure port a day or so ahead of time, you'll almost eliminate the likelihood of missing the boat. We all know, however, that travel, like life, can get mixed up in ways that we never anticipate.

If you purchase your air from the cruise line, the cruise line will do its utmost to get you on the ship. There are many, many documented cases of ship departures being delayed while awaiting the arrival of a delinquent flight full of cruise passengers. Likewise, cruise lines have flown passengers who actually missed the boat to rendezvous with the ship at the first port of call. The more passengers that are affected by late flights, the more likely the cruise line is to hold the ship. The most important thing to understand, however, is that the cruise is absolutely not under any legal obligation to hold the ship or to assist in any other manner. If you read the terms and conditions of your Passage Contract, you'll almost immediately encounter language like the following: "Under no circumstances does [X Cruise Line's] responsibility extend beyond the ship. All arrangements made for the guests with independent contractors [such as airlines] are made soley for the convenience of the guest and are at the guest's risk." What you *can* count on, exclusively as a matter of customer relations, is for the cruise line to do what is practicable. Do 30 late arriving guests on a weather-delayed flight from Cleveland justify delaying the departure of a 3,000 passenger cruise ship? Perhaps, but don't count on it. We know of at least one situation when the ship sailed while two busloads of flight-delayed passengers waited at the airport to be driven to the port 20 minutes away.

Sometimes, when air is arranged through the cruise line, and passengers miss the boat owing to flight delays, the airline will help out. Assistance usually comes in the form of a meal and perhaps a hotel room. If the airline flies to your first port of call, it will try to book you on a flight so that you can meet the ship. Because the airline is not responsible for weather or air traffic control delays, it has no legal obligation to help. Like the cruise line, any assistance rendered is primarily a matter of customer relations.

If you book your own travel arrangements to the departure port, you're on your own. As far as the cruise line is concerned, you're totally responsible for getting to the ship. If you miss the ship through no fault of your own, however, as in the case of a delayed flight, you will have that travel insurance we recommended to fall back on. Travel insurance is also your safety net if you miss the boat because of sickness, or because of bankruptcy of the cruise line. Missing the boat because of an airline strike is also usually covered by travel insurance, though the conditions for coverage vary from policy to policy. If you or your cruise line book you on an airline involved in a labor dispute, discuss the situation with your insurance carrier to determine under what circumstances you're covered. When it comes to travel insurance, don't, as the saying goes, leave home without it.

Problem 5 — Lost Luggage

If you book air through the cruise line, the cruise line will make every effort to get your luggage to you (once it's recovered), including flying it to meet you at a port of call. Once again, this assistance is purely voluntary as opposed to obligatory. If you handle your own air, you must depend on the airline (generally without any assistance from the cruise line) to get your recovered luggage to you. In such situations, the probability of your luggage catching up with you while on your cruise is slim. Minimize the chances of your luggage being lost by arriving in port a day early and/or eliminating connecting flights where possible. Buy travel insurance, and make sure it pays off if your bags are delayed more than 24 hours.

Problem 6 — You Get Sick during Your Cruise

Although most large cruise ships carry a physician and at least one registered nurse, they are really not equipped to handle anything much beyond sore throats and diarrhea. Additionally, because the vast majority of cruise ships fly under foreign flags, physicians are not required to be licensed to practice in the United States. From the cruise physician's perspective, shore-based facilities are better equipped to handle serious illness and emergencies. In practical terms, this means that the cruise physician will want to transfer you to a hospital on shore at the first opportunity if he anticipates your illness taxing the rather meager limitations of his clinic. As you would intuit, larger ships have the better-equipped clinics, though the patient-to-physician ratio is lower on smaller ships. What you might not intuit is that, according to the fine print in your passage contract, the cruise line is not responsible for medical care you receive while on board. As with the problems discussed earlier, travel insurance is a must. When you purchase your policy, be sure to make sure any pre-existing condition is covered. Also, familiarize yourself with the policy's medical evacuation coverage.

Problem 7 — Onboard Complaints

If your stateroom toilet backs up, the air conditioner conks out, or the showroom performers quit, don't expect a refund. If it's not resolved onboard when it happens, the best you are likely to get is a discount on a subsequent cruise. Once again, it's that pesky passage contract that purports to absolve the cruise line from all responsibility, anytime, anywhere. In point of law, however (as any attorney who specializes in travel will tell you), some of the language is nothing but smoke, totally unenforceable and made part of the contract as a bluff to inhibit you from taking legal action. Understand, however, if you decide to sue, that cruise lines operate under maritime law, and you might have to file the lawsuit in the country where the ship is registered. It's not an accident that so many cruise ships fly under the so-called flags of convenience, particularly those of Liberia and Panama.

Legalities aside, it's always preferable to settle problems on the spot. Usually, you will direct your complaint to the chief purser or to the hotel manager, and usually they will be quite responsive. Be polite and friendly, and keep your anger under control. As a last resort, if your complaint is not addressed, fax the president of the cruise line. Resend each day until your problem is resolved. Keep copies of your faxes in case the complaint goes unremedied for the entire cruise. As of this writing, Carnival is the only cruise line that will allow you to cancel your cruise and disembark once underway if things are not satisfactory, and this privilege is available only on certain itineraries.

If you are really unlucky, like when your cabin is for some reason uninhabitable and the ship is completely full, your only option is to negotiate the best deal you can or leave the ship on your own initiative at a port of call. If you jump ship, regardless of the reason, you're on your own. Consequently, we recommending contacting your travel insurance carrier for advice about how to best proceed before taking action.

Problem 8 — Itinerary Changes/Cancelled Ports of Call

You will discover that the cruise line has complete discretion in regard to changing the itinerary of canceling a scheduled port stop. Though occasionally abused, this discretion is necessary in order to insure the safety of the passengers, ship, and crew. It is this flexibility that permits a ship to circumvent storms or offload a passenger at a nonscheduled port for medical reasons.

Problem 9 — Shore Excursion Problems

Because shore excursions are conducted off the ship and produced by local tour companies, the cruise line will decline responsibility for any problem you have, however serious. Sometimes, however, as a matter of customer relations, a cruise ship might offer you a refund or assist you in obtaining satisfaction from the tour operator. Nevertheless, you should always register your complaint with the cruise line. Though of little comfort to you, so doing may result in the cruise line forcing an errant tour operator to clean up its act.

What's the Real Cost of a Cruise?

Some readers report being surprised by all the extras that are not covered by their cruise fare: items like port charges, beverages on board, spa services, photos taken by the ship's photographer, shore excursions, wine tastings, and even designer ice cream treats. Although all these things add up to a hefty sum, we don't consider them to be "hidden" charges. Except for port charges, such purchases are optional. Any travel provider will try to sell you stuff; it's like the popcorn or beer vendors at the ballpark. You know they'll be there and that what they sell will be expensive. Buy or not as you see fit, but don't be surprised by their presence. The cruise lines find these services to be very lucrative profit centers, which help them keep basic cruise prices down. Because most folks don't like to scrimp on their vacation, however, it's wise to anticipate these expenditures. Even the little stuff like beverages and photos can tack on $200–$400 to a week-long cruise. So be forewarned.

Concerning port charges, after some lawsuits in Florida seeking to redress the less-than-forthright ways that certain cruise lines represented port charges, almost all cruises from Florida to the Caribbean now include port charges in the cost of the cruise rather than tack them on as a separate charge. Still, watch out for port charges, particularly for Europe and Asia.

Preparing for Your Cruise

A cruise may be about the easiest vacation you can take when it comes to making preparations because so much is done for you, particularly when you buy an air/sea package. During the cruise, entry formalities are handled by the ship for its passengers in most cases, sparing them the need to fill out immigration forms or clear customs in each port of call.

In most ports you can simply walk off your ship after it has been cleared by local authorities; spend the day sight-seeing, shopping, enjoying a sport or other pleasant pursuits; and return to your ship without having to do anything more than pass through metal detectors for security reasons and show your boarding pass. It's remarkable, if you stop to think about it or compare it to a trip by air visiting similar locations.

The destination of your cruise will make some difference—the more exotic the location, the more you may have need for planning ahead, perhaps for inoculations, visas, and the like. And of course, the weather during your cruise will determine the wardrobe you select.

Such advice may seem obvious to those who have traveled, and if it does, let this information serve simply as a reminder or checklist. Even the most seasoned travelers have been known to pack their cruise tickets in their checked luggage or leave their traveler's checks at home.

Cruise Line Brochures

The easiest place to start your preparation is by reading the large compendium of the cruise line from which you selected your cruise. It has a wealth of useful information. To be sure, much of it is glossy pictures and promotional puff to entice you to take a cruise, but almost all contain several pages, usually toward the rear, aimed at answering the questions people ask most often.

They are the specifics about dining hours, smoking/nonsmoking provisions, paying for incidentals on board ships, embarkation and sailing times, and similar tips. In this book, too, each of the major cruise line profiles in Part Two includes a chart entitled Standard Features, which will answer similar questions pertaining to a specific cruise line and its ships.

Cruise Line Videos

Most cruise lines have videotapes of the cruise you are taking that they would be happy to send you—for a fee. Most cost about $15. Essentially, it is a promotional video, but it will give you an idea of what to expect, particularly if your cruise is to an area of the world in which you have not traveled previously. You will probably receive a flyer from the cruise lines to order the tape directly from a distributor. Some cruise line websites allow for purchasing the video online; some sites even feature virtual ship tours.

Travel Documents

You do not need a passport or visa for cruises in the Caribbean, Alaska, Mexico, Panama Canal, New England, Canada, Bermuda, or Hawaii—that's about 90% of the cruises sold in the United States. However, it's a good idea to carry your passport or some documentation that bears your photo because airlines—and many cruise lines—require a photo identification. What's more, it's always smart to have a passport for travel outside the United States—as much for your returning to the United States as for any reason. If you do not have a passport, you will need to have proof of citizenship, such as a certified copy of your birth certificate. Personally, we would never leave U.S. shores without our passports. It facilitates your travel wherever you are, and it's the best identification you can carry. Never pack your passport in your suitcase; carry it with you at all times.

Aliens residing in the United States need to have valid alien registration cards and passports. All non-U.S. citizens must have valid passports and necessary visas when boarding any cruise ship departing from and returning to U.S. ports.

Passengers on most other cruises—in Europe, former Soviet bloc countries, Asia, Africa, South America—are required to have a valid passport and in some cases may need visas. A valid passport usually means one that will not expire for at least six months.

Often, on cruises in these destinations, ship authorities will ask you to surrender your passport when you check in and will keep it until the end of your cruise. This enables them to clear the ship more quickly in foreign ports. In such cases, you do not need to worry about giving over your passport to the ship. The passports are locked away securely and are taken out only if local authorities ask to see them.

Travel Requirements

Specific requirements for visas and vaccinations depend on the ports of call on your cruise. Normally, this information will be provided by your cruise line or travel agent. However, obtaining the necessary visas and any other documentation required for embarkation, debarkation, and reentry into the United States is your responsibility; if you do not have the proper documents, you will be denied boarding. If you buy your cruise on the Internet or from a seller not located in your city, the seller may neglect to inform you of required travel documents and other pertinent information. Even when you purchase from your local travel agent, however, it's a good idea to independently confirm document, visa, and vaccination requirements for the countries you'll be visiting. Nobody likes a last-minute surprise.

U.S. passengers under 18 years of age are usually not allowed to board a cruise ship at initial embarkation without proper proof of identification. No refund of the cruise fare will be given to passengers failing to have such identification. Documents that will be accepted as proof of identification vary with each cruise line. You will need to inquire in advance if the information is not provided in the cruise line's brochure, which it usually is—in the fine print.

Children traveling with anyone other than their parents or legal guardian must have permission in writing for the child to travel. Failure to comply with this requirement can also result in denial of boarding.

Dress Codes and Packing

What to pack will be determined by your ship, its destinations, and, to some extent, the itinerary. An adventure cruise might be three weeks long, but not a single night will be formal or even very dressy. The dress code is usually explained in the cruise line's brochure; we also note it in the Standard Features in each cruise line's profile in Part Two.

There are no limits on the amount of luggage you can bring on board, but most cabins do not have much closet and storage space. More importantly, because you are likely to be flying to your departure port, you need to be guided by airline regulations regarding excess baggage.

As a consequence of the September 11th, 2001, terrorists attacks, all checked and carry-on luggage is carefully screened before being allowed on board. Even if you pack something in your checked baggage as seemingly innocuous as a corkscrew, knitting needles, or a pair of small scissors, the items might possibly be confiscated and not returned until you disembark. Moreover, none of your checked luggage will be delivered in the normal fashion to your cabin. After an hour or two of panic, thinking your baggage is lost, you'll be summoned to ship security. There you will be asked to identify the offending luggage and objects and to sign forms acknowledging that you brought such items aboard, and that they have been impounded for the duration of the cruise. While on your cruise, be aware also that purses, bags, and packs that you carried ashore will be searched before you're allowed back on board. Ditto for anything you purchased while ashore.

Despite the image you may have about fancy parties and clothes, the reality is that shipboard life is very casual. You will spend your days in slacks, shorts, T-shirts, and bathing suits. Lightweight mix-and-match ensembles with skirts, shirts, blouses or T-shirts, shorts, and slacks are practical. Colorful scarves are another way to change the look of an outfit. For women, cocktail dresses are appropriate for evening wear.

Men usually are asked to wear a jacket at dinner in the dining room. If you do not have a tuxedo, bring a dark suit and white shirt. Add a selection of slacks and sport shirts, and one or two sports jackets. If you are heading for a warm-weather cruise (Caribbean, Mexico, Hawaii, Tahiti), pack as you would for any resort destination. Lightweight, loose-fitting clothing is ideal, and cotton or cotton blends are more comfortable than synthetic fabrics for the tropics. Include two bathing suits if you are likely to be spending much time in the sun and at the beach. Don't forget a cover-up for the short jaunt between your cabin and the pool or other outside decks, as cruise ships ask passengers not to wear bathing suits in the public rooms.

Take along cosmetics and suntan lotion, but don't worry if you forget something. It will most likely be available in shipboard or portside duty-free shops. Sunglasses and a hat or sun visor for protection against the sun are essential. A tote bag comes in handy for carrying odds and ends, as well as plastic bags for wet towels and bathing suits on returning from a visit to an island beach. You might also want to keep camera equipment in plastic bags as protection against the salt air, water, and sand.

The first and last nights of your cruise are casual, and the nights your ship is in port almost always call for informal dress. At least one night will be the captain's gala party, where tuxedos for men and long dresses for women are requested but not mandatory.

Bring your most comfortable walking shoes for shore excursions. Tennis, deck, or other low-heeled rubber or nonskid shoes are recommended for walking about the ship, up and down gangways, getting in and out of the ship's tenders, and for sight-seeing. And you will need a sweater for breezy nights at sea or for the air-conditioning in the dining room or shore excursion bus. A small flashlight, a fold-up umbrella, and a light jacket are often handy.

Pack lightly. For a one-week or shorter cruise, you should be able to fit everything you need into one suitcase. But most of all, be comfortable. You do not need to rush out and buy an expensive wardrobe. Obviously, if your cruise is in a cool or cold climate, you will need to plan accordingly. A Baltic or Scandinavian cruise in summer is likely to encounter colder temperatures than you might think—similar to a New England fall—but then can quickly turn to a hot summer day. Plan for layers when the weather is uncertain.

As we mention elsewhere, it's a sound practice to have a small carry-on bag for your medications and cosmetics and to include a change of clothing for your first afternoon aboard your ship, in the event of a delay in the delivery of your luggage. Also, bring a foldaway bag to carry all those souvenirs, gifts, and duty-free bargains that probably won't fit in your suitcase.

Every evening, an agenda for the following day is delivered to your room; it states the dress code for the following evening. It may be:

Casual   Comfortable daywear, such as slacks, shorts, or jeans, but some cruise lines will state specifically that T-shirts, tank tops, or shorts are not allowed in the dining room for dinner.

Informal   Dresses and pantsuits are suggested for the ladies; jackets for the men, but ties are optional.

Formal   Cocktail dresses or gowns for the ladies, and tuxedo, dinner jacket, or dark business suit for men; jacket and tie are required.

As a general rule, the lineup will be like this:

3–4-night Cruises   One formal, one informal, and one or two casual.

7–8-night Cruises   Two formal, two informal, two or three casual.

10–14-night Cruises   Three or four formal; four or six informal; four or five casual.

You are asked to comply with the ship's stated dress code, if for no other reason than out of respect for your fellow passengers. Generally, the suggested attire is respected throughout the evening or at least until after the shows in the main showroom and the late-night buffet, when it is a gala event. Often, those who want to stay up late for the disco or casino change to more comfortable dress, if they prefer.

Costumes

Some ships still have one night as a masquerade party, and others have theme nights for which some people bring an outfit—for 1950s and 1960s night or country-and-western night, a musical instrument or props for the passenger talent show, or a costume for the masquerade parade. It's entirely up to you whether or not to participate. The cruise line's brochure usually tells you about theme nights, or you can ask your travel agent for theme nights featured on your cruise, if you want to join in. If you don't have space for a costume, the cruise staff can help you make one.

Sports Equipment

If you plan to play golf or tennis frequently, you might want to bring your own equipment, and of course, you'll need the appropriate clothes and shoes. Ships that have golf practice facilities sometimes supply the equipment for a nominal fee. Inquire.

Fins and a snorkeling mask (particularly if you have one fitted with your eyeglass prescription) are bulky, but might save you a $10–$20 fee each time you go snorkeling on your own. If you buy the ship's shore excursions, the equipment is included. Scuba gear is usually included in dive packages, too, and except for your regulator, is impractical to bring on a cruise.

Hiking boots, jogging shoes, riding attire, and other sporting gear will depend entirely on you and the nature of your cruise. For adventure or expedition cruises, such as to Antarctica, your cruise line will give you ample information about dress and the equipment you need.

Money Matters

Dollars are readily accepted throughout the Caribbean and indeed throughout most of the world, as are traveler's checks and major credit cards. In Europe or Asia, the ship's purser or front office usually offers foreign currency exchange facilities, or the ship brings someone aboard to provide the facility in each port of call.

If you do exchange money (it's a great opportunity to teach kids about other currencies—French francs in Martinique, Dutch guilders in Curaçao, pesos in Mexico), exchange only small amounts for your immediate use. Seldom will you have time to exchange the money back before returning to your ship, and you lose money every time you make the exchange.

Even with U.S. dollars, always carry small denominations—ones, fives, tens. Chances are, if you are owed change, it will be returned in the local currency. Incidentally, U.S. coins are seldom accepted in foreign countries and are impossible to exchange except in quantity at foreign exchange banks. Likewise with foreign coins when you want to exchange them back into U.S. currency. Most become souvenirs.

Major credit cards have become the currency of travelers worldwide. On a cruise, you will often find them the most convenient method of payment for settling your account aboard ship, for shopping at duty-free shops, and for payment of local restaurant or hotel bills. However, do not expect to use them in off-the-beaten-track locations. The Cuna Indians of the San Blas Islands—an exotic stop on Panama Canal cruises—want your greenbacks.

Prescription Medicine and Other Medical Requirements

As with any trip, whether on land or sea, you should have all your required medicine with you and carry it in your hand luggage, not packed in your suitcase. As a further precaution, bring copies of your medicine prescriptions—and for your eyeglasses, too.

If you have dietary requirements, you or your travel agent should communicate them to your cruise line at the time you book your cruise. Most ships can accommodate normal requirements of low salt and low fat, but more complex ones that require special stores be carried aboard require planning. Do not take anything for granted. Inquire. For example, many ships do not normally stock skim milk. In each of the cruise line profiles in Part Two under Standard Features, the amount of advance notice a cruise line requires to handle special diets is indicated.

Cruise ships that travel beyond coastal waters are required to have a doctor on board; most large ships have nurses and adequate medical facilities for normal circumstances. The doctor and nursing staff have daily office hours, which are printed in the ship's daily agenda, and they are always on call for emergencies. There are charges, generally reasonable, for most medical services.

Sunburns

You will need to take precautions against the sun when you are on a Caribbean, Mexican, or Antarctic cruise. The sun in these regions is much, much stronger than the sun to which most people are accustomed. Always use a sunscreen with an SPF of 15 or higher, and do not stay in the direct sun for long stretches at a time. Nothing can spoil a vacation faster than a sunburn.

Learning the Lingo

Cruise ships have a language all their own. Though it is not necessary to enroll in a Berlitz course to learn it, becoming familiar with a few terms will be worthwhile so you won't feel lost at sea, if you will forgive the pun.

Passengers don't reserve rooms on a ship, they book **cabins,** which cruise lines sometimes call by a fancier name, **staterooms.** The price level of a cabin is known as its **category.** The rate per person in a double-occupancy cabin is called **basis two.**

When you reach your ship, you will **board** or **embark;** when it's time to leave the ship, passengers **disembark.** If the ship arrives at a port where it cannot pull into the dock, the ship will **ride at anchor** and passengers are taken ashore in a **tender,** one of the small ancillary vessels that travel on board the ship.

Several terms will assist you in finding your way around the ship. The **bow** is the front of the ship, the aft is the rear, and the center portion is **midships,** or **amidships.**

Heading forward, toward the **bow,** the right side of the ship is known as the **starboard side;** the left side of the ship is called the **port side.** Ships have **decks,** never floors. Decks are named after such things as precious stones (Emerald Deck), activities (Sports Deck), places (Monte Carlo Deck), and planets (Venus Deck).

If you've built up an appetite from all this exploring, you can go to the **main seating** (or sitting) and eat early, or the **second seating** and dine late. Some ships have **single seating,** which means that all passengers eat at the same time for all three meals. Other ships have **open seating,** in which case you may sit anywhere—at any unoccupied table or join others. By invitation, you may even find yourself at the **captain's table.**

On board, there are people to help you decode ship lingo. The **purser's office** is the information center, usually called Purser's Square. The **hotel manager** is in charge of all passenger-related shipboard services, such as dining, housekeeping, and so on. The **chief steward** is responsible for cabin services, and **cabin stewards or stewardesses** take care of cabins; the **dining steward** is your waiter. The **cruise director** functions as the emcee, and the **cruise staff,** who are his assistants, runs all activities and entertainment and makes sure that you are having a good time. Finally, there's the **captain,** who is in charge of everything.

Cruise lingo is part of the fun, so don't take it too seriously. Here are the most common terms you are likely to encounter.

Add-on   A supplementary charge added to the cruise fare, usually applied to correlated airfare and/or postcruise land tours.

Aft   Near, toward, or in the rear (stern) of the ship.

Air/Sea   A package consisting of the two forms of travel, that is, air to and from the port of embarkation, transfers to/from the port, as well as the cruise itself.

Amidships   In or toward the middle of the ship; the longitudinal center portion of the ship.

Astern   Beyond the ship's stern.

Basis two   A cabin accommodating at least two persons; also referred to as double occupancy.

Batten down   To secure all open hatches or equipment for sea worthiness while the ship is under way.

Beam   Width of the ship (amidships) between its two sides at its widest point.

Berth   Dock, pier, or quay (key); also, the bed in the passenger cabins.

Bow   Front or forward portion of the ship.

Bridge   Navigational and command control center of the ship.

Bulkhead   Upright partition (wall) dividing the ship into cabins or compartments.

Category   The price level of a cabin, based on location on the ship, dimensions, and amenities.

Colors   A national flag or ensign flown from the mast or stern post.

Course   Direction in which the ship is headed, usually expressed in compass degrees.

Crow's nest   Partially enclosed platform at the top of the mast, used as a lookout.

Who's Who on the Cruise Ship

Captain	Chief Engineer	Chief Officer	Doctor

Electrician	Electrician Chief	First Engineer	First Officer

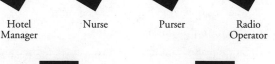

Hotel Manager	Nurse	Purser	Radio Operator

Second Engineer	Second Officer

Uniform designations of Seabourn Cruise Line; other cruise lines may vary.
Courtesy of Seabourn Cruise Line.

Deck plan   An overhead deck-by-deck diagram illustrating cabin and public room locations in relation to each other.

Disembark   Depart from the ship.

Dock   Berth, pier, or quay (key).

Draft   Measurement in feet from water line to lowest point of ship's keel.

Even keel   The ship in a true vertical position with respect to its vertical axis.

Fathom   Measurement of distance equal to six feet.

First seating   The earlier of two meal times in the ship's main dining rooms.

Fore   The forward mast or the front (bow) of the ship.

Forward   Toward the fore or bow of the ship.

Funnel   The smokestack or "chimney" of the ship.

Galley   The ship's kitchen.

Gangway   The opening through the ship's bulwarks (or through the ship's side) and the ramp by which passengers embark and disembark.

Gross registered ton   A measurement of 100 cubic feet of enclosed revenue-earning space within a ship (see **Space ratio**).

Hatch   The covering over an opening in a ship's deck, leading to a hold.

Helm   Commonly the ship's steering wheel, but more correctly the entire steering apparatus consisting of the wheel, the rudder, and their connecting cables or hydraulic systems.

Hold   Interior space(s) below the main deck for storage of cargo.

House flag   The flag denoting the company to which the ship belongs.

Hull   The frame and body (shell) of the ship exclusive of masts, superstructure, or rigging.

Knot   A unit of speed equal to 1 nautical mile per hour (6,080.2 feet), as compared to a land mile of 5,280 feet.

League   A measure of distance approximating 3.45 nautical miles.

Leeward   In the direction of that side of the ship opposite from which the wind blows.

Manifest   A list or invoice of a ship's passengers, crew, and cargo.

Midships   (see **Amidships**)

Nautical mile   6,080.2 feet, as compared to a land mile of 5,280 feet.

Open seating   Seating in the main dining room(s) is not assigned.

Paddlewheel   A wheel with boards around its circumference, and, commonly, the source of propulsion for riverboats.

Pitch   The rocking back and forth (bow to stern) motion of a ship that may be felt in heavy seas when the ship is under way.

Port   The left side of the ship when facing toward the bow.

Port charge   Port taxes, collected by the line and paid to a local government authority; it may include other miscellaneous charges, such as gasoline surcharge and fees.

Port tax   A charge levied by the local government authority to be paid by the passenger.

Prow   The bow or the stem (the front) of the ship.

Purser   A senior management position on board ship. In most cases, the purser is like the general manager of a hotel, but in some cases, he or she is more of the financial or administration officer.

Quay   pronounced "key") A dock, berth, or pier.

Registry   The country under whose flag the ship is registered and to whose laws the ship and its owners must comply; in addition to compliance with the laws of the countries at which the ship calls and/or embarks/disembarks passengers/cargo.

Rigging   The ropes, chains, and cables that support the ship's masts, spars, kingposts, cranes, and the like.

Roll   The alternate sway of a ship from side to side.

Running lights   Three lights (green on the starboard side, red on the port side, and white at the top of the mast) required by international law to be lighted when the ship is in motion between the times of sunset and sunrise.

Second seating   The later of two meal times in the ship's dining room(s).

Space ratio   A measurement of cubic space per passenger. Gross registered ton divided by the number of passengers (basis two) equals space ratio.

Stabilizer   A gyroscopically operated finlike device extending from both sides of the ship below the water line to provide stability for the ship and reduce its roll.

Stack   The funnel or "chimney" from which the ship's gases of combustion are released into the atmosphere.

Starboard   The right side of the ship when facing toward the bow.

Stateroom   Cabin.

Steward   Personnel on-board ship

Stem   The extreme bow or prow of the ship.

Stern   The extreme rear of the ship.

Superstructure   The structure of the ship above the main deck or water line.

Tender   A small vessel, sometimes the ship's lifeboat, used to move passengers to and from the shore when the ship is at anchor.

Transfers   Conveyances between the ship and other locations, such as airports, hotels, or departure points for shore excursions.

Upper berth   A single-size bed higher from the floor than usual (similar to a bunk bed), usually folded or recessed into the wall or ceiling by day.

Wake   The track of agitated water behind a ship in motion.

Water line   The line at the side of the ship's hull that corresponds to the surface of the water.

Weigh   To raise, for example, to weigh the anchor.

Windward   Toward the wind, to the direction from which the wind blows.

Time to Go

If you purchase an air/sea package, your cruise begins from the moment you arrive at the airport. Here's how.

Cruise Documents

Normally, you receive your travel documents—including tickets, transfer vouchers, boarding forms, and luggage tags—about two weeks before departure. Some cruise lines, particularly deluxe and smaller ones going to offbeat destinations, begin sending material a month or more in advance, and often include information on ports of call and on shore excursions sold on board ship. A "Welcome Aboard" brochure is intended to familiarize you with your ship. Read it.

Be sure to carry all documents and essential literature you receive from your cruise line or travel agent with you. Do not pack them in your luggage. You must show your cruise ticket when you check in at the dock.

The final documents will include your airline and cruise tickets. Your agent should have checked them before sending them to you. Check them yourself. If you buy your cruise late, documents may come directly to you from the cruise line. Check them, too.

Luggage tags show the cruise line's name and logo. They have spaces for your name and address and the name of your ship, cruise and cabin numbers, and departure date and port. Complete the luggage tags using information contained in your cruise ticket. Attach at least one tag to every piece of your luggage, including your handbags. (An amazing number of people in their excitement leave hand luggage behind on an airplane, in the airport, or on a motorcoach. If it's tagged, airline or port personnel will know immediately what to do with it.)

After you check in at the airport, you won't see your luggage again until you're aboard your ship. Assuming the bags are properly identified, they'll be in your cabin when you reach it or soon afterward. If not, do not panic. Cruise ships, especially large ones, have thousands of bags to load and sort as passengers arrive. In our experience, luggage is moved from the airport to your cabin with amazing speed.

Airport Arrival and Transfers

As you leave your airplane in Miami, Ft. Lauderdale, San Juan, Vancouver, or any major departure city, you will be met by uniformed cruise line representatives, usually holding a placard showing your ship's name. The representatives gather their charges and escort or direct them to a waiting motorcoach. Keep your transfer voucher handy; you must show it to board the bus.

If you do not spot your cruise line representative, ask airline personnel or other cruise lines' reps for help. Or go to an airport "red" phone and ask that your line's representative be paged. Or proceed to where motorcoaches pick up passengers for transfer to the pier.

You needn't go to the baggage claim area. Your luggage is being transferred directly from the airplane to cruise line trucks for transfer to the appropriate ship. Handling is based on information you wrote on your luggage tags; be sure it's correct.

Advance Arrivals or Delayed Returns

Almost all lines have hotel and sight-seeing packages for people who choose to arrive at their port of departure in advance of their cruise or linger there afterward. Packages are described in your cruise brochure. If your cruise begins after a long flight, lines normally schedule the first day for cruising to give passengers time to overcome jet lag. If the itinerary calls for immediate ports of call, you might consider arriving a day before departure.

Give the most serious consideration to a day-in-advance arrival when you buy the cruise by itself, are arranging your own transportation to the departure port, or your travel falls during busy travel periods when weather in the northern United States often turns bad and flights are delayed (such as Thanksgiving, Christmas, New Year's, and President's Day weekend).

If you're on an air/sea program, your line has a greater incentive— although not necessarily a legal one—to get you to the ship when you've been delayed, either by postponing the sailing or by arranging a hotel room and transporting you to the first port of call. In such instances, you're likely to be one of many stranded passengers.

Your name is on a passenger list, and the cruise line representative at the airport expects you. They are in touch with the airline and your ship and probably are setting strategy before you arrive. If you're traveling on your own and are delayed, your cruise ship has no record of your flight and no obligation to help, although most will try. If you arrive at least a day early, you can avoid this hassle. Some people advise arriving early to avoid standing in line for check-in. We view this as the least valid reason. Queues at the airport and dockside departure gates are a fact of life in mass-market travel. If you're so impatient that you cannot stand in a check-in line—even if it takes an hour—without having your blood pressure skyrocket, then you're probably on the wrong cruise. Megaships have mega-passengers, and they must be individually processed. (It would speed the process if everyone arrived with all their documents completed properly.)

At the Pier

If you're lucky, you will be among the first to arrive from the airport and the first in line for check-in. More likely, you'll be among several hundred others, and, depending on the cruise line, day of the week, size of the ship, and other contingencies, you will stand in line ten minutes to two hours. Pull out a magazine or book and start reading.

Large ships have a check-in system, asking you to line up behind your letter in the alphabet. Despite occasional glitches, this works well. If lines are exceptionally long, you would probably do better to relax in the nearest bar for an hour or so. You have until 30 minutes before departure to board the ship. Some lines let you board until 15 minutes before departure, but we don't suggest cutting it that close.

Normally, lines begin processing passengers at noon or 1 p.m. for a 4 or 5 p.m. departure. But they seldom allow passengers to embark sooner than two or three hours before departure, because time is needed for previous passengers to disembark and the crew to clean the ship and prepare your cabin.

Visitors

For security reasons, most lines do not allow visitors. If your friends or family want to send you off in style, they can contact your travel agent to arrange a party in your cabin, complete with flowers, wine, and champagne, or a birthday cake or anniversary surprise in the dining room.

Settling In

Boarding Your Ship

Most ships have uniformed cabin stewards/stewardesses at the gangway to take you to your cabin. Your escort may offer a quick orientation or ask you to wait for your regular steward, whose name is probably on a small tent card on your dresser. Also in your cabin is ship's literature, including an agenda for the day's events, a deck plan, and possibly stationery.

Checking Out Your Cabin

Take a quick look around the cabin to be sure everything is working—it usually is on new ships, not necessarily on old ones. Check how to operate air conditioning, lights, and the hot water faucets—some fancy new ones are tricky, and the water can scald you. Check the location of life preservers, blankets, and pillows—do you have enough? If anything is missing or not as you requested—twin beds instead of a double—report it now. If you cannot locate your steward, go to the purser or front desk. If you do not get satisfaction, work your way up to the hotel manager.

Hair Dryers/Electric Shavers

Almost all cabins on modern ships have standard 110 AC electrical outlets; your small hair dryer and electric razor won't need an adapter. A few older ships need them. Most new ships have hair dryers. We list this information in the ships' profiles in Part Two, in Standard Features, under Cabin Amenities.

Laundry and Dry Cleaning

Almost all ships have laundry service. Far fewer have dry cleaning facilities. Generally, laundry service is good and reasonable but tends to use lots of bleach. Give your articles to be cleaned or pressed to your steward. They usually are returned in a day, and same-day service is available for an extra fee. Price lists and laundry bags are in your cabin. For safety reasons, ships ask that passengers not use irons in their cabin, but many have public launderettes with an iron and ironing board, as well as coin-operated washers and dryers. The Standard Features section in our cruise line's profile details the availability of launderettes.

Telephones and Other Communications

All but a few ships have telephones in cabins with instructions for using them. Most phones have direct-dial to the United States 24 hours a day, but be aware of the price. Usually, you are charged $10–$15 per minute for a ship-to-shore call. Receiving a call or a fax may cost $3–$5 or more per minute. Policies vary. Some allow you to call collect or charge your call to your shipboard account. Celebrity Cruises has technology enabling passengers to dial toll-free numbers in the United States directly from their cabins. The price is $15.50 per minute. Crystal Cruises was among the first to enable passengers to send and receive e-mail with relative ease. Now, many cruise ships have added e-mail facilities. Also,

"Internet stores" in ports of call are becoming available around the world and are usually very inexpensive to use to send and retrieve e-mail.

If someone wants to reach you at sea, they can telephone the ship by calling (800) SEA-CALL, asking for the ship by name, and giving its approximate location. Charges for this call will appear on the caller's long-distance telephone bill. Ship-to-shore telephone and fax services are normally available only at sea. When the ship is in port, onshore communications must be used.

Cell phones work locally in ports and up to about two miles at sea, depending on the phone and the location. But beyond two miles, they seldom are effective, except perhaps for some very expensive models. With e-mail becoming so readily available on cruise ships, it is the best, least costly means to stay in touch with family and friends or to tend to business during a cruise.

Checking Out Your Ship

After you check out your cabin, tour the ship. Deck plan in hand, start at the top and walk the length of each deck. The ship will be your home for a while, and it's nice to feel at home as quickly as possible.

Checking on Your Dining Reservations

When you book your cruise, your travel agent should state your dining preference and request reservations. You may request first or second seating; tables for two, four, six, or eight; and smoking or nonsmoking areas, although most ships departing from U.S. ports now have smokeless dining rooms. Most lines say they honor requests on a first-come, first-served basis, yet few confirm them in advance. Generally, dining reservations are confirmed only by the maître d'hôtel on board.

Royal Caribbean International is among the few lines that print passengers' dining reservations on their cruise tickets. Why, in this computer age, all can't do the same is a mystery—unless it's to allow the maître d'hôtel to control last-minute shuffling and to ensure he gets his tips.

You may receive confirmation of your dining arrangements on check-in, or it may be in your cabin. If not, check on them. Even lines that give you a dining reservation in advance may ask you to confirm it with the maître d'hôtel.

If assigned arrangements are not what you requested, make a beeline for the maître d'hôtel. Most will accommodate you, though not necessarily on the first night. Rest assured, you won't be the only one. No other item causes more consternation than dining room reservations.

If you let the cruise line or maître d'hôtel place you randomly at a table and you are unhappy with your companions, do not hesitate to ask the maître d'hôtel to move you. Nothing is worse than spending a week dining with people with whom you have nothing in common and no basis for conversation. And you don't need to.

Dining Hours

All but the most luxurious or the most informal ships—and those with "freestyle" or "flexible" dining plans, like Carnival, NCL, and Princess—have two seatings for the day's main meals. Generally, they are:

Breakfast

First or Early Seating　7 or 7:15 to 8 or 8:15 a.m.

Second or Late Seating　8:15 or 8:30 to 9:15 or 9:30 a.m.

Lunch

First or Early Seating　Noon to 1 p.m.

Second or Late Seating　1:15 or 1:30 to 2:15 or 2:30 p.m.

Dinner

First or Early Seating　6:15 or 6:30 to 7:30 or 8 p.m.

Second or Late Seating　8:15 or 8:30 to 9:45 or 10 p.m.

Many ships have open seating for breakfast and lunch and assigned seats for dinner, in which case the hours are likely to be:

Breakfast

　8 to 9:30 a.m.

Lunch

　12:30 to 2 p.m.

Dinner

　First Seating　6:15 or 6:30 to 7:30 or 8 p.m

　Second Seating　8:15 or 8:30 to 9:45 or 10 p.m.

If you're an early riser, you probably will prefer the early seating. If you close the disco every night, you might choose the late one. You will not be confined to these meals, as there's usually an early-bird coffee, a buffet breakfast, midmorning bouillon, lunch buffet, ice cream on deck, afternoon tea, cocktail canapés, a midnight buffet, an alternative dining venue, and—if you're still hungry—room service, and on some ships, a fruit basket in your cabin.

Establishing Shipboard Credit

Most lines use a cashless system aboard ship. At check-in, you receive a card—like a credit card—which will be your identification card and probably your cabin door key. If you want to establish credit for purchases on board, drinks at the bar, wine in the dining room, and so forth, you must present a major credit card at check-in or the purser's office (you will be told at check-in) to have an imprint made and signed.

On the last night of the cruise, you receive a printout of your charges for review. You can pay the amount with cash or traveler's checks or have it billed to your credit card. In profiles in Standard Features in Part Two, we list credit cards each cruise line accepts.

Preparing for Time Ashore

Port Talks and Shopping Guidelines

All ships offer "port talks"—briefings on the country or island and port where the ship will dock. The quality of these talks varies enormously among lines and ships, depending largely on the cruise director's knowledge and the importance the line puts on such programs.

Most mainstream lines with large ships do a lousy job with port talks. On the other hand, adventure and expedition cruises offer superb talks. Small ships generally have a better track record than large ones.

In the Caribbean, particularly, talks on mainstream ships are given by staff with little or no real knowledge of the islands. They do little more than spill trite information and clichés.

The talks often are nothing more than shopping tips, some sponsored by local stores—a practice that has reached scandalous proportions. Cruise directors often receive commissions from local stores, even though they deny it. This vested interest could very well bias the recommendations.

Avoid being misled. If, during a port talk, the cruise director or anyone else recommends one store over another, shop around before buying. The store recommended may be the best place to buy—or it may not.

Also, be cautious of advice that fabulous buys are available in duty-free shops on board and in ports. Most often, you can do as well or better at discount stores and factory outlets at home. If you are considering sizable purchases of jewelry, cameras, china, or crystal, bring a list of prices from home and comparison shop. Be sure you are comparing similar products. Prices in shipboard shops are a good gauge; they usually are competitive with those in ports.

In the Caribbean, expect to save about 20% on such well-known brands as Gucci, Fendi, and Vuitton and on French perfumes, which must be sold at prices set by the makers. Any store caught undercutting the price will be dropped from distribution. The biggest savings are on cigarettes and liquor, not because the price is so much less, but because you save the hefty U.S. taxes imposed on them.

When preparing for your day ashore, be aware also that purses, bags, and packs that you carry along will be searched before you're allowed back on board. Purchases you make while shopping will likewise be inspected.

Shore Excursions: Some Pitfalls and Costs

"Shore excursions"—the sight-seeing tours passengers take at ports—are often the weakest element of the cruise vacation. That's unfortunate, given their importance to the cruise experience. Shore excursions are available at every stop on a ship's itinerary, almost always at additional cost. The exceptions are adventure and expedition cruises, on which shore visits are an integral part of the experience and one reason these cruises appear to be more costly than mainstream ones. Also, cruises in China usually include the cost of shore excursions, not because cruise lines are altruistic, but because the Chinese want it that way.

With rare exceptions, shore excursions cannot be purchased in advance, which is one reason they're a weak link. Usually, a pamphlet on shore excursions is included in the literature the cruise line sends you. Not all brochures list prices, but you can request them through your travel agent if you need them for budgeting purposes. We are happy to report that more lines are including prices in their literature. Also, more often pamphlets are specific to cruise itineraries, making it easier to select tours of interest.

Shore excursions are sold aboard ship either by a shore excursion office or, rarely, from the purser or cruise director. It has been assumed that people prefer to buy excursions on board because their interests and plans change once the cruise begins. However, that assumption may have no foundation in fact. After you have been subjected to the way shore excursions are sold aboard ships, you might say as we do: There must be a better way.

Often you must choose your excursions on the first night of the cruise. Unless you have done your homework in advance of your cruise, you will be buying blind. The shore excursion office usually has limited hours. For the first few days of a cruise, particularly on large ships, ticket lines are long. Therefore, it really pays to read your cruise literature plus books and magazine articles about your destinations in advance.

Shore excursions normally are operated by local tour companies. Motorcoaches seating 30–50 passengers are used; location and terrain are factors. Most tours assume that passengers are on their first visit to the locale—yet another reason they're a weak link. Shore excursions vary little among cruise lines and are, for the most part, dull, unimaginative, city and/or countryside tours to the best-known sights—a third reason they are a weak link. The few exceptions include excursions on Greek Isles cruises, where escorts are university graduates who must pass stiff examinations to qualify as guides. American Hawaii Cruises' excursions are commendable for their variety of sports and emphasis on nature and culture. Happily, many cruise lines are adding similar selections in an effort to appeal to younger travelers and in response to passengers' requests. The worst are excursions in the Caribbean. However, cruise lines, too, have been working with local operators to improve them and to be more creative with their selections.

As a rule for ordinary tours, expect to pay about $12–$15 per hour of touring. For example, a two- to two-and-a-half-hour city tour will cost about $25–$35, and a three-hour island tour will be $35–$45. Variables include the locale, the number of participants, local costs, and mode of transport.

As you study excursions offered by your line, look for options that keep things simple and reasonably short. Excursions longer than three and a half hours that involve multiple activities, sights, and stops will drive most people nuts. It's on the bus, off the bus, back on the bus, head counts. "Wait, Thelma's still in the rest room!" "Where are Harry and Louise?" "Gertrude's trying on a grass skirt. She'll be here in a minute." "I'll be right back. I left my credit card in the stuffed parrot shop!" With few exceptions, you'll spend more time driving among sites and loading and unloading the bus than you will touring or doing something interesting.

When you read descriptions of available excursions, check how long the primary activity or event is. If the written material doesn't say, ask the cruise director. You'll sometimes discover that the half-day "riverboat excursion" spends only an hour on the water. The remainder of the time is spent commuting and waiting for fellow passengers to shop.

In ports where most attractions you want to see are clustered in a small area, you may save time by taking a cab or walking. Rental cars are an another option. Two people forgoing the $48-per-person half-day excursion save $96, which they can apply toward cab fares, rental cars, and admissions. In most ports, you can see and do a lot for $96.

Ask probing questions about each port. Is it a good and safe place to explore on foot? What are the local people like? At many ports, tourists are subjected to swarms of in-your-face hucksters, peddlers, and beggars. In such places, escorted tours, though regimented and inefficient, can be a less stressful way to visit.

When the ship arrives in port, people who have purchased shore excursions are allowed to disembark first and are usually asked to follow a departure schedule to avert a traffic jam at the gangway. This is seldom a problem when the ship docks and passengers can disembark quickly. It can be a problem when the ship must tender, because it cuts an hour or more (depending on ship size) from the time you have in port if you plan to tour on your own.

At the End of Your Cruise

Tipping

There are no definitive rules about tipping, but because it causes so much consternation for passengers, cruise lines offer guidelines, distributing them aboard ship. Some even publish them in their cruise brochures, which is helpful if you want to budget for them in advance. In Part Two, the cruise ship profiles' Standard Features includes Suggested Tipping. The guidelines are similar: Tip slightly less on budget cruises, slightly more on luxury cruises. Follow guidelines or your inclinations. Ship officers and senior management are never tipped. For all service personnel, tips are their main source of compensation. Only a few deluxe ships include tipping in the cruise cost (noted in the cruise line profiles).

In a session at voyage's end, the cruise director will discuss disembarkation procedures and outline tipping guidelines. There no longer is anything subtle about tipping. On the final cruise day, your cabin steward will leave a supply of envelopes for distributing your tips, possibly with guidelines. Lately, the envelopes are crassly stamped with titles—Cabin Steward, Dining Steward, Waiter—in case you did not know whom to tip!

Normally, tips are given to individuals—your cabin stewards and dining room waiters. On ships with Greek crews and on many small vessels, tips are pooled for distribution to include those behind the scenes, such as kitchen staff.

The advent of alternative dining venues has confused tipping customs in recent years. Passengers tend to deduct from the amount given to their dining room wait staff in order to compensate for gratuities rendered at the alternative restaurants. To create a more uniform approach, a number of cruise lines have begun adding gratuities directly to your shipboard bill. Most of these offer the option of decreasing or increasing the amount on your bill depending on how you felt about the service. Whatever the tipping protocol on your cruise, you can be assured that it will be explained to you in detail, probably about a dozen times.

If tips are not added to your shipboard bill, custom dictates that you distribute tips the last night of the cruise. Some lines, particularly deluxe ones, will arrange prepayment of tips. Check our profiles for these lines.

Departing

To smooth disembarkation, your captain and cruise director will ask you to follow procedures outlined in the cruise director's final talk and repeated on closed-circuit television in your cabin and in the daily agenda. On the last day, your cabin steward will give you luggage tags to be completed and attached to your bags. You are asked to place your bags (except hand luggage) outside your cabin door before you retire. Times vary; some lines want it out by 8 or 10 p.m.—an unreasonable hour for passengers dining at the late seating. Such requests are for the ship's convenience, because no luggage can be unloaded until the ship docks. Do what's convenient for you and tell your cabin steward what to expect.

The last night of a cruise is almost always casual; plan your packing accordingly.

Luggage tags use a color-coded, alphabetic system that enables the ship to disembark passengers by cabin locations and airline departure times for those on air/sea packages. (Passengers on the earliest flights disembark first.) Tags also identify your airline so that your bags will go to the correct place at the airport.

Ships normally dock about 7 or 8 a.m. the last day and require about an hour to unload luggage, meaning no passengers will disembark before 9 a.m. The ship is very eager to unload passengers as quickly as possible. Some people find disembarkation so abrupt that it's unpleasant. Try to remember that the next group of passengers will arrive soon, and staff and crew have only about four hours to prepare the ship and be all smiles for them.

Breakfast is served either at normal hours with the full menu or at abbreviated hours with a short menu. Room service usually isn't available. You will be called to depart by the color of your luggage tags. After leaving the ship, you encounter chaos that varies depending on the port. Usually, you proceed to the baggage holding area, where your luggage has been placed according to the letter of your last name. You are responsible for finding it and taking it to Customs. In Miami, for example, baggage handlers help you, and the Customs official stands by the exit to take the declaration form you completed aboard ship. They may check your passport, so have it handy.

After clearing Customs, give your luggage to the airline representative. It will be trucked to the airport. Then find the motorcoach going to your airline's departure area, show your transfer voucher, and climb aboard. If you aren't on an air/sea package, you may be allowed aboard the motorcoach unless you have lots of luggage. Otherwise, taxis are nearby. Airlines with numerous passengers on their flights may set up desks at the port to enable you to check in at the dock and proceed directly to your gate at the airport. It's so sensible, you wonder why it isn't the norm.

Cruise Lines and Their Ships

The Heart of the Matter

Part Two consists of in-depth cruise line and ship profiles—the heart of this guide—serving the U.S. and Canadian markets. Listed alphabetically by cruise lines, each line has three parts: a company profile, its ships' standard features, and ship descriptions. Cruise lines profiled in this section are listed in the Table of Contents. For listings of specific ships, itineraries, destinations, or for a general subject index, refer to the respective indexes at the end of this book.

Cruise Line Profiles

The first three to four pages focus on the cruise line and the type of cruises it offers. At-a-glance summaries—Type of Ships, Type of Cruises, Cruise Line's Strengths, Cruise Line's Shortcomings, Fellow Passengers, Recommended For, Not Recommended For—help you select cruise lines of potential interest.

Summaries are followed by background on the line, its fleet, and cruise areas to reveal the company behind the cruise. The Style section defines the experience you can expect on any ship of that cruise line. Distinctive Features highlights amenities or facilities that are innovative or unusual.

Rates

The Rates section explains discounts, special fares, and packages and provides a range of per-person daily (per diem) costs. These figures were derived by averaging cruise-only (no airfare) brochure rates for each cabin class on every ship in the line. Calculations exclude owner's suites, presidential suites, and other extraordinary accommodations. The rate table aims to indicate the most and the least you would pay per day for a cruise if you paid brochure rates. Savvy shoppers almost certainly will be able to chip away 5% to 50% or more of the listed per diem by taking advantage of common discounts. (Our average rate is not calculated by adding the highest and lowest rates in the brochure table and dividing by two. Rather, the average per diem takes into account the number of each type of accommodation available in the line's cabin inventory. The per diem box averages rates for all ships of the line.)

Past Passengers tells what repeat customers can expect, and The Last Word is our summary of the line—the big picture.

Standard Features

Information on elements common to all ships of a line—including officers, staff, dining facilities, dress code, cabin amenities, and electricity— is listed in one chart for handy reference.

Cruise Ship Profiles

The cruise line's fleet, starting with its flagship (or the most representative) vessel, is covered in depth. Sister ships with identical design are clustered. Other ships that vary only in degree receive shorter treatment. We recommend that readers review the entire section for a given cruise line to have a complete picture of the cruise experience offered.

Quality Ratings   To differentiate ships by overall quality of the cruise experience and to allow comparison of ships from different lines, we give ships a rating of 1 to 10, with 10 being the best. The numerical rating is based on the quality and diversity of the ship's features and service, taking into consideration its state of repair, maintenance, and cleanliness; the design, comfort, décor, and furnishing of public areas; recreational and fitness facilities; meal quality and dining room service; entertainment, activities, and shore excursions; cabin comfort, décor, furnishings, and spaciousness; and hospitality, courtesy, and responsiveness of officers and crew.

We have opted for numerical ratings because some of our colleagues in the travel press have hopelessly muddled the more familiar star ratings. Traditionally, ships have been rated one to five stars. This system was easily understood by the cruising public and provided a quick way to compare critics' opinions. Several years ago, however, some writers changed the scale to one to six stars, precluding meaningful comparison. Although those guidebooks are no longer published and the writers are deceased, the practice continues, mainly because the cruise lines perpetuate it. We believe a standardized rating system helps consumers. But so long as the star system remains corrupted, we elect to abandon the star business.

Value Ratings   There is no consideration of cost in the quality ratings. If you want the finest cruise available and cost is no issue, look no further than the quality ratings. If, however, you seek both quality and value, consult the value rating, expressed in letters. All value ratings are based on brochure rates. Any discount you obtain will improve the value rating for a ship. Value ratings are defined as follows:

A	Exceptional value, a real bargain.
B	Good value.
C	Absolutely fair. You get exactly what you pay for.
D	Somewhat overpriced.
F	Significantly overpriced.

A Word about New Ships

We do not evaluate or rate new ships until they have been in service for at least one year. This allows the new ship to work out any kinks and settle into normal operation. If you are considering a cruise on a new ship, check our ratings and descriptions of other ships in the same line for a good idea of what to expect. If a ship has not completed a year of service at press time, it will be marked as a "preview" in the ship's ratings box.

American Canadian Caribbean Line

461 Water Street, Warren, RI 02885
(401) 247-0955; (800) 556-7450
fax (401) 247-2350
www.accl-smallships.com

Type of Ships   Small, no frills, budget.

Type of Cruises   Light adventure, destination-oriented, unhurried pace.

Cruise Line's Strengths

- innovative, small ships
- imaginative itineraries
- homey ambience
- friendly, diligent staff
- moderate prices

Cruise Line's Shortcomings

- minimal service
- spartan cabins with small bathrooms
- limited shipboard facilities
- sparse precruise information

Fellow Passengers   Mature, experienced travelers ages 55–85; retired couples, seniors; water sports enthusiasts. Not all are sporty, but all are good sports; friendly and unpretentious, most with modest means, college-educated, well-traveled. Even affluent passengers who care little for luxury and ostentation and are keenly interested in history, wildlife, and ecology. They are avid readers and play bridge and Scrabble. Most come from the northeast United States, Florida, and California.

Recommended For   Travelers seeking friendship, companionship, light adventure in unusual destinations; budget-conscious travelers favoring a small ship with family atmosphere. Those who abhor large ships.

Not Recommended For   Swingers, hyper superachievers, snobs, or night owls.

Cruise Areas and Seasons   Spring–fall, U.S. coastal waterways between Rhode Island and Florida; Hudson River/Erie Canal, New England/

Canada; small mid-America rivers and Mississippi byways to New Orleans; Great Lakes from Chicago, Lake Superior and Finger Lakes. Winter, Bahamas; Virgin Islands; Eastern/Southern Caribbean and Orinoco River; Belize, Barrier Reef, Honduras, and Guatemala.

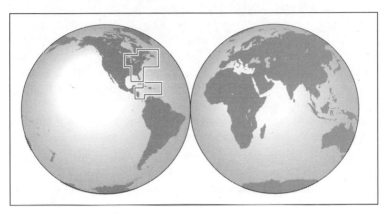

The Line   Shipbuilder and adventurer Luther Blount designed and built his first small ship in 1964 for cruising the Hudson River, Erie Canal, and Canada's inland waterways with his friends. A loyal following developed, and his hobby became a business that pioneered innovative itineraries and ship design.

With slightly larger ships, he expanded to the Bahamas, Virgin Islands, and small islands of the Eastern Caribbean, added "Caribbean" to the line's name, and again pioneered unusual itineraries in Central America, the Southern Caribbean, and other U.S. waterways.

Each vessel, built at Blount's shipyard in Warren, Rhode Island, has had design improvements, larger cabins, and better public space. Blount was a hands-on president, designing every aspect of the ships (with design concepts adopted by many small cruise ships), supervising the building, and scouting new itineraries. ACCL remains a family enterprise. Daughter Nancy Blount, who had been vice president and director of operations, took over as company president when Luther Blount retired in 2001 at the age of 84.

THE FLEET	BUILT/RENOVATED	TONNAGE	PASSENGERS
Grande Caribe	1997	99	100
Grande Mariner	1998	99	100
Niagara Prince	1994/1999	95	84

Style   Adventure at budget prices. Leave your Guccis at home—there's no one who would be impressed. Since its inception, ACCL has maintained an informal, unpretentious atmosphere with limited service and planned entertainment. Passengers receive an intimate look at places they visit. The ships' shallow drafts enable them to cruise small tributaries. Bow ramps, a Blount innovation, allow access to inaccessible places like secluded beaches for swimming and snorkeling. The ships carry a glass-bottom boat, small sailboats, and snorkeling equipment.

ACCL cruises, staffed by American officers and crew, are run like a family outing. Surprisingly good food is served family-style in a folksy atmosphere conducive to friendships. Limited table service is provided by cheerful, hard-working staff who are always ready to bring beverages or second helpings and deal with special requests.

New itineraries are offered every year, tapping pristine areas strong in natural beauty and history and providing frequent opportunities for exploring, swimming, and snorkeling.

Distinctive Features   Bow ramps; retractable pilothouse allowing vessels to sail under low bridges and the length of Erie Canal; underwater viewing cameras.

	HIGHEST	LOWEST	AVERAGE
PER DIEM	$310	$198	$245

Per diems are calculated from cruise line's nondiscounted *cruise-only* fares on standard accommodations and vary by season, cabin, and cruise areas.

Rates   Port charges are additional. Some shore excursions included.

Special Fares and Discounts   10% discount on certain cruises when two cruises are booked back to back; up to 20% discounts or more periodically on special promotions.

- **Third Passenger** 15% discount for each occupant of cabin.
- **Single Supplement** 175% for certain cabins, depending on season and time of booking.

Packages

- **Pre/Post** Panama, Belize, Bonaire, Trinidad, New Orleans.

Past Passengers   Loyalty is rewarded; after ten cruises, a passenger gets one free. Advanced mailings on new itineraries and special discounts.

The Last Word   Up to 68% of passengers are repeat, suggesting that ACCL has found the right formula for a certain type of passenger: one who doesn't want or need pampering and appreciates small ship cruising, preferring conversation and friendship to chorus lines and casinos. New itineraries usually sell out quickly. ACCL reflects the owners' hands-on philosophy and personal touch with customers. Passengers who understand the limitations of a small ship and the nature of these cruises enjoy themselves immensely; those who do not may discover they're on the wrong ship.

ACCL's chief shortcoming is the dearth of information on itineraries, ports of call, and shore excursions sent to passengers before their cruise. Tours are not published in advance, and passengers receive no literature describing places a cruise will visit. ACCL responds that itineraries and tours change, but experience shows they do not change that much. It is difficult to understand why ACCL handles such information haphazardly, particularly when its passengers are destination-focused. It's even more puzzling when you know that ACCL is one of the few cruise lines that does not profit on shore excursions. They're either included in the cruise price or sold at cost—one of many reasons ACCL cruises are a truly good value.

ACCL STANDARD FEATURES

Officers   American.

Staff   Dining, Cabin, Cruise/American.

Dining Facilities   One dining room with open seating; meals served at specific hours: breakfast, 8 a.m.; lunch, noon; dinner, 6 p.m.

Special Diets   Cruise line needs notice at booking, but chefs can accommodate basic requests.

Room Service   None.

Dress Code   Casual at all times; men never need a tie. Gentlemen might bring a jacket and women a dress in case they want to try a fancy place in a port of call.

Cabin Amenities   Air-conditioning/heat; upper-deck cabins have windows that can be opened. Very small bathroom with hand-held shower. Reading light; plug for hair dryers. Limited drawer and closet space.

Electrical Outlets   110 AC.

Wheelchair Access   No designated cabins; motorized chair between main and sun decks.

Recreation and Entertainment   Lounge with bar setup, books, and videos; informal entertainment, occasional lectures; bridge and parlor games. No casino, swimming pool, gym, or theater.

Sports and Other Activities   Glass-bottom boat and snorkeling equipment on board for warm-weather cruises.

Beauty and Fitness   No facilities. On request, cruise director will make appointments with beauty/barber salons in ports.

Other Facilities   Ships have no doctors; "BYOB" policy.

Children's Facilities   None. Children under age 14 not accepted.

Theme Cruises   Fall foliage.

Smoking   No smoking inside ships; allowed only in outside open areas.

ACCL Suggested Tipping $12–$20 per person per day. All tips are pooled and shared.

Credit Cards   None. Passengers may use travelers checks or personal checks.

NIAGARA PRINCE	QUALITY **2**	VALUE **A**
Registry: United States	Length: 175 feet	Beam: 40 feet
Cabins: 42	Draft: 6.3 feet	Speed: 12 knots
Maximum Passengers: 84	Passenger Decks: 3	Elevators: Chairlift
	Crew: 15	Space Ratio: NA

The Ship   The U.S.-flagged *Niagara Prince,* an innovative small ship with shallow draft, made her debut in 1994. She was designed to navigate the length of the Erie Canal and sail on coastal waters. The comfortable but basic ship has two passenger decks with homey décor and low ceilings.

The lounge and dining room, located forward on the top or sun deck, rather than on the main deck as on earlier ships, has windows at the bow and along the sides, providing enhanced views. The lounge, shaped by the bow, has the ship's only television set, books, and newspapers (updated as available in ports). The dining room is an all-purpose room between meals. The sun deck has cabins and a wraparound promenade with small sitting areas at each end.

A flight of steps at the bow accesses the patented bow ramp, used when a site of interest has no dock. Extensions lengthen the ramp and allow for dry shore landings. Stairs from the promenade deck lead to a partially covered rooftop deck with chairs.

Also atop is the retractable pilothouse, lowered to pass under bridges by lifting off its roof, folding back its three sides, and disconnecting all the equipment. The captain's chair, console, steering mechanism, and equipment then are lowered to the promenade deck and reconnected so the ship can resume operation. It's quite a scene to watch, leaving you with an I-had-to-see-it-to-believe-it feeling.

Niagara Prince's profile can be made even lower with a hull feature Blount likens to letting the air out of a tire. It enables the ship to pass under the Erie Canal's lowest bridges and traverse the waterway from Troy to Buffalo, the first boat to do so in over 120 years. (Previous ACCL ships traveled about three-quarters of the way.) The feature also is used to navigate the Chicago River through the heart of the Windy City, passing under its bridges.

Niagara Prince offers a motorized chairlift for passengers who have difficulty negotiating stairs, and during recent renovations, new hallway railings were added to improve capabilities for handicapped passengers. Other changes included opening the bow area to make it more accessible for passengers, relocating the bar to increase space in the dining/lounge area, and refurbishing with new furniture and rugs.

Itineraries   See Itinerary Index.

Cabins   Small, spartan, but functional cabins have twin beds on metal frames. Storage space is limited to four drawers, about one square foot of counter space, and a four-foot-tall cabinet for hanging clothes; luggage goes under the beds. Accordion doors close tightly but do not lock.

Bathrooms, ingeniously designed by Blount, are tiny but utilitarian; they were improved somewhat during the ship's most recent refurbishing. They're a deluxe version of a "head" on a sailboat or RV. A very small sink with spring taps lets water run for only a few seconds at a time. The hand-held shower is very efficient and can be left in its wall mount when showering; the shower curtain is the "door" to the head. A trap in the floor lets water out. The toilet has a fill-and-flush system that works very well. However, if you do not operate it properly—refilling the water in the bowl after each use—or close the trap in the floor, an unpleasant odor develops.

All but two main-deck cabins are outside. The largest and most desirable cabins are on the sun deck. Six cabins open onto the promenade; others have large sliding windows—a pleasant feature on U.S. waterways when fresh, cool air fills the room.

Cabins are cleaned daily; linens are changed every third day. Bath towels are replaced as needed. (The ship does not have laundry facilities.) There is no room service.

Specifications 40 outside cabins (6 opening onto the promenade); 2 inside; all have private facilities and twin lower beds; some can be converted to doubles. Four cabins have upper and lower berths. Standard dimensions are between 72 and 96 square feet.

Dining A big advantage on a small ship is its fresh food and homemade bread and pastries. Aboard *Niagara Prince*, well-prepared American fare is much better than expected for the ship's category and better than on more expensive lines.

Menus are posted daily. One of two entrées available is lighter, healthful fare. This reflects past passengers' criticism of the ship's tendency to serve high-cholesterol foods. New menus are an improvement, but we would prefer more salads and green vegetables and less gravy and sauces.

The main course of the hearty breakfast—eggs, pancakes, and so on— varies daily. Lunch usually includes a freshly made soup (the best we've had on any ship), salad, and dessert. Dinner features fish, chicken, or other meat; vegetables; and dessert. Meals are family-style; staff serves dessert, beverages, and second helpings. Coffee, tea, and cookies are always available in the dining room.

The dining room, which has an open kitchen, has tables for four, six, eight, and ten. The square tables for four are also used for card games. Passengers bring their own liquor and wine, and ACCL provides storage, setups, and ice. For the captain's dinners, ACCL supplies wine and an open bar. Likewise, for Celebration Night, when passengers collectively celebrate birthdays, anniversaries, and so on, the line supplies wine. Make-Your-Own-Sundae, with many varieties of ice cream and toppings, is another popular event.

Service   Most crew members—young, energetic, and terrific—are from Rhode Island or neighboring states. The teams that clean the cabins also attend the dining room. They are cheerful, hardworking, unfailingly polite, and particularly accommodating to their mostly older passengers.

Facilities and Activities   Except for television, videotapes, local talent at some ports, and visiting lecturers, there is no evening entertainment. Most passengers are in bed by 10 p.m. Although the ship has some paperbacks, avid readers should bring their own books.

Passengers gather in the lounge for predinner cocktails. A crew member helps prepare drinks. After dinner, some may linger for a film or bridge and other card and parlor games. ACCL's captains are very knowledgeable about places the ships visit and often provide running commentary.

The ship has no shop, but the cruise director does open his " boutique" to sell signature shirts, caps, and jackets at least once during each cruise.

Sports and Fitness   Onboard, a mile walk on the promenade deck usually starts the morning fitness activity for most passengers. Ashore, sports activities can include swimming, snorkeling, hiking, and birding, depending on the itinerary.

Shore Excursions   On the cruise's first day, the cruise director distributes descriptions of tours. Excursions vary with itineraries and cost $6–$30. ACCL uses local operators specializing in small special-interest groups. The line says it continuously checks tours and books the most appealing.

Postscript   The *Niagara Prince* is a one-of-a-kind ship, sailing unique itineraries through America's most historic waterways. It's both a great value and a great cruise experience.

GRANDE CARIBE	QUALITY **2**	VALUE **A**
GRANDE MARINER	QUALITY **2**	VALUE **A**
Registry: United States	Length: 183/182 feet	Beam: 40 feet
Cabins: 50	Draft: 6.6 feet	Speed: 12 knots
Maximum Passengers:	Passenger Decks: 3	Elevators: Chairlift
100/96	Crew: 15/17	Space Ratio: NA

The Ships   Built at Blount Marine in Warren, Rhode Island, the *Grande Caribe* and her near twin, *Grande Mariner,* are designed for coastal cruises from Labrador to the Amazon. Like other ACCL ships, they have shallow drafts and bow ramps to guarantee access to areas large cruise ships simply cannot reach. They also have a retractable pilothouse for passage under low bridges and a chairlift for passengers who have trouble negotiating stairs. On Caribbean and Central American cruises, the ships carry a Blount-designed glass-bottom boat and Sunfish.

Although the *Grande Caribe* is only slightly larger than her earlier sister ships, her layout varies in several ways. The dining room is on the main deck; the lounge, with wraparound windows, is on the top deck. A new feature is a stern swimming platform.

The *Grande Mariner,* which made her debut in 1998, has more comfortable cabins than her sisters do and unique features, including an acoustical "floating deck" between the engine room and main-deck cabins aimed at reducing engine noise and sound-deadening enclosures for the ship's main generators. (We did not find the ship quieter than her earlier sisters. In fact, our cabin, 44A, was actually noisier from the sound of the generators.)

In another first for ACCL, the *Grande Mariner* hull is ice-strengthened for cruising in Canadian subarctic waters of Labrador, Newfoundland, and parts of the St. Lawrence River. The ship's 24-passenger glass-bottom boat and shore launch are built with the same foam-based materials found in a life raft.

The *Grande Mariner's* "vista view" lounge, a multifunctional room located forward on the upper deck, has wraparound windows to showcase passing scenery. The room has a bar, piano, and large projection screen; it can be used for lectures by visiting experts, historians, and naturalists, or for business seminars. A self-service bar has storage shelves for passengers' liquor and a fridge for chilling wine and beer. Nightly, the chef prepares hors d'oeuvres for the cocktail hour.

Itineraries   See Itinerary Index.

Cabins   The *Grande Caribe* has a third, lower deck (the *Niagara Prince* lacks this) with six cabins fitted with upper and lower berths and no windows. There are three similar, inside cabins on the main deck. These 9 are the least expensive of the *Grande Caribe's* 50 cabins.

All other cabins are on the main and sun decks and have two beds, either side by side or in an L shape. Two cabins have double beds. Six cabins on the sun deck have doors that open to the outside promenade.

On the *Grande Mariner,* each cabin has its own air conditioner with air circulated outside through ducts. Unlike many other ships where air is recirculated, the Blount-designed system supplies fresh air continuously to the cabins, and stale air is removed.

Also, *Grande Mariner's* cabins are ACCL's most comfortable. Bathrooms, particularly, show marked improvement. Gone is the hole in the floor from which odors escaped. Toilets operate on the standard principle, but the design is more streamlined. Also new—cabins doors can be locked from the inside. However, passengers are not issued keys, and they don't need them.

Specifications   50 cabins (*Caribe* 9, *Mariner* 7 inside/no window; *Caribe* 8, *Mariner* 9 open onto promenade); all have private facilities and twin lower beds (except *Mariner* has 2 cabins with double bed); some converted to doubles. *Caribe* 8, *Mariner* 10 have upper and lower berths; 1 cabin has 1 double and 1 single. Standard dimensions, 80–110 square feet.

Service   The young and energetic crew members are outstanding. They are hardworking, smiling, and unfailingly polite. The same teams that clean the cabins also attend the dining room. They seem eager to please and are particularly accommodating to their mostly older passengers.

Facilities and Activities   There is no evening entertainment of the usual cruise variety. Passengers gather in the lounge for informal, predinner cocktails. After dinner, some may linger for card or parlor games or to watch a film. The lounge has a television and videotapes, and visiting lecturers or local talent may appear at ports of call. Most passengers are in bed by 10 p.m.

Postscript   ACCL's ships' best features are their staff, itineraries, and the camaraderie among passengers—the latter not found on a large ship. The ships are basic (at times, you feel you're camping), but passengers appear to be happy and having a good time. Clearly they are the type more interested in destinations than in creature comforts.

Note that no liquor is sold on board any ACCL vessels; BYOB basics with setups are offered.

Anyone planning a cruise on the *Grande Caribe* or *Grande Mariner* should read the entire section on ACCL to have a more complete picture of the cruise experience the line offers.

Carnival Cruise Lines

3655 NW 87th Avenue, Miami, FL 33178-2428
(305) 599-2600; (800) 438-6744
(800) 327-9501; fax (305) 406-8630
www.carnival.com

Type of Ships New, mod superliners and megaliners.

Type of Cruise Casual, contemporary mass market. "Fun Ships" hallmark makes the ship the destination—just as central to the cruise as the ports of call.

Cruise Line's Strengths

- lavish recreational and entertainment facilities
- new fleet with unusual, innovative interiors
- value
- clear, easy-to-use literature
- variety of dining outlets
- quality of cuisine for price category

Cruise Line's Shortcomings

- megaliner size
- little relief from crowds and glitz
- lack of outdoor promenade deck on some ships
- long lines for facilities and services

Fellow Passengers From all walks of life, ages 3 to 93. Although Carnival's image is shiploads of young swingers partying day and night (an image Carnival once cultivated to attract young people to cruising), the mix is more likely to range from Joe Sixpack and his Nike-shod kids to Lester and Alice celebrating their 50th wedding anniversary. The cruises lend themselves to families with or without kids, honeymooners, married couples, singles, and seniors. Average age: 43. On a typical cruise, 40% are ages 35–55; 30% younger than 35 (including 400,000 kids annually); 30% older than 55. Fifty percent are first-time cruisers. Most have medium income.

Recommended For First-time cruisers who want an active, high-energy, party atmosphere; families, young singles, and couples; young-at-heart of any age; those who enjoy Las Vegas glitz or similar ambience.

Not Recommended For   Small-ship devotees; sophisticated travelers who prefer luxury and individual travel; anyone seeking quiet or cerebral travel experience; those who consider Martha's Vineyard their ideal vacation spot.

Cruise Areas and Seasons   Bahamas, Caribbean, and West Coast and Mexican Riviera year-round. Panama Canal, Alaska, Hawaii, Bermuda, New England/Canada, seasonally.

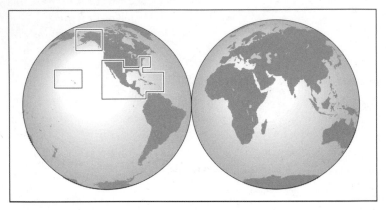

The Line   In 30 short years, Carnival Cruise Lines went from one ship that ran aground on its maiden voyage to the largest, most influential company in the cruise business, having revolutionized the nature of cruises along the way. Its story is the stuff of legends.

The late Ted Arison, a cruise executive in Florida, and a maverick travel company in Boston bought the *Mardi Gras* (formerly the *Empress of Canada*) in 1972. After three years of losses and near bankruptcy, Arison took over the company, assumed its $5 million debt, bought the assets—the *Mardi Gras*—for $1, and created the "Fun Ship" concept, turning a profit in his first year and adding two more ships.

Arison's aim was to take the stuffiness out of cruising, abandon the elitist image on which classic oceanliners had thrived, and make cruises fun and available to everyone, particularly to middle America, who never dreamed of a holiday at sea. He hit the right button. Through the 1970s, Carnival ships broke occupancy records while traditional companies were sinking all around.

Carnival continued to defy conventional wisdom. In the late 1970s, with spiraling shipbuilding costs and the oil crisis putting the future of cruising in doubt, Carnival ordered a new ship, *Tropicale,* whose technology set new industry standards, changed ship profiles, and enhanced Carnival's "Fun Ship" concept. Then, a decade after its inauspicious beginning, Carnival added three radically new ships—*Holiday, Jubilee,* and *Celebration*—which became trendsetters of the 1980s and beyond. These 1,800-passenger superliners were not the largest passenger ships ever built, but their design and madcap décor were profoundly different from oceanliners of the past.

To prepare for the 21st century, Carnival added eight megaliners, each for over 2,600 passengers, and lifted eyebrows with such names as *Fantasy* and *Ecstasy.* They were followed in late 1996 with the 101,000-ton, 3,400-passenger *Carnival Destiny,* the world's largest ship when it was launched. Carnival was so pleased with her performance and passenger response that it ordered four more like her, each costing $450 million or more.

Along with the Destiny class, Carnival started a new class of ships with the 86,000-ton *Carnival Spirit* and *Carnival Pride,* which debuted in 2001, and another new class of 110,000 tons starting with the *Carnival Conquest* in 2002. Carnival's new ship investment in the 1990s exceeded $5 billion; those so far for the 21st century have added more than $3 billion, bringing the fleet total to 22 ships by 2005. When the new ships for its sister companies—a total of 10—are added in, the expenditure reaches more than $6 billion.

Under Arison's son Micky, Carnival's young, aggressive team has marketed cruises as the universal dream vacation for everyone. A publicly held company since 1987, Carnival carries almost three million passengers a year, accounting for more than 37% of all cruise passengers boarding from U.S. ports. In 1989, it broadened its base (and buffed its image) by acquiring the classic Holland America Line and the upscale Windstar Cruises. Later, it acquired ownership of ultraluxurious Seabourn Cruise Line. In 1996, Carnival bought part-ownership in Costa Cruises, Europe's largest line (which Carnival later bought in total). The following year, Carnival stunned the cruise world by buying its competitor Cunard. And more recently, it outmaneuvered Royal Caribbean International for the purchase of Princess Cruises/P&O Cruises, adding another 18 ships to its inventory. These acquisitions give Carnival a total of 83 ships and a whopping 70% share of the world cruise market. All operate as separate companies, each with a sharp focus; together, they give Carnival tremendous clout.

In 1999, Carnival became the first major cruise line to launch direct booking on its website, which now accounts for 15% of its sales. In recent years, Carnival has introduced departures from new gateways, particularly new U.S. ports such as Jacksonville, advancing the "close-to-home" trend following the 9/11 attack that expanded its focus on families. Carnival also added a second children's playroom to all Fantasy-class ships. Its children's program employs one of cruising's largest staffs of trained personnel, with over 100 child counselors spread over 19 ships on a full-time basis; additional personnel are hired during peak periods. The line was also the first with a smoke-free ship.

"Vacation Guarantee," a Carnival innovation, allows a dissatisfied passenger, after notifying the purser's office, to leave a cruise at the first non-U.S. port of call and get a prorated refund. Another Carnival "first": a 24-hour, toll-free hotline—(877) TVL-HTLN (885-4856)—for passengers who encounter a travel emergency (such as severe weather or an airline strike) en route to or returning from their cruise. Passengers outside the United States can call collect (305) 406-4779. In 2001, it launched new, more flexible dining programs and introduced fleetwide Internet access for passengers.

Carnival's Skipper's Club is a VIP check-in system that enables the line to check in passengers from remote locations. For instance, passengers met at the airport in San Juan can be issued boarding passes electronically, so they can board the vessel immediately upon arrival at the pier. Guest booked in category 11 or 12 are automatically enrolled. Passengers may inquire at the cruise terminal about enrolling in the club.

THE FLEET	BUILT/RENOVATED	TONNAGE	PASSENGERS
Carnival Conquest	2002	110,000	2,974
Carnival Destiny	1996	101,353	2,642
Carnival Glory	2003	110,000	2,974
Carnival Legend	2002	88,500	2,124
Carnival Liberty	2005	110,000	2,974
Carnival Miracle	2004	88,500	2,124
Carnival Pride	2002	88,500	2,124
Carnival Spirit	2001	88,500	2,124
Carnival Triumph	1999	102,000	2,758
Carnival Valor	2004	110,000	2,974
Carnival Victory	2000	102,000	2,758
Celebration	1987/2000/03	47,262	1,486
Ecstasy	1991/2000	70,367	2,052
Elation	1998	70,367	2,052
Fantasy	1990/2000	70,367	2,056
Fascination	1994	70,367	2,052
Holiday	1985/94/98/2000	46,052	1,452
Imagination	1995	70,367	2,052
Inspiration	1996	70,367	2,052
Jubilee (until late 2004)	1986/1999	47,262	1,486
Paradise	1998	70,367	2,052
Sensation	1993	70,367	2,052

Style   Youthful and casual, "Fun Ships" have so much action and diversions that the ship itself is the cruise experience. An important part of creating Carnival has been Joe Farcus, an interior architect and decorator, unique in his role among the cruise lines. He believes people go on vacation to have fun, and his job is to create the surroundings and atmosphere for it. If you accept his flamboyant décor as entertaining, you will find it ingenious. But sometimes, so much bombards the senses that the impact is more exhausting than exhilarating.

The emphasis on fun aims to get people out of their cabins and into public spaces to become part of the action. The variety of activity and entertainment attracts a range of passengers, but the basic appeal is to the young and young at heart—at reasonable prices.

Another characteristic: Perhaps more than any line, Carnival has standardized features on its ships. If you see a water slide on one ship, you can count on its being on the others. A menu with four desserts on one ship will be on others. Even deck names are the same. The uniformity helps keep down costs, and consistency is reassuring to passengers—and to their travel agents.

Distinctive Features   Ships' design and décor, children's programs, 24-hour pizzerias, sushi bars on nine ships, alternative dining; state-of-the-art fitness centers, areas for topless sunbathing, tuxedo rentals, vacation guarantee, golf program, smoke-free ship, travelers' hotline.

	HIGHEST	LOWEST	AVERAGE
PER DIEM	$693	$108	$306

Per diems are calculated from cruise line's nondiscounted *cruise-only* fares on standard accommodations and vary by season, cabin, and cruise areas.

Rates   All include port fees.

Special Fares and Discounts   Super Savers early-bird program provides discounts ranging from up to $860 per cabin on three-day cruises to $2,200 on seven-day cruises.

- **Children's Fare**   Same as deeply discounted third/fourth person rates. Passengers younger than age 21 must be accompanied by a parent, grandparent, or legal guardian 25 years old or older in the cabin. Exceptions apply to married couples and to children traveling with parents in a separate cabin.
- **Single Supplement**   150% or 200%, depending on category. Singles matching program.

Packages

- **Cruise/Air Add-on with Transfers:** Yes.
- **Pre/Post** Yes. Wedding packages in U.S. home ports and eight Caribbean ports year-round, plus Vancouver.
- **Others**   Yes.

Past Passengers   No club. After first cruise, passengers receive a two-year free subscription to *Carnival Currents,* the line's onboard magazine, which includes discounts. Repeater's party on five-day or longer cruises.

The Last Word   Carnival has had an enormous impact on cruises, particularly those aimed at the mass market. The line wrote the book on marketing. Yet despite its success, a Carnival cruise isn't for everybody. The ships have more glitter than glamour. Some people love them; others think they redefine tacky. For the generation that grew up with shopping malls and Las Vegas–style glitz, Carnival's gargantuan, flashy ships may feel like home. But if big and boisterous is not your style, Carnival is probably not for you. Yet everyone should take at least one Carnival cruise to see for themselves. The ships are eye-popping and the atmosphere infectious. Even the most staid, buttoned-down party poopers are often turned on by the Carnival neon and end up having the time of their lives.

CARNIVAL STANDARD FEATURES

Officers   Italian.

Staff   Dining/International; Cabin/Central American, Asian, others; Cruise/ American and others.

Dining Facilities   Two main dining rooms/four seatings (except Spirit class, one dining room). Breakfast and lunch cafeteria-style and Seaview Bistro dinner service in lido restaurant; midnight buffet. Lido restaurant is four-in-one: pizzeria, Asian, trattoria, American grill. Alternative restaurants on newest ships.

Special Diets   Low-salt, diabetic, vegetarian, bland.

Room Service   24 hours, upgraded menu.

Dress Code   Casual; no shorts in evening; two formal nights on 7-day; tuxedos not required, semiformal dress is acceptable.

Cabin Amenities   Closed-circuit television; safe. Bath with shower; international direct-dial phones. Hair dryers on Destiny and Spirit class; other ships on request. Terry robes in all outside cabins.

Electrical Outlets   110 AC.

Wheelchair-Access   14–27 cabins, depending on ship.

Recreation and Entertainment   Casino, bingo, disco, library; 10 bar/lounges (16 on Spirit class; 18 *Destiny*; 22 *Conquest*); two-deck show lounges (three-deck on *Destiny*).

Sports and Other Activities   Three or four outside swimming pools, shuffleboard, jogging tracks (Fantasy, Destiny, Spirit class), Ping-Pong.

Beauty and Fitness   Barber/beauty salon, sauna. Spas on all ships; full gym, exercise classes, body treatments. Spa fare on menus.

Other Facilities   Boutiques, tuxedo rentals, infirmary, video of cruise souvenir ($39), and coin-operated laundry facilities; Internet cafés fleetwide.

Children's Facilities   Camp Carnival, year-round, with supervised activities for toddlers to teens. Video arcades, water slides, playroom, teen club/disco, children's menus, high chairs. Baby-sitting, 10 p.m.–3 a.m., for $6 per hour for first child, $4 for each additional child in same family; children under two years also welcome. Passengers under age 21 must be accompanied by adult older than age 25 in same cabin.

Theme Cruises   Some.

CARNIVAL STANDARD FEATURES *(continued)*

Smoking Smoke-free dining rooms and main show lounge. *Paradise*, totally smoke-free.

Carnival Suggested Tipping $9.75 per person, per day added automatically to passenger's on-board account, which can also be pre-paid when booking cruise. Otherwise, $3.50 for waiter, $2 busboy; $3.50 cabin steward, per person, per day, 15% added to wine and bar bill.

Credit Cards Cruise and shipboard charges: American Express, MasterCard, Visa, Discover, Optima.

FANTASY / ECSTASY	QUALITY **4**	VALUE **B**
ELATION	QUALITY **5**	VALUE **B**
FASCINATION / IMAGINATION	QUALITY **6**	VALUE **A**
INSPIRATION	QUALITY **6**	VALUE **A**
PARADISE	QUALITY **7**	VALUE **A**
SENSATION	QUALITY **4**	VALUE **B**

Registry: *Fantasy / Ecstasy / Elation / Paradise:* Panama	Length: 855 feet	Beam: 118 feet
Sensation / Imagination Fascination / Inspiration: Bahamas		
Cabins: 1,022/1,020	Draft: 26 feet	Speed: 21 knots
Maximum Passengers: 2,610/2,606	Passenger Decks: 10	Elevators: 14
	Crew: 920	Space Ratio: 34

The Ships Billed as ships for the 21st century, Carnival's eight megaliners were already bedazzling passengers of the 1990s. Their flashy décor and high-energy ambience are Las Vegas, Disneyland, and Starlight Express all in one. Atrium lobbies ascend seven decks at the heart of the ship and contain huge, specially commissioned art. Throughout the vessels, there are so many bars, lounges, and entertainment and recreation outlets—all imaginatively decorated—that they can't be absorbed in one cruise. No one cruises on one of these ships to rest; the senses work overtime.

Except for décor—each ship is themed—the vessels are identical, and as with all Carnival ships, even the deck names are the same. The *Fantasy*, first of the group, is dazzling with its towering atrium awash in lights dominated by a 20-foot-tall kinetic sculpture of rotating cylinders, created by Israeli artist Yaacov Agam. Here and in the entertainment areas, 15 miles of computerized lights are programmed to change color—constantly but subtly—from white to cool blue to hot red, altering the ambience with each change. *Fantasy* was given a multimillion-dollar refurbishing in 2000, and meeting facilities and a brand new promenade were added.

The second megaliner, *Ecstasy,* is designed as a city at sea. Carnival-watchers declared her the fleet's most elegant and sophisticated vessel, reflecting an effort to upgrade the style. But there's no mistaking this for anything but a Carnival ship, especially when encountering the 24-foot-tall plastic and steel sculpture in the Grand Atrium. Created by kinetic artist Len Janklow, it encompasses 12 huge cubes flooded in light, each holding 8 small cubes that appear to float in space.

Ecstasy's décor takes inspiration from Manhattan's Café Society, showcasing exotic woods, Italian marbles, rich carpets, sumptuous fabrics, and a vintage Rolls Royce on the lounge-lined City Lights Boulevard. The promenade's highlights are the **Neon Bar,** a piano bar with vintage neon signs, and Chinatown Lounge, guarded by huge lion-headed Foo dogs.

Sensation, third in the series, resembles *Ecstasy* with décor slightly more sophisticated than her mates'. Light, sound, and color create a "sensual" environment. Public rooms range from elegant to kitschy. Among them, the **Touch of Class Lounge** is a "hands-on" experience, with gigantic hands cupping the entrance, hands supporting tables, and chairs and bar stools shaped like hands.

Fascination takes Hollywood of the 1930s, 1940s, and 1950s as its theme, mixing homage and spoofs—and kitsch galore. On the entertainment promenade, Hollywood Boulevard, are **Puttin' on the Ritz Lounge, Bogey's Café,** and the **Passage to India Lounge.** But the showstoppers are 20 life-sized mannequins of movie legends posed as they might be in real life. At the **Stars Bar,** you find Gary Cooper and Rita Hayworth, and in the **Tara Library,** Vivien Leigh and Clark Gable. Purple neon dramatically edges each of the seven decks rising from the Grand Atrium's lobby, which is centered by an enormous sculpture, *Nucleus,* by British artist Susanna Holt.

Architect Joe Farcus's fertile imagination worked overtime creating the décor of the bars and lounges for *Imagination.* Images of space ships, space stations, and other futuristic technologies are incorporated into four rotating towers of stainless steel and clear plastic that are the centerpiece of *Imagination's* atrium. The 24-foot sculpture by Len Janklow is among commissioned works from five artists whose imaginations carried them from powerful seascapes to mythical tales of ancient lands.

The ship's 24-hour pizzeria is now a feature on all Carnival ships. Favorite nightspots include **Shangri-La,** for music and dancing, and **Mirage,** a sing-along piano bar.

Farcus's concept for the *Inspiration* was drawn from the arts. Décor incorporates musical icons, themes, and motifs—from a larger-than-life replica of Elvis's guitar in the disco to the elegant **Chopin Lounge** with a piano. The ship offers the Fantasy group's multideck, glass-domed atrium and dramatic centerpiece, a promenade of lounges and bars, and sports and recreation features.

Elation boasts significant improvements over her Fantasy sisters and incorporates some of the best design elements, including the atrium lobby bar copied from *Carnival Destiny*. *Elation* was the first cruise ship with the new Azipod propulsion system, which dramatically reduces engine noise and vibration. The system pulls rather than pushes the ship, eliminating the need for rudders or stern thrusters and increasing maneuverability and fuel efficiency.

Elation, the most sophisticated of the Fantasy-class ships, has a broader appeal than her older, glitzier sisters, although there is still plenty of glitter. *Elation's* theme is the mythological Muses. The ship's noticeably more elegant décor uses copper tones and inlaid woods. Prisms and fiber-optic lights create subtle lighting and mood changes. Among new features were a sushi bar, Carnival's largest children's center, a patisserie and coffee bar, a redesigned lido café area, a casino bar, and a conference center.

The eighth member of the group, *Paradise,* is the world's first and only smoke-free cruise ship. A bright red no-smoking emblem is painted on the hull. Even the staff does not smoke. Carnival takes the no-smoking policy very seriously. Passengers must sign an agreement binding them to the rules; anyone caught smoking is subject to a $250 fine and may be told to leave the ship.

Your first view on boarding *Paradise* is likely to be the atrium, centered by a large circular bar—a feature copied from *Carnival Destiny,* where it has been very popular. Immediately, you notice foot-tall Fabergé-like eggs. Used in décor throughout the ship, they have tiny lights to suggest the diamonds and rubies on Fabergé originals. From the bar, a stairway decorated with three kinds of wood winds upward to the Atlantic Deck, where every lounge recalls maritime history. *Paradise* immortalizes famous steamships in maritime history and evokes the era when travelers boarded famous vessels and headed to foreign lands.

Itineraries   See Itinerary Index.

Cabins   As with all Carnival ships, the 12 cabin categories include some of the largest standard cabins and junior suites of any ship in their price category. They are finished in light oak, and although color schemes vary among ships, the furniture and décor are essentially the same—basic and comfortable.

Almost all cabins have twin beds that convert to king-size—a Carnival innovation quickly copied by other cruise lines. Cabins have international direct-dial phones; a desk/dressing table; television with channels for movies, cartoons, and satellite programs (depending on ship's location); stereo music; and wall safes. Outside cabins have picture windows. Bathrooms are well designed and have roomy shower stalls. They have soap and some toiletries; hair dryers are available on request. Closet space is adequate for short, warm-weather cruises. All ships have self-service laundry rooms with washers, dryers, irons, and ironing boards—a big plus for families traveling with children.

Specifications   389 inside cabins, 564 outside; 54 suites with verandas (28 suites with bathtub Jacuzzi). Standard dimensions, 183–190 square feet; 953 with twins convertible to doubles; 19 inside with upper and lower berths; no singles. All ships have wheelchair-accessible cabins.

Dining   Each ship has two dining rooms with two seatings for breakfast and lunch, and four seatings for dinner at 5:45 p.m., 6:15 p.m., 8 p.m., and 8:30 p.m. The rooms are on an upper deck and have large windows with good views.

Restaurants have round tables for eight people in the center of the room; the sides are lined with rectangular tables, which are sometimes difficult to get in and out of. The *Ecstasy's* **Wind Star** and **Wind Song** and *Elation's* **Imagination** and **Inspiration** dining rooms get more kudos for stylish décor than their older sisters. All earn criticism for high noise levels. The ships no longer have wine stewards; wine is served by waiters often unfamiliar with the selections.

Breakfast, lunch and midnight buffet are served cafeteria-style on the Lido Deck. *Fantasy's* **Windows on the Sea** is one of the group's most attractive restaurants, with pastel parasols, brass highlights, and etched glass. On the *Ecstasy,* the **Panorama Bar and Grill** has floor-to-ceiling windows and a playful ambience with signal flags and blue neon lighting. *Fascination's* **Coconut Grove Bar and Grille** has imitation palm trees as columns and a bamboo bar and tables.

Seaview Bistros, alternative casual dining available fleetwide, serve specialty salads, pastas, steaks, and desserts in a café setting. They operate each evening from 6 to 9:30 p.m. in the lido restaurant. Tablecloths, pre-set silverware, and flowers on tables set the tone. Service is buffet-style, but waiters refill drink orders and food requests. Another winner is the around-the-clock pizzeria, offering delicious pizzas with varied toppings, fresh Caesar salads, and warm garlic rolls. *Paradise, Elation, Imagination, Inspiration,* and *Jubilee* have sushi bars.

Carnival initially was not known for its cuisine, but recent efforts to upgrade the quality, selection, and variety have yielded outstanding results. The line now offers menus fleetwide with lighter, more contemporary cuisine and an expanded wine list. A typical dinner menu offers three juices; four appetizers; three soups; two salads; two fish choices; three entrées of beef, chicken, or turkey; five desserts; and a variety of ice cream and sherbet, cheese, and beverages. At least one item per course is marked as spa fare, which has lower calories, sodium, fat, and cholesterol.

Service   Dining staff generally earn good marks, but cabin attendants get mixed reviews. Cruise directors and their staff are very professional, but the cruise director on ships of this size is in little evidence except when he is on stage. Recent passengers on Fantasy reported that contacting their room steward or the purser's desk by phone was nearly impossible. They also complained that they encountered orientation problems on boarding. Rather than being escorted to their cabins, they were handed ship diagrams and directed to find their cabins on their own. The bottom line: Megaliners offer many wonderful facilities and options, but personal service is not among them.

Facilities and Activities The ships' array of activities include bingo, a singles party, a newlywed game, a passenger talent show, horse racing, bridge, ballroom and country line-dance classes, masquerades, wine and cheese parties, and sing-alongs. There are tours of the galleys and bridge, first-run movies daily, and abundant boutiques. The library/lounge— especially the mahogany-paneled **Explorer's Club** on *Ecstasy*—is one of the loveliest rooms in the Carnival fleet.

The Fantasy group's most distinctive feature is an indoor promenade that serves as an "entertainment boulevard" of bars, lounges, disco, casino, and nightclubs. Called the Century Boulevard on the *Fantasy,* the promenade has the **Cats Lounge,** with décor inspired by the long-running Broadway show, and **Cleopatra's,** a piano bar with every conceivable cliché in ancient Egyptian art.

At one end of the boulevard, the spectacular, two-deck **Universal** show lounge stages nightly entertainment on the scale of a Las Vegas extravaganza. It's outstanding. At the stern is the opulent **Majestic Bar,** with a king's ransom in marble and onyx. Through the bar is the flamboyant **Crystal Lounge,** where red and white lights nearly blind you. Here you can catch the naughty comedy acts. The casinos, each with over 200 slot machines, blackjack tables, roulette, and other games, are among the largest afloat.

The most amusing place on the *Fascination's* nighttime array is **Club 88,** a piano bar named for the 88 keys on a piano and decorated with huge, neon-lit keys at the door and on the columns between piano-shaped tables. At the Passage to India Lounge, two life-size elephant figures are a prelude to the interior draped with elaborate Indian ceremonial cloth. Furnishings include British colonial-style mahogany chairs, a statue of a multi-armed Hindu deity, a domed shrine holding a Buddha, mosaic ceiling tiles, and floral carpets. The **Puttin' on the Ritz Lounge,** with décor inspired by Fred Astaire's top hat, offers late-night comedy acts and a vocalist.

Fascination's **Palace Lounge,** in shimmering golden beige and silvery pink with painted clouds decorating the walls, had the most technologically advanced stage at sea when she was introduced.

On the *Sensation,* the popular **Michelangelo Lounge** combines soft gray, yellow, and black in its furnishings and uses classic features, such as Ionic columns, Greek designs, and ceiling frescoes. The bar and dance floor are marble. The **Polo Lounge** was designed for those seeking a quiet spot—all the ships have at least one such lounge.

The *Elation's* **Mikado** showroom (named after the Gilbert and Sullivan operetta) strikes a Japanese theme with large fans, rice paper shoji screen walls, Japanese-motif upholstery, and gold-leaf bamboo and chrysanthemum designs sandblasted onto black fossil stone walls and tables. **Duke's** piano bar evokes Manhattan in the Jazz Age, paying tribute to Duke Ellington. Entry is via a replica of Washington Square Park's Triumphal Arch. Décor includes replicas of famous New York sights. A bar encircles a white baby grand piano on a turntable. The **Jekyll and Hyde Dance Club** has eight-foot-tall sculptures of Robert Louis Stevenson's fictional character with split faces, meant to convey benevolence and malice. The heads swivel to the music's tempo, and monitors set into the sculptures show live pictures of dancing guests and music videos.

On the *Paradise,* all public rooms are named for oceanliners, and the **Blue Riband Library,** namesake of the international prize awarded for the fastest transatlantic crossing, pays tribute to them in miniature models and old photographs. It contains a full-scale reproduction of the gold and onyx Hales Trophy, models of ships that won the prize, and memorabilia, including a signed photo of the duke and duchess of Windsor on the *Queen Elizabeth.*

In eye-popping contrast, the **America Bar** across from the library is named for the *SS America* and all but screams U.S.A. with its red, white, and blue color scheme, starred carpet, and stars and stripes on the walls. At the stern, the 1,300-seat, two-story **Normandie** show lounge carries an Art Deco theme and celebrates the French liner considered by some to be the best ship ever built. Another showroom, the **Queen Mary Lounge,** uses funnels from the great ship as the motif to line the bar and walls, frame the seats, and serve as table bases. From the Italian liner *Rex,* Farcus took the Latin meaning of rex (king) and conjured up the king of the jungle, giving the **Rex Dance Club** a jungle theme.

Sports and Fitness   Three swimming pools (one with a slide), Ping-Pong, shuffleboard, and volleyball are available, and pool games are staged almost daily. On Caribbean and Mexican cruises, depending on ports, you can play golf, sail, ride horseback, bike, hike, snorkel, scuba dive, and windsurf.

The 12,000-square-foot spa on the sports deck is a fully equipped gym with trained instructors, separate locker rooms, dressing rooms, and showers for men and women; six whirlpools, saunas, and steam rooms. Or one can choose from an array of exercise and aerobics classes, and a 500-foot outside jogging track-all included in the cruise price. Instructors will also create a fitness regimen for you to follow at home. All Carnival ships have a secluded deck area for topless sunbathing.

Carnival's golf program provides play at more than a dozen courses in the Bahamas, Caribbean, Hawaii, Europe and Mexico. It offers one-on-one, 30- or 60-minute instruction from PGA teaching pros aboard ship and on golf excursions. Shipboard lessons are in a netted driving range where golfers' swings are videotaped and computer-analyzed. A take-home video with voice-over instruction and stop-action/slow-motion analysis is provided with each lesson. Golf packages include greens fees, instruction, cart rental or caddie, and transportation to and from courses. Prices range from $50 for on-board lessons to $225 for golf excursions. Equipment rentals include Callaway clubs and Adidas "soft spike" golf shoes.

Spa and Beauty The beauty salon and spa, operated by the Steiner Group, a British-based company, has nine private rooms for body and facial treatments—including facials, pedicures, massage, and herbal packs. Services aren't free and can become an expensive indulgence.

Children's Facilities Camp Carnival, which handles 400,000 kids fleetwide annually, is a year-round program with a wide array of activities supervised by trained counselors for children in four age groups: Toddlers (ages 2–5), Juniors (ages 6–8), Intermediate (ages 9–12), and Teens (ages 13–16). Young children enjoy puppet making, finger painting, and learning the alphabet and numbers; older kids have pizza parties, scavenger hunts, and lip sync contests and play bingo, charades, and Twister. Teens have activities ranging from disco parties and star search contests to evening deck parties. All ships have video arcades, wading pools, water slides, playrooms (two on Fantasy class), teens' club/discos, children's menus, and high chairs.

One playroom is designed for kids ages 6–11, and is stocked with age-appropriate toys, games, and puzzles, including such popular pastimes as air hockey, foosball, and "pop-a-shot" basketball, along with the latest high-tech video games. The other playroom is geared toward toddlers.

Elation and *Paradise* have among Carnival's largest children's facility, the 2,500-square-foot **Children's World.** It is divided into three sections. One features an educational computer lab and computer games. The arts and crafts section has spin art, sand art, jewelry-making machines, easels for painting and drawing, and a gallery for displaying participants' creations. The third is an indoor play area with a climbing maze, toys, games, and a video wall where kids can watch movies, music videos, and cartoons. The outdoor play area has a schooner-shaped playhouse and a wading pool for toddlers. Teens get special attention, too, with **Virtual World,** photography workshops, late-night movies, and disco parties.

Camp Carnival operates from 9 a.m. to 10 p.m. At 10 p.m., babysitting in the form of slumber parties in the children's playrooms becomes available through the purser's office for $6 per hour for the first child, $4 for each additional child. Carnival has a "Fountain Fun-Card" for those younger than age 21, good for unlimited sodas from the bars (the card is $9 on a 3-day cruise, $30 on an 11-day cruise).

Shore Excursions   Recently, Carnival has tried to provide greater variety. Nonetheless, dockside in almost all Caribbean ports are plenty of vans with driver/guides eager for your business and ready to design a tour to your liking. Prices depend on your ability to bargain and the driver's eagerness for your business, but do agree on a fee before the tour begins.

An air/sea package is recommended for cruises departing from Port Canaveral combined with Orlando attractions because the Orlando airport, where most passengers arrive, is about an hour's drive from Port Canaveral, where the ships depart. There is no public transportation between the two; those traveling on their own must hire a taxi or rent a car. Or, those booking "cruise-only" can buy Carnival's transfer package. Also, if you buy the Orlando package, plan to take the Spaceport USA bus tour on the day you sail. That way, the full morning can be spent at Spaceport USA, about 20 minutes from Port Canaveral. A late lunch is available aboard ship until 3:30 p.m. In Alaska, the line offers excursions for teens, along with nearly 100 tours for all ages.

HOLIDAY / JUBILEE	QUALITY **4**	VALUE **B**
CELEBRATION	QUALITY **4**	VALUE **B**
Registry: *Jubilee, Celebration:* Panama / *Holiday:* Bahamas	Length: 727/733 feet	Beam: 92 feet
Cabins: 726/743	Draft: 25 feet	Speed: 21 knots
Maximum Passengers: 1,800/1,896	Passenger Decks: 9/10	Elevators: 8
	Crew: 660/670	Space Ratio: 32

The Ships   When the *Holiday* was unveiled in 1985, her décor was called zany. Micky Arison, Carnival's chairman, called it a "Disney World for adults." For those accustomed to the sleek lines of traditional ships, the boxy look of *Holiday* took some getting used to, but it was the innovations inside that revolutionized cruising, making the ship with its four decks for recreation and entertainment as much the destination as its ports of call. The most startling change was the main promenade deck. Instead of circling the ship, as had been typical, the deck runs double-width down only one side—a feature that became standard on all Carnival megaliners. Called Broadway on the *Holiday,* with nearly as much glitter as its namesake, it serves as a meeting place and thoroughfare, with bars, nightclubs, casinos, a disco, and reminders of Broadway: a traffic light, street lamps, an authentic 1934 bus, and Times Square.

A decade later, after larger and more flamboyant ships had been added to Carnival's fleet, the *Holiday* is regarded as traditional. That may be pushing credibility, but it's amazing how quickly passengers became comfortable with the new ideas the *Holiday* introduced. What's more, the innovations continue. The promenade was redesigned, and **Doc Holiday's** (a country-and-western lounge) was added. A separate section contains **Cyber City,** a virtual reality and game center. The fitness center was expanded, the casino renovated, and the lido restaurant remodeled, adding another dinner option and a 24-hour pizzeria.

The *Holiday* was quickly followed by the *Jubilee* and the *Celebration.* The trio are identical in almost all aspects except décor. Each is themed, with the *Jubilee,* inspired by historic, romantic England, having its main promenade called Park Lane, a Victorian gazebo bar, a Trafalgar Square, and **Churchill's Library.** Generous use of wood throughout makes it more mellow than other Carnival ships. Standouts are the Art Deco **Atlantis Lounge** showroom and the **Sporting Club,** a casino with golden slot machines, etched glass, and golden mirrors. In 1999, *Jubilee* was renovated, giving her a sushi bar and an expanded health and fitness facility.

The *Celebration* pays tribute to New Orleans and Mardi Gras, complete with Bourbon Street, an outdoor café, bistro, a New Orleans streetcar named, yes, Desire, and a Dixieland band playing nightly on Bourbon Street before dinner. Sculpture by Israeli artist Yaacov Agam greets passengers in the lobby, and his wall pieces decorate public areas. But the most dramatic art is by San Franciscan Helen Webber, whose sculptured aluminum kites hang on wires the full six decks of the stairwells. The *Celebration,* like the other ships, has its own quiet corner—**Admiral's,** a library and writing room dedicated to great oceanliners of the past. The *Celebration* recently completed a major refurbishment which included all cabins, public areas, dining rooms, purser's lobby, stairs, and elevators.

The *Holiday, Jubilee,* and *Celebration* set the course for Carnival for the decade and had an incalculable impact on cruising. Zany, yes. Successful? You bet. In late 2004, *Jubilee* will be transferred to P&O Cruises Australia, Carnival's newest acquisition resulting from the purchase of Princess Cruises.

Itineraries   See Itinerary Index.

Cabins   For all the unconventional elements on the ships' activity decks, cabins on the *Holiday* trio are downright sane and larger than most on other ships in the same price category. Outside cabins have picture windows; inside have backlit windows of the same size, making the cabin seem larger and less closed in. Cabins are furnished with twin beds that can be converted to kings and have ample closet and drawer space in cabinets of genuine wood. Artwork decorates the walls and adds a touch of class.

Specifications   279 *Holiday* / 290 *Jubilee/Celebration* inside cabins, 437/443 outside; 10 suites with whirlpool bathtubs. Standard dimensions, 180/185 square feet. 683/709 with twin beds convertible to kings; 27/16 inside, 10/8 outside with upper/lower berths. No singles. 15/14 wheelchair-accessible.

Dining   The Holiday group offers the same menus as other Carnival ships, with two dining rooms serving three meals. Carnival has upgraded and expanded lido-area food service on all its ships to meet passengers' preference for casual breakfast and lunch choices. Specialties are offered in addition to standard favorites, such as scrambled eggs, hot dogs, and hamburgers. Particularly popular are the made-to-order pasta stations and expanded salad bars. Ice cream and frozen yogurt are available all day, (cookies in the afternoon) in the lido. Staff in the area has been doubled for better service. Wine bars have been added on the promenade decks.

Facilities and Activities   The Lido Deck has acres of open space and a swimming pool with a 14-foot-tall spiral water slide, a signature on Carnival ships. A more secluded pool is at the stern; a kids' pool is a deck below. The ships have spas with separate facilities for men and women. Decks are covered with Burmese teak.

Activities are numerous, ranging from wine tastings to knobby-knee contests (you would be amazed by how many people join in!). In the evening, there's bar hopping and people-watching on Broadway, Park Lane, or Bourbon Street, and action in the casino or electronic game room. A favorite spot on all three ships is the piano bar, but *Celebration's* **Red Hot Piano Bar** wins the award for novelty. Red walls glow under red lights, and the bar is shaped like a red piano with the ivories as the bar counter. And the music is . . . red hot. A spiral staircase leads directly to the casino a deck above.

The ships have huge theaters spanning two decks, where Broadway-style musicals and Las Vegas–type shows are staged twice nightly. Seats are terraced on six levels, giving all 1,000 patrons unobstructed views.

The year-round children's program, Camp Carnival, offers supervised activities for four age groups. **Cyber City** incorporates cutting-edge electronic game technology.

Shore Excursions   All Carnival ships offer similar shore excursions at common rates. They are posted on Carnival's website. Many are off-the-shelf tours you often could take on your own. The main reason to book excursions through the ships is convenience. Recently, Carnival added a group of sports-oriented shore excursions for teenagers, such as horseback riding in Cozumel, biking in Key West, and cave tubing in Belize; these are discounted 20% off the regular price.

CARNIVAL DESTINY	QUALITY 8	VALUE A
CARNIVAL TRIUMPH	QUALITY 8	VALUE A
CARNIVAL VICTORY	QUALITY 8	VALUE A
Registry: *Destiny, Triumph:* Bahamas *Victory:* Panama	Length: 893 feet	Beam: 125 feet
Cabins: 1321/1379	Draft: 27 feet	Speed: 22.5 knots
Maximum Passengers: 3,400/3,470	Passenger Decks: 12	Elevators: 18
	Crew: 1,050/1,100	Space Ratio: 37/38

The Ships The *Carnival Destiny* was the largest cruise ship ever built when she made her debut in 1996 and was the first one too wide to transit the Panama Canal. When the ship was being planned six years earlier, Carnival employees were asked to submit their wish lists for enhancing the new vessel. Apparently, they got most of their wishes.

The *Destiny* has Carnival's first double-decked dining room; a show lounge spanning three decks; a double-width promenade lined with lounges and bars; a mall-style shopping area; a 9,000-square-foot casino; 18 bars and lounges; four swimming pools and an expansive spa; a retractable glass dome over the pool area; and sports and recreation facilities similar to the Fantasy group of ships. The pool area has a stage for entertainment and teak decks cantilevered in an amphitheater. **Virtual World** is a high-tech virtual reality game center.

Destiny's configuration is a departure for Carnival. Entertainment and recreation decks are between accommodations decks. The two lowest passenger decks have only cabins, followed by three decks of public rooms, then five decks of cabins and suites with balconies. To avoid big rooms and long corridors that would make the ship's huge size obvious, public rooms span two or three levels. The layout is often confusing, however.

Despite her size—nearly three football fields in length—*Destiny* does not seem as large from the inside as some of her Fantasy-class cousins. This is primarily because of the layout and the décor, which is softer and toned down—sometimes even tony—a change from Farcus's flamboyant creations on other Carnival ships.

The Rotunda (Capital Lobby on Triumph; Seven Seas Atrium on Victory) a nine-deck atrium with four glass elevators and a glass dome, is the ship's focal point. An enormous marble and onyx mural of geometric forms suggesting skyscrapers decorates the walls. But instead of the huge sculptures on Fantasy-class ships, *Destiny's* atrium has an attractive lobby bar at its base, creating a meeting place that helps humanize the huge space.

The *Carnival Triumph,* which debuted in 1999, builds on *Destiny's* success but incorporates new features. Sixty percent of cabins have ocean views with a sitting area, and more than 60% of those have verandas. The ship celebrates the world's great cities, with such venues as **Underground Tokyo** video arcade, the **Rome Theater, Vienna Café** coffee bar, and **Oxford Bar.** A huge golden globe dominates the atrium; it's inlaid with glittering fiber optics that mark the world's metropolises. Smaller globes are part of the décor shipwide. The new Panorama Deck, one level above the Lido Deck, has 42 ocean-view cabins, most with verandas, and 24 inside ones, adding capacity for 132 guests. *Carnival Victory,* whose theme is the seven seas, arrived in August 2000.

Itineraries See Itinerary Index.

Cabins *Destiny's* standard cabins are the largest and the most attractively furnished in the Carnival fleet. All have hair dryers and safes; some have interactive television. Cabin numbers pinpoint your deck and location (forward, aft, or midship). Each section has its own elevators. Sixty percent of standard outside cabins have small balconies, all with clear panels for unobstructed ocean views. Unfortunately, they do nothing to absorb sound. This and insufficient soundproofing make the cabins noisy. Particularly to be avoided are cabins on Deck 6 forward, which are directly above lounges that operate most of the night. Ocean-view cabins have a sitting area with sofa and coffee table. Veranda cabins create a new category of standard cabins for Carnival that, although larger, are comparable in price to standard outside accommodations on Fantasy-class ships. Family cabins are near the children's play facilities.

Specifications   515 inside cabins, 432 outside with verandas; 48 suites with verandas, some with bathtub Jacuzzi. Standard dimensions, 220–260 square feet; all cabins with twins convertible to kings; 4 inside with upper and lower berths; no singles; 25 *Destiny* / 27 *Triumph, Victory* wheelchair-accessible cabins.

Dining   Carnival's first bilevel dining rooms feel roomy, and the additional space allows wider separation between tables. But the restaurants are noisy. Both dining rooms enjoy ocean views.

The two-deck **Sun & Sea** (**South Beach Club** on *Triumph;* **Mediterranean** on *Victory*), the casual lido restaurant, is dressed in shades of green with yellow, hand-blown Murano glass and hand-painted ceramic tile decorating walls and countertops. Different settings create dining options: Trattoria for pasta and made-to-order Italian dishes; Happy Valley for Chinese cuisine, stir-fried to order; and The Grille for hamburgers and hot dogs. Service has also been upgraded; waiters carry dishes and beverages to tables. The **Seaview Bistro** alternative dinner venue in the lido restaurant offers specialty salads, pastas, steaks, and desserts—plus a daily special—in a café setting. The bistro operates each evening from 6 to 9:30 p.m. Also open are a 24-hour pizzeria and, on the promenade deck, a patisserie appointed with cherry wood counters and windowed banquettes. *Carnival Victory* has a New York–style deli.

Facilities and Activities   In the evening, you are likely to run out of energy before you run out of choices. The flashy **Millionaire's Club** (**Club Monaco** on *Triumph;* **South China Sea Club** on *Victory*), said to be the largest casino afloat, has 321 slot machines and 23 table games. In the lavishly decorated **Apollo Bar,** the piano revolves, enabling the pianist to shine a spotlight on anyone eager to test the microphone on each table.

At the whimsically decorated **Downbeat,** where a 20-foot trumpet and French horn are suspended above the bandstand, patrons sit on clarinet-shaped barstools or at glass tables supported by oversized sections of horns.

In the **Point After Dance Club,** tricolor neon lights snake across the ceiling above a bilevel floor, and over 500 video monitors flash pictures and computer-generated graphics around the room. A staircase by the dance floor leads to the elegant **Onyx Room,** a more sedate club where backlit alabaster panels glow softly beside a neon and glass dance floor.

The three-deck **Palladium** show lounge is one of the most technologically sophisticated afloat, Carnival says. The additional deck below seating levels allows the orchestra pit to be retracted, and the space above enables backdrops, lighting equipment, and performers to be "flown" offstage via cables. A Venetian glass chandelier hangs from the dome; at show time, it goes high-tech with fiber optics.

To achieve the three decks of seats for 1,500 people, some sacrifices were made. The main floor is almost level, making viewing more difficult the farther back one sits. Also, balcony rails partially block some views. The big production shows are top-notch.

Yet more entertainment is offered in **Virtual World,** a game center with virtual reality and electronic games, and **All Star Bar,** decorated with celebrity memorabilia, including tables bearing autographs of sports stars, and featuring seven big-screen televisions broadcasting sporting events.

Sports, Fitness, and Beauty   The *Destiny* has four pools, including a children's pool, and seven whirlpools. One has Carnival's trademark water slide—but here, it is three decks tall and 214 feet long. A retractable dome covers the aft pool.

The 15,000-square-foot spa and health club has two levels, one with a beauty salon, massage rooms, Jacuzzis, and sauna and steam rooms, the other with an aerobics room and a juice bar. The spa offers hydrotherapy baths, aromatherapy, and other body treatments. There is also a "Nouveau Yu Health Environment Capsule," an egg-shaped, temperature-controlled capsule designed to induce relaxation. The gym has an array of equipment, including bikes, treadmills, step and rowing equipment, and 16 Keiser machines. Instructors lead exercise classes and can be hired as personal trainers. An eighth-mile jogging track is on the sun deck. On the *Triumph,* more open space was provided on the Lido Deck for deck chairs, and the fore and aft pools were enlarged and bordered by "wading" areas.

Children's Facilities   The two-deck-tall, 1,300-square-foot indoor and outdoor play center includes a jungle gym and pool. See the *Fantasy* profile for information on Carnival's children's program.

CARNIVAL SPIRIT	QUALITY 8	VALUE A
CARNIVAL PRIDE	QUALITY 8	VALUE A
CARNIVAL LEGEND	QUALITY 8	VALUE A
CARNIVAL MIRACLE	(March 2004)	
Registry: Panama	Length: 963 feet	Beam: 105.7 feet
Cabins: 1,062	Draft: 25.7 feet	Speed: 22 knots
Maximum Passengers:	Passenger Decks: 12	Elevators: 15
2,667	Crew: 930	Space Ratio: 40

The Ships   *Carnival Spirit,* the first of a new class of ships for Carnival built at Kvaerner Masa-Yards in Finland, entered service in April 2001; her twin, *Carnival Pride,* followed in January 2002. The third member of this class, *Carnival Legend,* joined in August 2002, and a fourth, *Carnival Miracle,* is scheduled to arrive in spring 2004. They are among the longest ships in the Carnival fleet, but they still can pass through the Panama Canal. The ships have a number of environmentally friendly technical enhancements, and their technologically advanced Azipod propulsion system enables them to reach a maximum speed of 24 knots, and thus sail on innovative itineraries. The ships boast an exceptional space ratio of 40 (the Fantasy class is 34, Destiny group 37) with the usual Carnival array of amenities and facilities, and some new ones, such as the first Carnival ships with a wedding chapel.

The theme of *Carnival Spirit* is design, particularly architectural design which makes for an eclectic mix of décor, while that of *Carnival Pride* is icons of beauty which gave Farcus's active mind neverending inspiration—from architecture and artistic masterpieces to athletic achievement and the human body. The beauty icons start with Renaissance inspiration in the atrium lobby, elevator, and stairwell areas, where huge reproductions of murals by Botticelli, Raphäel, and other Italian painters adorn the walls. Here, too, the craftsmanship of the Italian Renaissance is reflected in rich details of wood, bronze moldings and dominated by gold, sienna and burnt-red tones.

The ships' interior promenade meanders through public rooms on two consecutive decks, linking the ship's two atriums with its dining rooms, more than a dozen bars, lounges and entertainment venues, and a shopping arcade that includes a tuxedo rental and flower shop. The ships also have a wraparound outdoor promenade on Atlantic Deck—the first for a Carnival ship in two decades.

Carnival Pride's theme is "Icons of Beauty," which is reflected in rococo, Renaissance and neoclassical details of the décor. *Carnival Legend's* motif is inspired by great legends of history, from the ancient Greeks in the atrium, to modern jazz in the New Orleans design of **Satchmo's Club,** and the Art Deco of **Billie's Piano Bar,** named for blues legend Billie Holiday. *Carnival Miracle,* being constructed at Kvaerner Masa-Yards in Helsinki and scheduled for launch in March 2004, has fictional characters as its theme—but Harry Potter is not among them.

Carnival Miracle will have Tampa as her home port year-round, taking over the seven-day western Caribbean itinerary of *Inspiration,* which itself will switch to year-round four- and five-day cruises from Tampa. *Carnival Miracle,* the fourth of the Spirit class, is expected to be the largest cruise ship based in Tampa on year-round basis. She also will be used to introduce a new seven-day round trip from Baltimore to Key

West, and the Bahamas series in spring and fall of 2004, adding further to the "close-to-home" cruising trend and bringing Carnival's total to 19 North American home ports.

Like her sister ships, *Carnival Miracle* has indoor and outdoor wrap-around promenades, an upscale supper club located atop a towering 11-deck-high atrium, and a large percentage of balconied cabins. She will have a two-level dining room; large poolside food courts offering casual breakfast, lunch, and dinner; a 24-hour pizzeria; and a sushi bar. There are sixteen lounges, ranging from an elaborate, multilevel showroom for Vegas-style revues to an intimate piano bar.

The ship will have a casino, shopping mall, wedding chapel, video game room, and Internet café. There are several swimming pools—including one with a spiral water slide, a spa and gym, a "Camp Carnival" program for kids ages 2–15, and a comprehensive golf program.

Cabins   The ships have several levels of suites with private balconies and have set a new standard for outside cabins, 80% of which have private balconies. Many cabins can accommodate up to four guests; other are interconnecting and are ideal for large families.

Specifications   213 inside cabins, 99 outside, 624 outside with balconies, 68 with French doors; 52 suites, 6 penthouse. 16 wheelchair-accessible.

Dining   Each ship has three restaurants. *Pride's* **Normandie Restaurant** (**Empir**e on *Spirit;* **Golden Fleece** on *Legend*), spanning two decks with wrap-around windows, has elegant décor based on the famous oceanliner *Normandie,* one of the most beautiful passenger vessel ever built.

Spirit's unusual **Nouveau Supper Club,** Carnival's first alternative restaurant (reservations only; $25 charge), is situated topside with one end bordering the ship's huge red-glass smokestack and the other extending out over the top of the ship's multideck atrium. Among the menu specialties are prime aged beef and stone crabs from the famous Joe's Stone Crab Restaurant in Miami Beach, a Carnival exclusive. The restaurant's counterpart on the *Pride* is **David's Supper Club,** with a full-size replica of the famous Michelangelo sculpture, *David,* celebrating the beauty of the human body.

The **Mermaids' Grille,** the ship's lido restaurant, has a variety of food stations, each offering a different type of cuisine and including a pizzeria. It is open almost around the clock.

Facilities and Activities   The ships seem to have a dance floor at every turn. From the **Beauties Dance Club** to the **Starry Night** jazz club and the grand **Taj Mahal** show lounge. On the *Pride,* a famous Van Gogh painting was the inspiration for the Starry Night jazz club (**Club Cool** on *Spirit*). The beauty of ideas and intellectual achievement is enshrined in the **Nobel Library,** with a portrait of Alfred Nobel who created the famous prize. The room also houses the Internet café. The beauty of experience is represented in the **Perfect Game** sports bar and the **Winner's Club** casino. **Butterflies Lounge** draws on natural beauty with faux windows decorated with colorful transparent fabrics that resemble butterfly wings which disappear under special lights to illuminate the flocks of butterflies behind. Four different butterfly patterns are seen in the upholstery. Architectural beauty is celebrated in the Taj Mahal show lounge (**Pharaoh's Palace** on *Spirit*) filled with intricate Indian designs and stonework sparkling with small jewels pressed into decorative designs. Infrared listening devices for hearing-impaired passengers are available in the *Spirit* main lounge.

Other highlights include a chapel suitable for weddings or religious services; multilevel **Nautica Spa;** ice cream/frozen yogurt bar, and a large conference center.

Sports, Fitness, and Beauty   The ships have a two-level health and fitness facility, along with huge open decks and three swimming pools, one with a two-deck-high water slide plus a children's wading pool. One of the pools is heated and has a sliding glass roof, known as a magradome— ideal for Alaska, where *Carnival Spirit* spent her maiden summer. A golf program, managed by Elite Golf Cruises of Florida, with private lessons, digital teaching technology, and packages for shoreside play starts at $45 for 30-minutes and $80 for one hour; each includes a video. Equipment rental is available for a fee. Advance reservations can be made at (800) 324-1106 or **www.carnivalgolf.com.**

Children's Facilities   A variety of new and expanded family-friendly amenities have been added to the fleetwide Camp Carnival and include choices from fun, educational geography classes and candy-making machines to special family activities on a private island, teens-only shore excursions, and "just-for-kids" port lectures. **Fun Club,** located forward on Upper Deck 5 and decorated with a colorful undersea motif, is divided into three areas, connected by a series of tunnels. The first area houses an arts and crafts center, the second has a computer lab, and the third, has a play room stocked with toys and games, a video wall displaying movies and cartoons, and kid-sized tables and chairs. An outdoor play area has a mini-basketball hoop and other playground equipment. **Real Virtuality,** a high-tech game room housing video and arcade games, is one deck below the Fun Club.

A turndown service offering freshly baked chocolate chip cookies on the first and last night of their voyage is available. So too is the fleetwide Fountain Fun Card, a soft drink program for unlimited sodas, costing from $9 for three-day cruises to $20 for seven-day cruises for those under age 21 (21 and over, $15 and $30 respectively); and there are kids' menus. Babysitting is available from 10 p.m. to 3 a.m. in the children's play room for $6 per hour for the first child and $4 for each additional child in the same family. Strollers are available for rent at $6 per day and $25 for the week.

CARNIVAL CONQUEST	**(Preview)**	
CARNIVAL GLORY	**(Preview)**	
CARNIVAL VALOR	**(Late 2004)**	
CARNIVAL LIBERTY	**(2005)**	
Registry: Panama	Length: 952 feet	Beam: 116 feet
Cabins: 1,486	Draft: 27 feet	Speed: 22.5 knots
Maximum Passengers:	Passenger Decks: 13	Elevators: 15
3,700	Crew: 1,160	Space Ratio: 37

The Ship   *Carnival Conquest,* which made her debut in New Orleans in 2002, is the largest vessel in the fleet and the first to have her interior décor tied directly to her home port. Using the ship's interiors as a huge canvas, designer Joe Farcus created something of an ode to Impressionist and post-Impressionist art and the Big Easy's French legacy.

The main atrium, called the Atelier, has Impressionist paintings on the central ceiling dome and wall; the Artists' Lobby is dominated by a large hand-painted mural collage of famous paintings. The collage effect is picked up in the promenade and in other public areas throughout the ship.

Her sister ship, *Carnival Glory,* which arrived in July 2003, takes colors as a theme, with each public room done in different shades of the rainbow and reflected in their name and décor. The kaleidoscope of colors begins in the Colors lobby, **Color Bar,** and the main atrium, named Old Glory after the United States flag. Each deck was given a different color; looking up through the atrium, it's easy to see the color definition of each deck. The Kaleidoscope Boulevard has one-square-meter light fixtures subdivided into geometric modules that are backlit with strips of color. The result is thousands of different tones in a slow-moving kaleidoscope.

Itineraries   See Itinerary Index

Cabins   By Carnival standards, the cabins are exceptionally low-key and understated, dressed in soft pastels and lovely rich wood that blends with the soft colors. A wall unit has a dresser/desk with drawers and cabinets; safe; minifridge; television with CNN, BBC, Discovery Channel, and other channels such as ABC, CBS, and NBC when available; and three closets that should be ample for most people on a week's cruise. All outside cabins have a sofa; most are sofabeds. The bathroom with a rather tight shower stall has a dispenser for shampoo and shower gel. All outside cabins get terry robes. There are a larger number of cabins with a small balcony with space for two chairs—and that's about all.

Specifications   10 penthouse suites, 42 suites, 504 outside with balcony, 343 outside without balcony, 18 outside with glass wall, 570 inside cabins.

Dining   Each ship has two two-level dining rooms. On *Conquest,* the **Monet** and **Renoir** dining rooms (**Platinum** and **Golden** on *Glory*) are identical architecturally and have panels of wood-veneered images of the Eiffel Tower in the walls and ceiling. The fabrics and colors are based on works by the two painters. *Glory's* dining rooms take their décor from their colors and are elegant in their simplicity—resembling, somewhat, the uncluttered lines of Japanese décor, with only a touch of color from a few handpainted bonsai and cherry-blossom trees on the walls and ceiling. The rooms are the most crowded of any dining rooms we've experienced on any Carnival ship. Off to each side of *Glory's* Golden dining room is a private dinning room, **Copper** (for 28 people) and **Silver** (for 36 people), which are among the most handsome rooms on the ship. *Conquest's* **Renoir Restaurant** was inspired by *Lunch at the Restaurant Fournaise,* a tranquil scene of boaters relaxing at a café overlooking the Seine, featured in the wall-covering fabric. In the **Monet Restaurant,** one of the artist's famous "Water Lilies" series sets the motif.

The bilevel **Restaurant Cezanne** (**Red Sail** on *Glory*) on the Lido Deck has the atmosphere of a 19th-century French café. In addition to Carnival's standard variety of Italian, Chinese, Mexican, and other food stations, you can enjoy hamburgers and hot dogs, a 24-hour pizzeria, and a self-service ice cream/frozen yogurt station. The restaurant is also the venue for the **Seaview Bistro** (**Fish and Chips** on *Glory*), a new dining outlet on the second level of the Lido restaurant. **Café Fans** (**Creams** on *Glory*) on Promenade deck is a patisserie serving a variety of coffees and rather pricey desserts; next door is a sushi bar. And there's 24-hour room service with new, expanded menus.

The Point, high on Panorama Deck, is *Conquest's* reservations-only supper club, named for the style of Georges-Pierre Seurat, known as pointillism, which renders images through thousands of individual dots, or points, of color. *Glory's* **Emerald Room** has light fixtures resembling giant emeralds and a huge medallion on the wall made up of hundreds of these light fixtures. In addition to being a steakhouse, the Point continues Carnival's relationship with Joe's Stone Crab in Miami Beach, featuring the stone crabs on the menu. For structural reasons, the Club is divided into two separate rooms (rather than the large open space by the funnel as on the line's Spirit class). The cost is $25 per person. In our experience, Carnival's alternative restaurants are excellent, with food and service top-notch and well worth the extra charge. Reserve early in your cruise, as they are very popular and fill up fast.

Facilities and Activities   The **Toulouse-Lautrec Lounge,** the main show lounge, takes its inspiration from the painter's sketches drawn from the subjects he saw in the cabarets, circuses, and brothels of Paris's Montmartre. To the sides of the stage are the famous windmill signs of the

Moulin Rouge cabaret; the windmill motif is repeated in the carpet. *Glory's* **Amber Palace,** the most extravagant room on the ship, is named after Russia's famous Amber Room (recently reconstructed and open to the public) in the palace of Peter the Great. The wall covering, for example, replicates the mosaics of amber as they are on the palace walls; hanging from the ceiling is an enormous crystal chandelier, with smaller ones at the sides of the room. The Russian eagle is designed into the room's carpet, and the cut velvet covering on the seats would seem to suit any czar's palace. For those who take a backstage tour, the state-of-the-art stage and equipment is on par with the latest of Broadway.

Two new shows debuted on *Glory: Livin' in America* and *Rock Down Broadway* in keeping with the Carnival tradition of fast-paced Vegas-style revues that blend choreography with elaborate sets and costumes. *Rock Down Broadway* is one of the best shows we have ever seen on any cruise ship—or on Broadway for that matter.

Conquest's **Tahiti Casino** and **Gauguin's Bar,** a sports bar, recall post-Impressionist Paul Gauguin's paintings of Polynesia. **Henri's Dance Club** takes its theme from the exotic jungle paintings of Henri Rousseau. Painted metal cutouts, meant to look like the coarse grass of Rousseau's paintings, are mounted on the wall, with occasional three-dimensional animal heads, similar to those lurking in the artist's works. *Glory's* **Camel Club Casino** is a bit incongruous. The camel color inspired Farcus to install statues of reclining camels (which kids love to climb, despite a sign reading "No one under 18 years of age is allowed in the Casino"), but from the camels it's a stretch to the main décor, meant to reflect the age of European rediscovery of Ancient Egypt and the Orient.

On *Glory,* the **White Heat Dance Club** has gigantic white candles, 12 to 18 inches in diameter, in silver candelabra bases from two to five feet tall and giving off imaginary white heat. One deck below, the multipurpose **Ivory Club** has an Indian theme set off with elephant tusk replicas, and the barstools and table bases replicate elephant feet. Across the way, the **Burgundy Bar** is a wine bar; **Cinn-a-Bar,** a piano bar; and the **Bar Blue,** taking its "blue" from giant peacock feathers in the motif, is the ship's jazz bar. The **Ebony Cabaret,** a multifunction show room with African décor, is one of *Glory's* most successful rooms, using ebony wood, African textiles, and handsome authentic wooden masks in the décor. **On the Green,** the sports bar, celebrates the game of golf with memorabilia from its legends. In all, the ships each have 22 bars and lounges. Daytime activity range from a Jazz & Bloody Mary Party to a Sing-a-Long or a Men's Hairy Chest Contest; art auctions, trivia quizzes, game shows, and adult comedy shows in the evening round out the offerings. They also have, libraries, multipurpose conference centers, boutiques, infirmaries and Internet cafés—$0.75 per minute or packages of 30 and 60 minutes for slight savings. Cruise e-mail available for a one-time activation fee of $3.95. Local calls are $9.50 per minute within the U.S.; additional charges may be applied to your credit card.

Sports, Fitness, and Beauty   Each ship has a spa with a large variety of treatments, sauna and steam rooms, a very small indoor pool with a most unusual half-moon-shaped Jaccuzi, a gym with state-of-the-art equipment, and a beauty salon. There are four swimming pools, including one with Carnival's signature slide; seven whirlpools (although often so many kids who should not be in them reduces the number by half); and a jogging track. You can start your day in the gym as early as 6 a.m. and be treated to classes in aerobics or abs or for $10 extra a session of yoga, Pilates, or seminars on body care, diet, or cellulite. Sports include basketball, volleyball, and golf.

Children's Facilities   The newest feature on the Conquest-class ships is the expanded teen recreation center housing a large, high-tech video game room and teen dance club with a DJ spinning the latest hits, a bar serving non-alcoholic specialty drinks, and a video wall along, with new activities and shore excursions for teen groups.

For younger children, *Conquest* and *Glory* have the largest play areas in the Carnival fleet. The Camp Carnival program set in **Children's World** is divided into four distinct areas: an arts and crafts center with spin and sand art and candy-making machines; an all-ages playroom with toys, games, and puzzles; a video room showing kids' movies and cartoons; and children's library, along with the latest PlayStation 2 game units. Children's World is also the venue for the ship's baby-sitting service, available nightly from 10 p.m. to 3 a.m. for $6 per hour for the first child and $4 per hour for the second child in the same family.

Adjacent to Children's World is an outdoor play area and a wading pool, and access to Carnival's trademark water slide. Stroller rentals are available for $6 per day and $25 per week.

Kids can also make their own culinary creations through new cake-decorating and pizza-making sessions, part of a full schedule of morning-to-night activities for children ages 2–15. Children receive their own printed activities program daily. Sample activities include storytelling, sing-a-longs, and "Play-Do Fun" for younger cruisers, and disco parties, scavenger hunts, and pool parties for older kids. The ships offer a variety of kid-friendly dining choices and a "daily junior special" in the main dining rooms. Kids are also provided with freshly baked chocolate chip cookies on the first and last night of the voyage; youth counselors host "children's only" meals poolside with a different cuisine featured each night.

Celebrity Cruises

1050 Caribbean Way, Miami, FL 33132-2096
(305) 539-6000; (800) 646-1456
fax (800)437-511; www.celebritycruises.com

Type of Ships   Stylish superliners and megaliners.

Type of Cruise   Moderately priced deluxe; ample activity at comfortable pace; emphasis on quality.

Cruise Line's Strengths

- cuisine

- well-designed, stylish, spacious ships

- dining room service

- children's program

- value for money

Cruise Line's Shortcomings

- lack of outside, wraparound promenade deck

- excessive promotion of onboard shopping

- boarding procedures

- loud deck music on some ships

Fellow Passengers   Moderately affluent, ages range from late 30s to 60s in high season; ages lower in off-season. Typical passenger is age 48, married, with household income of $50,000+. He/she tends to be an educated, experienced traveler, who understands quality, owns a house in relatively affluent suburb, and has college-age children. Fifty percent cruised before, and of this group, 20–30% are repeaters with Celebrity. Due to the line's regular departures from northeast United States in summer, a majority of passengers live on the East Coast; the balance come from the Midwest and West Coast.

Recommended For   Middle- to upper-middle-income travelers in their 40s and older, whether first-timers or experienced cruisers, who appreciate good service and cuisine and want recreation and entertainment of a large ship at an easy pace. Those with children during the holidays.

Not Recommended For   Small-ship devotees; those seeking adventure travel experience.

Cruise Areas and Seasons Bahamas, Caribbean year-round; Alaska, Canada/New England, Bermuda, Baltic in summer; Panama Canal, Hawaii, South America, east and west Mediterranean, and Europe, spring, winter, and fall.

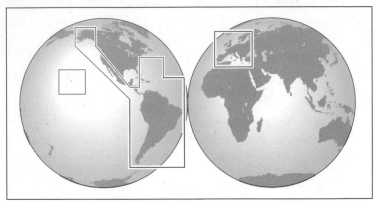

The Line From its inception in 1989, Celebrity Cruises' objective has been to offer deluxe cruises for experienced travelers at affordable prices. The plan was greeted with skepticism because the new line was being created by the owners of Chandris Cruises, an established company long associated with budget-priced cruises. But in less than three years, Celebrity achieved its goal and did so better than anyone imagined. Almost overnight, word spread that a Celebrity cruise was the best value among cruises, offering as much or more than many higher-priced cruises.

Quickly, too, it became apparent that Celebrity Cruises was more than just a new cruise line. It was a completely new product with a new generation of ships designed for 1990s travelers and new standards of service and cuisine in its price category. To their admirers, Celebrity's first vessels define the ideal size of a cruise ship and balance contemporary design and décor with traditional cruising.

In 1992, Celebrity took up another challenge, teaming with Overseas Shipholding Group, one of the world's largest bulk-shipping companies, to build a new class of cruise ships for the 21st century. Once again, Celebrity's ships were winners.

Known as the Century series, these ships—*Century, Galaxy,* and *Mercury*—accommodate 26% more passengers in 48% more space than Celebrity's first generation of ships and have the latest in entertainment and interactive communications systems. Even though the new ships are more spacious and deluxe, the midlevel price remains. The addition of these ships enabled Celebrity to expand beyond the Caribbean to Alaska and Europe.

No sooner were these ships in service than Celebrity began building yet another new class of ships, the 91,000-ton Millennium group. The first of the French-built ships, *Millennium,* made her debut in 2000, followed by *Infinity* and *Summit* in 2001 and *Constellation* in May 2002. Celebrity was merged with Royal Caribbean International in June 1997 but operates as a separate brand. The combination has resulted in a fleet of 20 ships. Royal Caribbean's Customer Service Center (phone (800) 529-6918) is a single point of contact to resolve problems prior to a cruise.

In 2002, Celebrity introduced four Celebrity Escape cruises, which are reserved for passengers age 21 and older. (No kids onboard!) The cruises are scheduled on Caribbean and Hawaii itineraries for the *Horizon, Mercury, Infinity,* and *Millennium* and have special activities designed for adults.

THE FLEET	BUILT/RENOVATED	TONNAGE	PASSENGERS
Century	1995	70,606	1,750
Constellation	2002	91,000	1,950
Galaxy	1996	77,713	1,870
Horizon	1990/1998	46,811	1,354
Infinity	2001	91,000	1,950
Mercury	1997	77,713	1,870
Millennium	2000	91,000	1,950
Summit	2001	91,000	1,950
Zenith	1992/1999	47,255	1,374

Style From the handsome, deep-blue-and-white exteriors with their signature stacks to the elegant interiors, Celebrity ships have style, combining the glamour of traditional cruising with a contemporary look. An example: Famous contemporary artists, such as David Hockney and Roy Lichtenstein, are displayed alongside ancient Greek artifacts. On its first ships, introduced when atriums were becoming standard on cruise ships, Celebrity chose instead to make more space for public rooms, giving passengers entertainment and recreation options similar to those on megaliners, but without the glitz. Small lounges, each with its own ambience and entertainment, appeal to a broad range of tastes.

The ships were also designed for passenger comfort and flow. For example, the **Rendezvous Lounge** amidships provides a place where passengers can mingle before and after dinner, reducing crowds waiting for the restaurant or show lounge to open.

Celebrity distinguished itself from competitors by giving top priority to superior cuisine, hiring as food consultant Michel Roux, an award-winning master French chef who operates a Michelin three-star restaurant and other food enterprises in England. Roux helped design the ships' kitchens, trained its chefs, and works with food suppliers to ensure year-round quality. He's created a sophisticated but unpretentious cuisine for refined palates, emphasized quality over quantity (although quantity is there, too), and he established a new standard for competitors. Recently, Celebrity added more deluxe amenities fleetwide and a "Concierge Class" for the premium cabins on Millennium-class ships.

Distinctive Features   Computer room on *Galaxy;* shipboard passenger-service manager. Children's program and specially priced shore excursions. Martini bars; cigar bars. Advance bookings for AquaSpa. Robes in all cabins. Butler service in suites. Alternative restaurant for casual dining. 24-hour room service. Internet cafés. Unique restaurants, music libraries, conservatories, and Concierge Class on Millennium-class ships.

	HIGHEST	LOWEST	AVERAGE
PER DIEM	$440	$127	$239

Per diems are calculated from cruise line's nondiscounted *cruise-only* fares on standard accommodations and vary by season, cabin, and cruise areas.

Rates   All published rates include port fees.

Special Fares and Discounts   Early-bird discounts, called Five Star rates, represent some of cruising's best values. Time-sensitive, capacity-controlled, advance-purchase fares offer up to 50% discounts on cruise-only rates (deluxe cabins and suites excluded). Base rates for seven-day cruises offer upgrades for a low fee.

Two itineraries—such as Eastern and Western Caribbean—can be combined at a special rate.

- **Third/Fourth Passenger** Yes.
- **Children's Fare** Yes.
- **Single Parents** Seasonally.
- **Single Supplement** 150–200%, depending on category. Guaranteed single rate.

Packages

- **Cruise/Air Add-on with Transfers** Yes.
- **Others** Anniversary, honeymoon, family.
- **Pre/Post** Yes.

Past Passengers   The Captain's Club is open to all passengers after their first Celebrity cruise. The club was recently revamped, with benefits determined by the number of times you cruise. Benefits for Classic level (1 to 5 cruises): one-category upgrade, custom air arrangements, presailing specialty restaurant reservations, priority embarkation/debarkation (where available) for founder classic members, exclusive party, welcome amenity gift with purchase at AquaSpa, certificates for Celebrity casino, golf clinic and special rate for simulator, wine tasting, reunion cruises, quarterly newsletter with exclusive offers. Select level (6 to 10 cruises): private event for Select and Elite members, behind-the-scenes tours, priority status for shore excursion waitlist, preferential debarkation (where available), plus all Classic member benefits. Elite level (11 or more cruises): private shipboard departure lounge with Continental breakfast, plus all Classic and Select member benefits.

The Last Word   Celebrity Cruises has been one of the industry's true success stories. It created the right formula at the right time: classic cruising updated for contemporary lifestyles and available at reasonable prices. Its immediate success resulted from exceeding everyone's expectations and reflected the extensive planning and testing that went into the ships. The line has maintained unusually high standards for its price range and continues to enhance the product by adding new deluxe amenities. The exception, which we criticized in earlier editions, were Celebrity's shore excursions. We're happy to report that they have improved, particularly in Alaska. There's still room for improvement in the Caribbean. But they do have a redeeming feature: reduced rates for children. Almost anyone would enjoy a Celebrity cruise, but first-timers with cultivated tastes and experienced cruisers who seek greater comfort and service than is common in this price range will be most appreciative of their value.

CELEBRITY CRUISES STANDARD FEATURES

Officers   Greek.

Staff   Dining, European; Cabin/International; Cruise/European, American.

Dining Facilities   One main dining room with two seatings for breakfast and lunch; midnight buffet; indoor/outdoor lido buffet breakfast and lunch. Century and Millennium class, two-level dining room. Alternative restaurant. AquaSpa, café in Millennium class.

Special Diets   Request at time of booking.

Room Service   24-hour menu; butler service in suites.

Dress Code   Casual but not sloppy during the day; informal in evening, with two nights formal or semiformal.

Cabin Amenities   Direct-dial phone; bath with shower; suites with marble bathrooms. Robes in all cabins. Television with CNN and music channels. Hair dryers, safes, minibars, on Century and Millennium classes.

Electrical Outlets   110/220 AC; 110 AC only on *Horizon* and *Zenith*.

Wheelchair Access   See Cabin section for each ship.

Recreation and Entertainment   Card room/library, casino, three–five-deck show lounge, bars/lounges, disco, video game room. Bingo, lotto, horse racing, culinary demonstrations, wine tasting, fashion show, dance lessons, art auctions, floral demonstrations on *Millennium*. High-tech entertainment center on Century class.

Sports and Other Activities   Two outside swimming pools; exercise classes, walks, golf putting, Ping-Pong, deck and pool games. Golf simulators on *Century*. and Millennium class; volleyball, basketball on Millennium class.

CELEBRITY CRUISES STANDARD FEATURES (*continued*)

Beauty and Fitness   Barber/beauty salon; health club, gym, and sauna; jogging track on sun deck; elaborate spa with beauty treatments.

Other Facilities   Boutiques, hospital, laundry and dry cleaning services, meeting facilities on Century, Millennium class; Internet on all ships. No passenger-operated washers or dryers.

Children's Facilities   Play room; teen disco; babysitters; year-round, age-specific programs with counselors.

Theme Cruises   Occasionally.

Smoking   Not permitted in dining room or theater. Other public rooms have designated areas.

Celebrity Suggested Tipping   Per person per day: waiter, butlers (suites only), $3.50; assistant waiter, $2; restaurant, 15% service charge added to all beverage checks.

Credit Cards   Cruise/onboard charges: American Express, MasterCard, Visa, Discover.

HORIZON	**QUALITY 7**	**VALUE C**
ZENITH	**QUALITY 7**	**VALUE C**
Registry: Liberia	Length: 682 feet	Beam: 95 feet
Cabins: 677/687	Draft: 24 feet	Speed: 21.4 knots
Maximum Passengers:	Passenger Decks: 9	Elevators: 7
1,374	Crew: 642/670	Space Ratio: 34.5

The Ships   The *Horizon* launched Celebrity Cruises in 1990, followed the next year by the *Zenith,* her near twin. The vessels' similarity aims to facilitate passengers' familiarity and comfort with the fleet and help keep down building costs. The German-built ships incorporate safety features that exceed national and international requirements. These safeguards added about $1 million to the cost of each ship.

Spacious and open, *Horizon's* ultramodern lines give it an almost futuristic look. Two design teams—from Greece and England—created its distinctive interiors. Original art on walls and displays of ancient artifacts add to the feeling of quality—a characteristic reflected fleetwide.

Public rooms are on four spacious decks. Those on the entertainment deck are connected by a promenade that, in one section, has floor-to-ceiling windows looking out to sea and flooding the area with light.

Building on the success of *Horizon,* Celebrity made a few enhancements on *Zenith,* which was completed in record time using computer-aided design. Michael and Agni Katzourakis, who created interiors for *Horizon* and many other luxury ships, designed the cabins. London-based John McNeece, another veteran of ship interiors, designed the public rooms. In contrast to *Horizon's* cool sophistication, *Zenith* has a warm, inviting ambience supported by lavish use of fine wood and rich fabrics in soothing colors.

In late 1998, nine public areas of *Horizon* received a $4.5-million makeover to add the signature elements of Celebrity's newer Century-class vessels: martini bar, cigar bar, chocolates and coffee café, and fancy spa. On Deck 8, the disco was replaced by a new rotunda with alabaster and bronze chandelier and wood flooring inlaid with a marble compass, and **Michael's Club,** a cigar bar echoing a private English club. Adjoining the club and with similar décor is a new library and card room, available for parties or meetings of up to 70 people. The library offers books plus electronic equipment for audio/visual presentations. Beside high-back chairs are wall units with headsets for listening to audio books and music. The **Business Center,** also in the library, has two computers and two printers for passenger use.

Under an exclusive agreement with the historic Milan coffeehouse, Pasticceria Confetteria COVA, the Plaza Bar on Deck 5 was transformed to the **COVA Café,** a coffee and chocolate bar. On Deck 7, the **Rendezvous Lounge,** the ship's most popular before-dinner area, was enlarged and given an expanded dance floor and redesigned window wall. The lounge has a small bar where a combo plays nightly for dancing and easy listening. Also on Deck 7 are a boutique, art gallery, and the Art Deco **Martini Bar.** The latter serves 26 types of martinis. *Zenith* was given a similar treatment in 1999.

Itineraries   See Itinerary Index.

Cabins   Handsomely fitted in light wood, the spacious, well-designed cabins reflect attention to detail that went into them. For example, all built-in furniture has been finished with rounded corners and edges for safety and durability. Décor is colorful and cheerful; space is generous, with two full-length closets (larger on *Zenith* than on *Horizon*) and plenty of drawers. Bathrooms, large for ships in this price range, have ample counter space. Almost 75% are outside cabins. Passengers can dial toll-free numbers in the United States directly from their cabins.

All cabins are equipped with the Celebrity Network, enabling you to order meals or wine for dinner, review your account, and request other services directly from your cabin television. Stewards can be summoned by phone. Cabins are cleaned and bathroom linens changed twice daily. Missing from these ships are passenger-operated washers and dryers. In-cabin dining—full breakfast and dinner off the restaurant menu—and massage are also available. Both are amenities normally found only on luxury ships.

On *Zenith,* lengthening the 9th, 10th, and 11th decks created space for ten suites and deluxe cabins more than on *Horizon,* and for larger royal suites. The roomy suites have marbled bathrooms with Jacuzzi tubs and excellent showers. Most have a king-size bed and sleeper loveseat. Suites have butler service, but unless you can easily afford the higher cost, the true value is in the standard cabins.

In summer and holidays when many children are apt to be aboard *Zenith,* avoid cabins on Europe Deck aft near the playroom—unless some are your own kids.

Specifications   144/146 inside cabins, 533/541 outside; 20/22 suites. Standard dimensions are 172 square feet; 473/462 with twin (273/260 convert to doubles); 64/74 double/king; third/fourth persons available; no singles.

Dining   Chef Michel Roux's highly praised cuisine was a major factor in the line's immediate success. Roux's credo is to use the best-quality products and keep menus seasonal. To maintain his high standards, Roux or one of his sous-chefs sail on every ship during the year. Food presentation receives as many accolades as preparation. A typical lunch menu offers a choice of four appetizers, two soups, two salads, two cold and three hot entrées, a selection of vegetables, and four desserts, plus ice creams, sherbet, and cheeses.

Dinners have even more choices plus a special menu by Roux. Every menu includes at least one lean-and-light dish. There is a separate, full-week's vegetarian menu. Wines are suggested on menus; prices are moderate to very expensive.

Celebrity eschews themed nights for dinner—common on other lines and often more show than authenticity. Rather, themes are given to the midnight buffets, when chefs are better able to do justice to ethnic cuisine. Another popular nightly feature is the presentation of "Gourmet Bites," a chef's sampling, in public rooms.

Dining room service is exemplary, and the gracious ambience is enhanced by piano music at lunch and dinner. Although the dining room seats 840, its H layout with raised center lessens the feeling of being in a huge room. Nonetheless, when the ships are full, which they usually are, tables are set close together, and the room is crowded. A few tables seat two; most accommodate four, six, or eight.

Alternative casual dinner service is available in the Coral Seas Café on *Horizon* (Windsurf Café on *Zenith*). The limited menu includes an appetizer, soup, salad, pasta, choice of meat, and dessert. Freshly made pizza is also available. The open rotisseries and large grills enable diners to see their food being cooked to order.

Breakfast and lunch in the Windsurf Café offer hot and cold selections. When the ships are full, long lines develop, particularly on days at sea when passengers don't need to be up for early excursions. To relieve the problem, waiters at the buffet lines carry your tray to your table. The most informal setting, the outside Grill, serves hamburgers and hot dogs cooked to order.

Service   Particularly in the dining room, service distinguishes Celebrity from other midprice cruise lines. Among their innovations is a passenger service representative, ready to help with problems that crop up and usually found in the main lobby.

Facilities and Activities   Scheduled activities are so numerous that it would be virtually impossible for one person to do them all. But the variety ensures there is enough to suit almost every passenger. Choices range from exercise and dance classes to contests and karaoke. The week's activities might include a singles' party, poolside Island Night, honeymooners' champagne party, a jazz concert, and seminars on cuisine, the stock market, stress management, and estate planning. Art auctions draw mild interest. First-run movies are shown daily in the show lounge, and older films play on cabin television; a week's schedule is provided in your cabin. The ships have lounges for peace or pleasure, with entertainment ranging from a sing-along piano bar and dance music to Broadway-style productions in the two-deck showroom. The popular Rendezvous Lounge, convenient to the dining room and crowded for cocktails, is great for people-watching anytime.

The *Zenith's* Fleet Bar (America's Cup on the *Horizon*), is among the most attractive rooms afloat. The top-deck, club-like piano bar has a small dance floor and an expanse of windows. It's everyone's favorite spot for drinks and dancing—light and cheerful by day, softly aglow at sunset, and sophisticated at night. The ships also feature champagne and caviar service in the observation lounge and martini bars.

Evening entertainment is balanced between specialty acts (acrobats, comedians, magicians) and big production shows, all of which are family-appropriate. In the bilevel show lounge, which doubles as a meeting room, most seats have good sight lines. During a week's cruise, two big stage productions are presented. From the upper level, passengers can walk aft to the casino, offering blackjack, roulette, and slot machines, or to the shops. An ATM is nearby, but each transaction costs $5.

Sports and Fitness   Wide, open decks have plenty of space for deck chairs, even when the ships are full, and quiet corners for reading, sunning, or snoozing, but shady areas are limited. At sea, there are swimming pool games, Ping-Pong, trapshooting, darts, shuffleboard, and golf putting. In port, golf, snorkeling, and other sports are offered, depending on location. The ships have large, well-equipped fitness centers and a one-fifth-mile jogging track on their top decks, but no outside, wraparound promenade deck. A full fitness program encompasses four or five activities daily. The cruise price includes use of the facilities, saunas, and exercise classes.

Spa and Beauty   A major addition to the ships in their makeover was an AquaSpa on the Sun Deck, replacing the Fantasia bar. Although smaller than those on Century-class ships and lacking their thalassotherapy pool, the spa offers many of the same treatments. It houses a beauty salon; six treatment rooms; sauna, fitness, and aerobics area; and separate changing rooms for men and women. All Celebrity ships offer the AquaSpa program by Elemis, a spa operator owned by Steiner of London. Services are expensive. Spas on all Celebrity ships have a barber shop and beauty salon and offer massage, facials, and body treatments for additional fees. Spa programs may be booked in advance. Beware: Steiner's staff pushes their products aggressively; you should not feel any obligation to buy.

Children's Facilities   During summer and major holidays, Celebrity ships offers supervised, daily programs for five age groups: Ship Mates (ages 3–6), Celebrity Cadets (ages 7–9), Ensigns (ages 10–12), and Admiral T's (ages 13–17). Younger children enjoy painting, drawing, songs, dances, movies, and other age-appropriate activities. Celebrity Summer Stock lets young actors participate in theatrical shows with dances and costumes. The Young Mariners' program showcases the operations of the ship and provides the opportunity to meet the captain and learn navigation by the stars.

Junior Olympics offer water volleyball and basketball, golf putting, Ping-Pong, and other games. At meals, kids can join their peers at the Celebrity Breakfast Club and at dinner, order from their own or the regular menu. The program also has family activities and a masquerade parade.

Shore Excursions   In summer, *Zenith* sails weekly from New York to Bermuda, where island tours, glass-bottom boat and snorkel trips, sailing, and nightlife tours are available. Most tours are one to three hours long and cost $13–$110. Children's rates are about 30–40% lower. Bermuda is also easy to tour on your own. You can visit historic forts, museums, art galleries, craft shops, duty-free shops, the aquarium, and the lovely botanic gardens. Tennis and golf can be arranged. The National Historic Trust has excellent walking tours. Rental cars are not available, but taxis are. Mopeds or scooters are the most popular modes of transportation. In October 2003, *Zenith* launched the cruise industry's first cruises from Jacksonville, Florida, to the Caribbean, ranging in length from 11 to 14 nights.

CENTURY	**QUALITY 7**	**VALUE C**
GALAXY	**QUALITY 8**	**VALUE B**
MERCURY	**QUALITY 8**	**VALUE B**
Registry: Liberia	Length: 815/866 feet	Beam: 105/105.6 feet
Cabins: 875/935	Draft: 25/25.5 feet	Speed: 21.5 knots
Maximum Passengers:	Passenger Decks: 10	Elevators: 9/10
1,750/1,870	Crew: 858/909	Space Ratio: 40

The Ships   Celebrity got a jump on the next millennium with the 1995 debut of the *Century,* first of a new fleet designed for 21st-century cruising.

The $320 million ship, built at the same German yard as the *Horizon* and *Zenith*, also had the same designers. *Galaxy* followed in 1996 and *Mercury* in 1997. More than ten teams worked with *Century's* builders to achieve a comfortable, inviting, integrated design. With 48% more space than their cousin ships but only 26% more passengers, this spacious trio has one of cruising's highest passenger-to-space ratios in their category. Public rooms range in style from an elegant wood-paneled bar to a futuristic disco. Sony Corporation of America designed a sophisticated, interactive communications and entertainment system, and the company's music, pictures, and electronic publishing divisions provide products and expertise.

Century's focal point is a three-deck Grand Foyer encircled by a staircase and topped with a painted glass dome lit as if by sunlight during the day and as a starlit sky at night. The piazza has marble floors, burled woods, brass trim, suede furniture, and a waterfall with changing fiber-optic images. Nearby are boutiques and the **COVA Café,** a floating version of Pasticceria Confetteria COVA, the Milan-based pastry shop famous for its exquisitely packaged chocolates, pastries, and signature coffees.

The *Galaxy* is essentially *Century's* twin in layout, but she is slightly larger with improvements over her sister ship, including the atrium, with a 40-foot-tall video panel projecting changing images and a high-tech center offering free computer classes. The atrium has been improved further on *Mercury* with a spiral staircase leading to the promenade deck, where the port side has the COVA Café (now found on all Celebrity ships).

The *Galaxy's* best new feature is a retractable glass dome covering a swimming pool and the surrounding deck. The **Oasis,** one of the ship's most popular areas, has an indoor/outdoor grill and bar that in the evening offers alternative casual dining, introduced fleetwide in 1998.

The ships have multilevel, multipurpose observation lounges that become discos in the evening. One of the ships' two atriums, positioned aft and spanning three decks, opens onto the casino, **Rendezvous Lounge,** the dining room's foyer, and a champagne bar.

Century-group vessels, like their predecessors, have multimillion-dollar art collections that are virtually contemporary art museums at sea. The focus for *Century* is contemporary masters; for *Galaxy,* the avant garde; and for *Mercury,* works by artists who emerged after pop art in the 1960s and 1970s. The collections were assembled by Christina Chandris, the ships' curator and former fine art advisor, in collaboration with the Marlborough Gallery of New York. The line provides information for a self-guided art tour.

Itineraries   See Itinerary Index.

Cabins   Each deck has its own color scheme, with cabins on each using complementary colors for carpeting and bedspreads. Windows in the spacious cabins are framed in rosewood, conveying luxury and comfort. All *Century* cabins have built-in vanities; generous closet and drawer space; large bathrooms with showers, hair dryers, and terry robes; telephones, safes, and minibars; and radios and televisions. Interactive cabin television enables passengers to order breakfast or room service, book spa appointments, buy shore excursions, gamble (charged to the room), order merchandise from shops, and watch pay-per-view movies (including adult selections). Interactive televisions located throughout the ship provide information and entertainment.

Although cabins on *Century* are similar to those on *Zenith* and *Horizon,* they were modified on *Galaxy* to accommodate more features. Some storage space was lost; drawer space, particularly, is inadequate. All have minibars, and upper-category cabins have VCRs. The ships have penthouse and royal suites, and all suites have marble bathrooms, whirlpool tubs, verandas, and butler service.

Century *Specifications*   304 inside cabins, 571 outside; 52 suites, 61 suites and deluxe cabins with verandas. Standard dimensions, 172 square feet; 806 with twin beds, all convertible to doubles; third/fourth persons; no singles. 8 wheelchair-accessible cabins.

Galaxy / Mercury *Specifications*   296 inside cabins, 639 outside; 50 suites and 170 mini-suites with verandas. Standard dimensions, 172 square feet; 877 with twin beds, all convertible to doubles; third/fourth persons; no singles. 8 wheelchair-accessible cabins.

Dining   *Century's* stylish **Grand Restaurant,** the main dining room, was Celebrity's first two-tiered dining room; a majestic staircase leads to a colonnaded center aisle reminiscent of the Karnak Temple in Egypt. Each of two galleys prepares food for half of the dining room, thus providing speedier service, consistent temperatures, and freshness. The **Orion Restaurant** aboard *Galaxy* has a larger second tier to accommodate the ship's greater capacity, and décor is lighter, more contemporary, and less pretentious than on *Century.* The room's focal point is an enormous, backlit ceiling panel of a hemisphere with continents superimposed. The *Mercury's* **Manhattan Restaurant,** with a backdrop depicting the Big Apple skyline, is completely different from those of its sisters. Food, however, is the same on all three ships and meets the line's high standards.

Other dining areas are the casual **Veranda Grill,** adjacent to the pool, and **Islands Café,** with four buffet stations and two bars. The café serves an afternoon tea buffet that's in addition to Celebrity's traditional Elegant Tea. *Galaxy's* **Oasis** (**Palm Springs Grill** on *Mercury* and the **Sky Bar** on *Century*) is a casual dining alternative restaurant. As something of an afterthought, the restaurant is a disappointment compared to the ships' other venues and to Celebrity's dining reputation. The outdoor section has a small swimming pool in a garden setting and is covered by a dome (particularly appealing on Alaska itineraries).

Among its latest innovations, Celebrity is the first line to offer complimentary pizza delivered to cabins.

Service   European-style service distinguishes Celebrity from other mid-price cruise lines. It's one of the ships' best and most rewarding features.

Facilities and Activities   The two-deck **Celebrity Theater** used for Broadway-style revues and cabaret shows has a sloping orchestra section and cantilevered balconies providing unobstructed sight lines. The venue has a revolving stage, the ability to handle multiple backdrops, an orchestra pit with adjustable height, sophisticated lighting, and other special effects.

The Art Deco **Crystal Room** (**The Savoy Nightclub** on *Galaxy;* **Pavilion** on *Mercury*), a low-key night club for evening dancing, has etched-glass panels, luminous alabaster dome ceiling, rotating bronze globe, and chic color scheme of red, black, and gold that recalls 1930s New York. The Savoy employs a jungle motif in its late-night cabaret, and **Fortune's Casino** has the full roster of games. Rendezvous Square, next to the dining room, is a lively place for cocktails or socializing before and after dinner.

High atop *Century,* **Hemisphere** (**Stratosphere Lounge** on the *Galaxy* and **Navigator Club** on *Mercury*) is an airy, sunlit observation lounge by day transformed into a futuristic "disco under the dome" at night, when window blinds lower automatically, etched-glass room dividers illuminate one by one, and a special table "glows." The hemisphere then rises—casting light from within—and the dance floor appears. Telescopes are placed around the room's edge for stargazing. On *Galaxy,* the Stratosphere has three sections. The outer one next to the floor-to-ceiling windows is a quiet zone for daytime viewing of scenery and reading. The middle level is ideal for cocktails at sunset, and the innermost can accommodate meetings during the day as pull-down screens separate it from other areas of the lounge. In the evening, the inner room becomes the disco, as sophisticated equipment transforms it and provides a terrific laser light show.

Michael's Club aboard *Century* is an intimate lounge fashioned after a private gentlemen's club, paneled in rich woods and furnished with leather chairs and couches. On *Galaxy,* the room is contemporary in décor and lacks the cachet of the club on *Century.* The clubs (one on *Mercury,* too) have been given over to the cigar-smoking fad; craftsmen demonstrate cigar making, an art Christopher Columbus learned from native tribes. The three ships also have martini bars. Flexible walls fold into pillars in a conference center, allowing it also to serve as cinema, meeting room, library, or card room. Keypads in the armchairs can be used for responses to questions or for interactive movies.

Activities are numerous and varied to appeal to a range of passengers and include exercise and dance classes, contests, singles' party, honeymooners' champagne party, and karaoke. Informational seminars also may be scheduled. First-run and adult pay-per-view movies are shown daily on cabin television; a schedule is provided in your cabin.

Sports and Fitness   The spacious ships have 62,000 square feet of open decks and sports, including simulated golf, Ping-Pong, volleyball, basketball, darts, and jogging. The *Century's* two swimming pools have cylindrical waterfalls and are rimmed with teak benches.

Spa and Beauty   AquaSpa, the ships' health and fitness center, is among the most popular feature on all three ships. It's one of the best-equipped gyms at sea, with a hydropool, saunas, steam rooms, cardiovascular machines, and weight stations. Personal trainers are available to create individualized training programs. Aerobics classes are ongoing. The spa offers a variety of beauty and health treatments. The most unusual is Rasul, based on an Oriental ceremony with a seaweed soap shower, medicinal mud pack, herbal steam bath, and massage.

Not to be missed is the tranquilizing thalassotherapy treatment taken in a 115,000-gallon pool with waterjet massage stations. Spa treatments are expensive; they may be booked in advance of your cruise.

Children's Facilities   With every new ship, Celebrity's children's facilities improve. The **Fun Factory** on *Galaxy* and *Mercury* is a 1,600-square-foot playroom, and there's also a kids' splash pool. As on other Celebrity ships, supervised daily programs are geared to five age groups. See previous section for details. Teens have a private lounge with a dance floor, plus a video game room. The program also offers family activities.

Shore Excursions   Passengers can look over and make reservations on line at www.celebritycruises.com. In the Caribbean, Celebrity premiered an excursion developed with the Nature Conservancy (Magen's Bay Nature Walk).

MILLENNIUM	QUALITY 7	VALUE B
INFINITY	QUALITY 8	VALUE B
SUMMIT	(Preview)	
CONSTELLATION	(Preview)	
Registry: Liberia	Length: 965 feet	Beam: 105.6 feet
Cabins: 975	Draft: 26.3 feet	Speed: 24 knots
Maximum Passengers:	Passenger Decks: 11	Elevators: 10
2,038	Crew: 999	Space Ratio: 46.6

The Ships   When the *Millennium* debuted in July 2000 in Europe, it launched a new class of ships for Celebrity—somewhat larger than her sister ships and with many of the same facilities, but even more spacious and with contemporary refinements sure to please maturing baby boomers. These include the line's largest spa, a unique specialty restaurant with a dine-in wine cellar, a large boutique of designer fashions, a music library, floral conservatories with full-service florists, and extravagantly large suites. The *Millennium,* the first of four sister ships, also enables Celebrity to expand its cruise horizons. *Infinity,* which debuted in spring 2001, has offered the line's first cruises to Hawaii. *Summit* has sailed in the Caribbean, Hawaii, and Alaska since debuting in October 2001; while *Constellation* entered service in Europe in May, 2002.

These ships are powered by environmentally friendly gas turbine engines, which reduce exhaust emissions by up to 90% and lower noise and vibration levels considerably. The way these ships glide out of port is reminiscent of the smooth sailing on board steam-driven, classic liners from the past. The only vibration noticed was in the aft section when the Azipod propulsion system was altering the ship's course. That same propulsion system also allows the ships to cruise at 24 knots, enabling them to sail to more destinations in shorter time. They are also able to transit the Panama Canal. Changes in the exterior design—a lean, chiseled profile with a new stack design and hull striping—makes the group look like the faster ships that they are. The interiors, created by some of the same design teams that worked on other Celebrity ships, are the line's most sophisticated and elegant to date and have something of a back-to-the-future décor, blending the glamour and grandeur of turn-of-the-century luxury liners with the amenities and state-of-the-art technology that passengers in the new millennium expect. They also hold Celebrity's signature features: museum-quality contemporary art collections, an enormous **AquaSpa, COVA Café di Milano, Michael's Club** piano bar, martini and champagne bars, and cuisine by Michel Roux.

Passengers are introduced to the *Millennium* via the Grand Foyer with a translucent, backlit onyx staircase. Opposite the shore excursion desk is a bank of four glass elevators—the first external-facing ones ever built on a cruise ship—that capture panoramic views as they rise. One passenger, enjoying her elevator ride with Amsterdam views, said, "It was almost as good as a shore excursion." Next to the elevators, a paneled wall of wood and metallic vinyl rises from the entry to the top of the ship through a series of atria.

In spring 2003, the line introduced "Celebrity Concierge Class," an enhanced level of accommodations with new amenities and priority services with the notion that little extras make a big difference. The new class is for premium outside with veranda cabins (category one) on Deck Nine of the four Millennium-class ships. The new amenities include a bottle of chilled champagne on arrival, fresh flowers and fruit, afternoon canapés, a leather key holder, personalized stationery, an oversized tote bag, and an umbrella to use during the cruise.

Sleeping comfort is enhanced with pillow-top mattresses; lush duvets; pillow selections, such as goose down, Isotonic, and others; and a new room-service breakfast menu. In the bathroom, this group of passengers will find oversized Egyptian cotton towels, Frette bathrobes, two hair dryers, a Hansgrohe shower head, and a selection of fine toiletries. On the veranda, they have a table for al fresco dining, cushioned chairs, and high-powered binoculars.

Priority service gives them priority luggage delivery, dining time and seating preferences, shoe-shine service, VIP invitations to exclusive shipboard events, priority shore excursion bookings, early embarkation/debarkation privileges, and a one-touch phone button direct to a Concierge Class desk representative.

Unique to the ships are their floral conservatories and the silk floral displays by Emilio Robba of Paris, renowned for his silk floral artistry, which add to the serene character of these beautiful vessels. The floral conservatories and boutiques—the first at sea—provide an attractive botanical environment, ideal for romantic occasions and reflective moments. Designed by Robba, they combine natural flora with his silk creations. The boutiques are operated by full-time florists who produce flower arrangements and corsages for passengers and hold classes in flower-arranging several times a week. Following the facility's success on *Infinity,* a small conservatory and boutique were added to *Millennium,* replacing the little-used teen center. On the three newer ships, the larger conservatories replace *Millennium's* sports bar. The Millennium-class ships also have **Notes,** a music library, **Online@Celebrity Cruises** Internet café, and meetings space with a business center.

Itineraries   See Itinerary Index.

Cabins   Of the 975 cabins, 80% are outside, and of those, 74% (or 56% of the total) have verandas. All cabins have air-conditioning, minibar, safe, telephone with voicemail, shower, hair dryer, and multifunction interactive television. The standard cabins are furnished with twin beds that are convertible to queen size. *Infinity, Summit* and *Constellation* have Connect@Sea and in-cabin Internet access. The spacious cabins are well appointed and beautifully finished. Added touches, such as a silver carafe of fresh water replenished regularly, heighten the level of service. There are no self-service launderettes—particularly missed on long sailings.

The Penthouse suites, measuring 1,432 square feet, plus 1,098 square feet of veranda, have marble floor foyers, separate living and dining rooms; baby grand piano; butler's pantry; master bedroom with generous closets; exercise equipment; dressing room with vanity; marble master bath with twin sinks; whirlpool tub, separate shower, toilet and bidet area; powder room; motorized draperies, lights and security system, two interactive audio/visual entertainment systems with flat-screen television, and a fax machine; veranda with whirlpool, wet bar, and lounges.

The Royal suites have floor-to-ceiling glass doors; separate living room with dining and sitting area; two entertainment centers with flat-screen TVs and VCRs; walk-in closet; bath with whirlpool tub and stall shower; and veranda with whirlpool tub. There are also Celebrity suites, each with themed décor and floor-to-ceiling windows; and Sky suites (including six wheelchair-accessible) also with floor-to-ceiling glass doors, sitting area with sofa bed and lounge chair, similar entertainment center, minibar, walk-in closet, and bathroom with whirlpool tub. All but a few suites have verandas and all have butler service.

Specifications   639 outside; 296 inside. 2 penthouse suites; 8 Celebrity suites; 8 Royal suites; 26 Sky suites, plus 6 wheelchair-accessible—all with verandas. Five inside and four outside cabins are wheelchair-accessible and have flat floors, cabin bathroom doorways 35 inches wide. Public elevator doorways are 39 inches wide.

Dining   The **Metropolitan Restaurant,** the main dining room, spanning two levels, features bold, geometric motifs in reds, blues, and golds based on French designs from the late 1940s/early 1950s, which the designers describe as "restrained exuberance." At night, panels with dramatic architectural scenes are lowered onto the room's expansive windows, with a quintet providing a quiet, elegant accompaniment. It's called **The Trellis** on *Infinity* and has an 18th-century-garden theme.

The **Olympic,** Celebrity's first specialty restaurant, is the *Millennium's* show-stopper. It takes its name from a rare maritime treasure—a section of the original Edwardian wood-carved paneling from the *Olympic,* the sister ship of the Titanic. First discovered in a private English residence, the exquisite French walnut paneling ornamented with gold leaf in Louis XVI style was bought at auction at Sotheby's. Seating only 134 people, the intimate dining room uses an Edwardian theme for its décor, to convey a nostalgic ambience of the elegant golden days of steamship travel. The Olympic restaurant also has the cruise industry's first demonstration galley (an open kitchen where guests can see their meals being prepared). The restaurant has its own menu of gourmet cuisine, and to make the dining experience even more memorable, some dishes are presented and finished table side. One treat is Waldorf pudding—a re-creation of an original dessert from the Olympic. There is a piano/violin duo entertaining. Memorabilia from the Olympic includes White Star Line china and the ship's bell, which is on exhibit in the foyer. Adjoining the room is a separate wine cellar, which can be used as private dining room for small groups of eight persons or so. The wine list has almost 200 international selections, some of them quite prestigious, and guests may also order Roux-recommended wines by the glass with each of the four courses. Wine and after-dinner espressos can increase the tab to $100 or more for a couple.

The same theme of honoring a different liner from the past, with superb design and décor and recreating the first-class dining experience of a past era, is found on *Millennium's* sister ships. *Infinity's* **S.S. United States** restaurant has etched glass panels from the famous American liner's first class ballroom. The French liner *Normandie* is featured in *Summit's* alternative restaurant and **Ocean Liners** on *Constellation,* saluting the classic ships of the past with memorabilia and paintings of famed liners and the original lacquered panels from the *Ile de France.*

At the entrance to each restaurant, glass cases containing memorabilia from the famous ships are found. The ambience of the great liner is enhanced by cutlery and china reproduced from the original ship's designs and the style of music performed throughout the evening. The three-hour dining experience is a unique opportunity to enjoy fine dining in the style of a bygone age. It is certainly worth the $25 per-person service charge added to your shipboard account when booking these restaurants.

The **Ocean Café,** an indoor/outdoor restaurant designed to resemble a Portuguese outdoor café, is the casual dining venue for breakfast and lunch buffet, while the **Ocean Grill,** with a separate entrance, is an alternative dining venue featuring steak, fish, rotisserie chicken, pizza, and pasta. There is no fee for this by-reservation, partial-waiter-service restaurant. Recently, Celebrity added fleetwide what it calls the "Casual Dining Boulevard" on the Lido deck, a nightly alternative to the more formal atmosphere in the main dining rooms. There, you will find a sushi café and a pizza and pasta bar.

Savvy travelers discover the **AquaSpa Café** where they can select light, healthy food and fruit plates, whole grain cereals and breads and yogurt at breakfast, and cold poached salmon and chicken and crudités at lunch. Smoothies and fresh vegetable and fruit juices are available for an extra charge.

Service   Service in the main dining rooms is very attentive and up to Celebrity's high standards. In the buffet-style café, you never have to carry your tray; waiters are ready to assist you. The alternative dining rooms have the highest level of service of any ship of this category and price range.

Facilities and Activities   The Celebrity Theater is the line's first three-tiered show lounge, seating 900 passengers in a classically inspired but contemporary setting with a full circular balcony. Designed by premier theater designers, the stage, orchestra pits, and lighting can accommodate most any Broadway-style show at sea. Sight lines are excellent and seats extremely comfortable with room between rows. The use of dazzling laser and lighting effects, movable stage levels, and the big-screen video is stunning, but they are frequently more remarkable than the quality of entertainers.

The ever-popular **Rendezvous Lounge,** an elegant cocktail lounge that leads to the dining room, has music for dancing, and the **Platinum Club,** on a balcony overlooking the lounge, is a martini bar and a champagne bar. **Michael's Club,** another Celebrity tradition, is a richly appointed piano bar with traditional English Georgian décor and natural cherry paneling. **Extremes,** at the top of the ship overlooking the pool deck, is Celebrity's first sports bar.

High above the ship on Sunrise Deck is a glass-sheathed observation lounge for panoramic viewing by day. It is transformed into an early evening cabaret and piano bar with a dance floor and a late night disco. The richly decorated **Fortune's Casino** has 228 slot machines, 23 game tables, and a huge selection of video casino games. Overlooking the Grand Foyer is a card and games area; the **COVA Café de Milano,** with a separate tea room and well attended classical music performances each evening; The café quickly becomes a favorite hangout for many, especially non-American travelers who enjoyed the European flair of this onboard version of the classic Milan coffeehouse. Passengers are served a variety of coffee drinks, champagne cocktails, and morning and afternoon pastries, often accompanied by music from a harpist or pianist.

Words, a two-level library; and **Online@CelebrityCruises,** the line's Internet café, with 18 individual stations enabling passengers to check their e-mail and other services. The charge is $0.50 per minute. Computer classes are available for $59 an hour. Similar facilities have been added fleetwide. (Many passengers find the special weekly rate for unlimited access is more affordable than the per-minute charge.) Nearby is **Notes,** a music library that has private listening stations with personal CD players and headsets and offers 1,500 selections of music in varying styles as well as musicology books.

The ship's conference/cinema is designed to hold more than 300 people in auditorium-style seating and offers the latest audiovisual technology, including seat voting/interactive systems and full control booth. The center also can double as the ship's cinema. Five flexible rooms, each offering television, monitors, computers, teleconferencing, Internet connections, fax machines, and private satellite telephones, are available for meetings and other functions.

The Emporium, the *Millennium's* European-styled shopping arcade, has designer boutiques, an art gallery, a signature Celebrity shop, a Michel Roux culinary shop, and COVA Café store.

Sports, Fitness, and Beauty   The Resort Deck has the Riviera pool with four freshwater whirlpools and plenty of areas for sunbathing as well as shaded spots. The deck also houses an entertainment area with a canopied stage and bandstand, a teakwood dance floor, two outdoor bars and the Grill. Forward is the **AquaSpa,** Aqua Dome, and the fitness area.

The Sunrise Deck overlooking the pool area has a running track and golf simulator (reserve at the Purser's deck), and the Sports Deck holds a full-size basketball court, paddle tennis, volleyball, and quoits, a game similar to horseshoes.

The 25,000-square-foot AquaSpa, which Celebrity says is the largest and most extensive spa of any cruise ship, is an impressive facility that includes a large fitness area; a gym with an enormous array of equipment (rowers, exercise bikes, recumbent bikes, treadmills, steppers), and an aerobics area, indoor hydropool with air beds, whirlpools, sauna, steam, tropical showers. The Persian Garden is a tranquil, aromatherapy oasis which can be booked by the hour. The AquaSpa has a beauty parlor and 16 treatment rooms, including a dry float room with shower, Alpha Massage Capsule, a disabled-accessible full-body treatment room, and other specialty rooms. The spa offers Celebrity's water-oriented treatments of Middle Eastern, Asian, and European origin, as well as such specialties as thalassotherapy, hydrotherapy, a new aromatic bath, and first-at-sea treatments such as hot stone therapy. Spa charges range from $33 for a 30-minute body composition test, $109 for a 50-minute well-being massage and fitness consultation, to $305 for a two-and-a-half-hour Haiku Ritual Facial and Aroma Stone Massage. You can save 20% on spa treatments by booking the first day of your cruise. Fitness consultants are on hand to assist with programs and assessments. In addition to the equipment in the fitness area, there are four daily classes, two of which, such as yoga and spinning, carry a $10 fee. Four decks down, the promenade does not completely circle the ship, as the lower level of the main dining room takes up the aft portion of Promenade Deck. Still, the long and wide promenade is a fine place for walkers and passengers for whom being on deck, close to the sea, is one of the great joys of cruising.

Children's Facilities   The **Fun Factory** for children ages 3–12 offers a variety of activities under an ocean travel and exploration theme. Children enjoy a puzzle wall, movie room, and colorful play area under the supervision of experienced councilors. A separate arts-and-crafts room are available for younger children, whereas the older children have their own broadcast room (though sometimes used by the younger children), video game arcade, dance floor, and CD jukebox.

Shore Excursions   A variety of tours from adventure activities to cultural experiences is available. In Alaska, they include the Mendenhall Glacier helicopter tour in Juneau, $216–$242; kayaking tours, $66–$89 or pan for gold, $30–$42. In Hawaii, there's a Hilo and Kilauea seven-and-a-half-hour volcano tour, $69–$79; or, two hours whale watching in Maui, $19–$35. In France, tours are often full-day trips to cities away from the port of call. From the Seine Valley, a ten-hour visit to Paris is

$68–$111; from Le Havre, an 11-hour excursion to Paris with a lunch cruise is $110–$185. On the Russia and the Baltic voyage, a 13-hour excursion by train to Berlin from Rostock is $295 and includes highlights of East and West Berlin, breakfast snack on the train, buffet lunch at a Berlin hotel restaurant, and dinner snack on the return trip.

Postscript   Each Celebrity ship has been an improvement on its predecessor. Gracious service combines with inviting décor, high-tech wizardry, and just enough glitz to keep the vessels competitive. The fleet will please travelers who prefer large ships for their high-energy entertainment, extensive facilities, state-of-the-art equipment, and elegant restaurants. The vessels' spaciousness is particularly appealing and unusual in their price group and provides a great deal of value for money.

Clipper Cruise Line

11969 Westline Industrial Drive, St. Louis, MO 63146-3220
(314) 655-6700; (800) 325-0010;
fax (314) 655-6670
www.clippercruise.com

Type of Ships   First-class small ships.

Type of Cruise   Destination-oriented, light adventure, low-key, intellectually stimulating cruises for nature- and culture-oriented travelers on the byways of the Americas and exotic, off-beat destinations.

Cruise Line's Strengths

- itineraries
- small ship experience
- cuisine
- accompanying naturalists and experts
- maneuverability of small ships

Cruise Line's Shortcomings

- lack of cabin amenities and service on oldest ships
- limited shipboard activities
- shallow-draft older vessels in turbulent waters

Fellow Passengers   Relatively affluent, educated, usually professionals, often retired or semiretired and part of a university alumni group. They come from throughout the United States and prefer small ships—often after trying a larger vessel—for the camaraderie, ambience, and small number of passengers. They are not looking for last-minute specials. They are mature, well-traveled, low-key, and, often, seasoned cruisers and Clipper repeaters. Most are environmentally minded and intellectually curious. Some prefer remote, relatively unknown areas; others seek destinations closer to home with strong cultural and natural history appeal, particularly places where small ships have access but large ships must pass by.

Recommended For   Experienced travelers who like the coziness of a country inn where people are called by name; big-ship refugees turned off by mainstream cruises and seeking quieter, more substantial travel experience; inquisitive minds who travel to learn.

Not Recommended For   Night owls, swingers, party seekers, unsophisticated travelers, people who want to be entertained, those with marginal interest in history and nature; and people who like to wear finery.

Cruise Areas and Seasons   Caribbean, South and Central America, Panama Canal, New Zealand, Antarctica in winter; Pacific from Australia, Polynesia, Far East to Alaska, Europe, eastern seaboard from Florida to Maine, New England/Canada, Great Lakes, West Coast from California to Alaska, Mexico/Sea of Cortés, Alaska, Russia/Alaska, Arctic/Greenland in spring, summer, and fall.

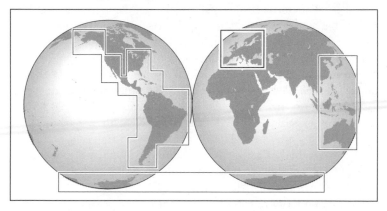

The Line   Clipper Cruise Line was created in 1982 to provide culture- and nature-oriented cruises on small coastal ships along historic byways of the United States and the Caribbean. Central and South America, Antarctica, and Asia were added as oceangoing ships joined the fleet.

The *Nantucket Clipper* and *Yorktown Clipper* are United States–built and registered and have American crews. Their shallow drafts and turn-on-a-dime maneuverability enable them to sail into places where larger ships cannot go. Destinations are as diverse as the Alaskan fjords and tours of the Antebellum South.

In 1997, Clipper Cruises was acquired by INTRAV, an established St. Louis–based group-tour operator, and acquired another vessel, the 122-passenger *Clipper Adventurer*. The ship's ice-hardened hull enables her to sail from the Arctic to Antarctica. The following year, the more deluxe, 128-passenger *Clipper Odyssey* joined the fleet. The ship added a completely new dimension to the cruise line, both in her style, offering more amenities, and in her destinations. In 1999, Kuoni, a prominent Swiss tour company, acquired INTRAV and Clipper Cruises.

THE FLEET	BUILT/RENOVATED	TONNAGE	PASSENGERS
Clipper Adventurer	1975/1998	4,364	122
Clipper Odyssey	1989	5,218	128
Nantucket Clipper	1984/95	1,471	100
Yorktown Clipper	1988/97	2,354	138

Style   Clipper cruises emphasize destinations rather than shipboard fun and games. The ships' size provides intimacy and a sense of place often missing on large ships, and cordiality resembling that in a country inn. There are passengers enough to ensure an interesting mix. It's easy to meet everyone in the course of a week and for camaraderie to develop effortlessly. The convivial crew members bolster the friendly atmosphere. Absent but not missed are casinos, discos, staged entertainment, and organized diversions of large ships.

The ships cruise mostly at night, stopping during the day for passengers to tour an island, hike in a rain forest, enjoy a secluded beach, or snorkel in reef-filled waters. Life aboard is casual, unregimented, and leisurely. The experience is enhanced by naturalists and experts who, in addition to presenting seminars, talk informally with passengers during shore excursions and cocktail hour.

Clipper is proud of its role in providing environmentally responsible travel, saying that ship size and the nature of the cruises have a minimal impact on destinations.

A consumer protection plan, pioneered by Clipper, places passenger funds in an escrow account monitored by the Federal Maritime Commission.

Distinctive Features   Historians, naturalists, and other experts travel as guides on ships; Zodiac landing craft aboard. Excellent precruise literature. Consumer protection plan.

	HIGHEST	LOWEST	AVERAGE
PER DIEM	$883	$287	$522

Per diems are calculated from cruise line's nondiscounted *cruise-only* fares on standard accommodations and vary by season, cabin, and cruise areas.

Rates   Published rates include port fees and most shore excursions, and frequently may include airfare and special events.

Special Fares and Discounts   Some advance booking discounts available and detailed in cruise line's brochure.

- **Third Passenger** Specific to each cruise, quoted in brochure.
- **Single Supplement** Specific for each category, quoted in brochure; otherwise, 150% of brochure rate on other cabins, when available.

Packages

- **Air/Sea** For some departures.
- **Others** No.
- **Pre/Post** Alaska; train tours combined with Sea of Cortés, northern California, and Pacific Northwest; Asia, among others.

Past Passengers In 2003, Clipper launched its Pinnacle program to reward past passengers for multiple cruises with special benefits, like travel certificates to be used for future cruises, in-room gifts, as well as acknowledgment by the captain and crew during the cruise. The program has three levels, with varying benefits: Explorers (2 to 5 trips), Grand Explorers (6 to 15 trips), and Elite Explorers (16 or more).

The Last Word Clipper has been transformed from a coastal cruise line to a worldwide operation since obtaining its new ships. Nonetheless, it continues to attract people who recoil at the notion of today's megaships. Yet anyone who does not fit into Clipper's country-club, somewhat academic atmosphere could quickly feel out of place. To compare Clipper's small ship cruise experience with that of large ships is comparing apples to oranges. In terms of the published prices, however, they are comparable. The difference is that Clipper does not discount its prices, even for early-bird bookings—a practice almost standard elsewhere. Prices, particularly for cruises on the two older ships, seem high given their lack of some shipboard services and facilities—no swimming pool, elevator, beauty shop, laundry room or laundry service, or cabin telephone and television. Clipper's two latest acquisitions with their amenities come closer to the mark. Precruise information sent by Clipper is thorough; some papers are the length of a book. These excellent reference materials reflect the line's commitment to making its cruises stimulating, enriching, and memorable.

CLIPPER CRUISE LINE STANDARD FEATURES

Officers American; *Clipper Adventurer*, European; *Clipper Odyssey*, Australian and European.

Staff *Nantucket, Yorktown*, Dining, Cabin/American; *Adventurer, Odyssey*, Dining, Cabin/Filipino; Cruise/American, all ships.

Dining Facilities Single-seating dining room for three meals with open seating, buffet breakfast and lunch in lounge, and occasional lunch buffet on sun deck or picnic on shore. Self-service juice, coffee, and tea in lounge.

Special Diets Accommodated with advance notice.

Room Service None.

Dress Code Casual but smart; coat and tie recommended for special occasions or going to fashionable restaurants in ports of call.

Cabin Amenities Radio, but no television or phones; bathrooms with showers; no other amenities. *Odyssey*, television for movies, safe, minibar, bathroom with small tub and shower. *Adventurer, Odyssey*, hair dryer.

CLIPPER CRUISE LINE STANDARD FEATURES
(continued)

Electrical Outlets 110 AC, except Adventurer, 220 AC.

Wheelchair Access One cabin and elevator, on *Odyssey* only.

Recreation and Entertainment Seminars by naturalists, historians and other experts; movies; occasional local entertainers. *Adventurer, Odyssey,* two lounges, bars, library.

Sports and Other Activities Gym and sauna on *Adventurer* only. Swimming, snorkeling, beach walks, wilderness and rain forest hiking. Swimming pool on *Odyssey* only.

Beauty and Fitness *Nantucket, Yorktown,* no beauty/barber shop; services generally available in port; *Adventurer* and *Odyssey* have both.

Other Facilities *Adventurer, Odyssey,* infirmary with doctor, gift shop, laundry service; e-mail service. *Nantucket, Yorktown,* no laundry service; no doctor aboard except Costa Rica, Sea of Cortés, and Orinoco cruises.

Children's Facilities None.

Theme Cruises None.

Smoking No smoking allowed in any interior areas, including cabins, at any time. Smoking permitted only on outside decks.

Clipper Suggested Tipping Tips pooled. $10 per passenger per day, deposited in a box at cruise's end. No service charge added to wine or bar bill.

Credit Cards For cruise payment: American Express, Diner's Club, Discover, MasterCard, Visa. On-board *Nantucket Clipper* and *Yorktown Clipper:* American Express, MasterCard, Visa; *Clipper Adventurer* and *Clipper Odyssey:* MasterCard and Visa.

NANTUCKET CLIPPER	QUALITY **5**	VALUE **C**
YORKTOWN CLIPPER	QUALITY **5**	VALUE **C**
Registry: United States	Length: 207/257 feet	Beam: 37/43 feet
Cabins: 51/69	Draft: 8 feet	Speed: 7/10 knots
Maximum Passengers:	Passenger Decks: 4	Elevators: None
100/138	Crew: 32-36/38-42	Space Ratio: NA

The Ships United States–built and flying the American flag, the *Nantucket Clipper* and the slightly larger *Yorktown Clipper* are almost identical. With their shallow drafts, the ships glide into small places as easily as they tie up in small ports, sailboat-filled harbors, and coves.

The *Nantucket Clipper* has three passenger decks and the *Yorktown Clipper* four, including a spacious top sun deck aft of the bridge—a comfortable place for watching the passing scene. Cabins and lounges are decorated with quality furnishings. No glitter, no glitz.

Both ships have a single forward observation lounge and bar on the center deck that serves as a social center. Three sides of the cheerful room have large windows trimmed with light wood. Textured fabric and neutral colors give the lounge a warm, contemporary look. During cruises, the room has the air of a club, with passengers conversing, reading, writing postcards, or simply watching scenery. It is also the scene for lectures, early breakfast buffet, afternoon cookies, and hors d'oeuvres at cocktail time.

Itineraries   See Itinerary Index.

Cabins   All six categories of cabins are outside, and all but the lowest category have picture windows. Cabins on the promenade deck open onto an outdoor, wraparound deck (as on river steamboats). Although these have an airy feel, some passengers might prefer cabins that open onto a central corridor. On the *Yorktown,* four cabins on the sun deck are the largest and most private.

The cabins are small but adequate, are well lighted, offer ample storage, and appear more spacious because of a large wall mirror. Beds are parallel or at right angles; the latter provides more floor space. The furnishings have a clean, modern look, with pastel curtains and bedcovers, closets and dressers in light wood, and landscape paintings on the wall. The bathrooms have showers only and are small, with limited shelf space. In an effort to let passengers get away from it all, cabins have neither telephones nor televisions. Radios, however, provide wake-up calls, ship information, and music. Some cabins get noise from the hydraulic lift that raises and lowers the gangplank in port. Also, there is no convenient place to dry wet clothes.

There is no room service. Laundry, beauty shop, and barber shop are usually available in port. The ships carry no nurses or doctors except on specific cruises. However, the vessels are almost always near shore in case of medical emergency. Lack of medical staff and the difficulty of walking on steep gangways make the ships unsuitable for physically disabled persons.

Specifications   All outside cabins; no suites. Standard dimensions range from 122–139 square feet on *Yorktown Clipper;* 106–123 square feet on *Nantucket Clipper.* All have two lower beds, some with pull-down third bunk; no singles. None are wheelchair-accessible.

Dining   The dining room, on the lower deck, has large windows and pleasant décor reflecting quality. Passengers dine at a single, open seating at round or square marble-topped tables, which are covered with cloths for dinner. The food is American cuisine overseen by a chef trained at either the prestigious Culinary Institute of America or at Johnson and Wales. Meals feature excellent soups, good-quality beef, fresh seafood, vegetables, and fruit. They're presented in a straightforward manner by the young, cheerful staff. Selections are not as extensive as on larger ships—dinner menus offer two entrées—but all menus include a regional specialty. A small but moderately priced selection of wines is available.

An early light breakfast is served in the lounge; lunch buffets are offered on the sun deck, weather permitting. Snacks, including fresh fruit, are available throughout the day. In the afternoon, freshly baked chocolate chip cookies are set out in the lounge, welcomed by passengers who have gathered in anticipation. The bar is open from 11 a.m. to midnight.

Service The clean-cut staff of young American men and women are cheerful, attentive, friendly, and unfailingly polite. Most are college students from the U.S. heartland, where Clipper is based, who sign on for a year of employment. They take care of the restaurant, bar, and cabins, working 12 hours a day, 6 days a week, and smile through it all.

Facilities and Activities Daily seminars by naturalists, historians, or other experts on places visited on the cruise precede follow-up discussions after the visits. The naturalist also acts as guide for nature walks, bird-watching, and study of the local environment. Afternoons at sea, a movie plays in the dining room. A local folklorist or other interesting characters may come on board for a lecture, discussion, or entertainment. The cruise director briefs passengers daily about upcoming adventures. Activity centers around the destination, whether it's a tour of a historic town, a golf game, or a forest hike. There are no organized fun and games. Deck space is adequate for a destination-oriented ship, and most people use it to sunbathe, read, or watch the scenery—often through binoculars. Evenings in port enable passengers to explore local nightlife. Otherwise, passengers gather in the lounge after dinner to visit, or they retire to the dining room to watch videos. Most are in their cabins by 10 p.m.

Sports and Fitness Walkers can circumnavigate the promenade deck, and when the ships tie up at night, as they often do, passengers walk into town. Depending on itinerary and weather, snorkeling directly from the ship is available, and scuba diving, windsurfing, deep-sea fishing, golf, or tennis can be arranged. The ships have no pools, whirlpools, exercise equipment, or fitness centers.

Shore Excursions Cruises usually call at ports seldom visited by other ships and often tie up at small, out-of-the-way marinas and yacht harbors, enabling passengers to explore remote islands and coastlines on foot. Where *Nantucket Clipper* cannot dock, passengers go ashore by Zodiac boat; *Yorktown Clipper* has dib launches. Generally, such excursions are included in the cruise price. In urban areas, ships often tie up within walking distance of cultural attractions and offer above-average tours at reasonable costs.

Postscript Although the adventures are light and seldom far from civilization, many itineraries entail walking, wet landings, and climbing in and out of Zodiac boats in remote areas. Some involve traversing open sea, and with the ships' shallow drafts, passengers may have a bumpy ride for several hours. Because the ships do not carry doctors and do not have elevators, they are not able to handle passengers with health or physical limitations.

CLIPPER ADVENTURER	QUALITY 8	VALUE C
Registry: Bahamas	Length: 330 feet	Beam: 53.5 feet
Cabins: 61	Draft: 16 feet	Speed: 14 knots
Maximum Passengers:	Passenger Decks: 4	Elevators: None
122	Crew: 72	Space Ratio: NA

The Ship The *Clipper Adventurer* is the former *Alla Tarasova,* a Russian expedition vessel with an A-1 Super Ice-class rating. Her itinerary is designed by Hasse Nilsson, the widely known former master of the *Linblad Explorer* and the first captain to take passengers through the Northwest Passage.

Built in 1975 in Yugoslavia, the ship received a $15-million renovation before joining Clipper's fleet in 1998. As a result, she is one of the most comfortable and stylish expedition ships afloat, designed to be more elegant than Clipper's older craft while retaining the feeling of an adventure ship. The renovations added a window-lined observation lounge, library/card room and bar, small gym, beauty salon, covered promenade, and observation platform directly below the bridge. To ensure comfort even further, stabilizers were added in 1998. The ship's public rooms are mahogany-paneled and the furnishings upholstered in handsome colors of deep blue, red, and aquamarine.

The handsome vessel with its refined décor and upgraded amenities helps the line merge INTRAV's more upscale passengers with Clipper's eclectic mix. The ship is well suited for exploration with her ice-class hull, great maneuverability, and shallow draft that enable her to sail near shorelines, in polar waters, or along scenic riverbanks.

Itineraries See Itinerary Index.

Cabins *Adventurer* has 61 all-new, all-outside cabins averaging 130 square feet, including three suites. All have large windows or portholes. There are eight categories. Cabins are designed to be comfortable rather than posh. Twin lower beds are in an L shape or parallel (no queens). Bathrooms are tiled, with showers. Closet and storage space is ample. The suites on Boat Deck have separate seating areas with desks and chairs.

Dining A window-lined dining room accommodates all passengers at one leisurely seating at tables for two to seven. American and regional dishes are prepared by trained chefs. Service is provided by a Filipino staff who are cheerful and pleasant as they are attentive and accommodating.

Facilities and Activities The main lounge and bar of the cozy, clublike ship is the center for informal talks by staff naturalists, historians, and other specialists. Also in the lounge are breakfast and lunch buffets, before-dinner hors d'oeuvres, and musical performances. The **Clipper Club** lounge near the dining room is the favorite spot for cocktails. One level up, the small library offers books on wildlife and literature. The quiet retreat, furnished with silk-covered armchairs, doubles as a card room, with board games and puzzles.

One of the ship's best features is a large observation platform directly below the bridge. It's ideal for viewing wildlife or scenery. (Also, the captain maintains a 24-hour open bridge.) Promenades on two decks provide additional viewing venues. The wide Boat Deck promenade has a partially covered area aft and provides teak benches perfect for scene-watching or conversation. The Promenade Deck has a wide, enclosed deck, allowing exercise out of the elements. Other facilities and amenities include a small gym, beauty shop, a full-time physician, gift shop, and laundry service—the first time such amenities have been available on a Clipper ship. *Adventurer* is equipped with ten Zodiac landing craft for exploring hard-to-reach places.

CLIPPER ODYSSEY	QUALITY 9	VALUE B
Registry: Bahamas	Length: 340 feet	Beam: 51 feet
Cabins: 64	Draft: 15 feet	Speed: 14 knots
Maximum Passengers:	Passenger Decks: 5	Elevators: 1
128	Crew: 72	Space Ratio: 83

The Ship   In September 1998, less than seven months after launching the *Clipper Adventurer,* the cruise line acquired a fourth ship, the deluxe *Oceanic Odyssey,* from Spice Islands Cruises. When Clipper took over operations in November 1999, the ship was renamed the *Clipper Odyssey.*

Designed in Holland and constructed in 1989 by Japanese craftsmen, the ship is beautifully built with quality furnishings and the detail of a deluxe yacht with an intimate and casual ambience. The décor is warm and comfortable with traces of its Japanese origins in the pictures and other art.

The center of activity is the main lounge and bar on the main deck, which is used for most activities—lectures, socializing, or waiting for the warm chocolate chip cookies served in the afternoon. At cocktail time, when most passengers gather in the lounge, the dining staff lays out generous hot and cold hors d'oeuvres. Usually, the expedition staff gives a briefing on the day's activity ashore and preparations for the following day. After dinner, passengers usually return to the lounge for a lecture by one of the expert guides accompanying the cruise. Adjacent to the lounge is a library with good collections of reference books for each of the areas the ship visits.

One deck up, the **Day Lounge,** when not in use for light meals, becomes the card and reading room. Here, a self-service counter has coffee, tea, and juices around the clock. Directly outside is an outdoor deck and swimming pool. In good weather, the outdoor deck is used for informal parties. All five passenger decks are served by a central elevator.

Itineraries   See Itinerary Index.

Cabins   Accommodations, spread over four decks, are spacious, all-outside cabins with sitting areas. All standard cabins are the same size—approximately 180 square feet—and have large windows, except for a few on the lower deck, which have portholes. Each cabin provides a high degree of comfort, with television for videos and movies, a safe, mini-fridge, music system, and hair dryer—amenities lacking from Clipper's older ships. Bathrooms have a small, Japanese-style tub and shower. The rooms are furnished with a blonde wood, built-in dresser/desk with shallow drawers, a refrigerator, and two small hanging closets, plus bedside night tables with drawers. Beds can be configured as twin or queen size. One cabin is designed for disabled travelers. The one suite and eight deluxe cabins on the uppermost accommodations deck have verandas. Instant News from London (faxed news) is available daily.

Specifications   60 outside cabins; 1 suite and 8 deluxe cabins with verandas. Standard dimensions, 180 square feet. All have 2 lower twin or queen beds; no singles. One wheelchair-accessible.

Dining   The attractive **Main Dining Room** offers open, single seating at set hours for three meals and serves high-quality, well-prepared cuisine with regional accents using fresh ingredients, often bought from local markets on the ship's route. As with other Clipper ships, the chef is a graduate of the Culinary Institute of America or another reputable culinary school.

Breakfast in the dining room is a buffet feast of fruits, cereals, breads, eggs cooked to order, and a specialty of the day. Lunch and dinner menus are varied and creative and offer a choice of two soups, fish, chicken, meat, or vegetarian entrée, and dessert. Dinner has similar selections with even more choices. In addition, there is a daily healthy menu. Passengers may order half-portions of any course. A wine is suggested for each course of dinner; wine is available by the glass for an additional charge. Continental breakfast and light lunch are also served indoors in the sunny **Day Lounge** or poolside. Dress is casual throughout the day and only slightly more fashionable in the evening.

Service   The service rendered by the ship's Filipino staff in the dining room, bar, decks, and cabins ranks at the top of the list of the ship's best features and is the equal of some of the most luxurious ships afloat. They are smiling, pleasant, thoughtful, hardworking, and gracious at every hour of the day. Dining room waiters make a point of learning passengers' names from the first day, and even though passengers sit where they choose, the waiters seem to remember their individual likes and needs.

Facilities and Activities   The ship has a swimming pool and Jacuzzi; a small, well-stocked reading room; and a boutique. The ship's band plays dance music in the main lounge. The INMARSAT telecommunications system permits worldwide, 24-hour telephone and fax communication, and there is a computer station for passengers to send e-mail. All activity is focused on and determined daily by the port or location and weather, docking and tender or Zodiac landing condition, whether it is sightseeing, hiking, water sports, or other sports.

Sports, Fitness, and Beauty   The small gym on the Bridge Deck has a treadmill, step machine, bicycle, and free weights. There is a jogging track on the top deck. *Odyssey* has ample teak-covered deck space and the broad upper deck for sunbathing.

At the beginning of the cruise, passengers are issued snorkel gear to keep for their entire trip. Depending on the area of the cruise, the expedition staff takes passengers in Zodiac landing craft on shore excursions in remote areas and for swimming and snorkeling. The staff will arrange scuba diving where it is available for an additional charge.

The tiny hair salon on deck three has two chairs; the attendant, who also manages the ship's tiny boutique, does simple wash and set or blow dry. Next door is the small clinic staffed by a registered physician.

Costa Cruise Lines

Venture Corporate Center II
200 South Park Road, Suite 200, Hollywood, FL 33021-8541
(954) 266-5600; (800) 462-6782; fax (954)-266-2100
www.costacruises.com

Type of Ships   New, modern superliners.

Type of Cruise   Mass market, designed for Europeans as much as North Americans—hence, more European in service and ambience.

Cruise Line's Strengths

- Italian style and service
- friendly crew
- itineraries

Cruise Line's Shortcomings

- noise level in dining rooms
- excessive announcements
- language problems

Fellow Passengers   Costa has two seasons: Caribbean from late fall to early spring, and Europe from spring through fall. It results in two sets of passengers. In the Caribbean, up to 70% of passengers are North Americans, depending on the cruise; average age is 54 years, with annual household income of $50,000+. A bevy of Italian American fans and newlyweds are attracted by the line's Italian style. Most have cruised before.

In Europe, 80% or more are Europeans likely to have traveled abroad, perhaps having even cruised before. Among the North Americans, average age is about the same as Caribbean cruisers, but they would be inclined to rent a car and drive through Europe on their own instead of taking an escorted tour. They enjoy traveling with and meeting people from other countries.

Recommended For   Italophiles; first-time cruisers and less experienced travelers who want to sample European ambience, but with facilities typical of a large ship; and repeat cruisers who want to try something different.

Not Recommended For   Those who like small ships as well as an all-American atmosphere or prefer to travel with Americans.

Cruise Areas and Seasons Caribbean, Mediterranean, Greek islands, the Holy Land, Black Sea, Northern Europe, Norwegian fjords, the Baltic, Russia, South America, and transatlantic cruises.

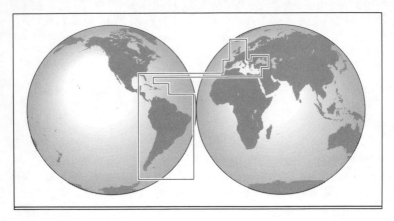

The Line Genoa-based Costa Crociere, parent company of Costa Cruise Lines, had been in the shipping business for over 100 years and in the passenger business for almost 50 years when it was bought jointly by Carnival Cruises and Airtours, a European tour company, in 1997. (Three years later, Carnival acquired Airtours' shares.)

Costa, Europe's largest cruise line, was among the earliest lines to offer one-week Caribbean cruises from Miami (1959) and the first to introduce an air/sea program (late 1960s). Despite its long Florida-Caribbean association, Costa changed course in the 1990s to become more Europe-focused. Of its eight ships, only two sail from U.S. ports, and they sail only in winter. The others, including the *Tropicale* transferred from Carnival in early 2001 and renamed *CostaTropicale,* and Holland America's *Westerdam* which joined the Costa fleet in April 2002 as *CostaEuropa,* are positioned in Europe and elsewhere.

Costa launched the 1990s with four new ships costing more than $1 billion and intended to serve a broad spectrum of passengers. The ships combine modern and classic qualities with new design features. The line added the larger *CostaVictoria* in 1996, followed by the even larger *CostaAtlantica* in 2000; the latter's sister ship, *CostaMediterranea,* followed in2003. Two 105,000-ton ships, *CostaFortuna* and *CostaMagica,* are due in December 2003 and in 2004, respectively. The last three ships alone will double the line's passenger capacity.

THE FLEET	BUILT/RENOVATED	TONNAGE	PASSENGERS
CostaAllegra	1992	28,430	808
CostaAtlantica	2000	85,619	2,114
CostaClassica	1991/2001	52,926	1,302

THE FLEET	BUILT/RENOVATED	TONNAGE	PASSENGERS
CostaEuropa	1986/1990/2002	53,872	1,476
CostaFortuna	2003	105,000	3,788
CostaMagica	2004	105,000	3,788
CostaMarina	1969/1990/2002	25,558	789
CostaMediterranea	2003	86,000	2,114
CostaRomantica	1993	53,049	1,344
CostaTropicale	1982/1998/2001	33,250	1,008
CostaVictoria	1996	75,166	1,928

Style   In the early 1980s, Costa coined the phrase "cruising Italian style" to celebrate its Italian basis in everything from design to cuisine. Its fleet is designed and built in Italy by Italians, with floors and walls of Italian marble, splendid wood cabinetry, designer fabrics and linens, and Italian art throughout. They reflect the sophisticated architecture and décor of modern Italian designers rather than the classic Italian look. The Finnish-built *CostaAtlantica* was the first to depart somewhat from the Italian style.

Life on board is made to seem molto Italiano, from the pasta and espresso to Italian language lessons, Italian cooking classes, Italian ice cream, pizzas in the pizzerias, and toga parties. Theme nights, such as "Festa Italiana," feature an Italian street festival with bocce ball games, tarantella dance lessons, pizza dough–tossing contests, Venetian mask making, and more. Yet for all the trimmings, the Italian ambience has been diluted, mainly because Costa ships no longer have all-Italian crews.

The ships are very much "today" with gyms, spas, and fitness programs, and Costa's Caribbean shore excursions emphasize outdoor activities. One of Costa's most popular innovations is its "private" beach on Isla Catalina off the Dominican Republic. The island is near the sprawling resort of Casa de Campo, which, among its many facilities, has a tennis village and three of the Caribbean's best golf courses. Casa de Campo recently opened a new marina village with restaurants and shops, enabling Costa's ships on Eastern Caribbean cruises to spend the day at the island and the evenings at the marina.

All dining and public rooms on Costa ships are nonsmoking.

Distinctive Features   Free hot pizza throughout day. On Caribbean cruises, couples can renew their wedding vows in a shipboard ceremony.

	HIGHEST	LOWEST	AVERAGE
PER DIEM	$538	$100	$269

Per diems are calculated from cruise line's nondiscounted *cruise-only* fares on standard accommodations and vary by season, cabin, and cruise areas.

Rates   Port charges are included.

Special Fares and Discounts   Andiamo Fares provide 12–25% discounts, depending on category, for bookings 120 days in advance in the Caribbean and 90 days in Europe. Additional discounts on Andiamo Fares are available in some categories for seniors and for friends and families traveling together. Combining Eastern and Western Caribbean or two Mediterranean cruises into 14-nighters offers savings, too.

- **Children's Fare**   Same as third/fourth passenger fares (works for single parents, too); also $199 for children age 17 and younger on some cruises.

- **Single Supplement**   150–200%.

Packages

- **Air/Sea**   Yes, for Europe; mostly as add-ons for Caribbean.

- **Others**   Spa, seniors, honeymoon, family.

- **Pre/Post**   Yes, in Amsterdam, Copenhagen, Genoa, London, Nice/Monte Carlo, Paris, Rome, Venice, Ft. Lauderdale, or Orlando, depending on cruise.

Past Passengers   No repeat passenger club. Past passengers receive mailings announcing new itineraries and offering discounts.

The Last Word   Costa has dared to be different in style and in the markets it pursues, preferring to be number one in Europe, where it has a strong base and years of experience, rather than struggling in the fierce competition of the Caribbean. The strategy virtually guarantees that when you take a Costa cruise, the experience will be European rather than catering to American tastes.

Some Americans welcome the opportunity to take a European vacation with Europeans. Others are turned off by cliques in lounges and bars and the steady stream of announcements-for bingo, shopping talks, and shore excursions—in five languages, even though English-speaking hostesses are aboard to cater to North Americans.

Areas are designated as smoking or nonsmoking on Costa ships, but some European smokers flout the restriction—defiantly.

COSTA CRUISE LINES STANDARD FEATURES

Officers   Italian.

Staff   Dining/Italian, other European, Asian, Central American; Cabin/International; Cruise/International.

Dining Facilities   One main dining room (two on *CostaVictoria*), two seatings for three meals, midnight buffet featuring Italian cuisine; indoor/outdoor buffet breakfast and lunch. Alternative dining; *Victoria, Atlantica, CostaMediterranea,* extra charge. Pizzerias and pastry cafes on most ships.

Special Diets   Should be requested four weeks in advance.

Room Service   24 hours, limited menu; butler service in suites with full service for meals from dining room menus.

COSTA CRUISE LINES FEATURES *(continued)*

Dress Code   Casual; informal evenings; two nights formal/semiformal.

Cabin Amenities   Phone, radio, private shower, hair dryer, safe, television; suites have whirlpool bath, minibar, and veranda (except *Victoria*).

Electrical Outlets   110/220 AC; adapters available on board.

Wheelchair Access   Six cabins on *Classica, Romantica, Victoria;* eight on *Allegra, Atlantica, Mediterranea.*

Recreation and Entertainment   Casino, bars and lounges with nightly entertainment, showrooms, disco, dance and Italian language lessons, bingo, bridge, horse racing, library, card room.

Sports and Other Activities   Three swimming pools, *Atlantica, Mediterranea* (one for children); two, *Classica, Romantica, Victoria* (plus one inside); one, *Allegra, Marina, Riviera.* Exercise classes, snorkeling lessons, paddle tennis, Ping-Pong, deck and pool games. *Victoria,* tennis/basketball. Golf Academy on *Atlantica, CostaMediterranea.*

Beauty and Fitness   Barber shop and beauty salon, spa, sauna, European beauty treatments, fitness centers, jogging track, whirlpools.

Other Facilities   Boutiques, medical facility, laundry and dry cleaning services, meeting room, chapel. Internet access on *Atlantica, Mediterranea, Victoria.*

Children's Facilities   Costa Kids year-round; babysitters. (No baby-sitting service in cabins.)

Theme Cruises   Golf, food and wine, others.

Smoking   Smoking in designated public areas; all dining and public rooms are nonsmoking.

Costa Suggested Tipping   *(Caribbean)* Per person per day: cabin steward, $3; waiter, $3; busboy, $1.00, head waiter; *(Europe)* Per person per day: cabin steward, $1.50; waiter, $2.50; assistant waiter (team), $2.50; Maître d' and head waiter, $2.50. 15% gratuity added to all beverage bills (including mineral water in the dining room).

Credit Cards   For cruise payment and on-board charges: American Express, Carte Blanche, Diners Club, Discover, MasterCard, Visa.

COSTAATLANTICA	**QUALITY 7**	**VALUE C**
COSTAMEDITERRANEA	**(Preview)**	
Registry: Italy	Length: 960 feet	Beam: 106 feet
Cabins: 1,057	Draft: 19.5 feet	Speed: 24 knots
Maximum Passengers:	Passenger Decks: 12	Elevators: 12
2,114	Crew: 920	Space Ratio: NA

The Ship   Costa's newest ships, *CostaAtlantica,* debuted in 2000, and her twin, *CostaMediterranea,* launched in June 2003, are the largest, fastest ships in the fleet and have drawn positive reviews from passengers. Now that Costa is under the Carnival Corporation umbrella, and with interior design in the hands of architect Joe Farcus, who is well known for creating the flamboyant décor of Carnival ships, there was considerable concern that he would "Carnivalize" these Costa ships. Farcus's imprint is unmistakable, but he has combined touches of his trademark fantasy and glitter with European elegance that seem to work and delight most—but not all—of the North Americans and Europeans who have sailed on them. It's safe to say that Farcus's décor is the antithesis of the modern spare interiors by Italian designers of Costa's other new ships.

Atlantica, because of her balconies and large windows, has a more open, lighter appearance than *Costa Victoria*. Most of the public rooms are on decks two and three, anchored by a spectacular glass-ceiling atrium. The décor of *Atlantica*, including the use of Murano glass and inlaid mosaic, is more playful than on other Costa ships. For example, the Glass Staircase near the spa gets traffic just for pleasure, and in public rooms, passengers take turns enjoying the Alice in Wonderland–style red-leather chairs with extremely high backs.

The Farcus touches are everywhere—the red leather benches near the theatrical multilevel fitness room have little boots on them; whimsical or fantastic motifs are worked into the carpets, the banquettes, and the tables, with subtlety and taste.

Atlantica is dedicated to Federico Fellini, the great Italian filmmaker, with her 12 passenger decks named for movies directed by him and huge blow-ups from his works placed in public rooms. Besides the impressive large public spaces, there are intimate quiet areas, like the small Italian garden by the chapel. It also pays homage to Venice with **Caffe Florian,** a replica of the 18th-century landmark in St. Mark's Square, with a menu and music from the original. Traditionalists will probably find these rooms the ship's most attractive area. *CostaMediterranea* is dedicated to the history, art, and architecture of Italy and the Mediterranean. The decks, for example, are named for historic figures—Medea, Pandora, Cleopatra, etc.

Atlantica was the first Costa ship to offer Internet access, available in a state-of-the-art center and in some staterooms and suites, where guests can bring their own laptop computer or rent one. Almost 65% of cabins and suites have verandas—a marked improvement over the *CostaVictoria,* which has none.

The ships are equipped with a dual Azipod propulsion system, new technology that was introduced on the *Carnival Destiny* and contributes to smooth sailing. They have received the Green Star from the Italian Register of Shipping for her innovative environmental protection design.

Itineraries   See Itinerary Index.

Cabins   The ships have 13 categories of cabins, most on decks 1 and 4–8. Of the total 1,057 cabins, 78% are outside. The 678 cabins with verandas have clear plastic barriers in front, enabling passengers to lie in bed and look out at the port of call or the sea. Another 68 cabins have French balconies.

Cabins are stylish in décor and very well designed, with an unusual amount of polished hardwood floors as well as carpets and fine leather. All cabins have direct-dial telephone, television, minibar, safe, hair dryer, amenities, and ample storage. Murano glass shades the bedside lamps with smaller, concentrated lights attached for nighttime reading and are exceptionally beautiful. Showers are much larger than on the line's previous vessels. The suites have plush robes, marble baths, double sinks, and Jacuzzi tubs.

Specifications 824 outside; 233 inside; 678 cabins (including 58 suites) with verandas. Cabins with verandas measure 210 square feet, inside cabins, 162 square feet, suites with verandas, 360 square feet. 8 wheelchair-accessible.

Dining The ships have several dining venues. The two-level **Tiziano Restaurant** (**Degli Argentierri** on *CostaMediterranea*) is the main dining room serving undistinguished Continental cuisine with some Italian specialties; the Botticelli Buffet offers breakfast and lunch in an informal setting with a rather limited, repetitive selection; and the **Napoli Pizzeria** serves a variety of excellent, fresh hot pizzas throughout the day. Surprisingly, there are no pasta stations in either the dining room or the lido buffet, as on Costa's other ships.

The dining rooms are quiet and comfortable. Healthful menus with low-fat, low-carbohydrate, low-calorie, and low-cholesterol courses are available in the dining rooms for lunch, dinner, and at the informal breakfast. A generous number of vegetarian dishes is offered, and there is a separate children's menu.

Club Atlantica by Marchesi, the alternative, by-reservation restaurant, is modeled after its namesake in Venice and has an extra charge of $23 a person—and it's worth it. It offers two appetizing single-choice menus and wines served amid candles, flowers, and live musical entertainment. If you come only once, you might want to mix and match selections from both menus.

Service Not everyone agrees about the service. Some say it's excellent, warm, and efficient; others say it's brusque and often haphazard. But for sure, longtime Costa fans will miss the verve of an Italian crew as the only Italians in the restaurants are the maître d'hôtel and his assistant. There are no wine stewards.

Facilities and Activities Daytime diversions include dance, gaming and golf lessons, port and shopping talks, art auctions, health and beauty workshops, bridge, handwriting analysis, tennis singles, arts and crafts, and quizzes. The library and card room are elegant and well used, but the multinational nature of the passengers means a somewhat limited number of books in English. Via della Spiga is the ship's shopping promenade, and there's a full-service conference center. The Internet center has five terminals.

Evening entertainment is designed for its multinational nature of the passengers with more dance, music, and magic than comic routines. The **Caruso Theater** (**Osiris** on *CostaMediterranea*), the impressive three-level main show lounge at the front of the ship, has very few columns to interrupt sight lines. En route to the theater, passengers pass the **Paparazzi Lounge** with bigger-than-life, black-and-white photographs of celebrities, such as Joe DiMaggio.

Caffe Florian, replicating the famous St. Mark's Square landmark, serves coffees, liqueurs, and aperitifs with background music evoking the romance of the Venetian legend that captivated such luminaries as Vivaldi, Dickens, and Stravinsky, among others. The **Madame Butterfly Grand Lounge** is complete with waitresses dressed in geisha style. The **Coral Lounge,** used for seminars and special entertainment, has an underwater quality with blue walls and huge white coral trees behind etched glass.

The glittering **Fortuna Casino** (**Grand Canal Casino** on *Costa-Mediterranea*) is well laid-out, with comfortable access to slots, roulette, and blackjack tables. It has its own bar—one of 12 on the ship—and is adjacent to the Madame Butterfly Grand Lounge.

Dancing in the evenings ranges from disco to swing, and bands playing for guests waiting to enter the dining room inspire impromptu dance sessions along the lounges. The two-level **Dante's Disco** with an outstanding sound system is positioned on the bottom two passenger decks—a good choice because the action tends to go to the wee hours of the night.

Theme nights are offered in the Costa tradition and include "Fiesta Italiana," a street festival-at-sea with bocce ball and tarantella dance lessons, and the always popular "Toga Party-at-Sea."

Sports, Fitness, and Beauty   Each ship has three outdoor pools plus Jacuzzis. One pool has a retractable roof that converts the central pool deck into an 11,000-square-foot solarium, thus providing all-weather swimming. Another pool has a water slide and is earmarked for children. The Aurora Pool, the third one located in the rear of the ship, is a quiet hideaway. It adjoins the dramatic two-level **Ischia Spa and Gym,** which has thalassic therapy treatment. A broad range of treatments, as well as sauna, steam, and whirlpools, are well used. Costa has full- and half-day spa packages as well as à la carte. Above the spa is a tennis court, where smaller-than-standard racquets are used; it converts to a basketball or volleyball court.

The workout area is theater-style with a main floor and balcony; it has an array of Technogym equipment like that found in a major health club, plus sophisticated electronic aerobic monitoring equipment. Exercise classes are offered for all fitness levels, including children's jogging and aerobics.

Costa's **Golf Academy-at-Sea** on Caribbean cruises offers on-board golf clinics, private lessons with a PGA pro, and play in port. Video swing analysis and lessons range from a 15-minute swing-check for $25 to a 60-minute golf lesson for $80. Other activities include golf seminars, putting competitions, tournaments, and range practice. Golfers can rent top-of-the-line clubs and shoes. Courses available are Mahogany Run (St. Thomas) and Teeth of the Dog (Casa de Campo, Dominican Republic), among others. Fees vary. The PGA instructor accompanies participants when they play in port.

Children's Facilities   The large and well-fitted **Pinocchio's Children's Room** is the center of children's activities. Costa Kids, a year-round program available on Caribbean and European cruises, offers daily activities geared to two age groups: Costa Kids Club, 3–12 years; and Costa Teens Club, 13–17 years. Two youth counselors are aboard each ship year-round; counselors are added when there are more than 12 children on a cruise. Youth Center activities include video-game competitions, bridge and galley tours, arts and crafts, a treasure hunt, Italian lessons, bingo, board games, karaoke contests, pizza parties, ice-cream socials, face painting, cartoons, and movies.

At sea, Kids Club hours generally are 9–11:30 a.m., 2–5:30 p.m., and 8–11 p.m. On Caribbean cruises, group baby-sitting for ages 3 (children must be out of diapers) and up is available on request from 6:30 p.m. to 11:00 p.m. In port, 8:30 a.m. to 12:30 p.m. and from 2:30 p.m. to 6:30 p.m. There is a charge. Costa also offers "Parents Night Out." On two different nights, parents can enjoy evenings alone while their children have the evening with their peers at a supervised buffet or pizza party with activities designed especially for them.

European cruises have three clubs: Baby Club, 3–6 years; Junior Club, 7–12 years; and Teens Club, 13–17 years. Baby Club offers a story hour, crafts, games, and ice-cream parties. Junior Club has aerobics, puppet theater, mini-Olympics, and team treasure hunts. Teens Club offers sports and fitness programs, guitar lessons, video productions, and a rock and roll hour. In Europe, free group baby-sitting for ages 3–6 is available, subject to staff availability. A disco and teen club offer a dance floor, video games, four computer stations, and a large television monitor.

Shore Excursions   On Eastern Caribbean cruises, the ship stops at **Isla Catalina,** where Costa developed facilities for a fun day at the beach with games and water sports. The ship also offers tours to **Casa de Campo,** one of the Caribbean's largest resorts, for tennis, horseback riding, and golf on world-famous Pete Dye courses. You must buy the ship's shore excursion to go to Casa de Campo; cruise passengers are not allowed to go there on their own. The ship offers diving and snorkeling at selected ports. With the completion of the new marina at Casa de Campo, the ship docks at Isla Catalina for the day and the marina for the evening, enabling passengers to enjoy the resort's elegant dining and nightlife. In Europe, shore excursions generally are as varied as the cruises and range from a glacier walk in Norway to a visit to Egyptian pyramids. Itineraries are port-intensive, rarely including more than one or two days at sea during a week.

Costa Cruise Lines European Fleet

COSTAVICTORIA	QUALITY 5	VALUE D
Registry: Italy	Length: 828 feet	Beam: 105 feet
Cabins: 964	Draft: 24 feet	Speed: 24 knots
Maximum Passengers:	Passenger Decks: 10	Elevators: 12
1,928	Crew: 766	Space Ratio: 38.9

The Ship Costa's first megaship made her debut in 1996. Designed by well-known naval architect Robert Tillberg, she was the largest passenger liner built in Germany when she was launched. Despite her size, her shallow draft provides exceptional maneuverability and gives the ship access to smaller ports and the Suez Canal. Her larger size makes possible more choices in dining and entertainment.

Ultramodern and sophisticated, the main entrance, the circular Planetarium Atrium, spans seven decks and has four glass elevators connecting the lobby with the pool deck above. It's capped by a large glass dome admitting sunlight that reflects off a colored glass sculpture by Milanese artist Gianfranco Pardi on the Boheme Deck (Deck 5). Deck 5 also has the purser's office, shore excursion desk, and a piano bar. All but one of the ten passenger decks are named after Italian operas.

The most dramatic room is the Concorde Plaza, an observation lounge at the bow. It spans four decks; a floor-to-ceiling glass wall provides spectacular ocean views. Opposite the windows is a marble dance floor adjoining a center stage; its backdrop is a waterfall inspired by Leonardo Da Vinci's drawings of the moon eclipsing the sun. Decorated in blues, silver, and gold, the lounge serves as an elegant area for socializing, special events, and evening entertainment, including cabaret shows, games, bingo, and port lectures.

Itineraries See Itinerary Index.

Cabins The majority of cabins are on the upper decks. Sixty percent are outside cabins with a porthole or large, square window. Cabins are small compared to those on *CostaRomantica,* and none has a private balcony. Victoria was the line's first ship to have a minibar, safe, hair dryer, and interactive television in every cabin. All cabins have direct-dial telephones and sliding doors that separate the living area and bathroom. Circular bathrooms have rounded showers and vanity areas.

The 6 top suites and 14 minisuites, forward on the pool and sports decks, are decorated with Laura Ashley fabrics and trimmed with pearwood. They have sitting areas, whirlpool baths, walk-in closets, and queen beds, plus one upper berth and a Murphy bed, thus accommodating up to four people. Butler service is provided.

The *Victoria's* unique "fan coil" system allows each cabin to be refreshed with its own recycled air or outside air. Thus, nonsmokers' air isn't mixed with smokers'. The ship does not have self-service laundromats for passenger use.

Specifications 391 inside, 553 outside; 20 suites; 6 wheelchair accessible. Standard cabins range from 120 to 150 square feet.

Dining *CostaVictoria* was the first Costa vessel to have two dining rooms: **Sinfonia Restaurant** aft and **Fantasia Restaurant** amidships. Both are decorated with marble and pine walls and glass chandeliers from Murano. Their picture windows are transformed from ocean views by day to Italian scenes by night by murals that drop in place like window shades.

Dinner menus have fewer selections than offered on some ships in Costa's price group, but choices are ample and of good quality, balancing Italian and European dishes with American favorites. A different pasta is featured at lunch and dinner; American audiences rave over them. A typical dinner menu offers three appetizers, two soups, two salads, three pastas, four entrées (one vegetarian), three or more desserts, ice cream, sherbet, cheese, and fresh fruit. The presentation is always attractive.

Ristorante Magnifico by Zefferino is modeled after the famous Zefferino's in Genoa. Passengers must make reservations and pay an extra charge of $23 per person, but given the uneven quality of the dining rooms' fare, it's worth it and has proven to be a popular alternative. Walls are hung with ten paintings of earlier Costa passenger ships by artist Stephen Card and contribute to the cozy atmosphere created by the addition of candlelight, flowers, soft music, and excellent service.

Passengers dine informally at an indoor/outdoor buffet serving breakfast and lunch. **Bolero,** the indoor buffet, is surrounded by glass windows and furnished with rattan chairs and marble tables. The outdoor **Terraza Café,** similar to one on *Romantica* but much larger, is protected by a large white canopy made by Canobbio, an Italian firm specializing in circus tents and sports arena coverings. Other dining options include two buffets, a pizzeria, ice cream bar, and grill.

Facilities and Activities Daytime diversions include lessons in dance, Italian language, and gaming; bingo; bridge; backgammon; culinary demonstrations; port and shopping talks; horse racing; and the Not-So-Newlywed Game. The teen center has a video game room, and there's a library, card room, and Internet center. Movies are shown on cabin television.

The two-deck **Festival Show Lounge** is decorated in rich reds with Tivoli lights twinkling in the ceiling. The stage can be raised for variety and production shows or lowered for dancing.

The **Grand Bar Orpheus,** with a bar trimmed in rare, blue Brazilian marble, is popular for cocktails and after-dinner espresso. It's connected by a curved glass stairway to the big, bright **Monte Carlo Casino.** Just outside the casino is **Capriccio Lounge,** an intimate piano bar decorated with floor-to-ceiling mosaics by Italian painter Emilio Tadini.

Theme nights may include Notte Tropical, the lively Festa Italiana, and the rollicking Roman Bacchanal. The full-service conference center offers meeting space, audiovisual equipment, movable leather chairs equipped with flip-top desks, and a board room for 20. The center has its own front desk, which meeting planners applaud.

Sports, Fitness, and Beauty   The Solarium, a top-deck viewing and sunning area, has pipes that continuously emit mists of cool water. The two outdoor pools are surrounded by six whirlpools and two shuffle-board courts. Nearby is the Wimbledon Tennis Court, a miniature court using smaller racquets and balls. It can be converted to a basketball or volleyball court.

The **Pompei Spa** has an indoor swimming pool centered with a large mosaic and surrounded by Roman columns and teakwood lounge chairs. The spa offers a Turkish bath, saunas, massage, thalassotherapy, hydrotherapy, and other beauty treatments. A 1,312-foot jogging track connects the spa to the gymnasium, which is equipped with weight-training equipment and an aerobics room. This is the first ship to carry products from Tuscany's chic Terme di Saturnia. There is a beauty salon.

Children's Facilities   Costa Kids Club for children ages 3–12 is further divided by age group depending on the number of children on a particular sailing. Activities include ship tours, video game competitions, arts and crafts, Italian language lessons, games, Coke-tail and pizza parties, ice cream socials, and kids' karaoke. The programs are not usually active when the ship is in port. Two nights of Parents Night Out (with free entertainment for children from 5 to 11 p.m.) are offered, and group baby-sitting for ages 3 and up is available for a fee.

Postscript   *Costa Victoria* is in the style of Costa's newest fleet, and the promise of "Cruising Italian Style" seems to be halfhearted when so many opportunities are missed. For example, each deck is named for an Italian opera, yet you can't hear Italian opera—or even Pavarotti—on the cabin radio, nor are any Italian movies (with or without English subtitles) shown on the cabin movie channel with run-of-the-mill films.'

Longtime Costa fans who expect this ship to be like the *CostaRomantica* or to have the ambience of the Costa cruises of old will be disappointed. It's a different product.

COSTAROMANTICA	QUALITY 7	VALUE B
COSTACLASSICA	QUALITY 7	VALUE C
Registry: Italy	Length: 722/869 feet	Beam: 102 feet
Cabins: 678/654	Draft: 24 feet	Speed: 19.5 knots
Maximum Passengers:	Passenger Decks: 11	Elevators: 8/10
1,356/1,998	Crew: 600/900	Space Ratio: 40/41.5

The Ships *CostaRomantica* and *CostaClassica* are almost identical. These spacious ships with public rooms on the upper four decks have ultramodern Italian interiors using a king's ransom in marble, dramatic window walls, futuristic sculptures, clean lines, angular shapes, and fine art to create a look that reflects modern Italian design and a radical departure from traditional European oceanliners.

Passengers are introduced to the ship in its dramatic Grand Lobby, set low on the Copenhagen Deck, which is dedicated entirely to cabins, as are the deck below and the two decks above. White-gloved room stewards escort passengers to their cabins. The background music of Vivaldi and other Italian composers is meant to underscore the start of a week of "cruising Italian style." The ships' layouts are easy to follow, with one lounge or public space flowing to the next, creating openness and harmony. Decks are named after European cities.

The dramatic centerpiece of *Romantica's* lobby is a moving sculpture by Japanese artist Susumu Shingu. Installed in 1992 to commemorate the Columbus quincentennial, it's a mobile whose panels move continuously and change color against the area's Cararra marble walls and floors.

Romantica's heart and social center is the Piazza Italia on the Verona Deck—an atrium furnished as a lounge, with a small bandstand and dance floor on one side and a bar on the other. The lounge is the favorite gathering spot for prelunch and predinner drinks, as it's a short walk from the dining room. Forward are meeting rooms, the library, chapel, card room, and the ground floor of **L'Opera,** the bilevel show lounge. From the Piazza, a double stairway leads up to the Vienna Deck and the popular **Romeo's Pizzeria** and **Juliet's Patisserie.** Forward are shops on the Via Condetti, named for Rome's fashionable shopping street.

Itineraries See Itinerary Index.

Cabins Spacious and well-designed, cabins are these ships' best feature. Standard cabins are fitted in cherry wood furnishings, including a dresser/desk unit with large mirror, bedside tables, a control panel for lights by the bed, ample closet space, and two chairs, one of which opens into a bed suitable for a child.

Elegant touches are the white curtain spanning the room, which can be raised and lowered to cover the oversized porthole; designer amenities; and high-quality bed and bath linens. All cabins have television, radio, safe, direct-dial satellite phone, and hair dryer. The 24-hour room service offers sandwiches and beverages.

Specifications   216 inside cabins, 428 outside, no singles. *CostaRomantica:* 16 suites, 18 minisuites. Standard dimensions are 175 square feet inside, 200 square feet outside. 242 take third and fourth persons. *Costa-Classica:* 291 inside cabins, 688 outside; 4 grand suites, and 16 with verandas. Standard dimensions are 150-200 square feet. 359 cabins take third and fourth persons. 6 singles. 6 wheelchair-accessible.

Dining   *Romantica's* **Botticelli Restaurant,** similar to *Classica's* counterpart, **Tivoli,** is beautifully laid out almost entirely in off-white and brown Carrara marble with coffered ceilings. Elegantly designed wicker-backed chairs encircle round tables, most seating eight, dressed in starched white cloths, fine china, glassware, and flowers. Movable side panels faced with a variety of scenes—a European city, landscapes, or Italian gardens—are changed each evening. They were designed by Giorgio Cristini, set designer for Milan's famous La Scala opera house.

The lovely room lacks carpeting or wall coverings, causing an extraordinarily high noise level that hinders conversation. Acoustical material was added, particularly in the ceiling, which helped—but not enough. Side tables toward the back of the room get less noise.

Il Giardino, the lido café for indoor breakfast and lunch buffets, is among the ship's prettiest informal settings, its rattan chairs dressed in English country fabrics against aquamarine glass walls and wood floors. At least two evenings per cruise, a dinner buffet is offered. The midnight buffet's setting changes depending on weather and the theme.

Adjacent to the lido café, the **Terrazza Café** reproduces the *Classica's* popular **Alfresco Café,** the ship's most pleasant location from dawn to dusk. Set with wicker chairs and tables under a high-peaked canvas canopy, it provides a cool, inviting outdoor setting for breakfast and lunch.

The other big hit is **Romeo's Pizzeria,** where pizza is served throughout the day. It's free, but you might want to buy a glass of wine or beer to wash it down. Romeo's neighbor, **Juliet's Patisserie,** open from 9 a.m. to midnight, serves pastries (without charge) and espresso. It's also the **Martini Bar.**

Afternoon tea, with fabulous desserts, is served daily; a cart dispenses Italian ice cream from 10 p.m. to midnight, and **Notte Tropical** is an outdoor tropical buffet.

Service In recent years, Costa has changed its crews' makeup, with major impact. No longer are the ships all-Italian but rather multinational, as most other cruise lines. As a result, Costa lost an edge that distinguished it. Italian officers still command the ships, and Italians supervise the restaurants, but the flair and fun that Italian waiters create is often missing.

Service is attentive, friendly, and good—often, very good—but for those who knew Costa before, the ambience isn't the same. The cruise staff cheerfully runs daily activities, but you're unlikely to see the cruise director except to open the nightly show.

Facilities and Activities Lessons in dance, Italian language, and gaming; bingo; bridge; backgammon; culinary demonstrations are some of the daytime diversions. Evening entertainment is planned to appeal to the multinational passenger mix. *Romantica's* main show lounge, the **L'Opera Theater** (**Colosseo** on *Classica*), is a modern interpretation of a classic, horseshoe-shaped concert hall. Creating a glamorous setting are red and royal blue carpets, blue velvet seats against a wall of blue mosaics, and brass accents. Most seats have good sight lines, and back pain sufferers will like the hard, stiff balcony seats. L'Opera has shows nightly.

Romantica's casino is spectacular, with stucco walls inlaid with gold accents and a large crystal chandelier. The **Tango Ballroom,** a multipurpose lounge with large dance floor, becomes a high-energy nightclub with live music. The room has window walls and is a lovely daytime retreat. The **Diva Disco** atop the ship, a daytime observation and cocktail lounge with floor-to-ceiling windows, is the late-night hot spot. Everyone's favorite is the toga party, when passengers create Roman garb from sheets provided by the ship. It's remarkable how many ways passengers find to make togas, and almost all passengers join in and have a great time.

Sports, Fitness, and Beauty Two outdoor pools are separated by Costa's distinctive yellow stacks. One has four Jacuzzis and is surrounded by three terraces of teak decks with lounge chairs. The second is inlaid with ceramic tiles; suspended above it is a Susumu sculpture in red metal, which changes shape in the wind.

The **Caracalla Spa** on the *Classica* has floor-to-ceiling windows. *Romantica's* smaller spa is beside the stack. In addition to weights, life cycles, and treadmills, the spa has sauna, steam, and massage rooms, plus a beauty salon offering personalized hair and body treatments. A partial deck above the swimming pools has a jogging track and sunbathing space.

Children's Facilities See *CostaVictoria* section.

Postscript After heavy criticism for seemingly endless shipboard announcements in five languages beginning at 8 a.m., Costa says it has trimmed the intrusion; however, we still hear complaints. Because most of this information is in the daily agenda, the broadcasts seem quite unnecessary.

COSTAEUROPA	QUALITY 7	VALUE B
Registry: Netherlands	Length: 798 feet	Beam: 95 feet
Cabins: 747	Draft: 75.5 feet	Speed: 20 knots
Maximum Passengers:	Passenger Decks: 9	Elevators: 7
1,773	Crew: 639	Space Ratio: 36.4

The Ship   The *CostaEuropa,* the former *Westerdam* of Holland America Line, joined the Costa fleet in spring 2002. She is not a new superliner, but she fits well with them. She is longer, more narrow, and has fewer decks than the newer ships, and a lower space-to-passenger ratio, nonetheless she's a spacious ship. (Moviegoers saw her in *Out to Sea,* the 1997 comedy starring Jack Lemmon and Walter Matthau.)

When she debuted in 1989, she was hailed as one of the decade's most magnificent ships. She combines the style and refinement of great liners with state-of-the-art facilities. To increase her capacity from 1,000 to 1,494 passengers and update some of her facilities, the ship was stretched. A 130-foot section was added, providing space for a two-tiered show lounge, more bars, a sports deck, fitness facilities, library, larger restaurant, and second buffet. Before entering service for Costa, the ship got a $6 million facelift.

Comfortable, classy, and contemporary, the *CostaEuropa* is dressed in pastels with lovely woods and interesting art and antiques. Most public rooms are on the Promenade Deck, anchored by the casino and several lounges forward and a bilevel lounge aft.

The **Dining Room** is on the lowest passenger deck. The main section has an interesting wood and Plexiglas dome. Dining is elegant and menu choices extensive; linen-covered tables are set with fine china, silver tableware, and fresh flowers.

The *CostaEuropa* has two lido restaurants, where buffets are available. You can have breakfast and lunch—as well as alternative dining several nights—in the pleasant settings of the veranda by the Sun Deck pool or the **Lido Restaurant** by the Upper Promenade pool.

Itineraries   See Itinerary Index.

Cabins   The ship has 21 cabin categories and boasts standard cabins with comfortable sitting areas. Minimum cabins are only slightly smaller, and suites are more than double average size. Most are fitted with twin beds; more than a third can be converted to queens. All have ample drawer and closet space. The comfortable décor employs the same soothing colors of public rooms. All cabins have telephone, closed-circuit television, multichannel music system, and fine toiletries; all outside cabins (except a few lower-priced ones) have bathrooms with a tub and shower.

Specifications 252 inside cabins, 495 outside. Standard dimensions, 200 square feet for outside cabins. Some upper/lower berths; no singles; 4 wheelchair-accessible.

Facilities and Activities The theater on Sun Deck is particularly pretty, with gray velour seats and deep blue carpets and walls. Current films are shown daily. The space is also used for religious services, meetings, and lectures. Other daytime activities include bridge tournaments, dance lessons, karaoke, and bingo.

Entertainment and activities are similar to those on her sister ships. Promenade Deck has a cluster of lounges and bars. In one, an orchestra plays for predinner cocktails. Later, the space becomes a disco. Next door is a sports bar, and across the way, another bar with a small dance floor.

The **Book Chest** is a delightful spot for those reading in quiet comfort. The nearby **Ocean Bar,** where every table has a sea view, is the best for people-watching because everyone passes en route to the main lounge, a multipurpose room with evening entertainment. The ship has a children's facility.

Sports, Fitness, and Beauty The Sports Deck has an unobstructed 40-by-40-foot jogging track, glass windbreaker walls, and two tennis practice courts. A retractable roof protects the Sun Deck swimming pool, two Jacuzzis, and bar. The fitness center on Navigation Deck offers exercise equipment, saunas, and massage rooms. The beauty salon and barber shop are on Promenade Deck.

COSTATROPICALE	QUALITY 3	VALUE C
Registry: Liberia	Length: 671 feet	Beam: 100 feet
Cabins: 511	Draft: 23.3 feet	Speed: 20 knots
Maximum Passengers:	Passenger Decks: 8	Elevators: 8
1,422	Crew: 540	Space Ratio: 36

The Ship The *Tropicale,* transferred from Carnival to Costa Cruises in 2001 and renamed *CostaTropicale,* was given a $25 million renovation before entering European service, taking over the itineraries of the venerable *CostaRiviera* which is no longer in service.

When she was launched in the 1980s, she offered trendsetting new features: all accommodations, except 12 suites, were the same size; all cabins had picture windows instead of portholes; there was expanded deck space for sports and other activities; and twin beds could be converted to kings-features copied throughout the industry.

In her most recent facelift, all public areas were completely updated from floor to ceiling, as were the cabins. Some decks were widened, and a pizzeria and a restaurant were added. The ship's funnel was replaced with Costa's signature yellow smokestack.

The forerunner of superliners, yet scaled down in size and activity, *Tropicale* is the right combination for many people. The ship has one dining room on a lower deck, seven bars and lounges, including a piano bar and showroom; and a casino. She also has three swimming pools, one of which is a children's pool, children's room, an Internet café, a fitness center and spa, and a specialty restaurant, **Club Bahia,** with a Brazilian theme.

The ship has 172 inside cabins, 307 outside; 10 suites; 11 cabins are wheelchair-accessible.

Itineraries   See Itinerary Index.

CostaAllegra and CostaMarina

CostaAllegra sails to South America from Europe, and *CostaMarina* is now dedicated to Costa's German market. Thus, they are not covered as these markets are outside the focus of this book.

Cruise West

2401 Fourth Avenue, Suite 700, Seattle, WA 98121
(800) 570-0072; fax (206) 441-4757
www.cruisewest.com

Type of Ships   Six small, informal, minicoastal cruising vessels, one luxury oceangoing ship, and one day-touring boat.

Type of Cruises   Casual, close-up, light adventure, with emphasis on scenery and wildlife in coastal areas.

Cruise Line's Strengths

- innovative itineraries
- enthusiastic crew
- itinerary flexibility allows extra time for wildlife viewing
- small ships

Cruise Line's Shortcomings

- small cabins; noisy lower-deck cabins on older ships
- small bathrooms with handheld showers on older ships
- limited shipboard facilities and evening activities

Fellow Passengers   Mature, physically active; mid-40s to mid-80s. Retired couples and seniors. Passengers somewhat older on Columbia River cruises; younger on Alaskan cruises. Up to 70% have college degrees or some college education; passengers are well traveled and more curious about nature, history, and ecology than typical passengers on mainstream cruise ships.

Passengers are outgoing; most would rather rise early to catch the sunrise than party late. Most are from California, Florida, New York, Great Lakes region, Pacific Northwest, and Texas; some from Canada. About 24% are repeaters. Regardless of age, they like the intimacy of a casual cruise to places larger liners cannot reach.

Recommended For   Small-ship devotees; people looking for light adventure, to experience a region up-close; those preferring wildlife to nightlife.

Not Recommended For   Travelers who need to be entertained; seek a lavish, resortlike experience with emphasis on nightlife; prefer facilities and activities of large ships; gamblers.

Cruise Areas and Seasons April–October, Alaska and western Canada, Colombia and Snake Rivers, Bering Sea; March–November, Pacific Northwest and California; September–May, Japan, South Pacific; December–April, Sea of Cortés, Costa Rica, Panama.

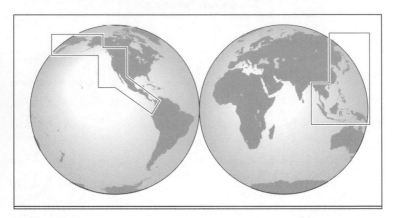

The Line After flying "The Hump" in the China-Burma-India theater in World War II, Charles B. "Chuck" West moved to Alaska to become a bush pilot. Flying over the northern wilderness, he recognized Alaska's great tourism potential. In 1946, he organized, sold, and piloted the first all-tourist air excursion north of the Arctic Circle. From that, he built the largest tour company in Alaska—Westours—which he sold to Holland America Line in 1971.

Starting over again at age 60, West built the tour company that became Cruise West. beginning in 1986, with a luxury cruiser for day tours on Prince William Sound. In 1990, adding its first overnight coastal cruising vessel sailing from Juneau to Glacier Bay, and six vessels in seven years, the line became North America's largest small-ship cruise company. Other ships followed as the company expanded its operations. In 1997, *Spirit of Endeavour,* the line's most luxurious ship to date, began offering a more upscale level of cruises. In 1998, the line took another major step, sending two ships to cruise Mexico's Sea of Cortés for the winter, thus becoming a year-round operator. The line's American-built and flagged vessels are subject to Federal Maritime Commission bonding and strict U.S. Coast Guard inspections.

In 2001, Cruise West added *Spirit of Oceanus* and launched a new era for the line, enabling it to develop new worldwide itineraries and attract new audiences. The all-suite ship, formerly *Renaissance V,* was the line's first oceangoing vessel and the most luxurious ship in the fleet by far. And in the autumn of the same year, it added the *Pacific Explorer* (formerly *Temptress Explorer*), offering cruises in Costa Rica and Panama.

THE FLEET	BUILT/RENOVATED	TONNAGE	PASSENGERS
Spirit of Alaska	1980/1995	97	78
Spirit of Columbia	1979/1995	98	78
Spirit of Discovery	1976/1992	94	84
Spirit of Endeavour	1985/1996	95	102
Spirit of '98	1984/1995	96	96
Spirit of Oceanus	2001	1,263	114
Sheltered Seas (day-cruiser)	1986/1994	95	70
Pacific Explorer	1995/1998	100	100

Style Cruise West believes that responsible travel means having enriching experiences that cause minimal impact on the environment. The company encourages environmental education and understanding through unusual, up-close experiences, while respecting wildlife and natural habitats.

The small, shallow-draft vessels can nose into shore for close views of scenery and wildlife and navigate intricate waterways, narrow locks, and small marinas inaccessible to larger ships. Their size and casual atmosphere inspire instant friendships not always possible on larger ships.

Two of the vessels have bow-landing capabilities, enabling them to pull up to wilderness beaches or shore-side parks. En route, narration and occasional talks by park rangers, historians, and other specialists inform passengers of the history, geology, and wildlife of areas they're visiting. Otherwise, onboard style is unstructured.

Passengers entertain themselves by immersing in the scenery and wildlife, reading, playing cards and games, or socializing with other passengers and the crew.

Cruise West's young, mostly college-age crew is recruited primarily from the Pacific Northwest and Alaska. Their caring attitude and enthusiasm are some of the line's strengths. Also notable is the cuisine, which is more sophisticated than is normally associated with small-ship, light-adventure cruising.

Distinctive Features Bow ramp on *Spirit of Columbia;* bow stairs on *Spirit of Alaska.* Open bridge. Dib launches (inflatable, Zodiac-like motorized launches with covers, seats, and railings) on *Spirit of '98* and *Spirit of Endeavour* provide shore access in Alaska and the Sea of Cortés. The latter also has Zodiacs to use.

	HIGHEST	LOWEST	AVERAGE
PER DIEM	$675	$150	$430

Per diems are calculated from cruise line's nondiscounted *cruise-only* fares on standard accommodations and vary by season, cabin, and cruise areas.

Rates   Port charges included.

Special Fares and Discounts

- **Single Supplement** Varies from 125% to 200%; single cabins on *Spirit of Glacier Bay*, *Spirit of '98*, and *Spirit of Discovery*. Twin rate available for singles on select cruises and all inside "B" cabins.

- Early-bird discounts and free air on 7-day or longer cruises when booked by specific deadlines.

- New Stowaway Program, if you are free to travel on 30 days' notice, you can become a last-minute "Stowaway" and save 25% off your cruise fare. You make your deposit for the cruise itinerary and the cabin category you prefer; the cruise line selects the exact date of departure within a 30-day window and notifies you at least 30 days in advance. If you decide not to go, the deposit can be applied to a future cruise.

Packages

- **Air/Sea** Air add-ons available from up to 75 gateways.

- **Pre/Post** Variety of cruise-tour Alaska packages with up to nine days of land touring.

Past Passengers   The Quyana Club (the name means "thank you" in Yu'pik Eskimo) offers passengers newsletters, shipboard credits, and 5% savings on all cruises and pre/post packages.

The Last Word   The company remains faithful to its founder's vision that small groups maximize travelers' enjoyment without overwhelming villages, small ports, and wilderness areas they visit, and that the focus should be outward, on nature and culture, rather than inward, on nightclubs and gambling. By focusing on wildlife—passengers are likely to see whales, bears, seals, and eagles—and the wilderness, Cruise West says it is increasing awareness and support for protection of natural treasures.

Most passengers try an Alaskan cruise first. If they like it, they graduate to cruises elsewhere. Baja California, Costa Rica or Panama give Cruise West alumni a complete contrast to Alaska or the Northwest. Yet the Sea of Cortés offers similar attractions—wildlife, beautiful scenery, and interesting culture—and much the same appeal. Now, they have new destinations, plus new ships in which to enjoy them.

CRUISE WEST STANDARD FEATURES

Officers American.

Staff Dining, Cabin, Cruise/American.

Dining Facilities One dining room with open seating; meals served at specific hours. Early Continental breakfast and 6 p.m. appetizers in forward lounge. Coffee, tea, fresh fruit available throughout day.

Special Diets Vegetarian, low-fat, low-salt, and other heart-healthy requests accommodated; notice required at time of booking.

Room Service None, except for owner's suite on the *Spirit of '98*.

CRUISE WEST STANDARD FEATURES
(continued)

Dress Code   Casual at all times. Most passengers wear jeans, chinos, and layer with shirts, sweaters, and windbreakers in cooler climates.

Cabin Amenities   Air-conditioning/thermostat; upper-deck cabins have windows that open. Most bathrooms on older ships are small, some with handheld showers; some have sink and vanity in room, separate from bathroom. Reading lights over bed; limited closets, storage on older ships. *Spirit of Endeavour, Spirit of '98, Spirit of Oceanus,* television, phone.

Electrical Outlets   110 AC.

Wheelchair Access   *Spirit of '98* and *Spirit of Oceanus* have elevators; *Oceanus* has two cabins accessible for disabled passengers.

Recreation and Entertainment   Forward lounge with bar setup, television, small library with reference books of area, informational videos, movies; informal entertainment by crew; occasional talks by historians, park rangers, and other experts. Bridge, other card and board games. Ships stock binoculars, but it's wise to bring your own. Musical entertainment on Sea of Cortés cruises.

Beauty and Fitness   Some fitness equipment, such as stair steppers and exercise bicycles. No beauty/barber shop.

Other Facilities   Doctor on Sea of Cortés cruises and on *Oceanus;* at least one crew member on each vessel is trained in "First Response."

Children's Facilities   None.

Theme Cruises   None.

Smoking   Not allowed in public rooms or cabins; smoking allowed only on outside, open deck areas.

Cruise West Suggested Tipping $10–$12 per passenger per day. All tips are pooled and shared by nonofficer staff.

Credit Cards   For cruise payment and on-board charges: American Express, Visa, MasterCard.

SPIRIT OF OCEANUS   **(Preview)**

Registry: Bahamas	Length: 295 feet	Beam: 50 feet
Cabins: 57	Draft: 13.25 feet	Speed: 14.5 knots
Maximum Passengers: 114	Passenger Decks: 5	Elevators: 1
	Crew: 65	Space Ratio: NA

The Ship   Cruise West took possession of its new ship, *Spirit of Oceanus,* in spring 2001 in Singapore. Built in 1991 as the *Renaissance V,* the ship was renamed *Sun Viva* when she was purchased by Sun Cruises, and later became *MegaStar Sagittarius* under Star Cruises, from whom Cruise West purchased her. After some cosmetic refurbishing, the ship sailed on a 32-day voyage from Singapore to Whittier, entering Alaska service in June—at which time she became the line's flagship, taking over that honor from *Spirit of Endeavour.*

The luxurious *Spirit of Oceanus* was Cruise West's first oceangoing vessel and, as such, opened up new horizons for the line, from new destinations worldwide to newer, more upscale cruises that would appeal to a completely new market. In addition to Alaska in summer, she sails on 4- to 13-night voyages to the Bering Sea from Anchorage or Nome.

Registered in the Bahamas-another first for Cruise West—the ship has American officers, an on-board naturalist guide, and an English-speaking crew whose numbers constitute the highest crew-to-guests ratio in the line's fleet.

Itineraries   See Itinerary Index.

Cabins   *Spirit of Oceanus* has spacious, all-outside suites, each with a large picture window or porthole, and ranging in size from 215 to 353 square feet. The 12 suites on Sun and Bridge Decks have private teak balconies—another first for Cruise West ships. Other cabin amenities include a walk-in closet, marble-topped vanity, and a lounge area separated from the bedroom by a curtain. All suites can be configured with two twin beds or a full queen-size bed and have a television/VCR, safe, minibar, satellite telephone, and private bathroom with a marble sink and shower. In the renovation, Cruise West added minifridges, safes, and hair dryers.

Specifications   57 cabins, ranging from 215 to 353 square feet; 12 suites with balconies; two wheelchair-accessible.

Facilities and Activities   The handsomely appointed *Spirit of Oceanus* has marble and polished hardwood interiors, sumptuous fabrics, and fine art. There are two large lounges (one with a grand piano) and several elegant bars, providing havens for conversation, reading, or playing board games. Among other new features passengers enjoy on a Cruise West ship for the first time are a hot tub on the aft Bridge Deck, a health facility, a patio bar, and a pool in warm climates.

The ship has a library, an elevator providing access to all five passenger decks, and spacious outside viewing areas and walkways on four of the five guest decks. The elegant dining room accommodates all guests at a single seating. Among the changes in the latest renovations, the casino was removed to make room for more public space and a small room with exercise equipment was added. The ship has a small clinic staffed by a doctor.

SPIRIT OF ENDEAVOUR	**QUALITY 3**	**VALUE C**
Registry: United States	Length: 217 feet	Beam: 37 feet
Cabins: 51	Draft: 8.5 feet	Speed: 13 knots
Maximum Passengers:	Passenger Decks: 4	Elevators: None
102	Crew: 28	Space Ratio: NA

The Ship   Built in 1983 in Jeffersonville, Indiana, *Spirit of Endeavour* (formerly *Newport Clipper* of Clipper Cruise Lines) was launched for

Cruise West in 1996 after a $5 million refurbishing. She was Cruise West's most luxurious ship at the time and added a new level of comfort to the line's fleet until the *Spirit of Oceanus* was added in 2001. One of the more deluxe small vessels sailing in Alaska and the Sea of Cortés, *Endeavour* has teak decks, a wide companionway, and comfortable lounges.

In the renovations, all cabins and public areas were refurbished, safety features were updated, and new engines and bridge electronics were installed. New bow and stern designs increase the ship's fuel efficiency by more than 22%. A "bulbous" underwater bow extension splits the water, reducing the bow wake and water resistance. A stern ferring forces water to flow closer to the surface, reducing drag.

Among Cruise West ships, the *Spirit of Endeavour's* clean lines and raked bow make it look most like a small cruise ship. Viewing breathtaking scenery in Alaska is a major activity on this ship, which appeals to those looking for quiet social life and a relaxed itinerary; in the Sea of Cortés, there are daily excursions that appeal to those eager for light adventure.

Passengers give high marks to the ship's educational programs, and they appreciate finding two pairs of high-powered binoculars and umbrellas in their cabins. The ship does not have an elevator. The décor throughout is understated and pleasing. The ship does not have a promenade deck completely surrounding the ship.

Itineraries   See Itinerary Index.

Cabins   Cabins are large compared to her older sister ships and have wide picture windows. They're equipped with phone, television/VCR, and tiled baths with showers. Refurbishing in 1999 added new closets, lighting and window treatments, wall coverings, artwork and furniture, as well as the upgrading of all the bathrooms.

Cabins are on three decks and of four types: The 100 series on the Main deck includes eight AAA category measuring 109 square feet, and four A's of about the same size. Lounge deck has 4 A's that open onto the outside deck, 12 AAA's, and 2 deluxe cabins measuring 155 square feet. Upper deck has 20 AA's and one deluxe cabin, all opening to outside veranda. The A and AA have twin or double, and some cabins take three passengers; most have large picture windows.

Specifications   51 cabins. The cruise line's brochures show precise layouts of each category.

Dining   The **Resolution Dining Room** accommodates all passengers at a single open seating; most tables seat six or eight persons, none are for two. Mealtimes may vary depending on the itinerary, but generally, breakfast served at 7:30 a.m., lunch at 1 p.m., and dinner at 7:30 p.m. The food gets high praise from passengers, and there's a good selection of wines. An unusual custom on board—the chef personally introduces the evening menu and invites passengers to dinner. As with most small ships, there is a great deal of camaraderie among passengers and friendly interaction with the ship's staff.

Facilities and Activities The spacious **Explorer Lounge** is a multipurpose room and the heart of the ship's activity, beginning with continental breakfast in the morning and coffee, tea, and cocoa available throughout the day. It is also used for most of the lectures. A wide selection of videos and magazines, are available in the library, along with a good selection of books and reference works pertaining to the area of the cruise.

The main activity on an Alaska cruise is sight-seeing, which Alaska offers like no other place in the country. A Baja California and Sea of Cortés cruise during the winter months offers more sports activities, such as hiking, swimming, snorkeling, and kayaking, as well as sight-seeing and spotting wildlife. Among the highlights are an opportunity to swim with sea lions, watching dolphins play, and photographing a colony of blue-footed bookies, but the most anticipated activity of all is whale-watching. From about mid-January to mid-March, large numbers of California gray whales assemble in the lagoons of Bahia Magdalena, which passengers visit.

SPIRIT OF '98	QUALITY 3	VALUE C
Registry: United States	Length: 192 feet	Beam: 40 feet
Cabins: 49	Draft: 9.3 feet	Speed: 13 knots
Maximum Passengers:	Passenger Decks: 4	Elevators: 1
96	Crew: 26	Space Ratio: NA

The Ship Added to Cruise West's fleet in 1993, *Spirit of '98* previously sailed as the *Pilgrim Belle, Colonial Explorer,* and *Victorian Empress.* The handsome vessel has the profile and interior of a turn-of-the-19th-century riverboat (she had a role in the 1994 movie *Wyatt Earp*).

Built in 1984, the décor recalls a Victorian country hotel. Accenting a handsome mahogany and mirrored bar in the forward observation lounge are fanciful wall lamps and wood columns trimmed with strip mirrors. Continuing the theme on her four decks are extensive use of wood, wingback chairs, leaded glass, and old-fashioned brass lamps. The ship has one elevator operating between the Main deck and Upper deck.

Itineraries See Itinerary Index.

Cabins All cabins are outside and have varied arrangements. They're roomy, with closet and storage space adequate for a casual cruise. All are decorated in rich Victorian-style colors and fabrics. All have TV/VCR combinations, are air conditioned, and have windows that open—a welcome feature. Cabins on lounge and upper decks open onto promenades. Main-deck, lower-priced cabins have windows on the outside hull, a benefit for those who like privacy but want to keep their curtains open.

The ship has an amazingly large, two-room owner's suite on the top deck with picture windows on both sides. The only cabin on the deck, just behind the bridge, it has a sitting area, a game and meeting area, complimentary bar, television, VCR, king-size bed, and bathroom with full-size tub. Occupants may have their meals served en suite.

Specifications 48 outside cabins; 1 suite. Dimensions range from 100–120 square feet. 40 with twins; 2 with upper/lower bunks; 4 with queen, 6 with doubles. 2 singles.

Dining The **Klondike Dining Room** provides seating at a variety of table configurations, including booths next to the picture windows. One open seating is offered at each of three meals. The cuisine is better than expected for this type of cruise. It's mostly Pacific Northwest fare encompassing fresh seafood, local produce, and Northwest wines and local specialty beers. In Mexico, meals have Mexican choices. Bread and pastries are baked onboard. Coffee, tea, cocoa, and fruit are available all day.

An early Continental breakfast is available in the forward lounge; full breakfast is at 7:30 a.m. in the dining room. Lunch features soups, salads, and sandwiches. Appetizers served between 6 and 7 p.m. may include Alaskan Dungeness crab and artichoke dip or baked Brie.

Entrées at dinner are attractively presented and surprisingly sophisticated. They may include fresh halibut in Dijon sauce, veal piccata with white wine and capers, or Oregon razor clams grilled with garlic aïoli.

Service The young, enthusiastic crew are friendly, caring, and especially considerate of older passengers. These "customer service representatives" perform a variety of duties, including cleaning cabins and serving in the dining room.

Facilities and Activities Unusual in coastal cruise ships, **Soapy's Parlor** is a second, quiet lounge with wraparound windows at the stern, a good spot for watching the vessel's wake. Tea is served in the afternoon. The bridge deck has ample space for sunning, viewing scenery, or lounging. A barbecue lunch is offered in good weather. A small area serves as a gift shop, where caps, mugs, and similar items are sold. A shuffleboard and huge checkerboard are on the bridge deck, along with two exercise machines.

The forward lounge is the ship's social center at night. Most entertainment is provided by the passengers interacting with each other in conversation, cards, or board games in the lounge or dining room. Absent are a pool, casino, aerobics class, bingo, midnight buffet, or napkin-folding classes. The crew provides informal talent and lively entertainment on Crew and Casino nights. Vegetable races are amusing—and can be lucrative for those who wager correctly on such entries as Percy Potato or the Lemon Sisters. A television shows evening movies. Occasional guest lectures, talks by the cruise coordinator/naturalist, and entertainment from the old-style player piano are offered.

SPIRIT OF DISCOVERY	QUALITY **2**	VALUE **D**
Registry: United States	Length: 166 feet	Beam: 37 feet
Cabins: 43	Draft: 7.5 feet	Speed: 13 knots
Maximum Passengers:	Passenger Decks: 3	Elevators: None
84	Crew: 21	Space Ratio: NA

The Ship   Built in 1976 as the *Independence* and renamed *Columbia,* this handsome vessel cruised the East Coast and Puget Sound before being acquired by Cruise West in 1992 and renamed *Spirit of Discovery.* The forward lounge of this three-deck vessel is the ship's social center and cool-weather retreat. Nicely decorated in blue, soft grays, teals, and mauves, it has a bar with standard spirits plus Pacific Northwest wines and specialty brews. Furniture is arranged in conversational groupings. These, along with mirrored ceiling and chrome accents, give it the look of a private yacht or small, European-style hotel.

The lounge offers good views to both sides and over the bow through vertical windows at the front. Passengers at the bow can almost touch the vegetation when the ship noses up to shore. The bridge has a wraparound viewing area and is open to passengers at most times. A stair stepper, exercise bicycle, and rowing machine are available.

Itineraries   See Itinerary Index.

Cabins   Cabins on all three decks are outside with large windows. Most are small but adequate and furnished with a vanity, desk, and chair. Bathrooms have showers. Closets could use more hangers. Two sought-after smaller cabins, sold as singles, are amidships on the bridge deck.

Four spacious, deluxe cabins on the top level have a queen-size bed, desk and chair, television/VCR unit, and fridge/minibar. All bridge-deck cabins and most lounge-deck cabins open onto a promenade. The two lowest-priced cabins are on the lower main deck forward, reduced in size to fit the hull's curvature.

Specifications   43 outside cabins; no suites. Dimensions range from 64 square feet (single cabin) to 127 square feet. 34 with twins, 1 with double, 4 queens, 2 with upper/lower berths, 2 singles.

Dining   The **Grand Pacific Dining Room,** aft on the main deck, is pleasant and airy, but a bit noisy because it's over the engine room. The food is imaginative and quite good, encompassing Pacific Northwest versions of classic American fare with fresh local produce and seafood. All passengers dine in one open seating; table configurations vary.

A continental breakfast is available for early risers. Sit-down breakfast, lunch, and 6 p.m. appetizers are served. Two entrées are offered at dinner; they may include lingcod baked in parchment or a superb rack of Ellensburg lamb roasted with Dijon rosemary crust.

Service Customer service, galley and engine crew, and deck hands are young Americans, most from the Pacific Northwest. They're attentive, enthusiastic, and outgoing. Friendships form between crew and passengers, and many crew members receive holiday greetings from passengers for years after they meet.

SPIRIT OF ALASKA	QUALITY 2	VALUE D
SPIRIT OF COLUMBIA	QUALITY 2	VALUE D
Registry: United States	Length: 143 feet	Beam: 28 feet
Cabins: 39	Draft: 7.5/6.5 feet	Speed: 12/10 knots
Maximum Passengers:	Passenger Decks: 4	Elevators: None
78	Crew: 21	Space Ratio: NA

The Ships *Spirit of Alaska* and *Spirit of Columbia* are identical in size, similar in layout, and are smaller versions of their sister ships. *Spirit of Alaska,* built in 1980 as the *Pacific Northwest Explorer,* was extensively renovated when acquired by Cruise West in 1991, and she was renovated again in 1995. *Spirit of Columbia* (formerly *New Shoreham II* of American Canadian Caribbean Line) joined in 1994 after being refitted in a "Western National Park Lodge" theme.

Both ships have four decks, with most cabins on the lower and upper decks and a forward lounge and dining room amidships on the main deck. The lounge is the center of social life and site of briefings. It has a small bar, gift shop, reference library focused on the cruise area, television, and movie videos. The upper deck has an unobstructed walking and jogging circuit and several exercise machines.

On *Spirit of Alaska,* the bridge deck provides open and covered seating and a good-weather venue for buffet lunches. Bow ramp stairs enable passengers to walk directly onto shore; some complain the stairs are steep and difficult to negotiate.

Besides décor, *Spirit of Columbia* differs in having a large owner's suite with windows overlooking the bow, three additional suites, a raised wheelhouse with 360° viewing, and a unique bow ramp. A hinged, V-shaped segment of the bow can be lowered to form a ramp, giving direct access to shore from the forward lounge.

Itineraries See Itinerary Index.

Cabins Cabins on both ships range from roomy—for ships of this size—to very small. *Spirit of Alaska's* suites and deluxe cabins have small sitting areas and open to promenades. Three bridge-deck suites have oversized double beds, windows on two sides, and accommodate a third person.

Spirit of Columbia's 11 suites and deluxe cabins have a television/VCR, refrigerator, side tables, and a chair. Suites have a double bed;

deluxe rooms, twins. The owner's suite has a queen-size bed, bathtub/shower, and complimentary bar. Upper- and bridge-deck cabins open directly onto promenades.

On both ships, main-deck cabins are on the short passage between the dining room and forward lounge, a high-traffic area, but convenient for those who want easy access to activities and facilities. Windows in these cabins are on the outside hull, ensuring privacy. Lower-deck cabins have portlights high on the bulkhead and not for viewing. Baths are small units with handheld showers and curtains on tracks. Most cabins have twin beds; all have reading lights, closets, and under-bed storage. They're just above the engine room and can be noisy when the ship is underway, but they are a good buy for budget-watchers.

Specifications   *Alaska:* 12 inside; 24 outside; 3 suites. Dimensions range from 81–130.5 square feet. 26 with twins; 13 with doubles; 7 cabins accommodate third persons; no singles. *Columbia:* 12 inside; 20 outside; 7 suites. Dimensions range from 73.5–176 square feet.

Dining   Meals are served at a single, open seating. Cuisine is good American fare, emphasizing fresh Pacific Northwest and Alaskan seafood and local produce. The *Spirit of Alaska's* Grand Pacific Dining Room was upgraded in 1994; long, family-style tables were scrapped for more intimate round and square ones. Upholstered banquettes run bow to stern underneath side windows.

Service   The young American staff helps set the friendly ambience and, despite the considerable workload, remains courteous, enthusiastic, and helpful, especially to seniors. Most retain a sense of awe about the magnificent region the vessel sails, often sharing passengers' excitement for wildlife sightings or glacier calvings.

PACIFIC EXPLORER	**(Preview)**	
Registry : Honduras	Length: 185	Beam: n.a.
Cabins: 50	Draft: 7 ft.	Speed: 12 knots
Maximum Passengers:	Passenger Decks: 4	Space Ratio: NA
100	Crew: 25	

The Ship   Built in 1995 and remodeled in 1998, the *Pacific Explorer* specializes in cruises of Costa Rica and Panama. The historic Panamanian port of Portobelo, dating from 1502, was added to its itinerary in 2003. The ship is staffed with English-speaking Costa Ricans and guides. A lounge and dining room are on the lower of four decks, cabins and a forward lounge are on Main and Upper decks, and the Bridge, Sun area, and outdoor bar are on the Sun deck.

All cabins have picture windows and are air-conditioned. They have television/VCR and private baths with showers. There are three types of cabins—deluxe (152 square feet), AAA/AA (122 square feet), and A (107 square feet)—and they are furnished with either twin or double beds. International cuisine and Central American specialties are served, along with breads and desserts made onboard by the pastry chef.

Recently, Cruise West has offered free airfare from Houston, Dallas, and Miami for new clients booking certain departures. Inquire from the cruise line.

Day Cruises

Sheltered Seas, a day-cruiser, is not covered here because her type of cruises are outside the scope of this book. For more information, contact the cruise line.

Postscript   Readers considering a cruise on any Cruise West ship should read the entire section for a more complete picture of the cruise experience the line offers.

Crystal Cruises

2049 Century Park East, Suite 1400, Los Angeles, CA 90067
(310) 785-9300; (800) 446-6620; fax (310) 785-9201
www.crystalcruises.com

Type of Ships   Modern, luxury superliners.

Type of Cruise   Modern version of glamorous, traditional cruising with a touch of California glitz, for upscale, sophisticated travelers.

Cruise Line's Strengths

- service
- beautifully designed ships
- alternative restaurants
- globe-roaming itineraries

Cruise Line's Shortcomings

- two seatings in main dining room
- some cabins with restricted views, except on *Serenity*
- limited closet space; some small bathrooms

Fellow Passengers   Professional, retired or semiretired, experienced travelers; likely to be business owners, entrepreneurs, and executives rather than staff; ages 45–70. Typical passenger is affluent, active, friendly, fashion-conscious, 55–60-year-old couple or mature single.

Recommended For   Quality-conscious travelers who appreciate style with flash and want large-ship facilities; urbane first-time cruisers who can afford it.

Not Recommended For   Anyone uncomfortable or uninterested in sophisticated ambience.

Cruise Areas and Seasons   Caribbean, Mexico, Panama Canal in fall, winter, and spring; South America, China/Orient, and Asia and world cruise, January–March; Europe, Mediterranean, and Alaska April–September. Fall, New York–Montreal.

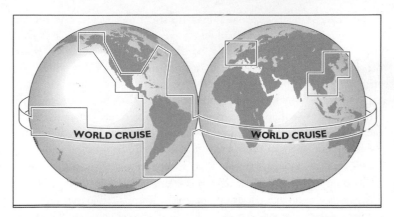

The Line Two years before her first ship debuted in 1990, Crystal Cruises promised it would return grand oceanliners' elegance and personalized service to modern cruises for the "upscale mass" market—an apparently inconsistent term. The line not only delivered on its promise; *Crystal Harmony,* its first ship, was even better than its advanced billing. It quickly became the ship by which others in her class—or aspiring to be in her class—were measured.

And therein lies the tale. There were no other ships in her class. Crystal Cruises created a niche all its own: *Crystal Harmony* is the size of most superliners but carries a third fewer passengers. (Some comparably sized ships carry twice as many passengers.) As a result, *Crystal Harmony* offers the best of all worlds: the facilities of a large, spacious ship with the personalized service of a small vessel.

The *Crystal Harmony* was built in Japan by Mitsubishi Heavy Industries, a subsidiary of Nippon Yusen Kaisha, the Japanese shipbuilding giant known for its technologically advanced ships—and incidentally, the owner of California-based Crystal Cruises. The ship incorporated state-of-the-art engines, radar, and navigational equipment. Comfort and amenities went far beyond the norm. Ironically, *Crystal Symphony,* twin of *Crystal Harmony,* was built in Finland, for cost-saving reasons. *Crystal Serenity,* a third ship which debuted in summer 2003, was built in France. Somewhat larger than her sister ships, *Crystal Serenity* appears to be setting a new direction for Crystal Cruises with facilities for greater focus on enrichment programs and enhanced onboard amenities.

THE FLEET	BUILT/RENOVATED	TONNAGE	PASSENGERS
Crystal Harmony	1990/2003	49,400	940
Crystal Symphony	1995	51,044	940
Crystal Serenity	2003	68,000	1,080

Style   Exceptionally spacious ships with superliner facilities and Rodeo Drive style are designed for affluent travelers willing to pay for luxury and personal attention and who appreciate quality in details. The cruises provide fine food and service in a gracious atmosphere; stimulating enrichment programs, a year-round roster of celebrity and expert speakers, and varied itineraries with more structure than ultraluxurious lines but less formality than luxury ships of old. Itineraries generally include more days at sea than is the norm, so passengers have time to fully enjoy the luxury and pampering that Crystal offers.

Distinctive Features   Computer University@Sea. Personal websites. Enrichment lectures. Two specialty restaurants at no extra cost; gentlemen hosts; close-captioned television for hearing-impaired passengers; free, self-service laundromat on each deck; business center with audiovisual equipment, fax machines, and office equipment; secretarial, translation, and e-mail services; take-out laptops; air-conditioned tenders with toilets.

	HIGHEST	LOWEST	AVERAGE
PER DIEM	$1,106	$427	$713

Per diems are calculated from cruise line's nondiscounted *cruise-only* fares on standard accommodations and vary by season, cabin, and cruise areas.

Rates   Port charges additional.

Special Fares and Discounts   Crystal has advance-purchase discounts ranging from 10% to 30% and more, depending on the cruise; they may be used with other promotional rates and Crystal Society savings. Another group marked with a **V** in Crystal's brochure offers two-for-one savings.

- **Third Passenger** Age 12 and older: minimum fare for cruise.
- **Children's Fare** Younger than age 12, half-fare with two full-paying adults.
- **Single Supplement** Crystal's single's fare begins at 125% of the double-occupancy rate for the lowest categories and is applicable to advance-purchase discount rates (130% for World Cruises).

Packages
- **Air/Sea** Yes.
- **Others** Honeymoon.
- **Pre/Post** Yes.

Past Passengers   Crystal Society past-passenger club offers amenities that increase with the number of cruises. These include business- and first-class air upgrades, confirmed stateroom and penthouse upgrades, shipboard credits, free cruises in staterooms and penthouses, limousine transfers, prepaid gratuities, and private luncheon and dinner parties.

Passengers are automatically enrolled after their first Crystal cruise and receive financial bonuses with every subsequent cruise. The higher reward levels are 5–30 cruises, 50, 70, and 100 cruises, but all members receive a 5% cruise discount, an additional 5% savings for reservations made while on a cruise, priority check-in, a Crystal Society travel bag, membership card, recognition pin, quarterly newsletter, and, beginning with the tenth cruise, a complimentary bottle of wine and fresh flowers on every cruise. Several cruises, including the annual president's cruise, are Crystal Society Sailings (marked with a C in the compendium) and feature a personal escort, exclusive events, and special gifts.

The Last Word　Crystal Cruises identified a market of experienced travelers (but not necessarily experienced cruise passengers) who weren't being served by other cruise lines and created a product that set new standards of luxury for large ships. Those who can afford the cruises get quality all the way. Compare Crystal's quality and extra amenities with those of other lines in the same price bracket, and you find Crystal's cruises are among cruising's best values.

CRYSTAL CRUISES STANDARD FEATURES

Officers　Norwegian and Japanese.

Staff　Dining/European; Cabin/International; Cruise/American.

Dining Facilities　One main dining room, two seatings for dinner with open seating for breakfast and lunch; buffet breakfast and lunch on Lido Deck; alternative dinner restaurants; cocktail hour; midnight buffet; tea.

Special Diets　Requests should be made when reservations are confirmed (or at least one month in advance).

Room Service　24-hour menu; butler service on penthouse deck.

Dress Code　Casual by day; casually elegant in the evening, with two formal evenings per week of cruising.

Cabin Amenities　Direct-dial phone with voicemail; television with CNN and ESPN, VCR or DVD; stocked minibar; safe; bathroom with tub, two hair dryers, robes; suites with marble bathrooms and whirlpool tubs.

Electrical Outlets　110/220 AC.

Wheelchair Access　Four cabins on *Harmony*; 7 *Symphony*; 8 *Serenity*.

Recreation and Entertainment　Casino, disco, nightclub, show lounge, piano bar, coffee/wine bar, cinema/theater, six lounges, observation lounge, card/meeting room, video game room, smoking room. Guest lecturers, area specialists, celebrities. Bingo, bridge, dancing, and crafts classes. Computer classes.

Sports and Other Activities　Two outdoor swimming pools, one with retractable roof; two Jacuzzis; teak deck for walking/jogging; paddle tennis; table tennis; golf clinics and practice corner; deck and pool games.

Beauty and Fitness　See text.

Other Facilities　Boutiques, concierge, hospital, laundry/dry cleaning, valet service, launderettes, photo processing center, video camera rentals, meeting facilities, business service center, e-mail facilities.

Children's Facilities　Playroom, babysitters, youth programs.

CRYSTAL CRUISES STANDARD FEATURES
(continued)

Theme Cruises   Food and wine; Asian art and literature, jazz & blues, others.

Smoking   Dining rooms nonsmoking; public rooms smoking in designated areas.

Crystal Suggested Tipping   Per person per day, cabin stewardess, $4; butler $4; waiter, $4, $5 for single travelers; assistant waiter, $2.50; $6 per person per dinner in specialty restaurants; 15% added to bar bills.

Credit Cards   For cruise payment and on-board charges: all major credit cards, cash, and traveler's checks. Ship uses a charge system, with the bill settled at the end of the cruise.

CRYSTAL HARMONY	QUALITY 10	VALUE B
CRYSTAL SYMPHONY	QUALITY 10	VALUE B
Registry: Bahamas	Length: 790/781 feet	Beam: 105/99 feet
Cabins: 408	Draft: 25 feet	Speed: 22 knots
Maximum Passengers:	Passenger Decks: 8	Elevators: 9
940	Crew: 545	Space Ratio: 52.6/54.3

The Ships   Gleaming white inside and out, *Crystal Harmony* is a symphony of Japanese technology and artistry, European service and tradition, and American flair for fun and entertainment. The elegance is in its simplicity, clean lines, and extraordinary attention to details. Its quality, luxury, and spaciousness—one of the highest ratios of passenger-to-space of any ship—are immediately evident. The décor has a bit of glitz but always in good taste. It was created by Swedish, Italian, and British designers influenced by Japanese artistic understatement. Quiet colors and quality furnishings harmonize. Fine fabrics and textures are set against marble and woods accented with brass and stainless steel. The generous use of glass gives interiors an airy ambience.

Passengers' introduction to the ship is the Crystal Plaza, an atrium lobby with cascades of Lucite lights, stairways, and railings that appear to float in space. They're outlined with brass fixtures against white marble walls. Deep green suede, fresh greenery, hand-cut glass sculpture, and a waterfall provide accents. Summing up the feeling of opulence is-what else?—a crystal piano. The beautiful vessel has lounges for many purposes and moods. The **Palm Court,** one of the most handsome lounges afloat, is an airy space in white and mint green with graceful palms under skylights. It wears the atmosphere of a traditional palm court in the afternoon when tables are set for tea with crisp linens and gleaming silver, and a harpist strums. Forward of the Palm Court is the fabulous **Vista Lounge,** a trilevel observation room with white leather chairs on sky-blue carpets and floor-to-ceiling windows that frame a 270° view.

In 2002, *Crystal Harmony* underwent extensive renovations from stem to stern, emerging with a reconstructed and expanded new spa and fitness center, a **Connoisseur Club** similar to the one on *Symphony,* and remodeled public areas, all designed in accordance with the principles of Feng Shui, the ancient practice of balance and harmony.

Crystal Symphony, introduced in 1995, is essentially a twin of *Crystal Harmony,* with some enhancements. The newly refurbished **Crystal Cove Lounge,** Crystal Plaza, and **Lido Café** were doubled in size; the casino and shopping arcade expanded; and a video room added. Also, a spiral waterfall highlights *Symphony's* atrium, and its color scheme is beige and light green, rather than *Harmony's* blue.

One of the most noticeable—but least successful—alterations is the combining of the popular Palm Court with the **Observation Lounge.** Other important changes are in the cabins—all outside, about a third more having verandas than on the *Harmony,* and all with larger, better-designed bathrooms. The two alternative restaurants were enlarged and moved.

Itineraries   See Itinerary Index.

Cabins   Large, comfortable, and handsomely appointed with fine fabrics and quality furnishings, the well-equipped cabins have sitting areas. All cabins on Decks 8, 9, and 10—more than half of *Crystal Harmony's* cabins and all penthouse suites—were recently refurbished. Quality European fabrics provide a warm combination of textured wheat colors. Mediterranean blue and yellow appear in Deck 8 cabins; coral and blue in Deck 9 cabins with verandas. Standard cabins have adequate closet and storage space, although some complain that hanging space is limited for long voyages. Large down pillows and comforters on beds, plush robes, fluffy towels, fine toiletries, and voicemail on the direct-dial telephone reflect attention to detail. All cabins have fresh flowers, two hair dryers, television with CNN and ESPN, when available, and Internet access.

More than half of all cabins have private verandas. Lifeboats obstruct views from some cabins (Categories G, Horizon, and promenade decks). *Crystal's* literature notes "limited" or "extremely limited" views and prices the cabins accordingly.

The ship's ultimate luxury is on the all-suite, concierge-attended Penthouse Deck. Suites have large bedrooms, large sitting areas, and luxurious marble bathrooms with Jacuzzi bathtubs. The four most extravagant suites encompass 974 square feet, including verandas. All were completely renovated and outfitted with new appointments in 2002.

The suites are attended by European-trained, white-gloved butlers and Scandinavian stewardesses. The young men, dressed in formal attire (some find this pretentious) are as competent as they are eager to serve. They will unpack your bags (and repack them at cruise's end), arrange a party or a dinner in your suite, and attend to other special requests.

Nightly at cocktail time, they serve hors d'oeuvres and pour drinks from your fully stocked bar.

During a day at sea, passengers are given a ship tour on which they visit all cabin categories—a useful sales gimmick! Should the impulse seize you to book your next Crystal voyage right there, a "cruise consultant" is aboard to make the arrangements—at a discount.

Symphony's standard cabins are roomier than *Harmony's*. All are outside, and 278—about a third more—have verandas and overall dimensions of 246 square feet. Other standard cabins cover 202 square feet and have large windows. All have a sitting area with love seat. Some Penthouse Deck suites are arranged to allow larger closets. Standard-cabin bathrooms have been enlarged. All have two sinks in a six-foot counter, bathtubs plus showers, and larger closets with more hanging space. All Penthouse Deck suites have verandas. In her 2002 renovations, *Symphony's* two 982-foot Crystal Penthouses were completley remodeled.

Specifications *Harmony:* 19 inside cabins, 461 outside; 198 with veranda. Standard dimensions, 196 square feet. 62 penthouse suites with verandas measuring 360 or 492 square feet. No singles. All twins convert to queens or kings. 4 wheelchair-accessible. *Symphony:* 480 outside cabins, including 64 penthouse suites with verandas and 278 deluxe cabins (246 square feet) with verandas; 138 deluxe (202 square feet) without verandas; 7 wheelchair-accessible.

Dining   Super in quality and stunning in presentation, cuisine is one of *Crystal Harmony's* best features, on par with good restaurants in New York and Los Angeles. Food is served on fine china by waiters who are as polished as the silver. The spacious peach-and-blue dining room with floor-to-ceiling windows and modern chandeliers is elegant and well designed. More space than usual is allowed between tables—helping keep noise down. Tables for two are more numerous than usual. *Symphony's* dining room is slightly more subdued than *Harmony's*.

Dinner menus, placed in cabins in advance, are greatly varied during a cruise. Typically, they include a choice of four appetizers; three soups; two salads; pasta; five entrées of fish, poultry, and meat; vegetables; and an array of desserts. Low-salt, low-fat, and low-sugar choices are available. The maître d'hôtel often asks passengers for their favorite dishes, which the kitchen will prepare with advance notice. The wine list has over 170 varieties. The ships' most innovative features—and the first for cruising—are the intimate, alternative dinner restaurants, available at no extra cost to all passengers. The alternative restaurants have a hidden charm: Dining in the same surroundings on a long cruise can sometimes become boring. The two additional restaurants offer a change of ambience and cuisine—a great bonus. On *Harmony,* the alternatives are **Kyoto,** which serves Japanese specialties and other Asian cuisine, and **Prego,** featuring Italian dishes. Each restaurant has its own kitchen;

dishes are cooked to order. Reservations are required; make yours early because both are enormously popular.

The *Symphony's* alternative restaurants—**Prego,** offering Italian cuisine, and **Chinois at Jade,** a new feature of the **Jade Garden,** are on Deck 6 instead of Deck 11 as on the *Harmony,* giving passengers easier access to the restaurants and entertainment areas on the same deck. Each has a separate entrance. Chinois at Jade, under the direction of Wolfgang Puck, known for his creative Chinese and French fusion cuisine, offers signature dishes from Puck's Santa Monica restaurant, Chinois on Main.

Symphony's Prego, twice as large as its *Harmony* counterpart, has a waiting list almost every night and probably ranks as the ship's main attraction. Decorated to suggest Venice, the room has banquettes and high-backed chairs around tables seating four or six. Dishes are outstanding. The Jade Garden has been redone, stressing Asian simplicity of design. Light-hued screens with bamboo patterns cover the windows and new multicolored carpeting and upholstery provide an upbeat and modern new look to this popular restaurant. The refurbishment eliminated the tiny water garden at the entrance. Food is excellent, prepared to order by an Asian chef and relying heavily on seafood, but beef and chicken entrées are also available.

The level of service and cuisine in the dining room and alternative restaurants is meant to compensate for the lack of the single-sitting dining room traditional on luxury ships. (Die-hards consider this Crystal's unforgivable sin.) The indoor/outdoor **Lido Café** serves breakfast, midmorning bouillon, and lunch. Luncheon and themed buffets set up around the pool are very popular. The **Trident Bar,** an extension of the Neptune Pool swim-up bar, offers hot dogs, hamburgers, and other snacks, and there's a bar for ice cream and frozen yogurt. By moving the *Symphony's* alternative restaurants to Deck 6, the Lido Café's size was doubled, a second buffet counter was added, and the café was connected to indoor/outdoor seating for breakfast and lunch. Crystal also offers casual dining on deck on select evenings, usually after a day in port, with an informal menu; passengers dress as they like in slacks, jeans, or shorts, and eat when they wish. A sumptuous tea is served daily in the **Palm Court,** and the Crystal Plaza is the setting for a weekly dessert extravaganza set to the music of Mozart. Should you still suffer hunger pangs, the fruit basket in your cabin will have been replenished, or your cabin attendant will bring any item on the extensive 24-hour room service menu. You also may dine in your cabin, with courses served one by one.

The attractive **Bistro Café** serves coffee and pastries for late risers and wine and cheese, coffees, teas, and desserts during the day. Charming French prints that decorate the wall are reproduced on the café's pottery. On several sailings, a wine and food festival features guest chefs and wine experts.

Service   Both ships have among the highest crew-to-passenger ratios in cruising. The well-trained staff is young, cheerful, and eager to please; service is thoroughly professional and consistently excellent. Dining room staff primarily are European; cabin attendants, European and Filipino; and the cruise and entertainment staff, American. A European-style concierge and purser service is available around-the-clock.

Facilities and Activities   Cultural and destination-oriented lectures by experts, political figures, and diplomats are a regular afternoon or after-dinner feature. Daytime pursuits include card and other games, dancing classes, golf clinics, and arts and crafts. The well-stocked library has added videos, DVDs, books, and periodicals.

Crystal has expanded its **Computer University@Sea** and upgraded the room's computers. Depending on cruise length, classes range from "PC Basics" to "How to Create Your Own Home Page." There is a $5 fee. The classroom aboard *Symphony* has 25 computer work stations and hands-on lab sessions. Passengers may also schedule private instruction in their cabins. Rental laptop computers are available. A similar room has been added in the **Compass Room/Business Center** on the *Harmony.* Crystal was among the first to introduce e-mail service on its ships. Passengers have their own e-mail address, which they receive with their cruise ticket. There's a $3 charge for first inbound/outbound and $1 charge thereafter. Recently, Internet access was added to all cabins for $1.25 per minute with a ten-minute minimum. Personal website classes have also been added. Laptop computers are available for rental.

The **Hollywood Theatre,** with high-definition video projection and hearing-aid headsets, runs films each afternoon and evening. Films and other programs also are available on cabin televisions. For further diversion, pricey temptations with designer names are sold in the pretty shops on Avenue of the Stars.

Predinner options include cocktails in the **Vista Lounge** or wood-paneled **Avenue Saloon** (enlarged on the *Symphony*), or a classical concert by a harpist or trio. *Harmony's* new **Connoisseur Club,** adjacent to the Avenue Saloon, is a cigar and cognac lounge with private club atmosphere.

A cabaret show in **Club 2100** and two Broadway-style, full-scale, high-quality productions in the **Galaxy** show lounge are offered at night. Local entertainers may perform at ports of call. One evening is a masquerade party.

"Repertory Theatre at Sea," introduced on *Crystal Harmony* and *Crystal Symphony,* is delightful innovation for the ships' entertainment and enrichment program. The new feature includes well-known comedy and light drama performed by professional actors on every cruise. The diverse roster offers 91 scenes, excerpts, or reading from larger works as varied as Shakespeare, Edgar Allen Poe and Henry James.

The **Starlite Club,** *Symphony's* Art Deco replacement for *Harmony's* Club 2100 and disco, is one of the ship's most attractive lounges. It's used for the captain's cocktail and past-passenger parties, pre- and postdinner cocktails, and dancing. In late evening, it becomes the disco, depending on passenger preference during each sailing.

Galaxy Lounge, the main show lounge, offers an array of first-rate productions that might range from classical ballet to a Broadway revue. Crystal has its own production team, Gretchen Goertz and Kathy Orme, who create all the production shows and are very original and very good. The talented show troupe includes former dancers from the Bolshoi Ballet and London's West End. The shows usually have spectacular costumes—some valued at $10,000 apiece—and sets by award-winning designers.

Crystal Harmony boasts the only casino at sea operated by Caesars Palace of Las Vegas. The casino (enlarged on *Symphony*) has Roman columns at the entrance, and offers blackjack, slots, and roulette. Before sailing, passengers receive an application for credit at the casino.

Sports, Fitness, and Beauty   A lap pool has adjacent whirlpools, and an indoor/outdoor swimming pool has a swim-up bar and a retractable roof. There's generous sunning space on deck, plus Ping-Pong, shuffleboard, pool games, golf, and the only full-scale paddle tennis court at sea. Deck 7 offers a wraparound, unobstructed route for walking or jogging.

Harmony's new spa has seven treatment rooms for a wide range services. A new dry-float bed suite, for one person or a couple, contains an innovative sensory bed to create a feeling of weightlessness, ideal for "Aroma Spa" and other treatments. The new fitness center has a dedicated room for yoga and Pilates instruction, as well as other classes and personal training sessions; a separate gym has a larger selection of fitness equipment, aerobics and exercise classes, and separate steam rooms and saunas for men and women. Personalized cuisine programs are available. **Crystal Spa** looks to the Orient for inspiration, using the basic philosophy of Feng Shui, the art of placement. Body and facial treatments are pricey and include a two hour massage and facial for $239, one-and-a-half hour aroma stone therapy for $175, and an hour lime and ginger salt glow and back massage for $141.

In association with Callaway Golf, Crystal offers a program on some sailings that enables participants to play historic courses worldwide. Callaway equipment includes right-handed or left-handed clubs for men and women. A golf pro is generally on board offering lessons and tips.

Children's Facilities   Supervised youth programs are provided only when the line knows in advance that a sizable number of children will be aboard. Fantasia, a children's playroom, is more of an entertainment center, with video games for children ages 3–16. In-room baby-sitting can be arranged with crew members for $7 per hour.

Shore Excursions   Shore excursions are sold onboard, but some may be available in advance. Details are in the shore excursion brochure passengers receive before their cruise.

Crystal's efficient tenders have air-conditioning—a much-appreciated amenity. Crystal provides good maps and information about each port. The concierge and excursion desk are helpful in suggesting and arranging independent port programs.

Crystal continues to add interesting and ambitious excursions, particularly on Alaska cruises. They range from hiking, kayaking, rafting, and horseback riding to wildlife viewing. One exotic option is a 70-mile float-plane ride from Ketchikan to Anan Creek, where only 48 people each day are permitted to watch black and brown bears feeding from the creek. Another is a wildlife tour in dugout canoes on a Botswana safari offered on the occasional Africa cruises.

CRYSTAL SERENITY	**(Preview)**	
Registry: Bahamas	Length: 820 Feet	Beam: 105.6 Feet
Cabins: 550	Draft: 25 feet	Speed: 22 knots
Maximum Passengers:	Passenger Decks: 9	Elevators: 8
1,080	Crew: 655	Space Ratio: 63

The Ship   Crystal's third ship, built at Chantiers de l'Atlantique in France, made her debut in July 2003. The ship combines the best features of her sister ships with new ones added, including more dining venues, more penthouse suites, more cabins with verandas and butler service, more entertainment lounges, and more fitness options, among others. The new ship is also almost 20% roomier and is richly decorated in very good taste.

Some of the new features are a new-style, alternative Asian restaurant and sushi bar, which is the third evening alternative; a boardroom with a wine cellar for special dinners and wine tastings at an extra charge; a second paddle tennis court; a new learning center for creative and educational hands-on classes; and a club lounge off the atrium for Crystal Society members, said to be the first ship to have a room dedicated specifically for its past passengers.

The familiar favorites from other Crystal ships include a contemporary rendition of the **Palm Court,** a spacious observation lounge with potted palms set into hexagonal skylights, the clubby **Avenue Saloon,** and the **Connoisseurs Club.** The **Computer University@Sea** classroom is more than 50% larger than the facility on the other ships and has a 24-hour Internet center, plus a private area for one-on-one computer instruction. The spa and fitness center, approximately 40% larger than on her sister ships, are quite lavish. Located high up and aft, the two sections have separate entrances and very good soundproofing—hence the thumping of exercise machines does not intrude upon the serenity of the treatment room or the **Lido Café** below. *Crystal Serenity* has an even greater space ratio (63) than her sister ships, with 34% more public space and one deck more than *Crystal Symphony*. The ship was designed by an international team headed by well-known Swedish naval architect Robert Tillberg, who worked on Crystal's other two ships. Tillberg says *Serenity* is a sister, not a twin, to the other Crystal ships. His team was responsible for most of the public rooms and all passenger and staff accommodations. Other firms designed the specialty lounges and restaurants, spa, and retail shops.

Itineraries See Itinerary Index

Cabins Like *Crystal Symphony*, the ship has no inside cabins, and approximately 85% of the outside cabins and suites have private verandas. None have obstructed views, as the lifeboats are stowed below the cabin decks. One and a half decks of *Serenity* are devoted to 100 Penthouse accommodations with verandas (56% greater than on *Crystal Symphony*). Of those, the most lavish are four Crystal Penthouses, each measuring 1,345 square feet-or 37% larger than those on sister vessels.

In addition to the suites, there are 368 outside cabins with verandas and 82 outside staterooms with large picture windows. The eight wheelchair-accessible cabins are found in various categories: two penthouses, two veranda cabins, and four cabins with picture windows.

The deluxe cabins with veranda (Categories A & B) are virtually identical to the penthouse cabins with veranda (Category P), all being 269 square feet, but the former do not have butler service. The cabins are furnished with a comfortable sofa with a pop-up coffee table for in-cabin dining and queen or twins beds with two night tables and lamps rather than preferred reading lights. The entertainment center has a remote-control television and DVD player. The minibar and refrigerator are stocked with complimentary soft drinks and bottled water. All cabins have a dataport for laptop computer hook-up. The veranda is furnished with two white plastic chairs and a table; chaise lounges can be requested. The bathrooms have full-size tubs and showers and twin sinks.

Dining Passengers on *Crystal Serenity* have the choice of five evening dining venues: the main **Crystal Dining Room** (two seatings); **Tastes,** an indoor/outdoor poolside area for casual evening dining; and three specialty restaurants: **Prego** for Italian fare; a sushi bar, a first for Crystal; and **Silk Road** for pan-Asian cuisine, featuring eclectic creations by famous master chef and Crystal consultant Nobuyuki "Nobu" Matsuhisa, known for his innovative blend of classic Japanese dishes with Peruvian and European influences. Two of the alternative restaurants operate on a reservations-only basis for no extra charge. No reservations are needed for the sushi bar. In general, service seems better and a bit less harried in Silk Road, perhaps because the menu is less extensive.

Serenity's Prego, the Italian specialty restaurant, is entirely different in style than on her sister ships. It is a long two-level room located aft on the starboard side, decorated in white and gold with bas-relief urns filled with fruit on the bulkhead pilasters. The decorative panels show Tuscan city scenes using two-dimensional depictions: the front panel low in height and the rear one in full height, with indirect lighting between to brighten the settings and create depth. Two Italian favorites on the menu are pumpkin ravioli flavored with apricot and filet of Angus beef topped with gorgonzola.

Among the "Nobu" selections on Silk Road's pan-Asian menu are lobster with truffle yuzu sauce, black cod with miso, and chicken with teriyaki balsamic. The airy portside setting is executed in lime green and soft blue lighting, with the sushi bar at the entrance.

During the day, passengers have choices similar to the sister ships, plus some new ones. Permanent hot-food stations aft of the ship's second pool serve luncheon buffets with a theme. The ship also offers stylish versions of its popular **Bistro,** a coffee and wine bar for morning and afternoon snacks such as cold meats, salads, cheeses and desserts; the **Lido Café** for breakfast and lunch; the **Trident Grill** for casual, poolside lunches throughout the afternoon; an ice cream/frozen yogurt bar; and 24-hour room service.

Facilities and Activities   The **Galaxy Show Lounge** is the main entertainment venue for production shows and has improved sight lines and state-of-the-art sound and lighting systems. Several new shows are being offered. A second cabaret lounge, the **Stardust Club,** provides a venue for daytime activities, such as dance classes and wine tasting, as well as for evening dancing and cabaret entertainment.

The **Palm Court,** with floor-to-ceiling 270° panoramic windows, is a splendid, roomy top deck lounge in blue-gray with rattan seating and used for afternoon tea with a menu of about a dozen regular and herbal teas. It's also a good spot for evening dancing and entertainment, special events, and for simply enjoying the changing scenery. New room extensions offer unusual views of the glass-enclosed bridge wings one deck below. Other public facilities include the Crystal Plaza and Crystal Cove, the lobby area with a two-story atrium and **Crystal Piano Bar;** the **Avenue Saloon,** Crystal's clubby signature piano bar; the **Connoisseurs Club,** a cigar lounge for after-dinner drinks; **Caesars Palace at Sea** casino; **Pulse,** a disco/nightclub for late-night dancing and karaoke; **Hollywood Theater,** a cinema-conference center with theater-style seating for day and evening movies, lectures, and religious services; a staffed library with books and DVDs and comfy reading bays, a card room for Crystal's avid bridge players; and a gallery of high-end retail shops.

Passport to Music, Crystal's latest innovation which debuted on *Crystal Serenity,* is a partnership with Yamaha to offer a program of music instruction as part of the line's new **Creative Learning Institute** (CLI), perhaps the most original experiential and interactive "edutainment," as Crystal calls it, offered at sea. Music instruction is offered in **The Studio,** *Crystal Serenity's* handsome, high-tech facility created expressly for CLI programs. The Studio is outfitted with 15 portable grand-piano keyboards—Yamaha's newest state-of-the-art model—and supported with the Clavinova digital piano. Certified Yamaha music teachers are aboard to teach groups of 12 to 15 guests. Depending on the length of the cruise, the average curriculum offers six, 60-minute sessions; guests receive a certificate at the program's completion. A selection of software created by Yamaha enables guests to continue their musical journey at home.

Other Crystal partnerships for the Creative Learning Institute allow well-known organizations and schools, such as Berlitz, the Cleveland Clinic, Society of Wine Educators, Pepperdine University, Tai Chi Cultural Center, *BOOK* magazine, and Barns & Noble, among others, to bring experts aboard to share their knowledge in a classroom setting. The CLI curriculum offers progressive levels of instruction on a single subject or several one-class sessions of related topics. The main categories are Arts & Entertainment, ranging from Asian woodblock printing to acting workshops; Business & Technology, estate planning to fundraising to patent applications; Lifestyle, dealing with topics such as book clubs, candlemaking, or menu planning; Wellness, with health and fitness topics; and Wine & Food. The CLI is very popular—a kind of Elderhostel at sea. Thus, when the ship is full, it's wise to sign up early. There is no charge for any of the courses.

Sports, Fitness, and Beauty   The new ship's 8,500-square-foot spa and fitness centers are approximately 40% larger, with more treatment rooms and a larger gym and aerobics studio than her sister ships. In response to passenger feedback, the ship has a second paddle-tennis court, an outdoor lap pool flanked by two whirlpools, a second indoor/outdoor pool covered by a sliding roof, a full promenade around the exterior of the ship for walking, jogging and shuffleboard, and a sports deck with two golf driving ranges, putting green, and table tennis.

Children's Facilities   *Crystal Serenity* has a **Fantasia** children and teen center with video games, both small and located high up and aft of the Palm Court foyer. Programs apply when there are children aboard, which is not often, especially on longer cruises.

Postscript   The *Crystal Serenity* is an evolutionary ship for the line. The recent refurbishment of the *Crystal Harmony* reflects the newer ship's lead. Roominess is probably the most obvious improvement, enabling Crystal to expand where the line excels, such as in the expansive and spectacular Palm Court, the Creative Learning Institute, Computer Learning Center, standard cabin size, more accommodations with butler service, and additional seats in the alternative restaurants. All in all, *Crystal Serenity* appears to go a long way to keep Crystal Cruises ahead of any competition.

Cunard Line, Ltd.

6100 Blue Lagoon Drive, Suite 400, Miami, FL 33126
(305) 463-3000; (800) 7-CUNARD; fax (305) 463-3010
www.cunardline.com

Type of Ships   Large, traditional ship; deluxe megaship .

Type of Cruises   Wide range of destinations and durations, from warm-weather vacations to transatlantic summer service for affluent, demanding travelers; distinctively British pedigree.

Cruise Line's Strengths

- name recognition
- distinctive ships
- itineraries
- accommodations and service
- single cabins on older ships

Cruise Line's Shortcomings

- mixed products on *QE2*

Fellow Passengers   Cunard attracts a broad spectrum of passengers—from first-timers eager to visit many ports to veterans who seldom leave the ship—but most are affluent, mature, experienced travelers. Depending on time of year, the makeup is American and British, with large contingents of Europeans and repeaters. *QE2's* world cruises attract a crowd—affluent and older, taking long winter vacations—very different from that on other itineraries, when passengers may be all ages, incomes, and professions, many families with children, and people eager to take an ocean voyage on famous ships.

Recommended For   Those who enjoy a certain amount of formality and tradition, and are accustomed to luxury and willing to pay for it.

Not Recommended For   Those uncomfortable in elegance who prefer a casual or nonstop party atmosphere.

Cruise Areas and Seasons   Around the world in winter; transatlantic, April–December; Europe, spring–fall; Caribbean, South America, Orient, Russia, New England/Canada, Panama Canal, and Africa seasonally.

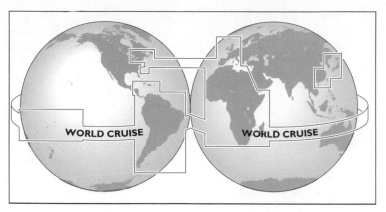

The Line Cunard Line, with a history stretching back to 1840, sailed into the new millennium with new owners, new management, and a new direction. But reinventing itself is nothing new for Cunard. With the postwar birth of the jet age and the demise of transatlantic passenger service, traditional steamship companies like Cunard had to adapt to the new realities to survive. Some converted their ships for modern cruising, some built new ships, and some bought or merged with other cruise lines. Cunard took all these steps and more.

During the era of the grand oceanliners, Cunard Lines was best known for its queens—the *Queen Mary* and *Queen Elizabeth*—which set the standard of elegance at sea for decades. *Queen Elizabeth 2* made her debut in 1969, when the future of transatlantic service was uncertain.

In 1971, Cunard was acquired by Trafalgar House, a multinational conglomerate headquartered in London, but doubts persisted throughout the decade on whether the line would survive. Having the only oceanliner on regular transatlantic service helped keep her going. In 1982, the *QE2* was pressed into Her Majesty's service during the Falkland Islands War. For Cunard and the *QE2*, it was a blessing in disguise, giving the ship a new lease on life with the publicity and a much-needed refurbishing by the British government before her return to passenger service.

In 1998, Cunard was sold to Carnival Corporation and merged briefly with Seabourn Cruise Line. The following year, Cunard's other ships were moved to other lines, leaving only the *QE2* and *Vistafjord*, renamed *Caronia* under the Cunard brand. The new owners spent millions renovating the *QE2* and *Caronia* and rebuilding Cunard with new ships.

The first, dubbed *Queen Mary 2*, and scheduled to be christened by Her Majesty Queen Elizabeth II on January 8, 2004, will be the "grandest and largest passenger liner ever built" according to Cunard, and will evoke the bygone era of seagoing luxury while representing the next era of oceanliner evolution, all to create "a new golden age of sea travel for those who missed the first." Her spa will be operated by the famed Canyon Ranch and her cuisine by the well-known New York-based French chef, Daniel Boulud. After the *Queen Mary 2* enters service, the *QE2* will be transferred to England to serve primarily the British market.

Cunard also has a 1,968-passenger, $400 million liner, *Queen Victoria,* under construction at the Italian shipyard Fincantieri, to be delivered in January 2005. The new 85,000-ton ship will be based in Southampton to serve the British market, part of Cunard's long-range strategy to target this growing cruise market. The new vessel will be built to Panamax standards so that she can be deployed on worldwide itineraries. The *Caronia* has been sold but will remain in Cunard service until November 2004.

THE FLEET	BUILT/RENOVATED	TONNAGE	PASSENGERS
Caronia	1973/1983/1994/1997/1999	24,492	665
Queen Elizabeth 2	1969/1987/1994/1996/1999	70,327	1,778
Queen Mary 2	2003	150,000	2,620
Queen Victoria	2003	85,000	1,968

Style   The legendary *Queen Elizabeth 2* has a style all her own. She is the only passenger ship sailing the Atlantic (until April 2004 when she is replaced by *QM2*) on a regular schedule, from April to December, with three levels of service. She also sails on an annual world cruise from January to April, and shorter cruises, usually in the Caribbean and Europe, fill the weeks between.

To many, the *QE2* has been the ultimate cruise experience, and the *QM2* is expected to follow in her wake, even more grand but more modern at the same time. A city at sea, she dwarfs all but the newest megaliners. The Queens are proud, elegant, formal, and as British as—well, yes—the queen. Throughout its history, Cunard has been an innovator in response to changing lifestyles. *QE2* was the first ship to have a full-fledged spa. Recognizing the impact of the electronic revolution, Cunard installed the first computer learning center, satellite editions of world news delivered daily to passengers, and a CD-ROM library on the *QE2*.

Distinctive Features   Year-round gentlemen hosts, computer learning centers, British nannies, driving range and putting green, florist, kennel, tuxedo rental, CD-ROM library, bookshop. *QE2:* 18-car garage. *QM2:* Canyon Ranch Spa, Royal Academy of Dramatic Art performance.

	HIGHEST	LOWEST	AVERAGE
PER DIEM	$762	$134	$458

Per diems are calculated from cruise line's nondiscounted *cruise-only* fares on standard accommodations and vary by season, cabin, and cruise areas.

Rates   Most port charges are included.

Special Fares and Discounts

- **Early-booking Discounts** Time-sensitive discounts called BEST fares range from 20% for booking and deposit a year in advance, 30% for payment in full a year in advance; 10% for Cunard World Club members; 15% for World Cruise Society members; and others when two or more cruises are combined.

- **Third/Fourth Passenger** Specific fares listed in chart in brochure.

- **Children's Fare** Children age 1 and 2 years travel free (plus port and custom charges). If the child is the second person, they are charged full published fare. If the child is the third or fourth person, third/fourth person fare applies.

- **Single Fares:** Single-occupancy cabins listed in brochure. Supplement for single occupancy of double cabin is 140–200%, depending on cabin.

Packages

- **Air/Sea** Yes.
- **Other Packages:** Yes.
- **Pre/Post** Yes.

Past Passengers   Cunard World Club, the past passenger program, has three levels: Bronze, two to four cruises; Silver, five to seven; and Gold, eight or more cruises or more than 100 days of cruising. Benefits include onboard credits and social events and discounts on published fares that may be combined with the 5% onboard discount. Onboard credits issued per cabin: Bronze, $100; Silver, $150; Gold, $200; may be applied toward purchase of goods and services, including spa treatments, shore excursions, and boutique items. Space-available upgrades offered to Silver and Gold members before sailing.

The Last Word   Cunard is known for luxury, but if you don't understand the differences in the levels of luxury, it can be somewhat misleading. For example, the popular image of the *QE2* is glamour, grand luxury, and haute cuisine. For those who buy the highest-priced suites and deluxe cabins and dine in the grills, this picture is accurate—but that's less than 30% of passengers. On her transatlantic run, *QE2* has three levels of service determined by cabin category, which is a polite way of saying three classes based on price. Each of three categories is assigned specific restaurants, and entry to the others is restricted accordingly. Try to dine or drink in the Queen's Grill or Bar, which is reserved for the top categories only, and you quickly learn what class distinction means. The redeeming factor is that all entertainment, sports, recreational facilities, and shops are available to everyone, regardless of class.

CUNARD LINE STANDARD FEATURES

Officers   British.

Staff   QE2, QM2, Dining, Cabin, Cruise/British and International. *Caronia*, Dining, Cabin, Cruise/Scandinavian and International.

Dining Facilities   QE2, single seating in five dining rooms for three meals, except Mauretania, two seatings on transatlantic; informal lido café for three meals and midnight buffet; snack bar. *Caronia,* one dining room, single seating for three meals. Casual indoor/outdoor café for breakfast and lunch buffets. Alternative Italian restaurant. QM2. Todd English restaurant, 3 dining rooms, pub and Lido.

Special Diets   Diabetic, low-calorie, low-cholesterol, low-salt, and vegetarian.

Room Service   24-hour room service. *Caronia,* full menus.

Dress Code   Formal/informal, for dining, depending on evening.

Cabin Amenities   Radio, direct-dial telephones, 20-channel television with CNN. Bathroom with tub and shower in mid and top categories. Refrigerators, walk-in closets, TV/VCR, terry robes, fruit baskets, nightly turn-down service and verandas. *Caronia,* VCR, hair dryer.

Electrical Outlets   220 AC.

Wheelchair Access   QE2, ramps; four cabins; bathtubs with grab bars, wide doors, low sills. *Caronia,* four cabins. QM2, 30.

Recreation and Entertainment   Casino, cabaret, revues. Life-enrichment seminars, guest lectures. Lounges, bars, disco, bingo, dance lessons, gentlemen hosts, computer learning center.

Sports and Other Activities   Indoor/outdoor pools, deck sports, golf putting and driving net, jogging track, paddle tennis, Ping-Pong. *Caronia,* golf simulator.

Beauty and Fitness   Spa, fitness center, gym, barber/beauty salon, exercise class. See text for more details. *Caronia,* saunas, walking/jogging deck.

Other Facilities   Cinema/theater, launderette, laundry/dry cleaning service, library, bookshop, shops, hospital. QE2, tuxedo rental shop, foreign exchange; Harrods; 18-car garage (transatlantic only), florist, board room, synagogue, kennel (transatlantic); *Caronia,* concierge, bookstore.

Children's Facilities   QE2, teen center, video, supervised children's playrooms, nursery, nannies, baby-sitting; special children's evening meal; served daily in the Lido at 5:30 p.m. *Caronia,* counselors seasonally.

Theme Cruises   Year-round selection.

Smoking   Designated areas in public rooms.

Cunard Suggested Tipping   QE2, $11–$13 per day added to bill, depending on cabin category; *Caronia,* $7 per day. Both ships include 15% gratuity for bar and salon services. Gratuities included in fare for cruises of 90 days or more. QM2, t.b.a.

Credit Cards   For cruise payment and on-board charges: American Express, Diners Club, Discover, MasterCard, Visa.

QUEEN ELIZABETH 2	QUALITY 7	VALUE C
Registry: Great Britain	Length: 963 feet	Beam: 105 feet
Cabins: 950	Draft: 32 feet	Speed: 28.5 knots
Maximum Passengers:	Passenger Decks: 12	Elevators: 13
1,791	Crew: 921	Space Ratio: 36

The Ship   *Queen Elizabeth 2,* Cunard's flagship, is the lone survivor of a long, rich history of ocean travel. After extensive facelifts in 1995, 1996, and 1999, her new look emphasizes her uniqueness: a grand oceanliner with the flexibility to provide a modern cruise experience.

Renovations included major remodeling of most public areas. Interiors were created by John McNeece, Britain's leading cruise-ship interior designer, and MET Studio, an architectural and design firm that worked with James Gardner, the *QE2's* original designer. They improved passenger flow and added new décor, facilities, and ambience that address today's lifestyle while retaining the ship's distinctive character. By integrating *QE2* and Cunard history into the décor, the designers created a floating museum named Heritage Trail as well as a ship as modern as the 21st century. Escorted tours of the 24 exhibits underscore her traditions.

Public rooms are on three decks—Quarter, Upper, and Boat—with new links and stairways to let traffic flow naturally and to reflect passengers' activities at different times of day. Promenades echo the earlier Queens. Passengers enter the *QE2* through the Midships Lobby, a two-story atrium on Deck 2 elegantly decorated in mulberry and green against honey-colored cherry wood trimmed in bronze, where a harpist is usually in residence during embarkation. A four-part mural by Peter Sutton depicting the history of Cunard and the *QE2* covers the atrium's circular walls. The bell from the first Queen Elizabeth and the Spirit of Atlantic statuette are displayed.

Itineraries   See Itinerary Index.

Cabins   Comfortable and convenient, all cabins were refurbished, their bathrooms retiled and given new fixtures in recent renovations, and two new Grand suites (QS category), including one wheelchair-accessible, and another enlarged, and two cabins in Princess Grill were added.

The *QE2's* complex arrangement of cabin categories is different for the world cruise and the transatlantic service. Because dining assignments are determined by cabin category, it's important to understand precisely what you're buying. In principle, when you pay more, you get more.

The top 6 among 23 categories—plus the 4 named suites—dine in the Queen's Grill. The next group, ultradeluxe, is split between the Princess and Britannia Grills. Assignments continue on down the line.

Categories don't completely reflect the variety of configurations. The top two decks, Signal and Sun Boat, have the largest, most luxurious suites with verandas and penthouse service, which includes butlers whose duties range from planning parties to arranging priority disembarkation and customs preclearance. Ultradeluxe cabins are amidships on Sun Deck, Deck 1, and Deck 2; other categories are fore and aft on Decks 2 and 3 as well as the two lower decks.

All cabins have television with 24-hour CNN, information, and movies. Cabins in grill and deluxe class have refrigerators, VCRs, and bathrooms with tub and shower; premium class has bathrooms with shower only. Bathrooms of 55 penthouse suites are in marble. *QE2* has a total of 136 single cabins covering five categories.

Specifications   97 single and 222 double inside cabins; 39 singles and 592 doubles outside; 700 with 2 lower beds. 7 ultraluxury suites. Some wheelchair-accessible cabins available. Standard dimensions not available.

Dining   Four of the dining rooms have single seating for each meal. The **Mauretania Restaurant** has an early and a late seating. Named for an early Cunard ship, this restaurant has vintage photographs and a 1907 telegraph from the vessel. As the centerpiece, *White Horses,* a sculpture by Althea Wynne, depicts four horses riding waves, emblematic of the British sailors' term for whitecaps. At the entrance is a 15-foot model of the *Mauretania* (one of the Heritage Trail's largest items) on display. On transatlantic service, this restaurant has two seatings.

The **Caronia Restaurant,** named for another Cunard ship of legendary opulence, got a complete makeover in the most recent renovations and is now one of the ship's most attractive rooms. In the style of a English country house, it has rich mahogany-paneled walls and columns and a white-painted ceiling with Murano glass chandeliers in a spreading leaf design. On the back wall behind the captain's table is a lovely Italian hill-country scene. It has a new stereo system and air conditioning intended to eliminate drafts.

The **Princess and Britannia Grills** have their own separate entrances from the **Crystal Bar.** The latter's name honors Cunard's first ship, *Britannia,* a model of which is displayed in the Heritage Trail group entitled "Samuel Cunard and the Paddle Steamers." The **Queen's Grill** is reserved for passengers booked in Queen's Grill class only. Among its latest renovations are etched glass doors and a completely new galley.

Menus are identical in all restaurants, except the Queen's Grill, where cuisine is meant to be of the highest gourmet standard and patrons enjoy tableside preparations. The rooms' sizes and ambience differ more than the food. Fare includes hors d'oeuvres, three soups, sorbet, five entrées, two salads, four or five desserts, cheese, ice cream, sherbet, and fruit. A spa menu is available.

The **Lido** is the ship's most obvious bow to current lifestyles. It was transformed into a buffet-style restaurant, providing an informal setting for breakfast, lunch, dinner, and the midnight buffet. Coffee and drinks are served all day. From our experience, with the exception of the Queens Grill, the food—and certainly the service—are the best aboard, surpassing even the Princess Grill. Floor-to-ceiling windows open to the outside deck, making the room light and airy. White, beige, and mint décor is set off by two murals by Italian artist Giancarlo Impiglia depicting the *QE2* cruise experience. Stairs lead from the café to the Deck 1 lido area and the **Pavilion** bar and grill.

Cunard recently engaged four-star chef, Daniel Boulud, one of New York's most creative French masters with three award-winning restaurants, to create a new repertoire for the line, starting with the *QE2's* 2003 world cruise. Boulud plans to draw from cooking traditions of the 35 ports at the ship will visit in creating his new dishes.

Service   Officers are British, but most hotel and cabin staff are European, many of them women. The level of dining room service rises with the dining room and price. In grill class, service is meant to be luxurious. For other passengers, it's, well, British. Most passengers say it's friendly and attentive. Unless you're in a top suite, do not expect cabin and dining service will be any different or better than most mainstream ships.

Facilities and Activities   Varied lounges and public rooms provide an array of activities. A day could begin with exercise in the fitness center or jogging, progress to a lesson in the computer center, and move to a seminar or workshop in the theater. The latter also functions as a lecture hall, conference room, and cinema. There is also a business center. Passengers can send and receive e-mail and faxes at more than a dozen computer stations. The Life Enrichment Program offers seminars, workshops, and lectures by experts. Bingo, horse racing, arts and crafts, and beauty demonstrations are available. Theme cruises add such attractions as jazz or classical concerts.

The *QE2's* is the only library at sea with a full-time professional librarian. Now doubled in size with a book shop, it has more than 6,000 books, hundreds of videos, and a multimedia reference library with material on CD-ROM. Red leather seats and desks are provided, but the library is so popular there's often no place to sit.

Lifestyle updates were central to the ship's renovations as evidenced in the Golden Lion, a large, classic English pub decorated in mahogany and plaid. It's the ship's informal social center with an upright piano, television, karaoke, and darts. Many lagers, stouts, and draught beers, plus local brews in port, are served. The classy **Grand Lounge** showroom has a fully equipped curtained stage, dance floor, a new audio system and improved sight lines. The latest addition brings fledgling Broadway and West End shows for development aboard ship. Passengers may attend rehearsals, workshops, and improvisation sessions performed by the cast that may appear on opening night.

The popular **Yacht Club,** aft, with handsome nautical décor and America's Cup memorabilia, is a lounge and bar by day and a sophisticated nightclub in the evening. The **Chart Room** on Quarter Deck showcases Cunard's nautical antiques. A piano from the *Queen Mary* plays for cocktails and after dinner. A bust of Queen Elizabeth II decorates the blue and gold **Queen's Room,** which has retained its dignified best with royal blue carpeting interwoven with gold Tudor roses. The royal connection is showcased in exhibits of the Queen's Standards, presented to the ship by Queen Elizabeth.

The room is the setting for afternoon tea with live music and evening ballroom dancing. (Gentlemen who forget their formal attire may visit the *QE2* tuxedo rental shop, and unescorted ladies may dance with gentlemen hosts.) Lounges offer varied dance music and celebrity performers, who in the past have included Bill Cosby, Peter Duchin and his orchestra, and Dick Clark, among others.

Sports, Fitness, and Beauty   The ship has indoor and outdoor pools. Deck sports include golf (putting and driving area), shuffleboard, Ping-Pong, and jogging on a track. Exercise classes are available daily in the fitness center and gym on Deck 7. The European-style spa on Deck 6 offers a sauna, massage, and beauty and body treatments. Steiner of London operates the barber shop and beauty salon on Deck 1. Among her extensive facilities, the *QE2* has one of the largest, best-equipped hospitals afloat.

Children's Facilities   **Club 2000** teen center is on Quarter Deck, and a supervised children's playroom and nursery are available high up on Sun Deck.

Shore Excursions   Booklets sent to passengers are cruise-specific, with thumbnail sketches of each port of call.

CARONIA	QUALITY 7	VALUE C
Registry: Great Britain	Length: 627 feet	Beam: 82 feet
Cabins: 375	Draft: 27 feet	Speed: 20 knots
Maximum Passengers:	Passenger Decks: 9	Elevators: 6
665	Crew: 379	Space Ratio: 35

The Ship   A spacious vessel designed for long cruises and gracious living, the *Caronia* (formerly *Vistafjord*) was launched by the now-vanished Norwegian American Cruises in 1973 and acquired by Cunard in 1983. She's a classic luxury liner, with the tasteful look of quiet grace and beautiful, distinctive interiors created when expensive hardwoods were used lavishly.

The ship is known for excellent European-style service and friendly officers and crew. Its consistent quality attracts discerning, well-heeled passengers, among them a high number of repeaters. Traditionally, Britons predominate, but there are Americans and other Europeans aboard, creating a cosmopolitan ambience.

A 1994 renovation gave *Caronia* 12 luxurious suites, a cozy Italian restaurant, a new public address system, a new purser's office with interactive scan map to help you find your way, and other improvements. Further updates in 1999 added a ten-station computer center and bookstore and gave the ship a more British essence with new British crew, Cunard colors, and some new names, such as the North Cape Bar remade into the paneled **White Star Bar,** and the new shopping area named Regency Shops.

In May 2002, the ship was transferred to her new home port of Southampton and became even more geared to British passengers with its onboard enrichment and entertainment programs; the currency is pounds sterling. *Caronia* was sold in 2003 but will remain in Cunard service until November 2004.

Itineraries See Itinerary Index.

Cabins *Caronia's* large, tastefully decorated cabins encompass 16 categories and 10 configurations. Some with connecting doors can combine to create a two-room suite with separate sitting area. Most cabins have twin beds (some convert to king), one or two chairs and a cocktail table, large mirrored dresser with locking drawers, minifridge, and generous closets. The ship has a large number of singles.

All cabins have television, radio, and soundproof walls and are equipped with safes, refrigerators, hair dryers, and VCRs. Telephones have caller recognition, a beeper system for calling stewards, an automatic wake-up-call system, and a 911 call button for emergencies. All cabins have new bathrooms, and 90% of them have tubs as well as showers. Terry robes are supplied, and your basket of fresh fruit is replenished daily.

Each of the 12 deluxe suites on the Bridge Deck has a private balcony. Two of the suites are duplexes with huge living rooms, as well as private Jacuzzis, saunas, and exercise rooms. Four cabins on the main and upper decks accommodate handicapped passengers. Cabins are attended by Scandinavian stewardesses who are as amiable as they are capable.

Specifications 19 singles and 35 double inside cabins; 54 single and 263 double outside; 12 suites, 11 with private balcony. Standard dimensions, 175 square feet. 73 single cabins. 4 for disabled.

Dining The bright, cheerful dining room, now called the **Franconia** after a former Cunard ship, holds all passengers at one seating. All meals have open seating. The sophisticated international cuisine consistently receives high marks from passengers for variety, preparation, and presentation. The highest-quality products—fresh when possible—are used. Fish is a feature; delicate pastries, a highlight. A typical menu has three appetizers, two soups, two salads, four entrées, four desserts plus a diabetic dessert, cheese, and fruit. Vegetarian and spa menus are available. American and European wines are stocked.

Waiters are excellent, but, surprisingly, no busboys help them. This may result in slow service, but on this type of ship, service is never rushed. Dining is a main activity of the day and is meant to be leisurely.

The popular, glass-enclosed **Lido Café** serves early-morning coffee and freshly baked rolls, as well as buffet breakfast and lunch, and there's an ice cream parlor. Midday buffets, frequently themed, feature hot and cold dishes, hot dogs, and hamburgers. **Tivoli,** an alternative restaurant serving fine Italian cuisine, is located on the top level of **Club Piccadilly,** a bilevel lounge and nightclub; outdoor seating under awnings was added recently. In oceanliner tradition, hot bouillon is served on deck daily at

11 a.m. Afternoon tea is offered in the ballroom, often with a fashion show, and at the Lido Café. A late snack is laid out at 11 p.m. in the dining room. Around-the-clock room service offers selections from dining room menus during meal hours and light fare at other times.

Facilities and Activities　The ship offers full days of activities. Gentlemen hosts are available for dance classes and afternoon teas, as well as for dining and ballroom dancing. Bridge instructors organize games. Other options include arts and crafts sessions, bingo, chess, Scrabble, backgammon, discussions on wines, astrology sessions, daily lectures by guest experts, a bridge tour, and recorded music on your cabin radio and television. The residential-style library, furnished with leather seats, has a video library, a CD-ROM search system, and a small business center with a credit card-operated fax machine, and a new computer learning center where classes are offered. The theater, near the library, shows current films or hosts guest lecturers.

Evening entertainment belies *Caronia's* somewhat staid image. The ballroom is the main showroom; nightly entertainment might be a Broadway-style revue or variety show, an updated version of a Gilbert and Sullivan operetta, or a guest performer. One night may bring a presentation of sea chanteys by the crew; another, a folkloric group from the port of call. The room's dance floor draws a crowd when big band music plays before dinner and after the show. A small casino next door offers blackjack and slot machines.

On the same deck, the **Garden Lounge** frequently hosts classical concerts, special parties, and dancing. The room has been refurbished to enhance its garden ambience. One flight up, the cozy Club Piccadilly, decorated in elegant black, red, and beige, offers piano music at noon, the ship's trio at cocktails, and a nightly cabaret. After the show, it becomes the disco.

Sports, Fitness, and Beauty　*Caronia* has one outdoor and one indoor swimming pool, Jacuzzis, shuffleboard, Ping-Pong, and a golf putting area. A wraparound deck invites walking and jogging (seven laps per mile), and the Sports Deck was recently roofed to expand activities. The spa organizes daily exercises. The beauty salon and barber shop offer mud wraps, massage, and other beauty treatments.

QUEEN MARY 2	**(Preview)**	
Registry: Great Britain	Length: 1,132 feet	Beam: 135 feet
Cabins: 1,310	Draft: 32 feet	Speed: 30 knots
Maximum Passengers:	Passengers Decks: 17	Elevators: 22
3,090	Crew: 1,253	Space Ratio: NA

The Ship The *Queen Mary 2* is not only the biggest, widest, longest, and most expensive ship ever built—her debut is expected to give birth to a new Cunard cruise line.

The oceanliner is meant to be reminiscent of great transatlantic steamships and, in Cunard's words, "relaunch the golden age of travel for those who missed the first one." However, the interiors will have a contemporary rather than a classic liner look, designed as an oceanliner for the 21st century and intended to appeal to baby boomers who Cunard sees as the ship's main market.

The *QM2*, costing upward of $800 million and constructed at Alstom Chantiers de l'Atlantique in Saint-Nazaire, France, is expected to be christened by Her Majesty Queen Elizabeth II on January 8, 2004. The 150,000-ton vessel's slick hull, with a height of 237 feet from keel to funnel top, travels at speeds of up to 30 knots, making her one of the fastest cruise ships and able to undertake unusual itineraries. She can carry up to 3,090 passengers in a "quasi-class system" similar to that on *QE2*, with the cabin category determining restaurant assignments.

QM2 has the first and only spa at sea operated by the world-famous Canyon Ranch health resorts; the world's first and only planetarium at sea; the largest ballroom at sea; the largest library at sea; the largest wine cellar at sea; and ten different dining venues, including the first and only shipboard restaurant by popular American chef Todd English.

There are 14 lounges and bars, a two-story theater, a casino, five indoor and outdoor swimming pools including a children's pool, an adults-only pool, another pool with a magrodome, hot tubs, boutiques, a pet kennel, and a children's facility, complete with British nannies. The learning center has guests lecturers from Oxford University. The ship's $5 million art collection includes over 300 original works of art.

The cuisine has been created by Daniel Boulud, New York's award-winning French chef famed for his originality. A floating microbrewery produces Cunard-brand beer. On departing the ship, passengers have four lounges—**Kensington, Chelsea, Knightsbridge,** and **Belgravia**—named for London's best-known upscale neighborhoods and tube stops; those in wheelchairs are transferred to tenders or docks by a hydraulic platform.

QM2 is following a similar pattern as the *QE2*, sailing on regularly scheduled transatlantic crossings between New York and Southampton from Spring to December and longer worldwide cruises at other times. Cunard has planned four maiden voyages: The first departs on January 12, 2004 from Southampton to Ft. Lauderdale and was sold out months in advance; the second, on January 31, is the initial voyage from the U.S. to the Caribbean. The others mark the maiden voyages of transatlantic service from Southampton on April 16 and from New York on April 25—an historic occasion for Cunard, as both *QE2* and *QM2* will depart

New York together, marking the first time two Cunard Queens have been berthed in the port together since March 1940.

Cabins   The three main cabin categories correspond to the ship's dining rooms—Britannia, Princess, and Queen. Britannia offers 17 cabin levels ranging from standard (194 square feet) to deluxe (248 square feet). Princess accommodations are 381-square-foot junior suites, while Queen encompass five levels of suites, ranging from 506 square feet to two-story Grand Duplex apartments at 2,249 square feet each.

Seventy-five percent of the 1,310 cabins have eight-foot-deep balconies. Thirty cabins for disabled passengers are available in various categories. All accommodations have interactive TV with multilanguage film and music channels, direct-dial phone, hair dryer, 110/220 volt outlets, and bathroom with tub and/or shower.

The five duplex apartments (Balmoral, Windsor, Holyrood, Buckingham, and Sandringham suites) are two stories high and cover more than 1,650 square feet. They have two-story glass walls overlooking the ship's stern, providing great sea views. The lavish suites have their own exercise area, veranda, two full bathrooms with tub and shower, a walk-in closet, a separate sitting area and refrigerator. Occupants in duplex apartments will be pampered by butler service and room-service dining prepared by chefs from the Queen's Grill. Apartments can be connected to a penthouse to create a 2,220-square-foot suite.

Four deluxe penthouses (Queen Mary, Queen Anne, Queen Elizabeth and Queen Victoria suites) overlooking the ship's bow measure between 861 and 1,076 square feet. Each features a marble bathroom with tub and shower, walk-in closet, refrigerator, separate dining area, and sitting area with large picture windows.

Suite amenities include two TVs, an entertainment system, a bon voyage bottle of champagne, personalized stationery, a bar with selected spirits or wine and soft drinks, plush terry cloth bathrobes, slippers, and daily fresh fruit and predinner canapés. Penthouses can also be connected with two of the suites to create more than 5,000 square feet of living space. In addition to dining at the Queen's Grill restaurant, suite passengers have an exclusive lounge for afternoon tea, cocktails, and an after-dinner aperitif. Several suites have a private elevator entrance.

Specifications   Duplex apartments, 5; deluxe penthouses, 4; penthouses, 6; suites, 82; outside standards with veranda, 782; outside standards, 138; inside standards with atrium view, 12; inside standards, 281. 30 wheelchair accessible.

Dining   Seating in the three main restaurants correspond to the level of the passenger's accommodation. All include menu selections created by French chef Daniel Boulud. The elegant **Queen's Grill** is reserved exclusively for luxury penthouses, duplexes, and suites, and the **Princess Grill** for passengers in junior suites. Both have single-seating dining and operate much like an upscale à la carte restaurant.

The **Britannia Restaurant** accommodates all other cabin categories with 1,347 seats and offers open seating for breakfast and lunch and two seatings for dinner. The three-deck-high room spans the width of the ship, with a dramatic central staircase meant to recall the grand dining rooms of past Cunard liners.

Another vast space is the **King's Court,** the lido restaurant serving buffet breakfast and lunch and four casual dining alternatives for dinner. At lunch, there are regional specialties and carved meats. In the evening, King's Court is transformed into sit-down restaurants: **La Piazza** for Italian specialties, **Lotus** offering Chinese and Asian cuisine, the **Carvery** serving carved meats, and the **Chef's Galley** for chef's selections. Here, passengers can watch and learn the preparation of their meal from Cunard or guest chefs sponsored by *Gourmet* magazine.

Other dining options include Todd English, featuring the innovative Mediterranean cuisine of its renowned namesake, open for lunch and dinner with indoor/outdoor seating overlooking the aft pool terrace. Reservations are required, but there is no charge. The **Golden Lion** and **Boardwalk Grill** are casual venues for fast food or pub grub, offering hot dogs, hamburgers, and other grills, a daily specialty, soups, and salads. Afternoon tea is served in the colonial-style **Winter Garden.**

Facilities   The **Royal Court Theatre,** the main showroom, has tiered seating for 1,100 passengers, concert hall acoustics, a hydraulic proscenium stage, and sophisticated lighting and sound equipment. The theater is the venue for full-scale, West End– or Broadway-type productions and other entertainers. The **Empire Casino** offers blackjack, roulette, and slot machines. The **Queen's Room** is the ballroom.

Illuminations, the first-of-its-kind planetarium-at-sea, has stadium-type seating where passengers are entertained with celestial shows, movies, lectures and other programs. Movies are also shown al fresco near the funnel high atop the ship.

ConneXions, the ship's enrichment program, has seven function rooms to use as classrooms or meeting rooms; they can be separated or joined to adjust for class sizes. The programs, ranging from wine appreciation and cooking to seamanship and navigation, are taught by expert guest instructors, some from Oxford University. Computer classes and business services are also available. The facility has the latest electronic equipment for passengers to send/receive email or access the Internet.

Also falling under ConneXions are the plays and workshops being conducted by England's famous Royal Academy of Dramatic Art, which supplies the actors and conducts the workshops.

The *QM2's* 8,000-volume library and the **QM2 Bookshop,** similar to those on the *QE2,* are furnished with comfortable leather sofas and armchairs and directed by full-time librarians. The library also has books on CD-ROM. Mayfair Shops, a shopping gallery, offer a myriad of items from sundries to fine leather goods and formal wear for sale and rental. Also in this area is the elegant **Champagne Bar,** created by the famous champagne house Veuve Clicquot Ponsardin, its first and only venture on a cruise line. In addition to a variety of champagne, the bar has a menu including caviar and foie gras.

Sports, Fitness and Beauty   The *QM2* boasts the largest spa afloat designed by the famous Canyon Ranch, which also operate it. The **Canyon Ranch SpaClub,** covering 20,000 square feet on two decks, has a staff of 51 to provide treatments and lead classes in yoga and tai chi as well as health-related workshops. The spa has 24 treatment rooms, a thalassotherapy pool, whirlpool, saunas, reflexology, an aromatic steam room, a gym with state-of-the-art equipment, a juice bar, and men's and women's locker rooms.

QUEEN VICTORIA	**(Preview)**	
Registry: Great Britain	Length: 951 feet	Beam: 105.8 feet
Cabins: 924	Draft: 24 feet	Speed: 22 knots
Maximum Passengers:	Passenger Decks: 13	Elevators: 14
1848	Crew: NA	Space Ratio: NA

The Ship   Cunard has a 1,968-passenger, $400 million liner under construction at the Italian shipyard Fincantieri, scheduled for delivery in January 2005, only one year after the launch of the *Queen Mary 2.* The new, 85,000-ton ship, to be based in Southampton to serve the British market, is part of Cunard's long-term strategy to target the growing British cruise market. Earlier repositioning of *Caronia* to Southampton was another move to in that direction. The new ship is tentatively planned to cruise from Southampton to the Mediterranean, Canaries, Northern Europe, and the Caribbean.

The *Queen Victoria,* one of the Vision-class ships slated originally for Holland America, is being built to Panamax standards so it can be deployed on worldwide itineraries. In the Cunard tradition, it will have a covered promenade deck encircling the entire ship, a forward observation lounge, and a large lido pool with a retractable roof. Exterior glass elevators will run ten decks on both sides of the vessel.

The ship will have a wide range of accommodations, and 67% of the outside cabins and suites have balconies. The onboard entertainment and lecture program will be designed for British passengers, and the onboard currency will be pounds sterling. Like *QE2* and *QM2,* the liner will have a **Queen's Grill** that will have single-seating, gourmet dining for passengers in upper-level cabins.

The ship will be powered by low-emission, diesel-electric motors and employ the Azipod propulsion system for greater maneuverability, enhanced operating efficiencies, and environmental benefits.

Delta Queen Steamboat Company

Robin Street Wharf, 1380 Port of New Orleans Place
New Orleans, LA 70130-1890
(504) 586-0631; (800) 543-1949; fax (504) 585-0630
www.deltaqueen.com

Type of Ships   Classic steamboats.

Type of Cruises   River cruises through America's heartland.

Cruise Line's Strengths

- the steamboats
- the setting
- turn-of-the-19th-century atmosphere

Cruise Line's Shortcomings

- limited shipboard activities
- small cabins on the Delta Queen

Fellow Passengers   Mix of ages, nationalities, families, couples, singles, and grandparents traveling with grandchildren. Group is likely to be cosmopolitan: Norwegians, Dutch, British, Germans, Canadians, and Americans. Average age is 62 years; it drops on shorter trips, which usually include more families. Most passengers are retired, with annual incomes over $35,000. There are young and middle-aged honeymooners and repeaters who have sailed on the steamboats many times. A surprising number of passengers live near the river and cruise to enjoy it in a different way. Fifty-five percent have been to Alaska; about 70% have cruised on an upscale, traditional line.

Recommended For   Anyone interested in American history, culture, and literature or just good, old-fashioned values regardless of age. Those who enjoy the relaxed pace and shoreline visibility that river cruises offer. Dixieland jazz fans. Anyone uneasy about ocean voyages or straying far from home.

Not Recommended For   Travelers expecting European-style elegance, elaborate cuisine, and polished service. Those who don't enjoy a certain amount of hokum. Families with young children (for lack of children's facilities). Those requiring large-ship amenities, such as cabin television.

Cruise Areas and Seasons Mississippi, Atchafalaya and Red (Louisiana), Cumberland, Tennessee, Ohio, Kanawha (West Virginia) rivers; intracoastal waterways of Louisiana and Texas year-round.

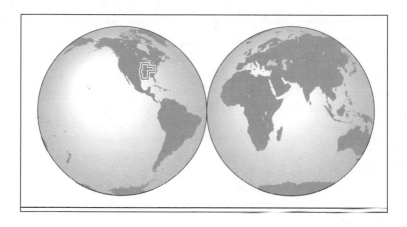

The Line The Delta Queen Steamboat Company is the oldest line of American-flagged ships. Of the six authentic, steam-powered paddle wheelers in the United States, Delta Queen's are the only ones offering overnight accommodations and traveling the length of inland rivers.

The forerunner of the cruise line was founded in 1890 by Capt. Gordon C. Greene, who pioneered riverboat vacations, and his wife, Mary, also an accomplished river pilot and steamboat captain. The couple and their sons owned and operated 28 steamers over the years. After World War II, Tom Greene purchased the *Delta Queen* in California, remodeled her, and inaugurated her with Mississippi River cruises in 1948. In 1973, new owners renamed the line Delta Queen Steamboat Company and added the *Mississippi Queen,* which is twice as large as her sister steamer; in 1995, they added the *American Queen,* which was the largest steamboat ever built.

Within a short time after the tragedy of September 11, American Classic Voyages, the owner of Delta Queen Steamship Company, as well as American Hawaii Cruises, United States Lines, and Delta Queen Coastal Voyages, declared bankruptcy. Then in May 2002, the Delaware North Company of Buffalo, New York, a privately-held hospitality and food service group of companies with annual revenues of $1.6 billion, bought three steamboats—*Delta Queen, Mississippi Queen,* and *American Queen*—of the Delta Queen Steamboat Company at auction for $80 million. All three ships were back in service before the year's end, along with 98% of the boats' staff and many members of the former management.

THE FLEET	BUILT/RENOVATED	TONNAGE	PASSENGERS
American Queen	1995	3,707	436
Delta Queen	1927/1984/1998	3,360	174
Mississippi Queen	1976/1996	3,364	416

Style   A cruise on one of the Queens differs from an ocean voyage. *Delta Queen* calls the experience "Steamboatin'," a unique visit with the American soul and character. While floating down the Mississippi on one of these "wedding cakes" at a lazy nine miles per hour, visions of Huck Finn and Tom Sawyer are sure to arise—as they have for thousands of folks who have come before you. Nostalgia is thick when a morning mist hangs over the shoreline and the only sounds are the low hum of engines and the red paddle wheel churning the river's muddy water. Mark Twain wrote that the Mississippi at morning has a "haunting sense of loneliness, isolation, remoteness from the worry and bustle of the world. The dawn creeps in stealthily, the tranquillity is profound and infinitely satisfying."

After breakfast, the cruise "Riverlorian" relates colorful bits of river history. Later, your boat, festooned in red, white, and blue flags, arrives in a port with its calliope (an organlike instrument with whistles sounded by steam or compressed air) in full song. Most likely, you'll be met by the mayor and other townfolk, who personally offer passengers directions. It's an experience not likely found on standard cruises.

Distinctive Features   Paddle wheel, calliope, *Delta Queen's* authentic interiors, Dixieland jazz, Southern specialties, immersion in 19th-century life on the Mississippi.

	HIGHEST	LOWEST	AVERAGE
PER DIEM	$671	$232	$407

Per diems are calculated from cruise line's nondiscounted *cruise-only* fares on standard accommodations and vary by season, cabin, and cruise areas.

Rates   Port charges included.

Special Fares and Discounts   Early-booking bonus available on most cruises.

- **Children's Fares**   One child age 16 or younger cruises free in some cabins on the *Mississippi Queen* when sharing a cabin with two full-fare adults.
- **Single Supplement**   150–200%, depending on vessel and cabin category.

Packages
- **Air/Sea**   Yes.
- **Others**   Theme cruises, such as Kentucky Derby.

- **Pre/Post** Packages in New Orleans, Memphis, St. Louis, Minneapolis/St. Paul, and other main ports.

- **3rd/4th** An adult sharing accommodations with two full-fare adults on the *Mississippi Queen* and *American Queen* will only be charged $100 per night.

Past Passengers Members of the Paddlewheel Steamboat Society of America receive a newsletter, champagne reception aboard ship, advance notice of schedules, and discounts in the ships' gift shops.

The Last Word For most passengers, the real destination of these cruises is the steamboats. Most people love this homespun, star-spangled slice of Americana, from the Huck Finn picnic to the foot-stomping Dixieland jazz. The riverboats have universal appeal and transcend age barriers. Aboard a recent cruise was an under-40 couple with sons 8 and 12 years old. The boys got a daily lesson in American history on the boat and in ports, but they also enjoyed romping on the Mississippi shoreline, à la Huck Finn. Then, one night in the lounge, the older boy was seen playing chess with a 96-year-old passenger.

DELTA QUEEN STANDARD FEATURES

Officers American.

Staff Dining, Cabin, Cruise/American.

Dining Facilities One dining room with two seatings for dinner; three meals daily, plus tea and moonlight buffet; open seating breakfast and lunch.

Special Diets Diabetic, kosher, low-calorie/cholesterol, and low-salt. Request with cruise reservations. Vegetarian and heart-healthy selections on menus.

Room Service Continental breakfast served in cabins on request.

Dress Code Casual but neat during the day; fashionable dress for evening—jacket and tie for men, dress or stylish suit for women.

Cabin Amenities Some cabins with brass beds, Tiffany-style windows, veranda, sitting area, baths with shower, writing area.

Electrical Outlets 110 AC.

Wheelchair Access Companion recommended. See text. Some cabins on *Mississippi Queen* and *American Queen*.

Recreation and Entertainment Jazz, big bands, cabaret, and Broadway stage revues in lounges; riverboat shows; bridge; bingo; calliope concerts; crafts and cooking demonstrations; sing-alongs. Riverlorian talks.

Sports and Other Activities Jogging on decks, kite flying, Ping-Pong; pool on *Mississippi Queen, American Queen*

Beauty and Fitness Small exercise room, whirlpool, aerobics, beauty salon on *Mississippi Queen* and *American Queen*.

Other Facilities Gift shop; *Mississippi Queen, American Queen*, conference centers, fax service, library, theater.

Children's Facilities None.

Theme Cruises See specific steamboats.

Smoking *Delta Queen*, smoking on outside decks only; *Mississippi Queen*, smoking section in lounges.

DELTA QUEEN STANDARD FEATURES
(continued)

Delta Queen Suggested Tipping   Per person per night, $15, detailed information is sent with cruise documents; $2.50 per bag for on and $2.50 per bag off for the porter. Porter's tips are left at purser's office; cash only.

Credit Cards   For cruise payment and on-board charges: American Express, Discover, MasterCard and Visa. Only gift shops and gratuities are accepted in cash. Traveler's and personal checks can be cashed at purser's office.

DELTA QUEEN	**QUALITY 3**	**VALUE D**
Registry: United States	Length: 285 feet	Beam: 60 feet
Cabins: 87	Draft: 9 feet	Speed: 9 knots
Maximum Passengers:	Passenger Decks: 4	Elevators: None
174	Crew: 80	Space Ratio: 19

The Ship   The *Delta Queen* is the only remaining authentic example of the thousands of overnight paddle-wheel steamers that once plied the nation's rivers. She has the warmth of a bed-and-breakfast inn, and her small-town friendliness mirrors the heartland ports she visits.

From the outside, this waterborne piece of history looks rather ordinary, except for her paddle wheel. Inside, however, she enchants with Tiffany-style stained glass, brass fittings, and rich, polished woods from another era. Simply knowing the *Delta Queen* is the real thing makes you appreciate every ceiling molding and creak in the floor. There's no other cruise vessel like her, and there never will be, because passenger vessels can no longer be built of wood. Indeed, *Delta Queen's* elaborate superstructure, which adds so much to her character, was almost her undoing.

In the 1920s, the ship was one of two steamers commissioned by the California Transportation Company for luxury overnight travel on the Sacramento River between Sacramento and San Francisco. Their steel hulls were fabricated in Scotland, then dismantled and shipped to California for reassembly. The wheel shafts and cranks were forged in Germany. Her American-built superstructure was crafted from pine, oak, teak, mahogany, and Oregon cedar.

The *Delta Queen* and her twin, *Delta King*, were launched in 1927 at the astounding cost of $875,000 each and became famous for their deluxe appointments. The *Delta Queen* might have died as other steamboats did, but at the outbreak of World War II, the navy commandeered her, painted her battleship gray, and used her to ferry troops across San Francisco Bay.

At war's end, the U.S. Maritime Commission auctioned the boat. Tom Greene, president of Cincinnati-based Greene Line Steamers, forerunner of the Delta Queen Company, bought her for just $46,250. Greene had the vessel towed 5,378 miles in a 37-day trip to New Orleans via the Panama Canal. From Louisiana, she steamed on her own up the Mississippi and Ohio Rivers to Pittsburgh, where she was refitted to her original state. She made her Mississippi River debut in June 1948.

By 1962, the ship's demise seemed imminent, but publicist Betty Blake revived the tradition of steamboat races to draw attention to the venerable steamer. It worked. In 1969, the *Delta Queen* returned to death's door when the federal safety standards banned wooden vessels as fire hazards. Blake organized a letter and petition campaign that won a congressional exemption the ship still enjoys. The riverboat was made fire-resistant, but in November 1970 she again faced demise. Another act of Congress, however, saved the *Delta Queen,* placing her on the National Register of Historic Places. More than a million dollars was spent to enhance fire resistance. In 1989, she was designated a National Historic Landmark.

To ocean veterans, a cruise on the *Delta Queen* requires reorientation. Large cruise ships take at least a day to figure out; *Delta Queen* requires under an hour. The small, intimate boat is like an inn. Arriving passengers are greeted by riverboat dandies and Southern belles in hoop gowns, the reception setting the cruise's tone.

At the speed of 6–8 miles per hour, the ship averages 100 miles a day (an automobile covers that distance in 90 minutes), but after a day, distance and speed become irrelevant. Life aboard is a tonic for stress. Seasickness is no issue. The steamboat's hush—scarcely a murmur—is immediately apparent.

Passengers settle in to watch the passing scenery—forested banks, marshy coves, and high bluffs—and a lively parade of barges and towboats heaped with grain, coal, scrap iron, and fuel. (Binoculars are helpful.)

Approaching port becomes a major event. The *Delta Queen's* throaty whistle and cheerful tunes from her 93-year-old calliope announce her arrival and draw people to the river. During docking, people ashore and passengers at the rails chat.

The engine room, open to passengers at all hours, is a marvel—immense pistons pushing huge beams that cause the giant red paddle wheel to turn. Engineers keep fresh coffee ready to welcome visitors.

Itineraries   See Itinerary Index.

Cabins   Cabins fall into eight categories, all outside with private showers. Hair dryers are allowed. Four of six suites have picture windows framed by stained glass, a conversation area, queen-size bed, bathtub, and shower; the other two have smaller sitting areas and shower only. Suites are furnished with antiques, while the homey furnishings in standard cabins range from good reproductions to collectibles and include patchwork quilts and wooden shutters. A few standard cabins have double beds; the remainder have twins.

The lowest-priced cabins have upper and lower berths. All are small but comfortable and clean. They range from 44 square feet for the smallest quarters to 68 square feet for mid-priced cabins to 135 and 156 square feet for top accommodations.

Cabins on two of the three decks face wide promenades dubbed the "front porch of America." Rooms on cabin deck open inside onto the quiet **Betty Blake Lounge,** but they have outside-facing windows. Bathrooms are small but functional; many have sinks outside the bathroom door. There's a dresser, and instead of a closet, an open rack with brass rods.

Specifications   87 outside cabins; 6 suites. Standard dimensions, 100 square feet. 56 with twin beds; 4 with double; 8 queens; 19 with upper and lower berths.

Dining   The **Orleans Dining Room** offers two seatings. Most tables accommodate four, although some seat two or six. Wide windows on two sides frame a river panorama. A pianist entertains throughout dinner.

A continental breakfast is served in the **Forward Cabin Lounge.** All other meals are in the dining room, with choices from the menu or buffet at breakfast and lunch. The breakfast buffet offers oatmeal, grits, fruit, ham, eggs Benedict Cajun (with crawfish sauce), and flavored pancakes. Southern specialties like biscuits and gravy can be ordered.

Menus feature American favorites—steak, stew, ribs, catfish, fried chicken, roast duck, and roast lamb—and Southern recipes. Portions are relatively small, yet sensible for those who sample all five courses. Preparation ranges from good to excellent. One of the four entrées at each meal is labeled Traditional River Fare. Possibilities include creamy red beans, rice with Cajun sausage and ham chunks, and crawfish pie. The Forward Cabin Lounge has coffee and iced tea available all day, afternoon tea, and a moonlight buffet at 10:30 p.m.—not as elaborate as aboard seagoing cruise ships, but offering desserts, fruits, and several hot items.

Service   Fresh-faced young Midwesterners provide cheerful service. The staff seems to be a well-integrated, clean-cut, happy family. Their attitude is infectious and genuinely appreciated by passengers. Cabin attendants keep everything neat as a pin.

Facilities and Activities   The laid-back *Delta Queen* offers simple pleasures. Televisions are absent, and the only telephone is for ship-to-shore communication. Despite images of riverboat gamblers, there's no casino; passengers must settle for bingo.

Days aren't packed with activities, but there's enough to do, including some things you'd never encounter on an oceanliner: flying kites from the deck, for example. The musically inclined—or curious—can try their hand at the calliope. Everyone who tries the keyboard gets a commemorative certificate.

Other daytime activities include card tournaments, lessons on *Delta Queen* history, radio trivia games, pilothouse tours, wine and cheese parties, sing-alongs, a Mardi Gras costume party, champagne receptions, and walking and jogging to calliope music. Riverlorian talks are well attended. The softly lighted **Betty Blake Lounge,** furnished with armchairs, sofas, desks, and bookcases, is fine for reading, board games, or writing postcards (a *Delta Queen* postmark is available in the adjacent purser's office).

The **Forward Cabin Lounge,** distinguished by mirrors and wooden pillars, is a popular place to prop your feet and watch the passing scenery through the windows. The lounge also has tables for card games and dining. Loaner binoculars are available free from the shore excursion desk.

The *Delta Queen's* centerpiece is the Grand Staircase, which links the Forward Cabin Lounge to the **Texas Lounge** upstairs. An ornate bronze filigree railing, scrolled latticework, and hardwood paneling accent this impressive stairway, which is crowned by a Tiffany chandelier. The ship is casual, but a lady in flowing skirts could make a grand entrance on the staircase.

At the Texas Lounge entrance is plaque recognizing the *Delta Queen's* landmark status. The wood-paneled lounge's piano bar is a magnet for the sing-along crowd. Passengers come here for popcorn, hot dogs, or hors d'oeuvres at cocktail hour. Wide windows provide the ideal setting for watching the river and sunsets.

The **Orleans Dining Room,** the boat's largest room, doubles as the entertainment lounge after the second-seating dinner. Tables are rearranged to accommodate a stage. Entertainers dazzle audiences with ragtime piano, Dixieland jazz, or banjo artistry. After the show, many passengers retire to the Texas Lounge for dancing and music. The wholesome entertainment is in keeping with the boat's character, and passengers get involved in festivities and hokey contests. By 11 p.m., most of the crowd has turned in.

Shore Excursions   Rural and urban ports offer visits to an array of heartland attractions, including Antebellum Southern plantations, Mark Twain's boyhood home, Gateway Arch in St. Louis, Civil War sites, and many museums.

Theme Cruises   Perennial themes are the Kentucky Derby in May, Great Steamboat Race in June, Fall Foliage in October and November, and Old-Fashion Holidays in December. Cruises with educational themes have been enhanced to appeal to travelers seeking a learning vacation.

Postscript   The *Delta Queen* has been called a romantic anachronism; there is nothing like her. To cruise on her is to experience another time. Her small size and leisurely pace are conducive to meeting and chatting with fellow passengers. It's a small-town atmosphere that might not suit everyone.

MISSISSIPPI QUEEN	QUALITY ⬛	VALUE ⬛
Registry: United States	Length: 382 feet	Beam: 68 feet
Cabins: 208	Draft: 9 feet	Speed: 7 mph
Maximum Passengers:	Passenger Decks: 7	Elevators: 2
416	Crew: 157	Space Ratio: 8

The Ship   If the *Delta Queen* is a floating country inn, her larger sister, *Mississippi Queen,* is a stately Victorian showboat. Proud and pretty, she rolls down the river like the grandest float in a parade. On board, it's the Fourth of July—a red, white, and blue celebration of Americana amid Victoriana. And for good measure, one day's lunch is always an old-fashioned barbecue picnic with all the trimmings.

Polished brass railings, beveled mirrors, crystal chandeliers, and Victorian style chairs evoke the turn of the century, yet the *Mississippi Queen* offers seven decks of comfort and many modern cruise ship amenities, including bathing pool, six lounges and bars, a small gym, library, gift shop, elevators, cabin telephones, some private verandas, and a beauty salon.

Modern comforts aside, this ship is a true steamboat, powered by an authentic steam engine. Her huge paddle wheel is not just for show. Visit the **Paddle Wheel Lounge** on Texas Deck and watch through floor-to-ceiling windows as the paddle wheel's bucket planks churn to drive the vessel.

Itineraries   See Itinerary Index.

Cabins   The *Mississippi Queen's* modern side is best appreciated in her cabins. All accommodations have air-conditioning, wall-to-wall carpeting, telephones, and private bathrooms. Standard cabins are compact and have tiny bathrooms with showers. Suites and outside deluxe cabins have private verandas, but only suites have bathrooms with tubs and showers. Each cabin displays historical art pertaining to its name. Cabin staff attend rooms twice daily to replenish towels and ice.

Specifications   73 inside cabins, 135 outside; 26 suites (114 with verandas). Standard dimensions are 123 square feet. 151 with twins; 36 with double; 21 with upper and lower berths; one wheelchair-accessible.

Dining   Two seatings are offered at dinner; open seating for breakfast and lunch. Menu choices are similar to the *Delta Queen's* and change daily. Five-course dinners include appetizers, soup, salad, entrée, and dessert. Grazers find a light lunch buffet in the **Grand Saloon,** a late-night snack in the **Upper Paddlewheel Lounge,** and hot dogs and ice cream all day at the open-air **Calliope Bar.** A room-service Continental breakfast may be ordered the previous night, although delivery may not be prompt.

Facilities and Activities   Entertainment is G-rated and genuine, emphasizing big band hits of the 1940s and 1950s, Broadway favorites, ragtime, and Dixieland jazz. The band plays nightly for dancing in the

Grand Saloon. The *Mississippi Queen*, like her sister ships, features a Riverlorian who regales passengers with tales from the past, historic tidbits about the river, and explanations of river activity.

Shore Excursions   Land tours cost extra and are purchased onboard unless arranged beforehand by a tour group. Tours in port last about three hours and cost from $10 to $52 per person per excursion.

Theme Cruises   Topics are listed in the line's literature.

AMERICAN QUEEN	(Preview)	
Registry: United States	Length: 418 feet	Beam: 89.4 feet
Cabins: 222	Draft: 8.6 feet	Speed: 10 mph
Maximum Passengers:	Passenger Decks: 6	Elevators: 2
436	Crew: 180	Space Ratio: NA

The Ship   The *American Queen* returned to service in January 2003. Constructed in Amelia, Louisiana, *American Queen* was the largest passenger vessel built in a U.S. shipyard in more than four decades when she made her debut in 1995. No expense was spared in re-creating the luxurious setting of yesteryear. The vessel merges the best features of the *Delta Queen* and the Victoriana of the *Mississippi Queen*, both of which are smaller, and the grand style of 19th-century steamboats with modern shipbuilding technology and selected cruise ship amenities. Her white exteriors are laden with gingerbread filigree, and a 45-ton red paddlewheel turns at the stern. Inside are a bathing pool, gym, conference center, movie theater, and elevators.

The vessel is powered by two 1930s Nordberg steam engines salvaged from the Kennedy, a dredge belonging to the U.S. Army Corps of Engineers. Each of the rebuilt engines generates 750 horsepower.

The *American Queen* rises 97 feet from the waterline to the top of its fluted stacks, making quite a show. The stacks and pilothouse can be lowered to enable the vessel to pass under low bridges.

The boat has a new program that combines a three- or four-night cruise with a three- or four-night stay in New Orleans, during which you have a choice of top-rated restaurants, hotels and tours.

Itineraries   See Itinerary Index

Cabins   A Victorian theme employs period wallpaper, floral carpets and fabrics, brass fixtures, etched glass, and antiques or good reproductions. Even modern plumbing and electrical fixtures are disguised as antiques. Each cabin is named after a river town or historic steamboat.

Seven categories are distributed on all but the lowest passenger deck. Some cabins have bay windows; 98 have verandas. Three-fourths are outside; some have windows or private verandas, but most have French doors. Mid-range standard cabins are considerably larger than on her sister ships.

Cabins are more "senior friendly," with larger bathrooms, emergency call buttons by each bed, and levers (rather than handles) on doors. As on *Delta Queen,* several cabins open onto promenade decks. Although *American Queen* is much larger, such touches provide a sense of community and make it easy for passengers to meet.

Specifications   54 inside cabins, 168 outside; 27 suites and cabins with veranda. Standard dimensions are 141 and 190 square feet. 208 with twin beds; 2 with doubles; 4 queens; 8 singles; 8 wheelchair-accessible.

Dining   Interior designers borrowed liberally from historic steamboats, particularly the 1878 *J. M. White,* called the most graceful and spacious steamboat of her time. Her dining saloon—which Mark Twain described as "dainty as a drawing room; when I looked down her long, gilded saloon, it was like gazing through a splendid tunnel"—has been copied and named the **J. M. White Dining Room.**

Located on main deck, the lowest passenger deck, the dining room spans two decks. Tall windows have ornate fretwork arches. A dropped ceiling divides the room and gives each half a soaring appearance. Each side has a vaulted space with huge mirrors in spectacular gilt frames dating from the 1880s. Providing music is a custom-built mahogany Victorian piano accenting the vessel's Victorian décor.

Facilities and Activities   The **Mark Twain Gallery** around the upper level of the dining room honors the author whose Life on the Mississippi captured the essence of steamboating. Books and curio cases contain exhibits on regional wildlife and steamboat history and river memorabilia. Furnishings include Tiffany-style lamps and writing tables. Window areas provide cozy nooks for reading, writing, or watching the scenery.

Forward from the gallery to starboard is the **Gentlemen's Card Room,** a masculine room meant to resemble Teddy Roosevelt's library. Cases are filled with books typical of late-19th-century homes, with many first-person accounts of exploration and vintage how-to books. One of the ship's two television sets is tucked behind cabinet doors.

To port is the **Ladies Parlor,** a Victorian drawing room where afternoon tea is served. From the gallery to amidships is the purser's lobby and grand, gilded staircase under a spectacular filigreed ceiling, also harking to the *J. M. White.* Beyond is the **Grand Saloon's** upper level and the lively **Engine Room Bar** overlooking the paddle wheel. The engine room viewing area is open to passengers around the clock.

Forward on Texas Deck is the cruise line's signature "Front Porch of America," complete with swings and rockers. Above, the Promenade Deck has a full-circuit walkway and the **Calliope Bar.** Stairs behind the bar lead to the topmost sun deck, small exercise room, and bathing pool (essentially a large hot tub). The Observation Deck also has a full-circuit promenade (seven laps equal a mile).

A lounge and bar at the dining room entrance links the lobby and Grand Saloon below, used for nightly entertainment and dancing. Designed as an idealized 1880 opera house, the theater has a proscenium stage and is ringed with private boxes on the second-story balcony.

The **Chart Room** on Observation Deck has authentic old piloting instruments and navigational charts as well as the boat's 1,500-pound bronze bell. At the end of the ship's first season, names of all inaugural passengers were engraved on the bell.

Disney Cruise Line

P.O. Box 10238, Lake Buena Vista, FL 32830 (407) 566-3500;
(800) DCL-2500; fax (407) 566-7739
www.disneycruise.com

Type of Ships   New megaliners.

Type of Cruises   Family-oriented mainstream cruises combined with a Walt Disney World vacation, designed for all ages.

Cruise Line's Strengths

- Disney name recognition
- new, innovative ships
- dining venue variety and presentation
- friendly, conscientious staff
- outstanding private island
- children's facilities
- family cabins

Cruise Line's Shortcomings

- intrusive, loud public announcements
- Disney overdose
- over-regimentation of children's programs
- uneven cuisine
- unnecessary pressure to vacate ship on disembarkation

Fellow Passengers   A cross-section of the nation—similar to patrons at Disney theme parks.

Recommended For   Families with children or grandchildren. But, like the Disney parks, a Disney product for kids of all ages.

Not Recommended For   Anyone who isn't enraptured by Disney.

Cruise Areas and Seasons   Bahamas, Caribbean year-round.

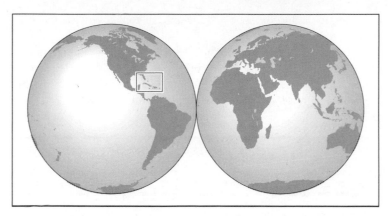

The Line   When Disney does something, it does it big, in a spare-no-expenses way. So, we were ready for the Disney Cruise Line to make a huge splash when its first ship, *Disney Magic*, was launched in 1998. What you see here and on her twin, *Disney Wonder*, is the result of three years of intensive planning by cruise industry veterans, Disney creative talent, and dozens of the world's best-known ship designers. Their task was to design a product that makes every adult feel the vacation is intended for them, while at the same time giving every child the same impression. The results may surprise people, including adults without children.

The ships are both classic and innovative. Exteriors have traditional lines, reminiscent of great oceanliners. Inside, they're up-to-the-minute technologically and full of novel ideas in dining, entertainment, cabin design, and entertainment facilities. Even Disney's exclusive cruise terminal at Port Canaveral is part of the overall strategy, aiming to make enjoyable even embarkation and disembarkation.

Disney offers a "seamless vacation package," combining a three- or four-day stay at Walt Disney World with a three- or four-day cruise. Disney Cruise Line passengers are met at the airport by Disney staff and transported to the terminal in easily identifiable buses. During the hour's ride, they watch a cruise video. When your cruise is packaged with a stay at a Disney hotel, you check in once. The key that unlocks your hotel room door also opens the door to your cruise cabin.

The major innovation is in dining. Each evening on board, you dine in a different restaurant with a different motif, but your waiters and dining companions move with you.

To cater to varied constituencies, some facilities, services, activities, and programs were designed specifically for adults without children, seniors, and honeymooning couples. For example, in addition to the themed restaurants, each ship has an alternative restaurant, swimming pool, and nightclub for use by adults only, as well as entertainment for all the family. Overcoming the hassle of tendering passengers was an important consideration when Disney selected its private Bahamian island visited on all cruises; deep water enables ships to pull dockside. In 2000, the line started a new seven-day Eastern Caribbean itinerary for the first time; and in May 2002, it added an alternating Western Caribbean one.

THE FLEET	BUILT/RENOVATED	TONNAGE	PASSENGERS
Disney Magic	1998	83,000	1,750
Disney Wonder	1999	83,000	1,750

Distinctive Features   Three themed restaurants with "rotation" dining, sports bar in a funnel, children's facilities, cabin design, port terminal. Pagers for adults to locate their kids participating in programs.

	HIGHEST	LOWEST	AVERAGE
PER DIEM	$616	$118	$327

Per diems are calculated from cruise line's nondiscounted *cruise-only* fares on standard accommodations and vary by season, cabin, and cruise areas.

Rates   Price includes port charges.

Special Fares and Discounts   Early booking can save on three-, four-, and seven day packages; consult Disney's brochure for details.

- **Children's Fares** Prices start at $229–$899 on three-/four-day cruises; $399–$1,399 on seven-day; ages 3–12. $99–$139 for 3 and under.
- **Single Supplement** 175–200%.

Packages Weeklong packages pair a visit to Walt Disney World in Orlando with unlimited admission to the theme parks and a three- or four-night cruise. A seven-day, cruise-only package is available. Most people buy the cruise/park package. Consult the Disney brochure for these prices.

- **Air/Sea** Yes.
- **Others** Honeymoon.
- **Pre/Post** Yes.

The Last Word   Cruise experts questioned whether Disney could fill its ships when kids are in school, but Disney estimated that if 1–2% of the estimated 40 million annual visitors to Disney's resorts and parks bought a Disney cruise vacation, the ships would sell out. The vessels are complex and innovative, breaking the mold of traditional cruise ships.

DISNEY CRUISE LINE STANDARD FEATURES

Officers European.

Staff Cabin, Dining/European, Cruise/American.

Dining Facilities Three themed family restaurants with "rotation" dining; alternative adults-only restaurant; indoor/outdoor café for breakfast, lunch, snacks, and buffet dinner for children; pool bar/grill for burgers, pizza, and sandwiches; ice cream bar.

Special Diets On request; health-conscious cuisine program.

Room Service 24 hours.

Dress Code Casual by day; resort casual and informal in the evenings. Jacket requested for men in Palo, Lumiere's, Triton's in evening; one formal night on *Magic* 7-night cruises.

Cabin Amenities Direct-dial telephone with voicemail; tub and shower, two-in-one bathrooms; television, safe, hair dryer, minibar stocked for fee. In-room massage for Deck 8 suites, beachside massages, all for a fee.

Electrical Outlets 110 AC.

Wheelchair Access Yes.

Recreation and Entertainment Showroom, theater, family nightclub, adult nightclub, sports bar, lounges.

Sports and Other Activities Sports deck, basketball, paddle tennis, family sports, adult pool, Ping-Pong, shuffleboard, biking and water sports on Castaway Cay (extra charge).

Beauty and Fitness Spa with sauna, steam rooms; beauty salon.

Other Facilities Self-service launderettes; digital photographic services and camera and video recorder rentals; dry cleaning, valet services; satellite phone services; medical facilities; guest services desk; 24-hour front desk service; fax and secretarial services; conference facilities.

Children's Facilities Age-specific supervised children's program, year-round youth counselors; group baby-sitting; teen club; nursery for ages 12 weeks to 3 years.

Smoking Smoking not allowed except in designated areas.

Disney Suggested Tipping Per guest per cruise for a three-night, four-night, and seven-night cruise: dining room server, $11, $14.75, $25.75; assistant server, $8, $10.75, $18.75; head server, $2.75, $3.75, $6.50; cabin host/hostess, $10.75, $14.50, $25.75. 15% service charge added to bar, beverages, wine, and deck service bills.

Credit Cards For cruise payment and on-board charges: all major credit cards.

DISNEY MAGIC	**QUALITY** 8	**VALUE** C
DISNEY WONDER	**QUALITY** 8	**VALUE** C
Registry: Bahamas	Length: 964 feet	Beam: 106 feet
Cabins: 875	Draft: 25.3 feet	Speed: 21.5 knots
Maximum Passengers:	Passenger Decks: 11	Elevators: 12
2,400	Crew: 950	Space Ratio: 35.4

The Ships   *Disney Magic* and *Disney Wonder* are modern cruise ships with long, sleek lines, twin smokestacks, and styling that recalls classic liners but with instantly recognizable Disney signatures. Colors—black, white, red, and yellow—and the face-and-ears silhouette on the stacks are clearly those of Mickey Mouse. Look closely and you'll see that *Magic's* figurehead is a 15-foot Goofy (Donald Duck on *Wonder*) swinging upside down from a boatswain's chair, "painting" the stern.

Interiors combine nautical themes and Art Deco inspiration, but Disney images are everywhere, from Mickey's profile in the wrought-iron balustrades to the bronze statue of Helmsman Mickey at the center of the three-deck Grand Atrium. Disney art is on every wall, stairwell, and corridor. Some works are valuable old prints of Disney cartoon characters. A grand staircase sweeps from the atrium lobby to shops selling Disney Cruise–themed clothing, collectibles, jewelry, and sundries; classic Disney toys; and souvenirs. (The shops are always full of buyers; some people speculate that the cruise line derives as much revenue here as other lines do from their casinos, which the Disney ships do not have.)

The ships have two lower decks with cabins, three decks with dining rooms and showrooms, then three decks of cabins, and two sports and sun decks with separate pools and facilities for families and for adults without kids. Signs with arrows point the way to lounges and facilities, and all elevators are clearly marked forward, aft, or amidships. (More deck plans mounted on walls would help newcomers get their bearings.) Passengers receive a Disney Passport, a purse-size booklet covering just about everything you need to know for your cruise. Daily in your cabin, you receive "Your Personal Navigator," listing on-board entertainment and activities separated into options for teens, children, adults, and families, plus shore excursions.

Itineraries   See Itinerary Index.

Cabins   Cabins and suites are spacious with generous wood paneling throughout. About three-fourths are outside, almost half with verandas. The 12 cabin categories range from standard to deluxe, deluxe with veranda, family suite, one- and two-bedroom suite, and royal suite. Categories are similar to those at Walt Disney World hotels. Passengers who spend three or four days at a Disney hotel are matched with a cruise cabin in a comparable category.

Note: If you're staying at a Disney resort before your cruise, be sure to complete and return your cruise forms at the hotel. By showing your shoreside room key card at the cruise terminal, you can bypass lines and board directly. Cruise-only passengers may encounter a wait at check-in.

Cabin design reveals Disney's finely tuned understanding of the needs of families and children and offers a cruise-industry first: a split bathroom with bathtub/shower and sink in one room and toilet, sink, and vanity in another. This configuration, found in all but standard inside cabins, allows any member of the family to use the bathroom without monopolizing it entirely. All bathrooms have both tub and shower. *Note:* For added convenience, couples or families should pack two of essentials like toothpaste, providing one for each sink.

All cabins sleep at least three; many accommodate up to six. In some, pull-down Murphy beds provide additional daytime floor space. Storage space is generous. Bureaus are designed to look like steamer trunks. Cabins have direct-dial telephone with voicemail messaging; television; hair dryer; and minibar (stocked for a fee). The room key also opens the minibar and safe. Keys are marked Adult or Child. The latter cannot open the minibar or safe.

Specifications 252 inside, 625 outside; 378 suites with verandas, 82 family suites, 16 1-bedroom suites, 2 2-bedroom suites, 2 royal suites; 16 wheelchair-accessible. All cabins accommodate 3; inside up to 4; deluxe with verandas up to 4; family and 1-bedroom suites up to 5; 2-bedroom suites up to 7; royal suites up to 8.

Dining Disney's most innovative area is dining. Ships have three different family restaurants, plus an alternative restaurant for adults only. Each night passengers move to a different family restaurant, each with a different theme and menu, taking along their table companions and wait staff. In each restaurant, tableware, linens, menu covers, and waiters' uniforms fit the theme.

On *Magic,* **Lumiere's**—named for the candlestick character in *Beauty and the Beast*—is a handsome, Art Deco venue serving continental cuisine. A mural depicts Beauty and the Beast (the equivalent restaurant on *Wonder* is called **Triton,** themed after *The Little Mermaid*). **Parrot Cay** dishes up Caribbean-accented food in a fun, tropical setting and seems to be the most popular for breakfast. But it's **Animator's Palate** that reflects the creative genius of Disney animation. Diners are given the impression they have entered a black-and-white sketchbook. Over the course of the meal, the sketches on the walls are transformed through fiber optics into a full-color extravaganza. Waiters change their costumes from black and white to color. The first course is a montage of appetizers served on a palette-shaped plate, and dessert—a tasteless mousse in the shape of Mickey—comes with a parade by waiters bearing trays of colorful syrups—mango, chocolate, and strawberry—used to decorate it. It's entertaining, but the food is less than inspired, and hot dishes are likely to arrive cold, but no ones seems to care—they are too absorbed in watching Disney perform its magic.

Palo, the Italian restaurant named for the pole gondoliers use to navigate Venetian canals, is the intimate, adults-only restaurant. It's the best aboard. The lovely, semicircular room has a sophisticated ambience with soft lighting, Venetian glass, inlaid wood, and a backlit bar. Northern Italian cuisine is featured. Food and presentation are excellent. More than two dozen kinds of wines are available by the glass ($5.50–$25). There's a $5 per-person cover charge. Reservations are required; make them as soon as you board or risk being shut out. (Disney underestimated demand for this venue.) Other dining options include **Topsiders** (**Beach Blanket Buffet** on *Wonder*), an indoor/outdoor café serving breakfast, lunch, snacks, and a buffet dinner for children; a pool bar and grill for hamburgers, hot dogs, and sandwiches; **Pinocchio's Pizzeria;** an ice cream and frozen yogurt bar; and 24-hour room service.

On seven-night cruises, the dining options are expanded. They include a "Captain's Gala" dinner with wine and French continental cuisine, and "It's A Small World dinner" as a final-night farewell, featuring dishes from throughout the world.

On the Eastern Caribbean itinerary, passengers have a "TROPICAL-ifragilisticexpialidocious" Caribbean-flavored dinner and deck party to salute the rich heritage of the Caribbean with island tunes and dancing servers. On the Western Caribbean one, it's "MEXICALifragilisticexpialidocious" dinner of Latin-inspired cuisine, deck party, and late-night buffet with Disney characters and a mariachi band. There's also a champagne brunch on sea days, high tea, and character breakfasts hosted by Chip and Dale, the latter offering kids a chance to meet and pose for pictures with popular Disney characters in Caribbean attire.

Service Passengers lavishly praise Disney cast members, as cruise and park staffs are called. Staffs are among the most accommodating you will encounter in travel, and they try hard to smooth your way. More than once when I stopped to get my bearings, a staff member was beside me in seconds to help.

Facilities and Activities Disney diversions are geared to children, families, and adults. A day at **Castaway Cay,** Disney's 1,000-acre private island, is meant to be the ultimate escape. The natural environment has been preserved. Miles of white-sand beaches are surrounded by beautiful water. A pier allows access without tendering. A four-car, open tram (like those at Disney World) conveys passengers from the ship to **Scuttle's Cove** family beach. The shuttle runs every five minutes. You could walk the quarter-mile to the beach, but it's inadvisable in the blistering heat. (Bring sunblock and wear a hat.) Strollers are available, as are rental bikes, floats, and kayaks. Lounge chairs under pastel umbrellas are plentiful, and some hammocks swing under the palms, but otherwise there's very little shade.

Disney Imagineers have created shops, rest rooms, and pavilions that give the impression they have been there for years. A supervised children's area includes a "dig" at a half-buried whale skeleton. Water sports are offered in a protected lagoon. One snorkeling course is near shore; the other, farther out, requires more endurance. On the distant course, snorkelers see a variety of fish they identify from a waterproof card provided with rental equipment. Lifeguards watch snorkelers all around the courses. The cruise line has also planted several "shipwrecks." On one in about ten feet of water, snorkelers can see Mickey Mouse riding the bow of the ship. There's also a treasure chest, its contents guarded by large fish. Rental equipment costs a pricey $25 for adults and $10 for children (ages 5–9). A combination of snorkel equipment and float for the day plus a one-hour bicycle rental is also available for only $6 more. Nature trails and bike paths are provided. The main beach offers kids' activities, live Bahamian music, and shops. **Cookie's Bar-B-Cue** serves a buffet lunch of burgers, pork ribs, hot dogs, baked beans, slaw, corn on the cob, fruit, and potato chips.

A second tram connects to **Serenity Bay,** the adult beach on the island's opposite side. The adult beach is a long sweep of sugary sand. A bar serves drinks, and passengers can enjoy a massage in one of the private cabanas with shuttered doors opening on the sea. Passengers must be back on the ship by 3:15 p.m. Most say they would have liked more time on the island.

Nightly entertainment is unlike any other cruise line's and features quality, Disney-produced shows. The 1,022-seat **Walt Disney Theater** stages a different musical production each night, with talented actors, singers, and dancers. These family musicals are on the level of Disney theme parks' live entertainment rather than Broadway and may appeal more to children than to adults.

Disney Dreams has about every Disney character and song ever heard and offers a light plot wherein Peter Pan visits a girl who dreams of Disney's famous characters. It's pure schmaltz, but audiences give it a standing ovation.

Another night offers *Hercules, The MUSE-ical,* a comedy that's the least saccharine of the lot. A Disney-themed trivia game show with a stylized set and host has passengers competing in front of an audience and getting some idea of what it's like to be on a television one. In the smaller **Buena Vista Theater** with full-screen cinema, passengers watch first-run movies and classic Disney films.

Studio Sea, modeled after a television- or film-production set, is a family-oriented nightclub offering dance music, cabaret acts, passenger game shows, and multimedia entertainment. The Art Deco **Promenade Lounge** is a daytime haven for reading and relaxation and a nightspot for cocktails and piano music. **ESPN Skybox,** a sports bar in the ship's forward, decorative funnel, has a big screen for viewing sporting events and a small viewing area with stadium seating.

Beat Street on *Magic* (Route 66 on *Wonder*) is an adult-oriented evening entertainment district with shops and two themed nightclubs: **Rockin' Bar D,** with live bands playing rock and roll, top 40, and country music;

and **Sessions,** a casual yet sophisticated place to enjoy easy music. Disney ships have no casinos. (Research showed its target markets weren't interested in gambling at sea, Disney says.) They also don't have a library or offer afternoon tea (a highlight on many cruise ships).

Sports, Fitness, and Beauty Of three top-deck pools, one has a Mickey Mouse motif and water slide and is intended for families. Another is set aside for team sports; the third is for adults. At night, the pool area can be transformed for deck parties and dancing.

The 8,500-square-foot, ocean-view **Vista Spa** and salon above the bridge offers Cybex exercise equipment, an aerobics room, exercise instruction, thermal-bath area, saunas, and steam rooms. It's supervised by a qualified fitness director. The spa, run by the British-based Steiner group, offers pricey beauty treatments along with a sales pitch for Steiner products. Despite high prices, the spa has proved to be very popular; it's generally booked for the entire cruise within hours of embarkation. Passengers in Deck 8 concierge level suites can have a private massage in their suite or veranda. Some examples: A full-body massage for 50 minutes, $89; oxygen facelift for 55 minutes, $89; back massage for 80 minutes, $144.

The Sports Deck has a paddle tennis court, Ping-Pong, basketball court, and shuffleboard. A full promenade deck lures walkers and joggers; Magic now has deck chairs.

Children's Facilities Playrooms and other kids' facilities occupy more than 15,000 square feet. Programs of age-specific activities are among the most extensive in cruising. They include challenging interactive activities and play areas supervised by trained counselors. Also offered is a children's drop-off service in the evening at the **Oceaneer's Club or Lab.** This service is available from 9 a.m. until midnight or 1 a.m. and is included in the cost of the cruise. Children in the drop-off program are taken to dinner at Topsiders.

The ships' **Flounder's Reef Nursery** has been expanded and improved with a new reception area and enhanced lighting that creates the look of being under the sea. There are new toys from Hasbro, Disney's partner. The toddler area, doubled in size, has a special porthole for parents to check on their kids without the little ones seeing them. The ships provide parents with pagers.

The nursery holds up to 30 children (10 infants and 20 toddlers). The child/counselor ratio is one babysitter to four children (ages 12 weeks to 1 year); one babysitter to six children (ages 1–2 years); and one babysitter to 11 children (2–3 years). On embarkation day, the nursery is open 1:30 p.m. to 3:30 p.m. to take reservations for the cruise. Space is limited and available on a first come, first serve basis, based on sitter availability. Group baby-sitting in the nursery operates from 1 to 4 p.m. and 6 p.m. to midnight, nightly. Cost is $6 per child, per hour; $5 per hour for each additional child. A two-hour minimum is required.

The Oceaneer's Adventure program encompasses Oceaneer's Club (ages 3–7), themed to resemble Captain Hook's pirate ship, with plenty of places for activity; and Oceaneer's Lab (ages 8–12), with high-tech play, including video games, computers, lab equipment, and a small room for listening to CDs. Kids wear ID bracelets, and parents receive pagers for staying in touch with their playing children. Both parents and children give the youth programs high marks.

Common Grounds (Deck 9) is a teen area themed after a coffee bar. It has a game arcade and organized activities, including volleyball at Castaway Cay. The program is a hit, as teens enjoy having a large part of the upper deck to themselves in the evenings. Quite appealing is the **Internet Café,** also reserved especially for them.

Shore Excursions The ships dock in Nassau for 15 hours, ample time to explore the island, enjoy a sport, visit Atlantis Resort on Paradise Island, and take in a show and casino. The ship offers 11 excursions for Nassau, most of them fairly standard tours. Among choices are the Historical Harbor Cruise ($20 for adults; $14.50 for children), the Blue Lagoon Beach Day ($38/$23), Blue Lagoon Dolphin Encounter ($113.50/$88.50), and a Historic Nassau city tour ($22/$16). Children's prices apply to ages 3 through 9. Booklets on excursions for the Eastern and Western Caribbean itineraries are also available, and now, all excursions can be booked with the line in advance of your cruise.

Postscript The Disney Cruise Line attracts a high percentage of first-time cruisers, thanks to Disney's reputation for quality, service, and entertainment, which helps dispel doubts about cruise vacations. At the same time, great effort is made to ensure that the ships appeal to adults—with or without children—as much as to families. Adults without children are catered to in myriad ways and presented with an extensive menu of adult activities. The presence of hundreds of children onboard does not diminish the adult experience.

More difficult to escape than children, however, is Disney's sugary, cute entertainment, which permeates every cruise. Expressed differently, you don't need to adore children to enjoy a Disney cruise, but you'd better love Disney. Instead of the usual ship's horn, you hear the first seven notes of "When You Wish Upon a Star."

Our main criticism of the ships' design is that all outdoor public areas focus inward—toward the pools rather than seaward, as if Disney wants you to forget you're on a ship. There's no public place on any deck where you can relax in the shade and watch the ocean (at least not without a Plexiglas wall separating you). If this quintessential cruise pleasure ranks high with you, book a cabin with private veranda.

A second characteristic, expected but nonetheless irritating, is the extent to which the ship is childproofed. There's enough Plexiglas on these ships to build a subdivision of transparent houses.

Some bothersome areas could quickly be improved. Examples: Public announcements are loud and intrusive. Bar bills include a 15% gratuity, then have an empty space marked "gratuity" below the total. This amounts to a second tip. Guest Services says the space enables passengers to reward "extraordinary" service with something "extra." But most passengers, especially first-timers, won't know that or may be too shy to ask and will add a second tip. Food and service is uneven. At Palo, food is excellent, but service is very slow. At Topsiders, food is mediocre, selections limited, and tables very crowded, but service is outstanding.

On the plus side, passengers booked on airline flights can check in for them shoreside. (Too bad all cruise lines can't provide this service.)

Glacier Bay Cruiseline

107 W. Denny Way, Suite 303, Seattle, WA 98119
(206) 623-7110; (800) 451-5952; fax (206) 623-7809
www.glacierbaycruiseline.com

Type of Ships Four small, no-frills coastal ships.

Type of Cruises Casual; active and light adventure, loosely structured itineraries; emphasis on nature, wildlife, and local culture.

Cruise Line's Strengths

- small, highly maneuverable ships
- Alaska Native culture and off-vessel activities
- all excursions included in cruise price
- friendly shipboard atmosphere
- enthusiastic staff and crew
- naturalists on every cruise

Cruise Line's Shortcomings

- small, spartan cabins with minimal soundproofing
- tiny, head-style bathrooms
- lack of shipboard diversions
- ships not very stable in rough waters

Fellow Passengers On active-adventure *Wilderness Explorer* and light-adventure *Wilderness Adventurer,* age ranges from 40s to 70s, with 80-year-olds and 30-somethings in the mix. Passengers are active and interested in nature and wildlife, attracted to the ships' itineraries, which favor wilderness areas. Many are veteran hikers and kayakers—two activities central to these cruises. All seek a trip heavy on experience and information and light on formality and glitz, and they are happy with flexible itineraries that free the captain to sail wherever passengers will get the best Alaska experience. Spartan cabins and lack of diversions suit them fine—in fact, the homey atmosphere draws many passengers.

Recommended For Outdoors enthusiasts; people interested in Alaska Native culture; escape from television, traffic, and the daily grind; people eager to reach less accessible waterways; those seeking an informal experience with camaraderie between passengers and crew.

Not Recommended For   People who need entertainment or casinos or would be bored without television or shopping; people wanting to remain anonymous aboard ship; those requiring large cabins and normal bathroom facilities; people taller than 6'3" (ships' ceilings are low).

Cruise Areas and Seasons   Alaska, May–September

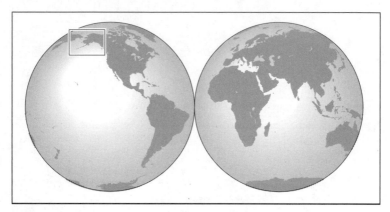

The Line   Formerly owned by the late Seattle entrepreneur Robert Giersdorf (founder of the America West Steamship Company), Glacier Bay Cruiseline and two of its ships were purchased in 1996 by Juneau-based Goldbelt, Inc., an Alaska Native corporation set up under the Alaska Native Claims Settlement Act and representing over 3,000 Tlingit and Haida shareholders. Two additional ships were purchased in 1996 and 1997 from American Canadian Caribbean Line. At press time, the cruise line was being purchased by a group of Seattle investors. The line's shipboard programs that focus on understanding Alaska Native culture and the environment will continue. Glacier Bay Cruiseline is the official concessionaire for Glacier Bay National Park and provides the only overnight accommodations in the park at Glacier Bay Lodge. Goldbelt will retain ownership and operation of the lodge.

THE FLEET	BUILT/RENOVATED	TONNAGE	PASSENGERS
Executive Explorer	1986/1999	98	49
Wilderness Adventurer	1984/97/99	89	72
Wilderness Discoverer	1992/99	95	88
Wilderness Explorer	1969/97	98	34

Style   Glacier Bay emphasizes experiences made possible by the small ships' ability to navigate in shallow waters and narrow passages, nose up to shore for wildlife watching, and get closer to whales. On their U.S.-registered adventure ships, Glacier Bay places heavier emphasis than other lines on putting passengers in contact with nature. Through kayaking, hikes (often directly from ship), and naturalist lectures, passengers spend much more time enjoying Alaska's natural wonders than shopping in ports or being distracted by shipboard activities. The adventures are offered on three levels: low, medium, and high.

One naturalist sails with every cruise and may lead a group no larger than a dozen on an excursion into the rain forest, explaining flora and fauna and natural features, while another heads a kayaking trip. On a recent Alaska cruise, a Native Aleut naturalist told Tlingit legends in a traditional manner. Native storytellers occasionally come aboard to provide cultural background.

All the ships are casual. The informality of the passenger/crew relationship results in off-duty crew members watching nature videos with passengers and naturalists sitting topside at night with passengers, watching the stars. Most crew members are from Alaska and the Pacific Northwest; a number are Native Alaskans. In fact, some Native crew members are stockholders in the line's parent company, adding noticeable pride of ownership to the way they comport themselves. The casual atmosphere and small number of passengers allow easy camaraderie. Passengers commonly know one another by name within days and maintain friendships long after the cruise.

Distinctive Features Shore excursions, kayak, and Zodiac adventures included in cruise price; Native culture-oriented excursions. Dry-launch platforms on *Adventurer* and *Explorer* enable passengers to step directly into their kayaks from ship. Shallow drafts and bow ramps allow ships to nose up to dockless place, allowing passengers to walk out of ship's nose onto dry land.

	HIGHEST	LOWEST	AVERAGE
PER DIEM	$695	$356	$457

Per diems are calculated from cruise line's nondiscounted *cruise-only* fares on standard accommodations and vary by season, cabin, and cruise areas.

Rates All port charges, airport transfers, and shore excursions included.

Special Fares and Discounts

- **Single Supplement** 175% of twin rate.

Packages

- **Air/Sea** Air add-ons available.

- **Others** One-, two-, and six-day independent tour packages include high-speed ferry transport from Juneau; Glacier Bay whale-watching cruise; and, with two-day package, overnight at Glacier Bay Lodge. Six-day "Air, Land, & Sea" includes air transportation from Juneau to Glacier Bay; day excursions in Glacier Bay, Icy Strait, and Tracy Arm; and overnights in Juneau and Glacier Bay Lodge.

■ **Pre/Post** Optional four- to nine-day Alaska packages. For example, six-day "Gates of the Arctic" visits Fairbanks, Gates of the Arctic National Park, Athabascan, and Inupik Native village of Evansville, and includes a float trip on the Koyakuk River.

The Last Word Two words—adventure and informality—sum up this line's cruise experience. The cruises are for people who want to do something really different. When your ship enters wilderness areas, you can imagine you are on an expedition into the unknown. Kayaking on a quiet lagoon or hiking through rain forest will do that to you. There is no better holiday than Alaska for children interested in wildlife and the environment. The *Wilderness Adventurer* and *Wilderness Discoverer*—which accept children—are ideal for families, particularly those who hike and camp together.

GLACIER BAY CRUISELINE STANDARD FEATURES

Officers American.

Staff Dining, Cabin, Cruise/American.

Dining Facilities One dining room with open seating, set meal times. Early Continental breakfast and cocktail hour with snacks in lounge or on top deck, weather permitting. Coffee, tea, cocoa, fruit, dry snacks throughout day.

Special Diets Notice required at booking. Accommodates vegetarian, low-fat, low-salt.

Room Service None.

Dress Code Casual at all times. Jeans, polos, and flannels the norm in Alaska. Many bring dress shirts, chinos, or dresses for the captain's dinner.

Cabin Amenities Windows that open in upper-deck cabins. Tiny "head-style" bathrooms (toilet is in shower stall). Reading lights over beds; small closets, limited drawer space.

Electrical Outlets 110 AC.

Wheelchair Access None.

Recreation and Entertainment Lounge with bar, television/VCR with nature, Native-culture videos, films; small library with nature books and field guides; board games. Binoculars available, better to bring your own. Nature and culture talks by naturalists and occasionally other experts.

Beauty and Fitness None.

Other Facilities No doctor. Crew trained in first aid and CPR.

Children's Facilities None.

Theme Cruises None.

Smoking Prohibited in cabins or public rooms; allowed outside on open decks.

Suggested Tipping $12–$15 per person per day. Tips pooled and shared by nonofficer staff and crew.

Credit Cards For cruise payment and on-board charges: American Express, Visa, MasterCard, Diners Club, Discover.

WILDERNESS ADVENTURER	QUALITY ■	VALUE ■
WILDERNESS DISCOVERER	QUALITY ■	VALUE ■
Registry: United States	Length: 157/169 feet	Beam: 38 feet
Cabins: 34/46	Draft: 6.5 feet	Speed: 10 knots
Maximum Passengers:	Passenger Decks: 3	Elevators: None
72/88	Crew: 22	Space Ratio: NA

The Ships   Wide and low-slung, the ships reflect a function-over-form sensibility. The quiet, maneuverable vessels (formerly *Caribbean Prince* and *Mayan Prince* of American Canadian Caribbean Line) are equipped with innovative features for which ACCL founder Luther Blount is known, including his patented bow ramp, which allows a ship to crawl right up to shores where there is no dock and off-load passengers for hiking and exploration.

Furthermore, the *Wilderness Adventurer* is outfitted with stable, two-person sea kayaks and a dry-launch platform that allows passengers to take their kayaks directly from the ship. Several outside areas—an open bow space, a half-covered top deck, and a small stern area—are ideal for wildlife watching.

Caution: Due to their shallow drafts, these vessels tend to pitch and roll uncomfortably in rough water, but because they ply the mostly protected waters of Alaska's Inside Passage, the going is usually smooth. Also, ceilings are low-only about 6'4".

In 1999, after *Wilderness Adventurer* ran aground near Juneau, it underwent a quarter-million-dollar repair and renovation, upgrading the comfort level at the same time. All cabins were refitted with new doors and refurbished, and the soundproofing was improved. Public rooms, including the dining room, were also refurbished.

In 2001, *Wilderness Discoverer* was given a multimillion-dollar renovation that included painting and refurbishing public areas and all cabins with new furniture and new doors; remodeling the dining room and lounge; and the addition of four suites on the Observation Deck, the only cabins located on this deck. They have large picture windows and are furnished with a queen bed, television/VCR, table, and chairs.

The ship also has a new hot water system, new sprinkler system, and new sound system enabling passengers to hear the naturalist, captain, and cruise director from any location on the ship. The vessel was rewired for wireless access. More rail space on decks for wildlife and glacier observation have been provided and there are additional two-person sea kayaks, a launching platform which allows passengers to embark easily on wilderness excursions directly from the ship, and a new custom-designed inflatable excursion craft.

Itineraries   See Itinerary Index.

Cabins   Very basic cabins come in three categories (five on *Discoverer*) determined by size and location. All have private bathrooms, and all but those on the lowest deck have picture windows that open-almost as good as having a balcony. Deluxe cabins (*Discoverer* only) and AA cabins on the Sun Deck have twin beds; some accommodate a third person. Deluxe cabins have more floor space. A-level cabins on the main deck, aft of the dining room, offer twin beds (double bed in three). B-level cabins, on the lowest deck, have no windows. They are furnished with two twins or one twin and one double bed. Storage in all cabins except deluxe is minimal.

Wilderness Discoverer's bathrooms are "marine heads;" Toilet, shower, and sink are in one small space separated from the main cabin area. A solid door has replaced the curtain that separated them before the renovations. Deluxe cabins on *Discoverer* and cabins 303–306 on *Adventurer* open onto the outside deck, rather than inside corridors.

Specifications   *Adventurer:* 30 outside, 4 inside cabins. Eleven cabins with double beds, 23 with twins. *Discoverer:* 37 outside, 5 inside cabins. Six cabins with queen-size beds, 8 with doubles, 28 with twins. No suites. Dimensions, 99 square feet. Some accommodate third passenger. No singles.

Dining   All meals are served in single, open seatings. Cuisine is basically American, with regional specialties and international touches, all freshly prepared. Snacks are served during predinner cocktails; cookies are baked fresh daily.

Service   Friendly, cheerful, and capable service is one of the ship's best features. Most staff members are young and come from Alaska and the Pacific Northwest. They do it all: cleaning cabins, serving meals, as well as toting luggage.

Facilities and Activities   Each ship has a single lounge with a full-time bartender. Entertainment is do-it-yourself, with naturalist lectures and occasional parlor games. Occasionally, a nature video or feature film plays on the lounge VCR, or the crew may challenge passengers to a board game. Passengers spend most shipboard hours reading, conversing, or watching for wildlife. Binoculars are available; most passengers bring their own. The open-bridge policy attracts passengers to the wheelhouse. Activities are typically hiking and kayaking.

WILDERNESS EXPLORER	**QUALITY 3**	**VALUE C**
Registry: United States	Length: 112 feet	Beam: 21.1 feet
Cabins: 17	Draft: 7.6 feet	Speed: 9 knots
Maximum Passengers:	Passenger Decks: 3	Elevators: None
34	Crew: 13	Space Ratio: NA

The Ship   The line's oldest ship (another former American Canadian Caribbean Line vessel, built in 1969), *Wilderness Explorer* offers perhaps the most active cruise experience in Alaska.

The ship is tiny, accommodating only 32 passengers in miniscule cabins, but it's the adventure—exploration and the line's respect for the natural environment—that's the big drawing card. Underscoring this concept, the line refers to the ship as its "cruising base camp." It's a means to take passengers into the Alaskan landscape rather than be a floating hotel. Nevertheless, interiors are surprisingly bright and cheerful, and the lounge has a piano.

All meals are served in single, open seatings in the dining room on the main deck. Snacks are served during the cocktail hour. Service is consistently friendly and professional.

Itineraries   See Itinerary Index.

Cabins   Except for one deluxe cabin behind the wheelhouse on the top deck, all cabins are tiny, offering upper and lower bunks, head-style bathrooms, and minimal storage. Tiny "portlights" in A- and B-class cabins admit light but can't be called real windows. AA-class cabins, next to the dining room on the main deck, have slightly more space and real windows. The deluxe cabin is considerably larger than others and has windows on both port and starboard sides.

Specifications   17 outside cabins, all with upper and lower berths. No inside cabins, suites, or singles, and none accommodate a third passenger.

Facilities and Activities   There is no shipboard entertainment or exercise facility. Passengers amuse themselves with board games, a small library, a television/VCR, and a piano in the lounge. A bar operates on the honor system except during cocktail hour, when it is staffed by a crew member.

Activities center on off-vessel exploration. Passengers who take this cruise through Glacier Bay and Icy Strait focus on nature exploration and wildlife observation and need to be in good physical condition to handle the three- to four-hour kayaking and hiking excursions. The only planned activities aboard are informal nature, culture, and history lectures by the ship's naturalists and the Glacier Bay park naturalist who accompanies the ship within park boundaries.

Postscript   A *Wilderness Explorer* cruise is a good choice for those seeking active, ship-based outdoor adventure. The port-free itinerary and small number of passengers mean your Alaska experience will be very personal and completely different from that of a large ship and most small ships. People requiring a lot of personal space should look elsewhere.

EXECUTIVE EXPLORER	QUALITY 3	VALUE B
Registry: United States	Length: 98.5 feet	Beam: 38 feet
Cabins: 25	Draft: 8 feet	Speed: 10 knots
Maximum Passengers:	Passenger Decks: 6	Elevators: None
49	Crew: 18	Space Ratio: NA

The Ship   Though odd-looking with its catamaran hulls and three-deck-tall, wedge-shaped superstructure, the *Executive Explorer* is Glacier Bay's most luxurious ship, sailing less adventurous port-to-port itineraries and featuring larger, better-appointed, more inviting cabins and public areas than the line's other ships. Streamlined and powerful, she's able to zip between ports faster than any other small passenger ship on the Alaska scene.

Public areas are pleasantly furnished, and like the line's other vessels, are decorated with Native Alaskan art. The **Vista View Lounge** and Vista cabins above it have a wall of windows overlooking the bow. An open top deck and covered area on the middle deck are best for wildlife viewing. An open area at the stern is another option.

The ship was out of service for the last two years, but it is expected to return to the fleet for the summer of 2004. Prior to that, she will be given a complete renovation.

Itineraries   See Itinerary Index.

Cabins   The ship has the largest, best-appointed cabins in the line's fleet. All have large windows, refrigerator, TV/VCR, considerable closet space, and solid cabin doors rather than the accordion-style doors of the other ships.

The bathrooms are small, arranged in the line's space-saving "head style" (toilet is in the shower stall); sinks and vanities are in the main cabin area.

All but Vista Deluxe and B cabins have twin beds that convert to queen size. One B cabin, smaller than the others, has upper and lower berths and accommodates two people but is suggested as a single. The two Vista Deluxe cabins (aft middle deck, below the bridge) face the bow and have a sitting area, queen-size beds, larger closets, and a wall of windows providing a wraparound view.

Specifications   25 outside, including 2 deluxe cabins. Two Vista Deluxe with queens; 22 standard with twins (convertible to queens), measure approximately 135 square feet; 1 with upper/lower bunks.

Dining   Meals are served in single, open seatings in one dining room. Cuisine, all freshly prepared, tends to be standard American fare with regional specialties, but galley staff often comes up with surprising gourmet touches. There are usually two or three entrées for dinner; Alaska salmon is a staple.

The galley staff bakes fresh cookies at midafternoon and serves a snack at the predinner cocktail hour. One dinner per cruise is designated as the captain's dinner, with lobster and free champagne. With advance notice, the galley staff can accommodate special diets.

Service   Service is one of the line's best features—cordial and warm, capable and professional. Members of the hotel staff, most of them young and mostly from Alaska and the Pacific Northwest, do double and triple duty, cleaning cabins, serving meals, and helping carry luggage on and off the ship. All in all, the service is more like that found at a friendly bed-and-breakfast than at a resort.

Facilities and Activities   The ship has only two public rooms—one lounge with the vessel's only bar, small library, board games, and videotapes; and one dining room. It has no exercise or entertainment facilities. A full-time bartender tends bar in the lounge.

Shipboard activities are focused mainly on observing nature and wildlife. In the evenings, the naturalists and the ship's cruise director give talks on wildlife, Native culture and history, and occasionally host participatory games. Other than this, entertainment is provided by Alaska itself and by passenger interaction.

Holland America Line/Westours, Inc.

300 Elliott Avenue West, Seattle, WA 98119
(206) 281-3535; (877) 932-4259; fax (206) 281-7110
www.hollandamerica.com

Type of Ships Modern superliners.

Type of Cruises Traditional yet modern, high-quality mainstream cruises.

Cruise Line's Strengths

- tradition and experience
- easy-to-like ships
- consistent quality and style
- worldwide itineraries
- impeccable condition of ships

Cruise Line's Shortcomings

- show lounge entertainment
- shore excursion cancellation policy
- communication problems with dining staff due to language

Fellow Passengers Experienced travelers and families who seek comfort and consistency, quality, a refined environment, and a high level of service and who choose cruises by their destinations. Many are retired business owners with some college education, executives, and professionals, but the range includes young nurses and secretaries on their first cruise, affluent seniors who cruise often, honeymooners, young families, and some disabled travelers. They're social-minded, well mannered, and outgoing, but not loud. They enjoy traveling with old friends and making new ones. They're conservative, careful with money, and seek good value. They often cruise to celebrate a special occasion, such as an anniversary or a family reunion.

The average age is mid-50s in winter, younger in summer, but varies by cruise length and itinerary. A seven-day Alaska and seven-day Caribbean cruise on the same ship attract different ages and incomes. More than 55% are couples; 50% are groups—as different as business or tour groups, or square dancing and stamp collecting clubs.

Recommended For Those who enjoy cruise traditions and want a quality experience in a refined environment, but like the facilities and choices available on superliners. Small-ship devotees open to trying a larger ship. Budget cruisers able to move up to higher quality.

Not Recommended For Swingers, party seekers, late-night revelers, trend seekers, or pacesetters.

Cruise Areas and Seasons Caribbean, year-round; Panama Canal, fall to spring; Asia, South Pacific, Africa, fall/winter; Alaska, Europe, Canada, New England, transatlantic, summer/fall; Mexico, Hawaii, Pacific coast, spring and fall; South America, world cruise, winter.

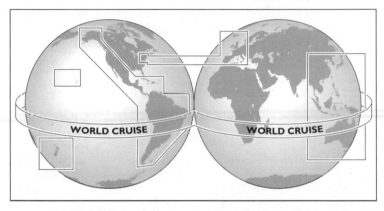

The Line Holland America has carried passengers since 1871. It's among the few lines to make a successful transition from a classic steamship company to a modern cruise line, and it did so better than most, managing to keep its identity and traditions intact while developing a fine mainstream product.

The turning point came in the early 1980s when the line introduced the *Nieuw Amsterdam* (sold in 2000) and *Noordam*, forerunners of today's superliners. They were revolutionary because of such features as a square stern that provided 20% more open deck; two outdoor heated pools; a fully equipped gym, spa, and whirlpool; coded cards rather than keys for cabins; and cabin television—all features that have become standard on new ships.

In 1988, HAL acquired the unusual Windstar Cruises, and the following year, Holland America, Windstar, and Seattle-based Westours, which pioneered Alaska tours and cruises, were acquired by Carnival Cruise Lines. The marriage proved to be brilliant, enabling Holland America to continue its expansion (four stunning new ships were introduced in the 1990s, and another four came in the first three years of the new millennium) and allowing the line to expand in Alaska, return to Europe after nearly two decades, and increase its number of longer cruises. All were factors critical to HAL's retaining its many loyal fans.

The Statendam-class ships resulted from a wish list drawn up by their designers and Holland America staff. The vessels combine classic elegance with state-of-the-art technology, offering such features as multideck atriums, fountains, Jacuzzis, jogging tracks, and theaters Broadway would envy. They were the first HAL ships to have private verandas. The faster *Rotterdam,* introduced in 1997, and her sister ship, *Amsterdam,* in 2000, with a top cruising speed of 25 knots, gave the line new flexibility in creating itineraries. Slightly larger twins, *Volendam* and *Zaandam,* were delivered in 1999 and 2000, and a brand-new class of four 85,000-ton cruise ships, dubbed the Vista series, began arriving in 2002 and 2003. Now the line is working on plans for another new class designed specifically for longer cruises.

In 1998, HAL introduced University at Sea, an enrichment program with seminars as diverse as Caribbean art and strategic investing. Developed with Eckerd College in St. Petersburg, Florida, and operated by Continuing Education, Inc., the courses are available on some Caribbean, Panama Canal, and Alaska cruises. No degrees or prerequisites are required. To widen its audience and meet the market's demand for short vacations, HAL offered cruises of five days or less for the first time. In 2001, the line introduced wheelchair-accessible tenders and Internet access for passengers fleetwide. More recently, the line has added a shore excursion booking facility to its website.

THE FLEET	BUILT/RENOVATED	TONNAGE	PASSENGERS
Amsterdam	2000	61,000	1,380
Maasdam	1994	55,451	1,266
Noordam	1984/2000	33,930	1,214
Oosterdam	2003	85,000	1,848
Prinsendam	1988/93/96/99/2002	38,000	794
Rotterdam	1997	59,652	1,316
Ryndam	1994	55,451	1,266
Statendam	1993	55,451	1,266
Veendam	1996	55,451	1,266
Volendam	1999	60,906	1,440
Westerdam	2004	85,000	1,848
Zaandam	2000	60,906	1,440
Zuiderdam	2002	85,000	1,848

Style   HAL cruises are classic but contemporary, blending Old World traditions with modern lifestyles. They offer the full range of activities expected on large, mass-market ships. The pace is leisurely, designed for experienced, mature travelers and families.

To attract younger passengers, the line expanded on-board sports and fitness facilities, added sports bars and ESPN programming, alternative dining, Internet access, and beefed up its children's program. The line has added sports and adventure shore excursions for active passengers on Alaska and Caribbean cruises and "Just for Kids" adventure and learning excursions in Alaska.

In 1997, Holland America bought the uninhabited 2,400-acre Bahamian island of Little San Salvador, renamed it Half Moon Cay, and developed it as HAL's private island destination on Caribbean itineraries. Located between Eleuthera and Cat Island, less than 100 miles southeast of Nassau, the 45-acre facility fronts a gorgeous white-sand beach. Three areas, connected by walkways and a tram, are an arrival marina and plaza built to resemble ruins of a Spanish fort, a shopping area styled as a West Indian village, and a food pavilion. The market has shops, an ice cream parlor, coffee shop, bar, and art gallery. There is a children's playground, wedding chapel, and post office selling Bahamian stamps—including one issued to commemorate the island. Passengers get a barbecue lunch of West Indian selections. The sports center offers snorkeling and diving on nearby reefs, Sunfish sailing, other water sports, volleyball, and basketball. Nature trails feature a bird sanctuary designated by the Bahaman National Trust. Passengers can sign the cost of all services and sports to their cabins; cash is required for island stamps.

Holland America's vessels feel like ships, not floating hotels. The fleet shares characteristics that reinforce the line's traditions: art and antiques reflecting Holland's association with trade and exploration in the Americas; Dutch officers and Indonesian crews, linking Holland's historical ties to Asia; and the Crow's Nest, an observation bar inspired by the lookout on the main mast of the company's old sailing ships.

Distinctive Features Escalators on newest ships, self-service laundries, good libraries, fresh flowers shipwide, fruit basket in cabins, hot hors d'oeuvres at cocktails, chimes played by a uniformed steward to announce dinner, private Bahamian island, alternative dining, Internet centers; world cruise specials: robes and personalized stationery.

	HIGHEST	LOWEST	AVERAGE
PER DIEM	$717	$90	$317

Per diems are calculated from cruise line's nondiscounted *cruise-only* fares on standard accommodations and vary by season, cabin, and cruise areas.

Rates Port charges are included. *Note:* HAL advertises "tipping not required." Yet, tips are not included in the fare. Hence, tipping is permitted, and has come to be expected.

Special Fares and Discounts   Save up to 45% for early booking under the Caribbean Savings program. A similar Alaska program offers 25% off. Membership Miles, a program with American Express, offers mileage redeemable for upgrades and discount dollars.

- **Third/Fourth Passenger** Low rates.

- **Children's Fare** Reduced rates for ages 2–18; specific rates for younger than age 2. Age 19 and older are billed as third/fourth persons sharing parents' room.

- **Single Supplement** 135–200% of double rate or specific rate on certain cruises; guaranteed share program.

Packages

- **Air/Sea** Yes.

- **Pre/Post** Yes.

- **Others** Renewal of vows and other pricey packages for special occasions. "Just for us,", $410, includes couple massage and chilled Cordon Rouge champagne at embarkation, a guarantee for table for two in the dining room, framed photo and more. Packages range from $79–$410. "Romantic Voyage," bon voyage flower bouquet upon arrival, champagne, private card lesson with $25 in chips, chocolate truffle dessert after farewell dinner, and spa day for one.

Past Passengers   Mariner Club members receive discount and upgrade offers about five times a year, amenities, recognition, theme cruises, and occasional cruises with HAL's president. New enhancements include baggage tags, separate check-in, party hosted by the captain, certificates for third to tenth cruise, and medallions for 40,000 miles to 250,000 miles.

The Last Word   Holland America puts itself in the premium category, between luxury and economy, but it's at the high end of premium, a hair's breadth from luxury, and deluxe by any standard. The refinements and thoughtful touches it offers are unavailable on most comparably priced ships. HAL's consistency—even the names of most public rooms are the same fleetwide—has built a large, loyal following that doesn't find the predictability boring; rather, reassuring.

We continue to be dismayed by Holland America's ambiguous tipping policy. HAL says the crew is not allowed to solicit tips, yet, they are allowed to accept them—and they expect them. In all our years of cruising, we have never had a cabin steward or waiter ask (i.e., solicit) us for a tip. Is HAL implying that when other cruise lines publish a "suggested tipping" scale and print envelopes that appear in your cabin for each person whom passengers are expected to tip, it's done by the crew?

HOLLAND AMERICA LINE STANDARD FEATURES

Officers Dutch; *Veendam,* British.

Staff Dining/Dutch supervisors, Indonesian and Filipino staff; Cabin/Indonesian and Filipino; Cruise/American and others. Bar, deck/Filipino.

Dining Facilities One dining room, two seatings. Indoor/outdoor lido restaurants for casual buffet breakfast, lunch, and alternative dining; taco, pasta, and ice cream bars.

Special Diets Kosher; low-sodium, low-cholesterol, low-fat; vegetarian; sugar-free desserts; baby foods. Request 30 days in advance.

Room Service 24 hours.

Dress Code Casual or informal with two formal/semiformal nights per week of cruise. Tuxedo rental service available.

Cabin Amenities Television with CNN, TNT; multichannel music system; hair dryers, direct-dial telephone. Suites and deluxe cabins have VCR, whirlpool bath, and minibar.

Electrical Outlets 110 AC.

Wheelchair Access 21 cabins on *Amsterdam,* 21 on *Rotterdam;* 22 on *Volendam, Zaandam;* 28 on *Zuiderdam, Oosterdam;* 4–6 on others.

Recreation and Entertainment Theater for movies and lectures; show lounge; nightclub; casino, bars, and lounges; karaoke; masquerades; crew show; culinary demonstrations; kitchen tours; bingo, card games, bridge; pool games; dance classes; library. Sports bars with ESPN.

Sports and Other Activities Two outdoor pools, tennis, golf putting, volleyball, Ping-Pong, shuffleboard.

Beauty and Fitness Beauty/barber shop, saunas, massage, fitness program, gym with professional instructors, jogging track, practice tennis. New spa treatments and fitness programs added recently.

Other Facilities Religious services, medical facilities, laundry/dry cleaning service, laundry rooms, meeting room. Credit-card phones. Wedding ceremony and amenity packages for vows renewal, honeymoons, and anniversaries at additional charge. Internet centers.

Children's Facilities Club HAL year-round youth program with counselors and age-specific activities for three age groups; "Just for Kids" adventure and learning shore excursions.

Theme Cruises See specific ships.

Smoking Designated smoking areas in public rooms; some, such as dining rooms, card room, library, and theater, are designated nonsmoking.

Holland America Suggested Tipping Not required; crew cannot solicit tips, but allowed to accept them. No gratuity added to bar bills.

Credit Cards Cruise and on-board charges: American Express, Discover, MasterCard, Visa; no cash.

MAASDAM	QUALITY **8**	VALUE **B**
RYNDAM	QUALITY **7**	VALUE **C**
STATENDAM	QUALITY **8**	VALUE **B**
VEENDAM	QUALITY **8**	VALUE **B**
Registry: *Maasdam/Ryndam/ Statendam:* Netherlands/ *Veendam:* Bahamas	Length: 720 feet	Beam: 101 feet
Cabins: 633	Draft: 24.6 feet	Speed: 22 knots
Maximum Passengers: 1,266	Passenger Decks: 10	Elevators: 8
	Crew: 602	Space Ratio: 43.4

The Ships   The *Statendam* and her sisters introduced a new class of ships in the 1990s that set the style and standard for Holland America into the next century. They combine Old World tradition with state-of-the-art technology and provide an imposing yet inviting ambience. The spacious ships differ in décor but are identical in layout and offer almost identical facilities and activities.

Interiors of the Italian-built ships were designed by De Vlaming, Fenns, and Dingemans (VFD), the Dutch firm responsible for earlier HAL ships and who helped establish the line's signature look and layout.

In the new group's public areas, designers drew from Holland America's history to capture the golden age of Dutch shipping, but in a contemporary context. Multimillion-dollar collections of art and artifacts from the 17th to 19th centuries are integrated in décor. These combine with contemporary art to enhance the ships' modern image. Together, they make the ships floating art galleries.

In materials, the world was VFD's emporium. Designers used whatever was interesting: woolen fabrics from Holland; leathers from Germany, France, and England; glass from Italy. Cabins were made in Finland, a Danish company supplied teak, and furniture was built in Slovenia. Galley equipment came from the United States.

Public rooms span two decks on the Promenade and Upper Promenade in an asymmetrical pattern, allowing for bars and lounges of different sizes.

The *Maasdam,* fifth ship in the company's history with that name, is a far cry from the first *Maasdam*—a double-masted iron steamship that carried 8 first-class and 288 steerage passengers. It sailed the Atlantic monthly from 1872 to 1884 at a speed of ten knots. Today's computer-piloted *Maasdam* has only one class and moves at more than twice that speed.

Passengers are introduced to the *Maasdam* by a three-deck atrium on the Lower Promenade Deck. Under a ceiling of mirrors and fiber-optic lights, the atrium sparkles with a 30-foot glass sculpture, *Totem,* by Italian artist Luciano Vistosi. The sculpture contains thousands of pieces of glass that catch the light and cast specks of color on nearby surfaces. The best place to see it is from the stairs that rim the atrium.

To one side of the atrium are the **Java Café** for espresso and cappuccino and the **Wajang Movie Theatre** for movies, lectures, and religious services. Adjacent meeting rooms offer audiovisual facilities.

Atrium sculptures on *Statendam* and *Ryndam* are classic in style but out of scale with their setting. On *Statendam,* it's a huge fountain with a bronze statue of three enormous mermaids rising from the sea. On *Ryndam,* it's a tribute in marble (five tons!) to sea legends. An oversized sea dragon twines around the sculpture's top and an undersized boat at the bottom, an improbable mermaid on its bow. The décor of the *Statendam,* also the fifth HAL ship to bear the name, is more baroque than the other ships and often eclectic. Interiors range from conservative to bizarre, blending textures and earth tones with classic European and exotic Indonesian motifs.

The *Veendam,* most stylish of the group, has the same layout as *Maasdam* but with different color schemes, furnishings, and art. The atrium features a glass sculpture, as on *Maasdam,* but of different design. Adjacent is the Crystal Terrace.

Itineraries   See Itinerary Index.

Cabins   Comfortable, contemporary furnishings in light wood are combined with continental touches. Standard cabins are almost 30% larger than comparable ones on ships of similar category. Large mirrors lighten the rooms, and in many, curtains separate the sleeping and sitting areas. Seventy-seven percent are outside cabins.

The décor uses two color schemes: peach and blue. Customized patterns reminiscent of Indonesian batik fabrics are used for curtains and bedspreads. Original art portraying Dutch themes accents standard rooms. Suites have original paintings and serigraphs depicting Dutch scenes.

All cabins have hair dryers, direct-dial telephone with computerized wake-up service, multichannel music system, and closed-circuit television. Full-length double closets and deep chests of drawers-nice features for long cruises-provide ample storage.

Standard cabins have sofas; 70% have sofa beds. All outside cabins have a bathtub and shower. Suites and deluxe cabins have a veranda, minibar, VCR, and whirlpool bath. Each suite also has a small private dining area; laundry and dry cleaning service is free.

Specifications   148 inside cabins, 485 outside (including 120 deluxe cabins and 29 suites with verandas). All with twin beds convertible to queen. Standard dimensions are 186 square feet, inside cabin; 196 square feet, outside cabin. 16 deluxe/36 standard outside have connecting doors for family suites. Some upper/lower berths and single cabins; 6 wheelchair accessible cabins.

Dining   The ships' crowning glories are their dazzling **Rotterdam Dining Rooms.** Surrounded on three sides by floor-to-ceiling windows that embrace the scenery and span the Promenade and Upper Promenade Decks, the rooms are a harmony of elegant tradition and modern technology. An impressive curved staircase connects the two levels.

On the *Maasdam,* a fountain of antique Argentine marble is the lower level's centerpiece. A ceiling canopy of a thousand morning glories is made of blown glass from Murano, Italy. Between the decks is a border of fiber-optic "florets" programmed to change color, altering the room's mood. The room is decorated in red accented by blue. Four large, colorful linen screens depicting day and night cover the walls on both decks.

One passenger's verdict: "The room is so beautiful it takes your breath away." The room is large but remarkably quiet; diners can converse in normal voices and hear chamber music playing on the balcony. The secret: Glass ceilings look spectacular—and absorb sound.

Many tables have either window or balcony seats. A microphone at the captain's table on the main floor allows him or other speakers to address the room; upper-level guests view the speaker on television monitors. Small, upper-level dining rooms—the **King's and Queen's Rooms**—are available for private parties.

Dining here and on all Holland America ships is more elegant, and menu choices more extensive, than on most of mainstream cruise ships. Tables are set with white Rosenthal china bearing a gold HAL logo, silver tableware, wine coolers, and fresh flowers on starched tablecloths.

A typical dinner menu offers a choice of seven appetizers (six cold, one hot); three soups (two hot, one cold) and three salads (five dressings); six entrées, including a vegetarian selection and a light and healthy one, plus selections of cheese and fruit; six desserts; pastries; ice cream; and light and sugar-free desserts.

Responding to passengers' preference for casual, flexibly timed breakfast and lunch—and the recently added alternative dining in the evening— Holland America has worked to perfect the lido buffet, outdoing competitors in quality, choice, and presentation. The best example is the *Maasdam's* **Lido Restaurant,** with its floor-to-ceiling windows and warm teal and coral interiors. Buffets offer hot selections, prepared to order, and cold treats. *Ryndam's* **Lido Restaurant** has a cheerful setting with colorful abstract ceramic paintings and a ceiling stripe of whimsical yellow neon.

More lunch choices-hot dogs, hamburgers, pasta, satay, and tacos-are available by the lido pool. A free ice cream bar is open daily. Sandwiches, desserts, coffee, and tea are available here around the clock. Hot hors d'oeuvres with Indonesian tidbits are served in public rooms before dinner, and a weekly Indonesian lido buffet is popular. And should you still be hungry, the 24-hour room service menu has been expanded, and your cabin's fruit basket is freshened daily.

Service HAL's efficient Dutch officers and friendly Indonesian and Filipino crew are a good combination. Unobtrusive service by a gracious and attentive staff is a hallmark—and a reason the line has so many loyal fans. Dining room supervisory personnel are officers; many crew members have been with Holland America for many years.

Unlike aboard most cruise ships, a uniformed steward passes through the ship playing chimes to summon passengers to dine. (Older passengers will be reminded of the pageboy in Philip Morris cigarette ads.)

It grieves us to report that HAL's service slipped as the introduction of eight ships in seven years required an army of new employees who need more training. We hope this situation will improve as they settle in. Some employees' limited knowledge of English is a problem, particularly in the dining room.

Facilities and Activities The *Maasdam* and her sisters each have five lounges, often with the same names and similar entertainment. The Promenade Deck is anchored by the two-deck main show lounge designed by Joe Farcus, who is known for his innovative, flamboyant ship interiors for Carnival Cruise Lines. Daytime activities include lectures, bridge tournaments, dance lessons, bingo, golf putting contests, kite flying, movies (with popcorn), religious services, and, the most unusual-guided tours of the ship's art and antiquities.

University at Sea, a series of personal and professional enrichment seminars, spotlight topics including nursing issues, memoir writing, and Caribbean culture and history. The programs are offered (extra fee) on some Caribbean, Panama Canal, and Alaska cruises. Ask HAL for specifics. The ships have large, comfortable card and puzzle rooms, a shopping arcade, and libraries with floor-to-ceiling windows. The ships hold auctions of contemporary art. Be wary of the sales pitch. If the bargain sounds too good to be true, it probably is.

In the *Maasdam's* **Rembrandt Show Lounge,** Delft ceramic tiles are set against brocade, gold-tinted mirrors and mahogany paneling to recall the 17th-century Dutch master whose portrait is etched into glass doors at the entrance. The **Vermeer Lounge** on the *Ryndam* honors the 17th-century Dutch master Jan Vermeer. It's Art Nouveau in style, reminiscent of great movie palaces of the 1930s, with lacy mahogany woodwork and silver columns amid dozens of luminescent tulips.

For the **Van Gogh Lounge** on the *Statendam,* the artist's *Starry Night* is the inspiration in computerized special effects, fiber-optic lighting, and curtain drawing. Staircases frame the stage, whose revolving platform facilitates set changes. The *Veendam's* **Rubens Lounge** is named after the celebrated 16th-century Flemish painter Peter Paul Rubens and features glass sculptures in his style.

The lounges offer Broadway-style shows similar to entertainment on other mainstream cruise ships. Big production shows had never been

Holland America's strong point until 1998, when the line introduced Barry Manilow's *Copacabana,* a production based on Manilow's popular song.

The **Ocean Bar** on the Upper Promenade showcases music by a combo. Here Matthys Roling, one of Holland's best-known artists, created her signature "drapery" art, decorating ceilings and walls in beige and red fabric. The oddly shaped **Piano Bar,** adjacent to the casino and popular for sing-alongs, is designed around a piano, with two semicircles of tables and curving sofas. Lights are programmed to change, altering the cozy room's ambience.

The casino offers blackjack, Caribbean poker, roulette, dice, and slot machines. Outside it, kinetic artist Yaacov Agam created a computer display wall that shows thousands of constantly changing images. The **Explorer's Lounge** farther aft is a pleasant spot for an after-dinner drink. The *Ryndam's* lounge displays a stunning mural of a 17th-century Dutch harbor filled with ships. The cigar ceremony in the Explorer's Lounge— a long-time HAL exclusive—is no more. The irony is that it was extinguished just as cigar bars became the latest fad.

By day, the **Crow's Nest** is an observation lounge, its angled windows overlooking the bow. It's ideal for viewing a Panama Canal transit or Alaskan scenery. At night, the lounge becomes the disco. Joe Farcus designed this room on the *Maasdam, Ryndam,* and *Statendam.* On the *Maasdam,* his interiors reflect the Pacific Northwest and Alaska scenery. Dark green "ubatuba" granite on walls is capped by white marble with jagged edges simulating snowcapped mountains; triangular lighting resembles evergreen trees. Large sections of the floor are made of slices of oak trees pieced together like a mosaic; the pattern is repeated in tabletops. A wavelike ceiling pattern suggests the northern lights and gives the evening disco a fantasy atmosphere. Light fixtures have a sketch of the *Halve Maen* ("half moon"), the sailing ship of Dutch explorer Henry Hudson and Holland America Line's corporate symbol.

On the *Veendam,* the **Crow's Nest** was designed by Dutch architect Frans Dingemans as a multipurpose area divided into three spaces—a garden-like room with rattan chairs and greenery, for afternoon tea; the nautical **Captain's Area** with leather armchairs, which can be partitioned off for private parties; and the disco.

Sports, Fitness, and Beauty   The ships' upper decks cater to active passengers. At the center of a teak expanse on Navigation Deck is one of two outdoor swimming pools. On the lido, a second swimming pool, with whirlpools and wading pool, has a retractable glass roof for use in cool weather-a great asset on Alaskan cruises. A tiled wall with a bronze sculpture of dolphins frames the area.

The topside Sports Deck has two practice tennis courts (on *Statendam,* the space is a jogging track). A teak deck encircling the Lower Promenade

Deck has space for deck chairs, walkers, and joggers (four laps equal one mile). The fleetwide Passport to Fitness program awards points for daily exercises and activities that can be redeemed for prizes, such as a belt pack or T-shirt.

The **Ocean Spa** has a beauty salon and fitness center with steam rooms, saunas, rooms for massages and facials, and a juice bar. The ocean-view gym is equipped with treadmills, step machines, rowing machines, life cycles, and a Hydra fitness circuit with ten resistance machines. In front of the spa is an outside deck for exercise classes.

Children's Facilities All ships have year-round, full-time youth coordinators (one for every 30 children, more during holidays and summer). They organize and supervise programs for three age groups: 5–8 years, 9–12 years, and teens.

Daily activities for children ages 5–8 may include storytelling, candy bar bingo, games, arts and crafts, charades, and ice cream parties. Those age 9–12 might learn golf putting, have dance lessons or theme parties, or participate in deck sports or scavenger hunts, Ping-Pong, or karaoke. Older children have a teen disco, dance lessons, arcade games, sports, card games, trivia contests, bingo, and movies. All have pizza and Coke-tail parties and ship tours. The ships have wading pools, activity rooms with video games, and children's menus listing such favorites as hamburgers, hot dogs, fish & chips, chicken fingers, and pizza.

"Just for Kids" shore excursion on **Half Moon Cay** offers a variety of activities, including beach parties, treasure hunts, water sports, scuba diving, and more; prices are $9–$119, and rental equipment costs $9–$19.

On the first night of each cruise, kids and their parents meet the youth coordinator, who outlines the program. At sea, there is at least one activity in the morning, afternoon, and evening; none are scheduled on port days. Baby-sitting by staff volunteers (availability isn't guaranteed) costs $7 per hour for the first child and $5 more per hour for additional children from the same family.

Shore Excursions Holland America/Westours has been a leader in Alaska travel and offers programs ranging from cruising near glaciers on dayboats to rail travel on the domed McKinley Explorer. In Ketchikan, you can have a four-and-a-half-hour sight-seeing/flight-seeing combination or you can kayak, fish, or pan for gold. Alaskan cruises that include the Inside Passage are highlighted by a visit to Glacier Bay National Park. Every Glacier Route cruise offers visits to Sitka's Alaska Raptor Rehabilitation Center, dedicated to returning injured bald eagles to the wild. Holland America Line/Westours recently donated $1.2 million to help the center buy 17 acres of land and lease a building from the University of Alaska.

In the Caribbean, the line offers 175 shore excursions at 30 Caribbean ports. Most are standard offerings with moderate to moderately expensive rates. Flight-seeing is available frequently, and certified divers are offered scuba excursions. Twenty tours designated "environmentally sensitive" are ecotours focusing on the islands' nature, history, and culture. These tours, designed to help passengers understand the islands better, range from guided rain forest hikes to air tours to view the archaeological sites. European shore excursions can be expensive on any line, but HAL's seem to cost more than its closest competitor. Save money by taking standard city tours on your own and buying only those excursions that are unique or that visit attractions difficult to reach on your own.

Note: Be very sure of your tour choices before you buy. In addition to the industry's standard policy of no refunds for cancellations 24 hours before a tour, Holland America charges a 10% fee for any cancellation.

ROTTERDAM	QUALITY **9**	VALUE **C**
AMSTERDAM	QUALITY **8**	VALUE **C**
Registry: Netherlands	Length: 780 feet	Beam: 105.8 feet
Cabins: 658/690	Draft: 29.8 feet	Speed: 25 knots
Maximum Passengers:	Passenger Decks: 10	Elevators: 12
1,316/1,380	Crew: 647	Space Ratio: 47/44.2

The Ships   The *Rotterdam,* the line's sixth ship bearing that name, upholds Holland America's tradition in contemporary style but little resembles *Rotterdam V.* She's more like the Statendam quartet, with almost the same layout and with many of their most popular features. Passengers recognize immediately that they are on a Holland America ship. Her slightly larger sister, *Amsterdam,* followed in 2000. Both have been designated as the line's flagships and introduced new features. They are intended to be the fastest cruise ship afloat, giving HAL new flexibility in itineraries. They also each have more deluxe cabins with verandas, an alternative restaurant, extensive facilities for the handicapped, and a private lounge and concierge desk for suite passengers.

F.C.J. Dingemans, principal architect of the Rotterdam and Statendam group, describes the *Rotterdam's* interiors as an evolution from the other four ships. There are a three-story atrium (oval instead of octagonal), a larger lido restaurant, and a dome over the lido pool. But *Rotterdam* differs from Statendam-class ships: She's longer, wider, and more spacious, as well as faster. Because she's designed to be speedier, the hull is longer and more tapered. Like *Rotterdam V,* she has two funnels aft. Passenger capacity is higher—1,316 versus 1,266 passengers. Three staircases instead of two put passengers never farther than about 125 feet from access to the public rooms.

Rotterdam's interior was inspired by (not a replica of) her predecessor, though some of her namesake's rich interiors and 1930s Art Deco style have been incorporated. The new ship uses more woods and darker colors to achieve a classy as well as classic ambience. Artworks commissioned for the new vessel and museum-quality antiques evoke the Dutch maritime tradition. A huge sculpture fills the three-deck atrium. More a curiosity than a work of art, it represents a Flemish clock tower with 14 timepieces and is embellished with mermaids, dolphins, and snakes. All HAL ships have valuable art collections, but *Rotterdam's* is the most varied. Works include glass wall sculptures, an 18th-century French oil painting, 17th-century Japanese armor, 18th-century Chinese silk scrolls, and antique furniture. The most memorable are life-sized replicas of the terra-cotta warriors found at Xi'an, China.

HAL invested $1 million to add a closed-loop system for the hearing impaired, Braille directories and directional buttons in the elevators, and large-print menus for the visually impaired. In cabins, light-flashing telephones and bed-shaker alarm systems are available. The *Rotterdam* has 21 wheelchair-accessible cabins (*Amsterdam,* 23); 4 have connecting doors for accompanying companions. The *Rotterdam* was the second ship of the fleet to install an Internet center.

The *Amsterdam* has distinctive features of her own. The atrium centerpiece is an ornate "Astrolabe" clock tower with a carillon in its base and four different faces: an astrolabe, world clock, planetary clock, and astrological clock. On display near the **Crow's Nest Lounge** is *Four Seasons,* a gold-plated sculpture of four pieces, originally created for the *Nieuw Amsterdam* of 1938 and bought from a private collector. At the lido pool, passengers will see a trio by British sculptor Susanna Holt—two brown bears fishing and their cub nearby.

The *Amsterdam* has 15 more suites than her sibling; and the **Web Site,** an Internet center, is in an accessible location adjacent to the **Java Café,** off the atrium.

Itineraries   See Itinerary Index.

Cabins   Standard cabins, a roomy 185–195 square feet, are similar to those in the Statendam group. Another 120 deluxe cabins with 245 square feet, have whirlpool bathtubs, VCRs, minibars, refrigerators, and verandas with chaise longues.

Navigation Deck 7 has 40 suites, all with verandas, a private lounge accessed by key card, and concierge where passengers may settle accounts, book shore excursions, and make special requests. The area's glass walls overlook the corridor, but when privacy is wanted, an electric current makes the high-tech glass opaque. Each of four penthouse suites offers living room, dining area and kitchen, bedroom and dressing areas, and steward's entrance. Two suites are wheelchair-accessible.

Specifications   133/117 inside cabins, 385/381 outside; 50/36 suites; 160 cabins with verandas; some adjoining cabins. 498 standard cabins with twin beds; 618 with convertible twins or queen beds; 284 with third and fourth berths. No singles. 21 wheelchair-accessible.

Dining   The elegant, two-level **La Fontaine Dining Room** spans the Promenade and Upper Promenade Decks. Décor mingles Venetian, contemporary, and baroque designs. Panoramic windows overlook the stern. The ceiling represents a star-filled night sky broken by circles of colored glass. Around the balcony are hundreds of individually lighted Venetian-glass morning glories. On the back wall are two giant murals of water-birds, recalling *Rotterdam V's* famous Ritz-Carlton room.

At **Odyssey,** a specialty Italian restaurant, passengers dine by reservation at no extra charge. The opulent room is reminiscent of a Venetian villa. The room is dressed in black with gold-framed mirrors in the ceiling, black and gold columns along the walls, and glass candelabras in alcoves. About 90 people can be seated in three intimate areas. Tables have a movable top that slides forward to ease access to banquettes. The restaurant also serves lunch on days at sea.

In the large, informal **Lido Restaurant,** passengers can enjoy a full breakfast and lunch or have hot dogs and hamburgers grilled to order and make-it-yourself tacos. An ice cream sundae bar, tea, and coffee are available all day. Alternative evening dining is offered several days of every cruise.

Facilities and Activities   The **Ambassador Lounge and Tropic Bar** (Upper Promenade Deck) has a movable wall allowing different configurations. After dinner, the lounge is a large room for dancing; in late evening, it's an intimate piano bar with the piano on a turntable.

Repeat passengers will recognize the ships' traditional collection of small public rooms. The adjoining **Half Moon and Hudson Rooms** accommodate up to 115 people for meetings or parties. **Ocean Bar** has replicas of items from the old Holland America building in Rotterdam; a copy of the sculpture of Henry Hudson's ship, *Halve Maen* ("half moon"), crowns the roof. The larger **Explorers' Lounge** focuses on maritime heritage of Italy and Holland in a large mural of Renaissance Venice. The dance floor is made of Italian marble in a floral pattern.

The **Crow's Nest Lounge** is on all Holland America ships, but this by far is the most successful. Floor-to-ceiling windows wrap around three quarters of this delightful daytime observation lounge. The room has three sections. To one side is a **Tea Area** decorated with porcelain and silver. To the other is a **Captain's Area,** with leather chairs and old ship models. At center is a circular bar and dance floor that become the nighttime disco.

Queen's Lounge, the two-level main show lounge, has state-of-the-art sound and lighting equipment, a rotating stage, hydraulic lifts, and a dance floor. Deep red, burgundy, and orange décor reflects the opulent age of sea travel. Huge, gold-etched Murano glass chandeliers resemble upside-down umbrellas. Along the room's sides, statues of Moorish guards hold large candelabra. The theater curtain is hand-painted satin in maroon, gold, and black.

Children's Facilities The Sports Deck has a children's playroom with craft-making areas, video games, and a teen disco. When only a few youngsters are aboard, the space can be used for morning coffee or afternoon snacks.

VOLENDAM	QUALITY 8	VALUE C
ZAANDAM	QUALITY 8	VALUE C
Registry: Netherlands	Length: 781 feet	Beam: 105.8 feet
Cabins: 720	Draft: 24 feet	Speed: 23 knots
Maximum Passengers:	Passenger Decks: 10	Elevators: 12
1,440	Crew: 647	Space Ratio: 42

The Ships Sister ships *Volendam* and *Zaandam*, built at the Fincantieri in Italy, are a new generation of luxury cruise ships. The *Volendam*, delivered in 1999, and *Zaandam*, in 2000, combine features from the Statendam group and the *Rotterdam*. The new ships are about as long and wide as *Rotterdam*, but their tonnage is greater because they have more passenger cabins—1,440 compared to *Rotterdam's* 1,316 passengers.

The principal architect, Frans Dingemans, who has worked on most of the HAL fleet, has created interiors in keeping with HAL's tradition and passenger preferences. The theme of *Volendam's* décor is flowers—from the 17th to 21st centuries—which are featured in public rooms' fabrics, art, doors, and other design elements throughout the ship. Music is the *Zaandam's* theme, with music-related décor throughout.

Layout of the ships' public rooms is the same as that of *Rotterdam*, including three staircases, an alternative restaurant, a lounge with additional dance floor, and a children's room on Sports Deck that can be used for meetings or receptions.

In the *Volendam's* three-deck-tall atrium is a monumental crystal sculpture by Luciano Vistosi, one of Italy's leading contemporary glass artists. He also created the towering atrium sculptures of the *Maasdam* and *Veendam*. The centerpiece of the *Zaandam's* atrium is an impressive pipe organ with mechanical figures of dancing musicians. The organ may be played by hand or operated automatically. Both ships showcase multimillion-dollar art collections, including works created specifically for the vessels by world-class artists.

Cabins The ships have more deluxe veranda cabins than their sister ships. The penthouse, 28 deluxe suites, and 168 minisuites and deluxe cabins have large verandas, VCR, whirlpool bath, and minibar. All cabins have a sofa, hair dryer, telephone with voicemail and computerized wake-up service, music system, and television. They are furnished with twin beds, convertible to a queen size.

Specifications 1 penthouse and 28 suites with verandas; 168 deluxe cabins (120 deluxe minisuites) with verandas, 384 standard outside; 139 standard inside; 21 wheelchair-accessible cabins.

Dining The *Volendam's* impressive bilevel **Rotterdam Dining Room,** located at the stern, has huge windows and an elegant staircase connected the two levels. Overhead, six large wrought-iron chandeliers designed by Italian artist Gilbert Lebigre hang from the ceiling; they are lighted by fiber optics. The **Marco Polo,** the *Volendam's* alternative restaurant, evokes a California-style "artists' bistro." Italian fare, including pastas and pizzas, is served in a relaxed setting. Its beechwood walls hold the drawings and etchings—reproductions and originals—of artists ranging from old masters to new talent. The restaurant has its own kitchen and staff and serves lunch and dinner daily; there is no extra charge.

Facilities and Activities The Art Deco design of the two-level **Frans Hals Lounge,** the *Volendam's* main show lounge, was inspired by the city of Amsterdam's famous Tuschinski Theater. The multicolored ceiling and colonnades contrast with dark wood walls and huge, colorful ceramic vases. The **Casino Bar** is the ship's sports bar, showcasing cinematic memorabilia. On *Zaandam,* the **Casino Bar** spotlights music.

There are HAL's traditional **Explorer's Lounge, Ocean Bar, Piano Bar, Library, Half Moon Room,** and **Hudson Room,** the last of which serves as a card or meeting room; **Wajang Theater,** which is equipped with writing tables and headphones to be used for meetings; **Java Café,** where complimentary espresso drinks are available; and **Crow's Nest,** which doubles as an observation lounge and nightclub.

The Navigation Deck was extended aft to accommodate additional cabins, and the outdoor swimming pool moved to the Lido Deck. The arrangement provides direct access between indoor and outdoor swimming pools and the **Lido Restaurant.** For *Volendam's* lido pool area, British artist Susanna Holt created a bronze sculpture of arcing dolphins, similar to those found on other HAL ships.

Another change on these ships that frequent HAL passengers will notice is the funnel design that resembles more closely those of the *Noordam* rather than the *Rotterdam* or the Statendam group.

The *Volendam* was also the first of the fleet to have an Internet center with eight computer terminals and a printer where passengers can send and receive e-mail. Open 24 hours, it is staffed from 9 a.m. to noon, 2 to 6 p.m., and 9 p.m. to midnight. The basic charge is $0.75 per minute with a five-minute minimum. Instructions for use are posted on each computer terminal.

Sports, Fitness, and Beauty   The ships have a large Steiner-operated spa and fitness center with beauty salon/barber shop, dual saunas and steam rooms, six treatment rooms, juice bar, and a glass-walled exercise room with the latest equipment. The Lower Promenade Deck is a wraparound teak deck, ideal for walking or cooling off in the line's traditional wooden deck chairs.

PRINSENDAM	**QUALITY 7**	**VALUE C**
Registry: Netherlands	Length: 673 feet	Beam: 95 feet
Cabins: 398	Draft: 23.5 feet	Speed: 21.8 knots
Maximum Passengers:	Passenger Decks: 9	Elevators: 4
794	Crew: 443	Space Ratio: 48

The Ship   The *Prinsendam* comes to the line with an illustrious history as the *Seabourn Sun* and *Royal Viking Sun,* having been the prize of Cunard's purchase of Royal Viking Line in 1994. After Carnival bought Cunard in 1998, Cunard and Seabourn Cruise Line merged, the *Sun* was given a $15 million renovation, renamed and moved to Seabourn, which turned out to be a misfit.

When the ship was transferred to Holland America Line in April 2002, Swedish architect Tomas Tillberg, the vessel's original interior designer, and Holland's F. C. J. Dingemans, the architect who has created handsome interiors for all HAL ships in the last two decades, were engaged to oversee major renovations that transformed her into a HAL ship. The *Prinsendam* emerged with a redesigned interior, new décor, and renamed decks and public rooms to correspond with the other ships in the HAL fleet. Artwork was added, including a frosted and sculptured glass cylinder and wall murals by Bolae for the circular atrium. Now, she carries the name of a sentimental favorite of HAL's loyal passengers that was lost several years ago in Alaskan waters after an accident. The sleek vessel has a sharply raked bow and a beautiful profile, which distinguishes her from the rectangular shape of later ships. The Finnish-built *Prinsendam* is one of cruising's most spacious ships. Penthouse and deluxe veranda suites are palatial; standard cabins are as large as other ships' suites. Treats include walk-in closets, comfortable lounges, a swim-up bar in the main pool, a lap pool, a spa, and a golf simulator of famous courses; and some unusual features like same-level jetways for easy access to docks or tenders; air-conditioned tenders with lavatories and catamaran hulls for stability; and two high-speed, man-overboard boats. Clean lines and uncluttered décor reflect the ship's Scandinavian origins. Fine wood and high-quality fabrics are used throughout. Public rooms and facilities are on three center and two top decks.

A major change was the switch from one- to two-seating dining, which means the main dining room no longer needs to seat all passengers at once, while the Lido restaurant required expansion. As a result, the dining room area on Deck 7 forward was reconfigured to include the **Ocean Bar;** the **Pinnacle Grill at the Odyssey,** an alternative, specialty restaurant; an art gallery; and an Internet center (which replaces Seabourn's computer center).

The lido restaurant on Deck 11 now includes service areas on both port and starboard sides with indoor and outdoor seating, plus the **Terrace Grill** for burgers and hot dogs, poolside. The aft lounge on Deck 8 was replaced with new lanai cabins complete with private deck area and whirlpool—a new concept for HAL not found on their other ships. The change raised the passenger capacity and slightly lowered the space ratio.

Itineraries   See Itinerary Index.

Cabins   Cabins are spread over eight decks. Seventeen categories offer four accommodation types: suites, deluxe veranda outside, outside with a large window, and standard inside cabins. All suites and deluxe cabins (more than a third of accommodations) have verandas. HAL spent millions of dollars upgrading cabins. Soft goods, draperies, and carpets were replaced with a new look featuring blue and gold floral pattern fabrics. Dark wood cabinets have a mirrored dresser/desk. Bathrooms received new sinks, tile, and plumbing repairs, while verandas have new doors, new teak decks, and stylish rattan furniture.

All cabins have television with CNN, TNT, and ship's programming; phone; minifridge; locking drawers; safe; hair dryer; refrigerator; and walk-in closets (cruising's first, but not found in wheelchair-accessible cabins). Most bathrooms have tub and shower. All but a few have twin beds convertible to kings, and most have a small sitting area with love seat, table, and chair. Two decks have launderettes. Room service is available 24 hours a day.

Suites have also been refurbished. The largest, most luxurious suites are on the top two decks. Dividers separate the bedroom and sitting areas. Additional amenities for deluxe cabins and suites include bath robes, extra-luxurious towels, DVD and video library access, personalized stationery, veranda, and floor-to-ceiling windows. In addition, penthouse and deluxe veranda suites have a private lounge, staffed by a concierge, for their exclusive use. They receive afternoon tea and hors d'oeuvres before dinner upon request; a private cocktail party with the Captain; an exclusive Indonesian rijstaffel luncheon hosted by the Captain and hotel manager; and complimentary corsages and boutonnieres on the first formal night, among other amenities.

The sole Penthouse Veranda suite was one of the first on a cruise ship to have a whirlpool bath surrounded by picture windows facing the sea. The new lanai cabins on Promenade Deck aft share a private deck area and whirlpool.

Specifications 25 inside cabins, 373 outside including suites; 68 suites; 1 penthouse suite; 151 with verandas; 82 deluxe. Standard dimensions, 191 square feet. 344 outside cabins and suites with 2 lower beds, convertible to kings; 19 suites with 2 lower beds convertible to kings and a sofa bed; 3 single cabins (2 outside, 1 inside); 8 wheelchair-accessible.

Dining *Prinsendam's* dining room on Lower Promenade Deck has two sections. The most desirable section, aft, has large windows on three sides, providing a panorama of sea and scenery. The forward section is smaller and more intimate, with tables for two by the windows. Both sections have raised center areas that offer sea views regardless of table location. The area is connected by a winding staircase to the popular **Explorer's Lounge** one deck above. Passengers are served in two seatings with assigned tables for dinner, and in open seatings for breakfast and lunch. Tables seating two, four, six, or eight are set with fresh flowers, fine china, crystal, and silverware. Menus are similar to those on other HAL ships, with specialties added from the region of the cruise. Dinner includes five courses with a flambé desert featured every night.

The **Pinnacle Grill at the Odyssey,** the handsome alternative restaurant in Mediterranean style, features Pacific Northwest cuisine and wines. Entrées are prepared on a very hot grill to guarantee tenderness and taste. Reservations are required, and a charge of $20 is added to your shipboard account.

The new **Lido Restaurant** is the venue for casual buffet breakfast, lunch, dinner, and late-night snacks. The variety of food here is impressive and includes a salad bar, soups, hot entrées, carvery, pizzeria, café, taco bar, ice cream bar, and dessert area; 24-hour coffee and tea are available. The restaurant, located aft on Lido Deck, has been expanded to both sides of ship with two service lines. A wall of windows overlooks the deck and sea. There's outdoor seating on the terrace, which resembles a sidewalk café with a teak floor. Poolside, the **Terrace Grill** serves hot dogs and hamburgers.

Facilities and Activities Promenade Deck holds most of the public rooms, including a casino, cigar lounge, **Java Bar and Café,** the **Explorer's Lounge,** a movie theater showing first-run films, a card room, the library, boutiques, shore excursions office, the 24-hour front desk, and the show lounge. *Prinsendam* offers a program of port and theme lectures similar to those on other HAL ships. "

The redesigned **Queen's Lounge** showroom has a new stage and state-of-the-art sound and light room added to bring the facility up to par with newer HAL ships. Production shows feature a cast of seven top-notch entertainers. In front of the stage is a sizable dance floor. Typical of ships built in the 1980s, the lounge has a low ceiling and poor sight-lines from seats in the rear. The **Ocean Bar** with bandstand and dance floor is action central in the evening. Forward of the Ocean Bar is the new **Internet Center,** with 11 flat-screen computer stations; and opposite the center, there's a new art gallery.

The casino offers slot machines and roulette, craps, and blackjack tables. Just outside the casino is the **Java Bar and Café,** one of the ship's most popular spots. It leads to the handsome **Oak Room,** reminiscent of a men's club, with leather chairs in a wood-paneled setting. It's a cozy daytime retreat and popular for after-dinner drinks.

The popular Explorer's Lounge is situated opposite the casino and beside the Java Bar and Café. One of the *Prinsendam's* loveliest rooms, it has a wall of windows with sea views and is decorated with Dutch etchings. In keeping with the Holland America fleet, there is a massive painting of 17th-century Dutch ships—in this case, being given a royal send-off on a voyage of exploration. Classical music is piped in during the day, and a trio plays classical favorites every evening. The lounge's comfortable leather chairs are popular with passengers who want to read, since the nearby **Erasmus Library** only seats four. Stairs lead to the dining room below. Above the bridge is an observation lounge with 180° of wraparound windows facing the bow. It's a popular perch for watching the world go by wherever the ship may roam. A pianist plays here in the evenings.

Sports, Fitness, and Beauty   A wind-sheltered swimming pool on Lido Deck has a whirlpool and swim-up bar and is ringed by a sunning area. Outdoors are shuffleboard, Ping-Pong, and quoits. A teak deck for walking 'wraps the Lower Promenade Deck, and an Astroturf jogging track encircles the Sports Deck. The wood-paneled **Golf Club and Pro Shop** on Deck 5 is a cozy hangout for golfers, with comfortable seating and magazines. It has a new, sophisticated golf simulator of 22 courses including many on the PGA tour (similar to the high-tech simulator on the *Zuiderdam*). A large golf cage is found on Sports Deck (12), but the putting area on that deck has been replaced by a versatile sports court for volleyball, basketball, and tennis.

The **Ocean Spa** has a lap pool with two whirlpools and a glass-enclosed fitness facility with toning and cardiovascular equipment. Spa treatment areas, designed with a classic Roman theme, boasts nine treatment rooms and an array of body treatments. Also available are sauna and beauty salon.

NOORDAM	QUALITY 5	VALUE C
Registry: Netherlands	Length: 704 feet	Beam: 89 feet
Cabins: 605	Draft: 26 feet	Speed: 21 knots
Maximum Passengers:	Passenger Decks: 9	Elevators: 7
1,214	Crew: 566	Space Ratio: 28

The Ship   The *Noordam* was the forerunner of the Maasdam group and is similar to them, particularly in features for which Holland America is known. The spacious trendsetter has square sterns and 20% more outside deck space than was customary for ships of her size, and she introduced many features now common on today's cruise ships. The ship offers doorsills flush with the floor, rather than the then-common toe-stubbing raised ones and was the first to use energy-saving fluorescent light bulbs (9 watts instead of 70 watts).

The décor, created by the Dutch design firm responsible for the Maasdam group, laid the basis for the Holland America look, tastefully blending traditional and modern styles and using museum-quality art and artifacts to underline Holland and Holland America's history. The theme of *Noordam's* art collection is the Dutch East India Company. Huge floral displays add a touch of class.

A great deal was borrowed from the *Rotterdam V*—HAL's flagship until her retirement in 1997. Notable is the teak promenade with the unusual 15-foot width that encircles the Upper Promenade Deck. It's wide enough for old-fashioned, cushioned deck chairs while leaving ample space for two or three people to walk abreast or joggers to pass. Often absent on new ships, this feature is thoroughly appreciated by people who love to cruise. The promenade, particularly in nice weather, is something of a Main Street, with passengers strolling, lounging, reading, napping, people-watching or watching the world go by.

Most public rooms are on the Promenade and Upper Promenade decks. They're always as spotless and efficient as they are comfortable and inviting. To give the interiors intimacy, designers created many lounges and bars and arranged them asymmetrically. In spring 2000, the ship was renovated from stem to stern.

Itineraries   See Itinerary Index.

Cabins   The *Noordam* has 15 cabin categories of 5 basic types, found on eight of nine passenger decks. Rooms are among the largest on any cruise ship in their category. They're homey, with light wooden cabinets and fabrics inspired by Indonesian batik.

All have phones, closed-circuit television, multichannel music, combination makeup/writing table, built-in corner or night tables with drawers, light controls at the bed, full-length door mirror, and ample closets. Walls and floors are insulated for soundproofing. Four cabins accommodate disabled passengers. In the recent renovations, 20 deluxe cabins were upgraded with a new layout, minibar, and new furniture. The bathrooms of most cabins were re-tiled, in addition to being refurbished.

Specifications   194 inside cabins, 411 outside cabins; 20 suites with picture window and king-size bed. Standard dimensions are 152 square feet inside and 178 square feet outside. 485 cabins with 2 lower beds (87 convert to queen); 50 with queens; 72 with 2 lower/2 upper beds; 142 have bathtubs and showers; no singles; 4 wheelchair-accessible.

Dining   The **Amsterdam Dining Room** on the Main Deck, with floor-to-ceiling windows overlooking the sea, is a class act, with many HAL touches: fresh flowers, soft lighting, heavy silverware, starched linens, fine china and crystal, a super Indonesian crew, and dinner music by the Rosario Strings. The dining room generally has one seating at breakfast and lunch and two at dinner with elaborate menus.

The indoor/outdoor **Lido Restaurant** overlooks the Promenade Deck pool and offers breakfast and lunch buffets, plus alternative dining several nights. Along with its refurbishment and new furniture, the restaurant now has a new salad bar, dessert counter, tea and coffee counter. Lido Terrace outside serves hamburgers, hot dogs, and tacos, and offers do-it-yourself sundaes-all at no additional charge. The lido also hosts the midnight buffet and weekly Indonesian buffet. Lest you worry about feeling hungry, a Royal Dutch Tea is served in the afternoons, 24-hour cabin service is available, and your steward freshens your cabin's fruit basket daily.

Service   Indonesians form most of the dining room and cabin crew, whereas Filipinos—generally more outgoing—provide musical entertainment and bar service. Many have long years of service, and all are unfailingly polite and efficient. They are HAL's biggest asset.

Facilities and Activities   Daytime activities include pool games, dance classes, movies in the **Princess Theatre,** bridge, horse racing, and bingo. Active travelers find the Passport to Fitness program; a jogging track; and a health spa where new equipment included treadmills and step machines, along with rowing machines, bicycles, weights, and other exercise equipment. Supervised children's programs are available year-round.

With so many lounges, almost everyone finds something to enjoy. In the stunning **Admiral Lounge,** a replica of the stern of a 17th-century Dutch East India Company ship forms the stage's backdrop. The spacious lounge hosts nightly shows and many daytime activities. Unfortunately, sight lines aren't great.

Canal Street, named for a well-known street in New York, leads to **Henry's Bar** and the **Hudson Lounge**—popular late-night gathering spots with floor-to-ceiling windows, live music, small dance floors, and bars. As on all HAL ships, a favorite room is the **Explorer's Lounge,** where passengers enjoy afternoon tea and after-dinner coffee to the music. The **Crow's Nest Lounge** atop of the Sun Deck is a daytime observation perch and late-evening rendezvous. The **Hornpipe Club,** adjacent the casino, doubles as a disco.

Postscript   Holland America appeals most to traditionalists who remember—and those who imagine—the era of grand ocean travel. Her cruises are fairly dressy. Men are asked to wear jackets in public areas after 6 p.m., and there are usually two formal evenings a week, more during long cruises. Readers considering a cruise on any HAL ship should review the entire section for a full picture of the cruise experience the line offers. HAL has a tipping-not-required policy, but so many passengers leave tips that it calls the policy into question. If you want to tip, use the guidelines for other ships in its category ($3.50–$5 per day for your dining steward and a similar amount for your cabin attendant).

ZUIDERDAM	**(Preview)**	
OOSTERDAM	**(Preview)**	
Registry: Netherlands	Length: 951 feet	Beam: 105.8 feet
Cabins: 924	Draft: 24 feet	Speed: 22 knots
Maximum Passengers:	Passenger Decks: 13	Elevators: 14
1,848	Crew: 800	Space Ratio: 46

The Ships Holland America has completed two of the four Vista-class 85,000-ton cruise ships that it is building. The first two ships, *Zuiderdam* and *Oosterdam*, take their names, respectively, from the south and east "vista" points of the compass. The "-dam" suffix follows the line's century-old tradition for its passenger ships.

The Vista-class name, selected from an employee contest, is meant to represent the ships' forward-looking design and HAL's future direction with ships that are the most advanced and most luxurious Holland America has ever built. Constructed at the Italian shipyard Fincantieri Cantieri Navali, the ships were delivered in 2002 and 2003. A third is due in April 2004. The four ships will increase Holland America's passenger capacity by 55%.

A more contemporary image—with the use of bright colors (orange, purple, and magenta), suede walls, and jazzy patterns in Holland America's first disco—and such 21st-century amenities as dataports in cabins and a high-tech golf simulator are signals that the new *Zuiderdam* is the line's determined effort to attract younger passengers, broaden its base, and lower the average age of its customers.

Zuiderdam definitely is a departure from past Holland America ships. Reactions have been mixed. Some people see in it the influence of Carnival Cruises and say it was time for updating the HAL look; others prefer the line's traditional style. On balance, there's no mistaking that the ship is a Holland America product.

The traditional fresh flowers are still everywhere, and so is the multi-million-dollar art collection and signature HAL rooms like the **Explorers Lounge, Java Café, Half Moon, Hudson Room,** and **Ocean Bar.** There's also a three-deck-high atrium with Art Deco styling and a fascinating Waterford crystal seahorse suspended from the ceiling.

Zuiderdam and *Oosterdam* are HAL's largest ships but carry only 25% more passengers. Passengers benefit by having bigger cabins and more (but not necessarily larger) lounges and other public areas in an asymmetrical layout that reduces the impression of an immense ship.

The vessels' propulsion system includes a full-scale diesel-electric power plant, backed up by a gas turbine as an additional power source, enabling the vessels to operate on diesel or gas turbine power. The ships use the Azipod propulsion system, allowing for greater maneuverability, operating efficiencies, and environmental benefits. The ships have innovative exterior elevators on both sides of the vessel, serving ten decks and providing passengers with panoramic sea views. Other new features include a cabaret-style show lounge as well as a new three-deck main show lounge; a casual "around-the-clock" café, an Internet café and Internet/e-mail dataports in all cabins, the largest spa facilities in the fleet, an extensive **Club HAL** children's facility with inside and outside play areas, two interior promenade decks, an exterior covered promenade deck encircling the entire ship, a large lido pool with a retractable dome, and the signature **Crow's Nest** observation lounge.

Cabins   One of the most significant differences in the Vista ships is their large number of veranda cabins. Eighty-five percent of the accommodations are outside, and two-thirds of them have balconies. (By comparison, on the Statendam-class ships, only suites have verandas.) The deluxe veranda outside cabins, the largest category, have 200 square feet, plus a roomy, 54-square-foot veranda. All cabins are furnished with sofas, minibars, hair dryer, safe, and telephone with voice mail and dataport. Most cabins have tubs, an amenity normally found in more costly suites on other lines. There is a concierge lounge for the exclusive use of penthouse and deluxe veranda suite passengers. In addition to 28 wheelchair accessible cabins, there is a dedicated elevator for wheelchair users, assistance with tender embarkation, and two tenders equipped with wheelchair accessible platforms.

Specifications   924 cabins, 623 with verandas. 2 penthouse suites (1,318 square feet), 60 deluxe suites (510–700 square feet), 100 superior suites (398 square feet), 461 deluxe outside (254 square feet). Standard 165 outside (185 square feet), 136 inside (170–200 square feet). 28 wheelchair-accessible cabins.

Dining   The two-story **Vista Dining Room,** the main restaurant, has floor-to-ceiling windows on three sides and two grand staircases. Each level has its own galley, which makes for faster service.

The large, bright **Lido Restaurant** has been expanded and designed in food-court style, with specialty areas offering made-to-order omelets, deli sandwiches, Italian and Asian specialties, salads, etc. Outside, the large Lido pool area is covered by a retractable dome; a sculpture of polar bears is a reminder of Holland America's role in Alaska cruising.

Odyssey, *Zuiderdam's* specialty, reservations-only restaurant, is twice the size of those on her sister ships, but the décor with elaborate silver chairs and overhead lights is in keeping with their Rococo style. The tables are set with Bulgari china for dining on the Pacific Northwest cuisine that is featured. There is a $15 per-person cover charge.

Facilities   *Zuiderdam's* new additions are the **Queen's Lounge,** a versatile venue where cabaret-style shows are staged and movies shown; the new **Windstar Café,** which is open 20 hours a day, offering specialty coffees, smoothies, pastries, and snacks; HAL's first disco; and the three-tier, bright red **Vista Lounge,** with a bar near the entrance, an orchestra pit, and $10 million of the latest sound and light equipment, where big production shows are staged. Currently playing are *Stage & Screen* (based on movie musicals) and *Under the Boardwalk.*

Passengers on the new *Oosterdam* see *Tommy Tune's Paparazzi,* a multi-million-dollar musical extravaganza created by the nine-time Tony award–winning director, choreographer, dancer, and singer, Tommy Tune; it's the first show he has created specifically for a cruise ship. The show, which pays homage to our fascination with celebrities and the photographers who chase them, will be added to the third Vista-class ship, *Westerdam,* when she is launched in April 2004.

As popular as ever is the **Crow's Nest,** the topside observation lounge where passengers escape for quiet by day and for dancing by night.

Sports, Fitness and Beauty   The **Greenhouse Spa,** operated by the Steiner Group, is more than twice the size of the spas on the Statendam-class ships. It has 11 treatment rooms (including one for couples), a large hydrotherapy pool, and offers features such as a unisex thermal suite with aromatic steam and sauna chambers. It's also another HAL first, as Greenhouse is a Steiner landside brand.

Zuiderdam has a golf simulator (as does *Prinsendam*) that displays 22 renowned golf courses, such as Pebble Beach and Pinehurst No. 2, on a giant projection screen, while a sophisticated computer system tracks players' shots; aspiring linksters actually play the course virtually hole-by-hole and shot-by-shot. Fees start from $30 per person for an hour of golf in a group of three or four. Private lessons are available from the onboard golf pro, with packages starting at $45 for a 30-minute session. Clubs and balls are included. Golf packages for play on the best courses are also available on all Caribbean itineraries.

Norwegian Cruise Line/NCL America

7665 Corporate Center Drive, Miami, FL 33126
(305) 436-4000; (800) 327-7030; fax (305) 436-4120
www.ncl.com

Type of Ships   Modern superliners and new megaliners, plus unique oceanliner.

Type of Cruises   Contemporary, mainstream, emphasizing "Freestyle Cruising."

Cruise Line's Strengths

- sports activities
- "Freestyle" dining options and flexibility
- nonsmoking cabins
- innovative ships

Cruise Line's Shortcomings

- loud deck music
- small bathrooms on some ships
- disparate fleet

Fellow Passengers   Norwegian Cruise Line is everyman's cruise line, with attractive ships where anyone can feel comfortable. Passengers, mostly from the United States and Canada, represent all walks of life, including young professionals, families, and seniors. Average household income ranges from $50,000 to $70,000.

Recommended For   First-time cruisers, active travelers of all ages who want a fun vacation and like the facilities of a large ship. Repeaters and middle-income travelers. Those who seek an unstructured atmosphere.

Not Recommended For   Snobs or seasoned travelers with five-star expectations. Sedentary travelers.

Cruise Areas and Seasons   Bahamas, Caribbean, Hawaii, New York–Caribbean year-round; Asia, South America, winter; Bermuda, Alaska, Europe, spring and summer; New England/Canada, Mexico, Mediterranean, fall; Panama Canal, May–March and September–October.

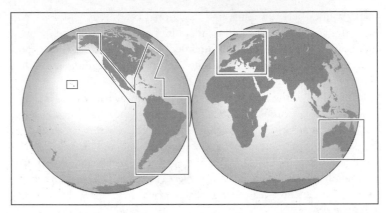

The Line On December 19, 1966, the *Sunward* sailed from Miami with 540 passengers on the first of three- and four-day cruises to be offered year-round by Norwegian Caribbean Line between Miami and the Bahamas. With this trip, NCL was born. Those cruises—the first packaged for the mass market—are credited with launching modern cruising. Since then, NCL, renamed Norwegian Cruise Line, has played a major role in shaping today's cruises. Within five years of startup, NCL had acquired three brand-new ships, pioneered weekly cruises to many Caribbean destinations, and introduced a day on a private island in its itineraries-a feature quickly copied by many competitors.

Yet for all these innovations, nothing equaled in excitement and impact NCL's purchase of the *Norway* in 1980. After buying her as the *France* for $18 million, NCL spent $100 million to transform her from a great oceanliner to a Caribbean cruise ship, setting in motion trends that transformed cruising completely.

Later in the decade, a series of costly expansion decisions, including the acquisition of Royal Viking Line and Royal Cruise Line, weakened NCL's debt-encumbered parent company, opening the way for more aggressive lines to take over its pacesetting role. However, by the 1990s, NCL had reinvented itself with a fleet of new ships, introducing super-liners with innovations that made NCL a trendsetter once again. Among the most notable were alternative dining; sports bars with broadcasts of ESPN and major sporting events; and separate sitting areas in standard cabins—which is an amenity usually reserved for deluxe accommodations. These innovations have become standard on new large ships.

In 1997, NCL became the first line to base a ship in Houston for year-round cruises to the western Caribbean. The following year, it became the first mainstream cruise line to base a ship in southern South America (which NCL dubbed Alaska South) for the winter season, sailing on

14-day cruises between Chile and Argentina. NCL also took over two ships of the defunct Majesty Cruise Line; ordered a 2,000-passenger ship; bought an unfinished hull intended for Costa Cruises (since completed as the *Norwegian Sky*); stretched three ships; streamlined the fleet with new names; and bought Orient Lines.

At the dawn of the new millennium, a bidding war between Carnival Cruises and Star Cruises, Asia's major cruise line, ended with Star Cruises as the sole owner of NCL. By 2001, NCL's new owners had launched "Freestyle Cruising," an innovative concept challenging many cruise traditions, and were building a series of megaships. *Norwegian Sun* debuted in September 2001, followed by the *Norwegian Star* in December 2001, launching NCL's new year-round Hawaii cruises; her sister ship, *Norwegian Dawn,* arrived in 2002.

Now Number Three in the lineup of big cruise lines, NCL once again astonished the cruise world by acquiring Project America's unfinished ships (left abandoned after America Classic Voyages declared bankrupcy in 2001), agreeing to finish their construction. With the help of Hawaii's powerful Senator Daniel Inouye, NCL gained the right to sail them as U.S.-flagged vessels with U.S. staff and crew and to base them in Hawaii for year-round cruising of the Hawaiian Islands.

As a next step, NCL locked up the deal even more completely by buying the two remaining U.S.-flagged ships—the *Independence* and the *United States*—saving the latter from the scrapyard and undertaking a total reconstruction of the vessel that had sat idle for almost two decades. Meanwhile, NCL has created NCL America as a new brand to manage the new operation and is expanding its Homeland Cruising program with more and more new departures from U.S. ports, such as seasonal cruises from Baltimore and Charleston and year-round cruises from New York and Houston. Even with all these development, NCL is not finished and at press time was concluding a deal to build two more 2,400-passenger, 93,000-ton ships to be delivered in 2005 and 2006.

THE NCL FLEET	BUILT/RENOVATED	TONNAGE	PASSENGERS
Norway	1962/79/93/2001/03	76,049	2,032
Norwegian Crown	1988/2000/03	34,250	1,026
Norwegian Dawn	2002	90,000	2,240
Norwegian Dream	1992/1998	50,760	1,748
Norwegian Majesty	1992/1999	40,876	1,462
Norwegian Sea	1988/2000/03	42,000	1,518
Norwegian Sky (to Fall 2004)	1999	77,104	2,002
Norwegian Star	2001	91,000	2,240
Norwegian Sun	2001	77,104	2,002
Norwegian Wind (to May 2004)	1993/98/2001	50,760	1,748

NCL AMERICA FLEET	BUILT/RENOVATED	TONNAGE	PASSENGERS
Pride of America	2004	88,000	2,144
Pride of Aloha	1999	77,104	2,002
(formerly Norwegian Sky)			
Norwegian Star (to April 2004)	2001	91,000	2,240
Norwegian Wind	1993/98/2001	50,760	1,748
(from May 2004)			

Style   NCL has always been at the heart of mainstream cruising. Attractive ships reflect contemporary lifestyles and offer a variety of activities for all ages almost around the clock, emphasizing sports, music, and entertainment with theme cruises year-round. NCL ships have thoughtful amenities and "signature" items, including a full luncheon buffet served on embarkation, expanded room service menus, and ice cream parlors and alternative restaurant at no extra charge; the Chocoholic Buffet, a weekly dessert extravaganza; wine stewards (some of NCL's competitors have eliminated them); and pool and beach attendants to provide chilled towels. All dining rooms are nonsmoking. In some casinos, some blackjack tables are reserved for nonsmokers. On the newest ships, cabins are equipped for the hearing-impaired. An extensive, year-round children's program includes supervised activities.

Fitness centers—open 24 hours/7 days a week fleetwide—offer fully equipped exercise facilities, aerobics classes, basketball/volleyball courts, and golf practice facilities. Water-sports instruction is combined with experience in ports. All ships have a "Dive-In" snorkeling program and can arrange scuba excursions for certified divers—even in Alaska. Great Stirrup Cay, NCL's private Bahamian island, offers varied activities.

Under its new owners, NCL introduced "Freestyle Cruising" to replace some of cruising's time-honored traditions with flexibility and options. The goal has been to broaden cruising's appeal. Gone are rigid dining hours, assigned seating, and dress codes. Instead, NCL's ships' dining venues (its newest ships offer ten restaurants) have open seating and open dining with continuous service like in a restaurant. Passengers can dine when, where, and with whom they want. The dress code is also optional, from casual to formal, depending on the venue. Other elements of Freestyle Cruising include increased service with a ratio of almost one crew member per cabin; upgraded cabins; more relaxed disembarkation at the end of a cruise; enhanced enrichment from computer classes to yoga and mountain biking; and a simplified gratuity system.

The *Norwegian Sun* and the *Norwegian Star* were the first to incorporate specific facilities for the new program during their building. The program has been phased in throughout the fleet. As an early reflection of the Asian influence of Star Cruises on NCL, Mandara Spa has replaced Steiner to handle the ship spas, introducing treatments that stem from Mandara's Southeast Asian roots, such as Javanese honey steam wraps, among others.

Distinctive Features Chocoholic buffets, dive program and offbeat excursions in Alaska, single/open seating for many meals; alternative dining; full-scale Broadway shows; and sports bars. Nonsmoking cabins, cabins for hearing-impaired. 24/7 fitness centers, Internet centers, including wireless access.

	HIGHEST	LOWEST	AVERAGE
PER DIEM	$486	$96	$213

Per diems are calculated from cruise line's nondiscounted *cruise-only* fares on standard accommodations and vary by season, cabin, and cruise areas.

Rates Port charges are included.

Special Fares and Discounts NCL's LeaderShip fares, available through travel agents, are capacity-controlled with discounts up to 50%. Other early-booking fares are also available. NCL's Premium Air Service handles requests for upgrades, stopovers, and flights on specific airlines and air/sea bookings. Requests for deviations must be written or faxed 60 days in advance and carry a nonrefundable service fee, plus fare differential, if applicable.

- **Children's Fare** Third/fourth person's fares. Children under age 2 free with two accompaning, paying guests.
- **Single Supplement** Guaranteed singles rate, subject to availability.

Packages

- **Air/Sea** Yes.
- **Pre/Post** Yes.
- **Others** Yes.

Past Passengers Latitudes, NCL's past passenger club, provides expedited check-in and embarkation at selected ports, captain's reception, *New York Times* news by fax, special cruises with $200 onboard credit, members' events, gifts, upgrades, discounts on selected cruises, newsletter, and customer service phone line. Members-only promotions are listed on NCL's website.

The Last Word In the 1990s, NCL had a litany of problems and financial woes that caused its competitors to outpace it in expansion and innovations. Now, with its new owners, which have very deep pockets, its future has brightened and once again, NCL is a trendsetter with its new direction, new ships and many new features.

NORWEGIAN CRUISE LINE STANDARD FEATURES

Officers Norwegian.

Staff Dining and Cabin/International; Cruise/American.

Dining Facilities *Sea, Majesty, Sky,* two; *Wind, Dream,* four; *Sun,* nine; *Star, Dawn,* ten—all with open seating. Embarkation lunch; Chocoholic, midnight buffets; Le Bistro, Sport Bar & Grill; ice cream parlors; pizzerias; array of specialty restaurants on newest ships.

Special Diets Vegetarian, low-salt/calorie, kosher; must be requested 30 days in advance.

Room Service 24 hours.

Dress Code Casual for day, informal in evening. One formal night on short cruises, two on seven-day with formal/semiformal attire.

Cabin Amenities Phone, refrigerator in suites, some bathrooms with tub, sitting areas in standard cabins on newest ships, television with CNN and ESPN. Hair dryers. *Majesty,* ironing board.

Electrical Outlets 110 AC. *Majesty,* 110/220 AC.

Wheelchair Access All have cabins, bathtubs with grab bars. *Dream, Wind,* 11; *Majesty,* 4; *Sky,* 5; *Star, Dawn,* 20.

Recreation and Entertainment Six or seven lounges, sports bars; Broadway shows, Las Vegas–style revues, comedy; nightclub; disco; casino ; library (except *Sea*). Wine tastings; singles, honeymooner parties; video arcade. Gentlemen hosts on long voyages.

Sports and Other Activities Sports Afloat program with golf practice, basketball, volleyball, Ping-Pong. Snorkeling; scuba for certified divers. Private island with rental equipment. Two swimming pools; jogging track.

Beauty and Fitness Aerobics, fitness center, sauna, jogging track, barber/beauty salon. Spa on *Dream, Wind, Sky, Sun, Star, Dawn.*

Other Facilities Medical, dry cleaning/laundry. Conference. All ships have 24-hour Internet café and wireless access; cost is $0.75 per minute; $3.95 per e-mail. Video e-mail, $4.95 per transmission; computer games, $3.95 per computer game application. Laptop rental, $20 per day.

Children's Facilities New and enhanced year-round program for ages 2–17 in four age-specific levels with youth counselors. Children's menus; fares; baby-sitting. *Majesty, Sky,* kids' splash pool; play room; *Dream, Majesty, Wind, Sky, Star,* soda packages $8–$16; backpack packages, $28–$40.

Theme Cruises See text.

Smoking Nonsmoking dining room. Nonsmoking sections in public rooms.

NCL Suggested Tipping NCL automatically applies a service charge to passenger's shipboard account: $10 per passenger per day for those 13 and older, $5 per day for children (ages 3-12); no charge for children under age 3. These tips can be increased, decreased, or removed. 15% added to bar tabs and spa services.

Credit Cards For cruise payment and onboard charges: American Express, Visa, MasterCard, Discover.

NORWEGIAN DREAM	QUALITY 5	VALUE C
NORWEGIAN WIND	QUALITY 5	VALUE C
Registry: Bahamas	Length: 754 feet	Beam: 94 feet
Cabins: 874	Draft: 22 feet	Speed: 18 knots
Maximum Passengers:	Passenger Decks: 10	Elevators: 11/10
1,748	Crew: 614/689	Space Ratio: 29

The Ships   The twin ships, *Norwegian Dream* and *Norwegian Wind,* were designed for people who want to know they're on a ship at sea. At almost every turn, glass walls frame the ocean and connect with the out-doors—a link that many modern cruise ships have lost. But these ships, breaking the mold on design, have unusual features inside and out. All five upper decks are open and slant downward to create a profile more sleek than those of most large new ships.

The ships have identical interiors; even names of decks, public rooms, and suites are the same. The comfortable, contemporary settings are the work of well-known Norwegian designers Petter Yran and Bjorn Stor-braaten. Quality fabrics, fine woods, marble, and brass trim translate to casual elegance. Windows and use of glass make the outdoors part of indoor décor. Light floods the interiors, giving them a lively atmosphere.

In early 1998, both ships were stretched 130 feet, and all cabins and most public rooms were refurbished. Lengthening resulted in a sleeker, more hydrodynamic profile, one captain says. The new sections increased the ships' lengths to 754 feet, their passenger capacity from 1,246 to 1,748, and added 251 cabins, but the space ratio decreased, surrendering some of the ships' spaciousness.

Lengthening also resulted in a new entrance and lobby and 12 new owner's suites; expansion of the **Four Seasons Dining Room;** a larger casino and nightclub; an enlarged fitness center and spa; new children's playroom; new coffee bar and lounge; splash pool, wet bar, and two Jacuzzis; outdoor café and pizzeria; and three new passenger elevators. Show lounges and bars received additional seating, and the shopping arcade nearly doubled.

The striking new entrance on the Promenade Deck has a Nordic motif in blue and gray with wood blinds, marble accents, and Art Deco light-ing. Here are a 24-hour reception desk, information and concierge desks, the purser's office, and shore excursion and "Dive In" desks. Most inno-vative are the dining rooms—four instead of the traditional one or two. The rooms have multiple tiers, creating more intimate settings and enabling all diners to enjoy panoramas through acres of windows.

Topside, the tiered Sun Deck becomes an amphitheater for evening entertainment. The former Sports Bar on the *Norwegian Dream* has been replaced with a buffet restaurant.

Itineraries See Itinerary Index.

Cabins The ships offer 15 categories; almost all are on the lower five of the vessels' ten decks. All portside cabins are nonsmoking; 16 cabins are equipped for the hearing-impaired, and 11 are wheelchair-accessible. Unusual in the midprice ships, 85% of cabins are outside with large windows; standard cabins are larger than average; all have a sitting area with table and sofa chair or love seat that converts to a third bed; and a curtain separates sleeping and living areas.

There are some trade-offs. Bathrooms are small, particularly the shower stall, and storage space is insufficient. Space around beds is tight, but separate sitting and sleeping areas compensate. Almost all cabins have twin beds that convert into a queen; remote-control, multichannel television with CNN and ESPN; radio; telephone; and hair dryer.

Passengers in International Deck cabins, added when the ships were lengthened, must access them through the **Four Seasons Dining Room,** which was expanded across the ship's girth. Otherwise, these passengers must detour up or down a deck.

Owner's suites measure 385 square feet and accommodate up to five people. Located on the Sun Deck, each has a separate bedroom and living room with convertible double sofa, television, stereo system, refrigerator, and balcony. Bathrooms have a tub and shower and entrances from both hall and bedroom. Other top-category suites also have balconies; most have refrigerators and floor-to-ceiling windows. They're served by an attentive concierge who provides complimentary amenities, including wine and hors d'oeuvres.

Specifications 179 inside cabins, 695 outside; 18 owner's suites; 52 penthouse suites with balcony; 62 suites. Standard outside dimensions, 160 square feet. Most cabins have 2 lower beds convertible to queen; some have third and fourth berths. 1 single; 13 wheelchair-accessible; 16 hearing-impaired.

Dining Each of the three main dining rooms has its own personality and setting; the fourth is an informal dinner café. All have the same menus, and food comes from a central kitchen. The diverse, distinctive settings make dining more fun and interesting, and open seating enables passengers to meet.

The three levels of **Terraces** are separated by greenery and connected by twin stairways. Some passengers say the arrangement suggests a supper club in vintage Hollywood movies. A mural covers the back wall, and a wall of glass allows splendid views.

The **Four Seasons Dining Room,** extending side-to-side in the ship, is the largest dining room. Floor-to-ceiling bay windows extend over the water and offer spectacular views. Four terraced areas provide excellent sight lines. Sun Terraces, the smallest dining room, is casually appointed in light wood and wicker. It's set on three narrow terraces with walls of glass on three sides that extend overhead. Shades protect diners when the sun is above. The view is across the aft swimming pool to the sea.

Le Bistro, the alternative restaurant, is open to all passengers on a first-come, first-served basis. The cozy, informal café offers a daily pasta dish prepared tableside and other light fare. Wine by the glass is available. The **Coffee Bar and Lounge** is designed as a coffee house, with such memorabilia as antique coffee machines on display. Coffee and coffee-flavored drinks are served. The area, with curved walls and quiet niches, incorporates the ship's library and card room.

The former Sports Bar has been replaced with a buffet restaurant as part of the ships' transformation to incorporate "Freestyle" dining.

Free ice cream and frozen yogurt are available poolside each afternoon. If you aren't watching calories and are willing to stand in long lines, you can pig out at the one-night Chocoholic Buffet. The Sun Deck splash pool has a semicircular "wet bar." Nearby, the casual **Outdoor Café and Pizzeria** serves breakfast and lunch buffets and snacks.

Service   The ships are praised for good cabin service, but complaints about service in dining areas are common.

Facilities and Activities   Daytime activities include art auctions, bingo, dance classes, bridge tours, culinary demonstrations, and pool and parlor games. We repeat our warning: At art auctions, know what you're buying. Bargains are rare, despite the sales pitch. A conference center on Sun Deck accommodates 60 people and can be divided into two spaces. An Internet café with computer terminals is available on the International deck; fees apply.

Fabulous entertainment is the cruise highlight. Passengers often give the shows standing ovations. *Dreamgirls* was the opener for the *Norwegian Dream,* and the ship has featured *42nd Street* in the **Stardust Lounge,** the main showroom. On alternate nights there are Las Vegas–style variety shows. The room is well laid-out in four tiers, providing comfortable seats and clear sight lines. The lounge has a dance floor, and dance music may be provided.

The Art Deco casino is much larger than its predecessor. Dressed in hot magenta and black, it offers blackjack, Caribbean stud poker, craps, roulette, "Let It Ride," and 158 slot machines. Adjacent to the casino is **Dazzles** nightclub, which has a circular granite bar, a circular dance floor, and curved sofas in velvet Harlequin patterns. **Lucky's** piano bar has a dance floor and is popular after the show.

Other nighttime action spots are the Sports Deck, anchored forward by the **Observatory Lounge** with floor-to-ceiling windows, an ideal spot for viewing Caribbean sunsets or the Alaskan wilderness. Open decks are sometimes used for outdoor parties. The informal **Rendezvous Lounge,** next to Four Seasons Dining Room, is a good meeting spot.

Sports, Fitness, and Beauty   Sports and fitness programs are offered year-round. The Sports Deck is mecca for active passengers. Golf instruction and a driving range, plus two outdoor pools, are available. Upstairs on Sky Deck is the basketball and volleyball court. The International Deck offers a small pool.

The **Health Spa and Fitness Center** on the Sports Deck has been enlarged to a full-service spa with eight treatment rooms for massage therapy, herbal wraps, and facials. A weight room has Cybex training equipment. Aerobics and other exercise classes balance excesses at the Chocoholic Buffet. A wide walking/jogging track wraps around Promenade Deck. The beauty salon is next to the observation lounge.

Tiered teak decks, separated by decorative greenery, are a sunbathers' and people-watchers' delight at the forward pool. It's an innovative design, but it's noisy. On some evenings, the area hosts outdoor events and dancing.

Snorkeling instruction is offered at sea, and hands-on experience is available in ports of call. The Alaskan dive program is a hit. Sports theme cruises-among them golf, tennis, baseball, and running-feature specialists and sports celebrities. An active or retired NFL player is aboard most seven-day cruises.

Children's Facilities   Kids Korner playroom is the base for NCL's year-round "Kid's Crew" program. Coordinators plan and supervise daily activities year-round. An NCL brochure lists activities for four age groups: Junior Sailors (ages 2–5), First Mates (6–8), Navigators (9–12), and Teens (13–17). At sea, the hours are 9 a.m.–noon; 2–4:30 p.m.; 7:30–10 p.m. First evening of cruise, 8–10 p.m. Port days, 3–5 p.m.; 7:30-10 p.m.

Kids meet the captain at a Coke-tail party; for the masquerade ball, they receive help in making costumes. Activities include dances and arts and crafts. There are races, treasure hunts, and games are planned for the day at the beach. The ship publishes *Kids' Cruise News* and *Teen Cruise News* daily. Also available are ice cream bar and children's menus.

The Kids Soda package: unlimited soda fountain access costs $8 for a three-day cruise or $16 for seven days. A Kids Backpack provides baseball cap, luggage tags, T-shirt, and more and costs $28–$39.50, depending on cruise length.

Children under age 2 sail free. For baby-sitting, inquire from cruise line prior to departure.

NORWEGIAN SKY	QUALITY **7**	VALUE **C**
NORWEGIAN SUN	QUALITY **8**	VALUE **B**
Registry: Bahamas	Length: 853 feet	Beam:105.8/108 feet
Cabins: 900/1,000	Draft: 26 feet	Speed: 23 knots
Maximum Passengers:	Passenger Decks: 12/11	Elevators: 12
2,400	Crew: 750/800	Space Ratio: 38

The Ships   The unfinished hull intended as Costa Cruises' *Costa-Olympia* was completed by NCL as the *Norwegian Sky*. She debuted in August 1999 as the first of a new generation of NCL vessels, with her sister ship, *Norwegian Sun*, which arrived in 2001. Swedish marine architects Tillberg Design created the handsome interiors of these $300-million vessels. They are a rhapsody in blue, romanticizing the ships names, with sky-blue and sea-blue décor throughout the ships. The initial impression one has on entering the glass-domed, eight-deck atrium is one of cool elegance. There is no glitz or bright lights but rather, an airy, refined setting with a multimillion-dollar art collection integrated into the décor.

The reception and purser's desks, concierge, and shore excursion offices are on Atlantic Deck. Neptune's Court, a second atrium, has a grand staircase just outside the **Seven Seas Dining Room,** connecting Atlantic deck to Promenade and International Decks with the main show lounge.

The operative word on these ships is options—with three dining rooms, an outdoor buffet, an indoor garden buffet, pizzeria, and wine bar, the NCL signature **Sports Bar & Grill, Le Bistro,** and an ice cream bar. There are also champagne and cigar bars.

The Sky debuted NCL's first **Internet Café,** where passengers can go online 24 hours a day, an enhancement added to all NCL ships. Ship's photographers have digital cameras, enabling passengers to e-mail photos home (additional fee). A "Skycam" on the bridge is downloaded onto a website so family ashore can track the voyage. Other facilities include the Atrium Room, available for small private functions, and a medical center.

In a joint venture, dutyfree.com and Colombian Emeralds International manage *Norwegian Sky* gift shops. Passengers view patterns and designs at a kiosk, with home delivery available. Liquor selections, displayed in the shopping arcade, can be ordered through room service.

The *Norwegian Sun* was the first of the fleet to have NCL's new Freestyle Cruising elements included during the building. Among them are more dining options—nine restaurants (some with surcharge or pay-as-you-go).

Among other new features, *Norwegian Sun* has a "lifestyle area" for classes in computers, financial planning, yoga, and so on; a larger Internet café; a wedding chapel; a larger gym and spa; larger cabins, and a new cabin category—minisuites with balconies.

In October 2004, *Norwegian Sky* will be reflagged under U.S. registry and renamed *Pride of Aloha,* joining the new NCL America division to sail the Hawaiian Islands year-round.

Itineraries   See Itinerary Index.

Cabins   The *Sky* cabins are similar but smaller than those on *Norwegian Dream* and are furnished with two lower beds that convert to a queen, a sitting area, dressing table, refrigerator, safe, remote control television, radio, telephone, large circular windows, and private bathroom with duvet. Other than the penthouses and owner suites, all cabins are uniform in size and efficiently laid out. The glaring shortcoming is insufficient storage space—a leftover because the ship was already under construction when NCL took over the project. Most have only three shallow drawers. To compensate, NCL has installed more shelf and drawer space in all cabins. Closet space is adequate. About 20% of the cabins have teak-floored balconies; all have Internet hookups. Fourteen penthouses with teakwood furnished balconies have butler service and an exclusive room service menu for breakfast, lunch and dinner.

Some of the *Sky's* shortcomings were corrected on the *Sun,* with more than 100 additional outside cabins (67% in total), larger cabins, and 30 minisuites with balconies, measuring 267 square feet. Four Owner's Suites, located forward above the ship's bridge, have 502 square feet each. All cabins have extra closet and drawer space.

Specifications *Norwegian Sky:* 1,000 cabins. 574 outside, 427 inside; 14 penthouse suites; 258 cabins, including 21 junior suites, have balconies. 8 owner's suites have balconies with Jacuzzis. Standard cabins measure about 150 square feet; 6 wheelchair-accessible. *Norwegian Sun:* 675 outside (152–172 square feet), 325 inside (167–176 square feet), 52 suites with balconies (436 square feet); 16 doubles, 185 triples, 779 quads; 20 wheelchair-accessible.

Dining The *Sky's* two main dining rooms, **Four Seasons** and **Seven Seas,** have two seatings and are connected by the intimate Horizons, a third, small dining room. The latter has a dozen or so roomy gold banquettes along large windows looking on to panoramic ocean views on one side of the room. Suite passengers are given first preference at **Horizons'** banquettes and window seats.

Other dining options include the richly furnished **Le Bistro,** with floor-to-ceiling windows, serving French/Mediterranean cuisine with tableside cooking, and **Ciao Chow,** a funky Italian/Chinese eatery. Le Bistro, which serves dinner until 11 p.m., and Horizons require reservations; they are very popular, so book early in the cruise.

The casual **Great Outdoor Restaurant** and **Garden Café** have "food action stations" serving up paella, sushi, Norwegian waffles, pasta, and more, intended to eliminate long buffet lines. Both cafés offer breakfast, lunch, and snack specialties that vary daily. There is a pizzeria and **Sprinkles Ice Cream Bar.** The 24-hour room-service menu offers pizza, too.

Passengers give the ship's cuisine, especially the alternative dining options, good reviews. The only dining disappointment is breakfast and lunch in the pool deck café for their lack of variety.

Although the *Sky* was NCL's first ship to offer Freestyle Cruising, the *Sun* reflects the concept more with its dining options. On a seven-day cruise, passengers never need to eat dinner in the same restaurant more than once, if they care to pay extra in some of the eateries. Among their choices, they can enjoy either of two main dining rooms with open seating from 5:30 p.m. to midnight every evening; a more formal Italian restaurant by reservation; French fare at Le Bistro; a Pacific Rim restaurant complex with a sushi bar and teppanyaki room; a California/Hawaii/Asian fusion restaurant; a tapas bar with entertainment; a 24-hour indoor/outdoor café with food stations serving hamburgers, hot dogs, soups and salads; and a "healthy living" restaurant with *Cooking Light* dishes and spa menus. Note, however, that some of these restaurants have a surcharge and some are pay-as-you-go.

Facilities and Activities   Gatsby's, a wine and tapas bar, is one of the best-looking lounges on the ship, with deep burgundy carpets, plush gold chairs, and leopard-print ottomans set against lush foliage, wood paneling, and floor-to-ceiling windows. The **Atrium Bar,** another piano bar with large glass windows and a view of the white and gold lobby area, serves champagne and premium vodkas along with caviar and paté de foie gras. A modest but respectable half-bottle of Veuve Clicquot with pâté de foie gras accompaniment is a mere $40–$50; if you go for the works, a bottle of Dom Perignon with sevruga caviar and pâté will run you $150.

Nonsmoking guests can select from the martini menu in the **Windjammer Bar,** and cigar connoisseurs enjoy freshly hand-rolled stogies and premium brandy behind the glass walls of the adjoining but segregated **Churchill's Cigar Club** with humidor. The **Coffee Bar** has a great selection of coffees and liqueurs at fair prices.

Monte Carlo Casino offers blackjack, roulette, Caribbean poker, and slot machines. Now playing in the golden, two-deck **Stardust Lounge** with a proscenium stage is *Hey Mr. Producer: The Musical World of Cameron Mackintosh,* which highlights legendary musicals Mackintosh produced, including *Cats, Miss Saigon, Les Miserables,* and *The Phantom of the Opera.* With its sound, lighting, and audiovisual facilities, it's possible to transform the lounge into a disco.

Checkers Lounge in black, white, gold, and red colors and a checkerboard pattern floor has what NCL claims is the longest bar at sea. Passengers may choose cabaret acts, illusionists, comedians, and on some cruises, the wildly popular jazz and pop show of Jane L. Powell & Company. The entertainment is uniformly of high standard in keeping with the NCL tradition.

The *Sky* also has a wedding chapel for ceremonies in port, a library, and the **Victoria Conference Center,** which seats 100 and can be divided into three smaller rooms.

On the Pool Deck, the **Topsider's Bar** is a long poolside bar with stools and outdoor tables; on the Sports Deck, the **Sports Bar** offers televisions with videotaped and live broadcasts of sporting events. It combines with the **Zone,** the teen disco. The **Observatory Lounge** has floor-to-ceiling windows overlooking the bow.

Roaming the decks is a "Skymobile" beverage cart making drink deliveries to passengers. When *Norwegian Sky* sails in the Caribbean, pool attendants provide Evian water, suntan lotion, cold face towels, and fresh fruit.

Sports, Fitness, and Beauty   The two swimming pools are connected by steps and a central wading platform to four hot tubs and set off by dark wood decks and dark green lounge chairs. Also on the enormous Sun Deck is a **Mandara Spa** with therapists trained in a wide range of spa treatments. It has a unisex beauty salon and a gym/aerobics area with exercise equipment to be used while enjoying ocean views through floor-to-ceiling glass walls.

On Sports Deck, passengers will find two golf driving nets, a full-size basketball/volleyball court, a batting cage, and shuffleboard. A walking and jogging track circles the Promenade Deck.

Children's Facilities   **Kids Korner** playroom on International Deck offers "Kid's Crew," a year-round, supervised program divided into four age groups; see "Children's Facilities" in *Norwegian Wind* section for details. A children's splash pool is on Sports Deck. There is also a new program, "Teen Passport," for teens ages 13–17, enabling teens to purchase a coupon book for $30, used for up to 20 non-alcoholic specialty drinks, as well as enjoying exclusive dance and pizza parties, and a farewell "Frat Party."

Shore Excursions   In Alaska, NCL offers some of mainstream cruising's best offbeat excursions, such as glacier hiking, mountain biking, forest trekking, a six-hour hike outside Skagway, and three hours of sea kayaking from Juneau (you're likely to see a whale close enough to feel its spray). Flight-seeing from Juneau to a remote lodge showcases vast ice fields. The more exotic tours have few slots; book early. Among the most popular is "Dive Into Adventure," for snorkeling and scuba diving. It's active and attracts a variety of passengers. Plus, few people can say they have been diving in Alaska. At excursion's end, participants shiver out of wet suits and jump into the heated pool on Sun Deck.

Note: Alaska shore excursions are expensive on every cruise line because of the very short season in which operators have to make money and the very high costs of operating tours in Alaska.

NORWEGIAN STAR	**QUALITY** 8	**VALUE** B
NORWEGIAN DAWN	**QUALITY** 9	**VALUE** B
Registry: Panama	Length: 971/965 feet	Beam: 107/105 feet
Total Cabins: 1,120	Draft: 28 feet	Speed: 25 knots
Maximum Passengers:	Passenger Decks: 15	Elevators: NA
2.240	Crew: 1,100	Space Ratio: NA

The Ships   The new $400-million, 91,000-ton megaliner, *Norwegian Star* (formerly slated for Star Cruises as *SuperStar Libra*) is something of a prototype for future NCL ships. Prior to her arrival in Hawaii, she joined NCL's new *Norwegian Sun* for the first-ever dual cruise-ship christening in Miami in 2001. Her name, *Norwegian Star,* was meant to signify the link between NCL and its owners, Star Cruises. Her sister ship, *Norwegian Dawn,* was delivered in December 2002.

The trendsetting *Star,* built in Germany, was outfitted to NCL specifications, and as the line's first ship to be based in Hawaii year-round, tailored to the requirements of the Hawaii market—i.e., no casino. However, a casino will be added when the *Star* moves to Alaska in spring 2004; based in Seattle, *Star* will become NCL's largest ship sailing in Alaskan waters, featuring winter cruises from Los Angeles to Mexico. Built at the maximum size to pass through the Panama Canal, she and her near-twin are NCL's largest and fastest ships, with a maximum cruising speed of 25 knots. They have been fitted with pod drives, which improve maneuverability.

Itineraries   See Itinerary Index.

Cabins   The ships have set new cruise industry standards in their cabins, with rich cherry-wood finishing, tea- and coffeemakers in every cabin, and larger bathrooms than the line's other ships, with toilets, shower, and washstand compartments separated by sliding doors. Seventy percent of cabins are outside, and over 70% of these have balconies.

A steel-and-glass structure on top of the ships, aft from the main sun deck, is a fantasy world, unlike anything on any other vessel today. It has two six-room "villas," each covering 5,350 square feet and each with a roof terrace and private garden and offering open-air dining, Jacuzzis, and totally private sunning and relaxing areas—all yours for a mere $26,000 per week.

In addition, the ship has 2 owner's suites, 2 honeymoon suites, and 30 penthouse suites, and an entire deck of spacious minisuites with balconies. There are 20 cabins of various categories for disabled passengers.

Most cabins have a sofa bed or pop-up trundle bed for a third lower bed and many have a fourth pull-down berth. A large number of cabins (including suites and minisuites) interconnect to create a two-, three-, four-, or five-bedroom area suitable for families.

Specifications   372 standard cabins with balconies, 250 outside; 361 inside; 107 minisuites with balconies; 2 owner's, 2 honeymoon, 30 penthouse suites; 6 multiroom villas; 20 wheelchair-accessible.

Dining   In keeping with the line's trendsetting Freestyle Cruising, enabling passengers to dine where, when, and with whom they wish, the ships each have 10 different restaurants offering 11 different menus every night—more dining options than any other ships in the North American market. **Versailles** (**Venetian** on *Dawn*), an ornate main dining room with floor-to-ceiling windows, offering the traditional six-course cruise dining experience, and **Agua** (**Aqua** on *Dawn*), a contemporary-styled second dining room, with a lighter menu. Both rooms are open from 5:30 p.m. to midnight. On *Star,* **Endless Summer,** a Hawaiian-themed restaurant set around the second level of the central atrium, has become the third traditional dining room; on *Dawn,* it's **Impressions,** with a 1900s French bistro style. Dining in these three restaurants do not have additional charges.

Soho, a high-end Pacific Rim restaurant features California and Asian fusion cuisine; **Ginza** is a Japanese restaurant with an à la carte section, a sushi and tempura bar, and a teppanyaki room. On *Dawn,* the Japanese/Chinese/Thai complex is called **Bamboo,** and on both ships, the outlets in this group have a $10 per person cover charge or an à la carte charge of $10–$15. **Le Bistro** is a French restaurant with nouvelle cuisine and French classics on the menu. The charge is $12.50 per person. The three restaurants with chargesrequire reservations.

The Market (**Blue Lagoon** on *Dawn*) is a food court for hamburgers, fish and chips, pot pies, and wok dishes; and an indoor/outdoor buffet restaurant extending over a third of a deck with "action stations" preparing made-to-order omelets, waffles, fruit soups, ethnic specialties, and pasta as well as an extensive buffet. **La Trattoria,** which takes over a corner of the Market in the evening, offers popular Italian fare and has table service. **Las Rambles** is a Spanish tapas restaurant and bar with live entertainment, but on the *Dawn,* it has been replaced by **Cagney's Steak House**—NCL's first steakhouse—with a 1930s theme and a $17.50 per-person cover charge.

Salsa on *Dawn* offers a combination menu of Tex-Mex selections and Spanish tapas. **Garden Café,** a buffet with food stations offering prepared-to-order omlets, pasta, soups, and ethnic specialties, doubles as a kids' café with an area that has small seats and tables.The *Star* also has an outdoor grill, an ice cream bar, and a coffee shop, plus 24-hour room service.

Facilities and Activities   One of the ships' most distinctive attractions is the show lounge, spanning three decks without obstruction and seating 1,150 people. Currently playing on both ships is *Music of the Night,* highlighting the music of Sir Andrew Lloyd Webber from such hits as *Evita, The Phantom of the Opera, Sunset Boulevard, Cats,* and others. Passengers also get to watch *It's Fame* and *Cirque Asia,* with the incredible feats of Chinese acrobats showcasing the cultures and tradition of the Pacific.

On *Dawn,* passengers are treated to two brand new shows. *Ravel,* meant to reflect the energy and excitement of Miami's hot South Beach, has DJs from the popular Miami television show *Deco Drive* manning the controls plus, red-hot radio personality Nikki Night from Miami's

Y-100-FM. *Ravel* rocks as musicians appear from every corner of the theater together with horn players, guitarists, and drummers, combining for a pastiche of Latin sounds. *Bollywood* is a celebration of India's traditional film culture, founded on spontaneous song and dance. Bombay nights come alive when the audience enters the theater as the scents of spices, incense, and perfumes fill the air. Bright sarongs and turbans combine to create a tapestry of color as stilt-walkers, magicians, and jugglers assemble to present the story. Aerialists wrapped in silks, belly dancers, and snake charmers perform against the Taj Mahal in the background.

The forward observation lounge has a dance floor and windows in the floor that allow views of the bridge; two adjoining rooms are available for private parties or meetings.

The *Star* has a cabaret lounge, karaoke bar with a large screen, a cigar lounge, wine cellar, champagne bar, a beer garden, an atrium café for coffee and pastries, an English pub, an attractive card room and library, and an Internet café with 16 seats. There is also a cinema/auditorium, four adjoining meeting rooms, gift shop and department store, and a wedding chapel.

The *Norwegian Dawn* has these attractions too, but it's most distinctive feature is the high-quality art on loan from Star Cruises Chairman Tan Sri Lim Kok Thay's personal collection. These include paintings by Vincent van Gogh, Henri Matisse, Claude Monet, and Pierre-Auguste Renoir—all of which have been exhibited in such famous museums as the National Gallery of Art in Washington, D.C., and the National Museum in Stockholm, among others. NCL has taken the art one step further by featuring images on the hull of the *Dawn.*

Another distinction for the *Norwegian Dawn:* She is the only ship offering seven-day cruises from New York to the Bahamas and the Caribbean on a year-round basis. Highlighting this itinerary, the ship stages "Ifuacata!" parties with hot Latin rhythms and special food and drinks. "Ifuacata!" has been called the hottest party trend in Miami and is named after the Spainish word meaning "to be hit by the unexpected."

A new NCL distinction: The first cruise line to offer wireless Internet access (WiFi) fleetwide. Passengers who bring their laptops can rent a wireless network card for $10 a day; laptops can be rented for $20 a day. Wireless Internet access costs $0.75 per minute, though buying minutes in bulk—33-, 100- or 250-minute packages—can bring the cost down to $0.40 per minute. The wireless service function best in certain areas of each ship, but it normally enables poolside surfing as well as access in meeting rooms and some other public areas.

Sports, Fitness, and Beauty   The main pool is located amidship on Deck 12. Aft is the bilevel spa and fitness center, with a waterfall in the atrium of its reception area and an indoor pool that is said to be the longest on any cruise ship. The fitness center has state-of-the-art cardiovascular workout equipment, aerobic and boxercise area with a sprung wooden floor, steam and sauna rooms, a jet-current exercise pool, whirlpool and hydrotherapy facilities. The spa operated by Mandara, one of the world's leading operators of resort spas and featured on all of NCL's ships, is in charge of the pampering with an exotic menu of treatments combining Asian and Eastern techniques. On the *Dawn,* the 11,302-square-foot **El Dorado Spa** has 21 treatment rooms, with one designed exclusively for couples. There are private hydrotherapy baths, a lap pool, a Jacuzzi, two Japanese pools, sauna, and a steam room in both the men's and women's areas. Passengers may also have spa treatments in their cabins, poolside and on-deck massages on port days, and massage and de-stress treatments on secluded beaches during private island visits.

The Sports Deck has an outside jogging track, golf driving range, volleyball, and basketball court. To complement the *Star's* facilities, an array of active shore excursions in Hawaii and Fanning Island, including mountain biking, sailing, scuba diving, and even skiing down a volcano, are available.

Children's Facilities The ships have a huge children's center, complete with a playroom, outdoor pool, movie theater, computer rooms, teen center, video arcade, a nursery, and toddlers' nap room. There is even a special children's area in the buffet restaurant, with their own low-level serving counter and kid-sized tables and chairs. *Norwegian Dawn,* constructed with families in mind, has the **T-Rex Childcare Center,** a supervised facility with a jungle gym; a children's playroom; **Flicks Movie Theater; Clicks,** a computer learning center equipped with five terminals; **Doodles** arts and crafts area; and **Snoozes** sleeping area. A highlight is the T-Rex Pool, a Jurassic-themed children's pool with dino-riffic water slides, a kids-only hot tub, and a paddling and wading pool for the little ones. The **Teen Club** is a disco strictly for teens, with a video wall showing the latest music video hits, a cinema, and **Video Zone,** a huge arcade with 25 of the latest video games. NCL has eight special menus for the most finicky young eaters, including kid-size hamburgers, hot dogs, spaghetti, chicken fingers, and ice cream sundaes. See "Children's Facilities" in *Norwegian Wind* section for details on the age-specific programs.

NORWEGIAN CROWN	QUALITY 7	VALUE B
Registry: Bahamas	Length: 616 feet	Beam: 92.5 feet
Cabins: 552	Draft: 24 feet	Speed: 20 knots
Maximum Passengers:	Passenger Decks: 10	Elevators: 4
1,104	Crew: 525	Space Ratio: 32.6

The Ship The *Crown Odyssey* came home to NCL in 2003 and resumed its former name as the *Norwegian Crown,* following a multimillion dollar refurbishment that added three new restaurants and converted the ship into a Freestyle Cruising vessel with a new look—a white hull— on the outside and many changes on the inside. The ship had spent the last three years as *Crown Odyssey* (the ship's original name) with Orient Lines, NCL's sister company.

Built in 1988, the spacious ship was widely acclaimed for her quality décor by the highly regarded design team of A. and M. Katzourakis. A modern interpretation of classic architectural elements with stunning Art Deco details, the décor in public rooms uses generous amounts of marble, fine woods, original art, antiques, chrome, mirrors, stained glass, smoked glass, reflective ceilings, and brass finishes.

Prior renovations included a redesigned Lido Deck with the addition of an Internet and e-mail center, library, card room, and and main lobby. On Marina Deck, a central foyer houses the reception desk, shore excursion office, shop, and a small gallery with fine antique reproductions leading to **Seven Continents Restaurant.**

At the foot of a circular grand staircase connecting the reception area and Odyssey Deck is a six-foot spherical sculpture in bronze by Italian artist Arnaldo Pomodoro. A mosaic of backlighted stained-glass panels in geometric patterns extends the height the ship's stairwells.

The *Norwegian Crown* was scheduled in begin service as part of the NCL fleet in September 2003, sailing from Baltimore as part of the line's expanded "Homeland Cruising" program. The 11-day Canada/New England cruises are NCL's first regular cruises from Baltimore. Afterwards, she sails from Miami to Santiago, Chile, to repeat her former South America series between Santiago and Buenos Aires. In summer and fall of 2004, she takes over *Norwegian Sea's* Philadelphia and New York/Bermuda series.

Itineraries   See Itinerary Index.

Cabins   *Crown* offers 18 categories on seven decks. About 78% are outside cabins, and more than half of the bathrooms have tubs. Most cabins are large; even the smallest have 154 square feet and the same basic amenities. All have full vanities, two mirrored closets, tie and shoe racks, safe, hardwood furniture and cabinetry, locked drawers, good lighting, and contemporary art. Bathrooms are marble or tiled and have large mirrors, recessed shelves, and hair dryers. Many bathtubs are midsize. All cabins have direct-dial phones and television with CNN and satellite channels. Four new suites on the Penthouse deck were added in the most recent renovations, as well as nine new inside passenger cabins.

All penthouse suites have private verandas, sitting room with a convertible sofa bed, refrigerator, walk-in closet, queen or convertible twin beds; marble bathroom with whirlpool tub, and butler service. Four apartments can be combined with adjacent units to provide more than 1,000 square feet. Glass partitions separate sitting and sleeping areas. Beds in the Superior AB Suite category fold into the wall to create a meeting room. The suites on Penthouse Deck have butler and concierge service; those on the other decks have only concierge service.

Specifications 116 inside cabins, 319 outside; 20 penthouse suites with verandas; 20 deluxe suites; 34 junior suites. Standard dimensions, 165 square feet. 284 double cabins; 150 triples; 82 quads; no singles; 32 connecting outside cabins. 4 cabins wheelchair-accessible.

Dining *Norwegian Crown* now boast six restaurants. The new additions are **Le Bistro,** NCL's popular signature alternative restaurant on the Lido deck, decorated in coral, green and gold colors with large, comfortable wood banquettes, classic chairs from France, and etched glass; the **Pasta Café,** high up on the top deck, with modern Italian décor accented by cobalt-blue and cherry wood, and a blue-granite-topped bar where passengers can watch the chefs prepare Italian cuisine; and **Chopsticks,** an Asian-themed restaurant, next to the **Yacht Club** on Odyssey Deck.

The main dining room, the elegantly appointed **Seven Continents Restaurant,** is a two-level room with a sunken central section under Tiffany-style glass domes. It's trimmed with lacquered woods, glass panels, and picture windows. There are two seatings, with open seating for breakfast and lunch and assigned for dinner. Spa cuisine is available. The dining room can be noisy due to the glass ceiling that reverberates the sound. It does benefit from very large windows and has two recessed side sections—the most desirable seats.

The Yacht Club serves as a dining venue for buffet breakfast and lunch with both indoor and outdoor dining. **Café d'Italia** is an al fresco dining venue for lunch aft on Penthouse Deck.

Facilities and Activities Daily activities include the Discovery Lecture Series, deck sports, bingo, bridge, dance classes, art, cooking demonstrations, and wine-tasting classes. . In addition to Le Bistro, the renovated Lido Deck aft has new **Kids and Teen Centers,** as well as the **Internet Café,** library, and game room. The Lido Bar was expanded to include the original outside area.

Evening entertainment is offered in the multitiered, Art Deco **Stardust Lounge,** where smoky gray mirrors create a sound-wave design in the tiered ceiling. Opaque crystals in Lalique-style glass panels continues the effect on the back wall. A sloping floor gives almost every seat good sight lines. The stage can be lowered to become a dance floor, and the intimate **Rendezvous Bar** next door is popular for cocktails. The **Monte Carlo Court Casino** received a complete renovation, adding glass walls around the perimeter and new upholstery and carpets in rich maroon and gold. The casino offers blackjack, roulette, Caribbean poker, and slot machines.

The ship's crowning glory, you might say, is the **Top of the Crown,** a circular observation lounge and bar with glass domes and floor-to-ceiling windows that offer sweeping views in three directions. A daytime retreat for reading and viewing scenery, it becomes a nighttime disco with an illuminated glass dance floor. The lounge has been enhanced with a new bar topped with blue-pearl granite. The stools, tables and chairs were removed to create an open space and replaced with pull-up cocktail tables attached to a railing that encircles the room. Expansive solarium windows with high-tech stainless-steel support systems make for a modern, more airy space. The teak deck has been restored, complete with large, plush lounge chairs.

Sports, Fitness, and Beauty　The ship's **Mandara Spa,** beauty salon and fitness center on Penthouse Deck were completely rebuilt. Aqua, mint green, and creamy white colors of mosaic tiles and light wood accents on the walls create the spa's serene setting. The spa has nine treatment rooms with a full-time director and offers a wide range of beauty treatments. Passengers can work out in separate aerobic and weight rooms as well as on an array of fitness equipment. The salon features four stations all facing an expanse of floor-to-ceiling windows.

Children's Facilities　A new teen and children's center has been added. The teen center, with bold colors of metallic purples, greens, and oranges, has a dance floor with state-of-the-art sound and light system, juice bar, and large, multicolored banquettes. A video arcade separates the teen center from the children's center. Kid's Crew participants enjoy an arts and crafts center, a computer corner, and a theater with a plasma screen and beanbags for comfortable viewing.

NORWEGIAN MAJESTY	QUALITY 5	VALUE C
Registry: Panama	Length: 680 feet	Beam: 89 feet
Cabins: 731	Draft: 20 feet	Speed: 21 knots
Maximum Passengers:	Passenger Decks: 9	Elevators: 6
1,462	Crew: 570	Space Ratio: 28

The Ship　*Norwegian Majesty* was lengthened in 1999 by 112 feet through insertion of a prefabricated midsection that added 203 new cabins, plus new public areas and facilities, increasing the ship's capacity from 1,056 to 1,460 passengers. Interiors throughout were refurbished. The work added a second pool, second dining room, new casino, another outdoor bar, **Le Bistro** restaurant, coffee bar, and substantially more deck space. Crew cabins were expanded to accommodate increased staff. Two new elevators and a third stair tower were incorporated. Corridors and stair towers received new carpets shipwide. All decks and most public rooms were renamed.

The lengthening also gave *Norwegian Majesty* a sleeker, more hydrodynamic profile, enabling the ship to maintain its 20-knot speed with the same power plant, despite increased size. New buoyancy reduced the ship's draft, allowing her to call on all current ports and at some that were previously inaccessible because of shallower waters.

In November 2003, the ship was scheduled to start a series of cruises from Charleston, South Carolina to the Western Caribbean. The home-porting in Charleston reflects a continuing expansion of NCL's Home-land Cruising program and is intended to cater particularly to the drive markets in nearby states. Apparently, it has already proven itself because shortly after NCL announced the plan, travel agents were complaining about the ship being overbooked.

Norwegian Majesty debuted in 1992 as Majesty Cruises' *Royal Majesty* and was intended to appeal to affluent passengers with understated ele-gance. Stylish interiors create a refined, harmonious environment of sim-plicity and clean lines. Contemporary décor employs soft colors, natural wood, leather sofas, glass, mirrors, and fresh foliage. Models of old sailing vessels bow to tradition. The ship is well laid out with many quiet corners. Characteristic of NCL, forward lounges have walls of sloped windows.

Passengers step almost directly into the two-deck atrium that serves as the main lobby and contains the front desk and shore excursion office. Called Crossroads, the circular area has white marble floors and stairs to a white marble island centered with a baby grand piano and furnished with banquettes.

The Atlantic Deck is devoted entirely to public areas. Off the lobby is the new **Four Seasons Dining Room;** beyond, the **Seven Seas Dining Room.** Forward are boutiques, library, card room, and meeting room. Small lounges border **Rendezvous,** a large, V-shaped piano bar connect-ing to **Royal Fireworks,** a lounge with panoramic windows.

Itineraries   See Itinerary Index.

Cabins   Ten categories range from royal suites to inside cabins with lower and upper berths. About 71% are outside, and a high percentage are nonsmoking. Standard cabins are modest in size. They have clean, uncluttered lines and are finished in natural wood. Most have twin beds separated by a chest of drawers. A desk unit has drawer space and a dress-ing mirror, and three closets add to storage. Each cabin has a television carrying CNN, cable sports, shipboard notices, and movies. Bathrooms have showers and a large sink, with ample counter and shelf space and a hair dryer. All cabins have a built-in ironing board.

Upper-category suites and cabins have a minibar, queen beds, and large windows. Forward on Majesty Deck, a group of cabins spans an unusual half-moon contour overlooking the bow. The two Royal Suites on Norway Deck have marble baths and 24-hour butler service.

Specifications   203 new deluxe or standard outside and standard inside. 250 inside, 481 outside; 22 suites. Standard cabins, 108–145 square feet. 487 cabins with 2 lowers (134 convert to doubles); 291 with double beds; 73 with 3 berths; 367 with 4 berths; 22 suites accommodate 3 persons; 4 wheelchair-accessible.

Dining   The impressive **Seven Seas Dining Room** has wraparound, full-length windows. A white baby-grand piano plays on a small island at the center. Most tables are set for four or six, contributing to the room's intimate feeling. Seven Seas, the first smoke-free dining room on a major cruise ship, has new chairs and carpeting in soothing blues.

The **Four Seasons Dining Room** also offers ocean panoramas through floor-to-ceiling windows. Adjacent is the 58-seat **Le Bistro** alternative restaurant, which serves light Italian and continental cuisine in flexible dining hours.

Breakfast and lunch buffets are served inside the casual **Café Royale** on Sun Deck; outside space overlooks two pools. The room is attractively furnished in light wood and wicker chairs. It's tight for buffet lines. Buffets are average, offering a range of hot and cold dishes, daily specialties, and cakes, pastries, muffins, and breads. The café is connected to the **Royal Observatory,** a handsome observation lounge/bar below that doubles as a sports bar.

Piazza San Marco Grill, a second Sun Deck serving area, is partially covered. Burgers, hot dogs, pizza, ice cream, snacks, and late-night buffets (different from the nightly midnight buffet) are offered.

Service   The crew encompasses 34 nationalities, and except for the dining room, service shipwide has received generally good reviews.

Facilities and Activities   Daytime offerings include bridge tours, Ping-Pong tournaments, bridge and Scrabble, fruit- and vegetable-carving demonstrations, poolside fashion show, napkin-folding classes, wine tasting, and dance. The ship has a card room, well-stocked library, and small boardroom. The Internet café is also in the card room; fees apply.

The **Palace Theater** show lounge is on one level with a steeply tiered floor. Sight lines to the circular stage are excellent from almost every seat. The new midsection has the **Monte Carlo Casino,** offering blackjack, Caribbean stud poker, roulette, and slot machines. Next door, the attractive **Polo Bar** has piano music nightly. One deck below, a small coffee bar and lounge offers coffees, teas, and coffee-flavored drinks, plus bar service. **Royal Fireworks** is a quiet area or meeting space by day and a dance lounge before and after dinner.

In summer, when the ship is in Bermuda, she isn't allowed to stage big productions or open the casino. Instead, the ship offers excursions to local nightclubs. An evening cocktail cruise along Bermuda's pretty shores is another option.

Sports, Fitness, and Beauty   Fitness fans pair workouts and ocean views in the gym. Equipment includes Life Circuit machines and a Nordic

Track. Exercise and dance classes are held in a mirrored studio. The spa on Promenade Deck has saunas for men and women and offers massage. A small beauty parlor also offers facials and spa treatments. A jogging track circles Promenade Deck.

Top decks have been transformed by the addition of a second swimming pool and the **Topsider's Bar,** a second open-air bar. Sky Deck, a new space above the Sun Deck, provides more sunning area while shading the two pools and whirlpools below. It has lounge chairs, rest rooms, and showers.

Children's Facilities   Supervised program; see "Children's Facilities" in *Norwegian Wind* section for details. **Kids Korner** play area has a kiddies' pool, playground rides, ball slide, and puppet theater. Bathrooms have lowered kiddies' sinks. Older children have a video arcade.

Shore Excursions   The ship spends four full days in St. George's, in front of King's Square. Nearby are shops, historic St. Peter's church, and motor-scooter rentals (the island's most popular transport; no car rentals are available). The picturesque town is ideal for a walking and convenient to beaches, but not to Hamilton, a town at the island's opposite end. Among excursions available is a visit to the Bermuda Aquarium Museum and Zoo. The ship's sports program offers sailing, snorkeling, scuba diving, and deep-sea fishing.

NORWEGIAN SEA	QUALITY 4	VALUE C
Registry: Bahamas	Length: 700 feet	Beam: 93 feet
Cabins: 763	Draft: 22 feet	Speed: 20 knots
Maximum Passengers:	Passenger Decks: 9	Elevators: 6
1,518	Crew: 630	Space Ratio: 27

The Ship   NCL's preparation for the 1990s began in 1988 with the debut of *Seaward,* renamed *Norwegian Sea,* the line's first brand-new ship in two decades at the time. The vessel was a class act from her unveiling. Glass, chrome, and Formica, with an almost total absence of wood, gave her a contemporary look, fashionable at the time. A decade later, the interiors seem dated. Now after multimillion-dollar renovations in early 2003, *Norwegian Sea* is up-to-date once again. Enhancements range from the addition of a new restaurant, new carpet, and granite floors and countertops to wood floors and new upholstery in various public rooms on the ship.

Robert Tillberg and Petter Yran, the original designers, created spaciousness by employing floor-to-ceiling windows to open the ship and provide splendid seascapes in lounges and four novel, glass-enclosed stairways. Also appealing are the small lounges—pleasant corners for drinks, conversation, and relaxation..

Norwegian Sea, which has returned to weekly "Texaribbean" cruises that NCL pioneer in the 1990's, is the only cruise ship sailing year-round from Houston.

Itineraries   See Itinerary Index.

Cabins   The ship offers 16 categories, with the 6 pricier ones on three upper decks and the others on the three lower decks. Compared to NCL's newer ships, *Norwegian Sea's* cabins are small. Standard cabins don't have a sitting area. Most are fitted with twin beds in an L shape; all have hair dryers and television for movies and 24-hour CNN and ESPN. Storage includes two closets and lots of drawers. Bathrooms are small, with meager counter space and small showers. Views from most cabins on Deck 7 are obstructed by lifeboats; windows of those on Deck 6 overlook the Promenade Deck (the one-way glass doesn't work well when cabin lights are on). Some J category inside cabins with two lowers and two uppers are small—suitable as a quad only for those really watching their pennies. The ship's suites were completely redecorated.

Specifications   243 inside cabins, 516 outside; 7 suites. Standard dimensions, 122 and 140 square feet. 462 with 2 lower beds (convertible to queen); 290 with 2 lowers and third/fourth berths; no singles; 4 wheelchair-accessible.

Dining   The dining rooms—**Four Seasons** and **Seven Seas**—have new décor and furnishings. Both offer open seating with most tables for four, six, or eight; few tables seat two. Menu selections are varied, with two to four options per course, but the food generally is unremarkable. The best choices are lamb and steaks, which are consistently high quality. Espresso and cappuccino are available without charge.

The **Big Apple Café,** the small lido restaurant sporting new ceramic tiles and wood floors and furnished with marble-top tables, garden awnings, overlooks panoramic sea views. Open almost around the clock, it serves informal buffets at breakfast and lunch, pizza, afternoon snacks, and light suppers.

Le Bistro, NCL' signature alternative restaurant, was transformed with new colors of classic golds and greens and new carpet, curtains, and upholstery. The no-reservations café, open from 6 to 11 p.m., has its own kitchen and offers an eclectic menu with a daily specialty. It only seats 82, so arrive early or very late. The **Pasta Café,** the ship's new fifth restaurant, is decorated in burgundy and peach colors, and serves Italian fare.

Service   *Norwegian Sea's* best feature is service-warm, friendly, and efficient. Staff for dining rooms, **Le Bistro,** and cabins, in particular, is outstanding.

Facilities and Activities   Overall, the daily agenda has fewer options than usually are found on NCL ships. At the stern on Deck 10 are the little-used **Observatory Lounge** (curtains were drawn every time we looked in, defeating the room's purpose); **Gatsby's Wine Bar,** which has had a dramatic change from its former black and white to a more romantic room with reds and greens, along with new wooden paneling and Scandinavian-designed chairs and tables; and **Boomer's** disco on Deck 8.

The International Deck is entertainment central. The focus is the two-deck Crystal Court dominated by a crystal and marble water sculpture. To one side is **Oscar's,** a stylish piano bar that's frequently the scene of art auctions. 'At center deck is Everything Under the Sun, the large shopping arcade; bargains are few despite daily promotions. Forward is the refurbished **Cabaret Lounge** showroom. Seats are very comfortable, but sightlines are hampered by the room's many columns and uniform elevation.

The newly refurbished **Stardust Lounge,** with rich burgundy and gold décor, is used for dancing and entertainment. The room has concentric circles radiating from the large dance floor and remind some of old-time movie nightclubs.It's used during the day for lectures, port talks, and bingo (pricey). The large **Monte Carlo Casino** has much less glitz than gaming rooms on other cruise ships. Slot machines line the room's side promenade. Two years ago, NCL added an **Internet Café,** and now passengers have wireless access or WiFi. They also have a refurbished **Butterfly Card Room and Library.**

Sports, Fitness, and Beauty   Topside, the ship has a large sunning area with a 42-foot pool, one of the longest on any cruise ship. A second pool has overhead sprinklers, shallows for lounging, and twin hot tubs. Nearby is **Lickety Splits,** which serves ice cream in early afternoon. One flight up, a sun deck forms a balcony on the pools' periphery. Forward is a small fitness center (open 24 hours) and sauna, golf driving range, and another bar. An unobstructed, quarter-mile deck circles the Promenade Deck. The Pool Deck was sanded and refinished and given new deck carpeting and teak decking around the pool.

Children's Facilities   Supervised age-specific children's program available; see "Children's Facilities" in *Norwegian Wind* section for details. The Porthole playroom for NCL's "Kids Crew" activities is open certain hours when the ship is at sea, but it's mostly closed when the ship is in port.

Postscript   Readers planning a cruise on *Norwegian Sea* should review the entire NCL section for a full picture of the line's cruise experience.

NORWAY	QUALITY **4**	VALUE **C**
Registry: Bahamas	Length: 1,035 feet	Beam: 110 feet
Cabins: 1,016	Draft: 35 feet	Speed: 20 knots
Maximum Passengers:	Passenger Decks: 12	Elevators: 11
2,032	Crew: 920	Space Ratio: 38

The Ship   The *Norway* is one of a kind, a great lady with classic lines and lots of character. When NCL bought the *France* in 1979, she had been mothballed for five years, but at $18 million, she was a bargain. Her high-quality equipment and workmanship were unrivaled. To build such a vessel today would cost $1 billion.

NCL spent $100 million to transform her into the *Norway*—a city at sea. Another update for the 1990s restored some of the beauty that made her a legend as the *France*. Two glass-enclosed top decks, an observation deck, 124 luxurious cabins, a huge spa, fitness center, and jogging track were added. The work preserved some of her classic features, including irreplaceable bronze murals, gold and silver wall treatments, and art from the France. But a lot of haphazard make-overs have resulted in a hodge-podge of styles.

In 2003, the ship suffered extensive damage from a fire. Details of the renovations had not been revealed at press time; nonetheless, NCL says it expects to return the ship to service by spring 2004, pending a report from the German shipyard where the repairs are to be made .

Itineraries   See Itinerary Index.

Cabins   Twenty categories spread across ten decks. Most cabins are roomy with ample storage, but there are also some tiny minimum-rate cabins. The top six categories, most on the top three decks, offer concierge service. All port-side cabins are nonsmoking. All cabins have television with CNN and ESPN.

During the initial *Norway* rebuilding, some spectacular cabins were created along the old tourist-class promenade deck using the original floor-to-ceiling windows; they have recessed bedroom alcoves and separate sitting areas. Some of *France's* original cabins with gold leaf and bronze fixtures were left intact, and Art Deco vanities with three-sided movable mirrors were retained. Many cabins have exquisite, glass-inlaid armoires from the original first-class cabins. All cabins display posters issued in 1994 to celebrate the ship's heritage.

Of the two decks added in 1990, the Sun Deck houses 32 penthouse suites, and Sky Deck has 84 deluxe cabins and suites with floor-to-ceiling windows; almost half have verandas. Two owner's suites and two grand deluxe suites decorated in royal blue and white are at the bow. The suites differ; some have a Jacuzzi; all have living room, bedroom, dressing room, and refrigerator. The owner's suites on the Viking Deck, with two bedrooms and two full bathrooms, are original. Late risers or those who enjoy an afternoon nap should not book the forward cabins on International Deck, as they will hear constant pounding from joggers overhead.

Specifications   371 inside cabins, 475 outside; 170 suites. Standard dimensions, 150 square feet; 503 cabins with 2 lower beds; 369 with double/queen bed; 124 with upper and lower berths; 10 wheelchair-accessible.

Dining   *Norway* has two beautiful dining rooms. The **Windward Restaurant** was the first-class Chambord restaurant on France, noted for its unobstructed expanse, but now with much more crowded seating.

Patrons descend a glamorous staircase and are seated amid gold and bronze murals. The former golden dome was redesigned into a star-filled night sky. The contemporary **Leeward Restaurant** is as dramatic. A spiral staircase leads to a mezzanine, reopened in the 1990 renovations; here, a table at the railing is a prized position. Service and food are the same in both rooms; seating is based on cabin location rather than category. Forward-cabin passengers eat at Windward; aft, in Leeward. Theme nights include the popular "Viking Night," when costumed staff in elaborately decorated dining rooms offer Scandinavian specialties. "SS France Night" evokes the grand style of cruising's past.

The **Great Outdoor Restaurant** overlooking the stern has a teak ceiling and overhead fans. It's a congested and chaotic setting, with long lines at breakfast and lunch buffets and deck parties during some theme cruises. The food isn't up to the dining room's level. The Art Deco **Le Bistro** alternative restaurant serves dinner at no additional charge; $5 tip is suggested. Open to all passengers, it seats 140 on a first-come, first-served basis. Book early. Wines are available by the glass.

The *Norway* was the first to offer NCL's wildly popular Chocoholic dessert buffet. High tea is served in the Art Deco **Club Internationale** lounge. Late-night snackers may find a Caribbean deck party. Passengers do not seem to agree on the *Norway's* cuisine. Some say the food is excellent; others say it's good but not exceptional. Still other diners express disappointment.

Service   There's no agreement on service, either. Some say it's wonderful; others call it NCL's weakest link, particularly in the dining room. Most praise cabin attendants. On a ship this large, varying opinions aren't unusual. People come with their own experiences and expectations. One waiter or barman can make all the difference. The bottom line is that the service is uneven.

Facilities and Entertainment   *Norway* has facilities to handle big-time entertainment, such as Broadway shows and Las Vegas–style revues, There's also music for dancing, disco, a piano bar, and comedy. Most of the action is on the central International and Pool decks. The bilevel **Saga Theatre** hosts blockbuster shows. The **Sports Bar** is a multi-screen hubbub of activity, the first aboard NCL ships. The stylish, spacious **Club Internationale** best reflects what is left of the *France's* splendor, with floor-to-high-ceiling lounge windows, plush sofas, and Art Deco touches carefully preserved. It's a grand setting for afternoon tea and drinks and dancing before and after dinner.

The million-dollar **Monte Carlo Casino** has black granite floors, mirrored walls, and a palette of magenta, hot pink, crimson, and royal blue accents. Ten replicas of antique slot machines by the entrance join 200 of the latest models. Nearby is **North Cape Lounge and Bar,** popular all-hours for entertainment. The disco **Dazzles** (downstairs, replacing the indoor tourist-class swimming pool) parties into the wee hours.

Activities and Diversions *Norway* is said to offer 80 or more activities. That's likely, considering the schedule of art auctions, bingo, dance classes, culinary demonstrations, word puzzles, parlor games, fashion shows, bridge and more.

Sports, Fitness, and Beauty *Norway's* facilities are outstanding. The ship has more than 65,000 square feet of outdoor decks—a mecca for sun worshippers. Shade-seekers can find a covered lounging area behind the bridge on Fjord Deck.

The fitness center, basketball and volleyball courts, and one-sixth-mile jogging track are on Olympic Deck. The ocean-view fitness center—opened 24 hours, 7 days a week—provides workout equipment and daily exercise classes. Topside between the stacks is a tremendous open deck and pool with bar. A year-round sports program is tied to activities in port with an incentive program offering prizes such as fanny packs and T-shirts for participants.

The luxurious **Roman Spa,** evoking a luxurious Roman bath—the Romans never had it so good!—has a large central area where white columns support high-arched ceilings and leather lounges line the sides. There are 16 treatment rooms for body wraps, aromatherapy, and other beauty treatments; 4 herbal therapy baths (cruising's first), cardiovascular exercise equipment, steam rooms, saunas, a Jacuzzi for eight people, beauty salon, a spa menu in dining rooms, and more. The **Gladiators** training room offers Stairmasters, bikes, and computerized fitness analysis machine. Spa experiences range from an hour to all week—and none of it cheap.

Children's Facilities Coordinators plan and supervise daily activiites in the year-round children's program. An NCL brochure lists activities for four age groups. See "Children's Facilities" in *Norwegian Wind* section for details.

NCL America

In February 2003, NCL surprised the cruise world when it announced that it would have a U.S.-flagged ship in Hawaii by summer 2004, employing an all-American crew, and subject to all American laws. The announcement came soon after Congress had passed a federal spending bill, which included a measure allowing NCL to sail foreign-built ships (the former Project America vessels) under a U.S. flag in Hawaiian waters without having to visit a foreign port (as had been required by law), and marked the first major exemption to the Passenger Services Act, enacted in 1886.

The legislation enables the owner of the Project America vessels (NCL) to reflag the two Project America vessels, plus one existing foreign-flagged ship, under the U.S. flag, subject to certain terms and conditions (for example, the ships cannot operate in the Caribbean and Alaska).

NCL America is the line's new brand under which all of its U.S.-flagged and -crewed ships will operate. For now, that involves two NCL America ships sailing interisland cruises and two NCL ships sailing Hawaii/Fanning Island itineraries—the largest Hawaii deployment ever and representing a 40% increase in 2004 over the previous year.

Pride of America, NCL's first Project America ship, now under construction at the Lloyd Werft shipyard in Germany, is the first new ocean-going passenger ship in nearly 50 years to sail under the American flag. She begins service in Hawaii on July 4, 2004, offering seven-night interisland cruises round trip from Honolulu.

Pride of Aloha, the second Project America ship, will be the 2,000-passenger *Norwegian Sky,* the first NCL ship to offer Freestyle Cruising when she was introduced in 2000. Reflagged under U.S. registry, she will be 100% U.S. crewed and will begin her Hawaii service in October 2004, offering three- and four-night interisland cruises round trip from Honolulu.

Norwegian Wind returns to Hawaii in May 2004 and resumes her 10- and 11-day itineraries, including Fanning Island (Kiribati) from Honolulu year-round. By the time the first NCL America ship arrives in Hawaii, the *Norwegian Star* will have moved from its Hawaii–Fanning Island cruises to seven-day summer Alaska voyages from Seattle. NCL says Project America Three is likely to enter the Hawaii market in 2006.

On the heels of its Project America purchase, NCL bought the only two existing U.S.-built ocean-going cruise ships, the *United States* and the *Independence,* and says it plans to rebuild them completely. Transforming these 50-year old vessels into modern ships for U.S. cruises falls into the line's future strategy that some have called the "Americanization" of NCL. According to NCL, the purchase was a practical way for NCL to expand its three-ship U.S.-flagged fleet; others say it was a shrewd move to protect its Hawaii position from competition.

To rebuild the two U.S.-built ships, the minimum the law requires is to maintain the hull and superstructure as 100% U.S., so all the steel and structural work is done in a U.S. shipyard. Beyond that, NCL can chose a U.S. or European shipyard, or both, for interior work. NCL says renovations are likely to take several years.

PRIDE OF AMERICA	**(Preview)**	
Registry: United States	Length: 920.6ft	Beam: 105.6 feet
Cabins: 1,073	Draft: 26 feet	Speed: 22 knots
Maximum Passengers:	Passenger Decks: 15	Elevators: 10
2,144	Crew: tba	Space Ratio: 37

The Ship   *Pride of America* has as her theme the "Best of America," reflected in the décor and names of public reooms—you can't miss it, starting with the design of the atrium, called the Capitol Atrium, inspired by the Capitol Building and the White House. The eight dining outlets and many lounges have such names as **Liberty Restaurant, Lone Star Steak House,** and **Napa Wine Bar,** among others.

In addition to an abundance of public rooms, the ship has state-of-the-art entertainment venues, three pools, extensive children's facilities, and large meeting facilities. It also sports several NCL firsts, including a conservatory, a new category of family suites, a tennis court, and an art gallery—all named and decorated to reflect America's diversity. (*Pride of Aloha's* Hawaiian theme is to be incorporated during the *Norwegian Sky's* refurbishment in September 2004.)

Itineraries   See Itinerary Index

Cabins   *Pride of America's* extensive choice of cabins is highlighted by a grand Grand Suite, over 660 balcony cabins, 250 family accommodations in all categories, and NCL's new concept—family suites.

The five owner's suites, each with 870 square feet, are named after Hawaiian flowers; each of six deluxe penthouse suites cover 735 square feet, and 28 penthouse suites range from 504 to 585 square feet. The suites are funished with a king-size bed and walk-in closet, a bathroom with a separate shower and Jacuzzi bath, dressing area, and flat-screen television; a separate living room has a Bang & Olufsen entertainment center, television with a DVD player and CD/DVD library, and computer access with Internet connection.

Each of the eight new-style family suites covers 360 square feet and has a living room furnished with a double sofabed and entertainment center, separate den with a single sofa bed, and a private bedroom with twin beds convertible to a queen. Four additional family suites (330–380 square feet) are interconnecting cabins sleeping up to eight people. The larger of the two cabins is an oversized outside cabin with two single beds that can be combined for a queen-size bed, plus a sitting area with a double sofa bed. The cabin interconnects with another outside cabin that has two single beds and two upper berths. The eight-person family suites have two bathrooms.

The 1,400-square-foot Grand Suite, positioned high atop the ship forward of the main sundeck, offers sweeping views of the ocean and an impressive assortment of amenities. It has a large living room with a Bang & Olufsen entertainment center with television, CD, stereo, DVD player, CD/DVD library, computer access with Internet connection, and a wet bar. The suite also has a dining room with a polished teak table seating six, plus a private butler. The master bedroom has a king-size bed and bathroom with separate shower and Jacuzzi bath, a dressing area with a flat-screen television and a large walk-in closet, and a separate powder room. On the large, wraparound veranda, suite occupants and their guests can enjoy open-air dining, a Jacuzzifor up to six people, and private areas for sunbathing and for entertaining up to 50 visitors.

Dining *Pride of America* offers eight restaurants and nine different menus every night. These include two main restaurants and alternative gourmet, ethnic, and casual eateries.

On Deck 5, **Skyline**, a main restaurant, has décor inspired by the architecture and skyscrapers of the 1930's; **Liberty**, the second main restaurant one deck up, has colonial design featuring the Founding Fathers and large paintings depicting important moments in American History. Both offer traditional dining.

Also on Deck 5, **China Town**, an elegant Pacific Rim/Asian fusion restaurant, has a sushi and sashimi bar and a teppanyaki room with two tables accommodating 32 people and offering Japanese-style dining with food prepared in front of guests. **Jefferson's Bistro**, NCL's signature restaurant, has an à la carte menu of nouvelle and classic French cuisine and décor inspired by Thomas Jefferson's home, Monticello. (Jefferson was the U.S. Ambassador to France from 1785 to 1789.)

On Deck 6, the **Lone Star Steak House** is an upscale steakhouse with Texas décor and art depicting the Houston Space Center, Texas Rangers, and Dallas Cowboys, and serves Angus Beef and other grilled meat, seafood, and chicken. The indoor/outdoor **Cadillac Diner**, a 24-hour diner, has décor of 1950s pop stars complete with Cadillac seats and a video juke box. The fare includes hamburgers, fish and chips, pot pie, and wok dishes.

On Deck 11, **Little Italy**, a casual Italian eatery inspired by New York's Little Italy, serves pasta, pizza, and other Italian specialties; while **Aloha Café/Kids Café**, the indoor/outdoor buffet with a Hawaiin theme including outrigger canoes and Polynesian carvings and artifacts, has food stations for prepared-to-order omelets, waffles, fruit, soups, and ethnic specialties. It also includes a buffet with small chairs and tables to accommodate 48 kids.

Facilities and Activities The heart of the ship, the Capitol Atrium, signals her All-American theme and has a decorative stone floor, water feature, and a stunning backlit glass dome. Her seven lounges and bars are designed to reflect the diversity of the country, such as the **Mardi Gras Cabaret**, the ship's nightclub; the **Gold Rush Pub**; and two outdoor pool bars, **Key West Bar & Grill** and the **Waikiki Bar.**

The **Soho Art Gallery** will offer original works of art, while Newbury Street resembles New England shops in the early 1900s. There is NCL's first conservatory, with a tropical landscaped garden and live exotic birds; the **Washington Library**; and the **Hollywood Theater** with large, golden statues adorning the walls. The ship also has WiFi capability and an Internet center. Passengers can obtain an Internet access card for their laptops or rent a laptop with wireless Internet capability.

Pride of America's meeting facilities—among the largest at sea—encompass six meeting rooms ranging from boardrooms for 10 people to an auditorium that can accommodate over 250 persons. Five of the meeting rooms—named for Hawaii and her islands—can be used individually or combined. The **Diamond Head Auditorium** is a multilevel, circular room that boasts a state-of-the-art audiovisual system with multiple screens that lower from the ceiling to be viewed by all participants. The auditorium also splits into two amphitheater-style presentation rooms. The conference area has a business center, a separate large gathering and break area, and the **Lanai Bar and Lounge,** for group cocktail parties and other purposes.

NCL America expects the ship's meeting facilities to appeal to the business market on several accounts. As the only large U.S.-flagged ships regularly sailing the Hawaiian islands and visiting only U.S. ports, onboard meetings qualify for corporate and individual tax deductions for meetings expenses. With weekly three-, four-, and seven-day cruises, planners can book a week's cruise or combine the short cruises with a hotel stay.

Sports, Fitness, and Beauty The **Santa Fe Spa and Fitness Center,** a tranquil area decorated with natural elements such as stone, wood, and artifacts from New Mexico, is operated by Mandara and offers an exotic menu of spa and beauty treatments. The Fitness Center has Cybex exercise equipment and Lifefitness cardiovascular machines, each with its own flat-screen television; an aerobics room for yoga, power walking, and other fitness classes; and saunas and steam room.

The Sports Deck has a basketball, volleyball, and soccer court. The large South Beach sunning and swimming area, inspired by Miami's Art Deco district, has some novel distractions and activities capturing the energy and fun of Ocean Drive and Lincoln Road.

Children's Facilities The ship is particularly family-friendly. At the **Rascal's Kids Center** and Kid's Pool—supervised facilities designed around a theme of native animals of America—the little ones can be kept busy with their own age-specific activities throughout their cruise.

Orient Lines

1510 SE 17th Street, Suite 400
Ft. Lauderdale, FL 33316-1716
(954) 527-6660; (800) 333-7300; fax (954) 527-6657
www.orientlines.com

Type of Ships   Midsize oceanliner.

Type of Cruise   Affordable, destination-intensive, light adventure with first-class amenities, fine cuisine, and refined ambience.

Cruise Line's Strengths

- service by attentive crew
- itineraries
- singles policy
- price
- dock-level gangway door
- expert lecturers on longer voyages
- precruise information

Cruise Line's Shortcomings

- limited room service
- entertainment

Fellow Passengers   Orient Lines attracts mature, experienced, inquisitive passengers who are friendly and interested in the line's off-the-beaten-track itineraries. On longer cruises, passengers range in age from 50 to 70, have average annual incomes of about $75,000, and are retired or semiretired, business owners, managers, or professionals. Most are North Americans, but some cruises might include Brits and other Europeans, Australians, and South Africans, depending on the itinerary. Many are veteran cruisers, but several are first-timers who have traveled frequently and are drawn to an Orient cruise by its strong destination focus.

Recommended For   Orient Lines has two seasons, each with a different appeal. On longer, winter cruises, passengers tend to be seasoned travelers, not necessarily experienced cruisers, who have the curiosity to appreciate exotic destinations, seek a learning experience, but like to travel in comfort. Also, small-ship devotees wanting to sample a cruise on a larger ship but not a megaliner. From May–October, passengers tend to be first-time cruisers, families, honeymooners; those wanting a land and sea vacation in Europe.

Not Recommended For   Unsophisticated or inexperienced travelers and those seeking a high-energy, holiday-at-sea, party atmosphere.

Cruise Areas and Seasons   In winter, Antarctica, New Zealand, Australia, Africa, and South America, including the Amazon, Caribbean, and Panama Canal. In summer, Mediterranean, Greek Isles, Black Sea, Northern Europe, Scandinavia, and Russia.

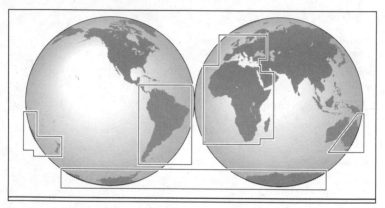

The Line   Orient Lines originated in 1991 when its former CEO, Gerry Herrod, a British entrepreneur and tour and cruise line veteran, bought the Russian liner *Alexander Pushkin* for about $25 million, when it had been in a Singapore yard for minor repairs and the Soviets couldn't pay their bills. The ship, built in East Germany in 1965 for the Soviets—who hoped to generate hard currency by cashing in on the growing cruise market—was one of four sister ships with ice-strengthened hulls. They served as Soviet troop ships.

At the cost of $75 million, Orient Lines transformed the vessel into a luxury liner and named her *Marco Polo*. At the same time, the cruise line was launched to offer upscale voyages for experienced travelers to exotic destinations at reasonable prices. In its second year, the mission changed somewhat when the line found great success in a summer Mediterranean program.

Orient Lines was purchased by Norwegian Cruise Line in 1998, but continued to operate as a separate entity. Meanwhile, NCL, including Orient Lines, was purchased by Asian-based Star Cruises.

THE FLEET	BUILT/RENOVATED	TONNAGE	PASSENGERS
Marco Polo	1965/1993	22,080	826

Style "Adventure in elegance" is one way Orient Lines' cruises have been described. From the start, Orient differed from most mainstream cruise lines by focusing on destinations, giving as much weight to developing unusual itineraries as to providing all the comforts and fine cuisine of a deluxe ship.

Meant to be an all-encompassing experience, the line's winter cruises include detailed port briefings, lectures by distinguished guest speakers and experts on destination areas, and extended pre- and postcruise hotel stays with sight-seeing. Some itineraries feature shipboard performances by local groups to showcase the culture of regions visited.

Like her sister Norweigan Cruise Line, an early indication of the Asian influence of Star Cruises on Orient Lines can be found with the introduction of Mandara Spa to operate the ship spa. Treatments stem from Mandara's Southeast Asian roots and include time-tested Balinese techniques, among others.

Distinctive Features Gentlemen social hosts (except on Mediterranean cruises); local cultural performances; helicopter and topside helipad; videotaping of lectures for replay on ship's television; low single supplement. One of only two luxury ships permitted to cruise Antarctica.

	HIGHEST	LOWEST	AVERAGE
PER DIEM	$719	$216	$385

Per diems are calculated from cruise line's nondiscounted *cruise-only* fares on standard accommodations and vary by season, cabin, and cruise areas.

Rates Port charges are additional.

Special Fares and Discounts Advance-purchase 10% discounts, 120 days before departure, depending on itinerary and cabin. Savings up to 28% for two or more cruises in sequence.

- **Single Supplement** 125% on all cabin categories except A and suites. For Mediterranean sailings, 50% for categories D–K, 75% for B and C, 100% for A and suites. The line frequently waives the supplement in special promotions.

- Guaranteed share program in specific cabin categories.

Packages

- **Air/Sea** Yes.

- **Pre/Post** Cruises are designed as cruise/tours with one- to three-day pre- and/or postcruise hotel stays in gateway cities. Several Mediterranean itineraries also include two- to six-day escorted motorcoach tours.

- **Others** Yes.

Past Passengers After their first cruise, passengers are enrolled in the Polo Club and receive information on new itineraries, the club magazine, cruise discounts, a travel bag, $25–$75 on-board credit (depending on cruise length), a bottle of wine in their cabin, and a VIP party with the captain.

The Last Word   The *Marco Polo* is midsize by today's standards, yet she is among the largest ships cruising to exotic destinations regularly. Her size enables her to provide upscale comfort and a full range of facilities, and her capacity provides a larger passenger base over which to spread costs. Hence, the line can offer cruises at prices considerably lower than its competitors with smaller deluxe ships.

Orient Lines cares about single travelers. In addition to having gentlemen hosts to dine and dance with unaccompanied women passengers, the line offers one of cruising's lowest single supplements as well as occasional singles promotions. Also, it's fastidious in matching participants in its guaranteed-share program.

Children are rare aboard the ship but are treated like royalty. On one cruise, a precocious 12-year-old—the only child on board—toured the engine room, was given a ship's uniform with officer's hat, name tag, and commander's stripes, and got the royal treatment from the staff.

ORIENT LINES STANDARD FEATURES

Officers   Scandinavian, European.

Staff   Dining, Cabin/Filipino; Cruise/American and British.

Dining Facilities   One dining room with open seating for breakfast and lunch and two seatings for dinner with assigned tables; lido restaurant for buffet breakfast, lunch, tea and specialty dinners.

Special Diets   30 days' advance notice.

Room Service   Continental breakfast, cabin attendants on call.

Dress Code   Casual by day; several formal/semiformal nights.

Cabin Amenities   Direct-dial telephone, safe, television with CNN when available, movies and ship programs, radio, hair dryer, toiletries. Bathrobes and slippers in upper-category cabins; small refrigerators in suites. Deluxe suites with sitting room, marble bathroom with tub and shower, and stocked minibars.

Electrical Outlets   110 AC.

Wheelchair Access   Two cabins.

Recreation and Entertainment   Four lounges, port/country lectures by experts, piano and/or string trio at cocktails and after dinner, folkloric dancers in port; library, card room.

Sports and Other Activities   Small outdoor swimming pool ; Ping-Pong.

Beauty and Fitness   Beauty salon/spa, massage, aerobics studio, exercise equipment, saunas.

Other Facilities   Medical unit. Zodiacs; helicopter and landing pad; meeting room. Internet access.

Children's Facilities   No special facilities.

Smoking   None in dining room; smoking permitted in designated wing of main lounge bar during shows, but not during lectures and briefings.

ORIENT LINES STANDARD FEATURES
(continued)

Orient Suggested Tipping Per day per person, $8 and 15% of bar bill. All tips are pooled and divided.

Credit Cards For cruise payment and on-board charges: American Express, MasterCard, Visa, Diner's Club, Discover.

MARCO POLO	QUALITY **7**	VALUE **A**
Registry: Bahamas	Length: 578.4 feet	Beam: 77.4 feet
Cabins: 425	Draft: 27 feet	Speed: 20. 5 knots
Maximum Passengers:	Passenger Decks: 12	Elevators: 4
826	Crew: 350	Space Ratio: 27.6

The Ship A lovely vessel with classic lines, *Marco Polo* has been enhanced by handsome Art Deco interiors created by A. and M. Katzourakis of Athens. Reminiscent of grand liners of the 1920s, pastel furnishings are set against etched and beveled glass, brass, chrome, and rich wood accented by Thai and Burmese antiques and prints, plus modern paintings.

Marco Polo is a comfortable ship designed for long cruises. Built for Arctic service, her hull is strengthened for icy waters and ice floes, with many extra frames added. A gangway door enables passengers to enter the ship at the same level as most docks and piers, averting a long walk up a steep gangway. A significant advantage is *Marco Polo's* superior stability. Twelve-foot waves and rough seas, particularly in such notorious waters as Drake Passage on an Antarctica cruise, are hardly noticeable.

Most cabins are on the main deck, one level below Belvedere Deck, which accommodates most public rooms and includes the lobby, three of four entertainment lounges and bars, the casino, and a library with over 1,000 volumes.

Outside vantage points—especially on the upper deck forward and Promenade Deck aft—are numerous for viewing scenery and wildlife or watching sunsets.

Itineraries See Itinerary Index.

Cabins Being an older vessel, *Marco Polo* has a variety of cabin sizes and configurations. Almost 70% are outside; those in upper A–D categories have picture windows.

Cabins are light and handsomely appointed with light wood furniture and pastel bedspreads, curtains, and carpeting. Most are comfortably sized for long cruises, with ample storage space, dressing table with pullout writing desk, and good reading lights. All have a telephone with international direct-dialing; radio; television with CNN in some areas, two channels for movies, and one for ship programs; safe; and a bathroom with shower, built-in hair dryer, and complimentary toiletries. Upper-category cabins provide bathrobes, slippers, and safes. Deluxe suites have a large sitting room, separate bedroom, large marble bathroom with tub and shower, and stocked minibar, replenished without charge. Junior suites and some deluxe cabins have a sitting area and bathroom with tub and shower. Family cabins have curtain-divided sleeping areas.

Views from accommodations on Sky Deck, including junior suites and deluxe cabins, and ten cabins on the upper deck, are partially obstructed by lifeboats. These are noted on the deck plan in the line's brochure. Two deluxe suites and some upper-deck and Promenade Deck cabins have windows facing deck areas; however, one-way glass prevents outsiders from seeing in.

Specifications 131 inside cabins, 288 outside; 6 suites. Standard dimensions, 140–180 square feet. 388 cabins with 2 lower beds (42 convertible to double beds); 28 accommodate third passenger; 10 accommodate 4 passengers. Suites and some upper-category cabins have double or queen-size beds, some have twin beds convertible to doubles. 2 cabins wheelchair-accessible.

Dining Fine cuisine and exemplary service in elegant surroundings with tables set in fine china, crystal, and fresh flowers make dining one of the ship's best features. The **Seven Seas Restaurant** is a large, formal room dressed in mauves and grays. Breakfast and lunch have open seating, but the two dinner seatings have assigned tables seating four, six, or eight.

Entry is from the central foyer graced with large abstract paintings and Oriental statues. A central, raised area with Art Deco circular ceiling is separated from lower sides by etched glass partitions. Floor-to-ceiling mirrors on inside walls help create a spacious feeling. Booths and tables for two to ten people are by windows at either side of the room. The room is designated nonsmoking.

Dinner menus offer three appetizers, two soups, four entrées, and two or three desserts, cheeses, and fruits. Lighter, low-fat, low-salt, or vegetarian selections are indicated. Wines from South Africa, Australia, Argentina, Chile, California, and Europe are offered at reasonable prices.

Raffles serves casual breakfast and lunch buffets, plus Asian food on some evenings; at lunch its aft corners have cooked-to-order pasta and specialty stations, and outside, there's a deck grill and an ice cream and dessert bar. Its large windows overlook the pool deck. Chairs and tables with umbrellas are set around the pool. Afternoon tea is served here and in the small **Palm Court.**

Twice weekly in the evenings, Raffles becomes an elegant, very popular bistro for 90 passengers (reservations required) with a changing menu of Chinese, Thai, and other Asian cuisine. A $15 charge per person includes wine and gratuities. On more casual Mediterranean sailings, Raffles' capacity increases to 370, and Italian and regional specialties are served all but one night of the cruise, when the Asian menu is featured.

Surprising for a deluxe ship, room service is unavailable, except for continental breakfast and in case of illness. The line maintains that the ship's fine-dining experience is best enjoyed in the dining room. Some passengers might disagree after a long, tiring day on tour. Despite the official policy, most cabin stewards will bring food to the cabin on request. Another point: On tour days, dress for dinner is casual, and the dining room atmosphere more relaxed.

Service   *Marco Polo's* tone is set by its friendly, service-oriented officers; lively British and American cruise staff; and most of all, its well-trained, hard-working Filipino crew, who win high praise for their attentiveness and cheerful dispositions. The dining staff seems to anticipate your every need, and the restaurant managers must have eyes in the back of their heads, always observing and rushing to correct even the simplest error. Cabin staff know passengers' names minutes after their arrival and address you by name throughout the cruise. This courtesy makes an indelible impression. Overall, the service on the *Marco Polo* is as fine as any we've had on a cruise ship, including the most luxurious ships at triple the price.

Facilities and Activities   Lectures by experts on the cruise region are well attended. Speakers might include such famous people as mountaineer Sir Edmund Hillary, wildlife expert Peter Alden, and anthropologist Donna Pido. Lectures are not presented on Mediterranean cruises because of itineraries' port-intensive nature. Among other diversions are bridge tours; origami (Japanese paper-folding); art classes, bridge and backgammon lessons and tournaments; workshops on magic; white-elephant sales; passenger talent shows; service club meetings (including Lions, Kiwanis, and Rotary); fashion shows; and joke contests.

The **Ambassador Lounge** showroom features local entertainment brought on board in various ports. These presentations and Filipino crew show are highlights of the cruise and much better than mediocre musical revues and variety shows staged on other nights. Other entertainment might include a classical concert or a piano recital. The lounge, divided into three curved sections, slopes gently toward the stage. Sight lines are good except behind pillars or when the room is completely full. Large windows span both sides of the room, and a marble-topped bar flanked by mirrors is at the rear. Diamond-shaped lighting fixtures, blue carpets and curtains, and pink décor give the room a 1930s look.

The **Polo Lounge** piano bar, with a cream-colored baby grand piano encircled by a bar, is popular for predinner cocktails and late-evening relaxing and sing-alongs. It's also used for afternoon bridge games. **Le Casino** offers roulette, blackjack, and slot and video-poker machines. To one side is an elegant white marble bar, black leather swivel chairs, and photos of famous entertainers. Off the casino are a small card room and a well-stocked library with comfortable leather armchairs and big windows. Guidebooks for the many countries visited by *Marco Polo* are provided. The **Palm Court,** a small room with marble-topped tables and wicker chairs, is a pleasurable retreat for afternoon tea or quiet conversation. Opposite are two small boutiques. Tucked away in a small area is the Internet service.

The **Charleston Club,** one of several multipurpose lounges, is used for bingo, painting lessons, cocktails, late-evening music and dancing, and midnight pizza. Glass doors open onto a lounge with a white baby grand piano and small bandstand, marble-topped bar, and dance floor. The lounge is a popular late-night gathering spot, though most passengers retire early.

Sports, Fitness, and Beauty   On the Pool Deck is a 15-foot-long swimming pool with teak benches on three sides. Ping-Pong and shuffleboard are available. A fitness center on the upper deck has a small, mirrored exercise room with treadmills, stationary bicycles, rowing machine, stair steppers, weight machines, and free weights. Aerobics and exercise classes are offered. Separate saunas for men and women and three outside Jacuzzis are available. The beauty salon, operated by Mandara, offers a full range of services, including facials, massage, and hydrotherapy.

An upper-deck jogging track ringing the ship consists mostly of a narrow, rubberized path behind the lifeboats. For walkers, Promenade Deck has a one-fifth-mile course between the Charleston Club and bridge gangway. It's all on teak decks with sea views.

Shore Excursions   All cruises feature pre- or postcruise packages and are particularly popular given the distances most passengers travel to the ship. Most cruises also include an unusual highlight ashore. For example, a cruise/safari in Kenya visits the home of Isak Dinesen (Karen Blixen), the author of *Out of Africa,* and wildlife-rich Amboseli National Park. Having the helipad is reassuring in case of an emergency in remote areas and for scouting ice conditions in Antarctica.

Note: Shore transport in some remote/primitive locations is not top of the line. Because of this, some shore excursions are inappropriate for passengers with limited mobility. Also, a fee may be charged for upgraded shore accommodations, but it is worth the cost in some out-of-the-way locations.

Postscript   Writing in 1298, *Marco Polo* opened his famous *Travels* with the words: "Ye kings, princes, nobles, townsfolk and all who wish to know the marvels of the world, have this book read unto you." If he were writing today, he might say, "All ye who wish to know the marvels of the world, take a cruise on the *Marco Polo.*"

Princess Cruises

24305 Town Center Drive, Santa Clarita, CA 91355-4999
(661) 753-0000; fax (661) 753-1535
www.princess.com

Type of Ships New superliners and megaliners.

Type of Cruises Modern, mainstream, worldwide, moderately upscale.

Cruise Line's Strengths

- worldwide itineraries
- Caribbean "private" island
- ScholarShip@Sea program
- spacious cabins, many with verandas
- 24-hour restaurant on most ships
- Scuba certification

Cruise Line's Shortcomings

- congestion in 24-hour restaurants
- uneven cuisine in 24-hour restaurants

Fellow Passengers Princess passengers are difficult to characterize because their ages and incomes vary with the ships, seasons, and destinations. Basically, passengers are age 45 and older with annual incomes of $40,000 and more. They tend to be experienced travelers who cruise frequently and enjoy Princess's mainstream vacations, but they can range from a California schoolteacher or a Midwestern computer systems analyst on a first cruise to affluent retirees on their 20th cruise. On longer cruises and those to "exotic" destinations, the average age is 55 or older; on one-week Caribbean cruises, the average age is younger.

Recommended For Modestly affluent first-timers, frequent cruisers who want easy-paced travel and prefer a balance between sea and land time, and those who understand *The Love Boat* was only a TV show.

Not Recommended For Swingers or first-time cruisers in search of The Love Boat; small-ship devotees.

Cruise Areas and Seasons Caribbean, year-round; Panama Canal, Mexico, Amazon, Orient, Holy Land, Australia/South Pacific, Hawaii/

Tahiti, Southeast Asia, Africa, Antarctica, winter; Bermuda, Canada/
New England, Alaska, Europe, Scandinavia, Mediterranean, Baltic,
summer.

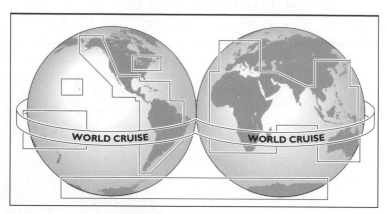

The Line   From its inception three decades ago, Princess Cruises helped
create the relaxed, casual atmosphere that typifies today's cruises.

P&O (Peninsular and Orient Steam Navigation Company), a British
firm and one of the world's oldest and largest steamship companies,
entered the cruise business in August 1844. In 1974, it bought Princess
Cruises, which had been an American company, acquired the *Island
Princess* (since sold to an Asian cruise line) and added the first *Sun
Princess*. The following year, P&O bought *Island Princess's* sister, *Sea Venture*, and renamed her *Pacific Princess*, better known to TV viewers as
"The Love Boat."

In the early 1980s, Princess became a trendsetter for modern mainstream cruising when it launched the *Royal Princess*. She was hailed as the
most stylish ship of the day, setting new standards in comfort and amenities. In 1988, Princess almost doubled its capacity when it acquired Los
Angeles–based Sitmar Cruises, another cruise pioneer, and integrated the
Sitmar ships into its fleet. The line continued to benefit from its involve-
ment in The Love Boat television series, which had an incalculable
impact on modern cruising, popularizing it for a generation of television
viewers—those who make up most of cruise passengers today—and
helping dispel cruising's elitist image

In the 1990s, Princess launched $3 billion worth of dazzling megaships.
Sun Princess ushered in the Grand-class concept and the line's largest vessel when it entered service in 1995. She was followed by triplets over the
following four years—all with the same architect, Njal Eide, as the *Royal
Princess,* and, like her, with significant new features, including cruising's
first 24-hour restaurant, two atrium lobbies, and two show lounges.

The 109,000-ton, $400 million *Grand Princess,* the largest cruise ship
ever built when she debuted in 1998, was the first of the Princess fleet

too large to transit the Panama Canal. The expansion tripled the line's capacity. The second ship of the Grand class, *Golden Princess,* arrived in 2001 and the third, *Star Princess,* in March 2002.

That appears to be only the beginning; two more ships made their debut in 2003. The 88,000-ton *Coral Princess* and *Island Princess* are a new class of ship and the best yet, combining the best features of the Sun- and Grand-class ships. They came with innovative power generation technology, combining diesel engines and gas turbines (the latter placed in the ship's funnel); and only 10% inside cabins and 80% of the outside ones with balconies. In spring of 2004, Princess will see its largest expansion to date with the addition of three super megaliners: The 113,000-ton *Sapphire Princess* in March, the 116,000-ton *Caribbean Princess* in April, and the 113,000-ton *Diamond Princess* in May.

Already a major player in Alaska and the Panama Canal, Princess will have increased its Caribbean presence by 75% by 2005, added itineraries throughout Asia and the Pacific, expanded in Europe, added safaris in Kenya and South Africa, sent the *Royal Princess* on her first around-the-world cruise in 2001 and her first Antarctic cruise in 2003, expanded its Scholarship@Sea program, and opened AOL Internet Cafés fleetwide.

Princess's Alaska role was enhanced in 1997 with the opening of the $20-million Mount McKinley Princess Lodge, featured on the line's cruise tours. The lodge, on 146 acres inside Denali State Park, has a spectacular view of 20,320-foot Mount McKinley and the Alaska Range. In 2002, Princess added its fifth Alaskan property with the opening of the new Copper River Princess Lodge, located at the entrance to America's largest national park, Wrangell–St. Elias.

On Caribbean cruises, the line offers Princess Cay, its private island in the Bahamas. Princess has one of the industry's best and most extensive selections of shore excursions. Almost all can be booked in advance of your cruise. Princess is also a leader in seasonal savings, deeply discounted advance-purchase fares, and two-for-one promotions. Just about everything you ever wanted to know about Princess Cruises is available on its enormous website, which was further enhanced with new features in 2003.

In 2003, the hard-fought battle between Carnival and Royal Caribbean to buy Princess/P&O Cruises ended in Carnival's favor. As a result, Carnival now owns 13 cruise lines with a total of 83 ships in the water or on their way by 2005. All, including Princess, continue to operate separately under their own brands.

THE FLEET	BUILT/RENOVATED	TONNAGE	PASSENGERS
Caribbean Princess	2004	116,000	3,100
Coral Princess	2003	88,000	2,000
Dawn Princess	1997	77,000	1,950
Diamond Princess	2004	113,000	2,700

THE FLEET (cont'd)	BUILT/RENOVATED	TONNAGE	PASSENGERS
Golden Princess	2001	109,000	2,600
Grand Princess	1998	109,000	2,600
Island Princess	2003	88,000	2,000
Pacific Princess	2003	30,277	680
Regal Princess	1991/97/99	70,000	1,590
Royal Princess	1984/1994	45,000	1,200
Sapphire Princess	2004	113,000	2,700
Sea Princess	1998	77,000	1,950
Star Princess	2002	109,000	2,600
Sun Princess	1995	77,000	1,950
Tahiti Princess	2002	30,277	680

Style   California modern in the mainstream, sedate but not staid, a Princess cruise is the essence of mass-market cruising: warm, inviting, and comfortable, suitable for a broad spectrum of people. The fleet has British officers, with their steamship tradition; Italian officers, with their natural charm; and a multicultural dining and hotel staff. Often trend-setters in facilities and amenities, the ships have the look of a well-bred, middle- to upper-middle-class environment—i.e., nothing too flashy or exaggerated—where almost anyone can feel at home. The line has worked hard to improve its entertainment and food, with menus featuring fresh, contemporary selections that had been missing in the past. Shipboard activities are varied and numerous. Ships fleetwide have gyms, saunas, and spa services and offer fitness and sports programs aboard and in port. Recently, Princess introduced telemedicine technology, giving ships' doctors worldwide access to medical specialists.

The New Waves scuba diving program, associated with PADI (Professional Association of Diving Instructors), offers snorkeling and scuba certification. Princess remains the only mainstream line to offer passengers the opportunity to become certified divers during a cruise.

All Princess ships have Internet access and alternative dining options. "Personal Choice Dining," a flexible dining room option, is available on Sun- and Grand-class ships. With it, an automatic gratuity system for the staffs went into effect on board, adding $10 per person per day to a passenger's shipboard account. "FlightChoice" provides passengers with information on their flight schedule 60 days prior to sailing with the option to choose a customized air schedule. Cruise Personalizers is an online service that enables passengers to book shore excursions, special occasion arrangements, and dietary requirements in advance of their cruise, while Alaska Outfitters links passengers with local guides who can help them customize their wilderness experience.

Distinctive Features   Scuba certification; 24-hour restaurants; terry robes and fresh fruit in cabins on request; fresh flowers in suites. CNN, ESPN, Discovery, Learning Channel fleetwide. Shore excursions literature; self-service laundries, private Bahamian island; Alaska lodges. Telemedicine technology; wedding chapels; wedding webcam on *Golden Princess*. Personal Choice Dining.

	HIGHEST	LOWEST	AVERAGE
PER DIEM	$487	$113	$288

Per diems are calculated from cruise line's nondiscounted *cruise-only* fares on standard accommodations and vary by season, cabin, and cruise areas.

Rates   Port charges included.

Special Fares and Discounts   Frequent two-for-one fares; savings and upgrades on combining consecutive cruises.

- **Third/Fourth Berth:** 50% of fare for suites to 30% of fare for inside cabins.
- **Children's Fare** Same as Third/Fourth Berth.
- **Single Supplement** 150–200%, Love Boat Savers discounts.

Packages

- **Air/Sea** Yes.
- **Others** Yes; wedding, honeymoon, anniversary, renewal of vows, and grand occasion.
- **Pre/Post** Yes.

Past Passengers   Captain's Circle past-passenger club members are invited to captain-hosted cocktail party and participate in activities including a club photo contest with prizes. Each receives a membership number to use when booking a cruise or corresponding with Princess, ensuring that they receive club benefits. Recognition pins are given, from the First Officer's pin for third and fourth cruises to a Commodore pin for ten or more. Quality gifts, such as Tiffany crystal, are presented at onboard parties to passengers who have sailed the most days with Princess. Members receive newsletters reporting new itineraries, new ship plans, staff profiles, chef's recipes, special discounts, and coupons for specific sailings and members-only sailings.

The Last Word   For millions of Americans, the popular image of cruising is a Princess cruise. It's perhaps not as luxurious or glamorous as the television image, but it's apparently close enough for the line to attract more than 750,000 passengers a year. Princess's strength is in its consistency, new fleet, itineraries and well-executed shore excursions. Little changes from ship to ship. Your ship will be comfortable, your cruise enjoyable, and you will get a lot for your money, if you have realistic expectations and plan ahead to take advantage of the line's heavily discounted fares.

To its credit, Princess has integrated seven enormous ships in six years smoothly—a gigantic job—and has been able to maintain the high standards, particularly of service, that has gained the line its loyal following.

PRINCESS CRUISES STANDARD FEATURES

Officers British and Italian.

Staff Dining/Italian, European, Filipino; Cabin, Filipino; Cruise/American, British.

Dining Facilities One main dining room, two seatings for three meals (Sun and Coral groups, two dining rooms; Grand group, three); Personal Choice Dining option on Sun, Coral, and Grand groups; alternative Bistro on *Regal* and *Royal*. Grand group: Italian, Southwestern restaurants. Sun group: Sterling Steakhouse. Coral, Italian and New Orleans, informal buffet breakfast, lunch in Lido restaurant; pizzeria; patisserie (except *Royal*). Grand, Royal, Coral, and Sun groups, 24-hour dining.

Special Diets Diabetic, low-calorie/cholesterol/salt, vegetarian.

Room Service 24-hour room service with light menu.

Dress Code Casual during day; evenings vary, usually there are two smart casual, three informal, and two formal in week's cruise.

Cabin Amenities CNN, ESPN, Discovery/Learning Channels and movies on television; fresh fruit daily and terry robes in cabins on request; direct-dial telephone; minifridges; hair dryers.

Electrical Outlets 220/110 AC.

Wheelchair Access 29 cabins on Grand group; 20 on Coral group; 19 on Sun group; 10 on *Regal;* 4 on *Royal*.

Recreation and Entertainment Las Vegas– and Broadway-style revues, music and dancing, casino, disco, wine and caviar bar, karaoke, theater, dance classes, bingo, bridge. Grand group, virtual reality center, three show lounges. Coral group, two show lounges, one with three revolving stages; demonstration kitchen.

Sports and Other Activities Two/three outdoor pools on all ships; Grand group, five; paddle tennis; jogging; scuba program; golf practice. Grand group, swim-against-current lap pool.

Beauty and Fitness Saunas, beauty/barber salon, spa, fitness program.

Other Facilities Library, hospital, boutiques; self-service laundry; meeting facilities; religious services; Grand group, wedding chapel; *Golden,* wedding webcam. Internet access.

Children's Facilities Princess Kids, Princess's youth program on all ships (*Royal,* only if 20 or more children are sailing for ages 3-17); special facilities and full-time youth coordinators: Grand, Sun groups and *Regal*. Group baby-sitting available 10 p.m.–1 a.m. for children ages 3–12 years for a $5 per hour charge. No in-cabin baby-sitting. See text.

Smoking No smoking in dining rooms and main showrooms; other public rooms have designated areas.

PRINCESS CRUISES STANDARD FEATURES
(continued)

Princess Suggested Tipping Ships with Personal Choice Cruising, gratuities automatically added to passenger's account at $10 per person per day for dining and cabin service. Passengers can add or reduce amount at pursers' desk. 15% is added to bar bills.

Credit Cards For cruise payment and on-board charges (settled at the end of the cruise): American Express/Optima, Carte Blanche, Diners Club, MasterCard, Visa, Discover; traveler's and personal checks; U.S., Canadian, and British currency.

ROYAL PRINCESS	**QUALITY 7**	**VALUE C**
Registry: Great Britain	Length: 757 feet	Beam: 106 feet
Cabins: 600	Draft: 26 feet	Speed: 20 knots
Maximum Passengers:	Passenger Decks: 9	Elevators: 6
1,200	Crew: 520	Space Ratio: 38

The Ship Launched in 1984, *Royal Princess* was christened by Diana, Princess of Wales. Both made an indelible mark on the 1980s. *Royal Princess* was at the time the most expensive passenger ship ever built. Her sleek lines and tapered bow looked traditional, but she had so many innovations inside that she was called revolutionary and set new standards in passenger comfort for the cruise ships that followed.

Royal Princess was the first cruise ship to have all outside cabins, television with remote control, minifridges, and full bathrooms with tub and shower in all cabins. She was first to have verandas in all suites, deluxe cabins, and some lesser categories, and large windows instead of portholes in every category. The biggest Princess ship when she debuted (but hardly a superliner by today's standards), she has two acres of open teak decks, three swimming pools, and a fully equipped spa. Her décor is refined. Interiors are defined less by walls than by art, sculpture, glass with brass railings, and live plants. The varnished wood hand rails are a rarity today. Muted colors and abundant windows create openness throughout the ship.

Royal Princess's layout is unusual. Most public rooms are on the two lower levels, and virtually all cabins are on upper decks. A large foyer on the lower Plaza Deck spans two decks—the first shipboard atrium, perhaps. The greenery-filled area is dominated by a large sculpture by David Norris consisting of a bronze spiral with seagulls rising over rocks. A dramatic staircase with glass balustrade curves in two wings upward to the Princess Court on Riviera Deck, where a portrait of Princess Diana hangs. The court, actually a balcony with piano lounge overlooking the foyer, is a gathering spot where passengers enjoy prelunch or predinner drinks, entertained by a pianist/vocalist. Riviera Deck also holds the main showroom, cabaret-style lounge, casino, boutique, card room, and a theater offering current movies daily.

Itineraries   See Itinerary Index.

Cabins   *Royal Princess* has 20 categories of cabins—all outside and spacious, and each with picture windows, a tiled bathroom with tub and shower, retractable clothesline, mirrored medicine cabinet door, and deluxe amenities, including terry robes. All cabins have minifridge, safe, multifunction phone, television with music channels, ship's information channel, shore excursion and shopping information, weather forecast, BBC World Service, CNN, ESPN, and other cable channels, four-channel music radio, and key cards for the door. Quality interiors and attention to detail are reflected in a large dressing table with makeup lights and mirrors, an easy-to-reach hair dryer, ample drawers, and large closets. In many cabins, a twin bed folds into a wall, providing extra sitting space by day. Some cabins on the Baja, Caribe, and Dolphin Decks have obstructed views, indicated on the deck plan.

Suites and cabins with verandas are very roomy; the outside deck accommodates a small table and chair; some have a chaise lounge. If you can afford a veranda, it's worth the additional cost. It's your private corner to enjoy breakfast, the peace and serenity of days at sea, and the fresh sea air day or night. The two largest suites have separate sitting and dining rooms, Jacuzzi bathtub, separate bedroom with queen-size bed, and large veranda. Minisuites are similar, but they don't have walls between bedrooms and sitting areas. Self-service launderettes offer washers, dryers, irons, and ironing boards at no charge. You pay for soap, bleach. and dryer sheets.

Specifications   600 outside cabins (150 with verandas, including 52 minisuites, 12 suites, 2 deluxe suites). Standard dimensions, 168 square feet. All cabins and suites with twin beds (convertible to queen); some cabins accommodate third person. 10 wheelchair-accessible.

Dining   The warm, pleasant **Continental Dining Room** has a raised perimeter level delineated with brass railings. Small islands of round tables break up the space, provide privacy, and help lower the noise level and allow easy conversation. Three meals are served in two seatings, usually with open seating on port days for breakfast and lunch and assigned seats for dinner. Most tables seat four to eight people; a few "twos" are available. The food is consistently high quality.

Senior dining staff is Italian and very attentive. Count on the maître d'hôtel or senior staff member to prepare fresh pasta tableside. Don't be shy if your favorite pasta isn't on the menu. Ask for it. The staff loves showing how well they can make it. Menus are posted at bars and elsewhere shipwide. They list five courses for lunch and seven for dinner. Typically offered are three appetizers, three soups, salad, pasta special, six entrées (at least one low-calorie), four desserts, and assorted ice cream, sorbet cheeses and fresh fruits. After the successful introduction of cruising's first 24-hour restaurant on *Sun Princess,* a 24-hour **Lido Café** was introduced on *Royal Princess,* followed by a pizzeria. The indoor/outdoor café with tile-topped tables is cheerful at any time. Here you'll enjoy informal buffet breakfast, lunch, snacks and 24-hour self-service coffee and tea. Since *Royal Princess* has just one main dining room, it does not offer Personal Choice Dining. To compensate, in the evening the Lido Café converts into two alternative dining areas: the pizzeria and the bistro. The latter has an à la carte menu with daily chef's specials. (Tipping is at your discretion in the bistro, as the standard charge has been eliminated.) Smokers and nonsmokers sit in separate enclosures. Also available are sheltered tables outdoors on Lido Deck and the stern's breezy deck. An elegant afternoon tea is served daily in the dining room, often with musical accompaniment. There is 24-hour room service with a light menu.

Service The dining room staff is the ship's most service-oriented group. They go out of their way for passengers and cater to special requests efficiently. There are no sommeliers in the dining room; wine is served by assistant waiters. The British officers socialize in the bars in the Riviera lounge.

Facilities and Activities A cruise staff of 40 present an enormous variety of entertainment. You might start your day's activities with bridge or dance lessons, or a craft demonstration. In the afternoon you might play golf or Ping-Pong, take a lesson in the casino, join a word or trivia game, or watch a culinary demonstration or horse races. Movies are shown three or four times daily in the comfortable **Princess Theatre.** And then, there's bingo. Books are available most of the day from the well-stocked library, but reading there is tough. The area, between two lounges, has comfortable sofas and chairs that make it a popular place for passengers to stop and chat. Four computers in the library have Internet hookups, and you can rent a laptop with wireless connection from the pursers' desk. Either method costs $7.50 for 15 minutes.

The **International Lounge,** used by day for bingo and other activities (concerts on European itineraries) and at night, for Broadway- and Las Vegas–style shows. The predictable fare meets Princess's high standards for shows. Seats are tiered in the semi-circular lounge; sight lines are generally good, except from the back. The **Riviera Club and Bar** and adjacent **Terrace Room** are the ship's most elegant lounges. They offer cabaret-style entertainment and a trio playing dance music every evening. Also available is the **Crown Casino** with slots, poker machines, and gaming tables.

Floor-to-ceiling windows in the **Horizon Lounge** provide a 280° panorama. The large room is quiet except during morning exercise class or evening karaoke. It's popular at cocktail hour (daily drink at a special price). After-dinner coffees and liqueurs are served here, and around midnight, the room becomes a disco.

Sports, Fitness, and Beauty A cluster of five small pools is the centerpiece of the Lido Deck, the main outdoor recreation area. On Sun Deck, passengers sunbathe on a raised platform, play table tennis and shuffleboard, swim in one of cruising's largest lap pools, and exercise in the spa. The fitness complex has a gym with Nautilus and other equipment, sauna and massage rooms, and a large Jacuzzi.

The **Lotus Spa** program features daily exercise and well-being classes as well as traditional and exotic spa and salon services. Start your day with a Lotus Walk on promenade deck followed by an energizing Dancing Lotus choreography session, aerobics and stretch classes. More leisurely classes include Aqua Aerobics, Pathway to Yoga, and the use of visualization, meditation, and relaxation techniques in the Mind, Body, and Soul classes. Joggers and walkers circle the wraparound teak promenade on Dolphin Deck (four laps equal one mile). The beauty salon offers hair and body treatments.

Shore Excursions Separate brochures describe each cruise's shore excursions, and they are listed on the Princess website. You can book online using your cruise booking number. Videos are available for purchase and cost $18 to $40. For *Royal Princess's* Baltic cruise alone, 40 tours are available, ranging in price from $25 for a half-day outing to over $1,000 for a full day of sight-seeing by private van. The lineup is fairly standard but varied, trips are well organized, and the guides first-rate. Princess offers hotel and tour packages that can be combined with European, Panama Canal, and South America cruises.

Postscript From launch, this classy ship was admired by competitors as much as her owners, and it's one vessel passengers request by name, rather than by itinerary. Like fine wine, she has mellowed nicely. Her passengers are older, more affluent, and less active than those on Princess's newer Caribbean fleet. Most are Americans. Her itineraries appeal to travelers with time and money for extended cruises. Those weary of glitzy megaliners will appreciate her most.

SUN PRINCESS	**QUALITY 9**	**VALUE B**
DAWN PRINCESS	**QUALITY 8**	**VALUE C**
SEA PRINCESS	**QUALITY 8**	**VALUE C**
Registry: Great Britain	Length: 856 feet	Beam: 106 feet
Cabins: 975	Draft: 26 feet	Speed: 21 knots
Maximum Passengers:	Passenger Decks: 14	Elevators: 9
1,950	Crew: 830	Space Ratio: 39.5

The Ships Before its launch, *Sun Princess*—at the time, the largest cruise ship ever built—was described by Princess as offering an intimate feel. Skeptics scoffed.

But guess what? Princess did it. Well, "intimate" is perhaps a stretch, but it certainly managed to diminish the interiors of this big ship to a human scale. The Italian-built ship made her debut in December 1995, the first of Princess's Grand class. Her mates, *Dawn Princess, Sea Princess,* and *Ocean Princess,* arrived between 1997 and 2000. (*Ocean Princess* left the fleet in September 2002 to join P&O Cruises.) From the outside, the gleaming white liners look colossal, towering 14 decks and stretching nearly three football fields in length. But inside, clever design has created a welcoming, accessible ambience.

The ships are spacious without being overwhelming. Warm colors and refined décor enhance the inviting atmosphere. The group sets new criteria for megaliners. Their layout is innovative in many ways. Rather than one cavernous atrium, these ships offer two. Instead of one enormous show lounge, there are two main show lounges. Two dining rooms are on different decks, and their layout, décor, and table arrangements help create an intimate ambience. Five dining outlets, including cruising's first 24-hour restaurant, provide options. Small spaces capture the intimacy of a small ship while creating options. Although other ships offer multiple lounges and dining alternatives, none has developed the concept to the extent of Princess's Grand-class ships. Whatever you choose to do, you can do, and whatever you miss one night, you can catch the next night.

The four-deck Grand Plaza is the ships' main atrium and social hub. It's a showcase of the exquisite Italian craftsmanship evident throughout the vessels and sets the tone for each ship. On the *Sun Princess,* in the elegant space, golden marble suggests the sun, and beige, bronze, and brown accents hint at shade. Sunbursts are set in the marble floors at every level of the atrium, and a backlit stained-glass dome overhead conveys an abstract underwater scene in aqua and turquoise. Glass elevators and a circular, floating staircase connect the decks and provide a stunning setting for the captains' parties.

Among the amenities are five swimming pools; a huge health center and spa; children's and teen rooms; a shopping arcade; computerized golf simulator; library and reading room with "audio chairs," each with its own bay window looking out to sea; and a business and conference center for up to 300 people. Each ship has a $2.5 million collection of paintings, sculptures, ceramic tiles, and Murano glass.

Another significant feature of the ships is their connection with the sea. A wraparound teak promenade lined with canopied steamer chairs provides a peaceful setting to read, daydream, or snooze.

Itineraries See Itinerary Index.

Cabins About two-thirds of cabins are outside; 70% of those have private balconies. There are 28 cabin categories. Nineteen cabins—among the most on any cruise ship—were designed to Americans with Disabilities Act specifications. Lifeboats obstruct views from 28 outside cabins on Promenade Deck. All standard cabins have a queen-size bed convertible to two singles, refrigerator, safe, ample closet, and bath with shower, terry robes, and hair dryers. All are well appointed and decorated in light, eye-pleasing colors.

Category A minisuites with private balcony are lavish in comfort, décor, and size—almost 400 square feet, plus the balcony. A marble-floored foyer with a mirror gives the illusion of a large apartment. Tastefully decorated in beige and butter tones accented by light woods and fine fabrics, each has a separate sitting area with leather chairs and a sofa that converts to a queen-size bed, and an entertainment console with television and music channels. A bar includes refrigerator.

The bedroom, separated by a curtained archway, has a queen-size bed, vanity/desk, and second television. Drawer space is ample, and the small walk-in closet has a safe. Sliding doors in the sitting area and bedroom lead to a balcony extending the length of the suite. Two lounge chairs and a table make it ideal for breakfast or napping. Etched glass divides the whirlpool tub from a shower stall, and a door separates the toilet and wash basin.

Specifications 372 inside, 603 outside cabins (410 with verandas); 32 minisuites and 6 suites with verandas. Standard dimensions, 135–173 square feet. All with 2 lower beds, convertible to queen; 300 with third berths; no singles. 19 wheelchair-accessible.

Dining Here are the choices: two dining rooms, cruising's first 24-hour restaurant, pizzeria, grill, patisserie, ice cream bar (there's a charge), 24-hour room service, and the newest addition, a steakhouse. And now, the option to dine where and when you want with Personal Choice.

The two main dining rooms are on Emerald Deck and Plaza Deck. They have an asymmetrical seating layout and small table groups in various sizes separated by etched-glass dividers. The design gives each group of tables a certain privacy. Separate galleys and service stations in every corner reduce traffic and help ensure that food reaches tables at the proper temperature. The walls are decorated with lovely scenic murals, adding to the gracious surroundings. Lunch and dinner menus offer a selection of appetizers, soups, salads, entrées, and desserts. A pasta special is offered every evening, although it is no longer prepared tableside. Healthy Choice selections, included on the regular menu, provide low-cholesterol, low-fat, and low-sodium alternatives. Wine list choices are reasonably priced, some under $20. Wines are also available by the glass.

Horizon Court on Lido Deck is an innovative 24-hour café with 270° ocean views through floor-to-ceiling windows, with seating on a trio of terraces. By day, buffets are served at two stations; at night, the center of the room becomes a restaurant with table service and a dance band. Reservations aren't needed, and there's no extra charge. Breakfast choices range from fresh fruit to hot dishes, with a different special daily. At noon, entrées include ravioli, roast beef, and a salad bar, but selection and preparation do not match the quality or variety in the dining room.

The pizzeria offers a sidewalk café setting with marble-top tables and wrought-iron chairs on the balcony overlooking the atrium. Open for lunch and from 6 p.m. to 2 a.m., it serves pizza hot from the ovens, which are in plain sight. Waiters take orders for drinks and pizzas. There's no charge for the pizza, but diners tip the waiters. The outdoor **Grill** serves cooked-to-order hamburgers and hot dogs; the patisserie on the Plaza Deck has espresso, cappuccino, and pastries. Sundaes, the poolside ice cream parlor, is a Häagen-Dazs concession, and there's a charge per scoop.

Service Officers are Italian, dining staff European, bar and cabin stewards Filipino, and reception and cruise staff American and British. Most of the crew are friendly and well trained, especially the dining staff, which consistently garners high praise. Service at the reception desk is uneven, and individual cabin stewards, ever smiling and eager to please, have received mixed reviews, often the result of insufficient training.

Facilities and Activities The wood-paneled library has a large selection of books, plus "audio chairs" with built-in headsets that are set by large bay windows overlooking the water. The **Card Room** is also used as a meeting room or for private parties. The ships offers a full schedule of daytime diversions, from art auctions and dance lessons to bridge tournaments and bingo. A tiny, computer-equipped **Business Center** with Internet access is next to the beauty salon.

Note: Art auctions have become ubiquitous on major cruise ships. Most of the art is terrible and terribly overpriced, despite claims to the contrary. One *Sea Princess* passenger recently wrote:

... the tacky, in-your-face display of art for auction [is] everywhere on the ship from embarkation to disembarkation—and it grew day by day ... on easels, hanging on walls, and even stacked up around the casino lobby, Atrium piano bar, and Wheelhouse and Horizon Court. Tacked on to many were auction announcements with the time and location highlighted in thick orange magic marker. Flyers also appeared in cabin mailboxes almost daily, and, after the "final" auction, another notice appeared announcing the "requested FINAL 'Rocky IV, Death Wish' absolutely final auction." Frankly, Princess has too much class to be using this sort of revenue-generating

scheme in the first place, but the carnival hawker's atmosphere and the total lack of knowledge or finesse exhibited by the auctioneer were almost comical. Sea Princess, *like her sisters, is an elegant ship with lovely décor, but even the "legitimate" artwork in many passageways and some elevator lobbies was obscured by the easels and announcements of art for sale.*

We couldn't agree more.

The Grand Plaza is the ships' hub. The Promenade Deck contains only public rooms and is anchored by the two showrooms. Forward is the **Princess Theatre,** with an enormous stage for Broadway-style productions. Graduated theater seating and an absence of pillars ensure fine sight lines.

Aft is the marble-walled **Vista Lounge** with tiered seating and floor-to-ceiling ocean views. Dancing and cabaret-style entertainment are offered. To one side, a large, free-form bar encourages mingling.

Shows in both lounges are repeated—four performances each for early and late seating over consecutive days. The ship's program suggests that passengers attend according to their dining room seating, but some passengers prefer to return to one show for an encore. This hasn't created seating problems because not all passengers attend all performances.

The **Grand Casino** has slot machines, video poker, blackjack, roulette, and craps. The stained-glass ceiling, lighted to simulate a spinning roulette wheel, is visible on the deck below, from where passengers access the casino via a staircase in the second atrium. On the *Sun,* a bronze tubular sculpture by Arizonan Lyle London decorates the lower level.

Flanking the ships' second atrium are the disco and the romantic **Rendezvous Lounge.** The disco's entrance glitters with fiber-optic lights and a video dance floor, rather than video wall. Rendezvous Lounge, an elegant refuge, serves caviar, imported wines, and champagnes by the glass. The **Atrium Lounge,** with a white baby-grand piano and dance floor, is particularly popular for predinner cocktails and late-night sing-alongs. Afternoon tea is also served there as well as in the **Horizon Lounge.**

The **Wheelhouse Bar** near the Princess Theatre is one of the ship's most attractive, inviting rooms. Resembling a British men's club, it's decorated in rosewood and dark burgundy with sumptuous, spruce-green leather chairs. Ship models and P&O memorabilia adorn the walls. Live dance music seems a jarring note in this room that could be ideal for quiet conversation. Yet passengers seem to enjoy the lively atmosphere, packing the dance floor before dinner and late into the night. On the *Sun,* a gallery outside the bar displays costumes worn by opera diva Dame Joan Sutherland.

Sports, Fitness, and Beauty   Some of the most innovative architectural designs benefit sports and fitness. One of the ship's pools is open to the sky, though set between two decks. On Riviera Deck are the main pools and the ocean-view spa. Half of this large area is a well-equipped gym; the other half is a mirrored room where aerobics classes are held. The spa has 11 massage and beauty treatment rooms, saunas, showers, changing facilities, and an ocean-view beauty salon. Next door, a computerized golf center simulates play on a half-dozen top courses ($36–$50 per half-hour).

Sunbathing areas are spread across three top decks with a pool and bar (live band during daytime) on one; another pool, whirlpool, and grill on another; and a splash pool, bar, and paddle tennis/volleyball/ basketball court on the third. A one-sixth-mile jogging track girdles the top deck; a broad teak promenade encircles the ship. (Three times around equals a mile.)

Children's Facilities "Princess Kids," Princess's fleetwide youth program, was expanded in 2002 to provide age-specific activities for three groups: Princess Pelicans (ages 3–7), Princess Pirateers (ages 8–12) and Off Limits (ages 13–17). It also includes in-port programs with lunch, running from 8 a.m. to 5 p.m. at no charge and learning opportunities through a partnership with the California Science Center and the use of National Wildlife Federation educational materials on wildlife and conservation. The program debuted on *Sea Princess* and *Star Princess* Mexican Riviera cruises and includes studies of the stars, ocean and coral reef, building and racing sailboats, among others. The new program complements Princess junior ranger program in Alaska and the fleetwide Save our Seas environmental program. Participants take home a "Pete's Pals" booklet reflecting the endangered species including white pelicans, manatees, sea turtles and panda bears in areas Princess sails. Group babysitting for ages 3–12 is available from 10 p.m.–1 a.m. for $5 per hour per child. Children can now travel on most itineraries at six months.

Sun Princess's **Fun Zone** is one of the most enchanting children's playrooms at sea. Here, kids romp in a splash pool, play in a castle and big-as-life doll's house, and perform in a little theater. Next door, **Cyberspace** (**Wired** on *Sea*), the teen club, offers video games, a disco, and refreshments. There's also new specialized teens spa program ranging from manicures to henna tattoos, body and hair glitter, face paint, and body art.

Postscript Of all the megaliners launched since the mid-1990s, *Sun Princess* and her siblings have best reduced behemoth interiors to human scale. They also prove that big can be beautiful, in large part due to their fine Italian craftsmanship. With choices 24 hours a day—in dining, activities, entertainment, and relaxing—anyone seeking less regimented cruising should find happiness on these ships.

CARIBBEAN PRINCESS	**(April 2004)**	
DIAMOND PRINCESS	**(May 2004)**	
GRAND PRINCESS	**QUALITY 8**	**VALUE B**
GOLDEN PRINCESS	**QUALITY 8**	**VALUE B**
SAPPHIRE PRINCESS	**(March 2004)**	
STAR PRINCESS	**QUALITY 8**	**VALUE C**
Registry: Bermuda/Britain	Length: 951 feet	Beam: 118/159
Cabins: 1557/1,296	Draft: 26 feet	Speed: 22 knots
Maximum Passengers:	Passenger Decks: 13	Elevators: 16
3,782/2,600	Crew: 1,200/1,110	Space Ratio: 37/42

The Ships   Saying the 109,000-ton, $450 million *Grand Princess* was the largest, most expensive cruise ship built when she debuted doesn't say much. But comparisons clarify the image: *Grand Princess* is about four times the length of New York's Grand Central Station. She's 28 feet taller than Niagara Falls, 49 feet taller than the Statue of Liberty, and too wide by 43 feet to transit the Panama Canal.

And what does "most expensive" mean? *Grand Princess's* price tag was almost twice the cost of the Pathfinder mission to Mars. Happily, there's plenty on this ship to suggest that Princess got its money's worth. Of the ship's 928 outside cabins, 710 have balconies—more than on any other cruise ship. She was the first with three main dining rooms and three main show lounges, each with a different show nightly. Her 13,500-square-foot casino is the largest afloat.

Get the picture? She's big, expensive, and has plenty of wow! But *Grand Princess* also comes with innovations even more exciting than those of the Sun group. For starters, she has cruising's first wedding chapel (Princess is, after all, the company of *The Love Boat*); the first virtual-reality arcade with a motion-based ride for up to 18 people, car races, and skiing; a blue-screen video production facility that lets passengers star in their own videos; and the first swim-against-the-current lap pool at sea. She was the first cruise ship with a Southwestern restaurant—one of three alternative restaurants—and the first to have 28 wheelchair-accessible cabins. At the time she debuted, *Grand Princess* was one of few cruise ships with duplicate operational and technical systems to ensure continued operation in emergencies. Her sisters, *Golden Princess* and *Star Princess,* have similar features.

Grand Princess's most unusual and noticeable design feature is the **Sky-walkers Nightclub,** an aluminum structure suspended 18 decks above the water at the stern like a skybox at a stadium. Accessed by a glass-enclosed moving walkway, it's an observation lounge by day and a disco by night.

The ship's enormous interior is diminished by being divided into many small spaces offering dozens of activities—so many choices that a week of cruising isn't enough time to try them all. The myriad options should be a comfort to first-time cruisers fearful of feeling confined or having nothing to do.

Among other distinctive features is the bridge, which extends beyond both sides of the ship. It's glass-enclosed to protect the computerized navigational instruments. A bow observation area gives passengers nearly the same view that officers have from the bridge. Balconies, outlined in blue glass, are built out from the ship's body of the ship in stair-stepped tiers. The design opens all balconies to the sun, but the negatives are a loss of privacy (cabins above overlook lower spaces) and noise traveling upward.

In spring 2004, the Grand class will more than double in cabin count when three more super megaliners are added: the 113,000-ton *Sapphire Princess* in March, the 116,000-ton *Caribbean Princess* in April, and the 113,000-ton *Diamond Princess* in May.

The 116,000-ton *Caribbean Princess,* built at Fincantieri shipyard in Italy, is the line's largest cruise ship to date. The ship, a slightly larger version of the *Grand Princess,* has the same features—three dining rooms, three show lounges, several alternative restaurants, a wedding chapel, **Lotus Spa,** nine-hole putting course and golf simulator, library, and Internet café. But it also has more cabins—261 more to be exact, in all categories. Like her sister ships, 80% of all outside cabins, or 881 cabins, have balconies. The *Sapphire* and the *Diamond* are like the *Grand* as well, with only minor differences.

A brand-new feature on *Caribbean Princess* is "Dive-In Movies," a splashy way for passengers to enjoy the latest movies under the heavens as they relax on deck. The movies are played on a giant, Times Square–style screen built into the superstructure of the vessel at the midship pool. The screen can also show special sports events and used for the Caribbean night parties held during every cruise. And true to any movie-watching venue, a variety of snacks will be available. Another new features is a Caribbean-themed alternative restaurant. Calling Ft. Lauderdale home and being true to her name, the *Caribbean Princess* will sail on Eastern and Western itineraries year-round.

Itineraries   See Itinerary Index.

Cabins   These three *Princesses* have 35 cabin categories each! Most cabins are on Decks 8–12, with a few on Deck 5 and 14. Of 710 outside cabins, 80% have verandas, and the majority range from 215–255 square feet, a spaciousness generally available only in deluxe suites. Décor uses pastels and renders a pleasant ambience. Closet and shelf space is generous; drawers are limited but adequate.

The ships' balconies offer several benefits. First, they entice passengers to spend more time in their cabins, reducing crowds in public areas. Second, with so many available in standard cabin, the amenity is affordable for a wider audience. The ships' wheelchair-accessible cabins are also available in all main categories. Cabins are more traditional in layout than those on the Sun group. Suites have tiled (not marbled) bathrooms and do not have Jacuzzi tubs. The two 800-square-foot Grand Suites (one on *Golden*) are aptly named. Each has a large balcony with whirlpool, a living room with fireplace, wet bar, three televisions, and walk-in closets.

Specifications   928 outside; 372 inside. 208 suites with balconies (325–800 square feet); 502 outside cabins with balconies (215–255 square feet); 218 standard outside (165–210 square feet); 372 inside (160 square feet); 28 wheelchair-accessible including 18 outside/10 inside (240–385 square feet); 609 with upper berths.

Dining   Each of the three ships have eight dining venues and offer the line's Personal Choice dining options. This enables passengers to choose between "Traditional Fixed Seating" dining with assigned seats and "Anytime Dining," thus providing passengers more flexibility in deciding when, where, and with whom they dine, as in a restaurant.

The main dining rooms, named for famous Italian artists—**Botticelli, Da Vinci,** and **Michelangelo** (on the *Star,* the rooms are named for famous Italian places: **Portofino, Amalfi,** and **Capri**)—have low ceilings and clusters of tables in a serpentine layout that breaks the space, so guests don't feel they're dining in a large room with many people. At least one of the three dining rooms is designated for traditional dining; one for Anytime Dining; and the third for either arrangement, depending on demand. Generally, it is wise to make a reservation if you want to dine at a specific time. Otherwise, you can just show up.

Horizon Court, the 24-hour lido café, has its own galley and a terrace for outdoor dining. The layout is different from that on *Sun Princess* and causes crowding and confusion. The food, which was sub-par for Princess Cruises on *Grand* in the beginning, seems to have been improved with more variety and selections. Open for brunch (on sea days only) and dinner by reservation are the popular **Sabatini's Trattoria,** an Italian specialty restaurant ($15 surcharge), and the **Painted Desert** (**Tequilos** on *Star*) ($10 surcharge), serving Tex-Mex fare and boasting the best service on the ship.

Outdoors are **Poseidon's Pizza,** where pizza is served all day; **Trident Grill,** providing hot dogs and burgers; and **I Scream Ice Cream** bar (**Sundaes** on *Golden* and **Scoops** on *Star*), a Häagen-Dazs concession where a scoop costs $2. The **Promenade Bar** overlooking the atrium on

Deck 7 doubles as a patisserie, serving a light breakfast of croissants and espresso, as does the **Lobby Bar** on Deck 5 on *Golden* and *Star*. Room service is available 24 hours. Because dining is available at all times, passengers do not need to plan shore time around mealtimes. The many dining options also reduce lines and crowds.

Facilities and Activities The *Grand Princess's* **Voyage of Discovery,** the $2.5 million virtual-reality center, is an eye-popper. The room has interactive games and a cyberbar, but its main attraction is a wild, motion-based virtual-reality ride that seats 18 people. Passengers buy a Voyager card for $20, which they use to start machines, and the cost of play ($0.75 to $3) is deducted. At the blue-screen **Limelight Studio,** passengers can star in their own video, inserted into an existing scene from a popular movie or historical event. Neither the virtual-reality center or blue-screen studio are found on *Golden Princess* or *Star Princess*. Rather, *Golden* has a digital studio which provides a face-replacement computer program. *Star* (and other ships) have a blue-screen portrait type of computer where they can photograph the subject against a variety of backgrounds (similar to the Limelight system). It's a portable system operated off a laptop computer.

Standard diversions are plentiful: bingo, karaoke, cards, board games, and writing room. The small business center has phone, fax, and computer facilities. (There's a charge to use of equipment.) In the 36-seat wedding chapel, couples can be married or renew their vows with the captain presiding. All three ships have webcams in their chapels, enabling folks at home to watch an on-board wedding live.

Shops sell sundries, clothing, jewelry, perfumes, and souvenirs. All are convenient to the Grand Atrium, the heart of the ship. In the **Art Gallery,** reproduction and original prints are for sale; the ubiquitous auctions are held almost daily and, unfortunately, often obscure the ship's $3 million museum-quality collection of contemporary art. The ship's library, **A Quiet Corner,** boasts an extensive book collection and the ever-popular private reading/listening chairs. The newest addition is the **AOL Internet Café,** which is open 24 hours daily; and a florist, who prepares fresh floral arrangements for purchase.

The ships offer a great variety of entertainment. Each of three showrooms has its own shows nightly. **Vista Show Lounge,** the midsize theater, presents cabaret-style entertainment that's quite varied. **Princess Theatre,** a two-deck showroom, stages large-scale production shows and revues and has the best sight lines and most comfortable seats of any shipboard theater we have experienced. The shows, all produced by Princess's production department, are outstanding. The **Explorer's Lounge** nightclub features soloists and bands playing a variety of music. The **Casino,** designed by the architects who created Caesars Palace Forum in Las Vegas, has one of the world's largest examples of holographic art. It also has 260 slot machines, 17 blackjack/poker tables, roulette, and craps. The ships have many other small entertainment places, some with music and dancing. The **Wheelhouse Bar,** with the ambience of a private club, offers music for dancing; **Snookers** sports bar has a bank of television monitors that broadcast sports programs, also available in cabins (the system can show events on Princess Theatre's big screen, too). **Calypso Bar** and **Oasis Bar,** outdoors and poolside, are frequently the scene of special events, including the Captain's Party. A retractable dome can be closed in bad weather. **Center Court Bar** is near the sports facilities; **Sea Breeze** and the **Mermaid's Tail** are mid-deck bars. **Alfresco's** bar overlooks the aft pool, which can be covered and converted into a stage for live concerts.

Sports, Fitness, and Beauty   Each of the Grand-class ships have five swimming pools—including one for children and one for crew—and nine whirlpools. The Princess Links computerized golf simulator lets passengers try some of the world's top courses. A landscaped putting green is available, as are paddle tennis, basketball, and volleyball courts. A swim-against-the-current lap pool is the centerpiece of the **Lotus Spa.** The gym has treadmills, Stairmasters, Lifecycles, weight machines, an area for exercise and aerobics classes, and new trainer-led options (all at a charge) like yoga, kickbox press, pulse group cycling, and Pilates, and an outside jogging track. There are changing rooms and saunas (no charge) for men and women. The beauty spa, operated by Steiner, has 11 massage rooms offering a range of pricey treatments, such as aromatherapy massage, mud and seaweed wraps, and reflexology. Also featured are new Asian-influenced treatments, such as Chakra stone therapy, a massage with hot, oiled stones. On *Star Princess,* the **Lotus Spa** is even larger than on her sister ships, with more treatment rooms and a thermal suite with steam rooms, heated lounge chairs, cool showers, and an ice bath for use by spa clients only, before or after treatments. A teak promenade encircles the ship; five and a half laps is just shy of a mile.

Children's Facilities   The two-level **Fun Zone Children's Center** offers a whale-shaped splash pool, life-sized doll's house, children's theater, ball jump, games, and more. Programs are age-specific and supervised. The **Off Limits Teen Center,** also bilevel, has a video disco, refreshment bar, video games, and private whirlpool. See "Children's Facilities" in the Sun group for Princess Kids' new expanded program.

Shore Excursions   Passengers receive a 64-page Adventures Ashore booklet describing shore excursions for their cruise. Most half-day trips cost $25–$55; full-day outings range from $65 to $125. Our experience is that Princess shore excursions are well organized, particularly given the size of ship and number of people touring. Excursions on Mediterranean cruises cover the most important attractions; we recommend them, especially for first-timers. Passengers familiar with the ports may want to arrange their own activities. During the *Star's* calls in Mexico, Princess has introduced a variety of new, adventure-type tours, such as "Dolphin Encounters" at $88 and kayaking, certified scuba diving and Sierra Madre excursions in all-terrain vehicles, at a range of prices.

Postscript Even with their many innovations and attractions, passengers who have sailed with the line before will recognize that these super-megaliners are very much Princess ships. They appeal most to those who see their size as a positive thing, providing options every hour of the day. They are sure to be popular with first-time cruisers. A big dividend of their size is a smooth ride. Those with health problems will be comforted to know the ships have a two-way video system (the first cruise ships to have it) that allows the ships' doctors to confer live with medical specialists and top hospitals ashore and in the U.S. *Golden Princess* and *Star Princess's* telemedicine facilities are even more state-of-the-art and include a digital x-ray machine, defibrillators positioned around the ship as well as in the ship's hospital, and other high-tech equipment.

REGAL PRINCESS	QUALITY **7**	VALUE **C**
Registry: Liberia	Length: 811 feet	Beam: 105 feet
Cabins: 795	Draft: 26 feet	Speed: 22.5 knots
Maximum Passengers:	Passenger Decks: 11	Elevators: 9
1,590	Crew: 696	Space Ratio: 44

The Ships Anyone familiar with the *Regal Princess* may not recognize her after her recent interior renovation and redesign that added a new 24-hour café, a children's center, and a remodeled atrium. The goal of the project, which comprised the largest refurbishment ever done on a Princess ship, was to bring the vessel in line with the newer Grand group, often using design, décor, and color schemes from them.

Regal Princess, whose godmother is former British prime minister Margaret Thatcher, was added in 1991 (Her twin, *Crown Princess,* was renamed and moved in April 2002, to Aida Cruises, a P&O company serving the German market.) Part of the inventory Princess received from its Sitmar purchase, the ship was very different from any other vessel. Designed by Renzo Piano, architect of Paris's Pompidou Center, the Italian-built super-liner has sleek lines that Piano says were inspired by the shape of a dolphin. Even now, the unorthodox design garners mixed reviews.

The good news: space and comfort. *Regal* is a superliner, but she carries 25–30% fewer passengers than some of her counterparts. This spaciousness is apparent in wide corridors, lounges with high ceilings, and large cabins. Even standard cabins are the size of some other ships' suites. The ship's appointments range from elegant, with top-quality fabrics, well-made furnishings, and museum-quality works by renowned artists (including Frank Stella, Robert Motherwell, and David Hockney) to the eclectic. Some bars display pop art, and 18th-century romantic landscapes hang in dining rooms. The result is an interesting, stimulating, and entertaining environment.

The main drawback of the interiors is that they look and feel like a hotel. Outside decks are few, and corridors with no ocean view border promenades and lounges. Unless your cabin has a veranda, you must go to the top deck or small, upper aft areas to see the seascape. The forward section, particularly, is closed off from the sea. And the Dome atop of the ship, meant to be a quiet observation lounge, is frenetic: Slot machines buzz in the casino, dance music spills from bars, and the area is thronged. The cavernous space might have been better used for outdoor decks.

The ship's new look is most evident in the three-deck atrium, the Plaza, which serves as the lobby and gathering place. Overall, it has been given a warmer, more inviting look. The backdrop of the main staircase is a large vertical water sculpture and a series of small, marble pools intended to create a restful atmosphere with the sound of water. Columns and railings are now covered with cherry wood, and greenery-filled marble planters at their base add warmth. There is a new marble floor at the base of the main staircase, and a large glass chandelier hangs above it. In the **Patisserie** on the first level, windows were added, helping give the space an airy appearance. Behind the newly paneled reception desk is a dramatic three-dimensional sculpture of swimming dolphins. On the upper decks, rich wood paneling was also added to the facades of the shops and bars around the atrium.

Actually, the most extensive aspect of the recent renovations is not visible. New stern thrusters were installed, increasing the ships' maneuvering capability and allowing them to visit ports without tug facilities.

Itineraries See Itinerary Index.

Cabins Spacious cabins are one of the ship's best features. They come in 26 categories and four basic arrangements: inside or outside standard doubles; outside double with a tiny balcony; outside minisuites with small veranda; and full suites with veranda. The 6 top categories plus the largest of the inside group are on three upper decks; the other 11 categories are spread across four lower decks. All have five-channel television with CNN, ESPN, and Discovery Channel; four-channel radio; direct-dial telephone; refrigerator; safe; walk-in closets, separate dressing area, and generous drawer space; and key card for door locks. Terry robes and fresh fruit are provided in all cabins. Standard outside cabins without balcony have oversized windows. Lifeboats are midway down the sides of the ship; 26 cabins on Dolphin Deck have obstructed views (they are indicated on the deck plan).

Specifications 171 inside, 440 outside cabins (134 with verandas); 36 minisuites, 14 suites with verandas. Standard dimensions, 190 square feet. All with 2 lower beds, convertible to queen; some have third/fourth berths; no singles. 10 wheelchair-accessible.

Dining The main dining room, which has two seatings for three meals, was extensively redesigned from floor to ceiling with new decorative touches, including new carpets and wall coverings, lighting and dimmer system, artwork, and treatment to the stainless steel surfaces to soften the room's appearance. Also changing the look is a new table arrangement, adapted from the Grand-class ships, that provides for greater privacy and better service.

Dinner menus are posted at bars and elsewhere aboard the ships. They're similar fleetwide, offering six courses for lunch and seven for dinner, with numerous selections for each course. Pizza lovers will enjoy the poolside pizzeria, complete with checkered tablecloths and Chianti bottles. It's open for lunch and in the evening, serving made-to-order pizzas at no extra cost. The patisserie has excellent espresso and cappuccino and assorted fresh pastries.

Regal's **Café del Sol** has been transformed into a 24-hour restaurant with increased seating capacity by an extension at the aft end of the café. It was remodeled with new seating arrangements and serving lines and given new décor; a new galley was added for bistro service in the evening. The extension also provided space for a dance floor and stage. On the open deck, there's a new salad bar and a hamburger bar.

Service Reports indicate that service and food have improved as Princess has worked to correct past flaws.

Facilities and Activities Another of the ship's best features is her lounges—greatly varied in size, décor, ambience, and entertainment. The largest is the handsome **International Lounge,** a bilevel show lounge with a horseshoe-shaped stage. Bacchus is a small wine-by-the-glass and caviar bar that was given a more intimate setting with lowered ceilings and glass partitions, along with new murals and other decorative accents. The **Bengal Bar** has a stage for a piano, a dance floor, and a mirrored bar. The room sparkles with brass and glass and has ceiling fans suggesting the days of the raj, complete with a brass statue of a Bengal tiger.

Next door, the intimate piano bar displays murals of fashionably dressed revelers from the 1920s. The **Adagio,** as it's called, also has an espresso machine. One flight up, the **Stage Door** cabaret and late-night disco offers a sunken dance floor. **Characters** on the Lido Deck is a colorful poolside bar serving innovative drinks. The huge, top-deck Dome with 19-foot ceilings is largely occupied by the casino. It has a dance floor, bar, and 100 trees! A cinema, library, and card room are available.

Sports, Fitness, and Beauty   The Sun Deck has two outdoor pools, one with a swim-up bar and the other with waterfalls and whirlpools; a paddle tennis/volleyball court; and a one-sixth-mile jogging track. There's no wraparound deck. Images, a beauty and fitness center, has an aerobics area, weight machines, exercise bikes, and a steam room.

Children's Facilities   During the latest renovations, a brand-new, 2,000-square-foot children's center was added to the top sports deck, directly above the café extension, replacing the basketball court. The multipurpose center can be divided into separate areas for children and teens or converted into a meeting or conference room. "Princess Kids," Princess's fleetwide youth program, provides supervised activities and facilities. See "Children's Facilities" in the Sun group section for details. Children younger than age 18 must be accompanied by an adult and have written consent from both parents or legal guardians to cruise.

CORAL PRINCESS	QUALITY 9	VALUE B
ISLAND PRINCESS	(Preview)	
Registry: Bermuda	Length: 964 feet	Beam: 106 feet
Cabins: 987	Draft: 26 feet	Speed: 21.5 knots
Maximum Passengers	Passenger Decks: 16	Elevators: 12
2,566	Crew: 900	Space Ratio: 44.6

The Ships   The 88,000-ton *Coral Princess* made her maiden voyage in January 2003 and was christened in the Panama Canal by the president of Panama—the first cruise ship ever to have such an honor. Her sister, *Island Princess,* debuted in July 2003, in Vancouver, also marking a milestone as the first cruise ship ever christened in the Canadian port city.

These twins are a new class of ships for Princess, built specifically to transit the Panama Canal, and they reverse the line's recent trend of building megaships of over 100,000 tons. Despite their smaller size, they are very spacious and include most amenities and services found on Princess's largest vessels, such as a wedding chapel, alternative dining options, a 24-hour restaurant, **AOL Internet Café,** and a substantial number of balcony cabins. Indeed, the duo appear to combine the best features of the Sun and Grand groups, plus having some great attractions that even the bigger ships can't boast.

Constructed at Chantiers de l'Atlantique, the ships are Princess's first French-built vessels. They are very well laid out, making it easy for passengers to get oriented quickly. Their refined and pleasing décor is sophisticated yet comfortable, interesting in detail, yet easy on the eyes. Among their newest features are the unusual high-tech facilities in the aft show lounge and their innovative power-generation technology—a gas turbine/diesel engine combination, with the gas turbines placed in the ships' funnels. The configuration not only has environmental advantages but also allows for additional space inside the ships used for enhanced passenger facilities. Then, there are the unique features: the first-ever cruise ship kiln—yes, a kiln—and a television-style demonstration kitchen. Emeril would feel right at home.

Itineraries See Itinerary Index.

Cabins Nearly 90% of the ships' cabins are outside, and most of these—83%—have private balconies. Although there are 33 different price levels, mostly resulting from location, season, and length of cruise, essentially there are only five types of cabins: suites with balconies (468–591 square feet); minisuites with balconies (323 square feet); outside standard with balconies (214–257 square feet); outside standard (168 square feet); and inside standard (160 square feet). The best value for money are the outside standards with balconies, which Princess calls "affordable balconies," and indeed, they are. The wheelchair-accessible cabins range from 217 to 374 square feet and are available in most categories.

Throughout, the cabins are decorated in easy-to-live-with warm colors and mellow wood. All cabins have twin beds that can be converted to queen; television with remote control, CNN, CNBC, ESPN, TNT, Discovery Channel, movies, and several radio channels; minifridge; ample closet and drawer space; two hair dryers; safe; telephone with voice mail; and bathroom with shower. Further amenities are added in the pricier categories: Minisuites have queen-size bed, separate sitting area with sofa bed, balcony, two televisions, bathroom with tub and shower, and robes (can be requested in standard cabins). Suites enjoy a larger balcony, walk-in closet, a wet bar, and bath with whirlpool tub. The pebbly nonslip surface of the bathroom floor is a welcome safety feature. There's a self-serve laundromat on every cabin deck—another appreciated amenity.

Specifications 879 outside (527 with balconies), 108 inside; 16 suites and 184 minisuites with balconies; 8 minisuites; 616 upper berths. 20 (16 outside/4 inside) wheelchair-accessible.

Dining The ships' Personal Choice Dining lineup offers two main dining rooms, **Provence** and **Bordeau,** which passengers can choose for either Traditional Fixed Seating (Provence Dining Room at either first or second seating each evening) or Anytime Dining (Bordeaux Dining Room between 5:30 p.m. and 10 p.m. or by reserving a specific time). Passengers may change from Traditional to Anytime dining during the cruise, if they find they prefer one style over the other. Further options are the 24-hour **Horizon Court** for breakfast, lunch, and bistro dinner for casual evening dining; the **Pizza Bar** where the specialties are varied and excellent; and the patisserie.

Two alternative restaurants carry a surcharge. The new **Bayou Café,** the first New Orleans–style dinner restaurant at sea ($10 per person, which includes a hurricane cocktail), offers Cajun specialties and live jazz. Reviews on this eatery are mixed. Some thought the food was excellent; we did not, and considering that New Orleans is noted for fabulous cuisine and some of the best restaurants in the country, we were disappointed with the Café's menu. The best aspect of the café is the jazz music in the evening, but be sure to avoid the seating at the side tables behind the orchestra; the sound level there is deafening.

Sabatini's ($15 surcharge), the popular Princess signature Italian restaurant, is open for dinner only except on sea days when it serves brunch. Dinner has a set menu of so many courses—all excellent—that it's almost too much food. The outstanding service is as good as the food. And if you are still suffering hunger pangs, there's a poolside hamburger grill, a Häagen-Dazs ice-cream bar(extra charge) near the pool, and 24-hour room service.

Service   The service throughout the ship is excellent. The friendly staff greets passengers at all times of day in all parts of the ship, and they are eager to help. The **Sabatini** staff is wonderful, and our Filipino room steward was superb, going out of his way to be helpful. We have never had a more cheerful, attentive, and professional room steward on any ship, including the most luxurious ones. Other passengers have reported enthusiastically the same kudos for the staff of *Island Princess.*

Facilities and Activities   The ship's design maximizes the public space for passenger activities, with some lounges spanning the ship from port to starboard. Most of the public rooms are on decks 6 and 7. Just as on the larger vessels, the new duo have three show lounges, but with an added dimension—the two-story interactive high-tech aft lounge. Known as the **Universe Lounge,** the décor has been inspired by Jules Verne's classic *20,000 Leagues Under the Sea* and sports three revolving stages with integrated lifts, giant projection screens, and the latest in lighting technology, digital sound, and video systems. The stages are designed for a diverse slate of entertainment, from Vegas-style shows to movie screenings and full television productions to small classroom-style demonstrations.

The Universal Lounge is also home to Princess Cruises' new enrichment program, ScholarShip@Sea, whcih Princess calls "edu-tainment." Considering the courses available—cooking, photography, ceramics, decorating, visual arts, computers, health, finance, and lectures on a wide variety of topics—the term is accurate. The lounge's demonstration kitchen can be moved into place for cooking classes by the ship's chef or visiting culinary experts. The room has network plug-ins for up to 50 laptop computers and an infrared headset system for the hearing impaired. Elsewhere on the ship is a kiln—a cruise-ship first—for firing the pottery made by passengers in their pottery class, one of the subjects available on ScholarShip@Sea. Each cruise offers a slate of up to 20 courses, with six options offered each sea day. For some there is a small fee, usually about $10.

Introduced on the *Coral Princess,* Princess Cruises plans to have the innovative ScholarShip@Sea available fleetwide by the end of 2004. Other daytime activities are the standard cruise-ship fare (which pale by comparison to the edu-tainment) and include the ubiquitous art auctions, bingo, horseracing, ice-carving demonstrations, and pool games.

Evening entertainment is as varied as the venues. Currently, *Coral Princess* has three new musical shows performed by a cast of 17 lively and very professional singers and dancers in the dual-level **Princess Theatre,** the main show lounge, or the multipurpose Universal Lounge. There is also a variety of music from jazz to country, singers, comedians and novelty acts in other lounges and bars, as well as classical concerts on some days. The **Wheelhouse Bar,** which spans Deck 7, is one of the most handsome rooms on any cruise ship and is very popular with passengers for cocktails and dancing before and after dinner. Further along the deck are some new gathering places, such as the **Churchill Lounge,** a cigar and spirits lounge with its own humidor, and the **Rat Pack Bar,** a 1960s retro martini bar—both firsts for Princess. One deck down is the casino with London-style décor and the **Explorer's Lounge,** which becomes the disco in the late evening. There's also a wedding chapel, an Internet café, a library and card room, duty-free shops, and an art gallery.

Sports, Fitness, and Beauty   The Lido deck (14) has a swimming pool, three whirlpools, and a poolside bar. In the **Lotus Spa,** meant to reflect the soothing aura of Bali, there is a swim-against-the-current pool, covered by a retractable glass magradrome, and two whirlpools. Further aft is the aerobics room and gym. Be prepared for a hard sell of the spa lotions and other products by the staff; your response should be equally firm if you have no interest in purchasing them. The new vessels offer a nine-hole putting course and golf simulator.

Children's Facilities   On Deck 12 aft is action central for Princess's supervised age-specific children's program. The outstanding facilities include **Off Limits,** the teen center with special activities for young adults ages 13–17, including video games and a teen disco. The **Fun Zone** is a special center for Princess Piloteers (ages 8–12), with regular activities designed for this age group. **Pelican's Playhouse** is the children's center for ages 2–7, where **Youth Center** staff host a daily schedule of age-specific activities. The Pelican's Pool is a dedicated children's pool.

TAHITIAN PRINCESS	(Preview)	
PACIFIC PRINCESS	(Preview)	
Registry: Gibraltar	Length: 594 feet	Beam: 83.5feet
Cabins: 344	Draft: 19.5 feet	Speed: 20 knots
Maximum Passengers:	Passenger Decks: 9	Elevators: 4
680	Crew: 373	Space Ratio: 44

The Ships   *Tahitian Princess* and *Pacific Princess,* the former *Renaissance III* and *Renaissance IV* of the now-defunct Renaissance Cruises, joined the Princess fleet in late 2002. The twin ships are midgets compared to the other ships in the Princess fleet, but many of the line's passengers who lamented the departure of the former *Pacific Princess* should be pleased with these ships. In addition to their more intimate cruise environment, the ships are quite new, having entered service originally in 1999, and they come with many modern features.

Both ships offer many of the Personal Choice Cruising options that have become Princess trademarks. These include a four restaurant choices: the main dining room, **Sabatini's Trattoria, Sterling Steakhouse,** and the 24-hour **Lido Café,** plus a poolside barbecue grill.

The ships each have a show lounge, eight bars, an observation lounge, casino, a library and card room, two shops, and a medical center. There is a swimming pool, a spa with two whirlpools and beauty salon, a fitness center, and jogging track.

Ninety-two percent of the cabins are outside and over two-thirds of these come with a private balcony. All have television with CNN, ESPN, and first-run movies, VCR, personal safe, refrigerator, and hair dryer. Passengers have a self-service launderette.

Specifications   344 cabins which includes 10 suites, 52 minisuites. 317 are outside; 27 inside. 232 cabins have balconies. 3 wheelchair-accessible cabins.

Postscript   *Tahitian Princess* sails year-round in Tahiti and the South Pacific on the region's only 10-day cruises. The three different itineraries round-trip from Papeete, Tahiti, call at Bora Bora, Moorea, and Raiatea, and either the Cook Islands, Samoa, or the Marquesas.

The *Pacific Princess* operates on a split deployment, sailing half the year throughout French Polynesia and the wider Pacific region for Princess Cruises, and the other half for P&O Cruises.

Radisson Seven Seas Cruises

600 Corporate Drive, Suite 410, Fort Lauderdale, FL 33334
|(954) 776-6123; (800) 477-7500;
(800) 285-1835; fax (954) 772-3763
www.rssc.com

Type of Ships   One-of-a-kind small ships and midsize vessels with big-ship facilities.

Type of Cruises   Quiet, luxury, destination-oriented cruises with personal service and sophisticated amenities.

Cruise Line's Strengths

- service

- itineraries

- cuisine

- single, flex-time/open-seating dining

- all-inclusive prices

- all-outside deluxe accommodations and amenities

Cruise Line's Shortcomings

- lack of promenade or outdoor wraparound deck on *Radisson Diamond* and *Song of Flower*

- limited lounges, entertainment and shipboard activities on *Radisson Diamond*

- disparate fleet

Fellow Passengers   Affluent, well-educated, well-traveled, 45 years and older, $100,000+ annual income. They cherish their individuality and shun group travel. *Diamond's* passengers are slightly more affluent, senior executives, professionals, and high-end resort vacationers. Typical age is 50+; over 75% are Americans. They usually have cruised before on luxury liners, have sophisticated tastes, and care about elegance and service. Some are likely to be special-occasion celebrators and incentive awards winners. *Paul Gauguin's* romantic destination, Tahiti, is an important factor in which passengers the ship attracts, particularly honeymooners and divers. The vessel also is popular with incentive groups. The typical *Navigator* and *Mariner* passenger is well traveled, 50+, with $125,000 average income; many own their company. Most are veterans of other upscale cruise lines.

Recommended For Upscale, independent, active, seasoned travelers accustomed to luxury and quality. Small-ship devotees who appreciate the advantages and accept the limitations of such vessels.

Not Recommended For Joiners; people who need to be entertained, want a full day of shipboard activity, or thrive in a Las Vegas atmosphere.

Cruise Areas and Seasons Round-the-world; Asia, Caribbean, transcanal, Mexico, South America in winter; Alaska, Mediterranean, Northern Europe, Norwegian fjords in summer; Tahiti year-round.

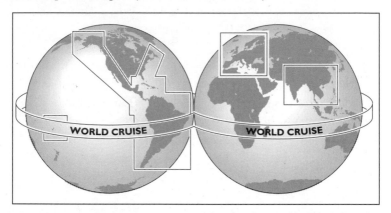

The Line In 1995, Radisson Diamond Cruises and Seven Seas Cruise Line merged to form Radisson Seven Seas Cruises. The deal represented an expansion into cruising by Radisson Hotels International, while the new line brought three market segments—contemporary, traditional, and light adventure—in the luxury cruise market under one umbrella.

The futuristic *Radisson Diamond,* planned primarily for the corporate meeting and incentive market, combines some of the amenities of a larger ship with the intimacy of a smaller one. When the corporate market failed to materialize sufficiently, the line changed course and sought affluent, seasoned travelers accustomed to luxury and fine cuisine who like to travel in a quiet, sophisticated environment.

Launched in 1990 by a wealthy Japanese businesswoman who established its high standards, Seven Seas Cruise Line's *Song of Flower* quickly made her mark by offering deluxe cruises at rates considerably lower than its competitors and winning accolades and awards after only its first year. Radisson Seven Seas introduced the *Paul Gauguin* in 1998, and in a joint venture with Monte Carlo–based V. Ships, it debuted the all-suite luxury *Seven Seas Navigator* in 1999 and the larger, all-suite, all-balcony *Seven Seas Mariner* in 2001, and her sister ship, *Seven Seas Voyager,* in spring of 2003. Each ship can boast some of cruising's highest space-to-passenger and crew-to-passenger ratios. Carlson Hospitality Worldwide, the parent company of Radisson Seven Seas Cruises, sold *Song of Flower* in 2003.

In January and February, the cruise line charters the *Hanseatic,* a 180-passenger German luxury ship known for adventure cruises, for a series of 11- to 17-day cruises of Antarctica which Radisson Seven Seas markets in North America.

THE FLEET	BUILT/RENOVATED	TONNAGE	PASSENGERS
Paul Gauguin	1998	18,800	320
Radisson Diamond	1992	20,295	350
Seven Seas Mariner	2001	50,000	700
Seven Seas Navigator	1999	30,000	490
Seven Seas Voyager	2003	49,000	708

Style For the smallest ships, their size, small number of passengers, and price ensure the cruises a certain exclusivity. They also help define the high level of service and personal attention passengers expect—and receive.

Shipboard life on *Diamond* is informal during the day but formal in style (though not necessarily in dress) in the evening. Surroundings are spacious and luxurious, the ambience sophisticated. The ship has loyal fans.

Paul Gauguin and the slightly larger *Navigator* fit the group well. *Seven Seas Mariner* and *Voyager* offer the same level of luxury but on a much larger scale.

Distinctive Features No-tipping policy. Water sports platform and marina. Extensive book and video libraries. *Diamond's* twin hull design. Cordon Bleu–directed venues on *Mariner* and *Voyager.*

	HIGHEST	LOWEST	AVERAGE
PER DIEM	$1,245	$165	$669

Per diems are calculated from cruise line's nondiscounted *cruise-only* fares on standard accommodations and vary by season, cabin, and cruise areas.

Rates Gratuities and wine with lunch and dinner included. All beverages or room bar initial setup included and non-alcoholic drinks restocked daily, depending on ship. Port charges are additional.

Special Fares and Discounts

- Second guest in suite categories A–H receive a 50% savings off *Seven Seas Mariner's* standard fares.
- **Single Supplement** Specific amounts per cruise in brochure.

Packages

- **Air/Sea** Yes.
- **Pre/Post** Yes.

Past Passengers Radisson Seven Seas Society, for repeat passengers, publishes a newsletter and offers members sailings with incentives and special prices. Some sailings are hosted by the line's president. Members receive quality gifts based on the number of days they cruise.

The Last Word The *Diamond* is so different, it's difficult to compare it with other cruise ships. Does the design provide advantages over conventional cruise ships? On balance, no. Alternatively, *Paul Gauguin* focuses on one destination and does it with great style; *Navigator* roams the world; *Mariner* and *Voyager* are the ultimate in luxury.

RADISSON SEVEN SEAS CRUISES STANDARD FEATURES

Officers *Diamond*/Scandinavian, European, Finnish; *Paul Gauguin, Mariner*/French, European; *Navigator/Voyager,* European, International, Italian.

Staff Dining and Cabin/European. *Diamond:* Cruise/American. *Paul Gauguin* and *Song of Flower:* Dining/European and Filipino; *Navigator, Mariner, Voyager:* European/International; Cruise/American and British.

Dining Facilities One dining room (*Paul Gauguin,* two; *Mariner, Voyager,* four) with open seating for three meals; informal indoor/outdoor café for buffet breakfast and lunch. Reservations-only alternative dining on *Diamond, Navigator;* three choices; *Mariner, Voyager* four choices.

Special Diets Accommodated with advance notice.

Room Service 24-hour service with full-meal, in-cabin dining.

Dress Code Casual by day; most evenings, jackets required for men. Formal or semiformal for captain's parties. Visits in some ports of call may require women to cover heads, legs, and arms.

Cabin Amenities Direct-dial telephone, hair dryer, television, VCR, radio, stocked minibar (on *Paul Gauguin* with nonalcoholic beverages); marble bathroom with tub and shower. *Diamond,* CNN, safe. *Diamond, Navigator,* all suites; *Paul Gauguin, Mariner, Voyager* all-suite, all verandas, terry robes, safe.

Electrical Outlets 110 AC.

Wheelchair Access Two cabins; *Mariner* 6; *Navigator, Voyager* 4.

Recreation and Entertainment Nightclub, cabaret, and piano entertainment in two lounges, small casino, dancing, card games, backgammon, book/video library, lecture program.

Sports and Other Activities One outside pool. See text.

Beauty and Fitness Beauty salon. Small gym. Spas on *Paul Gauguin, Navigator, Mariner, Voyager;* see text.

Other Facilities Business center on *Diamond;* boutique; hospital; *Mariner, Voyager,* Internet café, launderettes.

Children's Facilities None.

Theme Cruises Yes.

Smoking Smoking sections designated in public areas; no cigar or pipe smoking in dining room.

Radisson Seven Seas Suggested Tipping Gratuities are included in cruise fare; therefore, no-tipping policy; tips for special service on *Diamond.*

Credit Cards For cruise payment and onboard charges: American Express, Diners Club, MasterCard, Visa, Discover.

RADISSON DIAMOND	QUALITY **6**	VALUE **C**
Registry: Bahamas	Length: 420 feet	Beam: 103 feet
Cabins: 175	Draft: 26 feet	Speed: 12.5 knots
Maximum Passengers:	Passenger Decks: 6	Elevators: 4
350	Crew: 191	Space Ratio: 58

The Ship   If you were the first to fly the Concorde or are on a list to go to the moon, you may want to try the *Diamond*, which has the most revolutionary design of any cruise ship built in the last century. Sitting high above the water on twin hulls, this extraordinary ship is a traffic-stopper.

Diamond's design uses SWATH (Small Waterplane Area Twin Hull) technology intended to provide less motion, engine noise, and propeller vibration, plus greater stability than conventional ships. Does it? Maybe. The design also has trade-offs in terms of performance. Top cruising speed is slightly over 12 knots per hour, about 40% slower than most cruise ships. This limits the range and flexibility of *Diamond's* itineraries, and in a heavy sea, the waves slam up against the hull's underside, creating a loud boom. Moreover, both hulls contain machinery, and there's no underwater connection between them. To reach one from the other, staff must climb stairs to the main structure, cross over, and descend the other side.

The good news is that *Diamond* is unusually spacious, with roomy public areas and its cabins among the largest and most elegant at sea. Indeed, the interior is more like an understated luxury hotel, complete with meeting center and boardrooms. Interiors combine contemporary and Art Deco styles with fine wood, leather, and fabrics. A six-story atrium at the ship's entrance contains the reception desk, two glass-enclosed elevators, and an ebony-and-brass staircase leading to all decks, including the spa and gym, jogging track, and car room at the top.

Itineraries   See Itinerary Index.

Cabins   *Diamond* has six categories of cabins, although aside from the master suites, all are almost identical, with the main difference being a balcony or a picture window. All are large outside suites with a larger sitting area or a veranda with teak decking and solid steel partitions adding to the privacy. Four balcony suites connect to create a pair of two-room master suites. Most accommodations have twin beds convertible to queen size. The lounging area has a sofa and chairs, and large bay windows. Quietly elegant décor incorporates high-quality fabrics, including quilted wall-hangings.

Suites are very comfortable and have the amenities of a luxury hotel, including refrigerator stocked with beverages and complimentary initial minibar, two bottles of complimentary liquor, and fine Judith Jackson bath products. Closet space is minimal, although drawer space makes up for it. Bathrooms have a marble vanity, hair dryer, retractable clothesline, bathtub, and shower, but are small for this price range. All suites have entertainment systems with closed-circuit, remote-controlled, five-channel television with CNN, music channels, and VCR, stereo/radio, CD player, dressing table, international direct-dial telephone, and safe.

Two executive suites, which were recently renovated, offer a king-size bed, whirlpool tub, balcony, and bay window. Two wheelchair-accessible suites have been relocated to Deck 7 and refurbished. Room service, available 24 hours daily, is prompt and efficient. The extensive menu lists hot and cold items, including freshly baked pizza, and full-course meals during regular meal hours.

Specifications   175 outside cabins (121 with verandas); 2 executive master suites. Standard dimensions are 243 square feet including veranda or sitting area. All with twin beds, most convertible to queens. On Deck 8, some suites with a sofa bed can accommodate a third person; no singles. 2 wheelchair-accessible.

Dining   The spacious **Grand Dining Room,** with floor-to-ceiling windows embracing the sea, is one of the most elegant rooms afloat. Fine service, gracious ambience, and generous space between tables add to the luxury. Seating is open; neither times nor tables are assigned. Gourmet cuisine is the ship's most outstanding feature. Selections change daily and include fresh seafood and prime meats. Preparation and presentation are varied and sophisticated. Fresh pasta dishes are offered at lunch and dinner. Wine is included with dinner.

The informal **Grill** on the top deck offers indoor/outdoor dining from full menus and elaborate breakfast and lunch buffets. In the evening, it changes its name to **Don Vito's** and becomes a 50-seat Italian restaurant, complete with red-checkered tablecloths and singing waiters. The menu changes daily; delectable pastas are featured. Reservations are required (by noon), but there's no extra charge. It's very good, very popular, and very noisy.

Service   The ship's senior hotel and dining staff, many of them Italians, have years of luxury-ship experience. Most cabin and dining attendants are women from Austria, Germany, and Sweden; most are working on a ship for the first time. They are courteous and eager to please but sometimes lack polish.

Facilities and Activities   Some people like the lack of organized recreation; others could be bored. Depending on itinerary, offerings include educational and cultural lectures by guest experts, recent-release movies, bridge instruction and play, shuffleboard tournaments, bingo, card games, and backgammon. The library has a good selection of books and videotapes available 24 hours a day with no check-in/out required. The meeting/business center has audiovisual equipment, publishing facilities, fax and satellite communications services, and staff support.

A small computer center offers e-mail (through onboard accounts only; you cannot access your home account) but no Internet access. When not in use by business groups, the main meeting room is used for art auctions and movie screenings.

The largest lounge, **Windows,** takes its name from its sweeping wall of windows—which can only be appreciated at tea time, as the room is used mostly at night when the windows are covered. The lounge has an upper-level bar overlooking a small stage, dance floor and orchestra, and the main seating area. It's popular for cocktails when a combo plays and for after-dinner cabaret entertainment. Aerobics are offered in daytime, and late at night, it's the disco. The posh, windowless **Club** piano bar and lounge, decorated in sleek deco style, features a singer/pianist on most nights and is a comfortable rendezvous for conversation almost any time. The small **Chips Casino** offers roulette, blackjack, poker, and slots.

Sports, Fitness, and Beauty A European-style spa provides herbal wraps, massages, and beauty treatments for additional fees. There's no charge for the sauna and steam room, aerobics, yoga, stretch classes, and other exercise. Next door, the gym has exercise equipment, and an outdoor jogging track (13 laps = 1 mile). One deck below is a small swimming pool, and a single Jacuzzi. Shuffleboard and table tennis are available on the spacious aft deck. The original, hydraulically retractable water-sports platform that was part of the ship's design is currently not in use, following mechanical problems. Instead, a free-floating marina platform is lowered from the stern on calm days, allowing passengers to go swimming, kayaking, or Jet-Skiing directly from the ship.

Radisson Seven Seas is the Professional Golfers' Association's official cruise line. A "Golf Academy" and PGA-designated cruises in Europe are offered and include play at famous courses, a private lesson, and clinics with a PGA-certified pro. *Diamond* has a small driving net and, putting area. In the Caribbean, golf packages are available at 12 ports and can be booked prior to your cruise.

PAUL GAUGUIN	QUALITY 9	VALUE B
Registry: France	Length: 513 feet	Beam: 71 feet
Cabins: 160	Draft: 16.9 feet	Speed: 18 knots
Maximum Passengers:	Passenger Decks: 7	Elevators: 4
320	Crew: 211	Space Ratio: 59

The Ship Named for the French artist whose life and work embodied the romance of French Polynesia, the *Paul Gauguin* is the most deluxe ship to cruise the South Seas year-round. Its space ratio is among cruising's highest, and its shallow draft allows access to small, rarely frequented ports.

The French-built vessel is owned by French investors and operated by Radisson Seven Seas. *Gauguin's* clean lines, understated elegance, and attention to detail are immediately apparent. The yachtlike ship has an airy ambience with stylish touches, such as blond paneling and gray carpets.

Itineraries   See Itinerary Index.

Cabins   All accommodations are outside suites with separate sitting area; 50% have verandas. Each is furnished with a queen- or twin-size beds (convertible to queen), closed-circuit television and VCR, safe, direct-dial telephone, and refrigerator stocked with soft drinks, mineral water, and complimentary liquor on arrival. Interiors are enriched by crown moldings and wood accents. Finely crafted furnishings include a love seat and vanity/desk. Storage space includes two closets and built-in drawers. Marble bathrooms have a full-size bathtub and shower, plush towels and cotton robes, hair dryer, and assorted toiletries. Some passengers report being able to hear conversations next door. Cabins above the engine are noisy.

Specifications   160 outside cabins and suites; 80 with balconies. Cabins range from 202 square feet with picture window or portholes and 249 square feet with 56-square-foot veranda, to the 457-square-foot owner's suite with 77-square-foot veranda. 1 wheelchair-accessible.

Dining   Two restaurants offer single, open seating. Both have ocean views on three sides. An outdoor bistro, **Le Grill,** provides casual dining throughout the day and evening. Dinner for about two dozen people features freshly prepared steaks and seafood. An espresso bar and 24-hour room service are other options. **Restaurant L'Etoile,** the main dining room, features French and continental cuisine. The smaller **La Veranda** is a reservations-only dinner restaurant offering an Italian or a French menu. Passengers rate the French as being superior in food quality and service. Complimentary wine is served at lunch and dinner; the ship has an excellent wine list. Guests with reservations enjoy predinner cocktails and hors d'oeuvres in the **Connoisseur Club** (open after dinner for drinks and cigars). Evening attire is "country club elegant" (no ties).

Service   The crew generally succeeds in its quest to provide outstanding service. There are a few glitches in the dining room and in cabin maintenance, but the overall experience is fine.

Facilities and Activities   In tribute to Gauguin and French Polynesia, the **Fare** (pronounced "faray") **Tahiti Gallery** is a small library with books, videos, and other materials on the artist and region. A guest lecturer on every cruise discusses regional history and attractions. The ship has a card room and boutique stocked with Polynesian gifts.

   Le Grand Salon is the main lounge for early-evening dancing, entertainment, and daily lectures. Indoor/outdoor **La Palette Lounge** is used for afternoon tea, cocktails, and late-night disco. The small casino has blackjack, roulette, and slot machines, but local regulations bar use of the slots. Nighttime entertainment is minimal. Three movies are shown daily on the closed-circuit cabin system; the reception desk lends videos. A singer/pianist performs in La Palette before dinner, and the ship's Filipino band plays for dancing before dinner in Le Grand Salon and afterward in La Palette until 11:30 p.m., when the disco starts up.

Sports, Fitness, and Beauty The fitness center offers free weights and exercise machines that are in use constantly. Aerobics, hydro-calisthenics, and a walkathon are held daily. A separate **Carita of Paris** salon and spa offers a steam room, massage, facials, and beauty treatments, such as aromatherapy. Three- to six-day spa packages are available.

Paul Gauguin has an outdoor pool and splash bar on an upper deck and a retractable marina at sea level where passengers indulge in sports, including diving and snorkeling. Windsurfing and kayaking equipment is available. Snorkeling gear can be signed out at the cruise's start. Diving is a major attraction. The ship provides PADI-certified instructors and dive boats, as well as courses for novices (PADI certification available) and excursions for certified divers.

Shore Excursions Many shore excursions are water-oriented. Outings include a Jet-Ski tour of Bora Bora, outrigger/jeep combination tours, shark feeding, and helicopter tours. Weather permitting, a beach party is held on the line's private motu, a small islet.

Postscript Passengers concerned about seasickness should know that rough sailing isn't unusual for this ship, owing to her shallow draft and the sometimes rough Pacific waters. The redeeming feature: She travels mostly short distances between ports and is often at anchor in a sheltered bay at night.

SEVEN SEAS NAVIGATOR	QUALITY 8	VALUE B
Registry: Bahamas	Length: 560 feet	Beam: 81 feet
Cabins: 251	Draft: 21 feet	Speed: 20 knots
Maximum Passengers:	Passenger Decks: 8	Elevators: 5
490	Crew: 324	Space Ratio: 67.3

The Ship In a joint venture with Monte Carlo-based V. Ships, Radisson Seven Seas Cruises launched its all-suite luxury ship, *Seven Seas Navigator,* in August 1999. The Italian-built vessel, the fastest in the Radisson fleet at the time she entered service, has an ice-strengthened hull, giving her the ability to operate virtually anywhere in the world. *Navigator* was the second of five ships—one per year—that Radisson Seven Seas has been adding. V. Ships, established in 1984, is a company of the Vlasov Group, one of the world's largest providers of ship management and related services.

A small ship with a big-ship feel, the spacious *Navigator* (with one of the industry's highest space ratios) has half a dozen lounges, superbly appointed outside suites (90% with balconies, walk-in closets, and well-appointed bathrooms), single-seating dining, an alternative restaurant, a wide teak deck surrounding the pool, and a slate of worldwide, port-intensive itineraries.

Designed by Norwegian architects Yran & Storbraaten, *Navigator's* public rooms are strikingly contemporary and minimalist. Yet unusual lamps, exotic chairs, and varied materials and textures provide visual interest. The entire ship is well integrated, with light blue carpeting throughout and bold oil paintings (all for sale) decorating the corridors. A bank of glass elevators offers a bird's-eye view of the gracefully designed ship and a panoramic view of the pool area. Nonetheless, they seem out of place on a small luxury vessel, and the exposed machinery provides a jarring note.

The ship has an Italian captain and Italian and European senior officers. In her maiden year, she was the line's first venture to South America, where she spent part of the winter, and Alaska, where she cruised in summer. In 2002, she logged another milestone with the line's first world cruise.

Cabins Particular attention was lavished on the accommodations. They range from a roomy standard suites of 301 square feet plus veranda to Master Suites with 1,067 square feet plus a 106-square-foot balcony. All standard suites are identical; price varies by location. Ten suites are interconnected. Four suites are wheelchair-accessible with extra-wide doors and large, shower-only bathrooms.

The suites, like the rest of the elegant ship, are decorated in subdued colors with cherry wood accents. They have sitting areas, twin beds convertible to a queen, marble bathrooms with separate tub and shower, and walk-in closet with safe. Other amenities include a minibar with liquor set-up, bathrobes, hair dryer, television with VCR, and Judith Jackson bath products.

In standard suites, a coffee table rises to dining table height with the touch of a button, and upper-level suites have proper dining room tables. Passengers can dine en suite, ordering from the dining room menu during meal hours, with dishes served course by course. The ship offers 24-hour room service.

Master and Grand Suites, which come with butler service, have a foyer with a powder room, living/dining area, and a separate bedroom with bathroom that has a bidet. Two other top suite categories (A and B) also offer butler service—a posh touch that includes cocktails served daily.

Specifications 251 outside suites. Standard balcony suites measure 301 square feet plus balconies; 10 Grand Suites are 538 square feet plus balconies; 4 Master Suites measure 1067 square feet plus balconies. 4 wheelchair accessible.

Dining The open, single-seating **Compass Rose Restaurant** provides a gracious setting, with a small dance floor for occasional dinner dances. An alabaster compass rose skylight looks down on the pale yellow walls;

draperies in soft pastels frame the picture windows; and potted plants are interspersed among the widely spaced tables.

Passengers stroll across a parquet floor to enter the **Portofino Grill,** the alternative restaurant with its own galley. It provides a gorgeous setting of linen-draped tables, blue-cushioned chairs, and filmy white curtains, imparting a true Mediterranean flavor; this venue serves the ship's best dishes. At breakfast and lunch, the indoor/outdoor Portofino provides buffet dining; at night a wing of the spacious room is transformed into an à la carte restaurant featuring northern Italian specialties. Tables must be reserved for dinner, but there is no service charge here or elsewhere on this gratuities-included ship. Complimentary dinner wine is served in both dining venues.

Facilities and Activities   The two-tiered **Seven Seas** show lounge hosts varied entertainment, ranging from Broadway revues to concert pianists. The Stars Lounge is the disco/after-hours club where sleek, deep-blue leather chairs backed in wood line up along a glass-topped bar.

A few steps away, cigar lovers gather in the **Connoisseur Club's** tobacco-colored leather armchairs near a granite topped faux fireplace. Next door, the small **Navigator Lounge** serves coffee and cocktails throughout the day. At the large library stocked with books, periodicals, and 800 videos, there is a bank of nine computers where passengers can check their e-mail. Two boutiques sell designer wares.

A dark, rich-looking casino has tables for blackjack, stud poker, roulette, and craps; slots and poker machines are found in an adjacent room. High on Deck 11, passengers walk through a hall of marble and carpet to emerge in the light, attractive **Galileo's,** a piano bar and lounge with indoor/outdoor seating and a dance floor. One deck higher, forward, the Vista Lounge provides a hideaway of tambour chairs with thick yellow-and-green striped cushions (private parties welcome).

Sports, Fitness, and Beauty   Adjacent to the **Vista Lounge** are the spa, gym, and aerobics rooms, managed by noted aromatherapy practitioner Judith Jackson, whose programs are featured at resorts such as the Breakers and the Greenbriar.

The large amidships pool area offers a grill and two Jacuzzis, plus a venue for moonlight barbecues and dancing. Golfers get two driving cages and a putting green. A golf pro offers lectures and tips.

SEVEN SEAS MARINER	QUALITY ⑧	VALUE ⑧
SEVEN SEAS VOYAGER	(Preview)	
Registry: France/Bahamas	Length: 709/670 feet	Beam: 93//95 feet
Cabins: 328/353	Draft: 21/23 feet	Speed: 20 knots
Maximum Passengers:	Passenger Decks: 8/9	Elevators: 8
700/754	Crew: 445	Space Ratio: 71.4

The Ships   In another joint venture, Monte Carlo-based V. Ships and Radisson Seven Seas built cruising's first all-balcony, all-suite luxury cruise ship. Delivered in March 2001, the *Seven Seas Mariner* had the same architects and interior designer, Peter Yran and Bjorn Storbraaten of Norway, who designed *Song of Flower* and many other luxury cruise ships. Mariner's sister, *Seven Seas Voyager*, was delivered in April 2003. The stylish twins are the largest ships in the Radisson fleet, with the greatest space ratio of any cruise ships to date.

The two ships, which were built at different shipyards—*Mariner* in France, *Voyager* in Italy—are sisters rather than twins, with some major differences. The latter ship improved over her sister ship by taking some of the best features from *Navigator*, particularly regarding the larger size of its suites and the full bathtub and separate glass-enclosed shower stall, along with some extra marble touches in the bathroom. *Voyager's* hull is wider than *Mariner's*, and she has one additional deck. Two of the alternative restaurants, **Signatures** and **Latitudes**, have been relocated on Deck 5 and are serviced by a single galley, and Latitudes was completely redesigned to have a show kitchen visible to passengers from their tables and used for cooking demonstrations and classes. Also, *Voyager* is the first ship to have two independent propulsion and power-generation systems in two separate areas of the ship—a significantly enhanced safety measure.

On both ships, most of the pubic rooms are located on the first three and top two passenger decks and have as their focal point an eight-deck-high atrium with three glass-enclosed elevators and stairways curving up through the atrium. For some, the lounges on *Mariner* are so spacious they lack atmosphere; for others, the spaciousness of her public areas is the very essence of the ships' luxury. Significantly, the area of the public rooms on *Voyager* was reduced by 23%; two lounges on *Mariner* were combined into one lounge on *Voyager*.

The ships' spaciousness and sparseness are immediately evident in the atrium, whose sculpture décor and visible elevator machinery give it a raw unfinished look. The starboard side gallery leading off the atrium on Deck Six serves as a wide connecting boulevard running fore and aft past the open-plan library. The promenade deck windows provide natural light, and the generously proportioned space is furnished with wicker chairs, planters and greenery. Art auctions, with some decent paintings for sale, take place here.

The ships' facilities include a spa, a bilevel main show lounge, a small nightclub lounge with a dance floor; a large forward observation lounge; a library; and an Internet café. There is a **Club Mariner** for children. The ship has the standard Radisson features, such as all gratuities included in the fare, port-intensive itineraries, and single, open-seating dining with complimentary wine at dinner, but it's the choice of four restaurants that makes these ships quite different.

Also, the duo's innovative pod propulsion system eliminates the traditional shaft-and-rudder system, making the vessel up to 15% more efficient and reducing noise and vibration. The pods have forward-facing propellers that can be turned 360°, which optimizes maneuverability, fuel efficiency, and speed.

Itineraries See Itinerary Index.

Cabins The cabins are spread over five center decks and come in 13 categories of outside suites, all with balconies. The suites range from 301 square feet to 1,580 square feet. including the veranda and are paneled in light wood with fabrics in gold, orange rust, and light green. The deluxe suites are the most numerous and have a slightly partitioned and curtained bedroom with king-sized bed (convertible to twins) and lounge, walk-in closet and marble bathroom with a full tub and shower. Curiously, the bath and closet on *Mariner* are smaller than on the *Navigator,* something that was rectified on the *Seven Seas Voyager.*

The Penthouse Suites, somewhat misnamed, are larger than the deluxe category at 449 square feet, but not all are located on the top deck as the name might imply. They feature a roomy, partitioned lounge with L-shaped couch, two lounge chairs and a glass-top table. The 73-square-foot teak deck balcony has rather ordinary white plastic chairs and a low table. Accommodations increase in spaciousness in the higher categories, which also offer butler service. Some suites will take a third person, and the two bedroom master suites accommodate up to five.

All accommodations have satellite telephone; television with 13 channels, including CNN and ESPN, VCR for American and European systems, and A/V cable for personal video cameras; safe; bathrobes; hair dryer; in-suite bar set up upon embarkation; and complimentary replenished bottled water, soft drinks, and beer. The suites are attended by European stewardesses.

An expandable table top makes in-cabin dining a pleasure and is very popular, especially at the end of a busy day ashore. A full meal may be ordered from the **Compass Rose Restaurant** or from an in-suite menu 24 hours a day. Valet, dry cleaning and laundry service and tailor service for minor repairs and small alterations are available. The self-service launderettes on cabins decks are complimentary.

Specifications *Mariner* 328/*Voyager* 353 suites. 280 standard ocean-view suites, (*Mariner* 301 square feet; *Voyager* 356–370 square feet, including balcony); 80 suites (390–1,580 square feet). Limited number of suites accommodate 3 persons. 6 *Mariner*/4 *Voyager* wheelchair accessible. On *Voyager,* 24 suites are interconnecting.

Dining The choice of four dining venues gives the *Mariner* and *Voyager* their most distinctive quality, and all the venues offer a wide variety of high-quality cuisine. Two restaurants have open seating with no reservations necessary; two take reservations for specific tables; none have an additional charge. Complimentary wines are served with dinner in all four restaurants.

The spacious **Compass Rose Restaurant,** the main restaurant and the largest of the four, accommodates most passengers in open seating dining for three meals. The attractive room has a recessed arched ceiling and faux light-wood columns topped with a band of stainless steel capitals. The menu, changed daily, might offer homemade crab cakes as an appetizer, cream asparagus soup, two salad selections, pasta dish, and main courses, such as sautéed jumbo prawns and Black Angus beef. The choices also include vegetarian dishes and a *menu degustation* (a sampler of dishes appropriate to the cruising region).

La Veranda, an indoor/outdoor venue, serves a buffet with sheltered outdoor seating aft at wooden tables and chairs set under an awning. There is also an outdoor grill here. The buffet stations are cramped and limited in selection compared to the company's other ships, particularly the *Radisson Diamond,* which excels in this department. Inside the room's etched glass doors, the stylish high-back wooden chairs are set around tables under a coffered ceiling; the walls are hung with alluring black-framed Cote d'Azur travel posters. The unusual chairs have double rows of hollow vertical squares cut into the high backs, reminiscent of the work of Scottish designer Charles Rennie Macintosh. In the evening, a portion of La Veranda becomes a Mediterranean bistro for casual dining, offering a tapas, mezze or antipasti buffet, followed by table service for the soup of the day, salad, pasta, main course, and dessert.

Latitudes, the smallest of the four, is a reservations-only dinner restaurant with a set sampler menu and tableside presentations. Having started with a more Asian menu, the choices now might range from a foie gras mousse, crab and avocado in a light curry sauce, tomato bisque, pan-fried lobster in a lemon grass gravy, and beef tenderloin in salsa. The setting combines a South Seas and oriental décor with black lacquer chairs, walls decorated with wooden masks and headdresses, and large windows with slatted venetian blinds.

Signatures was the first permanent dining venue aboard a cruise ship directed by chefs from Le Cordon Bleu, the famed French culinary institute. The reserved-table restaurant is repeated on *Voyager,* offering a wide choice of entrées and main courses, and worth several visits on a long cruise. Marinated fillet of red snapper and roast breast of quail with turnips in a morel sauce are two examples from the list of six choices. The . appetizing dessert list included warm chocolate tart with cinnamon ice cream. The sophisticated setting features rust red chairs with gold tassels, an etched glass divider between the serving and dining area, and black glass against the aft wall. The chefs take their talents a step further by offering Le Cordon Bleu "Classe Culinaire des Croisieres" on certain voyages. Workshops, conducted by Le Cordon Blue–trained chefs, provide a hands-on introduction to the art of French cooking. Classes are limited to 16 guests in three two-hour sessions and cost $295 per person. Upon graduation, participants receive their own chef's apron and short toque, a tea towel, and a Le Cordon Bleu cookbook of classic recipes, as well as a certificate of participation. Inquire from the cruise line for future schedules.

Facilities and Activities Public rooms are varied in location from high up and forward to down low and aft. The **Observation Lounge,** located two decks above the bridge, offers comfy rust- and tan-colored seating to enjoy hot hors d'oeuvres and soothing piano music before dinner, while taking in a grand 180° view. From a perch along the horseshoe-shaped bar, the space takes on a magical quality at night.

The semi-circular **Horizon Lounge,** facing aft on one of the lowest passenger decks, is the handsome setting for afternoon tea, with music, and light after-dinner entertainment. Additional covered outdoor seating, which is little used, is a quiet spot for daytime reading. Nearby, the **Connoisseur Club** with tan leather chairs and an electric fireplace makes a sophisticated setting for smoking Cuban and Dominican cigars and sipping liqueurs and wines.

The liveliest venue is the **Mariner Lounge,** drawing a crowd before dining in the adjacent Compass Rose or Latitudes restaurants. The curvy Art Deco design is highlighted by deep blue fabrics covering the chairs and glass tabletops, embedded with a translucent star pattern and framed by raised wooden rims.

Stars nightclub-cum-disco, decorated with black and white photos of Fred Astaire, Ingrid Bergman, Katherine Hepburn, and other movie stars, is an oddly designed space with a spiral staircase in its midst that links to the midsize casino above. The semicircular two-level **Constellation Lounge,** with continuous brushed blue cotton banquette seating, is joined by staircases flanking the stage on each side. Here, full shows and cabarets acts are presented under a starlit ceiling of changing colors.

In the past, production shows have not been a strength of this line, but to their credit, that changed with the two shows that debuted on *Voyager.* The shows are performed by four primary singers plus a production cast of six. One, entitled *Lullaby of Broadway,* highlights Broadway shows from the fifties to today, with a multitude of numbers and costume changes. The second, a very innovative show, at least for a cruise ship, is entitled *On a Classical Note* and features opera, classical music, and light operettas. The four lead singers have a real opportunity to shine, especially when three different Gilbert and Sullivan operettas were staged in one production. A future addition on *Voyager* is to be a rock 'n' roll review.

The open-shelf library offers a generous selection of hardbacks, reference books, and videos with tables to spread out an atlas and comfortable seating for reading newspapers and magazines. The adjacent **Club.com** is the plainly decorated Internet center with 14 terminals (three more in the library) and offers very low charges for sending and checking e-mail. Passengers may also browse and enjoy computer games. Computer instruction, free and very popular, is excellent. A long rectangular card room also serves as a conference center.

Amidships on the same deck is a gallery of high-end shops, plus two specialty boutiques placed at two corners of the atrium landings.

Sports, Fitness, and Beauty The ships' spas are operated by Judith Jackson Spa with trained therapists available for a variety of treatments that include thalassotherapy, aromatherapy, seaweed and mud wraps, and a variety of massages. Adjoining the spa is an indoor/outdoor fitness center with treadmills, aerobic benches, Nautilus machine, Lifecyles, Stairmasters, free weights, and other exercise equipment. The center also has a beauty salon.

Deck space centers around the lido pool and three whirlpools, an outdoor bar and a mezzanine/jogging track above. Outdoor sports include paddle tennis, shuffleboard and golf nets.

Postscript *Mariner's* roominess has pluses and minuses. The latter becomes evident in the public lounges and bars, where except for the cocktail hour before meals, the ship's spaciousness often makes it seem empty of life. After dinner, the show lounge is a draw, but otherwise, most passengers retire to their suites. Occasionally, when younger passengers are on board, they may enliven the bars. On the other hand, it's good to note that the European-modern public rooms are lovely and varied in atmosphere and function. *Mariner* is testing a facility to enable passengers to book shore excursions in advance; check with the cruise line.

Royal Caribbean International

1050 Caribbean Way, Miami, FL 33132
(305) 539-6000; (800) 327-6700; fax (800)722-5329
www.royalcaribbean.com

Type of Ships   Superliners and megaliners.

Type of Cruises   Mainstream, mass market, modestly upscale, wholesome ambience.

Cruise Line's Strengths

- outstanding facilities and activities
- entertainment
- product consistency

Cruise Line's Shortcomings

- small cabins on older fleet
- limited storage in cabins on older fleet
- impersonal nature of big ships

Fellow Passengers   Moderately upscale couples, singles and families with household income of $40,000+ looking for wide variety in shipboard activities and destinations. Average age is 40s, slightly lower on three- and four-night cruises and slightly higher on ten-night or longer trips. In summer, the age drops because of large number of families traveling with children. About half have cruised at least once, and a quarter are Royal Caribbean repeaters. Genders split evenly, and nine in ten are North Americans. Up to 73% of men and 65% of women are married; 36% are professional, managerial, or proprietors. Educational level, occupations, and age differ on three- and four-night cruises, which are less expensive, shorter cruises appealing to younger people and first-timers.

Recommended For   Almost anyone taking a first cruise. Those who like large ships, want an array of options, want to be active, sociable, and don't mind large crowds. Ideal for families, particularly several generations traveling together, because there's something for every age.

Not Recommended For   Small-ship devotees; those who seek a quiet or intellectual milieu, hate crowds, and have no patience for long lines.

Cruise Areas and Seasons   Caribbean, Bahamas, Mexico, year-round. Bermuda, Europe, Alaska, in summer. Hawaii, spring and fall. Panama Canal, winter, May, and fall.

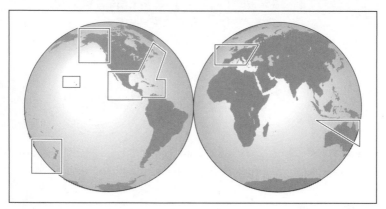

The Line   Founded in 1969 as a partnership of three prominent Norwegian shipping companies, Royal Caribbean Cruises Ltd. (the marketing name is now Royal Caribbean International) was the first line to launch ships designed for year-round Caribbean cruising. The vessels proved to be so popular that within five years more capacity was needed and two vessels were "stretched"—cut in half, then lengthened by inserting prefabricated midsections. For the 1980s, RCCL added superliners with unique designs. In 1988, *Sovereign of the Seas* was the first in a new generation of megaliners and the largest cruise ship ever built at the time. On *Sovereign's* arrival in Miami, traffic backed up for miles as people on shore tried to glimpse her. That year, too, RCCL merged with Admiral Cruises, a short-cruise specialist.

The line got a jump on the 21st century with Project Vision, a new generation of six megaliners. The first, *Legend of the Seas,* debuted in 1995 with acres of glass and cruising's first 18-hole miniature golf course. By 1998, all six ships had joined the fleet. The following year, RCCL launched *Voyager of the Seas,* the first of another new class and the industry's first 142,000-ton cruise ship. By 2003, five of the Voyager-class ships, with cruising's first rock-climbing wall and ice-skating rink, were in service, and another, yet to be named, is scheduled to be launched in 2004. The rock-climbing walls have proven so popular that they are being installed fleetwide. RCCL introduced the Vantage group, another new class of 2,100-passenger, 90,060-ton ships, with *Radiance of the Seas* in 2001; her sister ship, *Brilliance of the Seas,* in 2002; *Serenade of the Seas* in 2003; and *Jewel of the Seas,* expected in 2004. And now, not to let any other cruise line get ahead of it in the "largest ship" category, RCCL has ordered a 160,000-ton ship, dubbed *Ultra Voyager,* for delivery in 2006, with an option on a second one for 2007. Roughly 15% larger than *Voyager,* the *Ultra Voyager* will be 1,112 feet in length, 126 feet in width, and stand 18 stories high, carrying 3,600 passengers and 1,400 crew.

In a surprise move in 1997, RCCL bought Celebrity Cruises—a deal worth $1.3 billion that resulted in a combined fleet of 20 ships. Celebrity operates as a separate brand. In 2002, RCCL's attempt to buy Princess Cruises, one of its main competitors, did not succeed, however.

After two decades of focusing solely on the Caribbean, RCCL expanded to become a worldwide cruise line. To reflect its growth, the line changed its marketing name to Royal Caribbean International. It also created a new product, Cruise Hyatt, combining some three- or four-night hotel stays with a cruise departing from Puerto Rico and other locations where Hyatt has hotels. Recently, the line added a booking tool to enable passengers to book shore excursions in advance of their cruise. It also created Royal Celebrity Tours, a land-tour company in Alaska and the Canadian Rockies.

For all its firsts and innovative designs, RCI is still a conservative company that built its success on a solid, consistent product. Royal Caribbean is a public company, traded on the New York Stock Exchange. Majority ownership is held, however, by one of its founders, Anders Wilhelmsen and Co., and the Pritzker family of Chicago, who also hold controlling interest in Hyatt Hotels.

THE FLEET	BUILT/RENOVATED	TONNAGE	PASSENGERS
Adventure of the Seas	2001	142,000	3,114
Brilliance of the Seas	2002	90,090	2,100
Enchantment of the Seas	1997/1999	74,140	1,950
Explorer of the Seas	2000	142,000	3,114
Grandeur of the Seas	1996/1998	74,140	1,950
Jewel of the Seas	2004	90,060	2,100
Legend of the Seas	1995	69,130	1,800
Majesty of the Seas	1992/1997	73,941	2,350
Mariner of the Seas	2003	142,000	3,114
Monarch of the Seas	1991/1999	73,941	2,350
Navigator of the Seas	2002	142,000	3,114
Nordic Empress	1990/1998	48,563	1,602
Radiance of the Seas	2001	90,090	2,100
Rhapsody of the Seas	1997	78,491	2,000
Serenade of the Seas	2003	90,060	2,100
Sovereign of the Seas	1988/1996	73,192	2,250
Splendour of the Seas	1996/1998	69,130	1,800
Ultra Voyager	2000	160,000	3,600
Vision of the Seas	1998	78,491	2,000
Voyager of the Seas	1999	142,000	3,114

Style RCI ships are big ships that hum with activities almost around the clock, designed for high-volume, year-round, warm-weather cruises. That "C" in RCI could just as well stand for consistency. Whether you take a Royal Caribbean cruise in Europe or the Caribbean, the atmosphere is relaxed and activities are many and varied and designed primarily for U.S. and Canadian passengers. The ships have acres of sun decks, large pools, and lots of outdoor activity: games, competitions, the Ship-Shape fitness program, and sports, like golf, that often combine with sports in port. The ships have contemporary décor with themes related to Broadway hits, operas, and the circus. All vessels have extensive programs for children.

Distinctive Features **Viking Crown Lounge;** golf program; Labadee, RCI's private beach; Crown & Anchor lounges in San Juan and St. Thomas. Room service from dining room menus during lunch and dinner; children's program. Internet centers. *Legend's* and *Splendour's* miniature golf courses; rock-climbing wall; Voyager class, ice skating rink; *Explorer's* **Oceanography Center.**

	HIGHEST	LOWEST	AVERAGE
PER DIEM	$570	$132	$307

Per diems are calculated from cruise line's nondiscounted *cruise-only* fares on standard accommodations and vary by season, cabin, and cruise areas.

Rates Port charges are included.

Special Fares and Discounts

- **Breakthrough Fares** are capacity-controlled discounts (up to 40%) that change daily. The earlier you buy, the better the discount.
- **Third/Fourth Passenger** Yes.
- **Children's Fare** Third/fourth person rates.
- **Single Supplement** 200%; occasionally, from 150% on Royal Journeys.
- **Single Guarantee** Category and cabin assigned by RCI.

Packages

- **Air/Sea** Yes.
- **Cruise-Only/Air Add-Ons with Transfers** Yes.
- **Others** Honeymoon, golf, family, wedding. Crowning Touches and Royal Occasions packages (extra charge) designed for honeymooners or special occasion.
- **Pre/Post** In departure ports and some vacation spots. Cruise Hyatt combines three/four-night hotel with cruise.

Past Passengers The Crown and Anchor Society has three membership levels based on how many cruises you take: Gold membership, one–four cruises; Platinum, five–nine; and Diamond, ten or more. The biggest benefit is personalized attention by shipboard personnel. Members get *Crown & Anchor,* a quarterly magazine with information on new programs, itineraries, and ships; special offers and coupons; a color-coded landing card sticker; wine tasting, members-only web page, sweepstakes and shoreside events; and on cruises of seven or more nights, a cocktail party. Gold members also receive special offers on future cruises; Platinum, terry robes for use during the cruise, custom air arrangements, private departure lounge, special 800 number for reservations, and more; and Diamond, exclusive coupons, boarding privileges, concierge service on select ships, and priority on dining room seating, shore excursions, spa services, and disembarkation.

The Last Word   RCI is a cruise line of megaliners. It targets 80% of people buying cruises; only budget and luxury customers are excluded. There's no denying that the big ships are big and impersonal, and they have blurred and narrowed the quality that once separated RCI from the pack. If you don't like big ships, this isn't the line for you. But if you want a cruise vacation on ships that have everything, RCI offers good value.

ROYAL CARIBBEAN INTERNATIONAL STANDARD FEATURES

Officers   Norwegian, International.

Staff   Dining, Cabin/International; Cruise/American and British.

Dining Facilities   Two seatings for dinner plus midnight buffet; indoor/outdoor café with breakfast and lunch buffet; alternative dining for dinner with table service on all ships. Voyager class, three-level dining room, five alternative venues.

Special Diets   Low-fat, low-cholesterol, lean cuisine. Full vegetarian menus. Request kosher at time of booking.

Room Service   24 hours with light menu; dining room menus for lunch and dinner.

Dress Code   Casual but neat by day; informal in evening; one or two nights formal/semiformal. Tuxedo rental available.

Cabin Amenities   Direct-dial telephone; radio; television; daily world news update; bathtubs in suites; suites with marble baths on *Majesty, Monarch.*

Electrical Outlets   110 AC.

Wheelchair Access   Ramps on all ships; 4 cabins on *Majesty, Monarch, Nordic Empress;* 10 cabins on Sovereign; 17 on *Legend/Splendour,* 14 on other *Vision* and *Vantage* ships; 26 on Voyager class.

Recreation and Entertainment   Show lounge with entertainment nightly; disco, bingo, horse racing, movies, wine tastings, dance lessons. Viking Crown Lounge, bars/lounges, card room, library.

Sports and Other Activities   Two outdoor pools; sports deck with basketball, Ping-Pong, shuffleboard, skeet shooting. Miniature golf course on *Legend, Splendour,* and Voyager class. Rock-climbing walls fleetwide. Ice rink on Voyager class.

ROYAL CARIBBEAN INTERNATIONAL STANDARD FEATURES *(continued)*

Beauty and Fitness Beauty/barber shop; massage; sauna; ShipShape fitness program; jogging track; health club/gym. Solarium, elaborate spa on *Vision, Voyager,* and *Vantage* ships.

Other Facilities Boutiques; medical facilities; laundry/dry cleaning services; meeting rooms; Internet and e-mail service; cinema/theater on *Majesty, Monarch, Sovereign.*

Children's Facilities Year-round youth programs. Play rooms and teen centers on *Sovereign* and *Vision, Voyager,* and *Vantage* ships, plus *Nordic Empress, Viking Serenade;* teen nightclub on *Majesty, Monarch,* and *Vision* and *Voyager* ships.

Theme Cruises Jazz, country music, variety of sports.

Smoking Public rooms are nonsmoking except in designated areas.

RCI Suggested Tipping Per person per day, cabin steward $3.50; dining room waiter, $3.50; 15% added to bar/wine bill.

Credit Cards For cruise payment and on-board charges: American Express, Carte Blanche, Diners Club, Discover, MasterCard, Visa, JCB.

LEGEND OF THE SEAS	QUALITY **7**	VALUE **C**
SPLENDOUR / RHAPSODY	QUALITY **7**	VALUE **A**
ENCHANTMENT / GRANDEUR	QUALITY **7**	VALUE **A**
VISION OF THE SEAS	QUALITY **8**	VALUE **A**
Registry: *Legend/Grandeur/ Vision/Enchantment:* Liberia *Splendour/Rhapsody:* Norway	Length: 867–916 feet	Beam: 105–106 feet
Cabins: 902–1000	Draft: 24–25 feet	Speed: 22–24 knots
Maximum Passengers: 1,804–2,435	Passenger Decks: 10	Elevators: 11 or 9
	Crew: 735–784	Space Ratio: 38.32

The Ships *Legend of the Seas,* the first of six megaliners in the Project Vision series, arrived in 1995, and her five sisters followed over the next four years. Constructed in France and Finland, the megaliners were quickly labeled "the ships of glass." Each has two acres of windows, glass windbreaks, skylights, and walls of windows in public spaces. The Centrum, the centerpiece atrium, rises seven decks—two more than on the Sovereign-class vessels—and is topped by the **Viking Crown Lounge.** Bubble elevators whisk passengers to the lounge. The ships embrace the sea and vistas through windows and glass. Natural light sparkles, and open space is abundant.

Each has distinguishing features. At the Centrum's base is the **Champagne Terrace and Bar,** where fine wines and champagne are served by the glass. The elegant setting sets the tone for the ships. *Grandeur's* Champagne Bar covers the Centrum's entire lower level. A white baby grand piano stands next to a stairway to the second level. Decorative screens create conversation corners.

Works of art on *Splendour* were created by more than 50 artists and studios. The ship's atrium sculpture is the fleet's most dramatic. The work consists of three elements symbolizing the solar system. The dominant component, an 18-foot gilded disc representing the sun, hangs on a diagonal, silhouetted by rays from the skylight. Iridescent bulbs around the disc transmit and reflect colored light throughout the atrium. Hundreds of steel cords attached to the upper, outer rim of the disc gather at the top of the atrium and are illuminated, creating a glow.

On the Sun Deck is the Solarium, a landscaped indoor/outdoor area with a second swimming pool, whirlpools, and a café. Its Crystal Canopy provides cover in inclement weather. Unlike glass roofs on other ships, this one doesn't fold onto itself; instead it moves intact. The design uses much more glass, admitting maximum light into the Solarium when the roof is closed. The most celebrated features on *Legend* and *Splendour* are the world's first floating 18-hole miniature golf courses. The station where equipment and tee times can be obtained resembles a miniature clubhouse.

Itineraries   See Itinerary Index.

Cabins   A major improvement in the Legend class was the size of standard cabins- -153 square feet compared to 122 square feet in comparable Sovereign-group cabins. For two decades, Royal Caribbean said cabin size was unimportant because passengers spend so little time in their rooms, but in the Vision series, cabins are larger and more comfortable, with sitting areas and, for the first time, many balconies—one in four. Many more have bathrooms with tubs and showers, too. Pastels and light woods are used in décor. The Royal Suite has a baby grand piano, whirlpool tub, and veranda.

Specifications   327 inside cabins, 575 outside; 83 suites; 4 family suites; 231 with balconies; 388 third/fourth persons; no singles; 17 wheelchair accessible. *Grandeur/Enchantment,* 399 inside cabins, 576 outside, 18 suites; 4 family suites; 72 deluxe outside; 212 with balconies; 403 third/fourth persons; no singles; 14 are wheelchair-accessible. *Rhapsody/Vision,* 407 inside cabins, 593 outside; 18 suites; 72 deluxe; 4 family suites; 229 with balconies; 287 third/fourth persons; no singles; 14 wheelchair-accessible.

Dining   *Legend's* **Romeo and Juliet Dining Room** (the **King and I** on *Splendour* and **Great Gatsby** on *Grandeur*) spans two decks and has 20-foot-tall glass walls on each side—offering spectacular views from every table. The walls are virtually all glass—the load-bearing function is handled by interior columns. A revolving platform with a grand piano is framed by curving stairways to the balcony.

Décor in *Splendour's* King and I is noteworthy. A Thai temple facade has been replicated, and 16 historical paintings plus 2 epic murals were created by artists of Thailand's royal family. Each painting tells a story.

The nautical-motif **Windjammer Café** on Sun Deck is the indoor-outdoor area for breakfast and lunch buffets and alternative evening dining. Glass walls on three sides and a sloping skylight brighten the room. Each lunch has a theme, and ethnic food joins the regular array of hot dishes, salads, and sandwiches. Dinner, served 6:30–10:30 p.m., offers full table service. The café is a popular spot for reading, playing cards, and watching the water.

Service   Dining room service and room stewards are getting mixed reviews. Many workers know little English, and they lack training, the latter probably resulting from the line adding so many large ships in a short time.

Facilities and Activities   Vision ships are state-of-the-art at every turn. Computers helped design the bilevel **That's Entertainment Theatre** on *Legend* (**Palladium Theater** on *Grandeur* and **42nd Street Theatre** on *Splendour*) to ensure good sight lines for nightly, full-scale Broadway productions. The venue has a computerized system to move scenery, a device commonly used on Broadway, and an orchestra pit that can be raised and lowered.

The **Schooner Bar** is a piano lounge popular for its sing-along sessions. Décor includes authentic rigging and an aroma of tar. **Casino Royale** is next door. On *Grandeur,* passengers enter across a glass floor strewn with "sunken treasure" of jewels and gold coins. The cruise line has a beverage program for adults, which allows up to twelve drinks: non-alcoholic, $29.95, including service charge; fountain packages from $15–$65, depending on cruise length, plus 15% gratuity; and others.

The spacious **Anchor's Away Lounge** on *Legend* (**South Pacific Lounge** on *Grandeur* and **Top Hat Lounge** on *Splendour*) spans the ship's stern. It's a second showroom, used for parlor games, art auctions, daytime dance activities, and late-night shows and dancing. Topside, the glass-sheathed **Viking Crown Lounge** is an observation lounge by day and a nightclub and disco at night. Nightclub action is away from the room's quieter piano bar. On all the ships, the lounge is accessible from the atrium by glass elevators. Aft of the show lounge (to entice you coming and going!) is a mall with varied shops in attractive settings. For example, the **Harbour Shop,** selling liquor and sundries, recalls an old English vintner's shop through aged timber, antique barrels, and stone floors. The casino offers blackjack, Caribbean poker, roulette, craps, and 178 slot machines.

The conference center can be divided into four rooms, each with full audio/visual support. Adjoining is an attractive lounge that also can be divided. A card room can be divided into two sections, and there is a

2,000-volume library that on the *Grandeur* has an amusing lifelike sculpture titled *Snoozin.* **Explorers Court,** off the Centrum on the port side of Deck 8, is the place to relax, read, or converse. Starboard is the **Crown & Anchor Study,** a more formal gathering place.

Sports, Fitness, and Beauty   The Sun Deck has an outdoor pool. Contrasting is the quiet Solarium, the second pool area. When the **Windjammer Café** and main dining room are closed, the Solarium's café serves snacks, alcoholic beverages, sodas, and juices. The area can be covered by a glass canopy. Beyond the Solarium, the **ShipShape Fitness Center** and spa contain a beauty salon, aerobics area, gym, changing rooms, saunas, steam baths, and seven massage rooms (treatments are pricey). A sports deck is at the stern. Each ship has a padded promenade circling most of the ship.

Legend's much-publicized golf course, **Legend of the Links (Splendour of the Greens** on *Splendour*), is above the spa. It was designed by Adventure Golf Services, whose other miniature courses include one at the Mall of America in Bloomington, Minnesota. Each hole of the 6,000-square-foot Links is surrounded by rough to simulate a shoreside layout. The 18 holes range in size from 155 to 230 square feet, tees are 5 feet wide, and the longest hole is 32 feet. Each game costs $5; $40 buys unlimited play. The glass dome over the aft swimming pool can slide to the golf course, where it can be raised to provide almost ten feet of vertical clearance for golfers. A walkway along one edge of the course has benches to encourage spectators. Halogen lights illuminate nighttime play, and baffles redirect wind generated by the motion. A jogging track surrounds the course. Tournaments and children's tee times are available.

Children's Facilities   Outstanding Vision facilities for children complement RCI's supervised youth program, Adventure Ocean, available year-round, day and evening, and in port. Activities target ages 3 to 17, broken down into five age groups. Daily schedules are delivered to cabins. Among the most original activities is teacher-led Mad Science, which aims to make science entertaining and amusing. Group baby-sitting ($5 an hour per child) is available from 10 p.m. to 1 a.m. In-room baby-sitting is also available for $8/hour per room for a maximum of two children (minimum age six months). Family suites have separate bedrooms for children.

Club Ocean is the children's center. On *Grandeur,* it's submarine-themed and includes a tunnel, slide, pool of colored balls, and writing wall. Nearby is **Fanta-SEAS** (**Optix** on *Legend*), the space-themed teen center. The ships also have video arcades.

Note: If you or your children consume a lot of soft drinks, consider buying the "Ocean Potion Card." which allow children up to 18 to enjoy a dozen non-alcoholic drinks; ranging from $9–$40 depending on cruise length, plus 15% gratuity

ADVENTURE OF THE SEAS	QUALITY 8	VALUE C
EXPLORER OF THE SEAS	QUALITY 8	VALUE C
MARINER OF THE SEAS	(Preview)	
NAVIGATOR OF THE SEAS	QUALITY 8	VALUE C
VOYAGER OF THE SEAS	QUALITY 8	VALUE C
Registry: Norway	Length: 1,020 feet	Beam: 157.5 feet
Cabins: 1,900	Draft: 29 feet	Speed: 23.7 knots
Maximum Passengers:	Passenger Decks: 15	Elevators: 14
3,114	Crew: 1,185	Space Ratio: NA

The Ships   The $500 million *Voyager of the Seas* was the largest cruise ship ever built —142,000 tons—when she made her debut in 1999, and also the first of six similiar ships launched over the following five years.

Voyager is awesome. She's twice the size of the largest aircraft carrier ever built, twice as wide as Broadway in New York, and taller than a 20-story building. She has six diesel engines, each the size of a locomotive, and they produce 15,000 horsepower—the equivalent of 150 cars.

Twenty-one million hours worked by a crew of 10,000 people were needed to cut, shape, bend, and weld over 300,000 pieces of steel into the vessel's hull. Her 14 passenger decks cover 646,000 square feet. Furnishings include 538,000 square feet of carpeting, 15,000 chairs, and a $12 million art collection.

Voyager is cruise ship as entertainment. In contrast to other megaliners, where the goal has been to reduce the behemoth to human scale, RCI has made a virtue of *Voyager's* enormous size, touting her many options and features that only a ship of this size could offer. These include an ice rink, rock-climbing wall, inline skating track, five-story theater, and trilevel dining room.

Voyager also has a television studio, wedding chapel, and the largest youth facilities and largest spa and fitness center afloat. Fifty percent of cabins have balconies. Food and entertainment options and conference facilities rival those at major resorts.

At the heart of the ship, the Royal Promenade stretches the length of one and a half football fields between a 10-story atrium at one end and an 11-story grand atrium at the other. Stores, an ice cream parlor, champagne bar, and pub border the tree-lined boulevard. Around-the-clock entertainment, including jugglers, magicians, and mimes, brings a street fair atmosphere to the Promenade. Overhead lighting simulates day-to-night conditions outside. Three decks of inside cabins "with a view" overlook the boulevard. The rooms have window seats to watch the scene below, but the idea has not worked as RCI planned because the line failed to put one-way glass on the windows; hence, passengers in these cabins can see and be seen. To avoid being part of the peep show, they must keep their curtains closed.

Studio B is *Voyager's* pièce de résistance. It has a 40-by-60-foot ice-skating rink with arena-style seating for 900 spectators and is available for passenger use during the day (skates may be rented) and for ice shows at night. Fifty television monitors and a broadcast studio are adjacent to the area, which can also serve as a show lounge or conference facility, or be used for game and variety shows and musical concerts.

When I first heard about the ice-skating rink for a ship cruising the Caribbean, I was puzzled, to say the least. But I was pleasantly surprised when I saw it in action. The entertainment is wholesome, high-quality, and is certainly a welcome alternative, particularly for families, to the stale Las Vegas shows that have become the staple of most cruise ships.

Explorer of the Seas and *Adventure of the Seas,* as well as the newest, *Navigator* and *Mariner,* are almost twins of *Voyager* and have the same unusual attractions, including the ice-skating rink and rock-climbing wall. *Explorer* was the first ship to boast an interactive, state-of-the-art atmospheric and oceanography laboratory. She was also RCI's first ship with Internet access in the cabins.

Itineraries   See Itinerary Index.

Cabins   Large by RCI standards, cabins are similar in size and décor to those aboard Vision-class ships. Enhancements include larger closets and beds with rounded corners to leave more floor space. All cabins offer telephone, television, electronic minibar, hair dryers, and twin beds convertible to queen.

Specifications   Standard inside cabins, including the 138 Category G with atrium views encompass 150 square feet. The 757 cabins with private veranda (50% of the total) have 180-square-foot interiors plus a 4.5-by 8.8-foot balcony. 26 wheelchair-accessible.

Dining   *Voyager's* main dining room is actually three: the **Carmen, La Boheme,** and **Magic Flute** (**Mozart, Strauss,** and **Vivaldi** on *Adventure;* **Columbus, De Gama,** and **Magellan** on *Explorer*) restaurants connected by a grand staircase. Décor includes a 15-foot crystal chandelier, an antique harp, and gilded marble pillars. Seats—enough for almost 2,000 people—offer views of the staircase and main floor or the ocean.

Other dining venues are **Portofino,** an upscale Italian restaurant for dinner (reservations only); **Windjammer Café,** the lido restaurant for breakfast, lunch, and dinner; **Café Promenade,** for Continental breakfast, all-day pizzas, and specialty coffees; **Island Grill,** with a display kitchen, casual dinner; **SeaSide Diner,** a 1950s all-day/all-night eatery with indoor/outdoor seating and jukebox music; and **Sprinkles,** with around-the-clock ice cream and yogurt. There's a **Johnny Rockets,** of the fast food chain, which is wildly popular.

Facilities and Entertainment   In addition to the ice-skating rink and television studio, *Voyager* has one of the most impressive showrooms afloat. The 1,347-seat **La Scala Theater,** inspired by Milan's famous opera house, rises through five decks and has a stage trimmed with gold leaf, a dome with hand-painted murals, and boxes with satin bunting.

Voyager also offers the $1 million **Aquarium Bar** with 50 tons of water in four huge saltwater aquariums; **Spinners,** a revolving gambling arcade with an interactive roulette wheel that players sit in to play; and **Casino Royale,** cruising's largest casino. Also aboard are a cigar and brandy lounge, champagne bar, English pub, **Schooner Bar,** and a two-deck-tall library. The **Scoreboard** sports bar carries events live on large monitors. Alongside the glass bridge spanning the Royal Promenade is the **Vault,** a two-deck-high late-night disco. **Jesters,** the adults-only nightclub on *Adventure* (the **Chamber** on *Explorer*) is made to look like a gothic castle, with suits of armor, bats and gargoyles. Sitting atop of *Voyager* is **High Notes,** a jazz club offering nightly performances. Also high on the ship is a chapel where weddings are performed.

Voyager's conference center seats up to 400 people and can be converted into six smaller rooms and a boardroom. Also available are a multimedia screening room, video conferencing, classrooms, and space for exhibition/trade shows. Business services provide typing, copying, and computer access.

Sports, Fitness, and Beauty   The 15,000-square-foot health center offers exercise equipment. The Solarium and spa occupy 10,000 square feet. On the ship's smoke stack is cruising's first rock-climbing wall. Novices and experienced climbers alike are well briefed in advance, and participants work in teams. For most passengers, it's their first rock climbing experience, and they love it! Other outdoor facilities include a nine-hole golf course, driving range, golf simulators, inline skating track, and basketball/volleyball court. Also available are **Sea Quest** dive and snorkel shop and the **19th Hole** golf bar. Little wonder that one passenger, upon touring *Voyager* remarked, "This sure is a guy's ship."

Children's Facilities   **Adventure Ocean,** RCI 's expanded children's facilities, provides age-specific programs: Aquanauts (ages 3–5), Explorers (ages 6–8), Voyagers (ages 9–11), Navigators (ages 12–14) and Optix (teenagers, ages 15–17). The latter have a day/nightclub with computers, soda bar, DJ, and dance floor. **Paint and Clay** is a crafts area for young children; **Kids Deck** has deck checkers, shuffleboard, and tic-tac-toe; **Challenger's Arcade** is a virtual-reality game center; and **Virtual Submarine** provides underwater virtual-reality entertainment for all ages. The **Computer Lab** has 14 stations with games for amusement and education. Adventure Beach, for families, has swimming pools, a water slide, and water games and is convenient to **SeaSide Diner.** Adventure Ocean opens 30 minute before morning shore excursions depart to give parents some flexibility in planning for their day.

Postscript Passengers have responded to *Voyager,* and her sister ships enthusiastically, and almost anyone would enjoy a week on these ships. But you need to understand that it's not cruising in the traditional sense. The ship is the destination; her itinerary is almost immaterial. Like we said, these are cruise ships as entertainment.

SOVEREIGN OF THE SEAS	QUALITY **5**	VALUE **C**
MAJESTY OF THE SEAS	QUALITY **5**	VALUE **C**
MONARCH OF THE SEAS	QUALITY **5**	VALUE **C**
Registry: Norway	Length: 880 feet	Beam: 106 feet
Cabins: 1,140/1,177	Draft: 25 feet	Speed: 19 knots
Maximum Passengers:	Passenger Decks: 11	Elevators: 11
2,852/2,744/2,744	Crew: 833	Space Ratio: 30.8/32.3

The Ships When the *Sovereign of the Seas* was introduced in 1988, she was the largest cruise ship ever built and stirred unprecedented excitement and publicity. More important, she came with innovations that influenced the design of all superliners and megaliners that followed.

Her dramatic atrium, the Centrum, was a cruise-ship first. Located amidships and spanning five decks, the atrium opens the space to create a light and inviting environment. Stairs and balconies around the atrium and its glass-enclosed elevators seem suspended in air. A white piano set amid tropical foliage at the atrium's base plays soft music that carries to upper decks and sets the harmonious tone found shipwide. The atrium, similar to a hotel's lobby, provides a friendly focal point. Passengers are dazzled but not intimidated, and the notion of entering a behemoth dissipates. The atrium also separates the forward section of the ship, which contains the cabins, from the aft with all public rooms and dining, sports, entertainment, and recreation facilities. The arrangement has several advantages: Cabins are quieter; distances among public areas are shorter; and the ship doesn't seem so enormous.

Superb design features downplay *Sovereign's* gigantic size. The ship looks outward—few areas lack natural light or a view to the outdoors—a feature absent on many new ships. Together with an incredible array of facilities, they explain passengers' immediate acceptance of the megaliner. *Sovereign's* twins, *Monarch of the Seas* and *Majesty of the Seas,* arrived with few changes—a few more cabins, a family suite, and a redesigned **Windjammer Café.** Many public rooms carry the same names. Throughout, contemporary elegance creates a warm, inviting ambience.

The ships are floating resorts, making the most of their size by providing spaces for varying tastes. These include the signature **Viking Crown**

Lounge perched high on the stack; wide, outdoor promenades encircling the vessels; and sunny and shaded areas on three decks. They offer so many facilities and activities that even the most frantically active person can't participate in all of the options. Recently, *Monarach* was given a complete renovation, adding some of the features of the Voyager class.

Itineraries   See Itinerary Index.

Cabins   Each of the trio has 16 categories of cabins. Light décor helps compensate for standard cabins' smallness. Designed to make the most out of every inch of space, they're fitted with a vanity table, chair, and twin beds convertible to daytime couches. *Monarch* and *Majesty* cabins are similar to *Sovereign's* in size and décor, but have major enhancements. Verandas were added to 50 deluxe outside cabins, and suites and family suites sleeping up to six were created. The latter have two bedrooms, sitting room, two bathrooms, and veranda. *Majesty* has 146 cabins in the larger outside category, more comfortable than those on *Sovereign,* and the Bridge Deck contains only suites and deluxe cabins with private verandas. Bathrooms, though not large, are well designed with ample space for toiletries, thick towels, hair dryers, and excellent water pressure.

Specifications   *Sovereign,* 418 inside cabins, 710 outside; 12 suites. Standard dimensions, inside cabins 119 square feet, outside 122 square feet. 945 with twin beds (convertible to doubles); 196 third/fourth persons; no singles. 6 wheelchair-accessible. *Majesty* and *Monarch,* 444 inside cabins, 721 outside; 12 suites; 62 deluxe cabins and suites with verandas. Standard dimensions, 120 square feet. 917 with twin beds (convertible to queen); 260 third/fourth persons; no singles. 4 are wheelchair accessible.

Dining   RCI ships don't serve gourmet fare and don't intend to. Rather, galleys produce tasty food that's plentiful but not excessive, with ample variety. All ships have the same menus (consistency at work), although longer European cruises may feature local dishes. A typical menu offers seven juices and appetizers; three soups; two salads; five entrées with a choice of pasta, fish, chicken, veal, and beef; three desserts; and a selection of cheeses and ice cream.

In keeping with its ShipShape program, all menus have light selections annotated with nutritional information. You can also select vegetarian dishes or request the full vegetarian menu for an entire cruise. Wine lists include California, French, and other vintages. Prices are moderate.

Each ship has two dining rooms serving three meals, all with assigned seating. The *Sovereign's* **Kismet Dining Room** has elaborate columns and lighting fixtures; its twin, **Gigi Dining Room,** has columns styled after palm trees. *Majesty's* **Mikado Dining Room** has a Japanese theme, whereas the springtime theme of its twin, **Maytime,** is expressed in a mural of apple trees in bloom. *Monarch's* **Brigadoon Dining Room** has a

Scottish tartan motif; the **Flower Drum Song Dining Room** has sophisticated Oriental décor. Lunch and dinner can be ordered from room service from dining room menus.

A noticeable difference between *Sovereign* and her sisters is the two-deck, indoor-outdoor **Windjammer Café,** the place for casual breakfasts and lunches and alternative dinner venue. Breakfast and lunch buffets offer a variety of hot and cold dishes. Dinner offers full table service, and menus change daily. The Windjammer Café, wrapped on three sides by windows and spanning the ship's width, was redesigned, expanded, and lightened on the *Monarch* and *Majesty.* In place of the centerpiece on *Sovereign*—a two-story, mahogany-framed tree with crystal *bubbles*—*Monarch* and *Majesty* each have a mini-atrium with winter garden, waterfalls, and skylight.

Service RCI's crews, from the Norwegian captains to the mini–United Nations of the cabin and dining-room staff, are courteous and eager to please. An affable, largely Caribbean group of stewards tidy rooms twice daily and provide evening turndown service. Dining staff have many Europeans and provide attentive, efficient service. Indeed, the staff is so conscious of the constant evaluation of their work, as reflected in passengers' comment cards, that they sometimes overdo their attention. And it's likely that your waiter, when his supervisors aren't around, will all but beg you to praise him in your comments—his job may depend on it.

Facilities and Activities Among activities may be bingo; napkin folding; wine tasting; parlor games; dance classes; bridge; ice carving; parties for singles, children, and teens; a costume party; religious services; and a passenger talent show. The wood-paneled library resembles an English club; it can also be used for meetings. Two levels of sun decks provide peace, privacy, and a place to read.

Almost 24 hours a day, there's music to suit every mood—including big band, steel band, Latin, country, rock, strolling violins, and classical concerts. The **Follies Lounge,** *Sovereign's* richly decorated bilevel showroom, stages two shows nightly. The rooms have video walls with 50 television monitors on movable banks of 25 screens each. Comfortable seats have excellent sight lines, with a few exceptions. Other large lounges— **Finian's Rainbow** and the **Music Man**—have late-night entertainers and music. **Anything Goes** is the late-into-the night disco. *Monarch's* disco, **Ain't Misbehavin',** has a glass sculpture of Fats Waller.

Cantilevered from the funnel and encircling it is the extraordinary **Viking Crown Lounge.** The room, 12 stories above the water, provides a fabulous 360° view of the sea and sunset.

Among small lounges is the nautical-motif **Schooner Bar,** a favorite casual bar by day and a lively piano bar at night. **Casino Royale** next door offers blackjack, 170 slot machines, and American roulette. **Touch of Class** is a chic champagne bar where 50 people can clink flutes and scoop caviar. Décor lives up to the lounge's name with two lifelike bronze statues of 1920s flappers. Other options include **Flashes,** the teen nightclub, karaoke, a shopping boulevard, and a theater showing films daily.

Sports, Fitness, and Beauty   Fitness enthusiasts have a one-third-mile outside deck encircling the vessel and a second jogging track. The well-equipped health club offers saunas and locker rooms, a large exercise room with ballet bars, an array of exercise equipment, and a high-energy staff. The sports deck has twin swimming pools, two whirlpools, and a basketball court. ShipShape Fitness activities start with a sunrise stretch class or water exercises, low-impact aerobics, and walkathons, basketball, and Ping-Pong tournaments. Participants earn "dollars" for each activity, redeemable for T-shirts and visors. Vitality Unlimited is designed for senior citizens. All menus offer low-fat, low-calorie entrées, prepared to American Heart Association guidelines. The beauty salon/barber shop offers massage and beauty treatments at additional cost.

Children's Facilities   RCI was among the first lines to create a children's program with youth centers, play rooms, and counselors. The *Sovereign* group offers the program year-round. They also have video arcades and teen centers. *Majesty* and *Monarch* have teen nightclubs. Kids get their own daily agenda, slipped under the cabin door each night. Among the activities are ice cream and pizza parties, dance classes, golf putting, face painting, midnight basketball, autograph hunts, talent shows, and shore tours. Baby-sitters (extra cost), cribs, and high chairs are available. Captain Sealy's Kids' Galley, a menu for children ages 4–12, offers such favorites as peanut butter sandwiches, hamburgers, and pizzas, along with salads, fruit, and alphabet soup.

Shore Excursions   Descriptive booklets are included with documents mailed to passengers. Except for its golf programs and cruises that include Labadee in their itinerary, RCI's shore excursions are similar to those of other lines cruising the Caribbean. They include island tours, beach trips, and snorkeling and diving. RCI's private resort, Labadee, created in 1987 on the north coast of Haiti, offers the best day at the beach of any line. Its setting is beautiful—lush mountains rise behind a lovely cove with a series of crescent-shaped beaches. There are pavilions for dining, entertainment, water sports equipment, and a marketplace with Haitian crafts, which are the Caribbean's best. Music, dancing, and performances by a local folklore group are provided. Some itineraries call for a day at Coco Cay, a small Bahamian island. Diversions for a range of ages include beach games, pedal boats, shopping, steel-band music, visits to a shipwreck led by snorkeling instructors, a barbecue, palm-shaded trails, six sandy beaches for swimming, and hammocks and beach chairs for lounging. Children's programs are available.

NORDIC EMPRESS	QUALITY 5	VALUE C
Registry: Liberia	Length: 692 feet	Beam: 100 feet
Cabins: 801	Draft: 25 feet	Speed: 19.5 knots
Maximum Passengers:	Passenger Decks: 9	Elevators: 7
2,020	Crew: 685	Space Ratio: 30.4

The Ship Created for the short-cruise market, *Nordic Empress* dazzles with its design–from light that streams in by day to nighttime glitter. Passengers board at the nine-deck-tall atrium called the Centrum. Two of four elevators are glass and overlook a waterfall and greenery. Most public rooms flow from here. Two center decks contain the dining room, showroom, casino, and lounges. The Sun Deck topside is an all-day center of activities—from sunning and swimming to entertainment and dancing under the stars. It also contains the fitness and kids' centers.

The *Nordic Empress* continues RCI's consistency. There are no surprises except the ship itself, which has a very different look from other members of the fleet. The vessel offers a good sampler for those wanting to try a high-energy, activity-filled cruise and for busy people seeking weekend getaways.

Itineraries See Itinerary Index.

Cabins The dozen categories include many inside and lower-priced outside cabins. All are designed to be light and tropical in feeling. All have two lower beds, color television, three-channel radio, telephone, and private bath. Sixty percent are outside cabins with large windows. All suites and deluxe cabins have balconies.

Specifications 318 inside cabins, 483 outside; 6 suites; 69 deluxe cabins with verandas. Standard dimensions, 194 square feet. 495 with twin beds (all convertible to double); 358 with upper/lower berths accommodating third/fourth berths; no singles; 4 wheelchair-accessible.

Dining The two-level **Carmen Dining Room** has walls of floor-to-ceiling windows spanning two decks and providing panoramic views. There are two seatings for the three meals. Menus are the same as offered on other RCI ships and include theme dinners.

Meals and snacks are served around the clock, starting with early-riser's breakfast at 6:30 a.m. and ending with the midnight buffet. A typical seven-course menu lists a wide choice of juices and appetizers; soups; salads; pasta; entrées with fish, chicken, veal, and beef; desserts; cheese; and ice cream. All menus have health-conscious selections.

Breakfast and lunch buffets are served in the glass-domed **Windjammer Café.** It's also the alternative dinner restaurant, offering full table service between 6:30 and 10:30 p.m., and a midnight buffet. A Sun Worshipper's lunch and afternoon tea are served poolside. The full dining room menu is available for room service at lunch and dinner.

Service   *Nordic Empress's* crew are eager to please. Stewards, most of them Caribbean, make up rooms twice a day and provide evening turndown service. The friendly dining staff quickly learn your preferences. As on all other RCI ships, they will encourage good reviews on your passenger comment cards.

Facilities and Activities   Passengers on short cruises usually pack in as many activities as possible. *Nordic Empress* provides abundant choices. Topside by day are outdoor games and entertainment; elsewhere are dance classes, cards, crafts, bingo, and karaoke.

Nighttime entertainment is some of RCI's best, with good shows, music, and dancing for many tastes. Even a three-day cruise fits in the captain's cocktail party and a passenger talent show. Big, Broadway-style productions are staged in the impressive, tiered **Strike Up the Band** lounge. Sight lines are good from almost any seat. The lounge also has a dance floor. The ship's most dazzling feature is the trilevel **Casino Royale,** offering 220 slot machines, nine blackjack tables, roulette, craps, and wheel of fortune. Between the casino and Centrum is the festive **Carousel Pub,** designed with a merry-go-round theme. Under the tented ceiling is a mural with carousel paraphernalia. The larger, Art Deco **High Society** lounge features entertainment and dance music from the 1950s to 1990s.

The **Viking Crown Lounge** is at the stern on Sun Deck, rather than cantilevered from the stack as on other RCI ships. Nonetheless, with three walls of windows, it's a fine observation area. Late night, it's a disco.

Note: When the ship is in Bermuda during summer, much of this entertainment won't be available. Bermudan regulations don't allow ships to open their casinos or stage shows while they're in port. However, the ship offers Bermuda-by-Night shore excursions, or you can explore local nightlife independently.

Sports, Fitness, and Beauty   The large **ShipShape Fitness Center** has a glass-enclosed exercise area and an array of equipment, plus saunas, showers, and massage rooms. On deck are three whirlpools and two fountains that cascade into two pools (one for children). The beauty salon offers hair, facial, and beauty treatments (additional charge). Video golf in the **Golf Ahoy! Center** enables participants to try their skill at world-famous courses projected on the screen. A computer analyzes the stroke and scores the game. ShipShape activities range from aquadynamics to basketball free throws. "Dollars" earned for participation can be redeemed for T-shirts and visors.

Children's Facilities   **Kids' Konnection** is a multipurpose, 95-square-foot play room for children ages 5–12. Designed with a space-station theme, the room has an 11-foot ceiling, making room for the Tubular

Time labyrinth of suspended tubes that are lighted and carpeted inside. Children can crawl through the tubes to a slide and clubhouse platform. The youth program provides participants with a daily agenda, slipped under the cabin door at night. It's packed with activities, including ice cream and pizza parties, face painting, midnight basketball, talent shows, and shore tours. Menus designed for children ages 4–12 offer such favorites as peanut butter sandwiches, hot dogs, and pizzas, plus salads and fruit. Babysitters (extra cost), cribs, and high chairs are available.

Shore Excursions Descriptive booklets accompany documents mailed to passengers. Excursions target varied interests but essentially are off-the-shelf programs, among them island tours, beach trips, snorkeling, and diving.

RADIANCE OF THE SEAS	QUALITY **8**	VALUE **C**
BRILLANCE OF THE SEAS	QUALITY **8**	VALUE **C**
JEWEL OF THE SEAS	(2004)	
SERENADE OF THE SEAS	(Preview)	
Registry: Liberia	Length: 962 feet	Beam: 106 feet
Cabins: 1,050	Draft: 26.7 feet	Speed: 25 knots
Maximum Passengers:	Passenger Decks: 12	Elevators: 9
2,501	Crew: 859	Space Ratio: NA

The Ships With sunshine shimmering through walls of glass, Royal Caribbean's new *Radiance of the Seas* lives up to her name. The ship is so bright and airy you'll want to keep your sunglasses on when you come in from an outside deck.

Launched in 2001, *Radiance* has floor-to-ceiling windows on all levels of its nine-deck atrium and in 16 public areas, plus exterior glass elevators spanning 12 decks. Passengers never have to miss a minute of the beauty of Alaska and the Caribbean or the connection with the sea.

First of a new class of ship for Royal Caribbean—smaller than the giant Voyager class and larger than the Vision group—*Radiance of the Seas* is a classy lady. She incorporates the best of her predecessors: the many entertainment and activity options of *Voyager* (including a rock-climbing wall), the sleek profile of *Sovereign,* and glass galore. Her twin, *Brillance of the Seas,* debuted in Europe in 2002, prior to coming to her home base in Galveston, Texas, for year-round West Caribbean cruises. *Serenade of the Seas* followed in 2003 ,and *Jewel of the Seas* is expected in 2004. The ships are Panamax class, meaning they are narrow enough—just barely—to pass through the Panama Canal.

And these ships have highlights of their own: the most balconies of any RCI ships; Internet ports in every cabin; a bookstore/coffeehouse; and gas and steam turbines said to reduce emissions, noise, and vibration. *Radiance* reflects RCI's "resort-like" style, with the purser's desk called

Guest Relations, its staff wearing resort-wear (rather than officers-style uniforms), and a general manager and vacation experience director intended to foster guest satisfaction.

Radiance also boasts a first-at-sea: self-leveling pool tables. These high-tech tables are the big attraction in the **Bombay Billiard Club,** one of four lounges clustered in the **Colony Club.** The others are the **Calcutta Card Club; Jakarta Lounge,** an intimate bar with gaming tables; and **Singapore Sling,** a piano bar with floor-to-ceiling windows offering spectacular views aft. The Centrum, a dramatic, airy atrium and an RCI signature, is decorated in light woods and soft tones of sand, coral and aqua, set off with greenery, a waterfall, and colossal abstract sculpture, part of the ship's $6-million-plus art collection.

Another memorable area is the African-themed Solarium, with three life-sized stone elephants, a bronze of a lion cub dipping his paw in the water, a waterfall, stone relief art panels depicting gazelles and antelopes, greenery, and piped-in sounds of chirping birds. It also has a raised pool (with a counter-current), two whirlpools, a bar and pizzeria—all under a retractable glass roof.

Itineraries   See Itinerary Index.

Cabins   Accommodations are spacious and attractively decorated; 70% have verandas. The most lavish, the Royal Suite, is a palatial 1,035 square feet, with 173 square feet of balcony and such amenities as baby grand piano, wet bar, and entertainment center with 42-inch flat screen TV, stereo, and VCR, and bath with whirlpool, bidet, and steam shower. Veranda cabins measuring 179 square feet with a 41-square-foot-balcony are situated on Decks 7, 8, 9, and 10, with the ones on Deck 10 closest to the pools and other outdoor amenities. The lowest-priced cabins are inside cabins measuring 166 square feet.

All cabins are equipped with an interactive television, telephone, computer jack, vanity table with an extendable working surface for a laptop computer, refrigerator/minibar, hairdryer, 110/220 electrical outlets, two single beds convertible to double; and reading lights by the beds. There are wheelchair-accessible cabins are available in most categories.

Specifications   1,050 cabins; 237 inside; 813 outside (577 with balconies); 62 suites; 62 deluxe; 6 family suites; 65 third/fourth persons; no singles; 14 wheelchair-accessible.

Dining   Cascades, the elegant, two-level main dining room has a grand staircase, etched-glass mural-and, a cascading waterfall. The upper level has floor-to-ceiling windows; the lower level, large windows. Two smaller dining rooms, **Breakers** and **Tides,** are ideal for private parties. Breakfast and lunch are open seating; dinner is served in two seatings. ShipShape (or low fat) selections are offered for lunch and dinner. The casual **Wind-**

jammer Café serves buffet-style breakfast and lunch with a choice of indoor and outdoor seating. The **Seaview Café** cooks up burgers, hot dogs, and nachos. The food ranges from mediocre to delicious.

Alternative eateries include **Chops Grill,** serving steaks and other grills from an open kitchen; and **Portofino,** an upscale Euro-Italian restaurant with Tuscany-inspired décor. Fee is $20 per person at each which covers gratuities; reservations required.

Facilities and Activities   The three-level **Aurora Theatre,** the setting for Broadway-style revues, has Arctic-themed décor with sculptured balconies, side walls and parterre divisions resembling glacial landscapes. The futuristic **Starquest** (with a revolving bar) and **Hollywood Odyssey** are two night spots housed in RCI's hallmark **Viking Crown Lounge** perched high over the sea. The latter features jazz ensembles, comedians, pianists and vocalists. The ship has a large casino, several bars, and a library reminiscent of a traditional English study, as well as **Royal Caribbean Online,** the Internet center with 12 stations.

Fitness and Beauty   The ocean-view **ShipShape Spa,** the beauty and health center, has 12 treatment rooms including a Rasul and a thermal suite ($15–$42 for a half-hour); gym with 18 treadmills and an array of equipment; and fitness activities and exercise classes. Out on deck, passengers have more challenges at the rock-climbing wall with five separate climbing tracks, golf simulator and nine-hole miniature golf course, basketball court, and jogging track.

Children Facilities   The line's **Adventure Ocean** youth program offers supervised activities by age group (ages 3–5, 6–8, 9–12, and 13–17) in age-appropriate activity centers. Kids earn gift coupons for participating. Facilities include a computer lab, play stations with video games, and Adventure Beach with splash pools and a water slide. Teens have their own coffeehouse/disco with flat-screen televisions and soda bar. Children's menus and group baby-sitting are available.

Postscript   Royal Caribbean's reputation for delivering consistency holds up on all its ships. But remember, these are megaliners; you need patience for crowds and long lines, no matter how smoothly the ships operate. At the same time, their size and array of facilities and activities are treats in themselves and fuel the action-packed, high-energy atmosphere aboard.

Royal Olympia Cruises

805 Third Avenue, New York, NY 10022-7513
(212) 688-7555; (800) 872-6400; (888) 662-6237
www.royalolympiccruises.com

Type of Ships   Small and midsize oceanliners.

Type of Cruises   Quality, low-key, destination-oriented, short cruises in Greek Isles and longer cruises in Eastern Mediterranean and South America on less-traveled paths in homey ambience.

Cruise Line's Strengths

- friendliness and personal warmth of the crew
- Greek hospitality
- innovative itineraries
- cultural programs and quality guides

Cruise Line's Shortcomings

- dissimilar aging and new ships
- small cabins and limited facilities on smaller ships
- limited deck space and lack of promenade deck on new ships

Fellow Passengers   In winter, when the ships sail Western Hemisphere itineraries, 80% of passengers are age 55 and older and have the time, means, and inclination for long cruises. They are mature, modestly affluent, seasoned travelers, many retired or semiretired, with some sense of adventure. Destinations, quality experiences, and value are priorities. Most are college-educated and enjoy shipboard enrichment programs and shore excursions. Over 50% come from Florida, California, New York, and Texas and have annual household income of $75,000+. Most are frequent cruisers; up to 50% may be repeaters.

In summer, when the ships are in the Mediterranean, the passenger mix is international, with 40% from Australia, Mexico, South America, France, and Italy and 60% from the United States and Canada. They have household income of $50,000+. Average age is 40+ years. They range from newlyweds to retirees, plus families with children. Attractions of the Mediterranean appeal equally to honeymooners seeking romantic destinations, religious groups tracing the "footsteps of St. Paul," and amateur historians visiting places they studied in school.

Recommended For Moderately affluent, adventurous travelers seeking a different kind of experience in refined, conservative ambience, who expect the level of service, comfort, and amenities found in good hotels; value-conscious travelers who prefer to stay in cozy local hotels but want an English-speaking environment; people interested in Greek culture and cuisine; experienced cruisers who enjoy the style of traditional oceanliner.

Not Recommended For Party-seekers, night owls, those wanting big-ship action; unsophisticated travelers; people wanting to be entertained, and those with only slight interest in history.

Cruise Areas and Seasons South America, Amazon, Orinoco, Caribbean, Panama Canal in winter; Italy, Egypt, Greek Isles, Eastern Mediterranean, Black Sea spring–fall; transatlantic, April and November.

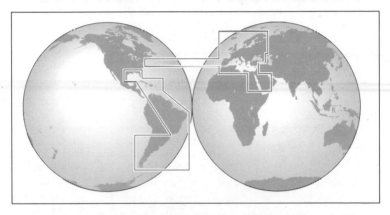

The Line In 1995, Sun Line Cruises, one of the most respected Greek-owned cruise lines, and rival Epirotiki Line, one of Greece's oldest and largest lines, merged to form a new company, Royal Olympic Cruises (later changed to Royal Olympia Cruises).

Sun Line, founded in the mid-1950s, was a pioneer, introducing some of the first ships designed specifically for cruising that eliminated class distinctions and provided large public rooms and outdoor areas for relaxation and sports. Itineraries included lesser-known islands of the Eastern Caribbean (a decade before other lines discovered them), and combined Eastern Caribbean islands with a cruise on the Orinoco or Amazon Rivers or the Panama Canal; they also offered cruises timed for the spring equinox at Chichen Itza in the Yucatán. Sun Line was first as early as 1985 to offer solar eclipse–watching cruises which were copied by almost everyone with a ship.

Many lines have added bigger ships, but Royal Olympia's remain small and intimate. Most crew members are Greek and Filipino; many count 20 or more years of service. The line has many repeaters. Traditionally, most of its cruises are sold in the United States through companies that package them as two-week vacations with tours of Greece, and the Eastern Mediterranean, combining hotel stays with a cruise.

The first of Royal Olympia's two 840-passenger ships, *Olympia Voyager,* debuted in 2000, and the second, *Olympia Explorer,* in 2002. Designed with an innovative "fast monohull," the vessels are meant to be the speediest (up to 29 knots), most time-efficient cruise ships afloat—an advantage in planning itineraries.

In 1999, having suffered serious dislocations due to the war in Kosovo, ROC found a white knight in Louise Cruise Lines, a Cyprus-based hotel, cruise, and ferry operator and ROC competitor in the Eastern Mediterranean. Louise now owns 70% of ROC.

THE FLEET	BUILT/RENOVATED	TONNAGE	PASSENGERS
Odysseus	1962/89/95	12,000	486
Olympia Countess	1976/91/96	18,000	814
Olympia Voyager	2000	25,000	836
Olympia Explorer	2002	25,000	836
Stella Solaris	1953/94	18,000	628
Triton	1971/76/91/96	14,000	676
World Renaissance	1966/91/96	12,000	474

Style   To sail on Royal Olympia's ships is to bide a while in a Greek town at sea. Staff and crew serve guests with the natural ease of people at home, and passengers are treated as valued friends, not tourists. The ships' moderate size contributes to the genial shipboard atmosphere. The ships are still traditional enough that you get a passenger list. The desire to experience Greek life and culture is delightfully contagious, and the ships offer many ways to satisfy it, from authentic Greek food to lessons in Greek dances and language. Every day, passengers can be heard practicing the latest tidbit of conversational Greek to the cheerful encouragement of crew and staff. The highlight of each cruise is Greek Night, with traditional Greek music and dancing by crew members.

In keeping with fitness trends, some ships offer spa cuisine. And for its high number of single women passengers, there's a host program on some long winter cruises.

Distinctive Features   Greek Night. Maya Equinox cruise. Host program on some longer cruises. Precruise purchase of shore excursions at savings. Fast monohull of newest ships.

	HIGHEST	LOWEST	AVERAGE
PER DIEM	$419	$126	$286

Per diems are calculated from cruise line's nondiscounted *cruise-only* fares on standard accommodations and vary by season, cabin, and cruise areas.

Rates   Ports charges are additional.

Special Fares and Discounts   Early-bird discounts. Low cruise-only rates, depending on itinerary and cabin category.

- **Third/Fourth Passenger** Yes.
- **Children's Fare** Yes.
- **Single Supplement** 150%, except suites; guaranteed share available.

Packages

- **Air/Sea** Yes.
- **Pre/Post** Yes. Summer Greek Islands/Mediterranean cruises can be combined with land packages for vacations of a week or longer.

Past Passengers   Passengers are registered as Royal Circle members after their first cruise and receive special mailings, discounts, and upgrades on selected sailings.

The Last Word   For travelers turned off by big, glitzy ships and their impersonal nature, Royal Olympia offers a refreshing option. The line provides the quality of traditional cruising with the comfort and warmth of Greek hospitality. Repeaters say it's like coming home; many return to the same ship year after year.

ROYAL OLYMPIA CRUISES STANDARD FEATURES

Officers Greek.

Staff Dining, Cabin, Cruise/Greek and Filipino.

Dining Facilities One main dining room for all meals; informal buffet breakfast and lunch served poolside. *Stella Solaris, Olympia Voyager/Olympia Explorer* have indoor/outdoor lido cafés with breakfast, lunch, and late-night buffets; and alternative dining.

Special Diets Low-salt, low-fat diets available. Kosher diets are accommodated with written request two weeks before departure.

Room Service 24 hours. Butler service in suites on *Voyager, Explorer.*

Dress Code Comfortable, casual during day; evening after 6 p.m. varies. *Stella Solaris* 10–12-day cruises: 3 formal evenings, 2 informal, remaining evenings casual.

Cabin Amenities Telephone, dual-channel radio, private bathroom, and a locking drawer for valuables. Television: *Stella Solaris,* top three cabin categories; all cabins on *Voyager, Explorer.*

Electrical Outlets *Countess, Voyager, Explorer,* and *Stella Solaris;* 220 AC (110 AC razors only); 110 AC, *World Renaissance, Odysseus,* and *Triton.* All ships are built with American and European outlets; the latter require plug adapter.

Wheelchair Access *Voyager, Explorer,* four cabins.

Recreation and Entertainment Lounge with nightly dancing to orchestra, cabaret acts, passengers' talent show, Greek Night, masquerade. Bridge, backgammon, bingo, dance classes. *Voyager, Explorer,* pizza bar, nightclub, casino, piano bar, cigar room, business center, library, card room.

ROYAL OLYMPIA CRUISES STANDARD FEATURES
(continued)

Sports and Other Activities   Swimming pool (two-section pool on *Stella Solaris*; two pools on *World Renaissance*), exercise classes, shuffleboard, Ping-Pong. *Countess*, paddle tennis, putting green, driving range; outdoor pool with Jacuzzi.

Beauty and Fitness   Beauty salon and barber shop. *Countess, World Renaissance, Voyager, Explorer*, fitness center, exercise equipment, exercise classes, and sauna. *Voyager, Explorer*, spa, whirlpools.

Other Facilities   Boutique; laundry service, no dry cleaning; medical services; religious service; ship-to-shore telephone service.

Children's Facilities   None.

Theme Cruises   Intermittently.

Smoking   No pipes and cigars in dining room or lounge during showtime. Smoking areas assigned in dining room.

ROC Suggested Tipping   Per person per day, $9. Tips are pooled and divided among ship employees. $3 cabin stewardess. On *Stella Solaris*, tips can be paid by credit card when passenger settles final bills. Personal checks not accepted for onboard charges. 10% added to bar /wine bill.

Credit Cards   For cruise payment and on-board charges: American Express, Discover, MasterCard, and Visa.

OLYMPIA EXPLORER	QUALITY 8	VALUE B
OLYMPIA VOYAGER	(Preview)	
Registry: Luxembourg	Length: 590 feet	Beam: 84 feet
Cabins: 418	Draft: 24 feet	Speed: 28 knots
Maximum Passengers:	Passenger Decks: 6	Elevators: 4
836	Crew: 360	Space Ratio: 30

The Ships   Royal Olympia's newest ships, built in Germany, were the first brand-new vessels for the line. *Olympia Voyager,* the line's new flagship, was launched in 2000, followed by her sister, *Olympia Explorer,* in 2002. The well-known Athens-based firm of A&M Katzourakis Architects & Designers created the interiors, with help from an impressive group of artists.

The ships' most distinguishing features are their hydrodynamic "fast monohull" design—a sleek bow and graceful profile that enable them to achieve a cruising speed of over 29 knots, permitting less time in transit, more time in port, and the ability to reach more ports on a weekly itinerary, thus creating itineraries that no one else can match. From a technical perspective, the hull's contour delivers significantly reduced fuel consumption, and despite the ships' high speeds, it's remarkably stable, with no more than a normal amount of vibration and engine noise for a high-speed ship.

Among the other highlights are that 70% of the cabins are outside; among *Olympia Voyager's* 48 suites are a group of unusual "Bay" suites with bay windows. The ship also has an extensive and unusual art collection with works of calligrapher Rosella Gaavaglia, ceramicist Ignazio Moncada, and painters Aldo Mondino, Erietta Vordoni, and Michaelis Katzourakis, among other notable artists. Each artist was commissioned to create works for specific public rooms and cabins. The décor and the predominately Greek staff and European clientele combine to create a sophisticated European-Greek atmosphere that is very appealing.

Understated elegance, sophisticated yet comfortable, *Olympia Voyager* interior décor is fresh and modern yet classic with extensive use of cherry wood paneling and glass. The decks are named for Greek gods. Helios, the top deck, has the swimming pool, an outdoor pizza bar, and the **Jade Spa** aft and the **Sky Lounge** forward, serving as an observation lounge by day and the disco by night. The deck also has the Sky suites.

Most of the public rooms are found on Apollo Deck and include the indoor/outdoor **Garden Restaurant** at stern and **Alexander the Great,** the main lounge, at the bow. Between, there are the **Cigar Club,** the casino, shops, the **Athena Library,** a card/game room, and a piano bar.

Selene Deck is anchored by the **Selene Dining Room** at the stern and ocean-view cabins and suites amidships, along with the reception area. Other facilities include a coffee bar, beauty salon, two shops, and a very large and well-equipped infirmary.

Olympia Explorer is similar to her sister ship but has new elements, including more cabins with balconies. The décor carries the theme "Precious Earth," for the precious stones that her lounges are named after, and complementary color schemes and art. For example, in the ship's main restaurant, **Aqua Marina,** gold and aquamarine colors are seen within the 2,000 ocean-colored crystals of the room's three chandeliers. The restaurant also has two triptychs designed by Greek artist Michalis Katzourakis. In the casual **Topaz Garden Lounge,** a brilliant blue topaz design dominates, inspired by the ocean. Entertainment is offered in the **Amber Lounge,** decorated with large paintings by artist Eiretta Vordoni.

Itineraries   See Itinerary Index.

Cabins   Accommodations include Sky suites on Apollo Deck, each encompassing 375 square feet, with floor-to-ceiling sliding glass doors leading to a private balcony; and on *Voyager,* Bay Window suites, 215 square feet, located forward on Selene Deck. Both categories have bathroom with tub and shower and butler service. The Junior suites, 183 square feet, have walk-in closets. Some of the Junior suites accommodate four people. Venus and Dionysus Decks hold the Junior suites and the majority of standard cabins. The balance are on the lower Neptune Deck.

Standard outside and inside cabins measuring 140 square feet seem small by today's standards on new ships, but they are well laid out and functional. However, *Olympia Voyager's* Bay Window suites are outstanding. They have an alcove with three large floor-to-ceiling windows projecting out over the sea. Alas, these suites have become veranda suites on *Olympia Explorer.* The 12 veranda suites on the top deck are very roomy and have deep balconies furnished with table and chairs, and two lounge chairs for sunning.

All cabins have twin beds convertible to doubles; minibar, safe, three-channel radio, direct-dial phone, interactive television, hair dryers, and 24-hour room service. The outside cabins on Neptune, the lowest deck, have large portholes. The aft cabins on Neptune and Dionysus Decks may be the least desirable because of possible noise from the engines.

Specifications   48 suites, including 12 with verandas; 20 Junior suites; and 16 Bay Window (*Olympia Voyager* only). 244 standard outside, including 4 wheelchair-accessible; and 126 standard inside doubles.

Dining   The **Selene Dining Room** at the stern has windows on three sides providing a lovely panorama of the ship's wake. Meals are served in two seatings at tables for two, four, six, and eight—all set far apart to ensure quiet, ease of movement, and a certain amount of privacy.

The **Garden Lounge,** the ship's attractive buffet restaurant with curving banquettes, large windows, and a rich red carpet, offers seating both inside and out and can double as a casual lounge during the day. In the pool area, there's a pizza station beneath a lovely tented awning.

The cuisine is good international fare with Greek specialties, such as stuffed vine leaves, marinated octopus, Greek salads with feta cheese, moussaka, souvlaki, and baklava. The meats come from the United States, so the steaks and roast beef are top-quality. Overall, the menus cater to both North American and European tastes, and the choices generally please most.

The lido is open for breakfast and lunch and some dinners, especially when shore tours return late from long days, like the Cairo excursion. The layout is efficient with double lines and separate stations for the drinks, fruit, and desserts. The outdoor grill produces some of the best pizza afloat, with a choice of four different toppings available throughout the day. Unfortunately, seating outdoors is inadequate on nice days.

A small annoyance that most ships catering to North Americans have eliminated but is still a custom on European ones: Passengers must queue for a table reservation on boarding. In this day of technology, it hardly seems necessary.

Service   Dining room service is usually quite efficient but can be somewhat matter-of-fact; and the friendliness varies from waiter to waiter, many of whom are Greek. Happily, there is a still a national feeling on this ship.

Facilities and Activities In keeping with Royal Olympia's tradition, when the ships offers Amazon and Orinoco River and Maya equinox cruises, an onboard enrichment program features distinguished experts and scholars in anthropology, archaeology, astronomy, and international politics to enhance the cruise experience. For example, Amazon cruises are accompanied by Loren McIntyre, who is credited with discovering the most remote source of the river. In summer, the line engages specialists for Europe and the Eastern Mediterranean and Greek guides who are among the best-educated, most knowledgeable professionals in the world.

Entertainment onboard is presented mostly in the modest, one-level **Alexander the Great Lounge,** where you'll find small-scale song-and-dance productions and music and magic acts, plus the always popular Greek night. An attractive **Piano Bar,** set amidships along a central winding corridor, is the ship's main social hub and offers a comfortable (if often smoky) spot to relax.

The **Anemos** nightclub, perched above the bridge on the topmost deck, serves as a 270° observation lounge by day. One level below, there's a comfortable **Cigar Room** with fantastic lounge-style couches. The ship's small casino, immediately next door, is bisected by the two-level reception atrium. On one side are 44 slot machines; on the other, a bar, four poker tables, and roulette—it's safe to say gamblers are not Royal Olympia's core audience.

A card room and a library with three computers round out the public rooms. There are no special facilities for children. The ship's deck space is limited; no promenade encircles the ship, and some deck space along the side with lifeboats is rather useless.

Sports, Fitness, and Beauty The small gym is equipped with steps, stationary bicycles, treadmills, and weights, but it's not particularly attractive (half the exercise machines face away from the room's few windows—which sort of negates the advantage of having the windows in the first place). Fortunately, the adjoining spa has a pleasant environment and an extensive range of treatments at prices that are lower than aboard most ships. These include massages, sauna, Swiss showers, facials, Turkish bath, mud bath, and other treatments. The ship offers a variety of full-day spa packages from $110 to $225.

Postscript While most cruise lines are building bigger and bigger ships for the mass market or more and more luxurious small ones for the most affluent travelers, Royal Olympia was willing to break out of the pack and deliver a truly unique, innovative, midsize cruise ship and offer cruises at reasonable prices. The line took a big gamble in building the *Olympia Voyager* and her sister ship, both for their size and their new technology. Judging from the positive response from passengers, it was a wise choice that has served the line well. All in all, the ships set a stylish new tone for Royal Olympia.

STELLA SOLARIS	QUALITY **5**	VALUE **B**
Registry: Greece	Length: 544 feet	Beam: 72 feet
Cabins: 314	Draft: 29 feet	Speed: 22 knots
Maximum Passengers:	Passenger Decks: 8	Elevators: 3
628	Crew: 320	Space Ratio: 29

The Ship   The *Stella Solaris* combines the facilities and amenities of a large ship with the atmosphere of a small oceanliner. She epitomizes traditional cruising with gracious service, quality, and warm Greek hospitality. Built in 1973, the ship has trim, flowing lines. You sense Old World charm when you step into the dignified, dark wood–paneled Main Foyer. No soaring atriums or lavish showrooms here. Rather, continental refinement is evident in furnishings and décor shipwide.

The cruise line has done a remarkable job of preserving *Solaris's* character over the years, replacing fabrics and fixtures as needed, but retaining original colors and patterns. The result is a comfortably sophisticated environment. Major renovations in 1995 and 2003 resulted in an enhanced and redecorated main show lounge, enlarged casino, upgraded boutique, enlarged and upgraded spa and gym, new carpets in public areas, and redecorated cabins—all while preserving the ship's personality. Televisions are found in the top three categories of cabins.

Passengers can orient themselves quickly because the main public rooms and dining room are on the Solaris Deck, which runs the full length of the ship. Most of the rooms are open and airy. Extra-high ceilings add to her spaciousness, and large windows connect passengers with the sea.

The Mediterranean-style main lounge is decorated in deep red and brown and hung with scenes from Greek mythology worked in bronze. The piano bar at the stern is a popular gathering spot for cocktails or private parties. A card and reading room on Boat Deck provides a quiet refuge; on Sapphire Deck, the large theater accommodates movies and concerts.

Itineraries   See Itinerary Index.

Cabins   Eleven price categories are distributed throughout the ship. Most cabins are large and decorated in pastels. Comfortable furnishings usually include twin beds, a dresser with lock drawers, large mirror, and coffee table. The three top categories include large, deluxe suites with separate sitting areas and bathrooms with tub and shower. All cabins and suites have telephones and multichannel music systems. Television is available in the top three categories. Nearly two thirds have bathrooms with tub and shower. Storage space is ample. Room service is available 24 hours a day from a limited menu.

Specifications   82 inside cabins, 232 outside; 66 suites (6 with double beds). Standard dimensions, 189 square feet. 225 with twin beds (none convert to double); 79 with upper and lower berths; no singles; no wheelchair-accessible.

Dining   The spacious dining room is first-class in décor, service, and cuisine. By day, light streams through windows on both sides of the long room. In evening, subdued lighting captures the spirit of the gathering. Tablecloth colors change with the evening's theme, but tables are always set with Royal Doulton china, Italian silverware, French crystal, and fresh flowers. Breakfast and lunch are open seatings; dinner has two assigned seatings. Most tables accommodate four or six persons. Food and service are continental but designed to cater to American tastes. Greek specialties, such as moussaka, are on the menu frequently, and genuine Greek salad is almost always available.

Topside, the indoor/outdoor lido café is the place for breakfast, lunch, and late-night buffets, midmorning bouillon, and afternoon tea. Passengers who prefer informality eat outside at umbrella-shaded tables by the ship's dual pools, or they take their trays one flight down to the Boat Deck and eat in old-fashioned wooden deck chairs. The deck has a wraparound promenade popular for jogging and strolling.

Service   One factor contributing immensely to *Solaris's* character is the remarkably large number of longtime crew members. The Greek staff delivers gracious, top-notch professional service with a personal touch, exemplifying Greece's tradition of hospitality.

Best of all are the pride and pleasure the crew take in their jobs—particularly in discovering and catering to passengers' preferences. For example: A recent passenger asked for a double cappuccino with breakfast the first morning, and the waiter delighted in bringing one each day without prompting.

Solaris's large number of repeat cruisers most often attribute their loyalty to the ship to its staff and crew and the warm atmosphere they create. Many request the same dining room and cabin attendants.

Facilities and Activities   Cabaret-style entertainment features vocalists, magicians, dancers, and comedians. There's dance music in the main lounge after the show and in the disco.

A highlight of each cruise is Greek Night, when dinner features Greek specialties; costumed officers and crew perform Greek song and dance (with passenger participation); and bouzouki music, along with the ship's excellent dance orchestra.

The daily agenda, delivered under the cabin door, includes the staples: fitness classes, bridge tournaments, arts and crafts, dance lessons, backgammon, bingo, and movies.

Sports, Fitness, and Beauty   The ship's two-section swimming pool is surrounded by an area for lounging, shuffleboard, and table tennis. Aerobics classes are offered for all ages and fitness levels. The gym has exercise bicycles, step machine, slant boards, and free weights. Walkers and joggers frequent the promenade deck (seven times around is slightly over a mile). Also aboard are a beauty salon, barber shop, sauna, and massage facilities.

Shore Excursions   Comprehensive shore excursions are described in literature accompanying cruise documents. Some can be reserved in advance. Tour companies working with *Solaris* are well organized and use comfortable buses with large windows. Tours generally allow time to explore on one's own. Most cruises highlight local culture and history. The line's guide, describing the places visited, is well written and illustrated and makes a fine souvenir.

Touring schedules in the Eastern Mediterranean are very full; cruises can be quite tiring. Time to linger over meals or lounge aboard ship is scarce, unless you pass up some sight-seeing and shopping. Two guides aboard each cruise prepare passengers for ports and to escort them ashore. Royal Olympia combines its cruise itineraries with land tours to create holidays of 7–21 days.

TRITON	QUALITY 2	VALUE C
Registry: Greece	Length: 486 feet	Beam: 71 feet
Cabins: 338	Draft: 21 feet	Speed: 22 knots
Maximum Passengers:	Passenger Decks: 7	Elevators: 2
676	Crew: 300	Space Ratio: 20

The Ship   Built in 1971 as the *Cunard Adventurer,* the ship was bought by Norwegian Cruise Line and renamed *Sunward II.* In 1991, she was acquired by Epirotiki Lines, which renovated her before introducing her as *Triton* in 1992. Public rooms, including the dining room and recreational facilities, are on the top decks.

The ship's facilities include a showroom, nightclub, four bars/lounges, casino, beauty/barber shop, boutique, and movie theater. *Triton* has wide teak decks and a large outdoor swimming pool with expansive deck area; adjacent is the fitness center.

A light and bright dining room offers two seatings for three meals and serves continental, Pacific Rim, and spa cuisine, as well as Greek specialties. The service is cheerful and attentive; the ambience is friendly.

Itineraries   See Itinerary Index.

Cabins   Most cabins are on the bottom three decks and are available in eight categories. Cabins are small and narrow but attractive. Standard outside cabins have two lower beds; most are convertible to a queen-size bed. All are furnished with desk/dresser and chair and have a bathroom with shower.

Specifications   110 inside cabins, 228 outside; 36 deluxe suites. 299 with twin beds, convertible to double; 2 with upper and lower berths; no singles; none are wheelchair-accessible.

Postscript   One of ROC's larger ships, *Triton* offers more facilities than most. She's a good value and is popular with budget-minded Europeans.

OLYMPIA COUNTESS	QUALITY **3**	VALUE **C**
Registry: Greece	Length: 537 feet	Beam: 75 feet
Cabins: 407	Draft: 19 feet	Speed: 18.5 knots
Maximum Passengers:	Passenger Decks: 7	Elevators: 2
814	Crew: 350	Space Ratio: 22

The Ship   Built by Cunard for informal, warm-weather cruising, *Cunard Countess* was acquired by Royal Olympia in January 1998 and renamed *Olympia Countess*. Aging but comfortable, she appeals to those seeking traditional cruising with port-intensive and unusual itineraries. Almost all public rooms are on the three highest decks. Lounges with tasteful, contemporary décor are large and geared to a busy program of daytime and evening entertainment.

The spacious Main Square lobby contains the purser's office, tour excursion office, and boutique.

Itineraries   See Itinerary Index.

Cabins   Accommodations are compact and comfortable but showing their age. There are 12 categories. About 60% of standard cabins are outside; all have phone, two-channel radio, baths with shower, and ample closet space. Twin beds are usually in an L configuration. Some cabins have a third lower bed, some a third upper berth; a few have one bed and one folding lower berth.

Higher-category cabins are roomier and have windows rather than portholes, sofa or chairs, television, VCR, minibar, twin beds, and bathrooms with tub and shower. Several cabins are equipped for the disabled, but some public areas, such as the pool, aren't wheelchair-accessible.

Specifications   136 inside, 271 outside, including 26 suites.

Dining   The windowed main dining room is pleasant but neither flashy nor elegant. The informal buffet, in an unusual arrangement, is on the same deck. The dining room has two seatings for dinner. The casual, open-air café serves early-morning pastries and a light breakfast, mid-morning bouillon, and light luncheon.

Facilities and Activities   Port-intensive itineraries curtail daytime shipboard activities. In the evenings, major production shows are presented in the comfortable main lounge, which also has a black marble dance floor and a large bar. An indoor/outdoor lounge on the same deck offers shows and dancing—popular with both passengers and the cruise staff. The nightclub showcases live bands and a DJ playing Top 40 hits. By day, when there aren't aerobics classes and craft lessons, the lounge is a quiet refuge. The topside lounge is a three-in-one nightclub, piano bar, and forward observation lounge. The piano bar has after-dinner entertainment nightly. The glass-enclosed Art Nouveau casino shares the space, offering slot machines, poker, and roulette. The ship also has a video game room, movie theater/meeting room, quiet library, and beauty/barber shop.

Sports, Fitness, and Beauty   Facilities include a paddle tennis court and golf driving range. The popular lido pool has two Jacuzzis, a bar, and a sunbathing area. Nearby is the fitness center, offering a Life Fitness Cardio-Fitness Center, mirrored wall, ballet barre, and sauna. A short jogging track is above the pool.

WORLD RENAISSANCE	QUALITY **3**	VALUE **C**
Registry: Greece	Length: 492 feet	Beam: 69 feet
Cabins: 237	Draft: 23 feet	Speed: 16 knots
Maximum Passengers:	Passenger Decks: 7	Elevators: 1
474	Crew: 230	Space Ratio: 27

The Ship   The *World Renaissance* was built in 1966 by Paquet French Cruises as its flagship, *Renaissance*. Royal Olympia's predecessor, Epirotiki, bought her. Small and yachtlike, she nonetheless has spacious rooms with wood paneling and generous deck space. The ship, renovated in 1996, has 237 cabins, including 15 suites. There are 178 outside doubles and 59 inside ones. Facilities include **El Greco Grand Salon,** the pleasant main lounge; two heated outdoor pools; **Xenia Tavern,** an intimate setting for classical concerts and nightclub entertainment; a casino; card room/library; theater/conference room; gym, sauna, beauty salon, and boutique; and an infirmary. Laundry service is available. The dining room serves three meals a day. Continental fare and Greek specialties are featured.

ODYSSEUS	QUALITY **2**	VALUE **C**
Registry: Greece	Length: 483 feet	Beam: 61 feet
Cabins: 226	Draft: 21 feet	Speed: 17 knots
Maximum Passengers:	Passenger Decks: 7	Elevators: 1
486	Crew: 200	Space Ratio: 19

The Ship   Before she appeared as the *Odysseus* in 1989, the former *Aquamarine* (launched in 1962), was virtually rebuilt by Epirotiki. She was refurbished again in 1995 when she joined Royal Olympia's fleet. Despite the renovations, the ship is a bit tired, and passengers complain the air-conditioning is inconsistent.

Odysseus combines the coziness of a small ship with the amenities of a large one. Most public rooms are on the Jupiter Deck. They include a main lounge, casino, bar/lounge, nightclub, and card room. An outdoor swimming pool and large deck area are nearby. Topside are an observation deck, small solarium, beauty salon and spa, and fitness center with exercise room. The ship has a sheltered teak-decked promenade. Other facilities include four Jacuzzis, four bars/lounges, shops, and library. Room service is 24 hours.

Itineraries   See Itinerary Index.

Cabins   Eight categories of varied shapes and sizes range from the top two suites to small and cramped inside rooms with upper and lower berths. About 80% are outside. Most are furnished with convertible sofabeds; a few have double beds. All have bathrooms with showers and limited hanging space.

Specifications   43 inside cabins, 183 outside; 2 deluxe; 143 with twin beds; 10 with double; 12 triples; 31 with upper and lower berths; no singles; no wheelchair-accessible.

Dining   The attractive **Aeolian Dining Room** has two seatings for three meals and open seating for breakfast and lunch. European cuisine with Greek specialties is served. Tables for four, six, and eight are set with china, crystal, and fresh linens. Breakfast menus include fruits and juices, yogurt, cereals, breads, pastries, meats, eggs, and five specials of eggs or pancakes or fruit. Dining room lunch offers two appetizers, two soups, a pasta dish, two entrées, a Greek specialty, salad, four desserts (one diabetic), fruits, and cheeses. Pacific Rim selections and spa cuisine are available. Dinner adds a vegetarian dish. Buffet breakfast, lunch, and afternoon tea are served on Lido Deck, and the **Marine Club** sets out a late-night snack.

Service   Most crew members are Greek or Filipino, and the atmosphere and service are friendly and attentive, particularly in the restaurant. The cruise director is English; the dance band, Eastern European; and singers, Latin and European.

Facilities and Activities   Daytime activity includes port and specialty lectures, aerobics, bridge visits, dance classes, backgammon, bridge, bingo, and arts and crafts, depending on itinerary. **Sirenes,** the main lounge, is used for daytime lectures and after-dinner entertainment. The ship's most popular gathering spot is the **Taverna.** The smaller **Naiades Lounge** is favored for predinner drinks; piano music often plays. The **Trojan Horse Night Club** has a tiny dance floor. Dancing and disco, and a repeaters' or singles' party also are offered. Greek Night is the entertainment highlight. Public rooms become a taverna, with Greek music, dance, and food. Passengers and Greek staff joyfully participate in the cultural immersion. The ship has no television; videos are shown daily in the **Marine Club.** The card room and small library are well used.

Postscript   *Odysseus* is well suited for those who prefer a small, comfortable ship and a friendly environment at modest price, and neither want nor need the dazzle of megaliners. She has returned to South America for the winter 2004, sailing between Buenos Aires and Chile and returning to the Mediterranean for the summer.

Seabourn Cruise Line

6100 Blue Lagoon Drive, Suite 400, Miami, FL 33126
(305) 463-3000; (800) 929-9391; fax (305) 463-3010
www.seabourn.com

Type of Ships   Small, modern, ultraluxurious oceanliners.

Type of Cruises   Top-shelf luxury cruises on worldwide itineraries.

Cruise Line's Strengths

- impeccable service
- luxurious accommodations
- exclusivity
- ship size/maneuverability
- open-seating dining
- cuisine
- worldwide itineraries

Cruise Line's Shortcomings

- limited activities
- limitations on use of water sports facilities
- room service breakfast
- disparate fleet

Fellow Passengers   Sophisticated, discriminating, well-heeled, experienced travelers; 80% from North America; others are from Europe and elsewhere. Age varies, depending on season and destinations. Most are age 50 and older; active business owners and professionals—doctors, lawyers, entrepreneurs—and honeymooners and some semiretired. They come mainly from the Northeast, Florida, California, and Chicago area. Fifty percent or more are repeaters. The mix could include a childless couple in their 30s or multigenerational families ages 4–70. Passengers are likely to have sailed on other luxury vessels and stayed in five-star hotels. They know and understand quality; their expectations are high, and their judgment tough.

Recommended For   Sophisticated, seasoned travelers accustomed to the best; affluent passengers whose first priority is service; those who seek exclusivity; yacht owners who want to leave the driving to others; those who shun big-ship, glitzy cruises; first-timers who seek and can afford small-ship ambience; honeymooners with rich parents; lottery winners.

Not Recommended For   Those unaccustomed to luxury or a sophisticated environment; anyone uncomfortable in a fancy restaurant or five-
star European hotel; flashy dressers, late-night revelers, inexperienced
travelers, children.

Cruise Areas and Seasons   Caribbean, Panama Canal, South America,
Australia/New Zealand, Fiji, Papua New Guinea, Southeast Asia in win-
ter. Europe, Mediterranean, Black Sea, Norwegian fjords, Baltic, British
Isles in spring/summer. New England, Canada, Caribbean, Red Sea and
Africa in autumn.

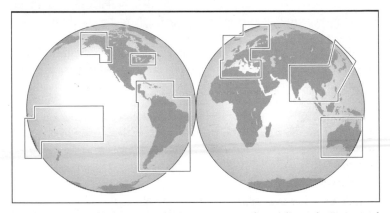

The Line   Founded in 1987 by Norwegian industrialist Atle Brynestad,
Seabourn Cruise Line's goal has always been to offer the world's most
luxurious cruises on the most elegant ships afloat for the most discriminating travelers. Seabourn quickly won enough fans with its first ship,
Seabourn Pride, to complete a second one. Seabourn's posh ships with
sleek, yachtlike profiles are small enough to be exclusive yet large enough
to be spacious and offer most facilities of a large ship. The ambience is
carefree elegance. Cruises follow the sun on worldwide itineraries that
circle the globe in a year's time.

In 1996, with the demise of Royal Viking and Royal Cruise lines,
Seabourn acquired the *Royal Viking Queen,* which was originally
intended to be the third Seabourn ship. In 1999, Carnival, which had
owned 50% of Seabourn Cruises, acquired 100% ownership. Seabourn
remains as a separate brand. With the purchase, Carnival became a major
player in the luxury market.

THE FLEET	BUILT/RENOVATED	TONNAGE	PASSENGERS
Seabourn Legend	1991/96/2000/03	10,000	208
Seabourn Pride	1988/97/2000/03	10,000	208
Seabourn Spirit	1989/99/2000/03	10,000	208

Style   Elegant but not stuffy, glamorous but not glitzy, Seabourn ships are like tony private clubs. Quality is key, starting with a nearly effortless embarkation and a white-gloved attendant to escort you to your suite (as luxurious as the brochure promises), where fruit and champagne await you. Décor exudes understated elegance. Service—always attentive, never intrusive—is as polished as the silver with which you dine. You will be addressed by name by the staff after your first appearance.

Seabourn attracts both old-money travelers who disdain mainstream cruise ships and newly rich who appreciate the line's status symbolism. It also caters to stressed-out professionals and others seeking privacy. Whatever their background, they're affluent enough to be accustomed to a high level of service and style without excessive fuss.

Days at sea are for relaxing. Dress and atmosphere are informal, and time is unstructured. The usual announcements, pool games, and contests are absent. In fact, a Seabourn cruise is so low-key, you may need to read your daily agenda to know what's happening. Each cruise has one or two special events meant to be highlights. It might be a special concert in an unusual location for Seabourn passengers only; a visit to a private island, marina, or estate; or a sporting event. Evenings aboard ship are more formal; fine dining is the day's highlight. On evenings when you prefer to relax, a full-course dinner will be served en suite.

"As You Like It," described as the ultimate in vacation flexibility, gives passengers freedom to choose from varied options. Passengers can tailor their cruise with separate and independently priced cruise fares, air-travel options, pre- and postcruise tours, hotel, and transfers. For air, the choices are Seabourn's air program with preselected carriers, economy, business, first-class; the cruise line's independent air program, booked through Seabourn; or a chartered Gulfstream to and from the ship anywhere in the world.

Distinctive Features   Unusual care for solo passengers. Foldout water sports marina. Personalized stationery, walk-in closets, complimentary self-service laundry/dryer. Golf program. Computer learning centers. Luggage shipping. Visiting chefs.

	HIGHEST	LOWEST	AVERAGE
PER DIEM	$1,421	$416	$962

Per diems are calculated from cruise line's nondiscounted *cruise-only* fares on standard accommodations and vary by season, cabin, and cruise areas.

Rates   Tips are included; port charges are additional. Prestocked minibar in cabins; wine with meals.

Special Fares and Discounts   Advance-purchase, capacity control discounts, know as BEST (Book Early Savings Tariff) rewards early birds with up to 30% savings. Repeaters get discount of 10% or more. BEST savings offers passengers up to a 30% discount. Cruises designated on the line's calendar with "$" offer price breaks; some may be positioning voyages. For the line's other special fares, consult its brochures.

- **Third Passenger** 25% of per-person published tariff.

- **Children's Fare** Same as third person rate.

- **Single Supplement** 110–200% of per-person double-occupancy basic suite, depending on cruise

Packages

- **Air/Sea** Yes. First- and business-class upgrades at extra charge.

- **Others** Yes.

- **Pre/Post** Yes. Many basic air/sea packages include one hotel night in the departure city; extensions available in all major gateways.

Past Passengers Members receive fare reductions for accumulated days of sailing, ranging from 25% after 28 days to a free 14-day cruise after 140 days. For a second Seabourn cruise, members get free trip cancellation/interruption insurance, plus other insurance and medical coverage. Up to 30% off for early payment.

The Last Word To compete in the growing ultra-deluxe market, Seabourn widened its price range and began offering much more flexibility. The per diems on some sampler and promotional cruises are no more than those of mainstream cruises. In any year, Seabourn visits more than 300 ports in over 100 countries. Very few cruise lines can match those numbers. If you can afford the price, you're unlikely to find any finer cruising—even on your own yacht.

SEABOURN CRUISE LINE STANDARD FEATURES

Officers Norwegian.
Staff Dining/European; Cabin/Scandinavian; Cruise/British, European, and American.
Dining Facilities Two open-seating restaurants-one more formal, the other a casual indoor/outdoor café. En suite dining. Complimentary wine.
Special Diets On request, four weeks prior to sailing.
Room Service 24 hours, cabin menu and full service.
Dress Code By day, casual but conservative, comfortable. Dinner is a dressy affair, informal (jacket and tie for men) or formal (two black-tie evenings on one-week cruise; four formal dinners on two-week cruise).
Cabin Amenities Television with CNN, ESPN; financial fax service; VCR, direct-dial telephone; marble bathroom with twin sinks (one on *Legend*), tub and shower, deluxe toiletries, hair dryer, bathrobes, walk-in closet, minifridge; safe. Stocked bar. Bose Wave radio and CD player.
Electrical Outlets 110/220 AC.

SEABOURN CRUISE LINE STANDARD FEATURES (*continued*)

Wheelchair Access Four suites.

Recreation and Entertainment Three lounges with entertainment/dance music nightly; cabaret, classical music concerts, folkloric performances in ports of call; weekly dinner-dance; casino; cruise-related lectures, bridge instructor/lessons; enrichment programs.

Sports and Other Activities Water sports marina, outdoor pool, deck sports; golf program.

Beauty and Fitness Several saunas, outdoor whirlpools, small gym, exercise classes, beauty salon, spa with massage, beauty treatments.

Other Facilities Self-service laundry, laundry/dry cleaning; library; boutique; hospital; nondenominational religious services.

Children's Facilities None; children under age 18 must be accompanied by parent or adult with written permission.

Theme Cruises Golf, classical music, food and wine, others.

Smoking Public rooms are designated as nonsmoking. One lounge is smoking after dinner.

Seabourn Suggested Tipping No-tipping-expected policy.

Credit Cards For cruise payment and on-board charges: American Express, Diners Club, Discover, MasterCard, Visa.

SEABOURN LEGEND	QUALITY **9**	VALUE **C**
SEABOURN PRIDE	QUALITY **9**	VALUE **C**
SEABOURN SPIRIT	QUALITY **9**	VALUE **C**
Registry: Bahamas	Length: 439 feet	Beam: 63 feet
Cabins: 106	Draft: 16 feet	Speed: 18 knots
Maximum Passengers:	Passenger Decks: 6	Elevators: 3
208	Crew: 150	Space Ratio: 49

The Ships In this age of glitzy ships, the Seabourn triplets (they are nearly identical) are the epitome of understatement. Clean lines, fine fabrics, and subtle styling are meant to soothe. Passengers board through a lobby that instantly reveals the ships' character. Quietly elegant, the small atrium spans five decks with a double circular stairway accented by brass railings and etched glass. A glass dome above illuminates the stairs and adjacent hallways with diffused natural light. Apricot and mauve carpeting complements blush marble and wood used throughout the vessel. The sense of space and serenity is immediate and is among the ships' most appealing features.

Public rooms occupy all of the two top levels and are aft on the two center decks. The dining room is on the lowest passenger level. In 2000, all three ships were given a stem-to-stern multimillion-dollar renovations, along with the addition of French balconies to 36 suites, a computer learning center, a cigar humidor, and an expanded gym, among other improvements. Again, in 2003, the ships have been refurbished and new amenities added.

The main showroom, **Magellan Lounge** (**King Olav** on *Legend*; **Amundsen Lounge** on *Spirit*), has a stage and dance floor. It is used for daytime lectures and evening entertainment. In the lobby area are the tour desk, cruise director's office, writing room, and computer center.

One flight up is a second entertainment lounge, which is cleverly glass-partitioned in three sections: a small casino; an informal bar; and a piano lounge used for activities, socializing, daytime parties, and predinner cocktails. After dinner, it's a nightclub. There's also a small book-and-video library.

The first of the two top levels contains the sports and spa deck and indoor/outdoor **Veranda Café**. Another flight up is the **Observation Lounge,** a beautiful room with sloping floor-to-ceiling windows. Early-bird continental breakfast and afternoon tea are served here-both stellar times for ocean panoramas. Reference material on shore excursions, board games, and puzzles are available. A bar outside serves morning bouillon and is a popular gathering spot in fair weather. A promenade used by walkers and joggers connects the bar to a sunning deck.

Itineraries   See Itinerary Index.

Cabins   Accommodations—all spacious, outside suites—are among the ships' finest features. Even standard Seabourn Suites are large. Their practical design maximizes space, and appointments—wall coverings, carpets, draperies, bed covers of fine, lightly textured fabrics—enhance harmony and elegance.

They have well-defined sitting and sleeping sections. The roomy conversation area has a sofa, two chairs, and a coffee table that can be transformed into a dining table. Two cushioned stools provide extra seating for guests. The sitting area is next to a five-foot-wide picture window placed low enough that you can lie in bed and watch the passing scenery. The window has a mechanical shade operated by a switch near the desk and a device to clean the outside automatically.

Now, 36 of each ship's 106 suites have French balconies in place of the five-foot picture window. The balconies consist of two full-length sliding glass doors opening onto a narrow, Riviera-style balcony with a waist-high glass balustrade. The sliding doors can be opened to enjoy sea breezes without cutting into the interior space of the room. In the ships' tariff, these suites are designated by categories B2 and B3, and their locations are shown on deck plans.

A curtain separating the sitting and sleeping areas can be drawn to put sleepers in darkness. Beds can be configured as twins or a queen. The bedroom section has a long dresser/desk and a large, lighted mirror. A wall-mounted minifridge and bar is stocked with two bottles of spirits or wine that you select when you book. Replenishments cost extra. Mineral water and soft drinks are free. The bar contains Norwegian crystal glassware. On the opposite wall is a pull-out writing desk, containing your personalized stationery and a small sewing kit. The cabinet conceals a television with CNN, ESPN, and other stations, plus a VCR.. The latest addition were a Bose Wave stereo radio and CD player in all suites. The walk-in closet contains extra shelf space and a safe.

The marble bathroom has twin sinks (*Legend*, one sink), mirrored storage shelves, a large tub, and a shower. Thick terry robes, a hair dryer, and toiletries are supplied.

Cabin doors have a thoughtful touch: a brass clamp to hold the daily agenda, messages, and menus. A hall-side door can be used to convert adjacent standard suites into doubles.

Sixteen larger suites are in four configurations. Classic suites have queen beds only, a larger sitting area, and a small veranda. Regal suites have a separate bedroom and living room, two bathrooms (one with shower and one with tub), a table with four chairs, two walk-in closets, and two sofas. Two owner's suites are the largest and have small private verandas.

Specifications   All suites: 88 are standard Seabourn suites (90, *Legend, Spirit*), 2 classic with verandas, 4 Regal (8, *Legend, Spirit*), 4 Owner's with verandas, 36 with French balconies. Standard dimensions, 277 square feet. 102 with twins (convertible to queen); no singles. 4 wheelchair accessible.

Dining   Fine dining is central to a Seabourn cruise, and the choices are diverse. For any meal, you dine when and with whom you like in the **Restaurant** dining room or the casual **Veranda Café,** an indoor/outdoor venue for buffet breakfast, lunch, and dinner. Both offer open seating. Or dine en suite, choosing from the 24-hour cabin menu or the dining room one, served course by course. Morning bouillon is served in the **Sky Bar,** afternoon tea with cucumber sandwiches in the **Observation Lounge.**

With Seabourn, the emphasis is on fresh ingredients, such as seafood, fruits, and vegetables, obtained in ports. Breads, pastries, and ice cream are prepared onboard. Menus, changed daily and repeated on a 60-day cycle, offer three appetizers, two soups, two salads, four entrées, four desserts, cheese, and ice cream. Generally, dishes are creative and sophisticated. You will find a familiar fettuccine alfredo, but you may be tempted by seared reindeer or grilled marlin with strawberry and cilantro sauce. Vegetarian and lean specialties are available.

Menu entrées are cooked to order, and presentation is outstanding. Suggested wines are usually moderately priced; the wine list is more elaborate. Wine is available by the glass. Caviar available by request.

The Restaurant is a pretty room dressed in pastels where tables are set with Wedgwood china, fine crystal, silverware, and fresh flowers. Most tables seat four or six, but two, eight, and tens are available. Breakfast and lunch appeal most to those who prefer a quiet environment and full service. Dinner is a lavish, somewhat formal affair. Two evenings each week call for formal attire, and for all but casual nights, dress suitable for fine dining in New York or Paris is expected.

Service is unfailingly superb. In fact, service in the Restaurant is the best, most professional we have encountered on any cruise ship. Alas, the food doesn't always match it. Signature dishes at dinner are fabulous, but breakfast and lunch are uneven, and cold croissants for breakfast are a disappointment.

Unlike on other cruise ships, singles are invited to join an officer's table or one hosted by management or a social-staff member. An invitation will be slipped under your door almost daily unless you indicate that you prefer to dine alone. At least once each cruise, a dinner dance is held in the Restaurant.

The informal, convivial atmosphere of the Veranda Café makes it the most popular choice for breakfast and lunch or for dinner after a long shore excursion. In the ships' most recent refurbishing, the Café got fresh new décor and new comtemporary menus. The lively café bustles with people and conversation indoors. Outside, tables are set under protective awnings. In fair weather, the deck is one of the most delightful dining places anywhere.

The breakfast buffet offers fruit, fresh breads and pastries, smoked fish, cheeses, and eggs, pancakes, and waffles are made to order. The lunch buffet includes salads, made-to-order pasta, hot and cold seafood, chicken and meats, or grilled fish or meat on request. Hard to resist are the daily surprises: guacamole, an Asian buffet, or a cheese and dessert bar. The homemade ice cream is a passenger favorite. But these aren't your ordinary self-service buffets. An army of attentive stewards take drink orders, assist you with your plate, and bring seconds.

Normally on one evening, Veranda Café becomes a trattoria with a special menu and lively music. The meal and the evening are wonderful and very popular. Reserve early.

Seabourn is continuing its highly appreciated "Chef's Circle," a guest chefs program that brings America's most creative and celebrated chefs onboard, features their signature dishes in the Restaurant, and has them give cooking demonstrations during the cruise.

Service Most passengers rate service as the single best feature—and with good reason: It's impeccable. Shipwide, the thoroughly professional staff is gracious and attentive, but never intrusive. The Norwegian captain and officers, European hotel staff, Scandinavian stewardesses, and

British and American cruise and social staff work harmoniously and are visibly proud of their ship. The ships' small size lends them to personalized service impossible on larger ships. The luxury setting offers more opportunities to provide good service, and the high crew-to-passenger ratio enables staff to deliver it.

The ship's no-tipping policy appeared to work very well, but we've recently been told that it's being modified to allow staff to accept tips. We thought it was the result of the line's lowering its cruise prices (20% or more), but we were wrong. Gratuities are still included in the cruise price. We hope the change won't impact service.

Facilities and Activities The daily agenda isn't taxing but might include a cooking demonstration; afternoon lecture by a well-known person from the arts, academia, politics, or show business; port talks; bridge lessons or play; a session with a golf pro; art class; galley tour, wine-and-cheese party; ice cream social; or folkloric show. A movie on one of Seabourn's other cruises—and a not-too-subtle sales pitch—may be presented. Not on the schedule are bingo, horse racing, pool games, or costume parties.

The library has movie videos as well as books. The boutique beckons to shoppers. The **Computer Learning Center** with five computers offers classes daily. In the **Observation Lounge,** a humidor cabinet was installed at the rear of the room and cigar tastings are held nightly.

Or you can do nothing at all. If the weather is fair, you'll probably be out on deck, relaxing, snoozing, or soaking in the Jacuzzi. Some places offer protection in hot or cool weather.

Evening entertainment is tony, designed for sophisticated people. The ship's small orchestra plays easy listening and dance music in the **Club,** or a pianist/vocalist performs at the cocktail hour. Evening cabaret and variety shows staged in the **Magellan Lounge** are usually very good. They feature the cruise director and three or four social-staff members. Lounge seats are slightly tiered, providing excellent sight lines. A classical concert or program by a young artist may be offered, or the **Restaurant** becomes a supper club with dancing. The casino offers roulette, blackjack, slot machines, and gaming lessons.

Sports, Fitness, and Beauty Decks have ample space for sunning and a teak promenade for walking or jogging. Whirlpools and a small, deep swimming pool are in a peculiar spot near the Veranda Café—the pool is often shaded by the ship's superstructure, inhibiting swimmers.

The ships have a water-sports platform with a 30-by-30-foot steel-meshed cage that drops into the sea, creating a protected saltwater pool. A teak border provides a launch area for paddleboats, windsurfers, and sailboats. Two high-speed boats pull water-skiers or transport snorkelers and divers to choice locations. Although the ships try to use these marinas at least once a week, rough water may preclude it.

In the 2003 renovations, fitness facilities were upgraded substantially, with the gym doubled in size and more state-of-the-art equipment added, along with new cabinets and lockers. Daily stretch and exercise classes at varied workout levels, individual training, sauna, and steam rooms are available. The cruise line also recently introduced the **Spa at Seabourn,** with enhanced selections of beauty treatments and services, along with new fitness classes in yoga, Pilates, and cardio Ki Bo Circuit training.

Seabourn has changed its golf program to provide participants greater flexibility. Now offered in conjuction with Elite Golf Cruise, the new program enables them to select only one golf course to play during their cruise or to play every day if preferable, rather than buying a preset package for several golf courses. Tee times and other information are available by calling (800) 324-1106 or by logging on to **www.seabourngolf.com.** Seabourn's ships visit 90 ports around the world where passengers have access to more than 100 golf courses, including most of the major and most famous ones.

Children's Facilities Although Seabourn doesn't offer the ideal family vacation, it's a testimony to staff that three children younger than nine years old reported having the time of their lives on a recent cruise.

Shore Excursions Excursions are well organized and orchestrated by an experienced, knowledgeable staff. On a Norwegian fjord cruise, the briefing was the most thorough heard on any but expedition-type cruises accompanied by specialists. There's no push to sell excursions, and even off-the-shelf motorcoach tours tend to be pricey. Information on excursions is sent to passengers before their cruise.

Each cruise offers one or two events designated as Signature Series shore excursions. They often are a cruise highlight but may have limited space. For example, a Norwegian voyage offered a concert of Edvard Grieg's music at his lakeside home near Bergen, presented by Norway's foremost pianist and interpreter of Grieg's music.

Postscript One of Seabourn's most useful innovations has been "Personal Valet Luggage Shipping," particiularly these days considering the frequent hassle travelers encounter at airports and customs. By teaming up with DHL Worldwide Express, it enables passengers to ship their luggage directly from their home to their ship. The service prepares all the shipping and customs paperwork, picks up the luggage, maintains 24-hour online tracking, insurance, and delivers the shipment. The cost is based on weight. As an example, 30 pounds from the U.S. to Seabourn's Scandinavia/Russia cruise cost about $200.

Silversea Cruises

110 East Broward Boulevard, Ft. Lauderdale, FL 33301
(954) 522-4477; (800) 722-9955; fax (954) 522-4499
www.silversea.com

Type of Ships   Ultraluxury, all-suite, small ships.

Type of Cruises   Luxury cruises on worldwide itineraries.

Cruise Line's Strengths

- luxurious all-suite accommodations, most with verandas
- open-seating dining
- cuisine
- impeccable service
- worldwide itineraries
- congenial atmosphere
- comprehensive, all-inclusive prices

Cruise Line's Shortcomings

- somewhat staid evening activities and entertainment
- shallow draft in rough seas

Fellow Passengers   Diverse demographically, experienced cruisers. Many have made the rounds of the luxury ships. Well-traveled and outgoing, passengers range from young professionals in their 30s to lively 80-year-olds. The majority are older than 50; couples are the rule. Passengers come from throughout the United States, and Silversea has a sizable European following. A high number of passengers are repeaters.

Recommended For   Sophisticated, knowledgeable travelers who prefer a finely crafted ship and low-key atmosphere to the glitz and games of big ships; those who appreciate exacting service in casual elegance.

Not Recommended For   Those for whom subtle luxury and attention to detail are unimportant, and anyone uncomfortable among non-Americans. Late-night revelers or children.

Cruise Areas and Seasons   Africa, India, Seychelles, Madagascar, Mediterranean, Baltic, Canada, New England, Far East, China, North-

446

ern Europe, South Pacific, Amazon, South America, Caribbean; world cruise voyage, seasonally.

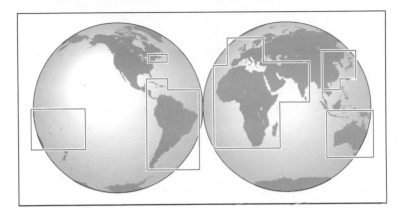

The Line   Silversea Cruises was created in the early 1990s by the Lefebvre family of Rome with the Vlasov Group of Monaco, commercial and passenger shipping families that previously owned Sitmar Cruises. The name was chosen to suggest quality, luxury, and the romance of the sea.

When the Italian-built fleet of identical twins was launched in 1995, Silversea took the luxury market by storm with reasonable pricing, uncompromising service, outstanding accommodations, and a space ratio of 55.74, among the highest of any cruise ship. The ultradeluxe, six-deck ships were substantially larger than most of their direct competitors, offering big-ship facilities and all-suite accommodations in a comfortable small-ship atmosphere. Their biggest advantage was their high number of cabins with verandas. Prices are the most comprehensive in luxury cruising and cover airfare, transfers, port taxes, travel insurance, beverage service (liquors and nonalcoholic drinks), selected wines at lunch and dinner, in-suite hors d'oeuvres and full meals, a special shoreside event on some sailings, baggage handling, gratuities, and deluxe precruise accommodations. The ratio of crew to passengers is 1 to 1.34.

Encouraged by its initial success, the line added another set of twins: *Silver Shadow* in 2000 and *Silver Whisper* in 2001. They are about a third larger and carry about a third more passengers than the line's first twins. The design is similar, but with enhancements based on passengers' comments: larger bathrooms and closets, more top-grade suites, 80% of cabins with verandas, poolside dining venue, computer center, cigar lounge, and larger spa and fitness center. The ships were built at the T. Marrotti Shipyard in Italy, where the first two ships were built. Also in 2001, the line debuted its first cruise around the world.

THE FLEET	BUILT/RENOVATED	TONNAGE	PASSENGERS
Silver Cloud	1994/2001	16,800	296
Silver Wind	1994/2003	16,800	296
Silver Shadow	2000	28,258	382
Silver Whisper	2001	28,258	382

Style   Sparkling clean, impeccably maintained, and luxurious in an understated way consistent with fine yachts, the ships offer elegance undisturbed by pretense or formality. From boarding to disembarking, passengers are attended by a crew that makes a genuine effort to know each individual and anticipate their every need. This attention is direct and friendly, but never obsequious.

Suites are exceptionally comfortable and exceed their representation in the line's brochure. Public areas are inviting and elegant. Structured activities are available, but they tend toward the relaxing and cerebral. Announcements, games, and contests are the exception rather than the rule.

At sea and in port, days are casual. Evenings are low-key but dressier. Most cruises include a "Silversea Experience" signature event—usually an excursion with dining and drinks in a beautiful setting, perhaps a private island, private club, or deserted coast.

Silversea attracts gregarious and adventuresome passengers. Although the atmosphere is social and conducive to meeting new friends, dozens of delightful nooks offer solitary time.

Distinctive Features   All-suite accommodations; comprehensive air/sea travel with personalized service at intermediate travel stops; all-inclusive prices. Silversea Experience on most sailings. Moderate single supplements. Golf program. Internet access. Personalized Voyage program.

	HIGHEST	LOWEST	AVERAGE
PER DIEM	$944	$440	$672

Per diems are calculated from cruise line's nondiscounted *cruise-only* fares on standard accommodations and vary by season, cabin, and cruise areas.

Rates   Tips, on-board beverages, including select wine and spirits, round-trip airfare with upgrades to business class available, all transfers, port charges, travel insurance, and deluxe pre-cruise accommodations are included.

Special Fares and Discounts   Early booking incentive savings range from 5–20%; they are capacity controlled and subject to availability. An additional advanced payment savings of 5% may be combined with the early booking savings when payment is made in full by specified date.

Silversea is continuing its "Silver Savings" program into 2004 and 2005 that enables passengers to save up to 50% off the cruise-only fares of Vista and Veranda suites on certain cruises. Generally, discounts are valid for some Caribbean, South America, South Pacific, Australia/New Zealand, Mediterranean, and Africa cruises and have set, pre-assigned savings on particular voyages. The Silver Savings offers are subject to availability; are valid only for new cruise bookings; and do not apply to land, hotel, and air programs.

- **Third Passenger** Approximately 50% of the Vista or Veranda Suite per-person published rate.

- **Single Supplement** 110%, 125%, 150%, 175% of per-person double-occupancy basic suite, depending on cruise.

Packages

- **Air/Sea** All cruises packaged with economy-class air; upgrades available for an additional charge, but still at special rates.

- **Pre/Post** Extensive pre- and postcruise tours. Many air/sea packages include one or more hotel nights in the departure or termination city; extensions available.

Past Passengers   Past passengers automatically become members of the Venetian Society, named to reflect the line's Italian ownership. On their second voyage, members receive a silver pin bearing the society's winged-lion emblem, a symbol of Venice. After they have sailed for 100-, 200-, and 500-plus days, they receive sapphire, emerald, and diamond pins, respectively. Members also receive a newsletter three times yearly containing information on special discounts. Other benefits include shipboard events hosted by the captain. Members get fare reductions of 5%, 10%, and 15%, combinable with early-booking incentives, advance-payment bonus, and consecutive-cruise savings. Members may bring friends in an additional suite at some savings. They also receive $250 or $500 shipboard credits and a credit to their Society account for the days their friends cruise. Members may accrue days toward a free cruise.

The Last Word   Silversea got off to a great start with its first two ships, setting exceptionally high standards for itself and the industry. Unfortunately, the second two, larger ships have not drawn the same level of praise uniformly. Nonetheless, it's hard to fault the accommodations, and not having to pay extra for beverages or worry about tipping is a big plus. Itineraries are creative, nonrepetitive, and worldwide, calling on some ports seldom visited by cruise ships. Officers and crew are actively involved in providing highly personalized service. If there are shortcomings, they are in the lack of innovative daily programs or evening entertainment that makes it worth staying up past 10:30 p.m.

Silversea Cruises remains a good value for those who can afford it, and recently, increased competition and the drop in travel worldwide have caused the cruise line to offer many of its cruises at substantially reduced rates, making them very good value for almost anyone planning to buy a cruise. Recently, too, the cruise line introduced a program entitled Personal Voyages which is being continued into 2004 and 2005. It provides prospective passengers with the flexibility and convenience to customize a cruise to suit their needs. In other words, for a minimum of five nights in a row, a passenger can cruise for as little or as long as they want.

Here's how it works: Passengers choose the length of their voyage (five nights minimum) and the embarkation and disembarkation ports from Silversea's list of approved ports of call in the Cruise Atlas or on its website (**www.silversea.com**), where there is a list of over 200 approved embarkation and debarkation ports, daily rates, and the complete terms and conditions of the program. To determine your cost, you select a suite category, then add up the daily rate for the days you plan to be onboard. You must arrange your own air transportation, but Silversea will assist you with hotel and/or transfers in select ports, as needed.

SILVERSEA CRUISES STANDARD FEATURES

Officers Italian.

Staff Dining/European; Cabin/European; Cruise/British and American.

Dining Facilities All meals served at one seating in restaurant; indoor/outdoor café for casual breakfast and lunch. Alternative dining specialty dinners on most evenings. In-suite dining.

Special Diets Available on request.

Room Service 24 hours, cabin menu and full-service dining room menu.

Dress Code Casual, informal, or formal. By day, casual but conservative; comfortable. Dinner is a more dressy. Informal (jacket, tie optional for men) or formal (two black-tie or dark suit nights on one-week cruise; four on two-week cruise).

Cabin Amenities Stocked bar, minifridge; interactive television with CNN, VCR, direct-dial telephone; marble bathroom with sink, tub, and shower, hair dryer, bathrobes, walk-in closet, safe.

Electrical Outlets 110/220 AC.

Wheelchair Access Limited.

Recreation and Entertainment Three lounges with entertainment/dance music nightly; cabaret, classical music concerts, folkloric performances in ports of call; nightly dancing; casino; cruise-related lectures. Internet access.

Sports and Other Activities Outdoor pool, deck sports; bridge instructor and lessons; enrichment programs.

Beauty and Fitness Two saunas, two outdoor whirlpools, small gym, exercise classes, beauty salon, spa with massage, beauty treatments.

Other Facilities Self-service laundry, laundry/dry cleaning; library with books and video; hospital; cigar lounge, computer center, nondenominational religious services.

Children's Facilities None; children under age 18 must be accompanied by parent or adult with written permission.

SILVERSEA CRUISES STANDARD FEATURES
(continued)

Theme Cruises Cuisine, wine, golf, music, and others.

Smoking Dining and public rooms nonsmoking except designated areas in lounges and bars.

Silversea Suggested Tipping No-tipping policy.

Credit Cards For cruise payment and on-board charges: American Express, Diners Club, MasterCard, Visa.

SILVER CLOUD / SILVER WIND	QUALITY 8	VALUE C
Registry: Bahamas	Length: 514 feet	Beam: 70 feet
Cabins: 148	Draft: 18 feet	Speed: 20.5 knots
Maximum Passengers:	Passenger Decks: 6	Elevators: 4
296	Crew: 210	Space Ratio: 56.8

The Ships Styled to soothe, the first Silversea twins are the antithesis of the huge floating hotels that dominate cruising. Elegance is anchored in simplicity, clean lines, earth-tone fabrics, and polished wood and brass.

The entry lobby surprises with its modest proportions. No six-story atrium here. The feeling is of boarding a yacht. The ship's layout is simple. On topmost Deck 9 are an observation lounge and jogging/walking track that circles the ship. It overlooks the pool and pool bar on Deck 8, which also contains the bridge, twin whirlpools, **Panorama Lounge** with indoor and outdoor seating, and the library which is open around-the-clock, unlike most other ships.

On Decks 4–7, all cabins are forward, all public areas aft. Elevators and a circular stairwell are aft of amidships. Deck 7 offers the fitness center, spa, and beauty salon and the **Terrace Café** for informal dining and breakfast and lunch buffets. Deck 6 has the main lobby, travel desk, reception desk, card and conference room, and showroom, which is large enough for small production shows but small enough to be intimate. Deck 5 has a sundries shop, casino, and the **Bar,** where the showroom audience gathers. The **Restaurant** is on Deck 4. Public areas are extensive for ships of this size. Dozens of quiet places throughout the ship invite reading or watching the water. *Silver Cloud* was completely refurbished in 2001 and additional renovations were being made before returning her to service in April 2004. *Silver Wind* had similar treatment in 2003.

Itineraries See Itinerary Index.

Cabins The spacious, all-outside suites are among the ships' signature features. Suites provide twin beds convertible to queen, walk-in closet, sitting area with loveseat, coffee table and side chairs, writing desk, dressing table with hair dryer, marble bathroom with full-size tub and shower, stocked refrigerator and cocktail bar, entertainment center with remote-controlled satellite, interactive television and VCR, and direct-dial telephone. A curtain separates the sleeping and living areas. Seventy-five percent of the suites have private, teak verandas; the remainder provide picture windows. All suites are decorated in light earth tones or pastel blues with nautical trim of polished wood and brass. Other ultradeluxe extras are fine, pure cotton bed linens and robes, down pillows, personalized stationery, fresh fruit, large umbrellas in the closets, complimentary shoeshine, and 24-hour room service.

Specifications   102 veranda suites (295 square feet); 34 vista suites (240 square feet, no veranda), 3 silver suites (541 square feet), 2 royal suites (1,031 square feet in the 2-bedroom configuration), 2 grand suites (1,314 square feet with 2 bedrooms), and 1 owner's suite (827 square feet). No singles. 2 wheelchair-accessible.

Dining   The main dining room, called the **Restaurant,** is reminiscent of an exclusive club. Tables are set with Eschenbach china, Christofle silver, linen, and Schott crystal. Draped picture windows flank the elegant room, and a domed center section adds to its spaciousness. A small marble dance floor allows for occasional dinner dances. Though formal, the Restaurant is also comfortable, relaxed, and unpretentious.

Passengers aren't assigned seating times or tables; they may eat any time during published hours. Lunch and breakfast buffets in the **Terrace Café** provide an informal option. No late-night buffet is offered. Room service is available 24 hours and is delivered with the same attention to detail characteristic of the dining room. Service is outstanding.

Carrying fewer passengers enables Silversea ships to cook dishes to order, as in a restaurant. (However, we have received complaints from some passengers that the kitchen isn't as accommodating as the line claims, or as it should be for this price, or as some competitors are.)

Silversea also provides for picky eaters, health-conscious diners, and the meat-and-potatoes set. Only the finest ingredients are used, regardless of how simple or complex the dish. Meat eaters in search of a cruise ship that can prepare a good steak, chop, or prime rib will find nirvana here. Menus offer three appetizers, a pasta, two soups, two salads, sherbet, three main courses, and usually a grilled selection. In addition are a "Light and Healthy" and a vegetarian entrée. The dessert menu is separate. Wines are included in the cruise price.

The food is excellent in quality and presentation, but for those unaccustomed to rich sauces and creams, it could be overwhelming—although you can order meals without creams or sauces. Freshness of ingredients is not a problem. One day, returning to ship aboard the tender, we were assaulted by an unexpected smell. Peering around the bulkhead, we discovered a grinning chef with a huge string of fish just purchased from local fishermen—a luxury that could never be provided on a large ship.

The casual Terrace Café high on the stern offers a commanding view of the sea. A wall of windows faces the sheltered outside dining area. Tables are always set with china, crystal, and silver. Buffet waiters take orders for drinks and hot entrées. Theme dinners take diners through eight delectable regions of Italy plus cuisine of the cruise's area. Several times each cruise, the Terrace Café offers a special multicourse meal on a reservations basis. These meals provide a change of scenery and let the chefs recreate traditional European fine dining.

Service Passenger rate service in a dead heat with accommodations as these twins' best feature. Without exception, the staff is professional and attentive, but never intrusive; friendly without being familiar; and thoroughly gracious in the European manner.

Working harmoniously, officers and crew form a highly effective and responsive team. A concierge is available for special services. These ships' size lends itself to more personalized service than larger ships can offer. There's no tipping. Period.

Facilities and Activities The next-day's programs, delivered nightly to your suite, are more mainstream than you might expect on an ultraluxury cruise, but they prove that even the pampered and sophisticated play bingo! A typical day might include an early power walk with the fitness instructor, a visit to the bridge, a lesson about computers or multimedia, aerobics, wine tasting by the sommelier, a bridge lecture; bingo, backgammon, shuffleboard competition; water volleyball; golf-putting competition; afternoon tea; team trivia; and line dancing lessons.

In conjunction with Relais & Chateaux–Relais Gourmands, Silversea has a series of culinary cruises highlighted by cooking demonstrations, gala dinners, signature dishes, and regional specialties created by master chefs from around the world.

Experts lecture on the cruise area, and a folkloric show might be staged by a local group. A morning port talk will include a sales pitch for tours. Doing nothing is an option. In fair weather, you'll probably be on deck, relaxing in a lounge chair or soaking in the Jacuzzi. There are ample places in shade or sheltered from wind. In foul weather, the library stocks books, magazines, periodicals, and videos; it's open around the clock, and sports computer terminals with Internet access. Also available are daily printed news and market-wrap reports.

In the evening, there's music for dancing before and after dinner and evening entertainment-a variety show, comedy, and magic. The ship's small orchestra plays easy listening and dance music in the **Bar,** and a pianist or vocalist duo perform in the **Panorama Lounge.** The casino offers roulette, blackjack, slot machines, and gaming lessons. Entertainment in the **Main Lounge** spotlights individual entertainers and production shows by a six-member group. All passengers can be accommodated in the steeply tiered, two-level room. Murals of sinuous women add an

Art Deco touch. Most sight lines are good. Late-night diversions consist of audience-participation games, dancing, and piano music in the Panorama Lounge.

Sports, Fitness, and Beauty   The pool deck has a large swimming pool, plentiful sunbathing space, two whirlpools, and a pool bar. Blue-and-white striped chair cushions create a nautical atmosphere. The uppermost deck has an Astroturf-carpeted promenade for walking or jogging. The modest fitness center is well equipped with life cycles, a Stairmaster, and free weights. One or more daily stretch and exercise classes for various workout levels is offered; individual training is available. Adjacent is the spa offering sauna, steam rooms, and beauty treatments and a comprehensive program of fitness, beauty, and spa treatments crafted for Silversea by Mandara Spa, an international spa specialist. It uses naturally blended treatments and Balinese techniques, incorporating its signature blend of exotic, traditional, and cutting-edge health and beauty programs, offering a wide array of treatments, including such unusual indulgences as a Hot lava rock massage and a Japanese honey steam wrap.

Children's Facilities   Children are rare on Silversea cruises, and no children's facilities or programs are offered. The occasional child receives lots of attention and generally enjoys the cruise. The nice pool and all-included drinks and snacks help.

Shore Excursions   Shore excursions are administered efficiently onboard, and the line has a good batting average with them. Silversea passengers' expectations that excursion operators will provide the same level of service they receive aboard ship may be unrealistic in some regions of the world, no matter how hard the cruise lines tries. This problem is, of course, not unique to Silversea; only that the contrast from the ship to the land operation is sometimes sharper.

Excursion sales are low-key, and some cruise directors do an excellent job of matching passengers with the tours most suited to their tastes. Even off-the-shelf motorcoach tours tend to be pricey. Passengers receive shore-excursion information before they depart.

Venetian Society cruises (about half of all) include one "Silversea Experience," a special shore excursion showcasing an area's culture. This may be a private tour or dinner in an extraordinary location. For example, the line has hosted wine tastings at private chateaux and dinner at a palace in St. Petersburg.

SILVER SHADOW	QUALITY **7**	VALUE **C**
SILVER WHISPER	QUALITY **7**	VALUE **C**
Registry: Bahamas	Length: 610 feet	Beam: 82 feet
Cabins: 194	Draft: 19.6 feet	Speed: 21 knots
Maximum Passengers:	Passenger Decks: 7	Elevators: 5
382	Crew: 295	Space Ratio: 73.9

The Ships   *Silver Shadow,* launched in 2000, was followed by her twin, *Silver Whisper,* in 2001. The noted Norwegian architectural team of Petter Yran and Bjorn Storbraaten, designers of *Silver Cloud* and *Silver Wind,* created the ships, which are slightly larger and accommodate 100 more passengers than the line's first ships. Otherwise, they are similar, more or less, to their sister ships in layout and contemporary décor. Throughout the ships, mellow wood furnishings and fine fabrics combine with marble floors and crystal chandeliers to create an elegant, stylish setting. Their passenger space ratio of 73.9 may be the highest of any cruise ship.

Silversea's hallmarks—veranda suites, single-seating dining, in suite dining, Christofle silverware, fine linens, down pillows—are found aboard the new ships. Among the new features are a casual poolside dining venue, a computer center, conference center, and cigar lounge, and a champagne bar. The ships also have an observation lounge, show lounges, boutiques, a larger spa, swimming pools and whirlpools.

Itineraries   See Itinerary Index.

Cabins   More than 80% of the suites have teak verandas. A standard Veranda Suite measures a spacious 345 square feet, including veranda. The smallest cabins measures 287 square feet. All cabins have a walk-in closet and large Italian marble bathroom with telephone, double-basin vanity, full bath and shower, and separate toilet, and are equipped with small refrigerators and cocktail bar; entertainment center with interactive television and VCR, and fresh fruit and flowers.

The largest suites range from 701 to 1,435 square feet and include the Owner's, Grand, and Royal suites in six variations. They have enlarged balconies, separate bedrooms and living rooms, large-screen televisions, and private bars. Owner's suites also have a guest powder room and CD stereo system. Larger suites are located amidships. Two Medallion suites, 501 square feet each, are extremely comfortable, with enough storage space for a family of five.

Room service, available 24 hours a day, offers a full room service menu. Passengers can order from the Restaurant's menu and have their meal served course-by-course in their staterooms. Self-service laundry facilities are available.

Specification   194 outside suites. 2 Owner's, 4 Grand, 13 Silver, 2 Medallion, 134 Veranda, 35 Vista (no veranda), and 2 wheelchair accessible cabins with verandas.

Dining   The **Restaurant,** the main dining room, has an elegant ambience with tables set with fine linens and Christofle silverware. It offers open seating and a variety of table configurations for two to six people. The popular bistro-style **Terrace Café,** with floor-to-ceiling windows opening onto panoramic views off the ship's aft deck, serves buffet breakfast and lunch, and makes a charming setting in the evening, when it is transformed into a casual alternative restaurant serving Asian, French and Italian fare. The **Grill** is a casual poolside dining venue.

The new **Le Champagne,** formerly a bar and available only for private parties, is now a top-of-the-line alternative restaurant seating about 25 for dinner. No surcharge or extra fees are charged. The restaurant, which debuted on *Silver Wind,* is now on *Silver Whisper,* and will be added to the other ships. Le Champagne, a Relais & Chateaux member, has met with passenger acclaim as a dining delight.

Facilities and Activities   In one corner of the **Terrace Café** is **Le Champagne Bar,** a elegant wine and champagne bar designed in collaboration with Moët & Chandon, the famous champagne maker, to be used for tastings and social gatherings for up to 24 guests, before- and after-dinner drinks, as well as a versatile venue for private parties. The décor of the room makes use of rich woods and warm tones and incorporates accents of Moët & Chandon's signature emblem—the crossed red ribbon which wraps the neck of each bottle of champagne; there's also a mosaic of etched glass with famous quotes about champagne from great figures in history, such as Winston Churchill and Voltaire.

Adjoining Le Champagne Bar is a cigar club, the **Humidor by Davidoff,** a Swiss-based purveyor of fine cigars and luxury merchandise. Designed in the style of a traditional English smoking club with rich wood floors and deep galley chairs, it has a walk-in humidor stocked with Davidoff products as well as a selection of Dominican, Honduran, and Cuban cigars. The lounge seats 25 and offers complimentary cognacs and cordials, along with cigars.

Of the ship's four bars, the **Casino Bar,** a small nook adjoining the casino, seems to be the most popular place. Simply furnished with a semi-circular cherry wood bar with ebony leather stools, it has two small leather sofas and modern-style halogen lamps and fixtures.

The ships have a shopping arcade, a library with books in varied languages, videos, and seven computer terminals with Internet access. Silversea is preparing to install keyboards into suites to provide in-room Internet access as well.

Service   The ships' size apparently makes a difference with service. They do not have as high a crew-to-passenger ratio as the smaller twins and can not deliver the same level of service. The shortcomings have been particularly noticeable to those familiar with Silversea's smaller ships on which its reputation was made.

Sports, Fitness, and Beauty   The ships have large health clubs and spas which occupy most of Deck 10 and are operated by Mandara Spa, specializing in Asian-type treatments. Decorated in a soothing combination of aqua and blue tiles and blonde carpets, the facility has a beauty salon and an aerobic and fitness center with weights, treadmills, stationary bikes and other equipment. There are separate steam rooms, saunas and changing facilities for men and women. The ships also have a heated outdoor pool and two whirlpools.

Postscript *Silver Shadow* and *Silver Whisper* are bigger—almost 70% larger—than their predecessors, but they may be proving that bigger is not necessarily better. Some passengers like the spaciousness and new facilities that the larger size provides; others prefer the more intimate experience that the smaller ships offer. Still, the new ships carry an enormous number of repeat passengers, and during the last two to three days of a cruise, many pasengers are seen in front of the Concierge desk waiting to book their next voyage.

Star Clippers, Inc.

4101 Salzedo Avenue, Coral Gables, FL 33146
(800) 442-0551; (305) 442-0550; fax (305) 442-1611
www.starclippers.com

Type of Ships   Replicas of 19th-century clipper sailing ships.

Type of Cruises   Casual, active, sports-oriented, sailing under canvas to out-of-the-way places.

Cruise Line's Strengths

- traditional sailing with some cruise ship comforts
- camaraderie
- ship size/maneuverability
- itineraries

Cruise Line's Shortcomings

- meager port information
- potential language/cultural collisions among passengers
- small cabins

Fellow Passengers   International mix. About half are American, Canadian, and Latin American; the other half are European, particularly Germans, including non-English speakers. The average age is 45, but some cruises have 20- and 30-year-olds. The majority are couples, usually including about a dozen newlyweds.

As many as 50% may be repeaters, attracted by sailing on a square rigger. Many appreciate the beauty and authenticity of the clipper ships and have no interest in nightclubs, casinos, and glitter aboard mainstream cruise ships, which they probably have shunned.

Recommended For   Independent, active travelers who seek light adventure and off-the-beaten-track itineraries, small-ship devotees, stressed-out urbanites, honeymooners and romantics captivated by the notion of sailing on a tall ship. Also, avid sailors, water sports enthusiasts, experienced cruisers weary of crowded large ships, and conservationists who appreciate environmentally friendly travel aboard ships that use their engines only when necessary. It's a great experience for children ages 7 and older who mix well with adults.

Not Recommended For Those seeking gourmet cuisine, pampering, around-the-clock activity, and resort facilities of a superliner. Physically impaired travelers.

Cruise Areas and Seasons Caribbean, South Asia, winter; Mediterranean, summer; transatlantic, trans–Indian Ocean, April and October.

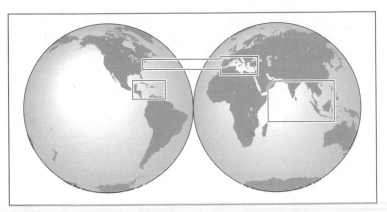

The Line Launched in 1991, Star Clippers is the dream come true of Swedish shipping entrepreneur Mikael Krafft, whose passion for sailing and building yachts and love of the clipper ship (one of America's greatest inventions, he says) led him to create an unusual cruise line with replicas of the sleek, mid–19th-century trading ships. Called greyhounds of the sea, they were the fastest ships afloat until the arrival of the steam age in the late 1860s.

About 100 feet longer than the original clippers and equipped with the latest marine technology, these clippers combine the romance of yesteryear's sailing with some modern amenities. They offer the excitement of manning an authentic square rigger and cruising out-of-the-way waters of the Caribbean, Mediterranean, or South Asia.

The success of Star Clippers's twins lead the line to build a third ship, which is reported to be the world's largest sailing vessel. She entered service in July 2000.

THE FLEET	BUILT/RENOVATED	TONNAGE	PASSENGERS
Star Clipper	1991	2,298	170
Star Flyer	1992	2,298	170
Royal Clipper	2000	5,000	227

Style Cruises have the freewheeling spirit of a private yacht and are intended to fit between budget-priced Windjammer Barefoot Cruises and pricey Windstar Cruises. They're designed for active, healthy folks who want their travel to be interesting, educational, and fun. Daytime dress is very casual (shorts and deck shoes); evenings are only a bit dressier. Cabins are average size and public rooms few, but the teak decks are roomy. Cruises offer island-hopping in a laid-back atmosphere with varied options at each port of call. The clippers can anchor in bays where large cruise ships cannot go. Launches take passengers to isolated beaches and places for scuba diving, snorkeling, and other water sports.

After a week's cruise, you will know on a first-name basis many passengers and most of the crew, who are both deck hands and sports instructors. You can help hoist the sails or laze about on deck watching the canvas and the sea. Itineraries ensure daylight cruising under sail. The environment is great for families with children ages 7 and up.

In 2003, the cruise line offered its first theme cruises on selected Caribbean itineraries which are being repeated in 2004. "Health & Wellbeing" provides for talks on weight management and healthy eating and a "healthy choice" selection on the menu of each meal, and other lectures concern managing stress and related matters. There are exercises and yoga onboard and excursions on foot or bike on shore. "Caribbean Discovery" introduces passengers to a Caribbean that most never know, with music, culture, and food of the region in focus. "Jazz & Blues" features music, dance, aerobic classes, jam sessions, and more to the tunes of Louis Armstrong, Ella Fitzgerald, and other jazz greats.

Its new promotion is even more exciting. For almost all departures of the *Star Flyer* from January to March 2004, Star Clipper Cruises has a great new 11-night Far East land/sea cruise. It includes seven nights aboard *Star Flyer,* plus four nights free hotel accommodations at the four-star Montien Hotel in Bangkok. The cruise-only prices start at $1,345 per person, based on double occupancy. The cruise lines will provide round-trip economy airfare from Los Angeles or San Francisco to Bangkok and continuing on to Phuket for only $595 per person—a savings of $600 per person over the normal add-on air charge. Rates from New York to Bangkok/Phuket are $945 per person; discounts are available from other gateway cities. Dates and itineraries for both the Caribbean theme cruises and the Asian special are available from Star Clippers.

Distinctive Features   The ship and helping sail it. Captain's daily briefings. PADI certification.

	HIGHEST	LOWEST	AVERAGE
PER DIEM	$399	$85	$212

Per diems are calculated from cruise line's nondiscounted *cruise-only* fares on standard accommodations and vary by season, cabin, and cruise areas.

Rates   Port charges are additional.

Special Fares and Discounts   10% discount on published rates for booking 120 days in advance on selected cruises.

- **Single Fare** Guaranteed rate, depending on season, with cabin assigned two weeks before departure.

- **Single Supplement** 150% for categories 2–6 (selected seasons) of published fare. 200% for highest-category cabins, deluxe suites and owners suites.

Packages

- **Air/Sea** Yes.

- **Others** Honeymoon.

- **Pre/Post** Yes.

Past Passengers   Membership cards for the Past Passengers Club are sent after your first voyage. Members receive special discounts and a bottle of champagne in their cabins on boarding and are placed on the ship's VIP list.

The Last Word   Star Clippers provides an unusual experience on unique ships that are modern and comfortable, yet steeped in tradition. More affordable than Sea Cloud and more upscale than Windjammers, Star Clippers's ships are more authentic than those of Windstar. Yet, they definitely aren't for everyone.

The ships cannot readily accommodate disabled passengers and aren't for people who want mainstream cruising's comforts and options. English is the ships' language, but announcements are likely in other languages, depending on passenger makeup.

Language can become a problem when English speakers are outnumbered by non-Anglophones, and some may feel left out of activities.

STAR CLIPPERS STANDARD FEATURES

Officers European.

Staff Dining, Cabin/International; Cruise/Swedish, Australian, and Hungarian.

Dining Facilities One dining room for three meals with open, unassigned seating. Light breakfast, occasional buffet lunch, hors d'oeuvres on deck at 5 p.m.

Special Diets Inquire in advance. Vegetarian, low-calorie standard on menus.

Room Service None.

Dress Code Relaxed and casual. Walking shorts, bathing attire with cover-up, skirts, slacks for daytime; slacks with polo or casual shirts, no jackets required for men in evening.

Cabin Amenities Radio, hair dryer, safe, cellular-satellite phone; movies, ports of call videos, and music; bathrooms with showers; upper category with whirlpool bath and minifridge.

STAR CLIPPERS STANDARD FEATURES *(continued)*

Electrical Outlets   *Star Clipper/Flyer*, 110 AC; *Royal Clipper*, 220 AC, American adapter needed.

Wheelchair Access   None.

Recreation and Entertainment   Piano bar with entertainer, outdoor deck bar for dancing and local entertainment, library/writing room, backgammon, and bridge.

Sports and Other Activities   Two outdoor pools; water sports and equipment; sailing dinghies, windsurfers, water-skiing, underwater viewing craft, waterjet launches, and inflatables carried onboard. Learn-to-sail and dive programs.

Beauty and Fitness   No beauty/barber service on *Star Clipper/Flyer*; spa, hair salon, gym on *Royal Clipper*. Exercise sessions.

Other Facilities   Dining room doubles as conference room with audiovisual equipment. Nurse on seven-day cruises; doctor and nurse on transatlantic. Ship's officers trained in emergency medicine.

Children's Facilities   None; younger than age 18 must be accompanied by adult.

Theme Cruises   On Caribbean cruises, three themes: Health and Well-being, Caribbean Discovery, and Jazz & Blues.

Smoking   No smoking in cabins. At first briefing, captain emphasizes that smoking is allowed on deck or in rear of dining room.

Star Clippers Suggested Tipping   Per person per day: cabin steward $3.50; waiter and busboy, $5; 15% added to bar bills.

Credit Cards   For cruise payment and on-board charges: American Express, MasterCard, and Visa.

STAR CLIPPER / STAR FLYER	**QUALITY 7**	**VALUE A**
Registry: Luxembourg	Length: 360 feet	Beam: 50 feet
Cabins: 85	Draft: 18.5 feet	Speed: 17 knots
Maximum Passengers:	Passenger Decks: 4	Elevators: None
170	Crew: 72	Space Ratio: 15

The Ships   *Star Clipper* and *Star Flyer* are identical, with four masts and square-rigged sails on the forward mast—a barquentine configuration—with a total of 16 sails (36,000 square feet of Dacron). They are manned, not computerized, and are capable of attaining speeds up to 19 knots. A diesel engine is in reserve for calms and maneuvering in harbors.

At 226 feet, they are among the tallest ships and the first true sailing vessels to be classified by Lloyd's Register of Shipping since 1911. Built in Belgium, they comply with the latest safety regulations for passenger vessels on worldwide service.

The ships have four passenger decks; all but eight cabins are on the lower two. Public spaces, which were recently refurbished, are on the top two. There, amid sails and rigging, every Walter Mitty begins to salivate with anticipation. They can help hoist the sails or watch in wonder. The ships are generally under sail from late evening to the following mid-morning. Under normal conditions, they use the engine only to maneuver in port. For true salts and romantics, balmy tropical air filling the white sails against a star-filled sky is the essence of bliss. Many stay up half the night savoring it.

Itineraries   See Itinerary Index.

Cabins   Small but comfortable, cabins are carpeted, air conditioned, and tastefully furnished with a counter/desk and built-in seat, large mirror, wood paneling, brass lamps, and prints of sailing scenes. Two portholes admit light. Under-bed storage holds luggage or scuba gear, and closet and drawer space is adequate for informal cruising.

Most cabins are outside and have twin beds convertible to a double. They have multichannel radio, phone, hair dryer, safe, ceiling-mounted television/video monitor (videotapes are available from the library in English and German), and 24-hour news prepared in British English, American English, Canadian English, and German. Each version includes news of interest to that group.

Bathrooms are very small. They have marble-trimmed fixtures and showers. Eight top-category cabins have whirlpool bathtubs, hair dryers, and minifridges stocked at cruise's start (occupants pay for restocks). These cabins open onto the deck; some people may feel that decreases their privacy. Cabin service is limited to cleaning. Inside cabins are sold only when the ship is full. Aft cabins on lower decks are the least desirable due to engine noise.

Specifications   6 inside cabins, 79 outside; no suites. Standard dimensions, 120 square feet. 66 cabins with 2 lower beds (convertible to queen); 18 cabins with fixed double beds; 8 cabins accommodate third passenger; 4 inside cabins have uppers and lowers; no singles.

Dining   **Clipper Dining Room,** resplendent with shining brass and etched glass, is rather formal for such an informal ship. Seating is at tables for six among or around a forest of columns, and banquettes along the walls by portholes. All passengers and officers are accommodated at one open seating. When the ship is full, the room is crowded.

The buffet breakfast has made-to-order omelets; lunch has a different pasta daily and a self-service salad bar. A light, early-morning breakfast and occasional lunch buffet are also served on deck.

Dinner selections include beef, chicken, and fish; vegetables; cheeses; and desserts. The food is plentiful but appeals mostly to those with minimal interest in epicurean delights. During a week, food can range from adequate to good, but not gourmet. The menu emphasizes fresh ingredients, fruit, salads, vegetables, and seafood. Wines are available at reasonable prices.

Service Officers and deck crew are friendly, energetic, and easygoing. They mix freely and easily with passengers, helping create the ship's relaxed atmosphere. The dining and hotel staff is low-key and congenial. An easy camaraderie between officers, staff, and passengers is one of the ships' appeal.

Facilities and Activities Passengers might be found playing backgammon or bridge. The teak-paneled library/writing room resembles an English club, with large brass-framed windows, paintings of nautical scenes, and a nonworking fireplace (snuffed by the U.S. Coast Guard). Furnished with card tables and comfortable chairs, it's a reception desk at boarding and a small meeting room. A good selection of popular fiction, travel, and coffee-table books is stocked. A tiny shop sells film and souvenirs. The dining room converts to a meeting room with screen projectors and video monitors for port lectures. The captain and cruise director hold "story time," an informal briefing, on deck in late afternoon or the morning before arriving in port. Passengers congregate around the open bridge, where they can hear the captain and his mates at work and watch the sails being raised and lowered. Many lend a hand with the rigging, but few hang in for the full cruise.

A small, U-shaped piano lounge wraps the landing of the stairway between the main deck and dining room. It has brass-framed panoramic windows and small tables with cushioned banquettes that seat about two dozen people. The skylight overhead is actually the transparent bottom of a pool on the sun deck. A pianist or vocalist entertains before and after dinner. Swinging doors connect to the outdoor **Tropical Bar.** Depending on the hour, it's a social center, meeting area, stage (where the captain speaks daily), spot for light breakfast or buffet lunch, or dance floor (taped music or electronic keyboard). There's no casino.

Sports, Fitness, and Beauty There are two tiny outdoor pools, one filled with fresh water and one with sea water. Beginning scuba lessons are offered at the forward pool.

Exercisers can walk from the stern to the bow around the open parts of the main and sun decks. At 8 a.m. daily, one of the water sports teams leads a half-hour aerobics session.

In the Caribbean and South Asia, water sports are a more important element of the cruise than in the Mediterranean. The ships carry sailing dinghies, windsurfers, underwater viewing craft, boats for water-skiing and skis, snorkel gear (issued for cruise duration), scuba equipment for certified divers, volleyballs, and oversized, solid-surface kadima paddles for beach sports. The ships might anchor in a remote cove or off a deserted beach and shuttle passengers to and from shore for snorkeling, sailing, windsurfing, and swimming.

The sports and recreational staff includes multilingual instructors. Snorkeling is organized almost daily in the Caribbean. Certified divers with C cards can join trips to reefs and underwater wrecks. A charge of $52 for a day-time dive or $60 for a night-time dive covers air tank refill, personal supervision, and transport by Zodiac.

Two dive programs are available: A PADI refresher course costs $75, for those whose certification has lapsed within the past year; and a full PADI certification course costing $415. For the latter, the line requires divers spread the course over a two-week cruise.

Shore Excursions   Guided tours (usually $25–$85) focus on a destination's architectural, historical, and environmental points of interest and are likely to be more interesting than those offered by mainstream ships. Fewer passengers and unusual itineraries help ensure more stimulating, personalized tours for participants.

The ships tie up in port as seldom as possible. Patented stabilizing tanks keep the ship steady at anchor. Tender service is offered every half-hour until sailing time, usually around 6 p.m.

ROYAL CLIPPER	QUALITY **9**	VALUE **A**
Registry: Luxembourg	Length: 439 feet	Beam: 54 feet
Cabins: 114	Draft: 18.5 feet	Speed: 20 knots
Maximum Passengers:	Passenger Decks: 5	Elevators: None
227	Crew: 106	Space Ratio: NA

The Ship   *Royal Clipper* made her debut in 2000 as the world's longest, largest sailing vessel ever built. Her gross tonnage of about 5,000 tons is more than twice that of *Star Clipper* or *Star Flyer*. Her appearance contrasts sharply with her running mates, which resemble large, white-hull racing yachts. *Royal Clipper* is a full-rigged ship, with square sails on all five masts; the earlier four masters are barquentine-rigged. *Royal Clipper* carries 56,000 square feet of Dacron sail, compared to 36,000 square feet on each of the small twins.

The vessel's interior, created by noted megayacht interior designer Donald Starkey of London, is more upscale than her sisters and has many new features. One of her three outdoor swimming pools—an oval, center pool—has a glass bottom, which allows light into the three-deck atrium below. A circular staircase links the atrium with lounges, cabins, and public rooms. **Captain Nemo's Lounge,** on the lowest passenger deck, has 16-inch portholes looking out on marine life day and night.

On the Main Deck below the bridge is an observation lounge with wraparound windows; it is used for meetings, informal talks, and Internet connections. The main deck also has the purser's office, a large piano lounge, an indoor/outdoor bar, and library.

The main lounge, located amidships, is as comfortable as they come with banquette, soft couch, and chair seating. It has a sit-up bar and a central well that look down into the dining room two decks below. Leaving via the aft doors, the covered **Tropical Bar** recalls the earlier *Star Clipper* pair; so too, does the paneled Edwardian library, though aboard *Royal Clipper* both rooms are on a much larger scale.

When there is no wind, the twin Caterpillar 2,500-horsepower diesel engines can drive the ship at up to 14 knots. When maneuvering in and out of port, the captain may put up most of the sails, then use a very quiet generator to turn the ship and drive it forward to leave the harbor.

Itineraries   See Itinerary Index.

Cabins   Standard cabins, each with 148 square feet, are 35% larger than those on sister ships; 26 have a third fold-down bed. There are two deck cabins of 125 square feet and six inside cabins of 100 square feet. The cabins are furnished in much the same style and vary mostly by location. They have marble bathrooms with shower, television, satellite telephone, radio channels, private safe and hair dryers.

The outstanding deluxe suites are located along a narrow central mahogany-paneled companionway with a thick sloping mast penetrating the corridor at the forward end. These luxurious cabins, measuring 255 square feet, are mahogany-paneled with rosewood framing and molding against an off-white ceiling and upper portion walls. Pale gold-framed mirrors enlarge the space, and brass-framed windows bring in light to bathe the far corner sitting alcove. Brass wall lamps and sailing ship prints round out the feel of an upward sloping ship's cabin, not a hotel-style room on a hull. One door opens to a huge marble bathroom with Jacuzzi bath—a nod to upscale cruise ship amenities. Another heavy wooden door leads to a private teak veranda with shrouds passing upward from the ship's side.

The two owner's suites at the stern are even larger at 320 square feet and have a private entrance and butler service. There are also two 175-square-foot deluxe cabins that open onto the after deck.

Specifications   114 cabins. 6 inside (double bed); 90 outside (all but 4 have two lowers, convertible to doubles; 27 convertible to triples); 2 owner's suites; 14 deck suites with verandas; 2 deck suites.

Dining   The handsome bilevel dining room accommodates all passengers at a single seating for all meals. The paneled room with brass wall lamps has rectangular, round, and banquette-style tables and is set low enough that in any kind of sea, the water splashes in washing machine fashion over the portholes.

An omelet chef cooks to order at breakfast and a carvery features roast beef, ham, and pork at lunch. The lunch buffets are the biggest hits on the menu for the first day at sea, providing jumbo shrimp, foie gras, artichoke hearts, herring, potato salad, lots of salad fixings, hot and cold salmon, meatballs, and sliced roast beef.

Service The international crew provides friendly service, though the pace can be slow at dinner when passengers order from the menu.

Sport, Fitness, and Beauty At least once during the cruise, passengers with a Walter Mitty fantasy may climb (wearing safety belts) the steel mast to a crows nest, 60 feet above the deck. They may also climb out on the netting that cascades from the bow sprit. Although passengers do not handle the sails as on Windjammers, they can enjoy being part of the navigation by collecting with the helmsmen on a raised platform above the bridge and chart room. They can also take lessons in sailing and rope tying.

The lower deck has an exercise room, spa, tiled Turkish bath, and beauty salon. A hydraulic platform stages the water sport activities, which include banana boats, water-skiing, diving, snorkeling and swimming from the 16-foot inflatable raft. An interior stairway gives access to the marina. Two 60-passenger tenders, resembling military landing craft, take passengers for beach landings. Two 150-passenger fiberglass tenders ferry passengers between the anchored ship and pier.

Postscript The ship has no special facilities for children, but when they are aboard, they are looked after well by the crew and staff, and there is much for them to observe, learn, and enjoy.

Although the overall experience and attraction of *Royal Clipper* is similar to the smaller clippers, comparisons are difficult. *Royal Clipper* is truly different. Her size, her 42 sails, the sheer amount of deck equipment, and her lavish Edwardian interiors are a sharp contrast to the smaller-scale, relatively simple, sleek sisters. As one passenger saw it, "For an ocean crossing, I would want the full-rigged *Royal Clipper;* for sailing the Caribbean or Mediterranean, I would be happy with either."

Windstar Cruises

300 Elliott Avenue West, Seattle, WA 98119
(206) 281-3535; (800) 258-7245; fax (206) 281-7110
www.windstarcruises.com

Type of Ships Deluxe sailing yacht/cruise ships.

Type of Cruises Low-key, laid-back, yet luxurious, for active, affluent travelers with cosmopolitan tastes for offbeat corners in sunny climes.

Cruise Line's Strengths

- appealing lifestyle
- private yacht exclusivity on small ships
- cabins
- romantic escape
- water sports

Cruise Line's Shortcomings

- evening activity
- port-intensive itineraries with minimal time under canvas

Fellow Passengers The mix is broader than generally perceived. Not all drive BMWs and Porsches: 40% have Jeeps and Fords, and 77% of those are the family version rather than sports model. Passengers range from 20 to 80 years in age, but the majority are 35–65 years old and the median age is 50. Incomes differ, and they might be first-time or experienced cruisers. Despite many differences, they share one aspect in common—a lifestyle preference, even if they cannot enjoy it 365 days of the year. Passengers are likely to be well traveled; from the United States, Europe, and Latin America; and about 75% are professionals—lawyers, doctors, business executives—and probably work in high-pressure jobs. The remainder are apt to be retirees from similar pressure cookers, plus a few honeymooners. They are active and enjoy individual and low-energy sports, such as golfing, walking, and swimming.

Recommended For Active, affluent, Type-A individualists, 25–75 years old, who really mean it when they say they want to chill out; those who abhor mainstream cruising; divers and others who enjoy water sports; experienced cruisers looking for something different; those attracted by the romance of sailing ships who want upscale luxury.

Not Recommended For   Anyone who prefers large ships, thrives on nightlife, or enjoys wearing fancy clothes; those who need to be entertained, don't relate to a sophisticated ambience; those who prefer a burger to brûlée.

Cruise Areas and Seasons   Caribbean, Tahiti, year-round;Bahamas, winter; Mediterranean, spring-fall; Baltic/Northern Europe, summer, transatlantic, April and October.

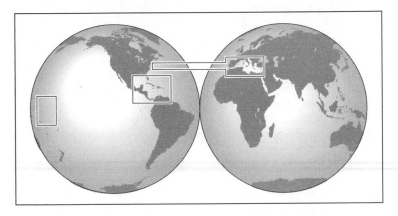

The Line   Four masts in a row, each with enormous triangular sails and as tall as a 20-story building, tower above a deck one and a half times the length of a football field and half its width. The great sails are manned by computers designed to monitor the direction and velocity of the wind to keep the ship from heeling more than 40°. The sails can be furled in less than two minutes.

These ships are windcruisers, which on their introduction in 1985 were called the most revolutionary vessels since the introduction of the steamship. The vessels use wind power alone up to 50% of the time at sea, depending on itinerary; electrical power and back-up propulsion are provided by diesel-electric engines. The ships marry the romance and tradition of sailing with the comfort and amenities of a cruise ship. Their all-outside cabins are larger, better designed, and better appointed than most standard cabins on mainstream cruise ships. The French-built vessels' shallow draft enables them to call at less-visited ports, private marinas, and secluded beaches.

Windstar Cruises was acquired by Holland America Line in 1987, and the next year both companies were purchased by Carnival Cruise Lines. Windstar continues to operate as a separate entity. In 1997, Windstar bought the five-masted *Club Med 1*, a larger version of the Windstar ships, and after remodeling, renamed her *Wind Surf.*

THE FLEET	BUILT/RENOVATED	TONNAGE	PASSENGERS
Wind Spirit	1988	5,350	148
Wind Star	1986	5,350	148
Wind Surf	1990/98/2000/01	14,745	308

Style   Laid-back, romantic, and informal, the cruises combine the atmosphere of a private yacht with the amenities and services of a cruise ship. From the outset, the ships have offered exclusivity because of their size, ambience, and the people they attract: upscale professionals who can afford a luxury cruise but want a less-structured environment and more unusual vacation than is available on traditional cruises.

The ships are wonderfully quiet under sail; you can hear the ocean wash the hull and the sails snap as wind fills them. Passengers visit the open bridge to see how everything works. The captains—their hands never far from the wheel—usually give eager passengers a few minutes at the helm.

There's a casual elegance and easygoing informality about the ship and its occupants. Regardless of age, passengers seem to blend easily; by week's end, they're good friends. Pressure to keep a schedule is nonexistent. You decide how to spend your day. Even ardent Type-A personalities can unwind.

Distinctive Features   The ship. Water sports platform; use of most sports gear free. A passenger lucky enough to hook a fish on a deep-sea outing can have it cooked by the chef.

	HIGHEST	LOWEST	AVERAGE
PER DIEM	$668	$336	$503

Per diems are calculated from cruise line's nondiscounted *cruise-only* fares on standard accommodations and vary by season, cabin, and cruise areas.

Rates   Port charges and tips are included.

Special Fares and Discounts   Booking six months in advance saves up to 50%. Windstar frequently offers two-for-one promotions. Other discounts are on a quarterly basis.

- **Single Supplement** 175% of the published per-person rate.

Packages

- **Air/Sea** Yes. Packages are available for Tahiti and some European cruises.
- **Others** Yes.
- **Pre/Post** Yes.

Past Passengers   The Foremast Club is open to all who take a Windstar cruise. They receive a quarterly newsletter, e-mails, and other literature highlighting new itineraries and special discounts, including alumni savings on select cruises.

The Last Word On our first Windstar cruise, having expected passengers on the level of royalty, the ones who seemed to be enjoying themselves most were a blue-collar couple from Massachusetts on their second honeymoon—and first cruise. A Windstar cruise is a relaxing, romantic escape, but the perception more than the reality seems to put it out of reach in price and ambience for most people. Although it's definitely a way to impress your friends, deciding whether this cruise is for you shouldn't be based on price (although you get a lot for your money), but on the type of cruise it offers. Those who relate to it think it's heaven; those who don't would probably be bored.

Our only complaint is that Windstar's itineraries are so port-intensive they leave little time for passengers to enjoy the ships, particularly under sail. Windstar recently added a day at sea to some Mediterranean cruises. We think two would have been better.

Windstar, like her sister company, Holland America Line, has a "no-tipping-required" policy. It supposedly means staff cannot solicit tips but can accept them. We think that's confusing, especially to first-time cruisers who already worry excessively about tipping. Further, tipping should never be "required." Period. It should be a passenger's prerogative. So, why does Windstar pretend? If they want passengers to tip, they should say so.

WINDSTAR CRUISES STANDARD FEATURES

Officers British

Staff Dining, Cabin/Indonesian and Filipino; Cruise/American, British, some European.

Dining Facilities One open-seating restaurant; indoor/outdoor café for breakfast and lunch buffet featuring traditional and tropical specialties; occasional barbecues on the beach. *Wind Surf,* lunch, dinner in Bistro.

Special Diets Sail Light menus with low-calorie, heart-smart, and vegetarian selections. Advance notice requested for others.

Room Service 24 hours.

Dress Code Casual and elegantly casual.

Cabin Amenities Color television, VCR, CD player, three-channel radio; international direct-dial telephone; safe; minibar and refrigerator; hair dryer and terry robe.

Electrical Outlets 110 AC (220 *Wind Surf*).

Wheelchair Access None. Seeing-eye dogs have been permitted.

Recreation and Entertainment Piano bar, casino, lounge with local musicians or ship's band, library, videocassette/CD library.

Sports and Other Activities Water sports platform for sailboats, windsurfers, motorized inflatables, water-skiing, scuba diving; snorkeling equipment carried onboard; saltwater pool. Charge for diving.

Beauty and Fitness Beauty salon; hot tub/Jacuzzi, sauna, masseuse, fitness room with weight-training equipment. Spa on *Wind Surf.*

Other Facilities Laundry; doctor, infirmary, e-mail/Internet access.

WINDSTAR CRUISES STANDARD FEATURES
(continued)

Children's Facilities   None. Children's videos.

Theme Cruises   Wine, culinary, life-enrichment on some repositioning cruises, which are packaged with airfare and pre-/postcruise hotel packages.

Smoking   Allowed in designated areas, but not in dining room.

Windstar Suggested Tipping   Tipping-not-required policy.

Credit Cards   For cruise payment and on-board charges: American Express, Discover, MasterCard, Visa, travelers checks.

WIND SPIRIT	QUALITY 9	VALUE C
WIND STAR	QUALITY 9	VALUE C

Registry: Bahamas	Length: 440 feet	Beam: 64 feet
Cabins: 74	Draft: 13.5 feet	Speed: 8–12 knots
Maximum Passengers:	Passenger Decks: 4	Elevators: None
148	Crew: 81/91	Space Ratio: 36

The Ships   The ships are identical inside and out. If not for their itineraries, they would be difficult to tell apart. Throughout, the tasteful appointments are well-designed and inviting. They have the feel of a sailing ship—wood and leather, portholes, and nautical blue and white—yet they're modern, with expanses of windows creating spaciousness and space-station-white walls adorned with contemporary art.

Because the number of passengers is small, boarding is speedy. You're greeted with a glass of champagne or chilled fruit drink and escorted to the main lounge to complete paperwork. Then, you're escorted to your cabin, where your luggage should be waiting.

The cabins, gym, and sauna are on the bottom two of four passenger decks. The third deck contains a main lounge and dining salon—both handsome. Through a lounge skylight, passengers have dramatic views of the majestic sails overhead. You'll also find a tiny casino, boutique, and beauty salon. The top deck offers a pool, bar, and veranda lounge.

Itineraries   See Itinerary Index.

Cabins   With the exception of the owner's suite, cabins are identical: large and outside. Larger than those on mainstream cruise ships, these well-designed, nicely appointed cabins make optimum use of space and are fitted with twin beds or a queen-size bed.

The marriage of tradition and technology is apparent in cabins. Each has twin portholes with brass fittings and wood cabinetwork, including a foldout vanity with makeup mirror. Modern amenities include remote-control television, VCR, international direct-dial telephone, CD player, safe, and minibar stocked daily with beer, wine, spirits, and soft drinks.

Note that drinks are expensive. A beer, for example, costs $5. However, Windstar offers several beverage packages: per person, per day, non-alcoholic, $18; all-inclusive, $45; and others.

Bathrooms have showers, teak decking, well-lighted mirrors, hair dryers, terry robes, and adequate storage.

Specifications 74 outside cabins; 1 suite with queen-size bed. Standard dimensions, 185 square feet. 73 with twin beds (convertible to queen); 11 (20 on *Wind Star*) with third berths; there are no singles and none wheelchair-accessible.

Dining The teak-lined dining room—nautical in design with rope-wrapped pillars—has low ceilings and subdued lighting, giving it an intimate atmosphere. Seating is open, restaurant-style. Cuisine continues to be uneven, ranging from super to ordinary. Generally, the smaller ships get better reviews.

Menus by celebrity chef Joachim Splichal of Patrina and Pinot Bistro in Los Angeles, whose French cooking incorporates light California style, match Windstar's casual style of cruising. The line serves California wines to complement the cuisine; tastings are offered. "Sail Light" menus by Jeanne Jones, who developed the spa menus for Canyon Ranch and the Pritiken Center, are also available.

Coffee, tea, juices, and breakfast rolls are served poolside for early risers. Breakfast in the glass-enclosed veranda offers tropical fruits and freshly baked breads. Afternoon tea on the pool deck with pastries and finger sandwiches is popular. Room service is available 24 hours a day. In the Caribbean, a highlight is the pool deck barbecue, serving grilled lobster tails, shrimp, and other seafood accompanied by local music.

Service The captain and European officers are affable, accessible, and visible, inviting passengers to watch the ship in operation, visiting with them, and participating in activities when possible. They welcome questions. Cabin staff and most restaurant personnel are Indonesian; deck stewards, bar personnel, and section captains are Filipino. All get very high marks.

Facilities and Activities Windstar ships don't have scheduled daily activities. You set your own schedule and make your own activities, independently or with new friends. That's what this cruise is all about. Days are passed sunbathing, reading, deep-sea fishing, swimming, and watching the ship's operation. (Readers should bring their books; selection aboard is limited.) Ship's television features two current movies daily, plus satellite news around the clock.

Nightlife is low-key and minimal. The tiny casino has blackjack tables, a Caribbean stud poker table, and slot machines. An easy-listening trio plays nightly for dancing in the lounge. Topside, rock videos play in the disco. You also can watch a movie in your cabin; a selection of videos is available at the reception desk. A Caribbean night showcases a reggae band, and passengers young and old dance on the pool deck.

Sports, Fitness, and Beauty　Water sports from the ships' foldout platform more than compensates for the absence of on-board sports. Furthermore, the ships' shallow draft enables them to stop at less-visited ports and secluded beaches and coves. On Caribbean more than Mediterranean cruises, water sports are a main attraction. Carried aboard are sailboats, windsurf boards, snorkeling and diving equipment (including tanks), and Zodiacs (inflatable boats) to take passengers snorkeling, scuba diving, water-skiing, and deep-sea fishing. Except for scuba, gear is available free of charge. Scuba (one-tank dive) costs $75 (divers must show certification). Beginning dive lessons are available. Dive masters and water sports directors are well qualified, personable, and eager to help. Snorkeling and scuba trips and lessons are organized daily. When the ships anchor off deserted islands, passengers often must wade from Zodiacs to the beach.

Each ship has a fitness room with some exercise equipment, sauna, and masseuse; Jacuzzis are on the pool deck. The salon offers aromatherapy.

Shore Excursions　Most excursions are half-day tours with an emphasis on tropical gardens, national parks, and other natural attractions. Prices are on the high side, costing $25–$150. Excursions at St. Kitts in the Caribbean, for example, include a rain forest hike and horseback riding. In the Mediterranean, sight-seeing is emphasized.

WIND SURF	QUALITY **7**	VALUE **C**
Registry: Bahamas	Length: 617 feet	Beam: 59 feet
Cabins: 152	Draft: 16 feet	Speed: 12 knots
Maximum Passengers:	Passenger Decks: 6	Elevators: 2
308	Crew: 191	Space Ratio: 48

The Ship　*Wind Surf,* acquired by Windstar Cruises in 1997, is the former *Club Med 1,* a larger version of the Windstar trio. After extensive remodeling, the ship was rechristened *Wind Surf* and entered Windstar service in 1998.

During renovations, 31 deluxe suites were created, reducing the ship's capacity some, although it remains double that of her Windstar sisters. Reducing the number of passengers was intended to offset the ship's larger size, which dilutes the intimate Windstar experience. The suites are double the size of already spacious standard cabins. A spa was also added.

In 2000, *Wind Surf* got another refit that corrected its most serious problem—the steep gangway was replaced by a new shorter one, lowering it from Deck 4 to Deck 2. To do so, two cabins (one from the port and one from the starboard side) were eliminated, thus lowering its passenger capacity from 312 to 308 and changing the ship's space ratio to 48. The new gangway has also improved the embarkation/debarkation process.

The ship has a new **Computer Center,** and the **Cinema/Meeting Room** was remodeled into a fully equipped conference center with meeting facilities for up to 60 people. The **Wind Surf Lounge & Casino** was completely redesigned with a new nautical design and color scheme and furniture, a beautiful teak bar, and relocation of the stage and dance area resulting in clear sight lines to the stage from every seat. The casino has additional gaming tables and slots. The new floorplan has enhanced passenger flow and allow for smaller, more intimate groupings.

Other public rooms include a library well-stocked with CDs, books, and videos; a signature shop; and fitness center. The captain maintains an open bridge. Also available are 24-hour room service, laundry service, and a doctor's office.

Itineraries   See Itinerary Index.

Cabins   The deluxe outside cabins encompass 188 square feet each and offer queen-size beds (convertible to twins) and a work/desk/vanity area. They are similar in layout and décor to standard cabins on Windstar's other ships. All have television, VCR, CD player, safe, minibar and refrigerator, and direct-dial telephone. The bathroom has a shower, hair dryer, toiletries, and terry robe.

The 31 new ocean-view suites in selected areas of top decks measure 376 square feet. Their décor, in maroon and cream, is accented by teak wood, linen wall coverings, and original art. Each suite has a queen bed convertible to twins and a sofa bed. A curtain can be pulled across the bedroom to separate it from the living room for dining or entertaining. In addition to standard amenities, suites boast his-and-her bathrooms with shower, teak flooring, plush towels and robes, and vanity lighting.

Specifications   31 deluxe outside suites; 123 outside cabins with queen beds (convertible to twins) and sitting area. Standard cabin dimensions, 188 square feet. Some cabins have third berth; some side-by-side have adjoining private door

Dining   The ship's two dining rooms—the **Restaurant** and the smaller **Bistro**—accommodate all passengers at one sitting with no assigned seats. Menus for both were developed by Joachim Splichal, chef and founder of the Patina group of top restaurants in Los Angeles. Passengers have the opportunity to dine in both during a cruise. Light and vegetarian menus are available. The **Verandah Café** serves breakfast and lunch.

The Bistro, Windstar's alternative restaurant, is modeled after Splichal's Pinot Bistro. Splichal and his partner, Octavio Becerra, developed 132 recipes for the Bistro..

All three venues have been improved with increased capacity. The Bistro has a new look with French- and Italian-inspired colors, fabrics, and furniture. The glassed-in Verandah had its aft wall pushed back to enclose a portion of the deck to allow for additional indoor seating, which is preferred by guests on hot or windy days.

Sports, Fitness, and Beauty The 10,000-square-foot **WindSpa,** operated by Steiner, has a staff of ten and offers three kinds of treatments. Health and exercise includes aerobics, yoga, and other exercise classes; a water aerobics pool; and a fitness room with trainers. Pampering includes Swedish, deep tissue, sports, and other massage; aromatherapy; hair care; manicures, pedicures, and facials; and hand, foot, and spa bath treatments. Purification treatments include herbal wraps, algae and fango body masks, and mineral baths. Services, with body treatment prices ranging from $40–$65, can be purchased in advance or onboard. The Windstar brochure outlines options.

Wind Surf offers a complimentary water-sports program'. The ship has a water-sports latform and equipment similar to that on the other Windstar vessels, two saltwater pools, and two hot tubs.

Postscript Affluent clients attracted to Windstar for casual elegance, small ships, fewer passengers, and the chance to sail with passengers of similar means and interests will find that *Wind Surf* is different. One passenger observed,

Wind Surf *is too large to get the true feeling of a yacht. It's more of a cruise ship experience than a sailing experience. Like so many ships sailing the Mediterranean in summer, the cruises are so port-intensive that there is little time—not enough time, in our opinion—to enjoy the ship, which as we said in the beginning is the best thing about Windstar Cruises.*

European and Smaller Cruise Lines

In addition to the cruise lines and ships in the American mainstream of cruising already profiled in this section, another group of lines, with ships based mostly in Europe, may be of interest to readers. Space doesn't allow the same in-depth treatment, but generally they're small to midsize ships operated in the European tradition. Their interesting itineraries often visit places many Americans would need an atlas to find. Ships have English-speaking staff, although the majority of passengers are Europeans speaking other languages. A few operate from U.S. or Asian ports. The degree of luxury varies widely. Some are luxury vessels launched only in the last year or so; others are renovated vintage ships forming a flotilla of new cruise lines.

Cruises appeal particularly to those who have traveled the main routes often and are looking for new destinations or a new environment in which to return to places seen previously. They also appeal to those who might never consider a typical cruise ship, preferring to explore less traveled waters.

Also described are a few lines and ships that cater mainly to the U.S. market but weren't profiled in depth for other reasons—such as the fact that they're sold mainly through tour companies in combination with larger tour programs, they're under charter much of the year, or we had difficulty obtaining information.

Note: In parentheses after each ship name is information about the number of cabins and passengers; officers and crew; and the ship's length and tonnage (cabins/passengers; officers/crew; ship length/tonnage).

Abercrombie & Kent, Inc.

1520 Kensington Rd., Suite 212, Oak Brook, IL 60523-2141 (630) 954-2944; (800) 323-7308; fax (630) 954-3324; www.abercrombiekent.com

Abercrombie & Kent is a prestigious international tour operator specializing in exotic journeys worldwide for affluent, sophisticated travelers with an avid interest in nature and wildlife. The cruise programs focus on Antarctica and barge and river cruises in Europe and on the Amazon, Nile, Yangtze, and Ayeyewaddy Rivers. All emphasize culture and ecologically sound tourism. Most passengers are professional, retired or semiretired, well-educated, well-traveled, usually age 50 and older, in good health, and fit enough to enjoy hikes in Antarctic snows or Zodiac rides on the Amazon. Singles make friends easily on these trips.

Marco Polo is a club for A&K veterans and offers a quarterly newsletter, "members-only" trips, a 5% discount on land arrangements on most tours, luggage tags, priority on new destinations, tailored itineraries, a free lending library of A&K videotapes, and eligibility to compete in the annual Marco Polo Photo Contest. Annual membership is $75; five-year, $200; lifetime, $750; and children's memberships are available.

Explorer II (194/300; British/International; 436 ft./12,500 tons)

In early 2003, Abercrombie and Kent replaced its venerable *Explorer I*, the world's first expedition cruise ship, with the new, spacious *Explorer II*, and with one stroke changed the nature of its adventure cruises, bringing a new level of comfortable and informal refinement to Antarctic travel. Gone are the small, spartan cabins and antiquated bathrooms of the old ship. Now passengers can enjoy modern, well-appointed and comfortable accommodations and public rooms on a ship with more facilities and greater flexibility than might have ever been imagined in the past.

Explorer II, the former *Minerva I* of Swan Hellenic launched in 1996, is a stylish yet unpretentious ship that has been likened to a country-house inn with gleaming brass, polished wood, fresh flowers, and original art decorating the walls. But beneath these amenities, there's strong steel, including an ice-strengthened hull, stabilizers, and bow thrusters that give the ship the power, stability and agility to handle open-water cruising and the icy channels of Antarctic seas.

The **Lounge** on Main deck forward is a favorite place for passengers to congregate before the day's Zodiac excursion, listen to talks by onboard naturalists and other experts, or join friends for after-dinner coffee. Two bars—the **Shackleton** and the **South Cape**—provide additional corners in which to relax. The ship's library is exceptional, with a wide range of books, as well as newspapers, games, and puzzles. The Main deck also has the dining room aft and a beauty salon (which also offers massage) at mid-ship. On Bridge deck is the swimming pool, a bar and informal restaurant, lounge, card room, cinema, library, exercise room, and sauna. The ship also has a gift shop, medical center, and four elevators.

Explorer II can carry up to 300 passengers, but on her Antarctica voyages, A&K limits her complement to 198 passengers. The smaller number enhances the comfort level for all passengers, including the use of outside cabins and suites only, so that all passengers have their own window onto the Antarctic landscape.

The atmosphere onboard *Explorer II* is informal, unregimented, and sports an easy camaraderie among the passengers and the experts (naturalists, geologists, zoologists, historians, and ornithologists) who accompany every cruise. Each day, passengers gather for informal pre-excursion briefings or post-trip wrap-ups in the ship's lounge or auditorium. Throughout the trip, they interact with the experts to exchange ideas and ask questions—at dinner, at the rail, or on a Zodiac. Staff and crew add to the experience with their informal talks and entertainment.

No formal entertainment or shows are offered; days are packed with intellectual and physical activities and the day's recap before dinner. Socializing resumes after dinner, sometimes continuing into the wee hours. A passenger may tickle the ivories or sing, but guests generally just converse. Slides, a film, or a Hollywood movie may be shown. The library is popular at any hour. Lectures are well attended. Most talks are accompanied by audiovisuals.

Explorer II offers among the most spacious and comfortable accommodations in Antarctica, many with private balconies. All cabins have vanity table/writing desk and chair, television and radio, refrigerator, direct-dial telephone, hair dryer, and binoculars. There are two owner's suites and 10 outside suites on Bridge deck forward, with floor-to-ceiling patio doors leading to a balcony and furnished with queen or twin beds, bathroom with tub, large double wardrobe, ample drawer space, and separate sitting area with sofa, chair, and table. The 12 outside deluxe cabins on Promenade deck forward have twin beds or queen bed and some have a pull-out sofa for triple occupancy; bathroom with tub; separate sitting area with sofa, chair and table; a large picture window mirrored for privacy. Promenade deck, midship and aft, also has 20 outside superiors with twins or queen bed, bathroom with tub, walk-in closet, armchair, and large picture window.

The standard categories (A, B, SA, and SSA) are spread on two decks: 30 on A deck, and 28 on B deck. All are outside and have twin beds or queen; bathroom with shower; single and double wardrobes; love seat; and a picture window or porthole. Four cabins are handicapped accessible, and four are single cabins. Laundry service is available on Deck A. For its 198 passengers, *Explorer II* carries a staff and crew of 146, who provide a high level of warm, personal service.

Explorer II has two dining rooms with open seatings and indoor and outdoor service. The menus offer international cuisine as well as selections of light fare and vegetarian dishes. Special diets can be accommodated with sufficient advance notice. "Smart casual" wear is the attire of the evening. Smoking is not permitted in most areas of the ship, but there is a dedicated smoking room on the Bridge deck and designated areas on the outer decks.

In addition to accommodations and meals, A&K's all-inclusive cruise prices include all bar drinks and house wines, onboard gratuities, and sightseeing. You receive a backpack, parka for Antarctica cruises, and very good precruise information.

Explorer II sails on diverse itineraries in Antarctica and neighboring islands. She claims to operate under guidelines to do all that is possible to protect the fragile Antarctic environment. Antarctic cruises are intended for serious travelers who cherish unusual opportunities and draw interesting, intellectually curious people, among whom many lasting friendships are forged. If you don't have a similar thirst for knowledge or the flexibility to deal with frequent changes caused by weather and sea, you could find yourself on the wrong ship a long way from home. Gadabouts and tourists wanting to add exotic destinations to their tally should look elsewhere.

A&K also markets some deluxe yachts, such as the famous *Sea Cloud* and the luxurious *River Cloud.* For A&K's river cruises, see Part Three.

American Canadian Caribbean Line

(See Part Two, Cruise Lines and Their Ships.)

American Cruise Lines

One Marine Park, Haddam, CT 06438; (800) 814-6880; (860) 345-3311; fax (860) 345-4265; www.americancruiselines.com

---

American Eagle (31/49 passengers; American/American; 165 ft.)
American Glory (31/49 passengers; American/American; 168 ft.)

The small coastal ship *American Eagle,* completed in 2000 at the owner's Chesapeake shipyard in Salisbury, Maryland, takes only 49 passengers on close-to-shore trips from New England through the Chesapeake Bay to the Deep South and Florida via the Intracoastal Waterway from March to December. For the eagle-eyed, some of the company ads and brochure photos might be familiar. American Cruise Lines first surfaced in 1974 with a previous *American Eagle,* and after operating six ships for 15 years, the company quietly went bust. Now ACL is back, competing head-on with other U.S. coastal lines. In 2002, the *Eagle* was joined by *American Glory,* which is three feet longer and three feet wider at the beam, but is otherwise similar.

The ships' public spaces are roomy, considering they have only four decks. The forward-facing **Nantucket Lounge** seats all passengers, and amidships, a shipwide foyer offers additional comfy couch seating. A library has television, VCR, and books. The décor is a bit plain, with utilitarian-looking walls and ceilings, but the carpets and fabrics help to dress it up. Both ships have an elevator with access to each floor, and equipment for the handicapped is available.

The dining room, glass-enclosed on three sides, has open seating at large round tables. The ships do not have a liquor license; instead, there is a complimentary bar and sumptuous predinner hors d'oeuvres for the very popular cocktail hour, and there are carafes of Almaden Chardonnay and burgundy on the dinner table.

Each ship has two chefs from the Culinary Institute of America and Johnson and Wales. Their expertise shows in the delicious, creative meals.

The food is uniformly excellent throughout the cruise. Lunch is light fare, such as crab cakes and chicken Caesar salad. The set dinner menus, with a choice of two entrées, might be grilled artichoke hearts, hearts of palm in balsamic vinegar, Cornish game hen with wild rice, grilled catfish, broiled live lobster, and desserts such as pecan peanut butter pie.

The fourth or Sports deck, open to the sky, has deck chairs for all passengers plus tables and chairs and a putting green. Additional covered deck space faces aft, and the open deck forward of the lounge is excellent for viewing ahead.

There are five cabin categories, all outside with windows that slide open to allow in fresh air. AA, the second grade up, measures 192 square feet and compares favorably to the line's competition. The six AAV cabins are 249 square feet, including veranda; *Glory* has 14 cabins with verandas. The average size of *Glory's* cabins is slightly larger at 220 square feet. Both ships have five single cabins priced at about a 50% premium over the AA category. Cabins are furnished with comfortable cane-style couches.

The American Cruise Lines' ships offers a low-key cruising experience with itineraries from New England to Florida that celebrate Americana, sometimes with the help of an enrichment lecturer. The passengers are mostly an amiable retired lot who like sailing in a small club setting. There may also be mothers, grandmothers, daughters and sons. The all-American crew includes college-age men serving as deck hands, and young women, some just out of high school, cleaning cabins and waiting tables. The level of service is friendly, if sometimes haphazard. The line offers Early Bird discounts to those who book four months in advance. Fares begin at $2,500 per person for a seven-night cruise.

American Safari Cruises

19101 36th Avenue West, Suite 201, Lynnwood, WA 98036; (425) 776-1911; (888) 862-8881; fax (425) 776-8889; www.americansafaricruises.com, www.amsafari.com

Safari Quest (11/22; American/9–10; 120 ft.)
Safari Escape (6/12; American/5–6; 105 ft.)

Formed in 1996, American Safari Cruises offers nature-oriented adventure cruises for affluent travelers on two small, luxury yachts. The Alaska itineraries are off the beaten track, close-up experiences of wildlife, or scenery viewing at a leisurely pace with the pampering of a luxury cruise. The line's three-, four- and seven-day fall and spring cruises sail on new itineraries in the Pacific Northwest and from San Francisco to the heart of the California wine country and tour private villas, dine in winery caves, and enjoy onboard wine tastings and lectures conducted by experts. There also is a winter series of weekly cruises of Baja California and the Sea of Cortés, departing from La Paz.

All cabins on the vessels are outside and deluxe. Each is furnished with a queen bed or two twin beds (except for one cabin with one twin on *Safari Quest*), television with VCR, and private bathroom with shower or tub. Amenities include evening turndown service, terry robes, and fresh flowers.

The main gathering spot is a salon furnished with comfortable couches and chairs. A self-service bar separates the dining area and salon. The salon opens onto the sports platform, where passengers can board a launch or two-passenger kayak or fish off the stern. A spiral staircase links all public decks, the library and lounge, and the bridge. A promenade circles the entire yacht. The yachts have a top-deck hot tub for an under-the-stars spa experience.

On Alaskan itineraries, binoculars, rain jackets, and rubber boots are provided. A skilled and personable expedition leader accompanies each cruise and serves in lieu of a cruise director. A trained naturalist—the expedition leader—organizes hikes and biking excursions, leads kayak explorations, and identifies wildlife en route. In the evenings and when appropriate during the day, the expedition leader lectures on the flora, fauna, geology, and the history of the areas visited. Praised by passengers as caring, enthusiastic, and knowledgeable, the expedition leaders elevate the experience from a luxury cruise to a horizon-expanding voyage of discovery.

Food aboard American Safari cruises is as good as it gets on a cruise ship. Each day, the chef joins the passengers to discuss the menu and to describe special dishes to be prepared. Early-bird breakfast of fresh fruit, pastries, cereal, juices, and hot beverages starts at 6 a.m., with a full-service cooked-to-order breakfast available at 8 a.m. A full-course lunch is served at 1 p.m. Hors d'oeuvres are offered nightly during the cocktail hour preceding dinner at 7 p.m. Two entrées are offered each evening—usually fresh local seafood as well as chicken, lamb, or beef. Wine with meals and all other alcoholic beverages are included in the price of the cruise. The wine selection is stellar, as are the upscale labels in the well-stocked bar. Beer drinkers will love the draft beers from a prize-winning Alaskan microbrewery.

The yachts travel in daytime for wildlife viewing and scenic exploration. In late afternoon, they anchor in a scenic, secluded cove or bay for the night, offering further discovery on foot or by Zodiacs. Sighting wildlife—whales, porpoises, harbor seals, black bears, brown bears, sea lions, bald eagles, cormorants, herons, sandhill cranes, oystercatchers, and gulls—is all but guaranteed. The yachts are small enough that the captain can change course immediately to approach something for closer inspection. Long Alaskan summer days allow kayaking, whale-watching by Zodiacs, and hiking until late evening.

All meals, excursions, and events on these cruises are strictly informal. Jeans, khakis, and shorts, along with outdoor gear appropriate to the cruise venue and time of year, are all you need. Though the expedition leader has lots of activities on tap each day, the decision to participate is yours. Soaking in the hot tub, reading, napping, and watching movies on your cabin VCR are some of the alternatives available. Each ship also offers an aerobic exercise machine.

The Alaska itineraries explore remote areas and small villages: 14-day cruise from Seattle to Juneau, prices per person, double start at $4,395; 8-day All-Alaska between Juneau to Sitka, from $6,495; and Southeast Alaska from Juneau to Prince Rupert, which sails the length of Tracy Arm and follows humpback whales to their summer feeding in Frederick Sound, from May–September, from $5,995. Prices cover shore excursions, including flight-seeing, unlimited use of kayaks, guided nature walks, fishing, all private transfers, open bar, and port charges. Tips are extra. The Sea of Cortés series are similiarly priced. Both vessels are available for private charter.

Although a luxury product, American Safari cruises represent a good value, offering a highly personalized and intimate private yacht experience for less than most upscale cruises of comparable length. Indeed, with early booking discounts and the inclusion of wine, liquor, and all shore excursions in the price of the cruise, American Safari cruises are among the most affordable luxury cruises afloat.

American Safari passengers are typically over 40 years old, well educated, and adventurous individuals who revel in learning and discovery and who enjoy making new friends. Life aboard is, after all, an intimate experience, one that practically ensures you will become well acquainted with your fellow passengers.

Itineraries   See Itinerary Index.

Classical Cruises

(see Travel Dynamics International later in this section)

The Cruise Broker

P.O. Box 342, New York, NY 10014; (212) 352-8854; (888) 875-5880; fax (212) 504-8057;

The Cruise Broker is a U.S. company specializing in European cruises. It represents several European-owned and -managed oceangoing ships Below are the lines and ships the Cruise Broker represents that offer ocean cruises, mainly of the Baltic, North Cape, Norwegian fjords, Mediterranean, and Caribbean. In all cases, the Cruise Broker can provide brochures on ships and itineraries; these include deck plans and ships' features.

Fred Olsen Lines (The Cruise Broker)

Black Prince (234/472; European/Filipino; 480 ft./11,209 tons)
Built in 1966 and renovated in 1999, the ship caters to Britons. It sails on 9–49-night cruises from Southampton, England, year-round, to South America and the Amazon, Canary Islands, Baltic Sea, Norwegian coast, Caribbean, Mediterranean, and Middle East. The ship—a good choice for gregarious travelers age 50 and older—has a gym, pool, sauna, beauty salon, disco, and casino and provides international entertainment and sports. On this and other Fred Olsen Lines cruises, early-bird discounts of 30% are available for booking six months in advance; last-minute values might be reduced 50%.
Itineraries   See Itinerary Index.

Black Watch (400/761; Norwegian/International; 674 ft./28,492 tons)
Formerly the *Royal Viking Star,* the much-loved *Black Watch* was judged too small and too old to compete in the U.S. market and was sold to Fred Olsen Lines and given an $8 million refurbishment.

Black Watch cabins come in a bewildering number of configurations. Thirty-nine are singles. Though most are small, all are nicely appointed. Ninety percent are outside with portholes, picture window, or private veranda. Baths are well designed but very plain. All cabins have televisions and phones, and many have refrigerators.

The ship's public areas are exceptional. The library is among cruising's largest and most splendidly appointed. (Unfortunately, it's only open a couple of hours each day.) Contiguous is an equally impressive card and game room. Both rooms display artifacts from earlier ships named *Black Watch.* Observation lounges overlook the bow and stern. Both provide live music well into the night. A third lounge adjoins the main showroom; décor honors the Scottish Black Watch Regiment.

The clubby **Braemar Room,** a large lounge adjacent to the dining room, is packed with brightly colored stuffed chairs. It's given over entirely to the British passion for tea, which is available around the clock.

Well-designed public areas continue outside with a promenade that encircles the ship. Also available are pools, Jacuzzis, bars, cafes, an Internet center, and outdoor areas (some covered) for sunning or relaxing.

Entertainment is professional, varied, and appealing to a range of ages and backgrounds. It puts to shame the offerings aboard many superliner competitors. During a recent voyage, we enjoyed Las Vegas–style production shows, an incredibly talented opera company, an illusionist, a comic, a celebrity vocalist, and classical music concerts. Lounges, the casino, and the **Star Night Club** dance venue bustle into the wee hours. Theme cruises are varied.

For an American, the greatest pleasure aboard *Black Watch* is meeting Britons—delightful, interested, and interesting. Many hours are spent with new English, Scottish, and Irish friends exploring the subtleties that make our cultures so similar yet so different. Some misunderstandings of idiom and accent are uproarious: Announcement of a "folkloric presentation" was heard by the Americans as a "full colonic presentation" . . . We couldn't wait! Because the British are gracious and friendly, being the minority was a special pleasure.

Itineraries   See Itinerary Index.

Braemar (377/820; European/International; 537 ft./ 20,000 tons)

The the former *Crown Dynasty* of Crown Cruise Line and *Norwegian Dynasty* of Norwegian Cruise Lines, she is one of the nicest ships in her size and price category in cruising. She is small enough to be cozy but large enough to offer modern cruise ship amenities and facilities.

Elegant but not stuffy, *Braemar's* décor communicates a sophistication that is apparent the moment you step onboard. Expansive glass windows throughout the ship, large open decks and terraces, and a five-story atrium with walls of glass create a feeling of space and openness. Polished woods, gentle lighting, and soft hues contribute to the stylish comfort.

Built in Spain in 1993 and originally designed by Scandinavian architect Petter Yran, known for his work on many luxury ships, the pretty *Braemar* was given a facelift by the eminent British ship interior designer John McNeese prior to beginning her new life in August 2001.

The layout of the eight-deck ship is unusual, if not unique. The five-deck, greenery-filled atrium lobby is aft, rather than amidships. Also, it's on the starboard side rather than at the center, with windows spanning Decks 4 to 8, admitting natural light and sea views, and helping connect passengers with the sea. Four of the main public rooms are stacked vertically at the stern, allowing for large windows in virtually every area. The decks are connected by outdoor stairways and open decks.

Deck 5 is devoted to public rooms. It's anchored at both ends by lounges oriented to the port side horizontally and facing large windows (rather than the usual arrangement of lounges facing the bow or stern). The multilevel show lounge, for example, is semicircular, with the stage and dance floor on the port side. Between the lounges are shops, a casino, and a bar.

Cabins are on five decks; about two-thirds are outside. They are nicely appointed in pastels with light wood furniture and brass fixtures. All have television, phone, safe, and card-key door lock. Closet space is good, but drawer space is minimal. Many cabins are fitted with twin beds that can be converted to a queen. Bathrooms are small but have large medicine cabinets, mirrored doors, and vanities. Deluxe cabins and suites have refrigerators and sitting areas with large windows. Ten suites have private balconies. Four wheelchair-accessible cabins have large bathrooms with grab bars and wide doorways. There are four elevators.

The dining room has a skylight and panoramic windows on three sides, providing natural light and sea views for all diners. Although tables are close, noise is low. The room, decorated in muted colors with lively, contemporary art, has a variety of table configurations separated from service areas by frosted glass.

Above the dining room on Deck 6 is a casual indoor/outdoor café— more elegantly decorated than usual for a lido café. It's also a lounge with a full-service bar and is used as the disco at night. Adjacent to the casino is a tastefully decorated bar separated from the main thoroughfare by frosted glass and wood paneling. The ship also has a cozy library with good sea views, a card room, an Internet center, and medical center.

The top deck has a swimming pool, Jacuzzis, bar, and the spa with large windows facing the bow. It is equipped with state-of-the-art exercise equipment, an aerobics area, and a juice bar. It also has a beauty salon with hair and body treatments, two saunas, and steam and massage rooms. A jogging track rims the pool on an overhang and windscreens line the deck's perimeter. A wide outside promenade circling Deck 5 provides an uninterrupted track for walking or jogging. The ship also has a golf program which is available on most Caribbean itineraries and on selected Mediterranean ones. It combines individual instruction onboard ship and play at clubs on shore.

Despite the increasing numbers of seasoned cruisers who prefer smaller ships, their choices in the midprice range are limited. As one of the few midsize ships built in the 1990s, *Braemar* helps fill the void.

Itineraries   See Itinerary Index.

Kristina Cruises (The Cruise Broker)

Kristina Regina (119/245; Finnish/Finnish; 327 ft./4,295 tons)

The ship, which has a receptive audience among well-traveled Americans, sails on three- to ten-night cruises from May to August in Scandinavia and Russia and does Baltic Sea cruises that include Lithuania, Poland, Russia, Estonia, Finland, Denmark, Germany, and Latvia. In spring of 2001, she underwent a million-dollar renovation. She has an English-speaking staff, several bars and lounges, library, sauna, and sun decks. Dining is at one seating; menus vary. Her small size enables her to dock within walking distance of town centers. One of her most popular cruises, White Sea–White Nights, sails to the Polar Circle from Helsinki in late June.

Itineraries   See Itinerary Index.

Discovery World Cruises

*1800 SE 10th Avenue, Suite 205, Fort Lauderdale, FL 33316 (866) 623-2689;
fax (954) 761-7768; www.discoveryworldcruises.com*

Discovery (351/650; Scandinavian, British,Dutch/ American, European,
Philippino; 553 ft./20,186 tons)

Founded in 2002 by well-known travel industry entrepreneur Gerry
Herrod, the new cruise line has been designed to offer deluxe cruises to
less traveled destinations at affordable prices, much like Orient Cruise
Line and other niche-market companies that Herrod headed in the past.
The cruises focus on giving passengers in-depth exposure to their desti-
nations, while providing the traditional comforts of a deluxe oceanliner.

From December to March 2004, *Discovery* will sail on cruises in South
America, Antarctica, New Zealand, the South Pacific, and leisurely
explore the South Seas and Hawaii. After visits to Mexico and Central
America, *Discovery* will sail through the Panama Canal, stopping in
Belize and the Yucatan before making a transatlantic voyage to England.
During the remainder of the year, the ship will be operated under charter
to Voyages of Discovery, a tour operator based in the United Kingdom.

Before entering service in 2003, the *Discovery*, built as the *Island Venture* in 1972 in Germany by century-old shipbuilder Rheinstahl Nord-
seewerke (and best known as Princess Cruises' *Island Princess*) underwent
extensive, multimillion-dollar renovations that, in effect, created a brand
new ship. She has retained her handsome, classic profile and grand
oceanliner ambience but now boasts modern safety features and amenities. At 20,000 tons—small compared to today;s megaliners—*Discovery*
is large enough for cruising to faraway places, yet small enough to enter
remote harbors that larger vessels must bypass.

Facilities on the eight-deck ship include three restaurants; five lounges;
lecture theatre/cinema; a well-stocked library; modest casino; modem
health club and beauty center; two swimming pools—one with a
retractable dome; two Jacuzzis; card room; Internet center, boutiques;
and four elevators. There is nightly entertainment, classical music concerts, and folkloric performances by local groups. The ship has 351 cabins and suites, equipped with televisions, safes, and built-in hair dryers.
Early-bird savings up to 50% are available.

Herrod has been joined in this venture by former principals from Orient Lines, Ocean Cruise Lines, and Pearl Cruises as senior management.
The ship's senior officers are Scandinavian, British, and Dutch; the cruise
staff is American and European; and the service staff, Filipino. In addition to founding Orient Lines, Gerry Herrod created the European tour
operator Travellers International and was former chairman of Ocean
Cruise Lines and Pearl Cruises.

Most itineraries are being marketed as cruise-tour vacation packages, which include extended stays and sight-seeing in embarkation and/or disembarkation cities, detailed briefings on each port of call, and local cultural performances on board. A hallmark of Discovery World Cruises is its enrichment program of lectures and workshops at sea, with noted expedition leaders and area experts on each voyage. When the ship is being operated by Voyages of Discovery, she will cruise the British Isles, the Baltic, Greenland, Iceland, and the Faroes Islands, Scandinavia, the Mediterranean, the Black Sea, Red Sea, Suez Canal, and North African.

All cabins have private facilities, air-conditioning, TV, hair dryer and safe. Cabins on Bridge and Promenade Deck have bath and a shower, cabins on other decks have showers. Outside cabins on Bridge and Promenade decks have picture windows (the view of the Owner's Suite is obscured by lifeboats).

All outside cabins on the Pacific Deck have two windows. All outside cabins on Bali and Coral Decks have two portholes. Cabins have two lower beds or a double bed. Some cabins have one or two upper berths or a sofa bed allowing for third or fourth person sharing (when only one or two passengers are occupying a cabin the upper berths are folded away). Most beds in twin cabins are arranged parallel to each other, although some are arranged in an L shape. A small number of cabins have an interconnecting door, which is kept locked unless otherwise requested. Outside and inside standard cabins measure 135 square feet; outside superior have 194 square feet.

Itineraries   See Itinerary Index.

First European Cruises

95 Madison Ave., Suite 1203, New York, NY 10016; (212) 779-7168; (888) 983-8767; fax (212)779-0948; www.first-european.com

Known in Europe as Festival Cruises, First European Cruises operates classic, midsize liners and new superliners year-round in the Mediterranean and northern Europe, and in the Caribbean in winter. Cruises are designed for the European, middle-income mass market of many nationalities. They will interest Americans who feel comfortable with other cultures or who speak one or two European languages. Staff is multilingual and speaks English, but most passengers do not.

First European maintains high standards of cleanliness and service. Some experienced American passengers have judged the food the best they have had on any cruise ship. Vessels are crowded and the cabins small, but the atmosphere is relaxed and unpretentious. Fare reductions and a children's program attract families during school vacations.

The cruise line added two brand-new 1,500 passenger ships in 2001 and 2002 and—has plans to build two 80,000-ton, 2,000-passengers ships.

In a joint venture with Hilton International in 2003, Festival Cruises (First European Cruises' parent company) made history with their ships becoming the first to offer Hilton's first cruise product. Under the trade name of "Hilton Floating Resorts on Festival Cruises" and sold in the U.S. by First European Cruises, the program adds concierge-style refinements to Festival's onboard product on the line's newest ships—*European Stars, European Vision,* and *Mistral*—and at the same time, broadens the cruise line's appeal.

The program offers special "Hilton Suites" and services, including suite accommodations with balconies, indoor and outdoor seating areas, queen-sized beds, bathrooms with bath tubs, Hilton-brand toiletries and robes, dedicated cabin steward and 24-hour room service; personalized check-in and priority embarkation/disembarkation with a special reserved waiting area; champagne, chocolate, and fruit in cabin upon embarkation plus daily sweets, cookies and canapes; special in-cabin breakfast service with freshly-squeezed juice; complementary after-dinner liqueur; free access to thermal suites in ships' health spas; VIP tour of ship's bridge, priority on shore excursions with limited numbers, and opportunities for private excursions with car and driver; 20% discount on wine list; 10% discount on bar drinks, excursions, purchases in onboard shops, treatments at the beauty center, photos, and sports activities. Fares for Hilton Suites average 8% higher than the normal price of a suite, beginning at $1,720 per person for seven-night cruises. Hilton Suite rates are also offered for third and fourth adults sharing the cabin, as well as for children ages 2–17. Inquire from First European for details and itineraries.

Azur (360/800; Greek/International/1330; 466 ft./15,000 tons)

Built in 1971 and refurbished in 1996, the Azur has seven passenger decks with one nonsmoking dining room, several lounges and bars, two swimming pools, a cinema, casino, sports and fitness center, disco, karaoke bar, and children's play room. Cabins have radio, phone, and bathrooms with shower. There are 12 suites.

Itineraries   See Itinerary Index.

Flamenco (401/800; Greek/European/350; 535 ft./17,000 tons)

Formerly the *Southern Cross* of CTC Cruise lines, she was acquired in 1997, given an $8 million refurbishing, and renamed *Flamenco*. The ship has one nonsmoking dining room, a variety of lounges and bars, showroom, casino, shop, library, and gym. Exercise classes and massage are available. Cabins are small but have private baths with shower, telephone, radio, and closed-circuit television for movies. She is currently under charter.

Mistral (598/1,200; French/International/500; 708 ft./47,900 tons)
European Vision / European Stars (783/1,500; Italian/International/711;
823 ft./58,600)

Delivered in June 1999, the French-built *Mistral* flies the French flag. She is based in Venice, sailing on cruises to the Greek Isles and Northern Europe from Kiel, Germany. Two similar ships—*European Vision,* which arrived in June 2001, and *European Stars,* in March 2002—each carry 1,500 passengers. *European Vision* sails in the Eastern Mediterranean from June to November and the Eastern Caribbean from the Dominican Republic from December to April. *European Stars* sails alternating Western and Eastern Mediterranean cruises year-round.

The eight passenger decks of the *Mistral*—named after European cities—have two restaurants, a theater, casino, conference center, piano bar, library/card room, beauty parlor, boutique, shopping arcade, show lounge, cigar bar, fitness center and spa with thalassotherapy center, sauna/massage, and two swimming pools. The ship also boasts a complete dialysis care unit.

The *Mistral's* 598 cabins include 80 suites with balconies. She has 297 standard outside and 221 standard inside cabins, and 2 are wheelchair-accessible. The ship's capacity can be increased by 490 passengers when Pullman or sofa beds are used. The crew numbers 480.

Built at the same shipyard and with the same interior decors as the *Mistral,* the *European Vision* and *European Stars,* each with 783 cabins, have some enhancements, such as a dedicated conference and Internet center, virtual reality games, golf driving range, children's splash pool, an additional outdoor restaurant, and double the number of suites with private balconies.

Itineraries   See Itinerary Index.

Global Quest Journeys

185 Willis Avenue, 2nd Floor, Mineola, NY 11501; (516) 739-3690; (800) 221-3254; fax (516) 739-8022; www.globalquesttravel.com

The line, formed in 1991 as OdessAmerica, is a joint venture between the Black Sea Shipping Company of Odessa, Ukraine, and International Cruise Center of Mineola, New York. BLASCO dates to 1833 and is the largest shipping company in the former Soviet Union, and one of the world's largest. It has 15 passenger ships and more than 300 cargo vessels.

Global Quest represents a variety of cruise lines and offers cruises of Africa and the Indian Ocean, Galápagos Islands, Adriatic Sea, Chilean archipelago, Antarctica, and European and Russian rivers. See further listings in Part Three.

Hebridean Island Cruises

Griffin House, Broughton Hall, Skipton, North Yorkshire, UK BD23 3AN; (011) 44 1756 704704; (800) 659-2648; fax (011) 44 1756 704794; www.hebridean.co.uk

Hebridean Princess (30/49; British/Scottish/38; 235 ft./1,420 tons)

Built in 1964 to carry 600 passengers, the ship was redesigned in 1994 to carry only 47 passengers in the style of a deluxe country inn. Accommodations vary from singles with shared facilities to suites. The ship has a lounge, restaurant, library of books and videos, and shop. She visits lochs, estuaries, and Scotland's Inner and Outer Hebrides islands on 4- to 14-night cruises from March to November, usually departing from the West Highlands port of Oban.

Itineraries See Itinerary Index.

Hebridean Spirit (49/80; British/Scottish/72; 300 ft./4,200 tons)

In 2000, Hebridean Island cruises bought the *MegaStar Capricorn* from Star Cruises, Asia's largest cruise line, and renamed her *Hebridean Spirit*. She was given a $4.7 million renovation and redesigned to accommodate 79 guests (down from 114 passengers) in a style similar to the *Hebridean Princess*. The crew of 72 (for a maximum of 80 passengers) includes seven chefs! Even her superstructure has been "aged" to give the ship the style and outline of ships from the "golden era of cruising".

The 49 cabins, decorated in a classical English yet contemporary style, include 18 singles (no supplementary charge). Each cabin has a sitting area and is decorated individually and named after familiar places. They have marble bathrooms with full tub and shower, a large or walk-in closet, and a tea and coffee maker. Eight cabins have balconies, and there are two suites.

The ocean-going vessel has enabled Hebridean Island to cruise in new waters and to offer itineraries for north European and Mediterranean destinations in summer, and from the Greek Islands through the Red Sea and the Indian Ocean to Sri Lanka in winter, on weekly cruises and normally with no repetition of ports of call. Passengers' departure points are reached by private charter to and from London. Prices for a seven-night cruise start at £5,740 per person for a single cabin and £5,140 per person double, and include air travel, transfers, entrance fees to attractions, gratuities, and port or passenger taxes. Brits account for 84% of the line's passengers, with 50% repeaters.

Itineraries See Itinerary Index.

Lindblad Expeditions

(See Part Three, Cruising Alternatives, "Adventure and Cultural Cruises.")

MSC Italian Cruises

250 Moonachie Road, Moonachie, NJ 07074; (800) 666-9333; fax (866) 338-9470; www.msccruisesusa.com

Part of a Swiss group operating a global fleet of 210 container ships and 36 fast ferries, Mediterranean Shipping Cruises acquired three of its four cruise ships in less than four years. One of the largest cruise lines in the Mediterranean, the firm also sails to South Africa and South America. With Italian staff and ambience, the ships offer classic cruises with good food and service. The line's new *Lirica,* built by the French shipyard Chantiers de l'Atiantique for $250 million, was delivered in 2003—the first phase of the line's expansion plans.

Lirica (795/1,590; Italian/International; 824 ft./58,600 tons)
Opera (795/1,590; Italian/International; 824 ft./58,600 tons)

MSC's newest flagship, the *Lirica* (or *Lyric* in English) made her debut in April 2003, with actress Sophia Loren doing the honors. Her twin, *Opera,* is scheduled to arrive in the spring of 2004. The ships are powered by a technically advanced propulsion system to reduce engine noise and increase comfort levels.

Among their amenities, the new ships each have two swimming pools, a fully equipped gym and jogging track, and two hot tubs and a sauna. They are equipped with a **Virtual Reality Center** and an Internet café with 16 terminals. Each has a disco and theater with new shows nightly, a supervised **Mini Club** for children, and a shopping gallery.

The 14-deck ships each have six elevators. Out of 795 cabins, 132 cabins have verandas. There are 387 outside standard cabins, 272 inside standard cabins, and 4 cabins for disabled passengers. All cabins have satellite television, minibar, safe, radio, and 24-hour room service.

Each of the twins have two restaurants as well as a grill and pizzeria; they serve authentic Italian cuisine. The staff and crew number 750.

For the 2004 winter season, the *Lirica* has replaced the *Melody*—an increase of 47% in capacity—departing from Fort Lauderdale to the Caribbean and Panama Canal.

Itineraries   See Itinerary Index.

Melody (549/1,076; Italian/International/535; 671 ft./36,500 tons)

Formerly the *Star/Ship Atlantic* of Premier Cruise Lines, *Melody* was acquired in 1997 by MSC. She has several lounges, a showroom, piano bar, disco, casino, fitness center, two outdoor pools, and beauty salon. Cabins are moderate in size and have radio, direct-dial telephone, and private bathrooms.

Itineraries   See Itinerary Index.

Monterey (290/576; Italian/International/200; 563 ft./21,051 tons)

Built in 1952 and refurbished in 1991 and 1997, *Monterey* once belonged to Matson Line and sailed for Aloha Pacific Cruises. The steam-operated vessel has been well maintained and is a pleasant older ship with a fine style and a friendly crew. She complies with new safety requirements. The classic Art Deco vessel gleams with brass and polished mirrors and has two swimming pools, fitness center with two whirlpools, sauna, hospital, library, beauty salon, boutiques, casino, disco, and two elevators. The attractive dining room offers two seatings. Cabins on the top three decks are large and have private bathrooms. Handicapped-accessible cabins are available. Most passengers are middle-income Italian and British, age 55 and older.

Itineraries See Itinerary Index.

Rhapsody (384/768; Italian/250; 541 ft./16,852 tons)

Built in 1977 as *Cunard Princess, Rhapsody* was refurbished in 1995 after purchase by MSC, and once more in 1997. Facilities include a swimming pool, whirlpool, fitness center, conference room, library, café, bars, casino, video arcade, cinema, beauty and barber shops, and medical center. Two elevators and dry cleaning services are available. A comfortable ship enhanced by a friendly atmosphere, she offers international cuisine with an Italian emphasis. It's served in the window-lined **Meridian Dining Room** at two seatings. Cabins are small with limited storage space and thin walls; all have private bathrooms. Passengers are middle-income Europeans older than age 50. They tend to be smokers. *Rhapsody* spends summer in the Mediterranean.

Itineraries See Itinerary Index.

Oceania Cruises

8120 NW 53rd Street, Miami, Fla. 33166; (305) 514-2300; (800) 531-5658; www.oceaniacruises.com

Insignia (342/684; European/European; 592 ft.; 30,077 tons)
Regatta (342/684; European/European; 592 ft.; 30,077 tons)

Oceania Cruises, launched in 2003 by two well-known cruise industry veterans, Frank Del Rio and Joe Watters, is aiming for a niche between the premium and luxury categories similar to that of now-defunct Renaissance Cruises, using two (and possible three) of the former line's ships, appealing to discerning, sophisticated travelers.

The new cruise line's goal is to create a five-star product with its cuisine, service, and destination-oriented itineraries, and offer it at reasonable prices. The relaxed onboard atmosphere is meant to resemble the casual elegance of a country club, neither stuffy nor pretentious. Formal wear is never a requirement for dining; passengers dress comfortably to enjoy their evenings.

The 30,277-tons ships—small in comparison to today's more typical megaships—provide an intimate atmosphere, while at the same time having the facilities of larger ships. For example, each ship has four restaurants with open seating, enabling passengers to dine when, where, and with whom they choose.

Each restaurants offers a different type of cuisine and a different ambience. Menus have been crafted by master chef Jacques Pepin, the line's Executive Culinary Director and one of America's best-known chefs via his numerous television appearances, food columns, and cookbooks. He has also served as the personal chef to three French heads of state, including de Gaulle.

Of the total 340 spacious cabins and suites, 92% are outside and almost 70% have verandas. The Owner's and Vista suites, encompassing nearly 1,000 square feet, have floor-to-ceiling glass doors that lead to a veranda. Prior to entering service for Oceania, the vessels were upgraded with luxury appointments such as fine linens and bedding, French-milled toiletries, and teak verandas.

The ships have spas where passengers can be pampered with aromatherapy massages and hot-stone treatments, along with other offerings. The fitness center has state-of-the-art equipment and an aerobic area. Personal trainers are available. **Oceania@Sea,** the 24-hour computer center, has Internet access, and there is a library, card room, medical center, self-service launderette, and four elevators. There is a high staff-to-guest ratio, with more than one crew member per cabin to provide the high degree of personal service the cruise line has promised.

The 684-passenger *Regatta,* inaugurated in July 2003, spent her maiden summer in the Mediterranean and Scandinavia and was scheduled to begin her winter Caribbean and Panama Canal cruises in November, sailing from Miami. The cruises are 7, 10, and 14 days; some itineraries have been tailored to include overnight port stays to allow passengers more time to to enjoy the locale. *Insignia,* which will debut in April 2004, will sail in Central and South America. Passengers are being registered in the line's repeaters club from their first cruise, making them eligible for travel rewards and other benefits.

Itineraries   See Itinerary Index.

P&O Cruises

Richmond House, Terminus Terrace, Southampton SO14 3PN, United Kingdom; (023) 80-525-252, fax (023) 80-525-253; www.pocruises.com

P&O Cruises stems from the original steamship company founded in 1837 whose principal routes served the British empire from India to New

Zealand. In 1974, P&O Cruises purchased Princess Cruises, and through it, had a big impact on modern cruising, particularly on the U.S. West Coast market. In 2003, P&O Cruises, along with Princess Cruises and the company's two other cruise lines, were bought by Carnival Cruises after an intensive bidding war with Royal Caribbean International for control of Princess Cruises.

The introduction of the *Oriana* in 1995, P&O Cruises' first brand-new ship in more than two decades, signaled the start of a modern era for the cruise line, replacing her old ships and building new ships designed for British passengers. *Oriana's* sister, *Aurora*, was delivered in 2000 with even more new features. In 2002, the *Oceana*, formerly the *Ocean Princess* of Princess Cruises, joined the fleet, followed by the *Adonia* (formerly the *Sea Princess*), which has a new twist—it's for adults only.

P&O's cruises are moderately priced, classic cruises and offer worldwide itineraries. Their British style cannot be overemphasized; it's what P&O passengers want. The atmosphere is very social, helped by friendly British officers who mingle with passengers and host tables at dinner—a popular feature. The ships are well-organized, aboard and ashore, with excellent programs that include outstanding lecturers on port history and culture, classical pianists, afternoon teas, Sunday religious services (Anglican) with a passenger/staff choir, and nighttime entertainment. The dress code tends to be more dressy than on similar ships catering to Americans. Men wear jacket and tie on most nights at sea and on formal evenings they wear tuxedos or dinner jackets and women don cocktail and long dresses.

P&O focuses on three programs: cruises departing from Southampton, those based in the Caribbean in winter, and annual around-the-world voyages. Most passengers are British, of all ages and incomes. Americans, Australians, and New Zealanders are a sizable minority on around-the-world voyages. P&O has expanded aggressively into the German market, creating a company and building ships specifically for that market.

Aurora (939/1,874; British/Indian and European/1850; 886 ft./76,000 tons)
Oriana (914/1,822; British/Indian and European/794; 853 ft./69,153 tons)

The *Oriana* is big and beautiful. New and modern, she nonetheless has the design and décor of a classic liner with traditional oil paintings, historic documents, and ship models on the walls. Interiors are as fine and refined as tea in a British parlor. No flashy neon or glitz here. The ship has an inviting calm and numerous nooks where it's easy to relax, read, write postcards, and let the world go by. It's cruising as it should be.

Aurora, a near twin of *Oriana* but with new features and a bit more glitz, made her debut in 2000 and brought with her some "firsts" for a ship dedicated primarily to the British market. These include two-deck penthouse suites, four decks of cabins with balconies, and interconnecting family cabins. She also had P&O's first 24-hour bistro-style restaurant, coffee and chocolate bar, champagne bar, tea- and coffee-making facilities in all cabins, a retractable dome over one swimming pool, and a virtual reality center. Her four-deck atrium has a waterfall and Lalique glass–style sculpture, and is surrounded by shops and a tour desk.

The size and spaciousness of these ships allow for a variety of public rooms and entertainment facilities, as well as some larger public rooms enabling passengers of all types to find comfortable and familiar surroundings. Vast amounts of open deck call to British sun worshippers and those who take a daily "constitutional."

Oriana's cabins are spacious and more luxurious than on previous P&O ships and come in a wide range of configurations with ample storage space. The ship has 114 singles—an unusually feature for today's superliner. Almost all cabins, including suites, are on the three middle decks. *Aurora's* cabin choices are even wider and range from two-deck penthouse suites to interconnecting cabins suitable for families. Over 40% of the cabins, including some standard ones, have balconies. Cabins on both ships have tea- and coffee-makers, safe, refrigerator, television, direct-dial telephone, air conditioning, and music system; some have bathtubs, hair dryers, and minibars.

Two main restaurants offer two sittings for three meals. The cuisine is very British: lots of meat and potatoes and sauces, excellent soups but few salads. The **Conservatory** on Lido Deck, with indoor/outdoor seating, serves a buffet breakfast and lunch. The area can become very crowded at peak lunch hours.

The ships' elaborate activities program ranges from bingo and crafts to bridge and dance classes. Port lecturers are very knowledgeable and generally have a dry, British sense of humor. They wouldn't dream of giving the shopping sales pitch heard on many Caribbean cruise ships. The comfortable library is well supplied.

Public rooms spread over two main decks offer a variety of atmospheres catering to class-conscious Britons. Many reflect in name and style the company's 165-year history, such as classical music in the elegant **Curzon Room,** cabaret in the **Pacific Lounge,** and large production show in **Theatre Royal.** There's **Lord's Tavern,** a cricket-themed pub; and the spacious **Crow's Nest** observation bar and lounge, with wraparound windows and a trio playing dance music before and after dinner. **Monte Carlo Casino** is small compared with those on big ships sailing the Caribbean.

On *Aurora,* a West End–style theater has the latest production technology and the new-concept main show lounge comes with a spacious bar, large dance floor, and retractable stage. Amidships is an intimate, futuristic nightclub with small dance floor and stage. One deck above, a large concert hall/cinema shows first-run films and stages concerts; there's also a business center with computers.

Activities of *Oriana's* vast open decks includes deck tennis, quoits, shuffleboard, golf nets, and trapshooting. Cricket matches between passengers and officers are popular. One of two adult pools is a generous 42 feet long. Passengers take daily walks on a wide promenade sprinkled with deck chairs shaded by lifeboats. A large spa offers aerobics, a gym, Jacuzzis, sauna, massage, beauty and therapy rooms, and a hair salon. On *Aurora,* a pool between decks 11 and 12 has a waterfall and is surrounded by tiered decks. Another pool can be covered by a dome in inclement weather; still another is reserved for families at certain times of year. A netted deck area is adaptable for cricket, soccer, and tennis, and golfers can practice on the golf simulator. A well-equipped gym and aerobics studio overlooks the forward pool. The spacious area is linked by stairs to health and beauty facilities.

P&O's children's program is highly praised. Four age-specific areas have separate, supervised well-designed programs. Children have their own pool and lido area, and they eat at an early sitting, with or without their parents. A staffed night nursery is available for children under age five and cabins have baby "listening" facilities.

Oceana (975/1,950; British; 856 ft./77,000 tons)
Adonia ((975/1,950; British; 856 ft./77,000 tons)

Oceana (formerly *Ocean Princess*) joined the P&O fleet in fall 2002; *Adonia* (formerly *Sea Princess*) in 2003. In a first for Britain, both ships were named—actually renamed—simultaneously in a joint ceremony in May 2003. The ships were part of Princess Cruises' Sun Princess group. (For a description of these ships, see Princess Cruises earlier in Part Two.) The major difference is with the new *Adonia,* which is a child-free ship. She was scheduled to spend her maiden autumn in the Mediterranean, followed by a 100-day cruise around-the-world.

Itineraries   See Itinerary Index.

Peter Deilmann Cruises

1800 Diagonal Road, Suite 170, Alexandria, VA 22314; (703) 549-1741; (800) 348-8287; fax (703) 549-7924; www.deilmann-cruises.com

Peter Deilmann Cruises' *Deutschland,* launched in 1998, was built as a traditional luxury liner in the grand European style. She has three restaurants and a promenade deck and accommodates 513 passengers in a variety of mostly outside staterooms. The ship is intended for German-speaking patrons. They will enjoy German food and German music and entertainment. All announcements and tours are conducted in German. There are some English-speaking staff members aboard. The ship made her first world cruise during the 2002–2003 winter season, sailing west.

(For Peter Deilmann River Cruises, designed for English-speaking passengers as well as European ones, see Part Three, Cruising Alternatives.)
Itineraries See Itinerary Index.

ResidenSea Ltd.

Regent Centre West, Building No. 2, Suite D; P.O. Box F-40967, Freeport, Bahamas;
(800) 970-6601; (305) 259-5151; fax (305) 269-1058; www.residensea.com

The World (88 suites, 110 apartments; Norwegian/320; 644 ft./
40,000 tons)

The World of ResidenSea, the first residential cruise ship ever built, was launched from Oslo on March 29, 2002 to begin her cruising odyssey and confounded the skeptics (us included), who said it would never happen. Five weeks later, she sailed to America on her maiden voyage

Billed as the world's first residential resort community at sea continuously circumnavigating the globe, *The World* has 88 guest suites, which can be booked by the general public, and 110 elegant, privately owned residences, many of which can be rented.

Here's what she offers on her 12 decks: private apartments ranging from 1,100 to 3,500 square feet, with décor by four top designers and fully furnished down to the flatware and china; the suites, ranging from 259 to 648 square feet; four theme restaurants featuring French, Italian, and Asian cuisine, plus a delicatessen; enrichment activities such as lectures and seminars; full-size tennis court; a retractable marina for water activities; two pools; a top-deck, open-air full-shot driving range, 40-course golf simulators, real grass putting greens, two artificial greens, a sand bunker, and a PGA-certified golf director; a fitness center; a Swiss spa, **Clinique La Prairie;** an art gallery, and several boutiques. Oh, yes, and three emergency wards and full-time doctor and nurse, as well as a telemedicine hookup with Mt. Sinai–Cedars Hospital in Miami Beach.

All this, while traveling the world: 140 ports in more than 40 countries with planned itineraries of six to 17 days in her first year, attending such special events as the Cannes Film Festival, the Grand Prix of Monaco, and the British Open in Scotland. She started the winter 2004 season cruising to the Falkland Islands and Antarctica. And the price (ah yes, if you have to ask): Apartments range from $2 million to $6.8 million, with an average price of $2.8 million. And then there's the annual maintenance fee, which includes housekeeping, of $160,000. More than 85 of the 110 apartments were sold before the ship sailed.

Who, you ask, would pay such a price? According to the marketing company, they are homeowners who have two or three residences, are 55, and first-generation entrepreneurs who have built their worth as computer chip-makers, real estate developers, or the like. They are very active, have an affinity with the sea, maybe own a yacht or have cruised a lot, and they guard their privacy.

North Americans constitute the largest number of buyers, followed by Norwegians, Brits, Germans, Australians and Swiss. Most owners, it is estimated, will stay aboard for three months a year, just as they would, say, at their condo in Aspen or their villa in the south of France.

The World's promoters say that the ship is for people who hate having to pack a suitcase to travel, who really miss sleeping in their own beds when they're away, and who long to see the world without ever having to leave the comforts of home. It seems such a simple idea that it's surprising no one ever floated it before.

Recently, 10 of 88 guest suites were made available for purchase for the first time. The suites, located together at the stern of Deck 7, span a wide range of size and price, and like the residential apartments, interiors of the four larger units were created by designers Nina Campbell, J.P. Molyneaux, Yran & Storbraaten, and Luciano Di Pilla. Each of these units measure 230 to 238 square feet and cost $1,350,000. The remaining six, each measuring 1,112 square feet, were done by Hirsch Bedner Associates, a design firm, and cost $680,000. All have satellite television with VCR; direct dial telephone; marble bathroom with separate tub and shower; Frette linens and feather-down pillows, luxurious bath amenities, and complimentary in-suite beverages.

The World operates on an all-inclusive basis: roundtrip economy air transportation, transfers, porterage, port charges and meals with beverages, including an extensive selection of fine wines and spirits. (No tips, please.)

ResidenSea Ltd., Freeport is the holding company of the Group. Its wholly-owned subsidiaries, ResidenSea AS (Oslo) and ResidenSea USA, Inc. (New York), are service companies for sales and marketing. The World of ResidenSea Ltd. is the ship-owning company operating the vessel. *The World's* guest accommodations and apartment rentals can be booked through travel agents or ResidenSea.

SeaDream Yacht Club

2601 South Bayshore Drive; Coconut Grove, FL 33133-5417; (800) 707-4911; www.seadreamyachtclub.com

SeaDream I / SeaDream II (55/110 Scandinavian/International/89; 344 ft./4,260 tons)

SeaDream Yacht Club, the new venture of Seabourn Cruise Line veterans, Norwegian entrepreneur, Atle Brynestad, who was Seabourn's founder, and Larry Pimentel, its former president, began operating in spring of 2002, offering seven-day summer Mediterranean and winter Caribbean cruises on the luxury twin ships, *SeaDream I* and *II* (formerly

Sea Goddess I and *II*). The twin mega-yachts, as the line calls them, were redesigned and refitted at Lloyd Werft's shipyard in Bremerhaven, Germany prior to their entering service.

The handsome twins are meant to provide a totally different experience from today's typical cruise, one that more closely resembles yachting. Like yachting, the ships offer an open and unstructured ambience and provide passengers the ability to move at their own pace and to make personal choices. "No clocks, no crowds, no lines, no stress" could be the company's motto.

These are the SeaDream differences the owners cite:

- **Flexible Schedules and Itineraries** *SeaDream's* yachts depart their first port and arrive at their last port as scheduled, but the ports in between are not run by a strict timetable. Captains have the authority to adjust for local opportunities. If they want to visit a small island fish market so the chef can pick up the catch of the day, that's fine. If the weather and the snorkeling are perfect in a small secluded bay and passengers want to remain longer, that's ok, too.

- **Overnight in Key Ports** Most cruise ships arrive at ports of call at about 8 a.m. and sail at 5 or 6 p.m. of the same day. *SeaDream* yachts overnight at such ports as Monte Carlo and St. Tropez where the action doesn't even get started until late in the evening.

- **Raid the Pantry** *SeaDream* passengers enjoy indoor and outdoor dining or room service, and they can raid the pantry 24 hours a day for cookies and milk or a sandwich—as they might at home.

- **Officers and Staff as Guides** Passengers might visit a small town pastry shop with the chef, go snorkeling with the captain, or go hiking, biking or golfing with the officers. What better guides to have, *SeaDream* says, than those who know their sailing regions like the backs of their hands?

- **No Tuxedos or Gala Gowns** *SeaDream* has no dress code; rather it stresses the casual nature of yachting.

The outdoor features of *SeaDream I* and *II* include alcoves for sunning on double sun beds, a private massage tent on deck, a large-screen golf simulator that can also be used to watch sports events or movies, captain's chairs with mounted binoculars, and a water sports marina at the stern where there is equipment for kayaking, water skiing, windsurfing, wave running, snorkeling, and Sunfish sailing. Tai chi, yoga, and aerobics classes are also offered.

Indoors, passengers have an Asian-style spa with a thalassotherapy tub into which warm filtered sea water is pumped; a health club with elliptical treadmills mounted with flat-screen televisions, free weights, and recumbent bikes. A personal trainer is available. The ships also have a Main Lounge with a 61-inch flat-screen television, a piano bar, casino, and a library with books, CDs, DVDs, and computer outlets. Laptop computers are available. Passengers are given their own onboard e-mail address.

Each ship accommodates from 47 to 55 couples, depending on the configuration. Of the 55 cabins, all but one are Yacht Club–category with 195 square feet. Sixteen of these are convertible to Commodore Club—cabins of 390 square feet with his and her bathroom facilities and a dining area accommodating four. The 450-square-foot Owner's Suite has a bedroom and bathroom with a tub and separate shower with a view of the sea, a living room and dining area, and a guest bathroom.

All cabins are Internet-ready and have an entertainment center with a flat-screen television, CD and DVD systems with an extensive selection of movies and other offerings, and a personal jukebox with more than 100 digital music programs. All bathrooms have multiple-jet massage showers and lighted magnifying mirrors.

Staff and crew number 89; most have been sailing on their respective ships for several years. The yachts, suitable for small meetings and incentive groups, are available for charter.

In November and December, the vessels offer a series of seven-day, round-trip cruises from St. Thomas to St. Thomas, priced from $2,200 to $3,199 per person, depending on the date.

Underscoring its focus on active adults, SeaDream is offering a seven-day Mediterranean golf cruise, September 11–18, 2004 ,that provides the opportunity for golfers to try their skill at six of the region's best golf courses.

Itineraries   See Itinerary Index.

Star Cruises

1 Shenton Way #01-02; Singapore 068803; (65) 226-1168; fax (65) 220-6993; www.starcruises.com

Malaysian-based Star Cruises, owned by Genting International, a publicly traded investment group, is a phenomenon in Far Eastern cruising. Launched in 1993 with 2 ships, it grew rapidly to a fleet of 11 ships despite the Asian financial crisis in 1998. By 2000, with its purchase of Norwegian Cruise Lines and Orient Lines and their eight ships, it was tied with Princess/P&O as the third-largest cruise line in the world. The line has captured 70% of the cruise market in Asia and the Pacific—carrying over 1 million passengers in the first five years—and has won eight awards for its cabins and facilities. On all ships, there is no tipping.

The Star fleet divides into several brands: Star, SuperStar, and Mega-Star, with more under construction or planned. The first of the new Libra-class 91,000-ton megaships, *SuperStar Libra,* was delivered to NCL in 2001 and renamed, and its sister, *SuperStar Scorpio,* is scheduled for 2002. The 112,000-ton Sagittarius class will follow in 2003 and 2004. By 2004, Star/NCL will have a fleet of 23 ships.

In 1997, Star bought the luxurious *Europa* for $75 million; she was renamed *SuperStar Aries* when she joined the fleet after a multimillion-dollar refit and refurbishment in 1999. In spring 2002, she was scheduled to be transferred to Orient Lines, but those plans are on hold. The all-suite, 37,000-ton ship carries 700 passengers and is suited to around-the-world cruises. She is considered to be one of the best cruise ships in the world.

Star Aquarius (713/1,900) / Star Pisces (829/1,264; Scandinavian/ International; 574 ft./40,000 tons)

The two Star ships are former Baltic ferries designed for the regional Asian market. The ships sail on short cruises from Hong Kong and Singapore, catering largely to families and first-time cruisers. The ships are exceedingly well maintained; each has no fewer than ten food and beverages options. Child-care facilities are extensive. Activities and entertainment are geared to the whole family, with karaoke, Ping-Pong and other sports, a library, spa, boutiques, and big-name performances. The line earns high marks for its food and incredibly friendly crew.

Itineraries   See Itinerary Index.

SuperStar Gemini (400/800; International; 532 ft./19,089 tons)

Built in 1992 in Spain for more than $100 million, *SuperStar Gemini* (the former *Crown Jewel*) was the first of the SuperStar group launched in 1995 and offers deluxe, traditional seven-night cruises from Singapore to Southeast Asian ports with a crew of 470. She is designed to appeal to the fly-cruise markets of Australia, Europe, the United States, and Canada. Her itineraries also appeal to experienced Asian cruisers, who prefer longer cruises. Most passengers are European and Australian; the balance are from Japan, Taiwan, and Hong Kong.

Itineraries   See Itinerary Index.

SuperStar Leo / SuperStar Virgo (983/980/1,966/1960; International/ 1,100; 887 ft./76,800 tons)

SuperStar Leo was added in late 1998, and her twin, *SuperStar Virgo,* in 1999. They were the largest and first world-class megaships in the Asia-Pacific market, and they set new standards with extensive facilities for those who prefer activity-filled cruises. The vessels have a high crew-to-passenger ratio of one to two. They have a standard dining room and eight other dining venues. Two serve Chinese and Japanese cuisine; another offers Southeast Asian specialties. Unusual features include a public observation area of the bridge, with videos detailing bridge and engine operations. They offer a casino, spa and fitness center, shops, and children's facilities. The ships' cruising speed is a zippy 25 knots, enabling them to include four to six ports of call on a seven-night itinerary.

SuperStar Taurus (formerly NCL's *Leeward*) offers short and long cruises from Japan, Korea, and China. *SuperStar Taurus's* arrival completed Star Cruises' Asian geographical coverage from Kobe in the north to Singapore in the south.

Itineraries See Itinerary Index.

MegaStar Taurus / MegaStar Aries (36/72; International/International; 270 ft./3,264 tons)

The MegaStars are the most deluxe of Star's brands. Formerly *Aurora I* and *II*, the ships were among the most luxurious small ships built in the 1990s. The ships operate on two- and three-day cruises, year-round from Malaysia, Singapore, and Kuala Lumpur. Each carries only 72 passengers and 80 crew members and is usually chartered to corporations, groups, or wedding parties.

Itineraries See Itinerary Index.

Swan Hellenic Cruises

631 Commack Rd., Suite 1A, Commack, NY 11725; (631) 858-1270; (877) 219-4239; fax (631) 858-1279; www.swan-hellenic.co.uk

Swan Hellenic, which was owned by P&O Line and now, by Carnival Cruises as a result of its purchase of P&O/Princess Cruises, has a large following in the United States as well as the United Kingdom, Australia, and Canada. The line caters to travelers (most age 50 or older) who are intellectually curious and interested in the art and culture of destinations they visit.

Minerva II (316/684; Italian/European; 594 ft./30,277 tons)

Swan Hellenic's new ship, *Minerva II,* was launched in April 2003. The ship originally debuted in 2001 as the *Renaissance VIII* of the now-defunct Renaissance Cruises. She is Swan Hellenic's most luxurious ship to date, with the most modeen facilities and amenities, although she has been given some country house–style touches to fit Swan Hellenic's image.

Minerva II's outstanding features include 93% outside cabins, of which 73% have private balconies. There also is a range of single cabins at affordable prices. Open seating dining in four restauranats with a wider choice of cuisine is also available. The ship has three bars, a library, spa facilities and fitness cener, and an outdoor swimming pool with a Jacuzzi. She offers a choice of venues for classical music recitals and other activities, such as art classes, tai chi, and music and dance performances by local groups.

The new ship is able to visit a wider range of destinations with the benefit of increased speeds. These itineraries continue to focus on well-known as well as off-the-beaten-track places, with a team of guest speakers on each cruise and a wide choice of excursions at ports of call. Prices will include excursions and all tips. The ship is making Swan Hellenic's first trip to Central America, departing from New Orleans in January 2004, as well as South America and the Amazon, the Bahamas, and the eastern seaboard of the United States and Canada. The cruise line offers substsantial early-bird savings, particularly for those booking two consecutive cruises.

Itineraries   See Itinerary Index.

Travel Dynamics International

132 East 70th Street, New York, NY 10021; (212) 517-7555; (800) 257-5767; fax (212) 774-1545; www.traveldynamicsinternational.com

The former Classical Cruises has been folded into its owners' operation, Travel Dynamics International, a long-established incentive-travel company. As in the past, the company continues to specialize in educational and cultural cruises, using a variety of well-known deluxe and luxury ships. Programs are designed for well-traveled, destination-oriented individuals who want a learning experience but don't want to forgo comfort. Itineraries span the globe and include exotic as well as familiar destinations. Lecturers and academics knowledgeable about the destination accompany the cruises. For 2004, the company will be using three ships: *Callisto, Clelia II,* and the brand-new luxury exploration ship, *Orion.*

Callisto (17/34; Greek/European; 164 ft./435 tons)

This small luxury yacht, built in Germany, underwent comprehensive renovation and refurbishment prior to her debut in 2000. The ship has 17 outside cabins, 11 with large panoramic windows and six with three large portholes each, a spacious lounge, a dining room accommodating all passengers at one open seating, and al fresco dining on two decks. There is piano bar, two broad decks for sunbathing, a swimming platform at the vessel's stern, and a gym. All cabins are air-conditioned and have full- or queen-sized beds, marble bath, radio, telephone, refrigerator, and television with VCR. The four-deck ship has a draft of eight feet and a speed of 14 knots. It is equipped with Zodiac landing crafts. The bridge is outfitted with state-of-the-art navigational and communications equipment.

Rates start at $6,495 per person and include a seven-day cruise. For 2004, the ship explores Sicily or the Amalfi Coast and sails in the Greek Islands and Crete.

Itineraries   See Itinerary Index.

Clelia II (42/84; Greek/European; 290 ft./4,077 tons)

Formerly *Renaissance IV,* the *Clelia II* is a small, all-suite luxury vessel with roomy public rooms, sophisticated décor, and ample facilities. The five-deck ship has two lounges, a well-stocked library, beauty salon, steam bath, pool, Jacuzzi, medical facilities, and gym. The elegant dining room, in light wood and marble, has open seating for all meals. Breakfast and lunch buffets are served outdoors. Also available are a room-service menu, in-cabin meals from the restaurant during dining hours, and an 11 p.m. snack. Evening entertainment may be lectures, music, movies, and videos. The spacious cabins, all with sea views, are paneled in dark wood and furnished with twin or queen-size beds. They have a sitting area or living room with vanity/desk, sofa, side chair, coffee table, minibar, television, radio, and VCR. Storage space is ample. Bathrooms are small and have showers only. Deluxe apartments and penthouse suites are available, some with two bathrooms and balconies. The ship was refurbished recently prior to being returned to service.

Clelia II's cruises explore the Mediterranean and Italy, focusing on history, archaeology, architecture, and nature. Guest lecturers are usually from leading U.S. museums and universities.

Orion (53/106; German/European; 337 ft./4,050 tons)

Billed as a vessel for a new age of exploration cruising, the new *Orion* was scheduled to have her maiden voyage in late November 2003. The new class of expedition ship combines the latest advances in ship design and communication technology with the style and comfort of a luxury cruise ship. From her ice-strengthened hull (rated E3, the highest rating available) to the remote viewing cameras atop its mast, no expense was spared in *Orion's* construction.

Built at the Cassens Shipyard in Emden, Germany, *Orion* is a model of German craftsmanship and engineering, with such features as technologically advanced stabilizers, bow and stern thrusters for easy maneuverability, a surround-sound audio system in the lecture hall, and direct Internet access in every cabin.

But it's *Orion's* luxurious accommodations that distinguish her most from other expedition ships. Each of the 24 standard cabins measure between 175 and 180 square feet, while each of the 29 suites measure from 215 to 345 square feet; eight have French balconies. All cabins are outside and include a sitting area or living room, direct Internet access, television/DVD and CD player, minifridge, private marble bathroom, ample closet space, and twin beds that can be converted to a queen. Large oval, rectangular, or sliding glass floor-to-ceiling windows offer panoramic views.

Orion's amenities include a spa, sauna, whirlpool, masseuse, hairdresser, boutique, several lounges, and a computer center equipped with Internet access. At the center of the ship is a glass atrium that wraps around the elevator and serves *Orion's* seven decks. The **Constellation**

Restaurant accommodates all guests at a single unassigned seating; an open deck off the main lounge is available for dining alfresco.

A spacious observation lounge on the top deck opens onto a wraparound deck for optimal viewing. The bridge also leads out to an open observation area. A "mud" room on the lower deck stores parkas, boots, and other equipment during and after a day of exploration. Ten heavy-duty Zodiac inflatable motorized boats are available for landing in shallow areas and to navigate small waterways, and several two-seater kayaks are available for individual exploration.

Classified with Germanischer Lloyd, *Orion* meets the latest international safety rules and regulations. The ship is served by 70 European officers and crew. She is spending her maiden winter on Antarctica cruises.

Part Three

Cruising Alternatives

River and Barge Cruises

A river cruise is not only a different way to see a country; it's a different country you will see. Whether you sail down the Danube or the Yangtze, up the Hudson or the Nile, or float on European channels or the Erie Canal, the cruise will be a new travel experience, even if you have visited the same area by land.

The river cruise most familiar to U.S. travelers is probably steamboating on the Mississippi, but there are many kinds of river cruises, their character shaped by the locale and nature of the waterway. An adventure cruise on the Amazon, for example, is quite different from barging in Burgundy. Nonetheless, river cruises share certain characteristics, and all are light years from an ocean cruise.

To begin with, boats (a vessel is a ship on the ocean, but a boat on a river) on river cruises are small. Most boats carry 100–200 passengers, although some of the new riverboats accommodate 250 or more, and Delta Queen's *American Queen* takes 400 passengers. Barges that glide along small canals and waterways are much smaller, usually taking about 12 and never more than 24 passengers.

The small size of vessels and the nature of the waterways provide an intimate look at the cruise locale, heightening the sense of place and history in a way oceanliners never can. The destination, not the boat, is the main attraction on a river cruise.

Cabins are small but comfortable. The ambience is informal, the dress casual. Except on some large riverboats, nightly entertainment is absent. Passengers are left to their own devices, and many rediscover the pleasure of conversation and friendship.

River and Barge Cruises in Europe

River cruises are available on major rivers worldwide, but the largest selection is in Europe—Rhine, Rhône, Seine, Danube, Volga—where rivers have been thoroughfares of commerce and culture for centuries.

European cruises—most between April and November—take you to the great cities through beautiful scenery laced with ancient forts, mighty cathedrals, and storybook castles. They dock in the heart of a different town each day. Tours are available, but most passengers can easily sightsee on their own.

River cruises reveal Europe the way it was meant to be seen. Almost all historic buildings were built facing the river, so when the boat docks in front of Pillnitz Palace on the Elbe, for example, passengers enter the way guests of Augustus the Strong would have entered centuries ago.

Some itineraries overnight in port, allowing passengers to attend local shows or dine ashore. Others sail at night so passengers wake refreshed for the next day of sight-seeing.

More than a dozen companies offer such cruises; the largest, Viking River Cruises, is typical. Its fleet of 26 ships sails the length of the Rhine, as well as the Elbe, Moselle, Seine, Saône, and Rhône. The Danube and Rhine-Main-Danube Canal were added in 1994, when the North and Black Seas were linked for the first time.

Riverboats and barges have completely different styles. Canals and smaller rivers deep in the countryside are traversed by barges gliding gently through some of the most beautiful and historic areas of England and Europe. The pace is so leisurely (three or four miles per hour) that passengers can get off to walk in the woods or bike in the village and not be left behind. The tortoise's pace, the utter peace and relaxation, are for some the best vacation they ever had. For others, it's like watching grass grow.

By day, passengers lounge on deck, play cards, read, and watch the boat navigate the locks. They can walk or bike, discovering interesting places and friendly people, and reboard at the next lock. The price usually includes a choice of guided tours by minibus or bicycle to nearby castles, wineries, and medieval towns.

Hotel barges, as they are known, are like floating country inns. They vary in size, carrying from 6 to 51 passengers on cruises of 3, 6, or 13 days. Cabins are small and bathrooms are tiny, but the barges, such as those of French Country Waterways, are luxurious. Many serve outstanding gourmet cuisine prepared by Cordon Bleu chefs. Regional wines, normally included in the cruise price, flow generously. The atmosphere is very informal—and very romantic.

Dozens of boats and barges cruise Europe. The season runs April through October. Here's a sampling with U.S. offices or representatives. Note that several companies offer the same boats; agreements may not be exclusive.

Note: In parentheses after each boat name is information about the number of cabins and passengers; officers and crew; and the boat's length (cabins/passengers; officers/crew; boat length).

Abercrombie & Kent International

1520 Kensington Road, Suite 212, Oak Brook, IL 60523-2156; (630) 954-2944; (800) 323-7308; fax (630) 954-3324; www.abercrombiekent.com

(Also see Abercrombie & Kent International under "Yangtze River Cruises," "Nile River Cruises," and "Amazon River Cruises," all later in this chapter.)

Actief (6/11; British; 100 ft.)
Three to six nights, upper Thames.

Alouette (3/6; French/British; 98 ft.)
Six nights in Burgundy and Franche-Comté.

Amaryllis (4/8; French; 129 ft.)
Six nights on various routes in France, including Burgundy, Franche-Comté, Loire Valley, and Midi.

Anacoluthe (25/50; French; 210 ft.)
Six nights, Normandy.

Caprice (11/21; French/British; 128 ft.)
Six nights in Southern Burgundy and Eastern Loire.

Chanterelle (14/24; British/French; 128 ft.)
Six nights, Park and Garden Cruise.

Chardonnay (27/50; French; 260 ft.)
Six nights, Beaujolais and Lyonnaise on the Saône.

Fleur de Lys (4/6; French/British; 129 ft.)
Six nights in Burgundy and Franche-Comté.

Hirondelle (4/8; French/British; 129 ft.)
Six nights in Burgundy and Franche-Comté.

L'Abercrombie (11/22; French/British; 128 ft.)
Six nights in central Burgundy.

L'art De Vivre (4/8; French/British; 100 ft.)
Six nights in the Upper Nivernais in Burgundy.

La Belle Epoque (6/12; French/British; 128 ft.)
Outdoor spa/pool as well as sauna and fitness area. Six-night cruises in Burgundy and Chablis.

Libellule (10/20; British/French; 128 ft.)
Six nights in Eastern Burgundy and the Franche-Comté.

Litote (10/20; British/French; 128 ft.)
Six nights in northern Burgundy.

Lorraine (11/22; French/British; 128 ft.)
Six nights in Alsace-Lorraine.

Marguerite (10/20; French/British; 128 ft.)
Spring Garden & Tulip Cruise, and Champagne Cruise.

Marjorie (4/8, Flemish ; 128 ft.)
Six nights in Northern Burgundy on the Yonne River and Canal du Loing.

Marjorie II (6/12; Flemish; 128 ft.)
Six nights in Northern Burgundy and Chablis.

Mirabelle (12/24; French; 128 ft.)
Six nights in Bordeaux-Dordogne.

Napoleon (6/12; French; 129 ft.)
Six nights on the Saône in Burgundy and Rhône in Provence.

Princess Royale (12/22; French; 166 ft.)
Six nights in Holland and Belgium.

Provence (27/50; English/French; 292 ft)
Six nights Provence and Camargue on the Rhône in France.

Roi Soleil (3/6; Dutch; 98 ft.)
Six nights in Provence, Camargue, Languedoc, and Canal du Midi.

Scottish Highlander (4/8; Scottish; 117 ft.)
Six nights on the Caledonian Canal and Scottish Highlands.

Shannon Princess II (5/10; Irish; 105 ft.)
Six nights on the Shannon River in Ireland and Lough Derg.

The Barge Lady

101 West Grand Avenue, Suite 200, Chicago, IL 60610; (312) 245-0900; (800) 880-0071; fax (312) 245-0952; www.bargelady.com

Variety of barges on canals of France, Holland, Belgium, Scotland, Ireland, Germany, and Great Britain; golf and wine-tasting cruises featured.

Etoile de Champagne

40 Broad Street, Boston, MA 02109; (800) 280-1492; www.etoiledechampagne.com

Etoile de Champagne (6/12; Dutch/6; 128 ft.), *La Nouvelle* (4/8, Dutch;/6;128 ft.)
Seven and twelve days, Holland, Belgium, France, Germany, and Mosel Valley; April–September.

Peter Deilmann Cruises

1800 Diagonal Road, Suite 170, Alexandria, VA 22314; (703) 549-1741; (800) 348-8287; fax (703) 549-7924; www.deilmann-cruises.com

This European line markets ten riverboats; a barquentine, *Lili Marleen;* and a luxury oceanliner, *Deutschland,* which made her debut in 1998. The line added its tenth riverboat, the *Fredric Chopin,* in 2002.

Casanova (48/96; German/European; 338 ft.)

Newly built in 2001, the deluxe boat offers spacious outside cabins with French doors on the upper deck and picture windows on the lower. All cabins have private bathrooms, telephone, radio, desk, and chair. Facilities include single-seating dining room, lounge, bar, library, dance floor, fitness area, conference room, boutique, and beauty salon. The boat sails seven-day cruises from Venice on Italy's Po River through mid-November.

Cézanne (See description under Provence Line.)

Danube Princess (94/198; European/German; 364 ft.)

Facilities include outdoor swimming pool, single-seating dining room, two bars, conference room, library, gift shop, and beauty salon. Cabins have private bathrooms, telephone, radio, and television. The ship sails seven-day Danube cruises March–early November from Munich to Austria, Hungary, and Slovakia; and 10- and 11-day Black Sea cruises.

Dresden (53/106; European/German; 320 ft.)

Facilities include single-seating dining room, bar, gift shop, beauty salon, fitness equipment, sauna, library, infirmary, and laundry room. All cabins have private shower and toilet, telephone, radio, and television. Dresden sails seven-day Elbe cruises from Hamburg or Dresden to Meissen, Magdeburg, and Wittenberg.

Frederic Chopin (41/79; European/German; 272 ft.)

The *Chopin,* a luxury vessel, debuted in March of 2002. Seven-night cruise that begins in Berlin and ends in Prague with overnight stays in Berlin, Dresden and Prague. Also, seven-night cruise Frankfort/Oderberg (Berlin), Germany, with overnight stays in Lunow, Straslsund, and Wolgast, Germany.

Katharina (41/79; European/German; 272 ft.)

Double- and twin-bedded cabins with French doors on upper deck, picture windows on lower deck. Various itineraries on the Elbe River between Potsdam and Prague. Seven-night cruise, Amsterdam to Amsterdam; Frankfort to Amsterdam; Munich and Basel to Munich (Passau).

Königstein (29/58; European/German; 221 ft.)

Seven-night cruise Berlin to Prague on the Elbe, Havel, Vltava, and Oder rivers to historic German and Czech cities and towns.

Mozart (97/200; European/German; 396 ft.)

The deluxe boat has large, all-outside cabins with spacious private bathrooms, television, minibar, hair dryer, and telephone. Facilities include an indoor swimming pool, whirlpool, sauna, and fitness center. From March to early November, the boat sails seven-day Danube cruises departing on Sunday from Passau and calling at Bratislava, Budapest, Kalocza, Esztergom, Duernstein, and Melk. Classical music summer cruises are scheduled.

Princesse de Provence (70/140; German/European; 363 ft.)

Large cabins have private bathrooms, hair dryer, telephone, and radio. Facilities include fitness equipment, single-seating dining room, two bars, conference room, library, infirmary, gift shop. March–November, the boat sails seven-day cruises round-trip from Lyon up the Saône River and down the Rhône to Arles, Chateauneuf-du-Pape, Viviers, Trevoux, and Avignon.

Prussian Princess (69/138; European/German; 363 ft.)

The deluxe boat offers spacious outside cabins with full-length French doors on the upper deck and picture windows on the lower. All cabins have private bathrooms, telephone, radio, desk, and chair. Facilities include single-seating dining room, lounge, two bars, library, dance floor, fitness area, conference room, boutique, and beauty salon. The boat sails seven-day cruises on the Rhine and Moselle rivers and Main-Danube Canal between Amsterdam and Basel; round-trip from Frankfurt or Amsterdam through German, Belgian, and Dutch canals.

European Waterways

53 E. 34th Street, New York, NY 10016; (212) 532-8356; (800) 546-7777; fax (212) 689-5456; www.ewaterways.com

Anjodi / Bonne Amie / Bonne Humeur / La Belle Epoque / L'Impressioniste / Rosa / L'arte de Vivre / Le Bon Vivant / Napolean / Nyphea / Papillon / The Sterling (3–6/6–12; French/French and English; 80–128 ft.)

Six nights, rivers and canals of France.

Marguerite (10/20; French; 128 ft.)

Six nights, between Amsterdam and Brussels during spring tulip season; and the Champagne region and Paris in summer and fall.

European Waterways also represents a medley of barges and riverboats for 6–14 passengers on the Shannon River in Ireland, Thames and other waterways of Britain, and Burgundy and other canals of France. Seven-day cruises on Shannon Princess can be geared to special interests, such as golf, sport fishing, equestrian, culinary, cycling, wildlife, and poetry. European Waterways also represents the luxury sailing ship *Sea Cloud* (see "Sailing Ships") and Temptress Cruises, which offers itineraries in Belize and Costa Rica (see "Adventure and Cultural Cruises").

French Country Waterways

P.O. Box 2195, Duxbury, MA 02331; (781) 934-2454; (800) 222-1236; fax (781) 934-9048; www.fcwl.com

Esprit (9/18; French/English/7; 128 ft.)
Cote d'Or wine region (Burgundy Canal, Saône River, Canal du Centre from Dijon to St. Leger-sur-Dheune).

Horizon II (6/12; French/English/6; 128 ft.)
Upper Burgundy (Burgundy Canal from Tonnerre to Venarey-les-Laumes).

Liberté (4/8; French/English/4; 100 ft.)
Western Burgundy region (Canal du Nivernais from Auxerre to Clamecy).

Nenuphar (6/12; French/English/6; 128 ft.)
Upper Loire region (Canal du Briar and Canal du Loing from Chatillon-sur-Loire to Samois-sur-Seine).

Princess (4/8; French/English/6; 128 ft.)
Champagne, Moselle Valley, and Alsace-Lorraine regions.

Global Quest

185 Willis Avenue, 2nd Floor, Mineola, NY 11501; (516) 739-3690; (800) 221-3254; fax (516) 739-8022; www.globalquesttravel.com

The company represents a variety of vessels which cruise in five general areas: Europe; Russia, Ukraine and Siberia; Danube; Galápagos and South America; and East Africa/Indian Ocean. Information on the latter two areas are found in the next section, "Adventure and Cultural Cruises."

"Europe by River" is the company's umbrella for 12 modern riverboats, all similar in size and holding 150-200 passengers and with all outside cabins, swimming pool, whirlpool, library, lounge, bar, and dining room serving international cuisine. They offer cruise/tour combinations of the Po, Elbe, Rhône, Saône, Rhine, Danube, Saar, Moselle, Main, Neckar, and Seine.

Kirov / Krasin (200–270 passengers; Russian or Ukrainian; 415 ft.)
All outside cabins, informal atmosphere, local entertainment, and guest lecturers on history and culture. On these 14-day voyages, passengers arrive in a different port each morning and have most of the day for sightseeing (guided tours optional). Boats sail from May to September on the rivers, lakes, and canals connecting Moscow and St. Petersburg. On three nights each in Moscow and St. Petersburg, passengers sleep aboard and can take guided shore excursions. Krasin sails on an eight day, seven-night cruise through four countries (Austria, Slovakia, Hungary, and Germany), visiting three capital cities—Vienna, Budapest, and Bratislav.

Kirov offers 12-day itineraries, from Moscow to St. Petersburg, linking the Imperial cities of czars, cruising along the Volga and Neva rivers.

Amadeus Rhapsody / Amadeus Symphony / Amadeus Viking / Viking Schumann / Viking Normandy (73–236 passengers; European; 347–370 ft.)

Danube cruises of 8 to 13 days, linking central and southeastern Europe, the Balkans, and Black Sea with cruise/tour options from Amsterdam to Prague for many of the nine countries sharing the waters. Itineraries include entertainment, guest lecturers, and shore excursions. Ships have all outside cabins, informal atmosphere, and regional cuisine. Ports may include Passau, Budapest, Vienna, Bratislava, Tulcea, and Weissenkirchen. *Amadeus Rhapsody* and *Amadeus Symphony* have a library, sun deck, and heated pools.

Peter the Great Cruises

2610 East 16th Street, Brooklyn, NY 11235; (718) 934-4100; (800) 828-7970; fax (718) 934-9419; www.cruise-russ.com

Peter the Great (157/280; Russian; 425 ft.)

Eighteen-day tour of waterways connecting Moscow and St. Petersburg. Nine ports of call, including four days in Moscow and four in St. Petersburg. May–September. Also available: Grand Russian Cruise.

Inland Voyages

Navigant International c/o Vacation Services; 112 Prospect Street, Stamford, CT 06901; (203) 978-5010; (800) 786-5311; fax (203) 978-5027; www.navigantvacations.com.

Luciole (8/14; Belgian, French/British, French; 100 ft.)

Six nights, Canal de Bourgogne or the Nivernais from Montbard.

Le Boat

45 Whitney Road, Suite C5, Mahwah, NJ 07430; (201) 560-1941; (800) 992-0291; fax (201) 560-1945; www.leboat.com

Le Boat specializes in barge charters and self-drive canal boats on canals in Britain, Scotland, France, Holland, Ireland, and Belgium; and yacht charters worldwide.

Elegant Cruises & Tours

24 Vanderventer Avenue, Port Washington, NY 11050; (516) 767-9302; (800) 683-6767; fax (516) 767-9303; www.elegantcruises.com

River Cloud (47/95; European; 360 ft.)

Launched in 1996, the splendidly appointed *River Cloud* is one of the finest boats on European waterways. Interiors convey 1930s luxury reminiscent of the Orient Express. She offers the impeccable service and fine cuisine for which her famous sister ship, *Sea Cloud,* is known.

The elegant dining room serves meals in a single, open seating in a relaxed, friendly atmosphere. Breakfast and lunch are buffet-style; dinner is served at tables. Menus feature continental specialties and complimentary fine wines, beer, and soft drinks. The centerpiece of the handsome lounge encircled by windows at the bow is a seven-foot Steinway grand piano. It's much in use during afternoon tea and music cruises when renowned pianists and opera stars are aboard. Amenities include a library, boutique, hair salon, exercise room, sauna, putting green, and large-scale chessboard. All cabins have telephone, radio, television, air-conditioning, safe, and marble bathrooms with showers and hair dryers.

The Dutch-built *River Cloud* sails on the Rhine, Main, Moselle, and Danube, April–October. The cruises are also sold through Dailey-Thorp Travel of New York, (212) 307-1555; Abercrombie & Kent, (800) 323-7308; European Waterways, (800) 217-4447; and other U.S. companies.

River Cloud II (45/88; European; 338 ft.)

Launched in late spring 2001, this boat sails on Italy's historic Po River between Cremona and Venice, on seven-night itineraries with the debarkation port alternating each week. Her public rooms include a lounge and library, restaurant, boutique, and hair salon. The air-conditioned ship has 15 junior suites with windows and 29 double-bed cabins with portholes. All have direct-dial telephone, television with video player, radio and music channels, minibar, emergency button, and bath with shower, hair dryer, bathrobes, and toiletries. A fruit basket, half-bottle of champagne, bottled water, and soft drinks are replenished daily.

A typical cruise would include two nights in Venice, cruising the lagoon to the islands of Murano, Burano, Torcello, and Chioggia, before entering the Po. Other ports and sites to be visited include Taglio di Po, the Abbey of Pomposa, Ferrara, Mantua, Verona, and Parma. Shore excursions include the Violin Museum in Boretto, where passengers hear a private Stradivarius recital. The line's other new ship, *Sea Cloud II,* an oceangoing sailing vessel, joined the fleet in April 2001.

Swan Hellenic Cruises

631 Commack Road, Suite 1A, Commack, NY 11725; (631) 858-1263; (877) 800-7926; fax (631) 858-1279; www.swanhellenic.com

River holidays (on the *Swiss Crystal*) are accompanied by expert guest speakers. Fares include excursions and tips. Summer cruises explore waterways of Russia and Central Europe in small, chartered riverboats. Cruises are 8–15 days and can be combined with pre- and postcruise tours. Reservations can be made through API, a U.S.-based consortium of travel agents, (800) 402-4API, or direct at Swan Hellenic's London office on its toll-free number, (877) 219-4239, between 4 a.m. and 12:30 p.m. EST.

Viking River Cruises

21820 Burbank Boulevard ,Woodland Hills, CA 91367; (818) 227-1234; (877)668-4546; fax (818) 227-1231; www.vikingrivers.com

A Switzerland-based company offering European and Russian cruises, Viking River Cruises has itineraries of 9 to 16 nights on the Rhine, Danube, Oder, Po, Seine, Rhône, Volga, and Dnjepr rivers. Its U.S. division offers all-inclusive programs created specifically for English-speaking passengers on the Elbe, Danube, Rhine, and Main ranging from 9 to 16 nights.

In 2000, Viking River Cruises bought Europe's largest riverboat company, KD River Cruises of Europe , bringing its total of riverboats in operation to 25. The former KD boats sail the length of the Rhine, Elbe, Moselle, Seine, Saône, and Danube rivers and the Rhine-Main-Danube Canal linking the North and Black Seas. Viking River Cruises also has boats cruising in Russia and the Ukraine. The following are some of the combined fleet.

Viking Normandie / Viking Burgundy (51–77/104–154; French/International; 295–365 ft.)

Two-seven night cruises; French Vineyard and Vistas, sail along the Rhone and Saône rivers through Burgundy, Provence and the scenery of the Ardeche region. Seven-night Paris and the heart of Normandy.

Viking Danube (75/150; 40/361 ft.)

Five nights, Rhine and Moselle between Basel and Amsterdam. Twelve nights, Rhine and Moselle exploration, Amsterdam to Basel.

Viking Europe (75/150; 40/375 ft.)

Seven-night cruise, Holland and Belgium (round-trip Amsterdam), and the Danube Explorer (Vienna to Nuremberg); 12-night cruise Vienna to Amsterdam; 14-night cruises, Danube River to the Black Sea and the Grand European Tour (Amsterdam to Budapest).

Viking Neptune / Viking Pride / Viking Spirit (75/150; 40/375 ft.)

Seven- to fourteen-night cruises: Holland and Belgium and Rhine, Main and Danube.

Viking Schumann (60/124; 28/311 ft.)

Six-night cruise on the Elbe (Berlin to Prague).

Viking Sky (75/150; 40/360 ft.)

Ten-night cruise, Antwerp to Basel.

Viking Kirov / Viking Pakhomov (103/199; 430 ft.)

From May to September, both boats sail on ten- and eleven-day "Waterways of the Czars" cruises between St. Petersburg and Moscow.

Yangtze River Cruises in China

The Chinese aptly call the Yangtze "Changjiang" (long river). Rising from the Tibetan plateau, it plunges through mountain passes into

Sichuan to form a border between Hubei and Hunan before reaching the fertile plains of Jiangsu and Shanghai, a journey of almost 4,000 miles. The Yangtze (a local name) is more than a scenic wonder. It was the site of epic battles in the second century B.C., and archaeological excavations suggest that the area was a cradle of Chinese civilization.

The river remains the great highway of central China, carrying passenger ferries, patrol boats, and barges piled with coal, limestone, timber, and cement. Small freighters deliver supplies to towns built into the cliffs and collect the fruit grown in terraced orchards.

The river is always busy, especially as it narrows into gorges. There, traffic control is essential, and cruise ship captains are in telephone contact with shore pilot stations as they steer the shallow-draft vessels between gravel shoals.

The Three Gorges: Qutang, Wu, Xiling

Qutang Gorge, also known as Wind Box Gorge, is five miles long, but never wider than 490 feet. Limestone cliffs erupt on either side in sheer walls up to 4,000 feet tall. The cliff face is pitted with caves, and the remains are visible of an old towpath—the only way through the gorge before the biggest boulders were cleared from the river.

Less than an hour after leaving the Qutang, cruise-ship passengers enter 25-mile-long **Wu Gorge.** Its cliffs are so high and steep that the sun rarely touches the water. Twelve peaks dominate. According to myth, they're a goddess and her handmaidens who chose to be turned to stone to stand sentinel over the river.

Midway through the gorge is the border between Sichuan and Hubei Provinces. The exit from the gorge is only 164 feet across, the narrowest part of the river.

It takes another day for cruise ships to reach **Xiling Gorge,** the longest canyon, which winds 47 miles through small gorges amid fierce rapids. On either side are examples of the mountains beyond mountains of classic Chinese scenery.

Three Gorges Dam

Three Gorges Dam is under construction at Sandouping, at the eastern mouth of the gorges. It's massive. The dam wall will be almost two miles long and 607 feet tall. Behind it, a lake will stretch 373 miles and cover 418 square miles, inundating most of the Xiling and half of the Wu Gorge. A million or more people are being evacuated in anticipation of the dam's completion in 2009.

Supporters say the $34 billion dam will control flooding and generate 84.7 billion kilowatt hours a year for Shanghai and the Lower Yangtze Basin. Opponents say it will destroy the environment and build a reservoir of toxic silt in an earthquake-prone region. Either way, it adds poignancy to a Yangtze cruise.

With Stage Two finished in June 2003, the eastern mouth of the gorges at Sandouping is virtually complete, and the reservoir continues to fill. The lake behind the dam will raise water levels in the Xiling and Wu

Gorge. Cruise boats journey through a brand-new, five-stage lock to go around the dam wall.

The first westerners to sail up the Yangtze River were British colonial administrators who established the inland port of Hankow (now part of Wuhan) in the 1840s. The most adventurous continued into the sparsely populated wilderness upstream and found the Three Gorges.

Transport was by sailing ships, which were hauled by teams of trackers through raging rapids and over great boulders until English trader Archibald Little pioneered steamship service from Wuhan, finally reaching Chongqing (formerly Chungking) in 1898. The voyage remained extremely hazardous until the 1950s, when the Chinese blasted away the largest boulders.

Regular cruises through the gorges were introduced in the early 1980s and became an established part of many all-China itineraries. The gorges are on the 120-mile (192-kilometer) stretch of river between Baidicheng and Yichang. Some itineraries between Chongqing and Yichang reduce the trip by a day and night. However, it has often proved difficult to arrange air or land transfers to or from Yichang. Most cruises thus cover the full 850-mile (1,370-kilometer) section between Chongqing and Wuhan.

Shore Excursions (Upstream or Downstream)

Shennong Stream/Daning River Gorges   All cruises offer a side trip up one of the Yangtze's tributaries for a closer look at the natural grandeur. Excursions feature fast-flowing, crystal-clear streams with shifting, pebbled shoals and sheer cliffs pocked with caves, clad in waterfalls, and encrusted with ferns. With the rising waters of the river, some of the lesser gorges are also now fully accessible by larger boats, and previously unexplored tributaries are available to visitors.

Shennong Stream is the better option, partly because the journey is taken in wooden longboats, which are steered, pushed, and sometimes hauled by husky young men of the Tujia minority. Shennong Stream is also a good option because it is one of the shallower tributaries.

The half-day excursion includes a visit to a Tujia-style house, where local dance is performed and worthwhile souvenirs are sold.

Zigui   This historic town, poised on the cliffs at the entrance to Xiling Gorge, exudes an air of ancient certainty, but it will be swallowed by the dam's reservoir. Only one building will be preserved: The temple dedicated to Chu Yuan, the scholar statesman who drowned himself in 278 B.C. in protest of his government's policy, will be moved downstream with the population. Travelers will lose a town whose main street is packed with sidewalk kitchens, vegetable stalls, al fresco hairdressers, one-room tailors, and an alley of pool tables.

Shashi/Jingzhou   Upstream from Wuhan, this bustling port contains the remains of a royal capitol from the seventh century B.C. Some original walls are maintained, and the museum contains a 2,000-year-old mummy.

Yueyang Tower   This gold-tiled pavilion on the Hunan banks of the river, upstream from Wuhan, was built in 716 as a military lookout. It was later expanded to provide a belvedere over scenic Dongting Lake.

Fengdu   Near the western entrance of Qutang Gorge, this ancient cliff town is reputed to be where people's spirits go after death. To placate unhappy and potentially dangerous phantoms, a temple sells "passports to hell" and other souvenirs.

Shibaozhai   The cliffside town, between Chongqing and the first gorge, has a 12-story red pagoda and hilltop temple. Built right into the cliff and called the "Pearl of the Yangtze," the temple is an architectural treasure from the Ming Dynasty, dating to the mid-16th century. Some excursions visit it.

Cruise Lines and Ships

About 40 ships offer cruises through the Yangtze gorges. The majority are Chinese-owned and marketed internationally by China Merchants Changjiang Cruise Company, with offices in Hong Kong (1607 Wing On Centre, 111 Connaught Road, Hong Kong).

A new generation of vessels caters to travelers whose interest has been fueled by reports that the gorges' days are numbered. These ships operate on regular itineraries designed to allow passage through the gorges during daylight. The timing concerns produce shore excursions that are conveniently located, interesting, varied, and appropriate to the area's history. The season lasts from late February to early December. Summer is extremely hot; in winter, the water level is low and temperatures are below freezing. There are almost weekly departures of the four-day, three-night downstream cruise from Chongqing and the five-day, four-night upstream trip from Wuhan.

However, those reports that the gorges' days are numbered are a bit exaggerated. Overall, the river will rise some 575 feet in total, but the gorges themselves are so deep that they will be less affected than some have claimed. While the landscapes will change, the reality is that the water will not submerge the gorges. In fact, since Stage Two of the dam is already complete, the river will rise only about another 131 feet at the dam's completion. In addition, the deeper water will open even newer vistas to cruisers, since the lesser gorges, which previously held little water, will now be fully navigable, and visitors will have the opportunity to explore previously inaccessible areas of the river.

Abercrombie & Kent International

1520 Kensington Road, Suite 212, Oak Brook, IL 60523; (630) 954-2944; (800) 323-7308; fax (630) 954-3324; www.abercrombiekent.com

East King / East Queen (78/156; Chinese; 300 ft.)

The twin boats *East King* and *East Queen* (operating March–November) are the fastest and most modern on the route. All cabins are a spacious 183 square feet and have picture windows, minibars, satellite television, international direct-dial telephones, safes, terry robes, hair dryers, and well-designed bathrooms. There are two suites, which can be combined with a tea lounge for seminars, groups, or small meetings. The main dining room serves western and Chinese meals. Public facilities include a nightclub, five karaoke rooms, an enclosed observation deck with café, a business center, and a 100-seat function room. Recreational facilities include a swimming pool, card rooms, gym, and sauna.

Regal China Cruises

57 West 38th Street, New York, NY 10018; (212) 768-3388; fax (212) 768-4939

Princess Sheena / Princess Jeannie / Princess Elaine (134 cabins, 10 suites/258 passengers; Chinese; 424 ft.)

These German-built boats—the longest on the river—are managed by Regal China Cruises, a Sino-American joint venture. They offer a ballroom, bar, sun deck, business center, and health club with sauna, gym, and practitioner of acupuncture and qigong. They have two dining rooms with river views: The main restaurant serves buffets of western and Chinese cuisine; the other offers Chinese table service or a buffet.

Standard cabins are rather small (121 square feet) but have direct-dial phone, radio, television, air-conditioning, and bathrooms with showers. Only superior-category cabins have a separate shower stall. The ten suites are spacious, with separate sitting areas, kitchenettes, and bathrooms with tubs. Ten cabins are specifically designated for single travelers.

The boats offer a variety of Chinese cultural programs, lectures, and activities, including mah-jongg, classical Chinese entertainment, and lessons in Chinese shadow boxing, tai chi, card games, and calligraphy. Local artisans demonstrate kite making, jewelry design, and other crafts daily. Passengers can also experience Chinese acupuncture or acupressure.

The ships have American cruise directors versed in Chinese history, language, and culture. They lecture throughout every cruise, particularly during sailing through the gorges and before shore excursions.

March to November, the ships sail upstream on five-night cruises from Wuhan to Chongqing and downstream on three-night cruises from Chongqing to Wuhan.

Victoria Cruises

57-08 39th Street, Woodside, NY 11377; (212) 818-1680; (800) 348-8084; fax (212) 818-9889; www.victoriacruises.com

Victoria Star / Victoria Queen / Victoria Rose / Victoria Prince / Victoria Empress (96–102/192–204; Chinese/112–125; 287 ft.)

Victoria Cruises, a New York-based Sino-American joint venture, sails vessels with the wedding-cake look and character of Mississippi riverboats. Each has four decks and an observation area and offers single-seating dining with Chinese and western cuisine. All standard cabins (155 square feet) are outside. They have two lower berths, picture windows, and private bathrooms with shower. Three grades of suites all have bathtubs. Facilities include a business center, cocktail lounge, game room, health clinic, beauty salon, gift shop, and reading room. In 1999, Victoria added the eastern Yangtze between Shanghai and Wuhan to its popular Three Gorges cruises on the western Yangtze. Stops at Nanjing, Yangzhou, Huangshan, and Lushan include numerous scenic and historic sites. Passengers can sail the river's entire navigable length or book segments (4–11 days). Western cruise directors lecture about China and the Yangtze, and a river guide offers narrative about sights.

Viking River Cruises, Inc.

21820 Burbank Boulevard, Woodland Hills, California 91367; (877) 66VIKING; (668-4546); (818) 227-1234; fax (818) 227-1237; www.vikingrivercruises.com

Century Star (93/186; European-Swiss/Chinese; 285 ft.)

Europe's largest river-cruising company is launching its first boat in China to sail on the Yangtze River cruise. Starting in March 2004, Swiss-based Viking River Cruises will offer five different seven-night cruise-tour itineraries on the newly-built, deluxe *Century Star.* With offices in Beijing and Chongqing, the cruise line, which aims to deliver five-star hotel service, will oversee all its program components, from ship operations and shore excursions to land programs, tours, hotel selections, meals, and cultural performances. Each program has English-speaking escorts and guides, helping to reinforce the on-site management.

The purpose-built *Century Star,* expected to be the most deluxe of the Yangtze cruise vessels, has all-outside cabins with balconies, baths with shower, telephones, and televisions. The boat has a restaurant, observation lounge and bar, gym, sauna, massage room, sun deck, business center, beauty salon, doctor, and laundry service.

Viking's Swiss hotel-management staff will oversee all food and beverage, hotel management, and service. A variety of food, from the traditional family-style Chinese cuisine to western selections and even an on-deck barbecue, will be available. English is the primary language onboard as well as during shore excursions and tours.

Passengers will be sailing during the last phase of the Three Gorges Dam project, and will have an adventure on a traditional Chinese sampan to the Lesser Three Gorges—formerly inaccessible to travelers. One itinerary includes a visit to Lhasa, Tibet. Pre- and postcruise land extension are available for Shanghai, Hong Kong, and Guilin. In addition to the river cruise, the 9–16-night programs include all shore excursions and tours, meals, five-star and deluxe hotels, intra-Asia flights, and English-speaking escorts. Prices start from $1,649 per person. With its policy of contributing to the regions in which it sails, Viking River Cruises is building a new elementary school in Jingzhou in the Hubei province. Passengers will have the opportunity to visit the school after it opens.

Other Yangtze River Cruises

Several other U.S.-based companies offer Yangtze cruises. All include the cruises as part of longer China itineraries ranging from 12 to 24 days.

Collette Vacations	(800) 340-5158	www.collettevacations.com
Grand American Travels	(800) 868-8138	www.china-vacation.com
Pleasant Holidays/	(800) 644-3515	
Japan & Orient Tours		
Maupintour	(800) 255-4266	www.maupintour.com
Orient Flexi-pax	(800) 223-7460	www.orientflexipax.com
Pacific Bestour	(800) 272-1149	www.bestour.com
Pacific Delight	(800) 221-7179	www.pacificdelighttours.com
SITA World Travel	(800) 421-5643	www.sitatours.com
TBI Tours	(800) 221-2126	www.generaltours.com
Travcoa	(800) 992-2003	www.travcoa.com
Uniworld	(800) 360-9550	www.uniworldcruises.com
Visits Plus	(800) 321-3235	www.visitsplus.com

Other Asian River Cruises

Orient Express Cruises

c/o Orient Express Hotels; 1155 Avenue of the Americas, New York, NY 10036; (800) 524-2420; fax (630) 954-3324; www.orient-expresstrains.com

---

Road to Mandalay (72/126; European/Burmese; 305 ft.)

The unusual cruises in Myanmar (formerly Burma) are offered by Orient Express Trains and Cruises, the company that operates the famous Orient Express. The boat sails from early September to mid-May on three- to seven-night itineraries on the Irrawaddy (Ayeyarwady) River between Mandalay and Pagan. The cruises are part of a package departing from Bangkok, Thailand, with round-trip flights to Yangon. The German-built *Road to Mandalay*, a deluxe cruiser, previously sailed the Rhine and Elbe. Before starting these cruises in 1996, the boat was renovated. Facilities include a pool, large sun deck, observation lounge, and several bars. The dining room accommodates all passengers in a single seating and serves international and Asian cuisine. The three cabin types include some singles. All have private bath and air-conditioning. Doubles have twin beds; larger cabins have a sitting area. Per person, double occupancy for three-night cruises range from $3,270 for a standard cabin to $4,580 for state cabin and include internal flights within Myanmar, transfers, and sight-seeing.

One 11-night and one 9-night adventure in mid-August visit a little-known region north of Mandalay to beyond Bhamo, stopping just short of the China border. Unlike the tranquil flood plains surrounding the lower Irrawaddy, the northern landscape changes as the ship enters the Three Narrows region, marked with lush forests and towering cliffs. Rates per person, double occupancy, range from $3,740 for a superior cabin to $4,600 for a state cabin.

Nile River Cruises

No trip to Egypt is complete without a cruise on the Nile. It is the perfect way to enjoy the Egyptian countryside as well as to see ancient temples and monuments because the most famous sites are clustered along the great river. Your first view of the Nile snaking through the desert will illustrate dramatically why the river has been so important throughout Egypt's history. Quite literally, Egypt would not exist without the Nile. Beyond the green ribbon—the land irrigated by the Nile—the desert stretches endlessly into the horizon. The Nile flows so gently that ships glide as though unmoving. Riverbanks, always near, give passengers an intimate view of rural life in upper Egypt. Along the riverbanks and in the fields of the green valley, Egyptians live today much as they have for thousands of years. Life and land have a continuity bridging the centuries, as visitors will see from the ancient drawings on the temple and tomb walls and the present scenes of the countryside. The sense of tranquility is an overwhelming sensation throughout the Nile cruise and is a total contrast from the roar and clamor of Cairo—the juxtaposition makes the pastoral setting of the Nile Valley all the more remote.

Nile Itineraries

Those beginning their cruise in Upper Egypt may travel from Cairo to Luxor or Aswan by plane, train, or road. They can begin their trip in Aswan and cruise to Luxor or do the reverse. We recommend the former, as the trip then saves the best for last: climaxing with sight-seeing at **Karnak** and the **Valley of the Kings** at Luxor.

Aswan was the capital of Nubia in ancient times and an important trading place. Today, it's primarily a winter resort and the administrative center for the **High Dam** and surrounding region. Aswan is dotted with antiquities. The most important is the **Temple of Philae**—one of many temples saved from the High Dam's waters-on an island in the river. The botanical gardens, also on an island, and the Agha Khan's mausoleum are standard stops on the popular excursion made by felucca, the graceful sailboats of the Nile.

From Aswan, Nile steamers sail downstream (north) to Luxor, stopping at **Kom Ombo, Edfu,** and **Esna**—sites of temples dating from the Ptolemaic or Greek period. One temple has a wall carving bearing the only known likeness of Queen Cleopatra. Luxor is the modern town next to the ancient city of Thebes, capital of Egypt for most of its illustrious early history. Boats dock on the east bank near the **Etap** and **Winter Palace** hotels, both walking distance from **Luxor Temple** and a short carriage ride to the colossal **Karnak Temple.** A full-day excursion visits the west bank to the Valley of the Kings, where tombs of Tutankhamen and other pharaohs were found; the **Valley of the Queens;** and the **Tombs of the Nobles,** which contain important art.

Many cruises also sail north to the **Temples of Dendera** and **Abydos,** considered the most important temple in Egypt for its artwork. A limited number of cruises sail beyond Abydos on longer itineraries, stopping at **Tel al Amarna,** capital of revolutionary pharaoh Akhenaten and his wife, Nefertiti; Minya, central Egypt's largest town; and **Beni Hassan,** site of tombs containing drawings showing ancient Egyptians at play.

Lake Nasser and Abu Simbel

Construction of Aswan High Dam created Lake Nasser, which stretches more than 300 miles south from Aswan to the Sudanese border. As waters rose, the famous temple of **Abu Simbel** was moved to higher ground in a colossal 1950s international project. For decades, visitors flew or drove to see Abu Simbel. Now, they can go by Nile steamer, departing from the south side of the dam. (See Misr Travel below.)

Nile Steamers

Nile steamers are small and cozy, friendly, and clubby. Some accommodate as few as 20; the largest carries 152 passengers. Cabins, smaller than those on standard cruise ships, are well appointed and comfortable. Most have twin lower beds (some have pull-down bunks for a third person), dressing table or night-stand, closet, and private bathroom with shower. Boats holding 80 or more passengers have lounges for reading and relaxing, a bar, sun deck, dining room with table service, and evening entertainment. Laundry service is available. Some offer Ping-Pong or a tiny swimming pool.

The boat's small size limits its recreational and entertainment facilities, but these aren't important on a Nile cruise, where antiquities and scenery are the attractions. "Roaming" room is surprisingly ample. Deck chairs invite lounging and watching history float by.

Newer vessels are four- and five-star and offer three- to five-night cruises between Luxor and Aswan. Some add **Abydos** and **Dendera** and feature cruises of six or seven nights plus optional land excursions.

Nile cruises are divided into three seasons (prices include all meals, service, taxes, and guided sight-seeing).

High season (October–April) per person per night: Five-star boats range from $190–$411; four-star, $150–$210.

Shoulder season (May and September): 15% off high-season rates.

Low season (June–August): 50% off high-season rates.

Although prices are lower in summer and many of the boats are air-conditioned, the heat in sight-seeing areas can be intense. Large groups walking generate dust in which it's difficult to breath; a dust mask or handkerchief over the mouth is helpful. Boat food usually is quite good. Be very careful to eat only fruits and vegetables that can be peeled. More than 200 boats or Nile steamers offer cruises. Unless you have the opportunity to inspect a vessel yourself, book only with established companies. Five-star boats operated by Hilton International, Mena House Oberoi, Meridian, Movenpick, Sheraton, and Sonesta are the main ones used by major U.S. tour companies.

If you arrive in Egypt without reservations and decide to cruise, make inquiries and reservations through the managing company's office in Cairo, where cabin space is controlled. If you wait until you arrive in Luxor or Aswan to find space, you must walk among ships and ask the boat manager if room is available.

If you have ample time, however, the latter method lets you see the ship, its cabins, and cleanliness (important, especially on boats of less than five stars) before booking. And, if you're good at bargaining, you may negotiate a price better than you might have received in advance in Cairo.

A selected list of companies and Nile steamers follows. *Note:* In parentheses after each boat name is information (where available) about the number of cabins and passengers; officers and crew; and the boat's length (cabins/passengers; officers/crew; boat length).

Abercrombie & Kent International

1520 Kensington Road, Suite 212, Oak Brook, IL 60523; (800) 323-7308; fax (630) 954-3324; www.abercrombiekent.com

Callisto (15 cabins), *Sun Boat III* (18 cabins), *Sun Boat IV* (40 cabins)

Cruises of five to eight days between Luxor and Aswan are part of an all-Egypt tour, plus Ancient Greece; Egypt and Kenya highlights tour of 10–20 days.

Esplanade Tours

160 Common Wealth Avenue, Suite L3, Boston, MA 02116; (617) 266-7465; (800) 426-5492; fax (617) 262-9829; www.esplanadetours.com

Monarch / Regency / Regina / Royale (30–70/50–102; Egyptian; 238 ft.)

The luxury quartet, owned and operated by Travcotels of Egypt, are fully air-conditioned. Each has 49 double cabins and 2 singles and suites. Also lounges, bars, panoramic windows, single-seating dining room, two sun decks, swimming pool, gift shop, beauty salon, and laundry facilities. Cabins measure 230 square feet; suites have 380 square feet. All have television, video, minifridge, and bathrooms with shower, toilet, bidet, and hair dryer. Three-, four-, and seven-night cruises between Luxor and Aswan or a Lake Nasser cruise between Aswan and Abu Simbel.

Mena House Oberoi Hotels / Misr Travel

Pyramids Road, Giza, Cairo, Egypt; 20-2-383-3222; fax 20-2-383-7777-12556;
www.oberoihotels.com

Sheherayar (74 cabins) / Shehrazah (74 cabins) / Oberoi Philae (58/105 cabins)
/ Nephtis (60/144 cabins)

These boats are operated by Oberoi Hotels, an international chain with
hotels in Cairo and Aswan. The *Oberoi Philae* resembles a paddlewheeler.
Each cabin has floor-to-ceiling sliding glass doors leading to private balconies. Jacket and tie are required for men at dinner. All ships sail on
three- to six-night cruises between Luxor and Aswan.

Misr Travel

630 Fifth Avenue, Suite 1460, New York, NY 10111; (212) 332-2600; (800) 223-
4978; fax (212) 332-2609; www.misrtravel.org

Eugenie (50/100) / Nubian Sea (60/120) / Kasr Ibrim (60/120)

Three and four nights on Lake Nasser. Boats have outside cabins with private baths. The four-night program sails south from Aswan on Monday
and ends at Abu Simbel on Friday; three-night cruises sail north on Friday
from Abu Simbel to Aswan. The highlight is a daylight visit to Abu Simbel.
A special feature is a candlelight dinner on deck in front of the floodlit temple of Ramses II. The price is about $150 per person, double occupancy, in
winter; lower in off-season. All meals and shore excursions are included.

Misr Travel, a quasi-governmental travel agency of Egypt, owns the
boats operated by Oberoi, Sheraton, and other companies with hotels in
Egypt. These include Movenpick's *Radamis* (67 cabins), Pyramisa's
Champillon (67 cabins), and Meridien Hotel's *Anni* (76/152) and *Aton*
(34 suites, 14 cabins). The latter is one of the most luxurious Nile boats.
All offer three- to seven-night cruises departing from Luxor and Aswan.

Nabila Nile Cruises

605 Market Street, Suite 507, San Francisco, CA 94105; (415) 979-0160; (800) 443-
nile; fax (415) 979-0163; www.nabilatours.com

King of Thebes / Ramses King of the Nile / Queen of Sheeba / King of the Nile /
Queen Nabila of Abu Simbel / Ramses II (36–72/78–154; Egyptian; 172–234 ft.)

Three, four, five- and eight-day cruises from Luxor to Aswan.

Sonesta International Hotels

200 Clarendon Street (41st floor of John Hancock Building), Boston, MA 02116; (617)
421-5400; (800) SONESTA-4; El Tayaran Street, P.O. Box 9039; Nasr City, Cairo, Egypt;
(011) 20-22-628111; fax (011) 20-22-635731; www.sonesta.com

Nile Goddess (63 junior suites/2 presidential suites/136; Egyptian); Sun Goddess (58 cabins/4 suites; Egyptian); Moon Goddess (54 junior suites /2 presidential suites; Egyptian)

Four–six nights between Luxor and Aswan.

United States and Canadian River Cruises

The Mississippi has the best-known river cruises, but there are others. Spectacular scenery is the main attraction. In the Northeast, the favorite season is autumn, with its brilliant foliage.

Note: In parentheses after each boat name is information about the number of cabins and passengers; officers and crew; and the boat's length (cabins/passengers; officers/crew; boat length).

American Canadian Caribbean Line

(See Part Two.)

American Cruise Lines

(See Part Two, under "European and Smaller Cruise Lines.")

American West Steamboat Company

2 Union Square, Suite 4343, Seattle, WA 98101; (206) 292-9606; (800) 434-1232; fax (206) 340-0975; www.columbiarivercruise.com

Queen of the West (73/163; American/47; 230 ft.); *Empress of the North* (112/235; American; 360 ft.)

The deluxe paddlewheeler *Queen of the West* was the first vessel of a company created by the former owners of Alaska's Glacier Bay Tours and Cruises. Inaugurated in 1995, the boat offers four- to seven-night cruises (March–December) on the Columbia, Snake, and Willamette rivers from Portland, Oregon. All shore excursions are included in the price.

In June 2003, the line launched a second paddlewheeler, *Empress of the North,* which has an important new feature—105 cabins 1 have balconies. The vessel has Seattle as her home port and offers Alaska cruises.

Cruise West

(See Part Two.)

Delta Queen Steamboat Company

(See Part Two.)

Ecomertours Nord-Sud

(See "Adventure and Culture Cruises" later in Part Three.)

International Expeditions

One Environs Park, Helena, AL 35080; (800) 633-4734; fax (205) 428-1714; www.ietravel.com

Spirit of Columbia (78 passengers, 152 ft.)

Spirit of Columbia departs from Juneau, Alaska, on 13-day cruises (June–August). The deluxe yacht approaches glaciers, explores inlets, and showcases Alaska's coastal wildlife. Naturalist/guides escort frequent trips ashore and excursions in small craft. The company also operates Amazon River cruises (see next section).

RiverBarge Excursion Lines

201 Opelousas Avenue, New Orleans, LA 70114; (504) 365-0022; (888) 282-1945; fax (504) 365-0000; www.riverbarge.com

River Explorer (99/198; American; 297 ft.)

Similar in concept to European barges, *River Explorer* was the first of its kind when it was inaugurated in 1998. She's a modern, American-built, American-flagged, and American-crewed hotel-barge; the vessel consists of two 295-foot custom-built barges connected and propelled by a 3,000-horsepower towboat. The forward barge contains public rooms, including a dining room accommodating all passengers at a single, open seating for all meals; a two-deck showroom; exercise and games area; library; gift shop; and Pilot House Lounge, a re-creation of a river pilot-house complete with equipment and windows overlooking the bow. Art depicting river exploration decorates public areas.

The aft barge contains all 99 cabins, each measuring 200 square feet. All are outside and have picture windows. Upper-deck cabins have balconies. All have twin or super queen-size beds, satellite television, VCRs, telephones with computer ports, minifridges, coffeemakers, irons, and bathrooms with tubs. Features include a never-empty cookie jar and 24-hour coffee service.

River Explorer sails from New Orleans on four- to ten-day excursions along the Mississippi River, its tributaries, and intracoastal waters. Each of seven itineraries focuses on a geographic region on the Mississippi, Ohio, Missouri, and Cumberland rivers; Atchafalaya basin; and Gulf Intracoastal Waterway.

Prices begin at $790 per person, twin, for a four-day excursion. Taxes, port charges, most shore activities, and tipping are included. Alcoholic beverages cost extra.

St. Lawrence Cruise Lines/Canadian River Cruise Vacations

253 Ontario Street, Kingston, Ontario, Canada K7L 2Z4; (613) 549-8091; (800) 267-7868; fax (613) 549-8410; www.stlawrencecruiselines.com

Canadian Empress (32/66; Canadian/14; 108 ft.)

Four, five, and six nights on the St. Lawrence and Ottawa rivers. Boarding ports include Kingston, Ottawa, Montreal, and Quebec City. Some cruises allow booking an additional whale-watching package in the Saguenay River area.

Amazon River Cruises

Many mainstream ships with South American itineraries include an Amazon River cruise. They enter on the Atlantic delta and sail upriver to

Manaus. The river is very wide; any intimate view must be obtained aboard small crafts on tributaries. More exotic regions of the upper Amazon are reached mainly from Iquitos, Peru. Many companies offering tours from the United States use the same boats on the Amazon; vessels' descriptions appear the first time they're named.

Note: In parentheses after each boat name is information (where available) about the number of cabins and passengers; officers and crew; and the boat's length (cabins/passengers; officers/crew; boat length).

Abercrombie & Kent International

1520 Kensington Road, Suite 212, Oak Brook, IL 60523; (630) 954-2944; (800) 323-7308; fax (630) 954-3324; www.abercrombiekent.com

Explorer II sails in April and May, leaving Belém, Brazil, on a 17-day cruise of the Amazon and its tributaries to Iquitos, Peru, and a second, upper-Amazon leg from Manaus to Iquitos. The latter leg also is available as a ten-day trip from Peru. (See Part Two.)

Ecotour Expeditions

P.O. Box 128, Jamestown, RI 02835-0128; (800) 688-1822; fax (401) 423-9630; www.naturetours.com

Tucano (9/18; Peruvian/7; 80 ft.)

The ship has wood-paneled walls, a large observation deck, a living room, and a balcony. Seventy-six windows showcase the forest. All cabins have private bathrooms with shower, toilet, and sink.

Seven- to eleven-day cruises depart Miami year-round. The trips on the Amazon and tributaries are accompanied by naturalists.

Explorers Travel Group

One Main Street, Suite 304, Eatontown, NJ 07724; (800) 631-5650; fax: (732) 542-9420; www.explorerstravelgroup.com

The tour company offers various Amazon adventures aboard the riverboats described below. They depart from Iquitos on two- to nine-night cruises on the upper Amazon. Explorers also uses the *Tucano,* listed under Ecotour Expeditions.

Amazon Clipper (10-20; Peruvian; 65 ft.)

Three-night cruises explore the tributaries to bird-watch, fish for piranha, and visit Ecopark, a wildlife rehabilitation sanctuary. Clipper's cabins have private bathrooms, bunk berths, as well as nighttime air-conditioning. Facilities include covered saloon, bar, dining area, library, and fully equipped kitchen. Local cuisine is served—mainly fresh fish. Mineral water is provided.

Amazon Explorer (8/16; Peruvian; 85 ft.)

Three- or six-night round-trip cruises upriver from Iquitos. The steel-constructed boat has a small air-conditioned lounge, dining room/bar, and sun deck. The cabins are outside doubles with bunk beds; all are air-conditioned and have private bath/shower.

Arca (13/32; Peruvian; 98 ft.)

Three to six nights, upper Amazon. The air-conditioned, steel-hull riverboat operates between Iquitos and the twin cities of Tabatinga, Brazil, and Leticia, Colombia. She offers ten twin-bedded cabins with upper/lower berths and three triples with lower beds. All cabins have private bathroom and shower. The boat has a lounge/bar and covered and uncovered deck areas.

Marcelita (26/52; Peruvian; 192 ft.)

New ship built in 1999 has dining room, bar, and library. All cabins are twins done in Amazon hardwoods with air-conditioning and private bathroom and shower. Ten-day cruise, with shore excursions including Leticia, Columbia, and Tabatinga, Brazil.

Rio Amazonas (20–40; Peruvian; 146 ft.)

Three- to six-night explorations of the upper Amazon, sailing downriver on Sunday from Iquitos to the twin cities of Tabatinga, Brazil, and Leticia, Colombia; upriver on Wednesday from Leticia. Itineraries can be combined. The ship has an air-conditioned dining room and library, covered and uncovered deck areas, and Jacuzzi/hot tub. Upper-deck cabins have picture windows and private bathroom with shower. Sun-deck cabins are larger, offering three twin beds, closet, and chair.

International Expeditions

1 Environs Park, Helena, AL 35080; (205) 428-1700; (800) 633-4734; fax (205) 428-1714; www.ietravel.com

La Esmeralda (11/22; 91 ft.) / *La Turmalina* (14/28; 115 ft.) / *La Amatista* (13/26; 125 ft.) *La Turquesa* (30/30)

These exploratory vessels sail from Iquitos, past the start of the Amazon, exploring its tributaries. These include the Ucayali, Marañon, or Tapiche rivers, viewed from excursion craft and on foot along jungle trails. Naturalists/guides accompany outings. All cabins have private facilities and air-conditioning. Eight-day cruises; weekly departures throughout the year.

Ladatco Tours

3006 Aviation Avenue, Suite 4C, Coconut Grove, FL 33133; (305) 854-8422; (800) 327-6162; fax (305) 285-0504; www.ladatco.com

Amazon Clipper (8; Peruvian; 66 ft.) / *La Amastista, La Esmeralda, La Turmalina* (11–14/22-28; Peruvian; 91–115 ft.)

Amazon Clipper is a two-deck riverboat refurbished for overnight touring. Cabins have bunk beds, private bath, and air-conditioning. Three-to four-day cruises, departing Monday and Wednesday from Manaus, on the Amazon and Negro rivers; or a six-day cruise combining the two. Multilingual local guide accompanies.

La Amastista, La Esmeralda, and *La Turmalina* offer six-day cruises, round trip, departing Sunday from Iquitos. Three-night cruises available. Itinerary includes bird-watching, jungle walk, and fishing in the Ataquari River.

Marco Polo Vacations / Galápagos Cruises

11440 West Bernardo Court, Suite 161, San Diego, CA 92127; (858) 451-8406; (800) 421-5276; fax: (858) 451-8472; www.marcopolovacations.com; www.amazonvacations.com

Three-night *Desafio* cruises depart year-round from Manaus to the Amazon and tributaries accompanied by multilingual naturalist. Continental and Brazilian cuisine served buffet-style. Three-day *Tucano* program includes jungle walk to explore flora. The four-day *Maguari* program visits the Samauma village in the Anavilhanas Islands and sails to the "wedding of the waters," where the Negro and Solimoes meet to form the Amazon.

Tara Tours

6595 NW 36th Street, Suite 306A, Miami, FL 33166; (305) 871-1246; (800) 327-0080; fax (305) 871-0417; www.taratours.com

Rio Amazonas (20/40: Peruvian: 146 ft.) / La Amastista, La Esmeralda, La Turmalina (11–14/22-28; Peruvian; 91–115 ft.)

Eight-night Amazon packages year-round from Miami to Iquitos include boat trips and one night at the Hotel Dorado, with jungle walks, visits to native villages, and English-speaking naturalists. Also new: the Amazon River expeditions aboard the *La Amastista, La Esmeralda* and *La Turmalina.*

Adventure and Cultural Cruises

Whether it is called an adventure or expedition cruise or an educational or cultural cruise is a matter of definition on which few people agree. And although there are differences, there are also similarities, particularly in the type of person to whom they appeal—namely, experienced travelers who prefer an intellectually stimulating or educational environment when they travel and do not need (or want) the activities and entertainment typical of mainstream cruises. They prefer the hands-on learning that adventure and educational cruises provide as well as the companionship of like-minded travelers.

Ships offering adventures or expeditions generally are informal and small, accommodating fewer than 150 passengers. Their small size enables them to visit places large ships cannot go. Vessels providing educational or cultural cruises might be larger and more formal. In all cases, the itineraries (which tend to be two weeks or longer), and the opportunity to learn from experts are the main attractions.

In the last two or three years, more deluxe ships have been added in the adventure and cultural cruises category, bringing with them a new level of comfort and expanded facilities. But the majority are still comfortable workhorses that safely ply icy waters or jungle rivers. They have cozy, functional cabins; friendly service; and good food, served at one open seating, often family-style. Dress is casual. Most ships maintain an open bridge.

Cruises are almost always seasonal to take advantage of optimum weather and wildlife conditions. On-board, passengers attend lectures by specialists and have time to enjoy fellow shipmates. Ports are likely to be remote and passengers travel by Zodiac boats to the most inaccessible areas, often making wet landings where no docks are available.

On shore, participants view wildlife and scenery, hike into coastal forests, or encounter remote cultures. Not all cruises require heavy exertion—many are light adventure, nothing more than a short walk. In the evening, staff naturalists and guest lecturers recap the day's excursion in well-attended sessions. On educational or cultural cruises, lecturers are more likely to be historians, anthropologists, museum authorities, and area specialists. Many such trips are sponsored by universities and museum groups, often as an alumni fund-raiser.

Destinations might be world-renowned sites visited by general tours, but participants on cultural cruises get in-depth information and excursions led by experts rather than the commercial guides that regular cruise lines use. Participants also are likely to attend cultural and folklore events. It isn't unusual for adventure and cultural cruises to overlap in their activities, particularly those offering light adventure (or "soft" adventure, the unappealing term the travel trade uses). Not only do these cruises appeal to the same type of people—they also may appeal to the same exact people.

If you've never tried an adventure/expedition cruise, there are a few things you need to consider. For starters, adventure cruises are not exactly laid-back affairs. You might be unceremoniously rousted out of bed at 5:30 a.m. to see a whale, a penguin, or nearly anything else within the purview of the cruise's educational program. Even if you're not rolled out at 5:30 a.m., you'll have to rise by 6:30 or 7 a.m. anyway to dress and have breakfast before the day's activities commence. If you have the temerity to try sleep in, you can count on an announcement every five minutes blaring from your cabin's public address speaker.

Similarly, such cruises tend to pack a lot into a day. On some ships, you scarcely have time for a shower and a change of clothes before dinner is served, and except for days at sea, naps are a rarity.

Before you book an adventure/expedition cruise, carefully scrutinize the itinerary and make some inquiries about the likelihood of rough seas. An Antarctic cruise, for example, must traverse the Drake Passage for a total of four days on a round-trip voyage from South America. The Drake Passage arguably serves up the roughest seas on the planet—not the place to be if you've never cruised before or if your experience is limited to the calm waters of the Caribbean.

Because many adventure/expedition cruises are at the ends of the earth or halfway around the world, you need to pay attention to all aspects of your travel plans. We recommend an intermediate layover both coming and going, as well as an extra day in the port of embarkation. If you're going to the Far East or Australia, try to arrange a night in Hawaii or California before continuing to your final destination. If you're headed to Antarctica, spend a night in Santiago or Buenos Aires coming and going. Once when coming home from Antarctica, Bob ignored his own advice. After two days bouncing like a marble in a spittoon crossing the Drake Passage, he disembarked the ship at 8:30 a.m., then had to wait until 1 p.m. for a four-hour flight to Santiago. He had another four-hour layover in Santiago before boarding a nine-hour flight to Houston and connecting on to his final destination. By the time he got home, he'd been traveling for 32 hours (not counting the Drake Passage). Believe us, it's just not worth it.

If you cruise package includes a stopover (and many do), it pays to check out the city where you'll be stopping. A Galápagos Islands adventure cruise included an overnight in Quito, Ecuador. Those folks who didn't check out Quito before leaving home were astonished to learn upon arrival that it sits in the Andes at an elevation of 9,300 feet. Not only did most not have warm clothing—they were heading for the equator, after all—but they discovered it was quite impossible to acclimate to that altitude in one day. After a restless night spent gasping for breath, they were exhausted as they began the final leg of their journey to the islands.

An equally compelling reason for an overnight stopover and an extra night in the port city is the opportunity to deal with lost luggage. Believe us, the worst time to have your luggage disappear is when you're about to embark on an adventure/expedition cruise. Chances are you've spent weeks rounding up the specialized clothing and gear required for the cruise, but if you have a day or more prior to boarding for your luggage to catch up with you, you'll be fine 90% of the time. In a worst-case scenario when your lost luggage stays lost, you'll still have time to re-equip in local stores before sailing.

Another precaution we take is to avoid luggage transfers between airlines. On an itinerary from Fort Lauderdale to Iceland for an expedition cruise out of Reykjavik, for example, we took an early Delta flight to JFK where we claimed our bags and then personally rechecked them with Icelandic Air. We were perfectly happy to suffer an extra hour or two at JFK for the peace of mind of knowing that our bags were safely checked with Icelandic Air to Reykjavik.

Expedition cruises don't require physical training, but participants should be in good condition and able to endure some exertion. More importantly, they need to be flexible in temperament as well as body. They should be good sports, keep a sense of humor, and be ready to forgo comforts occasionally. Adventure or expedition cruises take participants off the beaten path worldwide. They tend to be more expensive than mainstream cruises because fewer people share the cost and because it costs more to operate a ship in remote areas. Also, shore excursions are included, and lecturers must be accommodated in cabins that otherwise draw revenue.

Practically all adventure and cultural cruises are early-to-rise, early-to-bed affairs. The bar will be open late if you're nocturnal, but there's very little sleeping in. Many adventure cruises will rouse you at unspeakable hours if something interesting happens to materialize outside.

Participants tend to be strong environmentalists who expect fellow travelers to share their views. They like to be outdoors, are active, well traveled, well educated, intellectually curious, affluent, perhaps semiretired professionals age 50 or older. They belong to a museum or natural history group. They probably read Audubon, National Geographic, or Smithsonian magazine, watch public television, and support the local zoo.

Following is a representative list of companies offering adventure or expedition/educational/cultural cruises. They provide brochures, usually with deck plans of vessels they use, and descriptions of itineraries. Being specialists, they usually can answer questions with more firsthand authority than a travel agent or cruise line can.

Regarding Galápagos cruises, in an effort to prevent overcrowding at certain visitor sites, the Galápagos National Park Service has revised the itineraries of many tour boats. Check with the tour company for the latest information.

Note: In parentheses after each boat name is information (where available) about the number of cabins and passengers; officers and crew; and the boat's length (cabins/passengers; officers/crew; boat length).

Abercrombie & Kent International

(See Part Two.)

Explorer II sails to Antarctica, the Falklands, South Georgia, and the Chilean fjords in astral summer, and offers Amazon cruises in March and April. Small boats are chartered for Galápagos cruises.

Glacier Bay Cruises

(See Part Two.)

American Safari Cruises

(See Part Two. under "European and Smaller Cruise Lines.")

Classical Cruises

(See Part Two, under "European and Smaller Cruise Lines.")

Canodros, S.A.

Luis Canodros 2735, P.O. Box 59-9000, Miami, FL 33159-9000; (800) 327-9854; www.canodros.com

---

Galápagos Explorer II (50/100; Ecuadorian; 295 ft.)

The luxury, all-suite ship, built in 1990 as the *Renaissance III,* sails on three-, four-, and seven-night cruises weekly in the Galápagos Islands. Cruises can be combined with three or more nights at Kapawi Ecological Reserve, an unusual native Indian-owned and -operated base camp in the Amazon.

Itself Ecuadorian-owned and -operated, the ship has classic lines and interiors throughout. Cabins, all with sitting rooms, are air-conditioned and have queen or two twin beds, telephone, television for VCR use, refrigerator-bar, full-length wardrobe, marble bath, and 110-volt electric outlets. Also aboard are an outdoor pool and Jacuzzi, boutique, and doctor for minor illness or mishaps.

The elegant, nonsmoking restaurant offers one informal, open seating. International and Ecuadorian cuisine is served; special diets can be accommodated. A lunch buffet is served on deck. Staff will prepare additional dishes on request. All bar drinks—including bottled water—are complimentary; only name wines, champagne, and minibar contents cost extra. Cruise price also includes twice-daily tours escorted by naturalists.

The ship always anchors offshore, and passengers are tendered on dinghies for dry or wet landings. In keeping with the company's environmental commitment, all soaps, detergents, and shampoo used on board are biodegradable. The ship produces its own fresh water and is equipped with a sewage treatment system to minimize environmental impact.

Chlorine isn't used on board. Paper and nontoxic solids are incinerated, metal cans are compacted for recycling, and nonbiodegradable trash is returned to port.

Clipper Cruises

(See Part Two.)

Ecomertours Nord-Sud

260 Eveche-Est, Rimouski, Quebec G5L 1Y3 Canada; (418) 724-6227; (888) 724-8687; fax (418) 724-6230; www.ecomertours.com

Echo des Mers (20/44; Canadian/19; 170 ft.)

Ecomertours Nord-Sud offers five-, seven-, or eight-day nature-oriented cruises of the St. Lawrence River and estuary from mid-June to mid-September. The small, expedition-style boat departs from Rimouski-East, a port 188 miles east of Quebec City, for Anticosti Island at the mouth of the St. Lawrence and the Mingan archipelago. Travelers view marine mammals, birds, and flora of the islands and visit local villages.

A eight-day eco-cruise visits the national parks of Eastern Quebec on the St. Lawrence River to Saguenay–St. Lawrence Marine Park, the Mingan Islands National Park Reserve, and Forillon National Park in the Gaspe. A bilingual biologist leads talks, discussions, and observation of whales and birds. Ecomertours is a member of Bas-Saint-Laurent Marine Mammal Ecowatch Network, Biosphere de Montreal, and Environment Canada.

Two other itineraries—one for bird-watching and the other for whale-watching—depart in July. Seabirds of the St. Lawrence concentrates on the Mingan Islands, St. Mary's Islands near Harrington Harbour, the eastern point of Anticosti Island at Gull's Cliffs, and Bonaventure Island in Gaspe.

The three-deck *Echo des Mers,* built in 1966 and refurbished in 1997, has 20 cabins fitted with a double bed or two twin beds and 2 cabins with twins that bunk four persons. Twelve cabins have private bathroom with shower; eight have shared bathroom. Two small dining rooms accommodate all passengers at one open seating. Breakfast is buffet-style, but lunch and dinner have table service. Menus offer two main courses of regional cuisine highlighting seafood bought from local fishermen. The boat has a small lounge, bar, and a lecture/reading room. Massages are available. Prices range from about $687 per person quad to about $2,712 per person double in the best accommodation. Transportation at stopovers is included. The company can arrange itineraries of two to eight days for special-interest charters, such as bird-watching, kayaking, and diving.

In 2002, two new themed eco-cruises—Birds and Whales, and the Islands of the Gulf of the St. Lawrence—were added. They focus on the sea birds and marine mammals that spend the summer in the St. Lawrence and explore the islands along the lower north shore of Quebec.

Ecoventura S.A.

(See Galápagos Network.)

Esplanade Tours

(See "Nile River Cruises" earlier in Part Three.)

Galápagos Cruises c/o Adventure Associates

13150 Coit Road, Suite 110, Dallas, TX 75240; (972) 907-0414; (800) 527-2500; fax (972) 783-1286; www. metropolitan-touring.com

Adventure Associates is the U.S. representative of Quito-based Metropolitan Touring, Ecuador's leading tour company and the oldest company offering Galápagos cruises. Ships are well run and have excellent guides.

Isabela II (20/40; Ecuadorian; 166 ft.)

Completely renovated in February 2000, the ship's new look includes an enlarged reception area, a redesigned library, and a new multimedia system for briefings and lectures. The mahogany-paneled dining room and library were totally refurbished along with the bar-lounge and cabins. The redesigned sun deck now has a bar, observation area for whale- and dolphin-watching, and a solarium. The ship offers satellite telephone, fax service, and, in the future, Internet access. She sails from Baltra on Tuesdays and Fridays on three-, four-, and seven-night cruises of the Galápagos Islands; rates range from $1,140 to $2,660 in low season (March 16–June 14, September 1–October 31, November 21–December 20) and $1,270 to $2,955 in high season. Children under age 12 get a 50% discount year-round. Prices do not include Ecuador/Baltra flights or National Park entrance fee.

Santa Cruz (47/90; Ecuadorian; 230 ft.)

Three-, four-, and seven-night Galápagos cruises. The ship, renovated in 1998, is one of the largest and most comfortable sailing in Galápagos waters. Food and service are good, and the ship is well-run. All cabins were refitted and feature singles, doubles, or suites. The ship is carpeted and air-conditioned, with a large dining room, cocktail lounge, bar, library, Jacuzzi, and spacious decks. Three-day cruises visit the southern islands; four-day tours visit the central and northern groups. The two can be combined. Naturalist/guides, trained and licensed by Galápagos National Park, give nightly briefings on the next day's visit and accompany passengers on excursions. Groups are limited to 20 people.

Galápagos Network

6303 Blue Lagoon Dr., Suite 140, Miami, FL 33126; (305) 262-6264; (800) 633-7972; fax (305) 262-9609; www.ecoventura.com

The tour company, affiliated with a group of privately owned companies in Ecuador, offers year-round, three- to seven-night cruises in the Galápagos

Islands on its fleet of small vessels. Cruises are designed for the well-educated, well-traveled, and those eager to learn about nature, ecology, and environmental issues. The boats' size allows them to visit remote islands. Naturalist-guides lecture and lead walks. Passengers are ferried to the islands by launches.

Three-night cruises visit the southern islands of Española (Hood), Floreana, and Santa Cruz. Four-night trips visit the central and northern islands of Bartolome, Plazas, Santiago (James), Tower, and Santa Cruz. All vessels depart from San Cristóbal island and can be chartered. Passengers can snorkel year-round and scuba dive on designated cruises aboard *Sky Dancer.* Pre- and postcruise packages in Ecuador are available.

Life aboard a Galápagos Network cruise, especially on the *Letty, Eric,* and *Flamingo I,* is, well, familial. The small number of passengers and Ecuadorian crew connect almost immediately in a friendship that only ripens over the duration of the cruise. The whole crew—from the captain to the cook—is invested in sharing the rugged beauty and abundant wildlife of the Galápagos, and their enthusiasm is impossible to resist.

Dining features Ecuadorian specialties, which in spicing, aroma, and taste are always a surprise. Some dishes exhibit characteristics of provincial Mexican cuisine; others, remarkably, would be at home in an Indian (as in Bombay) restaurant. But it's all good, even if it keeps you guessing.

One of the Galápagos Network's greatest strengths is its land support. From the time you step off your international flight, there is literally someone to watch over you. Most itineraries include an overnight in either Quito or Guayaquil in quirky but totally wonderful (and totally Ecuadorian) local hotels. Be aware that Quito sits in the Andes at about 8,000 feet. Aside from being occasionally chilly, lowlanders often have problems breathing and sleeping in the rarefied air. Following an overnight, passengers continue on by plane the next day to the Galápagos.

Sky Dancer (8/16; Ecuadorian;100 ft.)

Built in the United States, the vessel has a spacious dining area which serves both Ecuadorian and international cuisine, fully stocked bar, main salon with entertainment center, allocated personal dive storage , and sun deck. Cabins are air-conditioned and have private bathrooms. *Sky Dancer* offers up to four dives per day on a preplanned, seven- or ten-night itinerary. Dive in the Northern Islands of Wolf and Darwin, famous for hammerhead sharks, giant manta rays, and whale sharks.

Eric / Flamingo I / Letty (10/20; Ecuadorian; 83 ft.)

Built in 1993, *Letty* is the newest of three luxury yachts. All are air-conditioned. Cabins have private bathrooms, VCR, and stereo equipment. *Letty* departs on Monday; the others depart on Sunday. At least four hours per day are spent on each island. The boats are well suited for families or groups. Three-, four-, and seven-night itineraries include the western islands of Fernandina and Isabela, as well as Española, Tower, Santa Cruz, Bartolome, South Plaza, Floreana, Santa Fe, and Santiago. In addition, passengers lunch at a ranch on Santa Cruz.

Galápagos Yacht Cruises

c/o Galápagos Inc., 7800 Red Road, Suite 112, South Miami, FL 33143; (305) 665-0841; (800) 327-9854; fax (305) 661-1457; www.galapagoscruises.net

---

Cruz del Sur / Dorado / Estrella del Mar (8/16; Ecuadorian; 75 ft.)

Cruz del Sur and *Estrella del Mar* sail from San Cristóbal; *Dorado* sails from Baltra with stops at the main Galápagos islands and others where larger ships don't go.

Yolita (6/12; Ecuadorian; 53 ft.)

Three-, four-, and seven-night cruises from San Cristóbal to Islas Lobos, Española, Punta Suarez, Gardener, Darwin Station, North Seymour, Baltra, Bachas, Rabida, Puerto Egas, Bartolome, Sullivan, Islas Plazas, Santa Fe, and Santa Cruz.

Global Quest

185 Willis Ave, 2nd Floor, Mineola, NY 11501; (516) 739-3690; (800) 221-3254; fax (516) 739-8022; www.globalquesttravel.com

---

Ambassador I (62/100; Ecuadorian/68; 296 ft.)

The ship has 40 outside cabins, 13 inside cabins, and is air-conditioned. It has a lounge, library, pool, lido bar, and single-seating dining room where American and continental cuisine with Ecuadorian specialties is served. The ship sails on three-, four-, and seven-night cruises year-round from Baltra to the Galápagos Islands and visits Española, Santa Cruz, Bartolome, Isabela, Santiago, and Floreana islands. Visitors go ashore in 20-foot boats carrying 20 people, including 2 crew members and a guide. Passengers may wade ashore. Twelve-day cruises include stayovers in Quito, Ecuador.

Eclipse (27/48; Ecuadorian; 210 ft.)

Built in 1998, the boat has a swimming pool, library/video room, shop, bar and observation deck. Sails on eight-day itinerary in the Galápagos.

Royal Star (111/200; German/130; 472 ft.)

Most cabins are outside, with air-conditioning, bathroom with shower, and phone. Some triples and quads available. One dining room with two seatings; cuisine is international with local specialties. Safari/cruise packages include 4–8 days to Kenya and 16–23-day cruise/land tour from Mombasa to Zanzibar and Mahe in the Seychelles.

New World Discoverer (86/160; International/90; 354 ft.)

See Society Expeditions in this section below for description of ship. Five expedition voyages of 21 days to Antarctica and to the Islands of the Scotia Sea and the Russian Far East and remote Alaskan wilderness are available.

International Expeditions

One Environs Park, Helena, AL 35080; (205) 428-1700; (800) 633-4734; fax (205) 428-1714; www.ietravel.com

Eric / Flamingo / Letty / Sky Dancer (See Galápagos Network)

Kleintours

Av. Eloy. Alfaro N 34-151, Quito, Ecuador; (888) 50-KLEIN; tel (593-2) 2267 000, fax (593-2) 2442 389; www.kleintours.com.

Two vessels, *Coral I* and *Coral II* (20- and 24-passenger capacity), offer three-, four-, and seven-day cruises. Three-day cruises depart on Sunday; four-day cruises, Wednesday. Three-night cruise start at $814 in low season (May, June, September) and $945 in high season.

The *Galápagos Legend* (90 passengers) offers three, four and seven day cruises. Three-day cruises depart on Mondays; four-day cruises depart on Thursday. All seven-day cruise for the three ships departs on Mondays.

Lifelong Learning Xpo America

101 Columbia, Suite 150, Aliso Viejo, CA 92656; (949) 362-2900; (800) 854-4080; fax (949) 362-2075; www.lifelong-xpo.com

The tour company offers cultural and adventure cruises for a well-traveled clientele on either part or full charter of well-known ships, such as Hapag-Lloyd's *Hanseatic,* to exotic destinations around the globe, on itineraries often designed by the company. The voyages are accompanied by lecturers who are experts on the regions visited and usually include several days touring in the departure city. An example for 2004 is a 14-day program on *Hanseatic,* one of the most advanced, environmentally responsible expedition ships cruising the Arctic waters to Falkland Islands, New Island, and the Drake Passage. Prices start at $8,595. Another explores Belize, Guatemala, and Honduras aboard the *Nantucket Clipper* on a 12-day adventure. Prices begin at $5,495.

Lindblad Expeditions

720 Fifth Avenue, New York, NY 10019; (212) 765-7740; (800) 397-3348; fax (212) 265-3770; www.expeditions.com

The globe-roaming, four-ship company was founded by Sven-Olof Lindblad, son of the late Lars-Eric Lindblad, who pioneered modern expedition cruising. In 1969 he launched the *Lindblad Explorer,* designed to take travelers to remote areas in comfort and safety. Lindblad Expeditions describes its mission as "providing travelers with a more thoughtful way to see the world, avoiding crowded destinations, and seeking out natural ones." A wide selection of light adventure cruises in various parts of the world are offered.

Endeavour (61/110; Scandinavian/International; 295 ft.)

This ship offers off-the-beaten-track cruises through Europe and Asia. May to June: Circumnavigating the British Isles; April to September: European Odyssey exploring the coasts of Spain, Portugal, and France, and ending at the Tower Bridge, London. In August, explore Scandanavia and the Baltics. September and October, the Azores.

Lord of the Glens (27/54; British; 150 ft.)

September, 12-day cruise, Heart of the Highlands, travels through the Scottish highlands, seeing historic places and extraordinary scenery. For a 14-day cruise, Heart of the Highlands is combined with a Royal Scotsman Train, a ride through countryside between Edinburgh and Inverness.

Polaris (41/80; Swedish/Filipino and Swedish; 238 ft.)

Polaris offers Galápagos cruises year-round. Ten-day land and sea itineraries are accompanied by outstanding naturalists, such as Dr. Lynn Fowler, who has conducted wildlife research in the area for over 20 years.

Sea Bird / Sea Lion (37/70; American; 152 ft.)

Four- to fifteen-day cruises, Exploring Alaska's Coastal Wilderness; Columbia and Snake rivers to Hells Canyon, Idaho; San Juan Islands; and an annual cruise to Baja California and the Sea of Cortés timed for optimum whale-watching; the Islands of the Pacific Northwest in September, and December only, a voyage through the Sea of Cortés.

The company occasionally charters other ships and operates cruises for universities or groups.

Sea Voyager (33/64; Costa Rican; 175 ft.)

Acquired in summer 2001 from Temptress Cruises, this ship has all-outside cabins with private bathroom and air-conditioning. She was completely refurbished in 2002 and sails on Costa Rica, Panama, Belize, and Guatemala cruises.

Melanesian Tourist Services Limited

Coastwatchers Avenue, P.O. Box 707, Madang, 511 Papua New Guinea; (310) 785-0370; fax (310) 785-0314; www.meltours.com

Melanesian Discoverer (21/35-54; New Guinean; 117 ft.)

Four- and five-night cruises on the Sepik River, five-night cruises to Irian Jaya, and seven night cruises of Melanesian islands, including the Trobriands, Rabaul, and Kavieng.

Metropolitan Touring

(See Galápagos Cruises.)

Orient Lines

(See Part Two.)

Quark Expeditions

980 Post Road, Darien, CT 06820; (203) 656-0499; (800) 356-5699; fax (203) 655-6623; www.quarkexpeditions.com

The tour company, a pioneer in Arctic and Antarctic expedition cruises, handles a group of Russian-built ships, all with Russian officers and crew. They're accompanied by an expedition leader, assistant expedition leader, lecturers, and Zodiac pilots who may be from the United States, Europe, or South America, depending on destinations and their expertise. Antarctica departures include a combination of Antarctic Peninsula, Weddell Sea, South Georgia, Falkland Islands, Chilean fjords, Ross Sea, New Zealand, and Australian subantarctic islands. Some depart from Cape Town. Some ships sail around the Arctic Circle and to the North Pole. New for 2003–2004 is "Solar Eclipse," the far side of Antarctica, on the *Kapitan Khlebnikov* in November, providing an ideal platform for viewing this unusual event.

Professor Multinovsky (28/49; Russian; 234 ft.)

The *Professor Multinovsky* has a lounge, bar, library, lecture room, two dining rooms, sauna, gift shop, and infirmary. December–March: Antarctic Peninsula, South Shetlands, South Georgia, and the Falklands round-trip to Ushuaia. June–August: British Isles, Faroes, Hebrides, Iceland, Greenland, Baffin, and Hudson Bay.

Orlova (62/90; Yugoslavia/53; 427 ft.)

The ship is fully equipped with a lecture hall, library, theatre, bar and lounge and a dining room. Upgrades are planned for the upcoming year, including the addition of a gym with panoramic views; a new forward bar and reception area; and renovations to the main deck, dining area, library, and bar. *Orlova* operates cruises to the Antarctic Peninsula, Falkland Islands, and South Georgia.

Kapitan Dranitsyn (54/112; Russian/Russian and European; 429 ft.)

This ship has a lounge, bar, library, dining room, lecture room, gift shop, infirmary, gym, sauna, pool, and two helicopters. From July to September, the icebreaker circumnavigates the Arctic, starting and ending in Murmansk. The voyage can be taken in one of four segments: Greenland, from Lonyearbyen, Norway, to Sondre Stromfjord; High Arctic,

Sondre Stromfjord to Resolute; Northwest Passage, Resolute to Provideniya; and Northeast Passage, Provideniya to Lonyearbyen. Voyages to the Antarctic Peninsula, Weddell Sea, and South Atlantic Islands from November through February.

Kapitan Khlebnikov (54/112; Russian; 428 ft.)

Antarctic icebreaker. Russia's Far East and Wrangler Island, the High Arctic. Also covers the Northwest Passage and Tanguary Fjord.

Yamal / Sovetskiy Soyuz (50/100; Russian; 491 ft.)

One of the world's most powerful icebreakers, the *Yamal* has a lounge, bar, library, gift shop, infirmary, dining room, lecture room, gym, sauna, pool, and two helicopters. She departs on 15-day expeditions round-trip from Murmansk to the geographic North Pole. Optional excursions beneath the polar ice cap aboard "Mir" deep-sea submersibles are available. *Sovetskiy Soyuz* is a sister ship to the *Yamal*.

Society Expeditions

2001 Western Avenue, Suite 300, Seattle, WA 98121; (206) 728-9400; (800) 548-8669; fax (206) 728-2301; www.societyexpeditions.com

New World Discoverer (86/160; International/90; 354 ft.)

After the line's ship, *World Discoverer,* had to be scuttled following an accident in the Solomon Islands in spring 2000, Society Expeditions purchased another expedition ship in summer 2000 and now offers a roster of exotic, nature-oriented worldwide cruises.

The new ship, originally built in 1990 and renamed *New World Discoverer,* holds 160 passengers. All cabins are outside with the standard ones starting at an unusual 215 square feet in size and ranging up to 538 square feet for the two-room owner's suite; seven junior. There are also eight veranda suites. The ice-hardened vessel sails with the same staff that was on the previous ship. The seven-deck ship has two elevators, a swimming pool, restaurant, lounge, library, sauna-whirlpool, hair salon, hospital, exercise room, and boutique. She is among the few passenger vessels in the world that can approach some of the most isolated and pristine island habitats.

The *New World Discoverer* may be the most luxurious vessel in expedition service, with public spaces and cabins more characteristic of upmarket, boutique cruise ships. In addition to their unusually large size, the cabins are richly appointed in polished woods and pastel soft goods. Baths are well designed and roomy by any standard. A number of cabins offer private balconies.

Dining is a signature specialty of Society Expeditions. In quality, selection, presentation, and service, Society proves definitively that expedition cruise dining can rise to the level of the finest ships afloat.

Cruises are designed for the well educated and well traveled. Passengers are welcome on the bridge at all hours, and zodiac operations are among the most efficient and best organized afloat. Interpretive programs and guided shore excursions (included in the cruise fare) are presented in both English and German, though Society Expedition clientele hail from North America and all over Europe.

Traditionally, Society Expeditions cruises, ranging from 10 to 25 days, are accompanied by experts who give daily shipboard lectures and act as guides. The line's fall season offers cruises to Papua New Guinea and the islands of the South Pacific, followed by Antarctica with South America from November to March and French Polynesia, and Society and Easter Islands in the spring. In the summer, the ship sails to Alaska and the Bering Strait, Russian Far East, and above the Arctic Circle.

Wilderness Travel

1102 Ninth Street, Berkeley, CA 94710; (510) 558-2488; (800) 368-2794; fax (510) 558-2489; www.wildernesstravel.com

The adventure tour company offers Galápagos programs almost year-round, some with up to three departures monthly. They combine cruises on small yachts with hiking in areas not usually covered by conventional excursions. The company also has a combination of the Galápagos and Upper Amazon River.

Norwegian Coastal Cruises and Cruise Ferries

The craggy coast of Norway, deeply indented like the fingers on your hand, was carved eons ago by massive glaciers. Crevices, which we call fjords, can be ten miles long. From their dark, mirror-like waters rise almost vertical cliffs, and awesome mountains climb to several thousand feet on each side. Often at the head of fjords are snow-capped peaks. In some places, glaciers inch toward the North Sea. Along the shores are Lilliputian fishing villages and isolated farmhouses. Farther up the mountains are lodges where hikers bed down in summer and Olympic hopefuls fine-tune their skiing in winter.

The setting is beautiful; late May through early autumn are ideal for cruising. Most major lines with ships in Europe offer Norwegian fjord cruises. Itineraries differs slightly, but the program is essentially the same: departing from Copenhagen, Oslo, Bergen, Harwich or Dover and going as far north as Trondheim, Norway's original capital and third-largest city, or Tromso, the largest town north of the Arctic Circle. Others continue to the North Cape, the northernmost point in Europe, and to Spitsbergen, a group of islands studded with massive glaciers. Another way to cruise the coast—the way Norwegians do—is on the Norwegian Coastal Express.

Norwegian Coastal Voyage

Eleven working passenger-cargo ships, known as the Hurtigruten ("fast route" in Norwegian), operate a daily passenger and cargo service from Bergen to 35 ports on Norway's coast, well beyond the North Cape to Kirkenes, near the Russian border.

A Norwegian institution since 1893, the ships operate year-round through all weather and are a lifeline for the people in small, often isolated communities along the way. The vessels, while increasingly cruise-oriented, provide transportation for locals and haul cargo ranging from automobiles and farm equipment to frozen fish.

The ships also carry tourists who may board and disembark at any port. Many visitors, however, take the 2,500-mile round-trip voyage as a 12-day cruise. Others sail one-way and return by road or air. (Some open-water passages can be rough; passengers should come prepared.)

Time in port varies from as little as 15 minutes to several hours. There are shore excursions (about $20–$40) at a few ports, and more costly trips leave the ship in one port, travel inland, and rejoin it in another.

The best time to make the trip is mid-May to July, the period with 24 hours of daylight. Some travelers prefer the quieter months of early spring and fall. Summer sailings fill quickly, although space is often available at short notice. During the off-season, cabins are plentiful.

In the height of summer, some stretches are crowded with deck passengers, especially between the mainland and islands. Generally, about half of the passengers are local commuters or those attending an onboard conference; the balance are an international mix. There are usually quite a few English-speaking people, and always many Germans. Announcements are made in the languages required by passenger makeup. Meals are served at two seatings when traffic warrants. Breakfast and lunch are buffet-style. Dinner is from a set menu; tables are reserved. Dietary requests should be made when booking. Continental and Norwegian dishes are served. Lunch offers the widest selection of hot and cold foods. Because of hefty taxes, alcoholic beverages are expensive—$6 or more for a beer is common. Entertainment is limited to the gorgeous scenery, enlivened by commentary, good conversation, cargo handling, and the festive occasion of crossing the Arctic Circle. The line provides an excellent guidebook. In summer, the newest ships might have a band for dancing.

Norwegian Coastal Voyage, Inc. markets the service in North America. The service has 11 ships in four classifications: Millennium, New, Mid-generation, and Traditional.

Millennium Ships

The *Finnmarken* and *Trollfjord,* completed in spring 2002, are 15,000 tons and take 643/674 passengers. Of the two new ships, the *Finnmarken* appears to be the more innovative with features such a Jugend-style (Art Nouveau) interiors, an indoor/outdoor café, wine bar, two panoramic lounges, an indoor pool, a racquet court and gym, four conference rooms, and 14 suites with private balcony. The *Trollfjord* has 21 suites, eight with balconies, glass elevators, sauna and fitness room, and eight conference rooms. The cargo is handled via ramps through the side doors. The standard amenities are the same as the New ships.

New Ships

The *Kong Harald, Nordkapp, Nordlys, Nordnorge, Polarlys,* and *Richard With,* all completed since 1993, add to the Hurtigruten the concept of the cruise ferry with its greater comfort (well established and popular in Baltic waters). Large and boxy (390 feet long and 63 feet wide), the ships take as many as 490 passengers in relatively roomy accommodations. Cargo is handled via ramps.

The modern cabins are mostly outside. They have foldaway beds and two lower berths, audio channels, automated wake-up calls, tiled baths with showers, and hair dryers.

Public rooms have the fashionable look of modern cruise ships, with rich fabrics, thick carpets, and ample use of brass, glass, and veneers. Norwegian art in the form of sculpture and painted seascapes are attractive features. A top-deck, wraparound observation lounge is for viewing and a midships lounge contains a cocktail bar. A middle deck offers a cocktail lounge, library/card room, conference rooms, souvenir shop, playroom, video arcade, 24-hour cafeteria, 240-seat restaurant, and private dining room. Also aboard are a sauna, small gym, and passenger laundry.

Mid-generation Ships

The *Midnatsol, Narvik,* and *Vesteraalen,* built in 1982–1983, then rebuilt and enlarged later in the same decade, carry up to 320 passengers. Cabins are smaller and decidedly plainer, but most are outside and all have private bathrooms with showers. The ships' have a forward-facing observation lounge and glass-enclosed top-deck lounge. Freight and vehicles are handled via roll-on ramps.

Traditional Ships

The 1956-built *Nordstjernen* is the sole remaining Traditional ship. She has 179 very small outside and inside cabins, some without private facilities. The best cabins sell out fast. The ship possesses rich character, teak decks, and a battered hull from thousands of dockings. There are two lounges (the forward facing one is nonsmoking), a restaurant and a cafeteria, the latter used by short-run passengers. Cargo and vehicles are loaded by crane. This ship is no longer in year-round service.

Since 2002, the *Nordstjernen* summer cruises around Spitzbergen are no longer marketed in the United States. Instead, NCV sells the 94-passenger *Polar Star* (see Svalbard Polar Travel, above), an expedition ship rebuilt from a Swedish icebreaker, on 10-day Spitzbergen circumnavigation packages from Longyearbyn. The company also markets the expedition ship *Brand Polaris* for a summer program of ten one-week cruises along the Greenland coast. North American passengers fly to the ship via Copenhagen.

On the Coastal Express

Billed as the world's most beautiful voyage, especially when the weather cooperates, the Coastal Express offers relaxed and informal adventure. Aboard the *Kong Harald,* the feeling is that of a small, modern, floating hotel. On the first morning at sea, a sheer mountain wall plunges into the narrow channel, and, to port, Norwegian Sea breakers pile up against low-lying islands. At a briefing, the courier reminds everyone that this is a working ship and that local passengers will be boarding and leaving at each port. The diesel engine throbs rhythmically in the background. At Bodo, a city at the northern end of Norway's main rail line, about 100 passengers board for the six-hour crossing to the Lofoten Islands. An automobile comes aboard and fork-lifts maneuver whole fish, bundles of evergreen saplings, and building materials.

During brief port calls, you can walk briskly to the main shopping street to buy souvenirs and newspapers. On one excursion, during the stop at Harstad, passengers attend a short worship service in a fortress church. There are visits to the North Cape promontory, an excursion from Kirkenes, turnaround port, to the Russian border, and a cruise into the **Trollfjord,** a one-mile passage between vertical rock cliffs bubbling with falling water. The new moon reflects in the turning basin as the captain revolves his ship in a tight half circle. During the warmer months, the ship sails well inland to take in the spectacular **Geirangerfjord.** By voyage's end, round-trip passengers have shared a 2,500-mile feast of dramatic scenery, shore visits, fresh—if somewhat repetitious—food, and constantly changing weather.

European Cruise Ferries

"Cruise ferry" is an inadequate term for a sophisticated breed of ship that takes passengers on overnight sea voyages but provides most of the comforts and amenities of a deluxe liner. Still, that's the name. And cars, recreational vehicles, and large trucks are indeed below deck.

Operating throughout northern Europe, the ferries crisscross the Baltic and North Seas, linking cities such as Copenhagen and Oslo, Stockholm and Helsinki, Newcastle and Bergen. Creative train-ferry itineraries often include the Eurail pass network. Most passengers are Scandinavians (Danish, Finnish, Norwegian, Swedish), are traveling to visit Scandinavian friends and relations, or are simply cruising. Germans are the second-most numerous among passengers. North Sea sailing attracts Britons.

Larger, newer ships offer varied restaurants. Options include quality à la carte dining, a 60-item smorgasbord, and simpler, cheaper cafeteria meals. The *Silja Europa* even has a McDonald's. After-dinner entertainment includes cabarets, dancing, gambling, and films. There are children's playrooms, video arcades, saunas, and on some ships, duty-free shopping (purchases roll to check-out in supermarket carts). English is widely spoken.

Cabins vary from well-appointed rooms with windows and cruise-ship amenities to large family cabins with private showers. Most accommodations are away from activity and noise of public rooms. Young Scandinavians come aboard to party on weekend sailings, so be prepared for some public drunkenness.

The following lines are represented in North America. They offer the most extensive routes and some of the newest and most sophisticated ships. However, they're only a sampling of a wider network spanning all European seas, including the Mediterranean. Most major intercity services are year-round. Ships occasionally may change routes or be sold.

Color Line

THE FLEET	BUILT/RENOVATED	TONNAGE	PASSENGERS
Bohus	1971	8,772	1,422
Christian IV	1982	21,699	1,860
Color Festival	1985/1986	34,314	2,000
Color Viking	1985	19.763	1,720
Kronprins Harald	1987	31.914	1,432

THE FLEET (cont'd)	BUILT/RENOVATED	TONNAGE	PASSENGERS
Peter Wessel	1981/1988	29,704	2,100
Princesse Ragnhild	1981/1992	35,438	1,875
Silvia Ana (fast day ferry)	1996	7,895	1,043
Skagen	1975/1982	12,333	1,200

Norwegian-based Color Line sails between Oslo, Norway, and Kiel, Germany; and between Oslo or Kristians, Norway, and Hirtshals in northern Denmark. In 1997, several fast, short sea routes opened between the northern Danish port of Skagen and southern Norwegian ports of Larvik and Moss.

The largest and most impressive of its ships are the *Kronprins Harald* and the *Princesse Ragnhild* on the Oslo–Kiel route, which leave daily from either port for the 20-hour overnight run. The ships enter and leave Oslo via the scenic Oslofjord, a two-hour stretch. Most passengers are German or Norwegian.

The departures from Newcastle that connect two to three times weekly in Bergen with Norwegian Coastal Express evening northbound departures are operated by the Fjord Line's 20,581-ton *Jupiter,* formerly the *Color Viking.*

Scandinavian Seaways (DFDS)

THE FLEET	BUILT/RENOVATED	TONNAGE	PASSENGERS
Admiral of Scandinavia	1976/1989	18,888	1,032
Crown of Scandinavia	1994	35,498	2,026
Dana Anglia	1978/1991	19,321	1,241
King of Scandinavia	1974/1990	13,336	972
Pearl of Scandinavia	1989/2001	40,012	2,090
Prince of Scandinavia	1975/1990	22,528	1,519
Princess of Scandinavia	1976/1991	22,528	1,534
Queen of Scandinavia	1981/1998	33,770	1,760
Skagen	1975/1982	12,333	1,200

Danish-owned Scandinavian Seaways (DFDS) operates cruise ferries between England and Denmark; England and Sweden; England and Germany; England and the Netherlands; Denmark and Sweden; Denmark and Norway; and Copenhagen and Gdynia.

The largest ships operate between Copenhagen and Oslo, with scenic departures from both cities at 5 p.m. and arrival about 9 a.m. the next morning. The northbound route from Copenhagen passes **Hamlet's Castle** at Helsingor, calls at Helsingborg (Sweden), and enters the **Oslofjord** at dawn. Two-night round-trip cruises are popular from Oslo and Copenhagen. They give passengers time ashore between the morning arrival and late-afternoon departure. The Copenhagen pier is adjacent to the central business district, and the Oslo pier is a short bus ride from the city's center.

DFDS departs year-round from Harwich, England, reached by boat train from London. It has three year-round overnight services to Esbjerg on the Danish west coast, with connecting boat train service to Copenhagen, Gothenburg (Sweden), and Cuxhaven near Hamburg, from where trains connect to all of Germany. Additional sailings operate from Newcastle to Gothenburg and Amsterdam.

Silja Line

THE FLEET	BUILT/RENOVATED	TONNAGE	PASSENGERS
Finnjet	1977	32,940	1,781
Silja Europa	1993	59,914	3,123
Silja Festival	1986/1992	34,414	1,916
Silja Opera	1980/1992/1995	25,611	1,400
Silja Serenade	1990	58,376	2,852
Silja Symphony	1991	58,377	2,852
SuperSeaCatIII	1999	NA	640
SuperSeaCatIV	1999	NA	722

Operating the world's largest cruise ferries, Silja Line is the best-known Scandinavian ferry company. The ships are cities at sea; some carry as many as 3,000 passengers.

Though busy, they're designed to avert crowding and long queues. Cruise ship–style atriums are the centerpiece; nearby are eateries, lounges, and bars for all incomes. The prestige route is Stockholm to Helsinki. A ship leaves each port at 5 p.m. every night year-round (the sun shines until 10 p.m. or later in summer, this being the Land of the Midnight Sun) and arrives the next day at 9:30 a.m. The extended passage time includes a middle-of-the-night call in the Aland Islands that permits the continuation of duty-free shopping, a major attraction for high-taxed Scandinavians. The two-hour passage through the Stockholm archipelago is a highlight; to enjoy the entire transit, be up about 7 a.m. The ship docks conveniently next to central Helsinki; passengers on the two-night round-trip have the day ashore. Extended stopovers are easily arranged. Arrival in Stockholm is slightly less with a subway connection to the city center.

The overnight Stockholm to Turku, Finland route is offered daily. A companion daylight service takes about 11 hours.

One of the fastest single-hull ships in northern Europe is the gas turbine *Finnjet*, whose 23-hour summer schedule between Helsinki and Rostock, Germany, calls for speeds of 30 knots. In the off-season, the ship operates a more relaxed schedule.

In 2000, the line introduced the even faster *SuperSeaCat IV* on Baltic daylight service between Helsinki, Finland, and Tallinn, Estonia. The new $30 million ship cruises at 37.8 knots and takes 1½ hours to make the crossing. The 328-foot monohull carries 752 passengers, 164 cars, and 4 motorcoaches. Facilities include a bar and cafeteria, 50-seat business-class lounge, shop, and observation area.

Viking Line

THE FLEET	BUILT/RENOVATED	TONNAGE	PASSENGERS
Ålandsfärjan	1972	n.a.	963
Amorella	1988	34,384	2,450
Cinderella	1989	46,398	2,500
Gabriella	1992	35,150	2,420
Isabella	1989	34,384	2,450
Mariella	1985	37,799	2,500
Rosella	1980	10,757	1,700

The red-hulled ships of Viking Line, Silja Line's main competitor, cruise similar routes. The Stockholm-to-Turku daylight voyage calls at Mariehamn in the beautiful Åland Islands, about halfway between Sweden and Finland. The Stockholm–Helsinki route may be taken as two-night round-trip cruises that include two dinners and two breakfasts. The berth in Stockholm is closer to the city center than Silja's while the Helsinki location is similar.

Information and Reservations

Norwegian Coastal Voyage and Silja Line
405 Park Avenue, New York, NY 10022
(212) 319-1300; (800) 323-7436; fax (212) 319-1390
www.coastalvoyage.com; www.silja.com

DFDS Seaways (USA) Inc.
Cypress Creek Business Park, 6555 NW 9th Avenue, No. 207
Ft. Lauderdale, FL 33309
(800) 533-3755; fax (954) 491-7958
www.seaeurope.com; www.europeonsale.com

Nordic Saga Tours (for Color Line)
4215 21st Avenue West, Seattle, WA 98199
(800) 848-6449; (206) 301-9129; fax (206) 301-9087
www.nordicsaga.com; www.colorline.com
The tour operator also represents Scandinavian Seaways, Fjord Line (Newcastle-Stavanger-Bergen), and other European cruise ferries.

Borton Overseas (for Viking Line)
5412 Lyndale Avenue South, Minneapolis, MN 55419
(612) 822-4640; (800) 843-0602; fax (612) 822-4755
www.bortonoverseas.com; ww.vikingline.fi

Freighters

The following information was adapted, with permission, from "Setting Sail by Freighter," by Dave G. Houser and Rankin Harvey, published as a special issue of *Cruises & Tours* magazine.

Introduction to Freighter Travel

Freighter travel may be the least-understood segment of the cruise industry. You don't read or hear much about it, and cargo lines that offer passenger service rarely advertise in the mainstream media. Many travel agents, too, lack experience and expertise in booking freighter cruises.

Freighters roam the globe, visiting ports both famous and exotic. They offer a carefree, informal environment conducive to total relaxation, and they cost much less than conventional cruise ships.

Before the post–World War II boom in air travel and cruises, freighters were a significant mode of international travel. Expanding air routes, lower fares, and the growth of the cruise industry gradually relegated freighter travel to a minor niche in the cruise market.

Cargo lines have recognized a revival of interest. A few have introduced combined container and passenger vessels that can accommodate larger numbers of passengers. More than 100 traditional freighters, which carry from 2 to 12 passengers, are currently in service. Many enjoy brisk bookings and operate at capacity during peak seasons. However, the extra regulations and general travel downturn resulting from the terrorist attacks of 9/11 (not to mention the ensuing wars) caused several freight lines to reconsider the practicality of passenger service. Call to confirm all information before making travel plans or reservations.

Freighters: Defining the Breed

What exactly is a freighter? First, let's say what it is not. A modern freighter isn't a rusty tramp steamer sailing on a mission of intrigue or romance as popularized in movies and novels. The vast majority of cargo vessels today are less than 30 years old. Trim and handsome, they're loaded with sophisticated navigation and communication equipment. Most are containerized, that is, their freight is carried in large metal containers resembling box cars systematically stacked below and above decks.

The International Conventions and Conferences on Marine Safety defines the passenger-carrying freighter as a vessel principally engaged in transporting goods that is licensed to carry a maximum of 12 passengers. Those licensed to carry more than 12 are defined as combination cargo-passenger ships. The latter must meet stricter safety standards and carry more staff, including a doctor, and they have the advantage of gaining preferred docking privileges over ordinary freighters.

Nowadays, nearly all cargo ships run on fixed schedules along established routes, except for those in so-called tramp service. Tramps don't sail regular routes or schedules and can be hired to haul almost anything, anywhere, anytime. A few take passengers.

Why People Choose Freighters

Traveling by freighter offers a rare opportunity to truly get away from it all. There are no crowds, no planned activities, no lines, no dress code, and no hoopla. The atmosphere aboard a freighter is relaxed and unstructured. Passengers can be as active or as lazy as they choose.

Freighters are for travelers who want to see the world on their own terms and at their own pace. Most are veteran travelers who have become bored or disillusioned with conventional tours, cruises, and popular vacation destinations. Their sense of adventure and yearning for discovery demand something different. A glance at freighter itineraries reveals ports that would be impractical or prohibitively expensive to visit any other way.

Freighter travelers recognize good value, and, on a per diem basis, there's no better travel value than freighters. With careful research and planning, you can roam the world for months aboard a freighter for roughly $70 to $130 per day.

Some people are attracted by the camaraderie they enjoy with fellow passengers. Sailing with usually no more than a dozen like-minded, well-informed veteran travelers in a low-key, relaxing atmosphere is their ideal travel environment and often leads to lasting friendships.

Is Freighter Travel for You?

Judging from the high rate of repeat bookings, once a freighter traveler, always a freighter traveler. If you haven't tried it but you've read this far, you may be a good candidate.

You must have plenty of time. Most folks just can't get away for a 30-, 60-, or 90-day voyage. For that reason alone, the majority of freighter travelers are retirees, teachers and professors, self-employed professionals, and occasionally an artist or writer. Common characteristics include an extensive travel background, love of the sea, preference for independent travel, and abhorrence of hoopla.

Wherever on this planet your imagination might roam, chances are you can go there on a freighter. Some of the more exotic and popular routes (round-trip from the United States) include South Africa from New York (46 days), East or West Coast to New Zealand/Australia (38–66 days), around the world from New York (90 days), Marquesas Islands from Tahiti (16 days), Mediterranean from East or West Coast (42–60 days) and South America from East or Gulf Coast (42–70 days).

Accommodations and Facilities

The majority of cargoliners have spacious, comfortable accommodations equal to, and often better than, those found on cruise ships. Normally they are located in a multistory superstructure at the stern. Cabins have showers and sometimes bathtubs. In most cases they're air-conditioned and tastefully furnished. Often, they have taped music, service phones, VCRs, minifridges, and picture windows rather than portholes.

Comfy, smartly decorated lounges invite card games, conversation, and evening cocktails. Most vessels have large-screen televisions and an extensive library of videos. Many cargoliners have small pools, exercise rooms, and saunas for officer and passenger use, and plenty of deck space for walks.

An open bridge policy seems to prevail among freighters; you're welcome to watch officers and crew in action except during critical maneuvers such as docking. On most freighters, in fact, passengers are free to go almost anywhere they please.

Pampering is not part of the program. Basic services are handled by a small contingent of stewards who usually double as cabin boys and waiters. A washer and dryer are generally available for passenger use. Phone and fax services are always available in emergencies, but policies on casual use vary.

Ships carrying more than 12 passengers have a doctor on board and generally have a small hospital or treatment center. But medical services aboard freighters carrying 12 or fewer passengers are limited. All, however, carry basic medical supplies and someone aboard will be trained in first aid. In case of serious illness, the captain will contact the nearest ship or shore station with a doctor available for advice. In a grave emergency, the victim will be transferred to a ship with appropriate medical facilities or be put ashore at the nearest port. Costs incurred in medical evacuation and treatment are the passenger's responsibility.

In view of this, you're advised to take out travel health insurance with medical evacuation coverage and to carry more than enough of any medications you require.

Dining and Food

Every freighter has a comfortable dining room shared by officers and passengers. Dining is the day's special event and an opportunity to socialize. Most officers are congenial, eager to please, and happy to share their knowledge of the ship, the sea, and the world. Most freighter food is of good restaurant quality, well prepared, and plentiful. Menus often feature the national cuisine of the ship's and/or officers' origin.

Breakfast and lunch are usually presented buffet-style while dinners are served at tables, often in four or five courses. Coffee and tea are available anytime, and between-meal snacks are provided. While beer, wine, and liquor is available on most ships, it may be necessary for you to BYOB.

Planning Your Freighter Voyage

The majority of freighters book up early, especially for peak summer months. Start early yourself—six months or more—to get your choice of ship and routing, and a year ahead is not unusual on popular voyages. Planning, booking and confirming your voyage can take much longer than you imagined. Depending on itinerary, you may have to obtain travel documents, such as visas, make arrangements concerning your home or business, get a physical checkup, and decide on trip and travel health insurance options.

First, consult a current issue of *Ford's Freighter Travel Guide* (19448 Londelius Street, Northridge, CA 91324; tel: (818) 701-7414), a comprehensive twice-a-year guide listing almost all passenger-carrying freighter itineraries. Your local university library may have a copy. A subscription costs $24 (plus $1.98 sales tax for California residents). Single copies are $15.95.

As a smart second step, join **TravLtips Cruise and Freighter Association** (P.O. Box 580188, Flushing, NY 11358; (800) 872-8584; **www. travltips.com;** membership costs $20 per year per couple or $35 for two years). You'll connect with this loose-knit group of 28,000 freighter and offbeat cruising buffs and receive bimonthly issues of TravLtips, the association magazine; periodic issues of *Roam the World by Freighter,* which includes member's reports of voyages; access to the association's travel planning and reservation services; and member-only invitations on special and unusual cruises. TravLtips and California-based **Freighter World Cruises** (180 S. Lake Avenue, Suite 335, Pasadena, CA 91101; (800) 531-7774) can help you select a vessel or voyage and book it, plus handle air and other travel arrangements. Printed twice monthly, *The Freighter Space Advisory* reports cabin availability, descriptions, departure dates from the U.S. and foreign ports, en route ports of call, and fares. You can subscribe online at **www.freightworld.com;** a one-year subscription costs $29.

Many cargo lines are represented by similar specialized agents. These services can be a real blessing, particularly to first-timers, because booking passage on a freighter is not quick and easy.

You need lead time. Because freighter schedules are prone to change, some lines require waitlisting (no charge) until firm schedules are released. Only then will waiting passengers be given an option on a cabin. A deposit—usually 10–20%—is required only after a cabin option is accepted. Final payment is usually due 45–60 days before sailing.

During the months before sailing, the departure date may shift a few days and the routing may change. (For example, you may be going to Wellington rather than Auckland.) This proves the value of having an experienced agent to keep you informed of changes and to help deal with them and your need for flexibility in schedule and attitude.

Every freighter company has its own policies affecting passengers. Most have literature outlining these policies and describing their ships and itineraries. Obtain such materials through your travel agent or directly from the line, and read everything thoroughly—including the fine print. Pay particular attention to the company's cancellation policy, and take it into account when you consider trip cancellation insurance.

Some lines offer single cabins; others charge a single supplement, usually less than 50%. Because freighters are working vessels, most lines won't accept preteen children for passage. Those that do usually charge the adult fare for children. Pets aren't permitted.

Fewer than 40 nations require U.S. citizens to carry visas, but those that do include Australia and Brazil—and both are countries frequented by passenger-carrying freighters.

Your Health

Cargo lines require passengers age 65 or older to present a certificate of good health from their doctor before booking can be completed. Review your itinerary with your physician regarding potential risk of disease or infection and any immunizations or protective medicines needed. Up-to-the-minute immunization recommendations are available from the **Centers for Disease Control's** 24-hour hotline in Atlanta: (877) 394-8747. You'll need a touch-tone phone and fax machine to receive faxed messages. You may also check for information on the CDC website at **www.cdc.gov.**

Clothing and Essentials

Packing for a 90-day freighter voyage should be no different from selecting your gear and garments for a 10-day trip. Nor should it weigh more; cargo lines, unlike cruise lines, aren't obligated to provide baggage service. Don't bring more than you can handle.

Casual attire is the rule. It's possible there might be a special occasion calling for dressier clothes, or that restaurants ashore may require them. For everyday wear, bring low-heeled, nonskid, rubber-soled shoes. They are essential for safe maneuvering aboard ship in rough seas. Be prepared for just about any kind of climate. Light wraps (even in the tropics) and rain gear are essential.

Foul weather is almost a certainty during any long voyage, and many freighter veterans pack a lightweight, two-piece rain suit (parka and pants), and rubber boots. They also are handy for wading through the dust and residue that cakes bulk-loading docks. Bring binoculars, some reading material (don't overdo; most ships have extensive libraries), washcloths, and facial tissue.

Electrical current on most foreign-flagged freighters is 220/250 AC. You'll need a voltage converter and plug adapter to use your appliances. Funds for shipboard expenses should be in U.S. currency. Traveler's checks are generally accepted, but very few lines take credit cards or personal checks.

Most lines say they have no policy on tipping. A few say that their stewards who serve passengers get extra pay and suggest that tipping be reserved for exceptional or special service. The norm seems to be $1.50 per person per day to the room steward and an equal amount to the dining steward.

Smoking is allowed on nearly all freighters because many officers and crew members smoke. A few lines bar smoking in dining rooms. The majority of officers and crew who smoke are courteous around non-smoking guests, and most passengers say smoking is not a big problem.

Freighter Travel Agents

The following is a sampling of freighter lines and routes. For more information, call the following agencies to request brochures and information about complete listings.

Freighter World Cruises
180 South Lake Avenue, Suite 335, Pasadena, CA 91101-2655
(626) 449-3106; (800) 531-7774; fax (626) 449-9573
www.freighterworld.com

TravLtips
25-37 Francis Lewis Boulevard, P.O. Box 580188,
Flushing, NY 11358-0188
(718) 224-0435; (800) 872-8584; fax (718) 224-3247
www.travltips.com

Freighter Travel Directory

The following directory is in two parts. The first part provides information on cargo lines, their vessels departing from United States ports, and their booking contacts. The asterisk (*) indicates the agent can arrange ancillary requirements, including air transportation (in some cases, air/sea package), hotel, transfers, hiring a car, sightseeing, and travel insurance. The second part, the Freighter Routing Directory, is organized by departure ports and gives a line's voyage duration and price range. Itineraries are available from cargo lines and sources cited previously in this chapter. Information is subject to change.

Note: Call to confirm all information. International freight regulations and routes are in a state of flux due to post-9/11 changes and tensions, and everything in this section is subject to change by the various companies and governments involved.

Blue Star Line

Four ships (registry: Bahamas; officers and crew: British/Filipino), regular service from U.S. ports to Australia and New Zealand.

Agent Freighter World Cruises, TravLtips *

American Star, Melbourne Star, Queensland Star, and *Sidney Star* (built 1972; 24,907 tons) each carry ten passengers in four double and two single cabins. All four ships have cabins with bath and shower; passenger laundry, pantry, bar/lounge, game room with television/VCR, and library. Age limit: 79 (medical certificate required).

CMA CGM, the French Line

Four ships (registry: Bahamas; officers and crew: French and international) in service from U.S. East Coast around the world. One ship (registry: French; officers and crew: French) in service from U.S. West Coast to Asia and Europe.

Agent Freighter World Cruises, TravLtips *

CMA CGM Matisse, CMA CGM Utrillo, CMA CGM La Tour, and *CMA CGM Manet* (built 1999 and 2001; 31,508 tons) each carry six passengers in one Owner's Cabin and two double cabins. All cabins have private bath/shower. Each vessel features a lounge/video room, fitness room, and indoor swimming pool. Age limit: 79.

Ville de Tanya (built 1998; 50,000 tons) carries four passengers in one double cabin and two single cabins. All cabins have sitting area, desk with chair and private bath/shower. The ship offers a passenger lounge, exercise room, laundry, and indoor swimming pool. Age limit: 70 (extended to 75 with good medical report).

Columbus Line

One ship (registry: Liberian; officers and crew: German), regular service from U.S. ports to Australia and New Zealand.

Agent Freighter World Cruises, TravLtips *

Columbus Canterbury (built 1981; 24,270 tons), two passengers in one Owner's Suite. The suite's bedroom has twin beds, sitting area, and private bath/shower. The suite's spacious dayroom features side windows, small refrigerator, and private bath. Large, nicely furnished lounge, library, swimming pool, deck chairs. Age limit: 79.

Hansa Shipmanagement

One ship (registry: Liberian; officers and crew: German) in service from U.S. East Coast to Africa.

Agent Freighter World Cruises *

MSC Florida (built 1997; 31,730 tons) carries six passengers in three double suites. Suites have minifridge, stereo with CD player, and private bath/shower. The vessel offers a lounge, exercise room, laundry, sauna, and indoor pool. Age limit: 79.

Hermann Buss and Oltmann

Three ships (registry: Germany, Antigua, and Barbuda; officers and crew: Polish, German, Ukrainian, and Filipino) in service from U.S. West Coast to the Mediterranean. One ship (registry: Panama; officers and crew: European and Filipino) in service from U.S. East Coast to the Caribbean and South America. One ship (registry: Antigua and Barbuda; officers and crew: Polish) in service from U.S. West Coast to South America and Asia. One ship (registry: German and Antigua; officers and crew: German, Polish, Ukranian and Filipino) in service from U.S. West Coast to Asia. One ship (registry: Antigua; officers and crew: German and Filipino) in service from U.S. West Coast to Asia and Europe.

Agent Freighter World Cruises, TravLtips *

MV Cielo d'America (built 1998; 30,300 tons) carries eight passengers in four double cabins. Cabins have sitting area and private bath/shower. The vessel offers a lounge, sauna, exercise room, and outdoor pool. *MV Cielo di San Francisco* (built 1998; 33,500 tons) carries three passengers in one Owner's Cabin and one single cabin. *MV Cielo del Canada* (built 1998; 33,500 tons) carries four passengers in one Owner's Cabin and two single cabins. Cabins on the *San Francisco* and *Canada* all have desk with chair, refrigerator, and private bath/shower. Both vessels offer exercise room, sauna, and indoor swimming pool. Age limit: 79.

Seaboard Pride (built 1998; 8,350 tons) carries two passengers in one Owner's Suite and one single cabin. Both cabins have minifridge and private bath/shower. Age limit: 79.

Maruba Trader (built 1998; 16,803 tons) carries five passengers in two double cabins and one single cabin. All cabins have sitting area, desk with chair, and private bath/shower. The vessel offers a bar/lounge and outdoor pool. Age limit: 79.

Trave Trader (built 1994; 22,250 tons) carries for passengers in one Owner's Suite, one single suite and one single cabin. All suites/cabins have sitting area, desk with chair, and private bath/shower. The suites each have a minifridge. The vessel offers a lounge/bar, sauna, and indoor pool. Age limit: 79.

Baltrum Trader (built 1999; 33,500 tons) carries five passengers one Owner's Suite and three single cabins. All suites/cabins have minifridge and private bath/shower. The vessel offers a pool and sauna. Age limit: 79.

Lykes Lines

Four ships (registry: British; officers and crew: Indian) in service from the U.S. Gulf Coast to South America.

Agent TravLtips *

TMM Sinola, TMM Hermosillo, Lykes Achiever, and *Lykes Challenger* (built 1985 and 1986; 40,744 tons) carry eight passengers in four double cabins. All cabins have sitting area, minifridge, and bath/shower. Ships have passenger lounge, passenger pantry, sun deck, and swimming pool. Age limit: 79.

Leonhardt & Blumberg

Four ships (registry: Liberian; officers and crew: German/South Sea Islanders from the Kiribati Islands) in service from the U.S. West Coast to Australia and New Zealand.

Agent Freighter World Cruises, TravLtips *

Direct Jabiru, Direct Condor, Direct Kestrel (built 2000; 23,587 tons), and *Direct Hawk* (built 2000; 18,587 tons) carry six passengers in one Owner's Suite and two double suites. Suites have twin beds, refrigerator, private bath/shower, sitting room with sofa, and desk. Each vessel has a lounge, exercise room, and swimming pool. Age Limit: 80.

Mare Schiffahrtsgesellschaft GmbH

Two ships (registry: German and Antigua; officers and crew: European and Filipino) in service from U.S. East Coast to the Caribbean and South America. One ship (registry: Antigua; officers and crew: German and Samoan) in service from U.S. West Coast to the South Pacific.

Agent Freighter World Cruises, TravLtips *

Mira J (built 1997; 8,500 tons) carries four passengers in two double suites. *Heinrich J* (built 1998; 6,850 tons) carries five passengers in one Owner's Suite and three single cabins. Suites/cabins for each vessel feature sitting area and private bath/shower. Both vessels offer a lounge. Age limit: 79.

Tausala Samoa (built 1998; 12,044 tons) carries three passengers in one Owner's Cabin (single) and one 3rd Engineer's Cabin (double). Both cabins have refrigerator, television/VCR and private bath/shower. The vessel offers a lounge, recreation room with Ping-Pong table and indoor pool. Age limit: 79.

Maritime Reederei

One ship (registry: Liberian; officers and crew: Croatian and Filipino) in regular service from U.S. East Coast to the Mediterranean.

Agent Freighter World Cruises, TravLtips *

P&O Nedlloyd Nina (built 1986; 28,948 tons) carries eight passengers in three double cabins and two single cabins. Cabins have refrigerators, sofa, desk with chair, and private bath/shower. The ship is completely air-conditioned and offers a lounge/bar and swimming pool. Age limit: 79.

Niederelbe Schiffahrtsgesellschaft Buxtehude

Ten ships (registry: Liberian and German; officers and crew: German/Filipino), four of which in service from U.S. West Coast to Asia and Europe, five in service from U.S. West Coast to Asia and the Mediterranean, and one in service from U.S. East and West Coasts to Asia and Europe.

Agent TravLtips *

Hanjin Amsterdam, Hanjin Copenhagen (built 1999; 69,050 tons), *Hanjin Athens,* and *Hanjin Bruxelles* (built 2000; 69,050 tons) carry five passengers in two double cabins and one single cabin. All cabins have sitting area, minifridge, and private bath/shower. The vessels offer a bar/lounge, exercise room, indoor pool, and sauna. Age limit: 79.

Ville de Taurus, Ville d'Orion, Ville de Mimosa (built 1997; 37,549 tons), Ville de Capella (built 1994; 42,673 tons), and *Ville de Libra* (built 1995; 42,673 tons) carry eight passengers in four suites. Suites feature minifridge, desk with chair, sitting area, and private bath/shower. Vessels offer laundry room, fitness room, bar/lounge, sauna, and indoor pool. Age limit: 79.

Hong Kong Senator (built 1993; 45,470 tons) carries eight passengers in three double suites and two single cabins, all with private bath and shower. The vessel offers a lounge, laundry, sauna, fitness room, indoor pool, and outdoor pool. Age limit: 79.

Projex Line

One ship (registry: German; officers and crew: German and Polish/Filipino) in service from the U.S. Gulf Coast to South America.

Agent TravLtips *

Lykes Falcon (built 1998; 23,897 tons) carries eight passengers in four double cabins with sitting area, refrigerator and private bath/shower. The vessel has a lounge/library, exercise room, and outdoor pool. Age limit: 79.

Reederei Bernhard Schulte

Two ships (registry: Cyprus; officers and crew: European and Filipino) in service from U.S. West Coast to Australia, New Zealand and South Pacific. Two ships (registry: Hong Kong; officers and crew: Polish, Indian, and Chinese) in service from U.S. West Coast to the Mediterranean.

Agent Freighter World Cruises, TravLtips *

MV Fesco Voyager and *Direct Kiwi* (built 1997; 22,300 tons) carry nine passengers in four double cabins and one single cabin. All cabins have sitting area, minifridge, television/VCR, tea/coffee and private bath with shower. Both ships offer a lounge, exercise room, laundry, and outdoor pool. Age limit: 79.

Caroline Schulte and *Elisabeth Schulte* (built 2001; 34,717 tons) carry three passengers in one double cabin and one single cabin. All cabins have private bath/shower. The vessels offer a lounge, exercise room, and pool. Age limit: 79.

Reederei F. Laeisz

Seven ships (registry: German; officers and crew: German and international) in service from U.S. West Coast to Asia and Northern Europe.

Four ships (registry: Liberian; officers and crew: German and international) in service from U.S. East Coast to Southern Europe and Asia.

Agent Freighter World Cruises, TravLtips *

Pudong Senator, Pusan Senator, Penang Senator, Portland Senator, Pugwash Senator, Portugal Senator, and *Peking Senator* (built 1997 and 1998; 63,645 tons) carry eight passengers in four double suites. Suites feature large living room, desk with chair, minifridge, bar, television/VCR, stereo with tuner, tape deck and CD, and private bath/shower. Each vessel offers a lounge, exercise room, sauna, and indoor pool. Age Limit: 79.

Pacific Senator, Patmos Senator, Palermo Senator, and *Shanghai Senator* (built 1992 and 1993; 45,000 tons) carry four passengers in two double cabins. Cabins feature sitting area, desk with chair, minifridge, bar, television/VCR, and private bath/shower. Each vessel offers a lounge, exercise room, sauna and outdoor pool. Age Limit: 79.

Reederei Nord

One ship (registry: Cyprus; officers and crew: European and Kiribati or Sri Lankan) in service from U.S. East Coast to India. One ship (registry: Cyprus; officers and crew: European and Kiribati or Sri Lankan) in service from U.S. West Coast to South America and Asia.

Agent Freighter World Cruises, TravLtips *

Indamex Taj (built 1994; 14,619 tons) carries six passengers in two double cabins and two single cabins. All cabins have private bath/shower. Age limit: 79.

Nordlake (built 1994; 22,450) carries six passengers in two double cabins and two single cabins. All cabins have private bath/shower. Age limit: 79.

Transeste Schiffahrt GmbH

One ship (registry: German; officers and crew: German and Filipino) in service from U.S. East Coast to South America.

Agent TravLtips *

Sea Tiger (built 2001; 25,608 tons) carries seven passengers in three twin suites and one single cabin. All cabins have private bath and shower. The vessel offers a bar/lounge, outdoor pool, and sauna. Age limit: 79.

Freighter Routing Directory

Because of space limitations, we have only included freighters departing from United States ports. However, many others depart from ports in other countries.

Atlantic and Gulf Coasts

Around the World

CMA CGM, the French Line   Four ships departing from New York, NY.

Duration is about 89 days. Rates: per person/double $8,947, single $10,500.

Africa

Hansa Shipmanagement   One ship departing from New York, NY. Duration is about 46 days. Rates: per person/double $3,910, single $4,600. Plus $241 per person for port taxes, deviation insurance, and U.S. Custom & Immigration fees.

Asia and Europe

Niederelbe Schiffahrtsgesellschaft Buxtehude   One ship departing from New York, NY. Duration is about 90 days. Shorter segments are available. Rates: Owner's Suite per person/double $7,650, Owner's Suite single $8,550, double suite per person/double $6,750, double suite single $7,875, single cabin $6,750. Plus $232.50 per person for port taxes, deviation insurance and U.S. Custom & Immigration fees.

Reederei F. Laeisz   For ships departing from New York, NY. Duration is about 91 days. Shorter segments are available. Rates: per person/double $5,005, single $6,370. Plus $201 per person for port taxes, deviation insurance, and U.S. Custom & Immigration fees.

Australia and New Zealand

Blue Star Line   Four ships departing from Savannah, GA. Duration is about 66 days. Shorter segments available. Rates: Fall/winter, per person/double $5,346–$6,138; single $6,402–$7,128. Spring/summer, per person/double $4,290–$4,950; single $5,148–$5,742. Plus $11 per person U.S. Custom & Immigration fees and $21 per person Australian movement tax.

Columbus Line   One ship departing from Savannah, GA. Duration about 66 days. Shorter segments available. Rates: high season (October 1–February 28), per person/double $8,250. Low season, per person/double $6,600. Plus $11 per person U.S. Custom & Immigration fees and $21 per person Australian movement tax.

Caribbean and South America

Hermann Buss and Oltmann   One ship departing from Miami, FL. Duration is about 14 days. Rates: Owner's Suite (single) $1,540, single cabin $1,400. Plus $261 per person for port taxes, deviation insurance, and U.S. Custom & Immigration fees.

Mare Schiffahrtsgesellschaft GmbH   Two ships departing from Port Everglades, FL. Duration is 12–88 days. Rates: Owner's Suite per person/double $1,800, Owner's Suite single $2,160, double cabin per person/double $1,260, double cabin single $1,330, single cabin $1,800. Plus $261 per person for port taxes, deviation insurance, and U.S. Custom & Immigration fees.

India

Reederei Nord One ship departing from New York, NY. Duration is about 55 days. Rates: per person/double $4,400, single $4,950. Plus $261 per person for port taxes, deviation insurance, and U.S. Custom & Immigration fees.

Mediterranean

Martime Reederei One ship departing from New York, NY. Duration is about 42 days. Shorter segments available. Rates: double cabin per person/double $3750, double cabin single $4,463, single cabin $3,780. Plus $230 per person for port taxes, deviation insurance, and U.S. Custom & Immigration fees.

South America

Lykes Lines Four ships departing from Houston, TX. Duration is about 42 days. Round-trip rates: double cabin per person/double $3,570, double cabin single $3,780. Plus $12 per person for U.S. Custom & Immigration fees.

Projex Line One ship departing from Houston, TX. Duration is about 42 days. Rates: double cabin per person/double $4,200, double cabin single $4,620. Plus $261 per person for port taxes, deviation insurance, and U.S. Custom & Immigration fees.

Transeste Schiffahrt GmbH One ship departing from Philadelphia, PA. Duration is about 42 days. Rates: double suite per person/double $3,780, double suite single $4,200, single cabin $3,780. Plus $261 per person for port taxes, deviation insurance, and U.S. Custom & Immigration fees.

Pacific Coast

Asia

Hermann Buss and Oltmann One ship departing from Los Angeles, CA. Duration is about 35 days. Shorter segments are available. Rates: Owner's Suite per person/double $2,975, single suite $3,150, single cabin $2,975. Plus $261 per person for port taxes, deviation insurance, and U.S. Custom & Immigration fees.

Asia and Europe

CMA CGM, the French Line One ship departing from Los Angeles, CA. Duration is about 83 days. Shorter segments area available. Rates: per person/double $6,736, single $5,781.

Herman Buss and Oltmann One ship departing from Long Beach, CA. Duration is about 80 days. Shorter segments are available. Rates: double cabin per person/double $7,600, double cabin single $9,200, single cabin $7,600. Plus $261 per person for port taxes, deviation insurance, and U.S. Custom & Immigration fees.

Niederelbe Schiffahrtsgesellschaft Buxtehude Ten ships departing from Long Beach, CA. Duration is about 84-90 days. Shorter segments are available. Four ships rates: double cabin per person/double $7,560, double cabin single $8,820, single cabin $7,140. Six ships rates: Owner's

Suite per person/double $7,225–$7,650, Owner's Suite single $8,550, double suite per person/double $6,375–$6,750, double suite single $7,225–$7,875, single cabin $6,750. Plus $232.50 per person for port taxes, deviation insurance, and U.S. Custom & Immigration fees.

Reederei F. Laeisz Seven ships departing from Long Beach, CA. Duration is about 83 days. Shorter segments are available. Rates: per person/double $6,640, single $7,055. Plus $201 per person for port taxes, deviation insurance, and U.S. Custom & Immigration fees.

Asia and South America

Hermann Buss and Oltmann One ship departing from Long Beach, CA. Duration is about 80 days. Shorter segments are available. Rates: double cabin per person/double $7,600, double cabin single $9,200, single cabin $7,600. Plus $261 per person for port taxes, deviation insurance, and U.S. Custom & Immigration fees.

Reederei Nord One ship departing from Long Beach, CA. Duration is about 70 days. Rates: per person/double $5,600, single $6,300. Plus $261 per person for port taxes, deviation insurance, and U.S. Custom & Immigration fees.

Australia and New Zealand

Leonhardt & Blumberg Four ships departing from Los Angeles, CA. Duration is about 48 days. Shorter segments available. Rates: Owner's Suite per person/double $3,600, Owner's Suite single $4,320, double suite per person/double $3,360, double suite single $4,032. Plus $11 per person U.S. Custom & Immigration fees and $21 per person Australian movement tax.

Reederei Bernhard Schulte Two ships departing from Los Angeles, CA. Duration is about 55 days. Shorter segments available. Rates: per person/double $3,740, single $4,345. Plus $11 per person U.S. Custom & Immigration fees and $21 per person Australian movement tax.

Mediterranean

Herman Buss and Oltmann Three ships departing from Los Angeles, CA. Duration is about 55 days. Shorter segments available. Rates: double cabin per person or single, $5,503. Plus $277 or $302 per person port taxes, deviation insurance and U.S. Custom & Immigration fees.

Reederei Bernhard Schulte Two ships departing from Seattle, WA. Duration is about 98 days. Shorter segments are available. Rates: per person/double $6,664, single $7,742. Plus $11 per person for U.S. Custom & Immigration fees.

South Pacific

Mare Schiffahrtsgesellschaft GmbH One ship departing from Los Angeles, CA. Duration is about 28 days. Rates: double cabin per person/double $3,060, double cabin single $3,600, single cabin $3,400. Plus $261 per person port taxes, deviation insurance and U.S. Custom & Immigration fees.

Sailing Ships

People choose to cruise for different reasons, and the primary motivating factors are as diverse as the amazingly wide range of ships, itineraries, and services available in the modern cruise market. For many, however, there is a longing that transcends midnight buffets, luxurious cabins, and myriad ports of call. These are individuals who are transfixed and enchanted by the lure of the sea itself. The feeling of being underway, the buffeting wind, the salt sea spray over the bow, and the twinkling phosphorescent wake are to them the stuff of dreams. There is no bingo, afternoon tea, or stylish air-conditioned lounge for these folks. Rather, you'll find them on deck leaning on the starboard rail, taking in every white-capped wave.

Almost all are landlubbers—individuals whose imagination draws them to the sea—and most of them first experience the sea aboard a large, modern cruise ship. It doesn't take long for them to realize, however, that no matter how grand a particular floating resort might be, they desire a much more intimate relationship with the sea. Opting for a smaller cruise ship does the trick for some, but for others it's not enough. Sooner or later, these last discover the wonderful world of cruising under sail.

Cruising under sail is cruising in concert with the sea. By definition, sailing uses currents, tides, and winds to the advantage of the sailor, always working with natural forces and never against them. Pursuing this harmony precipitates any number of outcomes (the elements are not always cooperative, you know), but it's always an adventure. Bringing home the reality of weather and sea conditions, sailing is for many a life-changing experience—an epiphany.

If you want to try sailing on for size, you have a wide selection of alternatives. Choices range from medium-sized cruise ships with computer-controlled sails and powerful, supplemental engines, to tiny schooners with no motor at all, where every passenger must help work the boat. Accommodations range from conventional cruise-ship staterooms to tiny cabins accessible only by descending a ladder through a hatch. Some voyages are veritable courses in sailing and seamanship; others demand nothing beyond normal cruise ship passenger passivity.

If you've not sailed before, enjoy the amenities of a larger cruise ship, or are uncertain how much of an adventure you want, consider sailing with either **Star Clippers** or **Windstar Cruises** (both described in detail in Part Two, Cruise Lines and Their Ships). Star Clippers operates four-masted, square-rigged ships with small (by cruise ship standards), air-conditioned cabins with private baths. You'll find a small pool, a library, and even a piano lounge. Star Clippers vessels carry a maximum of 170 passengers.

Windstar, which operates four-masted ships with triangular sails, costs about $580 per day before any applicable discounts, compared to an average non-discounted per diem of about $268 on Star Clippers. Most

Windstar ships carry about 150 passengers, with one ship, *Wind Surf,* carrying over 300. Cabins on all ships approximate the size of those of mainstream cruise ships. Truly cruise ships with sails, you'll even find a casino and a disco on Windstar vessels. Where a crew sets the sails in the traditional way aboard Star Clippers ships (you can pitch in if you want), sails on Windstar are computer-controlled. Ships of both lines have powerful diesel-electric engines. Windstar uses its engines for propulsion about 50% of the time, whereas Star Clippers employs its engines primarily to get into and out of port.

Similar to Windstar's *Wind Surf* is **Club Med's** five-masted, computer-controlled sailing ship *Club Med 2.* The length of two football fields, *Club Med 2* carries almost 400 passengers with a per diem ranging from $130 to more than $350 depending on season and itinerary. Smaller, luxury ships with large cabins and many main line cruise ship amenities are **Sea Cloud's** *Sea Cloud* (60 passengers) and *Sea Cloud II* (96 passengers), and **Peter Dielmann Cruises'** *Lili Marleen,* a re-creation of a 19th-century three-masted barquentine. The *Lili Marleen* accommodates 50 passengers. Facilities include lovely cabins decorated with burled wall finishes, three bars/lounges, and a library. The sailing cruise lines mentioned offer itineraries that can take you all over the world, except for the *Club Med 2,* which operates exclusively in the Caribbean.

Less expensive, but offering a more authentic, hands-on experience are the **Maine Windjammer Association** cruises and **Windjammer Barefoot Cruises.** The Maine Windjammer Association is the marketing arm for 14 individually owned and operated traditional tall ships, all schooners, ranging in size from 46 to 132 feet. The fleet operates exclusively along the midcoast region of Maine, with the majority of itineraries in the verdant, island-studded waters of Penobscot Bay. Most of the schooners were built between 1871 and 1945 as working boats for hauling cargo or fishing and were converted to passenger-carrying ships within the last 20 years. Eight of the fourteen schooners are designated National Historic Landmarks.

Cruises depart Camden, Rockland, or Rockport from May through October for three- to six-day itineraries which include short ports of call at small islands and at historic Maine coastal villages. Days, for the most part, are spent sailing. The schooners anchor in protected coves or tie up at small, picturesque maritime communities at night. Meals are served family style, sometimes in the galley and sometime on deck, and feature local produce and seafood among other things. A lobster bake on a forested island is a highlight of many cruises. While most the schooners accommodate 12–29 guests, the 60-foot *Mistress* carries only 6, and the *Victory Chimes,* the largest sailing vessel flying American colors, carries 44.

About a thousand miles south, the Caribbean is home water to Windjammer Barefoot Cruises. Though the names are similar ("windjammer" is nautical slang for a seaman on a sailing ship), Windjammer Barefoot Cruises is related to the Maine Windjammers in concept only. Windjammer Barefoot Cruises operates five sailing vessels and one motorized vessel year-round, on a variety of six-day Caribbean itineraries, including the Grenandines.

All of its sailing craft are larger than those of the Maine fleet, with the largest carrying 122 passengers and the smallest 64. Facilities are not as extensive as those of the Sea Clouds, *Lili Marleen, Club Med 2,* or Clipper and Windstar ships described earlier, but are more luxurious than those of the relatively spartan Maine fleet. Most Barefoot Windjammer cabins are air-conditioned and offer a private bath. Air-conditioning isn't generally needed in Maine, and schooner passengers usually share toilet and bathing facilities. Dining is of comparable quality in both fleets, with meals distinguished by fresh, locally available meat, seafood, vegetables, and fruit.

On both Maine Windjammer and Windjammer Barefoot vessels, you can help the crew sail the ship. On the Barefoot cruises, however, such activity is take-it-or-leave-it, while Maine schooner captains frequently count on passengers to help out. On ships of either fleet, you can avail yourself of a fairly extensive sailing education during your time aboard.

For all the similarities, however, there are likewise some striking differences. The Maine experience is all about sailing, while the Barefoot ships spend most of the day in port or anchored in a secluded cove, where diving, water sports, or sunning are the featured attractions. In fact, on a Barefoot cruise, most of the sailing is done between the hours of dinner and breakfast—the exact opposite of a Maine schooner.

If you take a moment to check out the respective Windjammer websites (**www.sailmainecoast.com** and **www.windjammer.com**), potentially critical difference will become immediately apparent. The Caribbean cruise line's site screams fun, sun, and partying down, with photos of young women in bikinis. The Maine Windjammers' site, in contrast, emphasizes the peace and serenity of sailing, rugged Maine coastline scenery, and maritime skills and history. Photos on the Maine site picture older patrons and families. On Barefoot cruises, morning Bloody Marys, afternoon Rum Swizzles, and wine with dinner are provided in the price of the cruise. On a Maine schooner, no alcohol at all is served or sold, though passengers are invited to bring aboard their own private stock. Days start early in Maine, while in the Caribbean, sleeping in is definitely an option.

Climate additionally differentiates the two sail cruise options. The Caribbean is a perfect destination during the cold-weather months of the year, while Maine offers a great escape from the heat during the summer and early fall.

Finally, regardless which cruise line you choose, you should know that seasickness is rare on sailing ships. This is because the wind stabilizes the ship in the water and prevents almost all of the side-to-side rolling motion that is the primary cause of seasickness.

Note: In parentheses after each boat name is information about the number of cabins and passengers; officers and crew; and the boat's length (cabins/passengers; officers/crew; boat length).

Classic Cruises of Newport

Christie's Landing, Newport, RI 02840; (800) 3951343; (401) 849-3033; fax (401) 849-3023; www.cruisenewport.com

Arabella (20/42; American; 160 ft.)

Favored by sailing enthusiasts, romance seekers, and travelers who enjoy soft adventure, *Arabella,* a new luxury schooner, offers cruises throughout the British and U.S. Virgin Islands from late December through early May, and the New England coast in summer and fall.

The Caribbean excursions, combining sailing, swimming and snorkeling with day trips and island dining, depart from St. Thomas on six-night sails to St. John, U.S.V.I. and Norman Island, Jost Van Dyke, Tortola, Virgin Gorda, and Peter Island B.V.I., and Culebra and Vieques, Puerto Rico.

Arabella has 20 air-conditioned cabins, each with satellite television, viewing portholes, and communications capabilities that allow guests to conduct business while at sea. She also houses an on-deck hot water spa, a lounge and bar, and water sports equipment for passenger use.

Rates range from $1,195 to $1,995 per person, based on double occupancy and include all daytime meals, four dinners ashore, and optional excursions. The cruise departs on Sunday at 4 p.m. and returns to St. Thomas on Saturday at or before noon. At the end of her Caribbean season, Arabella sails the New England coast for summer and fall cruises of four and six nights from Newport, stopping in Nantucket, Martha's Vineyard, Cuttyhunk, and Provincetown.

Arabella is part of the Newport-based Atlantic Stars Hospitality Group which has hotels in New York City, Newport, and Martha's Vineyard; a restaurant in South Beach, Miami; and operates cruise vessels on day trips around Newport Harbor and Narragansett Bay.

Club Med

75 Valencia Avenue, Coral Gables, FL 33134; (800) CLUB MED; (800) 258-2633; fax (305) 443-0562; www.clubmed.com

Club Med 2 (238/394; French; 613 ft.)

One of the world's largest cruise ships with sails offers casual, sports-oriented, all-inclusive vacations with an easy lifestyle for active, upscale vacationers. The ship sails on seven-day Caribbean cruises in winter, Mediterranean in summer, and transatlantic in spring and fall.

After two decades of spreading the gospel of all-inclusive resort vacations, Club Med applied its resort formula to a cruise ship, *Club Med 2*. Built in 1992, the 14,000-ton vessel marries today's technology to yesteryear's seafaring. She is as long as two football fields and rigged with five 164-foot masts and seven computer-monitored sails; there's no listing or heeling and no officers on deck—they are on the bridge monitoring computers.

Club Med 2 has an open, nautical feeling and is glitz-free, but loses much of the intimacy that makes the Windstar line's smaller version so appealing. She is spacious and has eight Burmese teak decks. Interiors by the well-known European designer Albert Pinto evoke understated luxury through meticulous craftsmanship and the use of fine mahogany, quality fabrics, and leather, reminiscent of classic sailing ships. A glass roof covers half the main lounge, bathing the area in light; walls of windows afford sea and shore views.

The cabins are large, comfortable, and handsomely decorated with hand-rubbed mahogany cabinetwork. All cabins are outside and have twin portholes. They're fitted with twin or queen-size beds, a mahogany desk, large mirrors, ample closets, television, radio, safe, refrigerator, minibar, and satellite telephone, which is also used to order room service. The teak-floored baths have showers, hair dryers, and fluffy bathrobes. Electrical outlets are 110/220 AC. In all, there are 191 outside cabins; 6 suites. Standard dimensions are 188 square feet. There are no singles.

The cruises are basically a French product with the same informal, carefree ambience of Club Med villages, but in deluxe surroundings with cruise ship amenities. Unique to both operations are GOs—gentils organisateurs—the social hosts and hostesses who keep the action and smiles going day and night. Most GOs are French, other Europeans, or Americans who speak very good French. Their first task when you board is to familiarize you with the ship and answer questions. They organize shipboard activities and can usually give valuable tips on the best bars and restaurants in ports of call.

Guests are welcomed aboard with a fruit basket in their cabin, along with complimentary champagne, fresh flowers, and bottled water. (Note: Only the first bottle of water is free.) Unlike at Club Med villages, breakfast can be enjoyed in your room. There is 24-hour room service, and laundry service is available for an extra charge.

The ship has two ocean-view dining rooms, each with a different menu featuring French cuisine. Le Grand Bleu, an open-air veranda café on the top deck, serves casual breakfast, luncheon buffets, and theme dinners featuring cuisine from around the world. Le Deauville is a more intimate, formal dining room. The à la carte menu offers several choices for each course.

Dinner is a serious affair lasting up to three hours. Complimentary wine from Club Med's private label, beer, and bottled water accompany lunch and dinner. Smokers are in the majority on board and have the run of the ship. Restaurants have nonsmoking sections, but smoking is allowed in all public areas.

Both restaurants have waiters and unreserved, unassigned seating at tables for two or more, with continuous service during dining hours. Officers and staff dine with passengers. Most seven-night Caribbean itineraries offer a lobster beach picnic.

The ship has three lounges, nightclub, casino, piano bar, and disco. The Topkapi Piano Bar, one of five bars, is the most popular for afternoon tea with French pastries and music and for after-dinner drinks (prices higher than average). The small casino offers roulette, blackjack, and slot machines. A lounge that doubles as a theater has a bar, stage, bandstand, and dance floor. A different show or program is presented here each evening by GOs—some more entertaining than others and all amateur. Some passengers say that luxury prices they paid merit more professional entertainers.

There's a small library, card tables with leather chairs in a lounge, and a boutique. Party-seekers make their way to the disco with its lighted dance floor, or the Fantasia nightclub, hidden on the bottom deck behind an unmarked door. One night in the Caribbean is Carnival.

Sports facilities include a teak sports platform at the stern that unfolds into the sea to become a marina when the ship is at anchor. The vessel carries sailboards, sailboats, snorkels, fins, and masks and provides free lessons in water-skiing, windsurfing, sailing, and snorkeling. Two ski boats with scuba equipment take certified divers on diving trips. The scuba program is one of the line's best values.

The less ambitious can retire to chaise longues around the two outdoor swimming pools—one fresh, one saltwater. Even when the ship is full, space to lounge is ample. The supervised fitness center has exercise equipment that passengers use while enjoying a panoramic view from the top deck. Aerobics and water exercise in the pool are offered daily. Several decks below is a sauna and massage room. *Club Med 2* has a golf simulator, a beauty salon and spa with massage therapists and treatments—all at additional cost.

The Club Med imprint is obvious. Officers are French; the crew, Filipino. The staff, dressed in impeccable white shirts, shorts, and socks, handle dining and hotel duties and earn praise for their friendly, professional service. The energetic, attractive GOs are managed by the Chef du Village, the cruise director. These cheery camp counselors do it all: the reception desk, run activities, teach sports, and entertain. During their off hours, they hang out with passengers. In the Caribbean, the ship visits a port each day and sails at night. Unfortunately, passengers get very little opportunity to experience the pleasure of sailing under canvas.

The ship attracts a range of passengers that changes with the cruise, season, and location. Typically, passengers are 30–60 years old. The majority are couples. Children younger than age 10 are not accepted. Most passengers like the informality and sociability of the GO concept. On the other hand, the constant interaction between the young, bouncy GOs and passengers creates a summer camp atmosphere that is not for everyone.

The GO team is bilingual in English and French, but French is the ship's primary language. That could be a problem for English speakers who aren't up to the language challenge, or who might feel there's unequal treatment. Club Med's attitude is: This is a French-European product. The cruise is, after all, an experience where Americans might lunch with people from Normandy, snorkel with Italians, and have cocktails with Austrians. That's part of the attraction.

Per diems range from $130 to $385 but may vary by season, cabin, and cruise areas. Tips, wine and beer at lunch and dinner, and most water sports are included in the fare; port charges are additional. Club Med offers specially priced cruises occasionally, but it does not discount prices.

Coastal Cruises

P.O. Box 798, Camden, ME 04843; (207) 785-5670; (800) 992-2218; www.schoonermaryday.com

Mary Day (15/30; American; 90 ft.)

This two-masted schooner sails on four- and six-day cruises along the Maine coast. New for 2004: lighthouse cruise, May–September.

Compagnie des Isles du Ponant

c/o Tauck World Discovery, 276 Post Road West , Westport, CT 06880; (203) 221-6891; (800) 788-8885; fax (203) 221-6828; www.tauck.com

Le Ponant (30/60; French/European; 290 ft.)

A luxury yacht like *Wind Star,* this ship is under charter by Tauck World Discovery, which offers cruises in the Caribbean in winter, including the Panama Canal, and Costa Rica and the Mediterranean in summer, usually sold in a land/sea package. The four-masted vessel's size allows entry into less-visited ports and bays.

Dirigo Cruises

39 Waterside Lane, Clinton, CT 06413; tel/fax (860) 669-7068; www.dirigocruises.com

The company has 16 sailing ships, which are found in Europe, the British Isles, Maritimes of Nova Scotia, Caribbean, Galápagos, New Zealand, Tonga, and other South Seas islands.

Cuan Law / Lammer Law (9/18; American/American and Chilean; 105 ft.)

Two of the world's largest trimarans sail six-night itineraries in the British Virgin Islands from Tortola *(Cuan Law)*, and seven-night tours of the Galápagos Islands from San Cristóbal *(Lammer Law)*.

Harvey Gamage (12/26; American; 95 ft.)

Seven-day winter cruises from St. Thomas to the United States and British Virgin Islands. In summer, three-night cruises between Bath, Maine, and Boston. Also offers a summer youth camp, a high school semester at sea for full credit and college credit terms.

Regina Chatarina (8/22; British; 105 ft.)

This two-masted lugger (schooner) sails from the Virgin Islands to Grenada on week-long Caribbean cruises. In summer, Seychelles Islands.

Soren Larson (9/18; British; 140 ft.)

The *Soren Larson* is a two-masted brigadine continuing its global odyssey from England to the South Pacific. This includes a series of cruises with continuing legs via Galápagos, Easter Island, Pitcairn, Tonga, Fiji, etc.

Maine Windjammer Association

P.O. Box 1144P, Blue Hill, ME 04614; (800) 807-wind; www.sailmainecoast.com

Formed in 1977, the Maine Windjammer Association is made up of 14 privately owned and operated traditional tall ships that once belonged to commercial fleets. They delivered everything from fish and granite to coal and Christmas trees along U.S. coasts. The two- and three-masted schooners range from 64 to 132 feet long. Eight are National Historic Landmarks, some older than 100 years.

The windjammers offer three- to six-day cruises from mid-May to October, departing Rockland, Rockport, and Camden in Maine. With more than 3,000 islands, the Maine coast is one of the best and most beautiful sailing areas anywhere. Ships sail by day, about 10 a.m. to 4 p.m., and anchor each night at a deserted inlet or quiet port or village where passengers can go ashore. Passengers may participate in all aspects of sailing, from hoisting sails and taking the wheel to helping in the galley.

Meals are served family-style and include fresh seafood, roasts, garden salads, chowder, and homemade breads and desserts. A lobster bake on an island is featured on every six-day trip and most three-day cruises. Accommodations are simple: single, double, or triple cabins with comfortable mattresses, fresh linens, and plenty of blankets. Shipboard life is relaxed and informal.

Each windjammer carries 6–44 passengers and a crew of 4–10. Cruises are ideal family vacations, appropriate for most ages. (Check with individual captains regarding children. The minimum age is 12 years old, unless you charter the whole boat. MWA also reserves the right to place 12–15-year-olds in certain sleeping quarters.) Some windjammers have theme cruises. The tall ships gather annually for an all-day race in which passengers can participate.

Cruise cost is about $90–$140 per person, per day. Charter rates are available. All vessels undergo rigorous U.S. Coast Guard inspections and carry ship-to-shore radios and electronic navigational devices.

Air transportation is available to departure ports via Portland International Jetport, with limousine service to the Rockland/Camden area. Commuter air service is available from Boston, and buses run from Boston and Portland. All vessels offer free parking.

Member vessels are *American Eagle, Angeligue, Grace Bailey, Heritage, Isaac H. Evans, J&E Riggin, Lewis R. French, Mary Day, Mercantile, Mistress, Nathaniel Bowditch, Stephen Taber, Timberwind,* and *Victory Chimes.* The association provides descriptive brochures.

Though all are schooners, each boat is different and special in its own way. The *Angelique,* for example, has a deck house salon—a passenger lounge above deck. This gives passengers a warm, cozy alternative to the galley on rainy days. The *Grace Bailey* offers a combination lounge/galley below deck large enough to accommodate an upright piano. Most toilet and bath facilities are shared. Some schooners, like the *American Eagle,* with hallways running fore and aft below decks, offer toilets and hot showers situated adjacent to passenger cabins. On other ships, the communal heads are accessed from the main deck. Cabins for the most part are very small—a place to sleep or change clothes, but not a place to hang out. Most cabins include reading light and a private sink, sometimes with hot and cold fresh running water, sometimes just with cold water. Storage space in the cabins is minimal, sometimes problematic when two or more share a cabin. A few ships offer 110-volt electrical outlets for hair dryers and such, but this is more the exception than the rule.

During fair weather, almost everyone hangs out on deck where lunch and sometimes other meals are served. Some ships have built-in benches on deck, while others provide collapsible chairs. On rainy days, a galley with a hot wood stove affords refuge from the elements during and between meals. While anchored, both in dry and wet weather, a canvas tarp is deployed over much of the deck.

Passengers should be reasonably agile. Access to lower decks is almost always by ladder, with the exception of the *Victory Chimes* and the *Heritage,* which substitute rather steep stairs. One ship, the *Stephen Tabor,* offers two main deck–level cabins.

Music in the form of informal jam sessions or sing-alongs are a favorite evening's entertainment on many schooners, including the *Stephen Tabor, J&E Riggin, Grace Baily, Victory Chimes, Angelique,* and *Mary Day.* Two ships, the *Grace Bailey* and *Angelique*, carry upright pianos, and the *Mary Day* carries an organ. Passengers are strongly encouraged to bring along any sort of acoustic (i.e. nonelectrical) instrument. On ships without captain or crew of a musical bent, storytelling is a preferred pastime. Regardless of the activity, it's a rare night when festivities go beyond 11 p.m.

In a rather marked departure from the rest of the cruise industry, no alcoholic beverages are sold or served on Maine Windjammer schooners (with the exception of educational wine tasting events on the *J&E Riggin*). Although guests are invited to bring aboard their own stash, most precruise instructional material makes it clear that excessive imbibing will not be tolerated.

Itineraries are quite flexible, with no particular urgency to be at a certain place at a particular time. Many captains ad-lib their itineraries en route, responding to the weather and the stated preferences of the passengers. And speaking of captains, they are as diverse as the ships. There are several husband-and-wife teams, some partnering gentlemen captains, and on the *Isaac H. Evans*, the fleet's only solo female captain. Some of the couple-captains bring their children along (amazingly socially acclimated and well behaved), including one couple with two preschoolers.

Summer weather in Maine is all over the map, although you can usually count on good wind. May and June are very unpredictable both in terms of temperature and rainfall. July is almost always warm, but with more rain than the predictably dry and warm August and September. Regardless of the time of year, good rain gear is essential.

Peter Deilmann Cruises

1800 Diagonal Road, Suite 170, Alexandria, VA 22314; (703) 549-1741; (800) 348-8287; fax (703) 549-7924; www.deilmann-cruises.com

Lili Marleen (25/50; German/European; 249 ft.)

Launched in 1994, the *Lili Marleen* is a re-creation of a 19th-century three-masted barquentine, a sailing vessel with one square-rigged mast and two gaff- or schooner-rigged masts. The ship has a lounge decorated with polished hardwoods and nautical paintings. The restaurant accommodates all passengers at one seating; cuisine is international with local specialties. There are three bars and a small library.

Lili Marleen has 25 outside cabins (7 standard, 15 superior, and 3 deluxe, which measure 108 square feet). They're decorated with burled wall finishes and pastel fabrics and have a sofa bed (convertible to double bed), upper Pullman berth, large wardrobe, safe, table and chair, sideboard, radio, and international dial phone. The tiled bathroom has a shower, hair dryer, and bathrobes. Laundry service, fax, and telex are available. *Lili Marleen* sails on seven-night cruises to Eastern Baltic to Sweden and Poland and Western Baltic to the Danish archipelago.

For the line's other offerings, see Part Two, under "European and Smaller Cruise Lines," and "River and Barge Cruises in Europe" earlier in Part Three.

Sea Cloud Cruises

32-40 North Dean Street, Englewood, NJ 07631; (201) 227-9404; (888) 732-2568; fax (201) 227-9424; www.seacloud.com

---

Sea Cloud (34/69; International; 360 ft.)

One of the world's most luxurious sailing ships, the *Sea Cloud* was built as a wedding present by financier E. F. Hutton for his bride, Marjorie Merriweather Post. The ship has 34 air-conditioned cabins with phone, safe, hair dryer, and bathrobes. The elegant dining room accommodates all passengers at one seating; complimentary wines are served at lunch and dinner. A library and boutique are available.

The four-masted barque sails on different itineraries year-round. She plies the Eastern Caribbean in winter and the Mediterranean during the remainder of the year, and she is marketed by several U.S. companies. Sea Cloud also owns the luxurious *River Cloud,* which sails European rivers (see "River and Barge Cruises in Europe" earlier in Part Three).

Sea Cloud II (48/96; International; 384 ft.)

The legendary *Sea Cloud* got a sibling in April 2001. The $40 million vessel is conventionally rigged with three masts (rather than *Sea Cloud's* four), and her more than 3,000 square yards of sail are manually operated. Modern with the highest safety standards, the vessel is traditional in appearance and offers opulent 1930s decor. Forty-eight luxurious cabins range from 130 to 236 square feet; two owner's suites each contain 300 square feet. Large deck areas and a swimming platform provide plentiful outside space. The ship has a bar, library with panoramic views, restaurant with large windows, sauna, and gymnasium.

Her all-weather cruising ability sets her apart from *Sea Cloud,* which is generally restricted to sunny climes. *Sea Cloud II* is cruising the North Sea and Baltic in summer, the Mediterranean in autumn, and South America in winter.

Star Clippers, Inc.

(See Part Two.)

Windjammer Barefoot Cruises

P.O. Box 190120, Miami Beach, FL 33119-0120; (305) 672-6453; (800) 327-2601; fax (305) 674-1219; www.windjammer.com

For sailors ages 7–70 with good sea legs and a Captain Mitty spirit, Windjammer Barefoot Cruises offers a chance to stand watch at the wheel or climb the mast and live out your fantasies. The line has a fleet of famous tall ships, including those once owned by Aristotle Onassis, the duke of Westminster, and financier E. F. Hutton. Most cabins have bunk beds, private facilities, and steward service. Itineraries are super, including the Grenadines (often called the world's most beautiful sailing waters) and less visited destinations in the Eastern and Southern Caribbean. Most cruises are six days; some have different southbound and northbound legs that can be combined.

Amazing Grace (92 passengers; British/West Indian; 257 ft.)

This is the fleet's only freighter. She offers 13-day cruises between Grand Bahamas and Trinidad, year-round.

Legacy (61/122; American/West Indian; 294 ft.)

Built in 1959, this ship was a meteorological research and exploration vessel for the French government. She was acquired by Windjammer in 1989, stripped to her hull, and converted into a four-masted tall ship, debuting in 1998.

The well-designed vessel has her original portholes, wide stairways, hand-carved South American wood, and custom interiors. All cabins are air-conditioned and have private bathrooms with showers. They're simply decorated and have wooden wardrobes, full-length mirrors, and either bunk, double, or twin beds (some have sofa beds). The most luxurious cabin, Burke's Berth, has a platform double bed, entertainment center, bar, and picture windows.

The top deck, with its large bar, local bands, and hermit crab races, is action central. The captain gives a morning briefing there on the day's activities.

Meals are family style in the dining room, which is air-conditioned. A small lounge contains the only television and VCR, along with books and games. *Legacy* is Windjammer's only ship to offer Junior Jammers Kids Club, a summer program of chaperoned activities for children age six and older.

Legacy departs from San Juan on alternating six-day itineraries in the spring and winter, calling at Culebra, St. Croix, St. John, St. Thomas, and Jost Van Dyke; or Culebra, St. Croix, Virgin Gorda (Spanish Town and Leverick Bay), St. John, and Vieques (a nighttime call for kayaking in the phosphorescent bay). She sails on four-, five-, and eight-day cruises in the Bahamas in the summer and fall.

Mandalay (72 passengers; British/West Indian; 236 ft.)

Mandalay is queen of the fleet. Formerly the yacht of financier E. F. Hutton and an oceanographic research vessel of Columbia University, she has three masts and 22,000 square feet of sail. Under Hutton's ownership, she was considered the world's most luxurious private yacht. When she retired in 1981 from Columbia, nearly half the existing knowledge of the ocean floor had been gathered by the ship.

Mandalay offers 6-day cruises from Grenada to Puerto la Cruz, plus 13-day cruises from Grenada to Blanguilla in the summer and fall, and other excursions to the Windward and Leeward Islands from Antigua to St. Vincent in winter and spring.

Polynesia (54/122; British/West Indian; 248 ft.)

This legendary fishing schooner has been featured in articles in *National Geographic* magazine and various television productions. She was added to the Windjammer fleet in 1975 after extensive remodeling, adding 12 deck cabins, 40 regular cabins, and 2 admiral suites, all double occupancy. All have private bathrooms and showers, wood paneling, and tile floors. Three bachelor quarters were built, each accommodating six. New plumbing, air-conditioning, and a teak deck were installed. The curved stern contains a specially designed dining salon with large tables, each depicting an island on Polynesia's itinerary. The mascot parrot oversees the ship's slot machine.

Probably the most popular Windjammer ship, *Polynesia* offers monthly singles' cruises, as well as other theme cruises. She sails six-day Caribbean itineraries from St. Maarten to St. Barts, St. Kitts, Saba, Nevis, Prickly Pear, Anguilla, and Montserrat, depending on wind.

Yankee Clipper (64 passengers; British/West Indian; 197 ft.)

In 1927, German industrialist Alfred Krupp built this ship as the *Cressida,* probably the world's only armor-plated private yacht. Adolf Hitler was aboard during World War II to award the Iron Cross to a U-boat captain. She was confiscated as a war prize and commandeered by the U.S. Coast Guard. After the war, she was acquired by the wealthy Vanderbilt family, renamed *Pioneer,* and sailed off the West Coast. Joining Windjammer's fleet in 1965, she was rechristened *Yankee Clipper.* Extensive remodeling gave her a third mast, continuous upper deck, and cabins with private bathrooms and showers. She's one of the fastest tall ships.

Yankee Clipper offers six-day Caribbean cruises year-round, leaving Grenada for Petit St. Vincent, Bequia, Mayreau, Palm Island, Union Island, Young Island, or Carriacou.

Windstar Cruises

(See Part Two.)

Zeus Tours and Yacht Cruises

120 Sylvan Avenue, Englewood Cliffs, NJ 07632; (201) 228-5280; (800) 447-5667; fax (201) 228-5281; www.zeustours.com

The Zeus Group, which marked its 50th year of operation in 1998, offers eastern Mediterranean and South American cruises in its own and chartered vessels.

Zeus I / Zeus II / Zeus III (24/48; Greek/European and American; 174 ft.)

These ships sail on seven-day Mediterranean itineraries in summer. The group also offers 12-day Greek Isles cruises aboard the sail-cruiser *Galileo Sun*. The yacht has a bar-lounge and 18 air-conditioned cabins with private bath and telephone. Windsurfing, snorkeling, and fishing equipment are available.

Cruise Ship Index

Key: A = Adventure, E = European Cruise Ferry, F = Freighter,
G = Galápagos, GR = Greek Islands, M = Mainstream,
NC = Norwegian Coastal, O = Others, R = River, SS = Sailing Ship

Itinerary Index

Abercrombie and Kent International, Inc.

Explorer II   **Home Ports**   Ushuaia, Port Stanley

November–February, 14–20 nights, Antarctica. Tour programs include flights between Miami and Santiago, Chile and between Santiago and the port of embarkation with one night hotel in Santiago. November, December, February, 18–20 nights, "Antarctica, Falkland Islands and South Georgia Island", between Ushuaia and Port Stanley; December, 16 nights, "Antarctica and the Falkland Islands" from Port Stanley to Ushuaia; February, 14 nights, round-trip from Ushuaia to the Antarctic Peninsula only.

Abercrombie & Kent also offers luxury and educational cruise packages aboard yachts, barges, river boats and sailing ships in South America, the Galapagos, Caribbean, Alaska, Mediterranean and on rivers in Europe, Russia, China, Myanmar and Egypt.

American Canadian Caribbean Line

Grande Caribe   **Home Ports**   Warren, RI, others vary with itinerary

November and May, 14 nights, Intracoastal waterway between Rhode Island and Florida.

May–October, 5, 12, 15 nights, Canada/New England on itineraries through the Erie Canal/Saguenay River; Saguenay/Gaspe/Nova Scotia/Maine; New England Islands; or, Erie Canal Fall Foliage.

Grande Mariner   **Home Ports**   Warren, RI, Chicago, others vary with itinerary

November and May, 14 nights, Intracoastal Waterway between Florida and Rhode Island.

December–April, 11 nights, Eastern/Western Caribbean and Bahamas to the Virgin Islands; Caicos/Exumas/Nassau; Bahamas/Eleuthera/Exumas; Belize/Barrier Reef/Guatemala; or, Belize/Roatan.

June–October, 6–15 nights, Colonial Coast, Great Lakes and Erie Canal, between Warren, RI and Chicago (15 nights); Chicago/Lake Michigan (6 nights); Lake Superior (8 nights); or, Erie Canal Fall Foliage (12 nights).

Niagara Prince **Home Ports** Warren, RI, others vary with itinerary
November, 14 nights, Intracoastal waterway from Warren, Rhode Island to Florida. Docks in Florida for the winter.

March, 7 nights, Intracoastal waterway, South Carolina to Jacksonville, Florida. Positions from Jacksonville to Tampa.

April–May, 11 and 14 nights, Tampa to New Orleans and between New Orleans and Chicago via rivers and waterways.

June–October, 6, 12 and 15 nights, Great Lakes/New England on itineraries to Lake Michigan (6 nights); Chicago to Warren, RI (15 nights); Canals of America Finger Lakes (12 nights); Erie Canal/Saguenay River (12 nights); or, Erie Canal Fall Foliage (12 nights).

American Safari Cruises

Safari Escape **Home Ports** Juneau, Friday Harbor
May–September, 7 nights, Alaska, between Juneau and Sitka calling at remote villages and coves with time for kayaking and whale watching, Tracy Arm, Sawyer Glaciers, Frederick Sound, Petersburg, Le Conte Glacier, Baranof Island. May and September, 14 nights, Inside Passage positioning cruises between Seattle and Juneau.

September–October, 7 nights, San Juan Islands and Fjords of Canada, round-trip from Friday Harbor, WA to Sidney, Victoria, Princess Louisa Inlet and Vancouver, BC; Roche Harbor, Jones Island WA.

Safari Quest **Home Ports** Juneau, Los Cabos, Astoria
December–April, 8 nights, Sea of Cortes, round-trip from Los Cabos, Mexico, calling at islands and bays including whale watching and Isla Partida, Isla San Jose, Isla Coyote, Loreto, Bahia Aqua Verde.

May–September, 8 nights, Alaska, between Juneau and Prince Rupert, BC calling at remote villages and coves with time for whale watching and kayaking, Misty Fjords National Monument, Ketchikan, Tracy Arm, Sawyer Glaciers, Frederick Sound, and Canoe Pass. May and September, 14 nights, Inside Passage positioning cruises between Seattle and Juneau.

September 22, 2004, 14 nights, Columbia and Snake Rivers from Lewiston ID to Astoria OR.

December resumes Sea of Cortes cruises.

Carnival Cruise Lines

Carnival Conquest **Home Port** New Orleans
Year-round, Sunday, 7 nights, Western Caribbean round-trip from New Orleans to Montego Bay, Grand Cayman, Cozumel.

Carnival Destiny   **Home Port**   San Juan
Year-round, Sunday, 7 nights, Southern Caribbean round-trip from San Juan to St. Thomas/St. John, Martinique, and 15-hour calls at Barbados and Aruba.

Carnival Glory   **Home Port**   Port Canaveral
Year-round, Saturday, 7 nights, alternating Eastern and Western Caribbean round-trip from Port Canaveral to either Nassau, St. Thomas/St. John, and St. Maarten; or, Key West; Belize City, Belize; Cozumel and Progreso/Merida, Mexico.

Carnival Legend   **Home Ports**   Ft. Lauderdale, New York
November–April, 8 nights, alternating Southern Caribbean or Panama Canal, round-trip from Ft. Lauderdale to St. Maarten, Barbados, Martinique; or, Belize City, Belize; Limon, Costa Rica; Colon, Panama (optional Panama Canal and Gatun Lake excursions available).
May–October, 8 nights, Eastern Caribbean round-trip from New York, calling at San Juan, St. Thomas/St. John and Tortola Virgin Gorda.

Carnival Liberty   Debuts Fall 2005

Carnival Miracle   **Home Ports**   Jacksonville, Tampa, Baltimore
March–April, 3, 5, 6 nights, round-trip from Jacksonville to Freeport (3 nights); Key West and Nassau (5 nights); or, Cozumel, Costa Maya, Freeport (6 nights).
April–May, September–October, 7 nights, round-trip from Baltimore, to Key West, Nassau, Freeport.
June–August, To Be Announced
November 2004, year-round, Sunday, 7 nights, round-trip from Tampa to Grand Cayman, Costa Maya, Cozumel, Belize City.

Carnival Pride   **Home Port**   Los Angeles (Long Beach)
Year-round, 7 nights, Mexican Riviera cruises, round-trip from Long Beach to Cabo San Lucas, Puerto Vallarta, Mazatlán.

Carnival Spirit   **Home Ports**   Miami, Vancouver   others vary with itinerary
November–March, 8 nights, alternating Western and Southern Caribbean round-trip from Miami to St. Maarten, Barbados, Martinique; or, Belize City; Limon, Costa Rica; Colon, Panama.
March and October, November, 16 and 14 nights, Panama Canal positioning cruises between Miami and San Diego.
April, May, September, October, 12 nights, Hawaii between Honolulu (overnight) and either Ensenada or Vancouver to Lahaina, Maui (overnight); Nawiliwili, Kauai; Hilo and Kailua Kona, Hawaii.
May–September, Wednesday, 7 nights, Alaska between Vancouver and Seward to Ketchikan, Tracy Arm, Juneau, Skagway, Lynn Canal, Sitka,

College Fjord northbound; College Fjord, Valdez, Hubbard Glacier, Juneau, Skagway, Lynn Canal, Ketchikan southbound.

May and September, Wednesday, 7 nights, Alaska Inside Passage round-trip from Vancouver to Juneau, Glacier Bay, Skagway, Ketchikan.

Carnival Triumph   **Home Port**   Miami
Year-round, Saturday, 7 nights, alternating Eastern and Western Caribbean, round-trip from Miami to San Juan, St. Thomas, St. Maarten; or, Cozumel, Grand Cayman, Ocho Rios.

Carnival Valor (Debuts December 2004) **Home Port**   t.b.a.

Carnival Victory   **Home Ports**   Miami, New York
November–May, Sunday, 7 nights, alternating Eastern and Western Caribbean round-trip from Miami to either San Juan, St. Maarten, St. Thomas; or, Cozumel, Grand Cayman, Ocho Rios.

May–June and October, 5 and 6 nights, round-trip from Charleston (5 nights) or Norfolk (6 nights) to Nassau and Freeport.

June–October, 4,5,7 nights, Canada/New England round-trip from New York, 4 nights on alternate Thursdays to Halifax, Nova Scotia; or, 5 nights on alternate Saturdays and Mondays to Halifax, Nova Scotia and St. John, New Brunswick. September–October, Saturdays, 7 nights to Boston; Portland, Maine; Sydney and Halifax, Nova Scotia.

Celebration   **Home Port**   Galveston
Year-round, 4 and 5 nights, Western Caribbean round-trip from Galveston, Texas, 4 nights, alternate Thursdays to Cozumel; or 5 nights, alternate Mondays and Saturdays to Cozumel, Calica/Cancún. Both have 2 days at sea.

Ecstasy   **Home Port**   Los Angeles (Long Beach)
Year-round, 3 and 4 nights, Baja from Long Beach. 3 nights, Friday, to Ensenada; 4 nights, Monday to Ensenada and Catalina Island.

Elation   **Home Port**   Galveston
Year-round, Sunday, 7 nights, Western Caribbean cruises round-trip from Galveston to Progreso and Cozumel, Mexico; Belize, City, Belize.

Fantasy   **Home Port**   Port Canaveral
Year-round, 3 and 4 nights, Bahamas cruises from Port Canaveral. 3 nights, Thursday to Nassau; 4 nights, Sunday to Freeport and Nassau. Both have one day at sea.

Fascination   **Home Port**   Miami
Year-round, 3 and 4 nights, Bahamas and Western Caribbean from Miami. 3 nights, Fridays to Nassau; 4 nights, Monday to Key West, Cozumel.

Holiday   **Home Ports**   New Orleans, Jacksonville
To October 2004, 4 and 5 nights, Western Caribbean, round-trip from New Orleans. 4 nights, alternating Thursdays, to Cozumel; 5 nights, alternating Saturdays and Mondays to Playa del Carmen, Cozumel.

From October 23, 2004, year-round, 4 and 5 nights, round-trip from Jacksonville, 4 nights, Thursdays, to Freeport and Nassau; 5 nights, alternating Mondays and Saturdays to Key West and Nassau.

Imagination   **Home Port**   Miami
Year-round, 4 and 5 nights, Western Caribbean round-trip from Miami. 4 nights, alternate Thursdays to Key West and Cozumel; 5 nights, alternate Mondays to Key West and Belize; 5 nights alternate Saturdays to Grand Cayman and Ocho Rios.

Inspiration   **Home Port**   Tampa
To October 2004, Sunday, 7 nights, Western Caribbean round-trip from Tampa to Grand Cayman, Costa Maya, Cozumel, Belize.

From October 30, 2004, year-round, round-trip from Tampa, 4 and 5 nights. 4 nights, alternate Thursdays to Cozumel; 5 nights, alternate Mondays and Saturdays to Grand Cayman and Cozumel.

Jubilee   **Home Port**   San Juan
To September 2004, year-round, Sunday, 7 nights, Southern Caribbean round-trip from San Juan to St. Thomas, Antigua, St. Lucia, Dominica, St. Kitts, Tortola.

October 2004, begins sailing from Sydney under a new name for P and O Cruises, Australia.

Paradise   **Home Port**   Miami
Year-round, Sunday, 7 nights, alternating Eastern and Western Caribbean round-trip from Miami either Nassau, St. Thomas/St. John and Casa de Campo Resort at La Romana in the Dominican Republic; or Belize, Isla Roatan (Bay Islands, Honduras), Grand Cayman, Cozumel.

Sensation   **Home Port**   Tampa, New Orleans
To October 2004, 4 and 5 nights, Western Caribbean round-trip from Tampa, 4 nights, alternate Thursdays, to Key West and Grand Cayman; 5 nights, alternate Mondays and Saturdays, to Grand Cayman and Cozumel. 2 days at sea.

From October 23, 2004, 4 and 5 nights, year-round, round-trip from New Orleans, 4 nights, alternate Thursdays to Cozumel; 5 nights, alternate Mondays to Cozumel and Calica; 5 nights alternate Saturdays to Cozumel and either Costa Maya or Calica.

Celebrity Cruises

Century **Home Port** Ft. Lauderdale
Year-round, Saturday, 7 nights, Eastern/Western Caribbean, round-trip from Ft Lauderdale to either San Juan, St. Thomas, St. Maarten, Nassau; or, to Ocho Rios, Grand Cayman, Cozumel, Key West.

Constellation **Home Ports** San Juan, Dover, New York
To April, Saturday, 7 nights, Southern Caribbean, round-trip from San Juan to St. Maarten, St. Lucia, Barbados, St. John's, St. Thomas.

April and September, 14 and 13 nights, transatlantic, San Juan to Dover; Dover to New York.

Round-trip from Dover, 14 nights, July 17, 2004 calls at Paris, Cork, Dublin, Glasgow, Copenhagen, Brussels and the Norwegian Fjords including Olden, Geiranger, Hellesylt and Bergen Norway.

September, October, 10 and 11 nights, Canada/New England, round-trip from New York to Newport, Bar Harbor, Sydney, Quebec City, Saguenay River, Halifax.

November 2004 to April 2005, Saturday, 7 nights, Southern Caribbean, round-trip from San Juan to Casa de Campo, Barbados, Grenada, Antigua, St. Thomas.

Galaxy **Home Ports** San Juan, Baltimore, Rome, Galveston
To March, 7 nights, Southern Caribbean, round-trip from San Juan to St. Thomas, St. Kitts, Barbados, Margarita Island, Aruba.

March–April, September–October, 10 and 11 nights, Caribbean, round-trip from Baltimore to either Key West; Cozumel; Belize City; Coco Cay, Nassau (10 nights); or, Charleston, St. Thomas; San Juan; St. Maarten and Nassau (11 nights). September, 11 nights, round-trip from Baltimore to Bar Harbor, Maine; Halifax and Sydney, Nova Scotia; Quebec City, Quebec; cruising through the Saguenay River and Portland, Maine.

May and September, 14 nights, transatlantic, Baltimore to Rome and reverse.

May–August, 10 and 11 nights, Mediterranean, round-trip from Rome to either Naples, Santorini, Mykonos, Malta, Barcelona, Ville-franche (Nice) (10 nights) ; or, Mykonos, Rhodes, Santorini, Istanbul (2 days) Kusadasi, Athens, Naples (11 nights).

November 2004–April 2005, 11 and 12 nights, Panama Canal, round-trip from Galveston to Cozumel, Belize City, Cristobal, Panama Canal partial transit, Puerto Limon, Grand Cayman plus Montego Bay on the 12-night.

Horizon **Home Ports** Tampa, Norfolk, Philadelphia
To April and November 2004–April, 2005, 10 and 11 nights, Panama Canal/Eastern Caribbean round-trip from Tampa to either Grand Cay-

man; Puerto Limon, Costa Rica; Colon, Panama; and Roatan, Honduras (10 nights) or, Turks and Caicos, San Juan, St. Thomas, St. Maarten, Tortola, Key West (11 nights).

April–May, September–October, Saturday, 7 nights, Bermuda, round-trip from Norfolk to Hamilton and St. George's and for 6 nights, May 29 and September 5, 2004.

June–August, Saturday, 7 nights, Bermuda, round-trip from Philadelphia to Hamilton and St. George's.

Infinity **Home Ports**   San Diego, Vancouver, Ft. Lauderdale, Honolulu others vary with itinerary

January, March, April, 14 nights, Panama Canal, between San Diego and Ft. Lauderdale via Aruba, Puntarenas; Acapulco and Cabo San Lucas.

January–March 2004 and 2005, 12–14 nights, South America, Ft. Lauderdale to Valparaiso; between Valparaiso and Buenos Aires; or, round-trip from Buenos Aires.

May and September–October, 9–12 nights, Hawaii, between Ensenada and Honolulu or Honolulu and Vancouver, via Kailua Kona and Hilo, Hawaii; Lahaina, Maui (2 days); and Nawiliwili, Kauai.

May–September, Sunday, 7 nights, Alaska, round-trip from Vancouver to Ketchikan, Juneau, Sitka and cruising the Inside Passage and Hubbard Glacier.

October–December 2004 and March–May, 2005, 10–15 nights, Hawaii or Panama Canal either between Ensenada and Honolulu; or, between San Diego and Ft. Lauderdale.

Mercury **Home Ports**   San Diego, San Francisco, Vancouver, Seattle

November–March, 10 and 11 nights, Mexican Riviera, round-trip from San Diego to Cabo San Lucas, Mazatlán, Puerto Vallarta, Acapulco, Xtapa/Zihuatanejo plus Manzanillo on the 11-night sailings.

March–May, October–November, 7–11 nights, Mexican Riviera/California Coast, round-trip from San Francisco to Monterey, Santa Barbara, San Diego, Ensenada, Catalina Island; or, Monterey, Catalina Island, Cabo San Lucas; or, Cabo San Lucas, Mazatlán, Monterey; or, Monterey, Catalina Island, Mazatlán, Puerto Vallarta, Cabo San Lucas; or, Monterey, Catalina Island, Mazatlán, Manzanillo, Puerto Vallarta, Cabo San Lucas, Mexico.

May and September, 6 and 9 nights, Pacific Coast/Alaska, San Francisco to Vancouver via Juneau, Ketchikan; Vancouver to San Francisco, via Juneau, Skagway, Hubbard Glacier, Ketchikan, Victoria; 12 nights, Alaska, round-trip from San Francisco, Ketchikan, Skagway, Icy Strait, Hubbard Glacier, Juneau, Victoria and either Vancouver (May 5 sailing) or Sitka (May 17 and September 12 sailings).

June–August, 7 nights, round-trip from Seattle to Juneau, Skagway, Hubbard, Ketchikan, Prince Rupert B.C.

November resumes Mexican Riviera cruises from San Francisco and San Diego.

Millennium **Home Ports** Ft. Lauderdale, Barcelona, Venice

To April and November 2004–April 2005, Sunday, 7 nights, Caribbean, round-trip from Ft Lauderdale, to San Juan, Catalina Island (Casa de Campo), Dominican Republic; St Thomas; Nassau.

April and October, 14 nights, transatlantic, Ft. Lauderdale to Barcelona and reverse.

May–October, 12 nights, Mediterranean, between Barcelona and Venice, calling at Villefranche (Nice/Monte Carlo), Livorno (Florence/ Pisa), Rome, Naples, Santorini, Dubrovnik, Athens plus Mykonos on westbound sailings.

Summit **Home Ports** Ft. Lauderdale, Vancouver

November to April, 10 and 11 nights, round-trip from Ft. Lauderdale to either St. Maarten, St. Lucia, Barbados, St. Kitts, St. Thomas (10 nights); or, Key West; Cozumel; Puerto Limón, Costa Rica; Colón, Panama; Aruba; Grand Cayman (11 nights).

May and September, 14 nights, Panama Canal between Ft. Lauderdale and San Diego; Pacific Coast/Alaska, between San Diego and Vancouver via Catalina Island, San Francisco, Seattle, Victoria, Hubbard Glacier, Juneau, Skagway, Sitka, Ketchikan.

June–September, 7 nights, Alaska, between Vancouver and Seward, via Hubbard Glacier, Juneau, Skagway, Ketchikan and either Icy Strait or Valdez and College Fjord. 7 nights, round-trip from Vancouver, September 10, 2004, to Juneau, Skagway, Hubbard Glacier, Sitka.

November resumes 10 and 11-night Caribbean from Ft. Lauderdale.

Zenith **Home Ports** Jacksonville, New York

To April, 14 nights, Caribbean, round-trip from Jacksonville, to either Labadee, Ocho Rios, Grand Cayman, Puerto Limon, Colon, Roatan, Cosa Maya; or, San Juan, St. Thomas, St. Kitts, Grenada, Barbados, St. Maarten, Tortola, Nassau.

April–October, Saturday, 7 nights, Bermuda, from New York to Hamilton and St. George with 2 days at sea.

November 2004–April 2005, 14 nights, Caribbean, round-trip from Jacksonville, to either Costa Maya, Roatan, Puerto Limon, Colon, Grand Cayman, Key West, Coco Cay; or, San Juan, St. Thomas, St. Kitts, Grenada, Barbados (1.5 days), St. Maarten, Coco Cay.

Clipper Cruise Line

Clipper Adventurer   **Home Port**   Varies with itinerary

January–February, November–December, 16 and 14 nights, Antarctica or Antarctica and The Falklands sailing between Ushuaia, Argentina and Port Stanley, Falkland Islands via Elephant Island, Antarctic Peninsula, Antarctic Convergence, Drake Passage and Cape Horn. Cruisetour, 14 nights, November 29, 2004, between Ushuaia and Santiago (hotel stay) sails round-trip from Ushuaia to Antarctic Peninsula, Deception Island, Drake Passage and Cape Horn.

April–June, 10–13 nights, Mediterranean and Western Europe, from Lisbon to Rome or reverse; Lisbon to Bordeaux; Bordeaux to Paris, 10 nights, May 16, 2004; special 60th anniversary Liberation of Europe cruises : Rouen to London; Calais to London; Paris to Dublin.

June–August, 11–16 nights, Celtic Isles, Iceland, Greenland, from Greenock to Dublin; Dublin to Reykjavik, Iceland; Reykjavik to Sonderstronfjord; or, Sonderstronfjord to St. John's, Newfoundland.

September, 10 and 14 nights, Newfoundland/ Labrador/ Nova Scotia and Colonial America from St. John's, Newfoundland to Halifax, Nova Scotia; or, Halifax to Savannah, Georgia.

September–November, 12–14 nights, Panama Canal/South America, from Puerto Morelos, Mexico to Balboa, Panama; Balboa, Panama to Trinidad; Trinidad to Belem, Brazil; or, Belem to Salvador;

Clipper Odyssey   **Home Port**   Varies with itinerary

January–February, 13 nights, Australia/New Zealand between Queenstown, New Zealand and Auckland, New Zealand via Milford Sound (Embark), Doubtful Sound, Dusky Sound, Dunedin, Akaroa, Lyttelton, Queen Charlotte Sound, Motuara Island, Picton, Wellington, Napier, Tauranga; Auckland to Cairns, Australia; Sydney to Brisbane, Australia.

March–June, 12–17 nights, Australia/Japan, round-trip from Sydney to Great Barrier Reef; Japan and Korea from Tokyo to Himeji; round-trip from Himeji; or, Himeji to Otaru.

July–August, 14 nights, Russian Far East/Alaska, from Petropavlosk, Russia to Nome, Alaska. 13 nights, Alaska/BC between Homer and Prince Rupert, British Columbia via Harriman Fjord, College Fjord, Chamberlain Bay, Valdez, Kayak Island, Gulf of Alaska, Elfin Cove, Point Adolphus, Juneau, Tracy Arm, Haines, Wrangell, Zimovia Strait, Petersburg, Wrangell, Metlakatla, Ketchikan, Mary Island.

September–December, 14–16 nights, South Pacific from Honolulu to Tahiti; Tahiti to Easter Island; Fiji to New Caledonia; New Caledonia to Wellington, New Zealand.

Nantucket Clipper   **Home Port**   Varies with itinerary

January and December–January 2005, 7 nights, Caribbean round-trip from St. Thomas to St. John, Jost Van Dyke, Tortola, Virgin Gorda, Salt, Norman Islands, Christmas Cove.

January–February, 7 nights, "The Rain Forests, Reefs, and Mayan Temples of Belize and Honduras" cruise tour, between, Puerto Cortes, Honduras and Belize City, Belize, via at Dangriga,

Cocoa Plum Cay, Rio Dulce, Punta Pichilingo, Puerto Barrious, Punta Sal Peninsula, Roatan Island, Cayos Cochinos.

March–May and September–December, 7 and 14 nights, U.S. East Coast on various itineraries including Antebellum South Along the Intracoastal Waterway from Jacksonville, Florida to Charleston, South Carolina; Colonial America and Civil War Battlefields from Jacksonville to Washington, D.C./Alexandria; Springtime on the Chesapeake Bay, Alexandria to New York City; or, round-trip from New York to Haddam, Block Island, Great Salt Pond, Newport, Nantucket, Martha's Vineyard, with 2 nights on board in New York City. Fall sailings operate in reverse.

May–September, 7–14 nights, Canada/New England and Great Lakes from New York to Halifax NS; Halifax to Rochester, NY; Halifax to Quebec City; Quebec City to Buffalo Y; between Rochester and New York or Quebec City; Lakes Erie and Huron from Buffalo to Port Huron; or, round-trip from Port Huron or Buffalo to Sault Ste. Marie.

Yorktown Clipper   **Home Port**   Varies with itinerary

January–February and December–January 2005, 7 nights, Caribbean, round-trip from Crown Bay, St. Thomas to St. John, Jost Van Dyke, Tortola, Virgin Gorda, Salt, Norman Islands, Christmas Cove.

February, November–December, 7 nights, Panama Canal/Costa Rica, Balboa to Puerto Caldera, from Colon, Panama to Puerto Caldera, Costa Rica, transiting the Panama Canal and calling at Bahia Garachina, Marenco, Quepos, Manuel Antonio National Park, Punta Leona and Curu.

February–March, 7 nights, round-trip, Sea of Cortez, from La Paz to San Carlos via Isla Partida, Los Islotes, Isla Espiritu Santo, Cabo San Lucas, Bahia Magdalena, Boca de Soledad, La Entrada.

April–May, October, 5 nights, California wine country round-trip from Redwood City to Sausalito, Sacramento, Vallejo and San Francisco.

September, 5 nights, Pacific Northwest, between Seattle and Vancouver to either Roche Harbor, Sucia Island, Matia/Puffin Island and Victoria; or Victoria, Friday Harbor, Roche Harbor, Sucia Island, Matia/Puffin Island. Optional Rockies Rail tour add on, Calgary/Vancouver available.

May–September 7 nights, Alaska, round-trip from Juneau to Elfin Cove, Glacier Bay National Park, Margerie Glacier, Bartlett Cove, Skagway, Haines, Sitka, Tracy Arm. May and September, 12 nights, positions between Seattle and Juneau.

Costa Cruises

Costa Allegra **Home Ports**, Santos, Amsterdam
December 2003–March 2004, 6–22 nights, South America, round-trip from Santos, Brazil.

June–August, 11 and 12 nights, North Cape/Iceland and Baltic/Russia round-trip from Amsterdam to either Bergen, Hellesylt, Geiranger, Trondheim, Honningsvag, Tromso, Gravdal and Olden, Norway; or, Ronne, St. Petersburg, Tallinn, Stockholm, Copenhagen.

CostaAtlantica **Home Ports** Ft. Lauderdale, Copenhagen
December 2003–April 2004, Sunday, 7 nights, alternating Eastern/Western Caribbean from Ft. Lauderdale to San Juan, St. Thomas/St. John, Catalina Island (Costa's private resort)/Casa de Campo/Santo Domingo and Nassau; or, Key West, Cozumel, Ocho Rios, Grand Cayman. April, 16 nights, transatlantic, Ft. Lauderdale to Genoa.

May–September, Sunday, 7 nights, Baltic/Russia and Norwegian Fjords, round-trip from Copenhagen to either Visby, Stockholm, Helsinki, St. Petersburg, Tallinn; or, Hellesylt, Geiranger, Flam, Bergen, Kristiansand and Oslo, Norway. May 13, 2004, 10 nights, positions from Genoa to Copenhagen.

CostaClassica **Home Port** Savona
April–November, Sunday, 7 nights, Tunisia/Spain/France round-trip from Savona to Palermo, Sicily; Tunis, Tunisia; Palma de Mallorca and Barcelona, Spain; Marseille, France.

CostaEuropa **Home Port** Amsterdam, Savona
January–April, 11 nights, Canary Islands, round-trip from Savona to Barcelona, Spain; Casablanca and Agadir, Morocco; Arrecife and St. Cruz de Tenerife, Canary Islands; Funchal, Madeira; Malaga, Spain.

May–September, 11–14 nights, Baltic and Russia or Fjords/North Cape round-trip from Amsterdam to either Ronne, St. Petersburg, Tallinn, Stockholm, Copenhagen, plus Oslo on the 12-night; or, Bergen, Hellesylt, Geiranger, Trondheim, Honningsvag, Tromso, Gravdal and Olden, Norway. July, 14 nights, adds Spitsbergen. May and September, 9 nights, positioning between Genoa and Amsterdam.

May and September–November, 8 and 11 nights, Spain/Portugal or Black Sea/Med, round-trip from Savona or Genoa to either Barcelona, Alicante, Cadiz, Malaga, Gibraltar, Lisbon; or, Naples, Istanbul, Yalta and Odessa, Ukraine; Bosporus/Dardanelles; Santorini and Katakolon, Greece.

CostaFortuna   **Home Ports**   Savona, Ft. Lauderdale
To April 2004, 11 nights, Canary Islands, round-trip from Savona to Barcelona, Casablanca, Arrecife, St. Cruz de Tenerife, Madeira, Malaga.

April to November, 7 nights, Tunisia/Spain/France, round-trip from Savona to Naples, Italy; Palermo, Sicily; Tunis, Tunisia; Palma de Mallorca and Barcelona, Spain; Marseille, France
November 2004–April 2005, 7 nights, Caribbean, round-trip from Ft. Lauderdale. November, transatlantic, Genoa to Ft. Lauderdale.

CostaMagica   Debuts Fall 2004. Itineraries t.b.a.

CostaMediterranea   **Home Ports**   Ft. Lauderdale, Venice
To April, 7 nights, Caribbean, round-trip from Ft. Lauderdale to either San Juan, St. Thomas/St. John, Catalina Island/Casa de Campo/Santo Domingo, Nassau; or, Key West, Progreso/Merida, Cozumel, and Grand Cayman.

April and November, 16 nights, transatlantic between Ft. Lauderdale and Genoa.

May–November, 7 nights, Greece/Turkey, round-trip from Venice to Bari, Katakolon, Kusadasi, Istanbul, Piraeus (Athens.

November 2004–April 2005, 7 nights, Caribbean, round-trip from Ft. Lauderdale.

CostaRomantica   **Home Port**   Savona
May–November, 10 and 11 nights, round-trip from Savona to either Canary Islands, Italy/Greece/Turkey, Spain/Portugal/Morocco or Turkey/Black Sea.

CostaTropicale   **Home Port**   Santos, Venice
To March, 3–11 nights, Brazil, round-trip from Santos.

May–November, Saturday, 7 nights, round-trip from Venice to Dubrovnik, Croatia; Corfu, Itea and Argostoli, Greece; Kotor, Montenegro; Ravenna, Italy

CostaVictoria   **Home Ports**   Savona, Venice
To March, 11 nights, Egypt/Greece, round-trip from Savona to Naples, Italy; Messina, Sicily; Alexandria, Egypt; Limassol, Cyprus; Marmaris, Turkey; Rhodes, Piraeus (Athens) and Katakolon, Greece.

April–November, Monday, 7 nights, Greek Isles, round-trip from Venice to Bari, Italy; Katakolon, Santorini, Mykonos and Rhodes, Greece; Dubrovnik, Croatia.

Cruise West

Pacific Explorer   **Home Port**   Los Suenos (Costa Rica)
January–April, November–December, 7–9 nights, Costa Rica and Panama, cruise-tours round-trip from San Jose (7 nights) or between San

Jose, Costa Rica and Colon/Panama City including the Panama Canal and San Blas Islands (9 nights).

July–August, 6 nights, Costa Rica eco–cruise-tours, round-trip from San Jose. Specially designed for families.

Spirit of Alaska   **Home Port**   Whittier, Portland

May–August 3–4 nights, Alaska, round-trip from Whittier, to College Fjord, Chenega Glacier, Knight Island, plus Cordova on 4-night sailings. Positions between Juneau and Seattle, 10 nights, May 8 and September 1, 2004.

September–October, 7 nights, Columbia River, round-trip Portland, to Hells Canyon, Walla Walla and wine country, Clarkston, Hood River, Maryhill, Astoria and transit the locks of eight dams including Bonneville Dam.

Spirit of Columbia   **Home Ports**   Seattle, Juneau

April–May, September–October, 7 nights, British Columbia and Pacific Northwest Islands, round-trip from Seattle to La Conner, Vancouver, Cruising Howe Sound, Princess Louisa Inlet, Nanaimo, Victoria, Friday Harbor and Rosario Resort on Orcas Island with shore excursion included in each port.

June–August, 8 nights, Alaska, round-trip from Juneau to Tracy Arm, Kake for wilderness exploration, Sitka, Icy Strait, Glacier Bay. May 9, 19, 29, September 7, 2004, 10 nights, between Juneau and Seattle.

Spirit of Discovery   **Home Ports**   Portland, Juneau, Ketchikan

March–May September–November, 7 nights, Columbia and Snake rivers round-trip from Portland to Bonneville, Hells Canyon, Walla Walla, Hood River, Maryhill, Astoria.

May–August, 8 nights, Inside Passage between Juneau and Ketchikan via Misty Fjords, Metlakatla, Petersburg, Frederick Sound, Tracy Arm, Sitka, Glacier Bay, Skagway and Haines; or, round-trip from Juneau to Tracy Arm, Kake for wilderness exploration, Sitka, Icy Strait, Glacier Bay. Positions between Juneau and Seattle, 10 nights, May 19 and August 21, 2004.

Spirit of Endeavour   **Home Ports**   La Paz, Juneau, Ketchikan, San Francisco

January–March, 7 nights, Sea of Cortez, round trip from La Paz to Bonanza Beach, Isla San Jose, Isla San Francisco, Loreto, Isla Partida and a day seeking whales and marine life. Optional Copper Canyon rail excursion, four nights, available.

May–September, 8 nights, Inside Passage between Juneau and Ketchikan. calling at Misty Fjords, Metlakatla, Petersburg, Frederick Sound, Tracy Arm, Sitka, Glacier Bay, Skagway and Haines. Positions between Juneau and Seattle, 10 nights, May 3 and September 2, 2004.

September–November, 3 and 4 nights, California wine country, round-trip from San Francisco to Sonoma, Napa Valley, Sacramento River Delta, Sausalito/San Francisco Bay.

Spirit of '98 **Home Ports** Portland, Ketchikan, Juneau
April and September–October, 7 nights, Columbia and Snake rivers round-trip from Portland to Bonneville, Hells Canyon, Walla Walla, Hood River, Maryhill, Astoria.

May–August, 8 nights, Inside Passage between Ketchikan and Juneau via Misty Fjords, Metlakatla, Petersburg, Frederick Sound, Tracy Arm, Sitka, Glacier Bay, Skagway and Haines. Positions between Juneau and Seattle, 10 nights, May 14 and August 26, 2004.

Spirit of Oceanus **Home Ports** Vancouver, Anchorage
May–September, 11–12 nights, Alaska, between Vancouver and Anchorage via Prince Rupert, Misty Fjords, Petersburg, Juneau, Tracy Arm and Sawyer Glaciers, Glacier Bay, Sitka, Kenai Fjords, Homer; or, June, between Anchorage and Nome via Homer, Kodiak, Katmai National Park, Shumagin Islands, Dutch Harbor, Pribilof Islands, explores the Bering Sea and crosses the Arctic Circle.

Sheltered Seas **Home Port** Juneau
May–August, 4–5 nights, between Juneau and Ketchikan. Cruising by day with overnight in hotels ashore.

Crystal Cruises

Crystal Harmony **Home Ports** Honolulu, San Francisco, Ft. Lauderdale, others vary with itinerary
January and October–December, 7–19 nights, Panama Canal and Caribbean from New Orleans to Honolulu; Los Angeles to Ft. Lauderdale; round-trip from Ft. Lauderdale; between Ft. Lauderdale and Caldera, Costa Rica; or, round-trip New Orleans.

January–February, 10 and 18 nights, Hawaii and South Pacific, round-trip from Honolulu to Nawiliwili, Kailua–Kona, Christmas Island, Hilo, Lahaina; or, Honolulu to Auckland, New Zealand.

March–May, 14–15 nights, Australia/Southeast Asia/China/Japan/Trans–Pacific from Auckland to Sydney; Sydney to Singapore; Singapore to Hong Kong; Hong Kong to Beijing; Beijing to Tokyo; or, Tokyo to San Francisco.

May–September, 12 nights, Alaska and Canada round-trip from San Francisco; September 28, 10 nights, Mexican Riviera, round-trip from Los Angeles.

Crystal Serenity   **Home Port**   Varies with itinerary
January and December, 14 nights, Mexican Riviera, round-trip from Los Angeles to San Diego, Puerto Vallarta, Manzanillo, Acapulco, Zihuatanejo, Mazatlán, Cabo San Lucas.

January–May, 106 nights, World Cruise, Los Angeles to New York available in segments of 22–29 nights: Los Angeles to Yokohama; Yokohama to Singapore; Singapore to Cape Town; Cape Town to New York. Ports of call are Hilo, Honolulu, Lahaina, Hawaii; Guam, Saipan, Hiroshima, Kobe, Nagoya and Yokohama, Japan; Shanghai and Hong Kong, China; Ha Long Bay, Da Nang and Ho Chi Minh City, Vietnam; Laem Chabang (Bangkok), Thailand; Singapore; Yangon, Burma; Cochin, India; Male (Maldives); Victoria (Seychelles); Mombasa, Kenya; Lamu Island; Durban and Cape Town, South Africa; Walvis Bay, Namibia; St. Helena, Rio de Janeiro, Salvador, Brazil; Barbados; Tortola and Fort Lauderdale.

May and November, 8 and 11 nights, transatlantic, New York to Southampton; Lisbon to Ft. Lauderdale.

May to October, 7, 11, 12 nights, Mediterranean and Canary Islands, from Southampton to Athens; Athens to Venice; Athens to Rome; Athens to Barcelona; Rome to Venice; Rome to Athens; Rome to Istanbul; Rome to Barcelona; Venice to Rome; Istanbul to Barcelona; Barcelona to Athens; Barcelona to Venice; or, Barcelona to Lisbon.

November–December, 7–15 nights, Caribbean and Panama Canal, round-trip Ft. Lauderdale; or, Ft. Lauderdale to Los Angeles.

Crystal Symphony   **Home Port**   Varies with itinerary
January–April and December, 7–14 nights, Panama Canal and Caribbean, between Ft. Lauderdale and Caldera, Costa Rica; round-trip from Ft. Lauderdale; Caldera to New Orleans; or, New Orleans to Ft. Lauderdale.

April and September, 9 and 16 nights, transatlantic, from Ft. Lauderdale to Lisbon; or, London to New York.

May, 9 and 12 nights, Mediterranean and Western Europe, from Lisbon to Rome; or, Rome to Dover.

May–August, 9–12 nights, Baltic, Norwegian Fjords, British Isles, between Dover and Stockholm; between Dover and Copenhagen; between Dover and Rouen; Rouen to Stockholm; Stockholm to Copenhagen; or, round-trip from Dover.

September–October, 11 and 12 nights, Canada/New England, Colonial America between New York and Montreal, then positions from Montreal to Ft. Lauderdale.

November, 17 nights, South America, from Ft. Lauderdale to Buenos Aires or reverse.

Cunard Line, Ltd.

Caronia **Home Port** Southampton, others vary with itinerary

January–February, 75 nights, South America, round-trip from Southampton, available in 15–50-night segments: Ft. Lauderdale to Valparaiso; Ft. Lauderdale to Rio de Janeiro; Valparaiso to Rio de Janeiro; Rio de Janeiro to Ft. Lauderdale; Southampton to Valparaiso; Southampton to Rio de Janeiro; Southampton to Ft. Lauderdale; round-trip from Ft. Lauderdale; Ft. Lauderdale to Southampton.

May–December, 4–18 nights, round-trip from Southampton to Channel Islands and Le Havre; Iberia; Western Mediterranean; Baltic; Iceland/Norway; Norwegian Fjords/North Cape; Scotland/Ireland/Guernsey; Canary Island/Madeira; or the Adriatic. Christmas cruise, 14 nights to the Canary Islands and Madeira.

November, 30 nights, transatlantic round-trip from Southampton to Lisbon, the Azores, Caribbean islands, Tenerife and Lisbon.

QE2 **Home Ports** New York, Southampton, others vary with itinerary

January 5–April 25, 110 nights, World Cruise, round-trip from New York. Sails via Panama Canal to Los Angeles, trans–Pacific to New Zealand and Australia with three days in Sydney, Japan, Hong Kong, SE Asia, India and Indian Ocean to South Africa, Canary Islands, Lisbon, Southampton. Available in segments of 8 to 91 nights from Los Angeles, Auckland, Sydney, Hong Kong, Singapore, Cape Town, Southampton.

April, 6 nights, transatlantic, Southampton to New York and reverse.

May–October, 3–19 nights, Europe round-trip from Southampton to Baltic, Norwegian Fjords, Channel Islands, England/Ireland/France, Iberia; Canary Islands; Western and Eastern Mediterranean; or, Egypt/Turkey.

October–November, 30 nights, South America, round-trip from Southampton to Rio de Janeiro, Montevideo, Falkland Island, West Africa.

December, 14 nights, Caribbean round-trip from New York.

Queen Mary 2 **Home Ports** Southampton, New York, Ft. Lauderdale

January 12, 2004, maiden voyage, 14 nights, from Southampton to Ft. Lauderdale via Madeira; Tenerife and Las Palmas in the Canary Islands; Barbados; St. Thomas.

January, March, May–June, November–December, 8–14 nights, Caribbean and Panama Canal, round-trip from New York or Ft. Lauderdale; or, between Ft. Lauderdale and New York.

February 2004, 12 nights, Rio for Carnival, between Ft. Lauderdale and Rio de Janeiro.

March, 17 nights, Three Continents Transatlantic, Ft. Lauderdale to Southampton via Barbados, Dakar, Las Palmas, Lanzarote, Madeira, Lisbon.

April–October 2004, 6 nights, transatlantic, between Southampton and New York, interspersed with several Europe, New England/Canada and cruises to nowhere.

May 7, 3 nights, round-trip from New York to nowhere (Mothers' Day Cruise).

May 24, 12 nights, Mediterranean, round-trip from Southampton to Vigo, Gibraltar, Palma de Mallorca, Barcelona, Marseille, Malaga, Cadiz and Lisbon.

July 11, 11 nights, Baltic/Norwegian Fjords, round-trip from Southampton to South Queensferry, Scotland; Trondheim, Bergen, Alesund, Hellesylt/Geiranger, Oslo, Norway; Hamburg, Germany; Rotterdam, Netherlands.

August, 9 and 12 nights, Southampton to Piraeus and reverse. Will serve as a hotel in Piraeus, August 12 – 30, 2004 during the Olympic Games.

September–October, 12 nights, Canada/New England, round-trip from New York to Portland, Maine; Sydney, Nova Scotia; Corner Brook, Newfoundland; Quebec City; Charlottetown, PEI; Halifax, Nova Scotia; Newport, RI.

October, 14 nights, Mediterranean, round-trip from Southampton to Vigo, Cadiz, Malaga, Palma de Mallorca, Barcelona, Rome, Livorno, Gibraltar, Lisbon.

Queen Victoria   Debuts March 2005; itineraries t.b.a.

Delta Queen Steamboat Company

American Queen   **Home Ports**   New Orleans, Memphis

January–April, 3 to 7 nights, round-trip from, or between, New Orleans and Memphis.

April–December, 3 and 4 nights, round-trip from New Orleans. 3 nights to Oak Alley, Baton Rouge; 4 nights to Oak Alley, St. Francisville, Baton Rouge.

Delta Queen   **Home Port**   New Orleans, others vary with itinerary

January–April, June, November–December, 3–7 nights, Mississippi, round-trip from New Orleans, between New Orleans and Memphis, or between New Orleans and Galveston.

Late April–November, 3–11 nights, Upper Mississippi, and Wilderness Rivers, from Chattanooga, Nashville, St. Louis, Minneapolis/St. Paul, Pittsburgh, Cincinnati, or Louisville.

Mississippi Queen   **Home Port**   New Orleans, others vary with itinerary

February–April, July–September, 3–7 nights, Mississippi, round-trip from New Orleans or between New Orleans and Memphis.

Late April–October, 4–11 nights, Upper Mississippi, and Wilderness Rivers, from Chattanooga, Nashville, St. Louis, Minneapolis/St. Paul, Pittsburgh, Cincinnati or Louisville.

Discovery World Cruises

Discovery **Home Port** Ft. Lauderdale

January–February, 13–21 days, Antarctica, Chilean Fjords, In the Wake of the Bounty; February–March, 14–18 days, New Zealand, Hawaii and Mexican Riviera, Mexico and Panama Canal; March–April, transatlantic. May–November, under charter by Voyages of Discovery (United Kingdom).

Disney Cruise Line

Disney Magic **Home Port** Port Canaveral

Year-round, 7 nights, Saturday, round-trip from Port Canaveral alternating Eastern and Western Caribbean to either St. Maarten, St. Thomas (with excursions to St. John), and Castaway Cay, Disney's private Bahamian island; or, Key West, Grand Cayman, Cozumel and Castaway Cay. Additional itineraries in 2004: August 7, 21 and September 4, 2004, to St. Thomas, San Juan, Castaway Cay. September 18 and October 2, 2004 to Antigua, St. Thomas, Castaway Cay. December 18, 2004, 10 nights to Key West, St. Maarten, St. Lucia, Antigua, St. Thomas, Castaway Cay.

Disney Wonder **Home Port** Port Canaveral

Year-round, 3 or 4 nights, round-trip from Port Canaveral on Thursday to Nassau, and Castaway Cay, (3 nights); or, on Sundays to Nassau, Castaway Cay plus Freeport (4 nights). Cruise can be combined with Disney World packages for a 7-night vacation.

First European Cruises

Azur **Home Port** Venice

Year-round, 10 nights, Eastern Mediterranean, round-trip from Venice to Dubrovnik, Katakolon, Alexandria, Limassol, Antalya, Rhodes, Athens, Corinth Canal. Subject to change

European Stars **Home Port** Genoa

January–March, 10 nights, Canary Islands and Morocco, round-trip from Genoa to Lanzarote, Madeira, Malaga, Marseille, Casablanca, Agadir. Subject to change.

April–December, Friday, 7 nights, Mediterranean, round-trip from Barcelona, to Marseille, Genoa, Naples, Messina, Tunis, Palma de Majorca. Subject to change.

European Vision **Home Ports** Venice, Santo Domingo

December–April, Sunday, 7 nights, Caribbean, round-trip from Santo Domingo to either Aruba; Curacao; Isla de Margarita; Grenada, Guadeloupe; or, Tortola; St. Maarten; Antigua; Barbados, Guadeloupe.

April and November, 13 and 14 nights, transatlantic between Santo Domingo and Genoa.

May–November, Sunday, 7 nights, Greek Isles, round-trip from Venice calling at Athens, Santorini, Rhodes, Corfu, Bari, Dubrovnik. Subject to change.

Flamenco Under charter.

Mistral **Home Ports** Santo Domingo, Kiel

January–April, Saturday, 7 nights, Caribbean, round-trip from Santo Domingo, Dominican Republic to Ocho Rios, Santiago de Cuba, Bahamas, Caicos, Cabo Samana. Subject to change.

May and September, 14 and 15 nights, transatlantic, from Santo Domingo to Kiel and Marseille to Santo Domingo. Subject to change.

May–September, Sunday, 7 nights, Baltic/Norwegian Fjords round-trip from Kiel to either Flaam, Molde, Andalsness, Hellesylt, Geiranger and Bergen, Norway; Copenhagen; or, Visby and Stockholm, Sweden; Tallinn, Estonia; St. Petersburg, Russia; Copenhagen, Denmark. Subject to change.

Fred Olsen Lines (The Cruise Broker)

Black Prince **Home Ports** Southampton, Greenock, Leith

January–March and October, 13–16 nights, Canary Islands round-trip from Southampton. February, 35 nights, 35 nights, Transatlantic, Amazon round-trip from Southampton.

April, 21 nights, Eastern Mediterranean/Greek Isles, round-trip from Southampton

April, October, 13–14 nights, Western Mediterranean, round-trip from Southampton.

June–July, 7–12 nights, North Cape from Greenock (Glasgow) Scotland, Norway or Baltic from Leith (Edinburgh)Scotland.

Black Watch **Home Ports** Southampton, Dover

January–April, 105 nights, World Cruise, round-trip from Southampton, available in 17–65-night segments, on a route from England to the Caribbean, Panama Canal, South Pacific, New Zealand, Australia, Mauritius, South Africa, Namibia, West Africa, Canary Islands, Madeira.

April–May, July, September–November, 4–21 nights, round-trip from Dover to Iberia; Adriatic; Western Med; or, Greek Isles.

May–September, 8–15 nights, round-trip from Dover to Norway; North Cape/Murmansk; Iceland/Greenland; or, Baltic.

Braemar   **Home Ports**   Barbados, Malaga, Dover

To March, 15 nights, Caribbean or Amazon, round-trip from Barbados. March–May, 10 nights, Canary Islands, round-trip from Malaga. March, 14 nights, transatlantic, Barbados to Malaga.

June and September–November, 4–15 nights, round-trip from Dover to France; Normandy Beaches for 60th anniversary of D Day; Western Med; Canary Islands; or, Italy.

June–September, 7–15 nights, round-trip from Dover to Norway; Baltic; North Cape/Spitsbergen.

Glacier Bay Cruiseline

Executive Explorer   **Home Ports**   Juneau, Ketchikan

Mid–May to late–August, 7 nights, Alaska, soft–adventure cruises between Juneau and Ketchikan aboard Alaska's only overnight catamaran. Visit Tracy Arm, Haines, Skagway, Pelican, Glacier Bay, Sitka, Wrangell, Metlakatla, Misty Fjords.

Wilderness Adventurer   **Home Ports**   Juneau, Ketchikan

Mid–May–early September, 7 nights, Alaska, active–adventure cruises between Juneau and Ketchikan, via Glacier Bay, Petersburg, Behm Canal, Misty fjords, Tracy Arm, Icy Strait; or, remote back–country cruise, round-trip from Juneau to Glacier Bay National Park, Tracy Arm Fjord, Endicott Arm, Point Adolphus and Icy Strait, Chichagoff, Baranof, and Admiralty Islands. Unlike standard itineraries, route takes ship mostly to uninhabited wilderness, where passengers use ship's sea kayaks or are ferried ashore in Zodiacs to hike. The itinerary is flexible and allows the captain to choose areas based on weather and water conditions, passenger interest, whale or wildlife sightings.

Wilderness Discoverer   **Home Port**   Juneau, Sitka

Mid–May–early September, 7 nights, Alaska soft–adventure cruises between Juneau and Sitka. Passengers overnight in embarkation port before boarding. Cruise includes "Adventure Activities" where passengers can learn to kayak using ship's sea kayaks or ferry ashore in Zodiacs for nature walks. Visit Haines, Skagway, Icy Strait, Frederick Sound, Tracy Arm Fjord, Glacier Bay, Chichagoff, Baranof, and Admiralty Islands.

Wilderness Explorer   **Home Port**   Glacier Bay

June–late August, 5 nights, Alaska, active–adventure cruises from Glacier Bay. Passengers fly to Glacier Bay to join the ship. Most daylight hours spent sea kayaking or hiking in Glacier Bay with one day in Icy Strait. Cruise price includes round-trip air transport between Juneau and Glacier Bay.

Global Quest

Royal Star   **Home Port**   Mombasa
Year-round, 14 and 21 nights, in East Africa/Indian Ocean, from Mombasa. Cruise/safari packages in conjunction with African Safari Club. Destinations include Kenya, India, the Seychelles, Mauritius, Reunion, Zanzibar, Mayotte, Madagascar.

Global Quest also offers packages aboard small ship expedition cruises to Antarctica, Russian Far East and the Arctic as well as cruise-tours to the Galapagos, the rivers of Europe and Russia and the Adriatic.

Hebridean Island Cruises

Hebridean Princess   **Home Port**   Oban, Invergordon, Greenock, Troon
March–November, 3–7 nights, Scotland's "Highlands and Islands" including the Inner and Outer Hebrides, Iona, Rum, Muck, Eigg, Harris, Lewis, Skye, Staffa and River Clyde, round-trip from Oban with several cruises from Troon (July), Invergordon (August) and Greenock (November).

Hebridean Spirit   **Home Port**   Varies with itinerary
December–April, 11–15 nights, Indian Ocean, including India, Seychelles, Madagascar, Tanzania. November and April positions via Egypt and the Suez Canal.

April–June and September–November, 6, 7, 9 nights, Mediterranean en–route between U.K. and Egypt via Turkey, Greece, Croatia, Italy, France, Spain, Portugal.

June–September, 3–9 nights, nights, Norway, Baltic, British Isles, from Trondheim, Tromso, Bergen, Helsingborg, Tallinn, Stockholm, Portland.

September–November, 3–7 nights, France/Spain, Western Med, Italy, Italy/Greece, Greek Isles, Greece/Turkey Turkey/Sicily from Bordeaux, Cadiz, Nice, Catania, Venice, Molfetta, Crete, Kusadasi.

Holland America Line

Amsterdam   **Home Ports**   Valparaiso, Rio de Janeiro, Seattle, others vary with itinerary
November–March, 12 and 17 nights, South America between Valparaiso and Buenos Aires via Stanley, Falkland Islands; Cape Horn; Ushuaia, Tierra del Fuego; Punta Arenas, Chile; Chilean Fjords; Puerto Montt, Chile; or, between Rio de Janeiro and Valparaiso, Chile, same route plus Montevideo and Buenos Aires (2 days).

January, 21 nights, Antarctica/South America, between Valparaiso and Rio de Janeiro, via Montevideo, Uruguay; Buenos Aires, Argentina; Falkland Islands, cruises past Elephant Island, Paulet Island, Deception Island, Errera Channel and Paradise Bay; Neumayer Channel; LeMaire Channel, and Petermann Island, Heading back to South America, cruises past Cape Horn to Ushuaia, Beagle and Cockburn Channels, Punta Arenas, Strait of Magellan, Chilean Fjords, Puerto Chacabuco and Puerto Montt.

March–April and October, 17–22 nights, positioning to/from South America, Valparaiso, Chile to San Diego or Seattle (March–April); Seattle or San Francisco to Valparaiso (October).

April, 18 nights, Hawaii, round-trip from Seattle, 18 nights, to Vancouver, Hilo, two days in Honolulu, Nawiliwili, Lahaina, Kona.

May–September, 7 nights, Alaska, round-trip from Seattle to Juneau, Hubbard Glacier, Sitka, Ketchikan and an evening call at Victoria, BC. 3 and 4 nights, September, round-trip Seattle to Victoria and Vancouver. November, resumes South America/Antarctica program.

Maasdam **Home Ports** Norfolk, Boston, Montreal

To April 2004 and from October 2004, 10 and 11 nights, Caribbean, round-trip from Norfolk to either Half Moon Cay, Tortola, Dominica, Barbados, Guadeloupe and St. Thomas (11 nights); or, San Juan, St. Maarten, Antigua and St. Thomas (10 nights).

May–October, 7 and 10 nights, Canada/New England, between Montreal and Boston, via Quebec City; Charlottetown PEI; Sydney and Halifax, Nova Scotia and Bar Harbor, Maine; or, between New York and Montreal, adding Newport, Gloucester and overnight on board in Quebec City; or, round-trip from Boston, via Portland, Bar Harbor, Saint John NB, Martha's Vineyard. Positions from Ft. Lauderdale to Montreal, 13 nights, May 9, 2004 and Montreal to Norfolk, Virginia, 14 nights, October 16, 2004.

Noordam **Home Ports** Tampa, Copenhagen, others vary with itinerary

January–March, 14 nights, Caribbean, round-trip from Tampa to San Juan, Tortola, Guadeloupe, Barbados, St. Lucia, Isla Margarita, Bonaire, Aruba, Grand Cayman.

April and November, 14 and 11 nights, transatlantic, Tampa to Lisbon; or, Lisbon to Ft. Lauderdale.

April–May and September–November, 9, 10, 11 nights, Mediterranean, between Barcelona and Rome, between Lisbon and Rome, or round-trip from Rome.

May–June and September, 14 nights, Western Europe, Rome to London; or Copenhagen to Rome. Special D–Day 60th Anniversary cruise, round-trip from London, 10 nights, June 2, 2004.

June–August, 10 nights, Baltic, round-trip from Copenhagen to Tallinn, Estonia; St. Petersburg; Helsinki; Stockholm and Kalmar, Sweden; Warnemunde (Berlin), Germany; Aarhus, Denmark. London to Copenhagen, 10 nights, June 12, 2004 via Norwegian Fjords.

Oosterdam **Home Ports** Harwich, Ft. Lauderdale, Seattle
To April 2004, Sunday, –7 nights, Caribbean round-trip from Ft. Lauderdale, to either St. Maarten, Tortola, Half Moon Cay; or, Half Moon Cay, Ocho Rios, Grand Cayman, Cozumel.
April and September, 14–22 nights, Panama Canal, Ft. Lauderdale to San Diego; or, Seattle to Ft. Lauderdale, available in segments.
May–September, 7 nights, Alaska round-trip from Seattle to Juneau, Hubbard Glacier or Glacier Bay, Sitka, Ketchikan and an evening call at Victoria, BC.
October–December, Sunday, 7 nights, Caribbean round-trip from Ft. Lauderdale, to either Half Moon Cay, Turks and Caicos San Juan, Tortola (Eastern); or, Half Moon Cay, Turks and Caicos, Grand Cayman, Cozumel (Western).

Prinsendam **Home Port** Varies with itinerary
January–April, 107 nights, World Cruise, Los Angeles to New York, via Honolulu; American Samoa; Fiji; Bay of Islands, Auckland, Christchurch, Dunedin, Milford Sound New Zealand; Port Arthur and Hobart, Tasmania; Melbourne, Sydney (two days), Hardy Reef, Whitsunday Islands, Cairns, Darwin, Australia; Komodo, Bali (two days) Indonesia; Sandakan, Malaysia; Manila, Philippines; Hong Kong (three days); Halong Bay, Vietnam; Bangkok (two days); Singapore; Kuala Lumpur, Langkawi, Malaysia; Thilawa, Myanmar (two days); Cochin, Mumbai (two days), India; Muscat, Oman; Istanbul, (two days); Pithagorio, Santorini, Greece; Venice (overnight on board); Gibraltar; Madeira; Ft. Lauderdale. Available in segments or 19 to 35 nights.
May and November, 10–13 nights, transatlantic, Ft. Lauderdale or New York to Lisbon; or, Lisbon to Ft. Lauderdale, 11 nights, November 9, 2004.
May, September–October, 12–14 nights, Mediterranean/Black Sea, Athens to Rome; Lisbon to Athens; Athens to Venice; Venice to Athens; or Athens to Lisbon.
June and September, 14 nights, Western Europe, Rome to Amsterdam; or, Copenhagen to Lisbon.
June–August, 14 nights, Baltic/Norwegian Fjords/Iceland, between Amsterdam and Copenhagen on various itineraries.
November 20, 28 nights, Amazon, round-trip from Ft. Lauderdale to the Caribbean and Amazon basin.

Rotterdam **Home Ports** Ft. Lauderdale, Baltimore, New York, others vary with itinerary
January–April, November–December, 10 nights, Panama Canal, round-trip from Ft. Lauderdale to Half Moon Cay, Curacao, Aruba,

Gatun Lake/Panama Canal and Puerto Limon, Costa Rica. New York to Ft. Lauderdale, 13 nights, October 30, 2004, same ports of call.

April–May, 10 nights, Caribbean, round-trip from Baltimore or Philadelphia, to San Juan, St. Maarten, Tortola, Half Moon Cay.

June, July, September, 16 and 17 nights, transatlantic, between New York and Amsterdam; New York to Copenhagen or London to New York City.

July–August, 15 and 16 nights, Copenhagen to Athens or Athens to London. Rotterdam will serve as a hotel during the Athens Summer Olympic Games.

September–October, 10 nights, Canada/New England, between New York and Montreal via Newport, Boston, Bar Harbor, Halifax, Sydney, Charlottetown and Quebec City. Round-trip from New York, 10 nights, October 20, 2004.

Ryndam **Home Ports** Vancouver, San Diego

October–April, 7 and 10 nights, Mexico/Sea of Cortez, round-trip from San Diego to Loreto, La Paz, Cabo San Lucas and cruising the Sea of Cortez. (7 nights); or, same ports plus Puerto Vallarta, Mazatlán, Santa Rosalia (10 nights.); or to Cabo San Lucas, Mazatlán, Puerto Vallarta (7 nights); or, same ports plus Acapulco, Manzanillo and Zihuatanejo (10 nights). Positions from Vancouver to San Diego, 14 nights, October 10, 2004 calling at Astoria, San Diego, Cabo San Lucas, Loreto, La Paz, cruising the Sea of Cortez, Puerto Vallarta, Mazatlán, Santa Rosalia

May–September, 7 nights, Alaska, between Vancouver and Seward. Northbound calling at Ketchikan, Juneau, Sitka and either Hubbard Glacier and Skagway or Glacier Bay and College Fjords. Southbound calling at College Fjord, Glacier Bay, Sitka, Juneau, Ketchikan. 7 nights, Inside Passage, round-trip from Vancouver May 7. September 17, 2004 to Juneau, Skagway, Glacier Bay, Ketchikan.

October, 21 nights, Panamerica/Panama Canal, round-trip from San Diego calling at Cabo San Lucas, Acapulco, Santa Cruz Huatulco, Puntarenas, Costa Rica; Amador, Panama City; Gatun Lake; San Juan Del Sur, Nicaragua; Puerto Quetzal, Guatemala; Zihuatanejo/Ixtapa and Puerto Vallarta.

Statendam **Home Ports** San Diego, Vancouver

January–February, 16 nights, Panama Canal between San Diego and Ft. Lauderdale.

October–April, alternating 7- and 10-night Mexican Riviera or Sea of Cortez and 15–16-night Hawaii cruises, round-trip from San Diego to Loreto, La Paz, Cabo San Lucas and cruising the Sea of Cortez (7 nights) plus Puerto Vallarta, Mazatlán and Santa Rosalia (10 nights); or, Hilo, Hawaii; Honolulu, Oahu; Nawiliwili, Kauai; Lahaina, Maui; Kona,

Hawaii and Ensenada, Mexico (15 nights) plus overnight in Honolulu or Molokai (16 nights). San Diego to Vancouver, 16 nights, April 19, 2004, same Hawaiian ports plus Victoria.

May–September, 7 nights, Alaska, between Vancouver and Seward. Northbound calling at Ketchikan, Juneau, Sitka and either Hubbard Glacier and Skagway or Glacier Bay and College Fjords. Southbound calling at College Fjord, Glacier Bay, Sitka, Juneau, Ketchikan. Inside Passage cruise round-trip from Vancouver September 12 and 19, 2004 to Juneau, Skagway, Glacier Bay, Ketchikan.

October, 21 nights, Panamerica, round-trip from San Diego, to Cabo San Lucas, Acapulco, Santa Cruz Huatulco, Puntarenas, Costa Rica; Amador, Panama City; Gatun Lake; San Juan Del Sur, Nicaragua; Puerto Quetzal, Guatemala; Zihuatanejo/Ixtapa, Puerto Vallarta.

November resumes Hawaii/Mexico cruises from San Diego.

Veendam   **Home Ports**   Vancouver, Tampa

November to March, 2004, Saturday, 7 nights, Western Caribbean, round-trip from Tampa to either Grand Cayman, Montego Bay and Cozumel; or, Key West, Belize City, Santo Tomas de Castilla, Guatemala, Cozumel.

May–September, 7 nights, Alaska, between Vancouver and Seward. Northbound calling at Ketchikan, Juneau, Sitka and either Hubbard Glacier and Skagway or Glacier Bay and College Fjords. Southbound calling at College Fjord, Glacier Bay, Sitka, Juneau, Ketchikan. Inside Passage cruise round-trip from Vancouver September 19 to Juneau, Skagway, Glacier Bay, Ketchikan.

April and September, 20–22 nights, Panama Canal positioning cruises between Tampa and Vancouver. Cruises can be taken in 14 to 20-night segments.

November, resumes 7-night Caribbean sailings from Tampa. One-time Southern Caribbean, 14 nights, November 20, round-trip from Tampa, to San Juan, Tortola, Guadeloupe, Barbados, St. Lucia, Isla Margarita, Bonaire, Aruba, Grand Cayman.

Volendam   **Home Ports**   Ft. Lauderdale, Vancouver

October–April, 10 nights, alternating Southern/Western Caribbean, round-trip from Ft. Lauderdale to Half Moon Cay, Turks and Caicos and either St. Thomas, Tortola, Dominica, Barbados (Southern) or Cozumel Grand Cayman, Cozumel, Veracruz, Key West (Western).

May–September, 7 nights, Alaska, round-trip from Vancouver to Juneau, Skagway, Glacier Bay, Ketchikan.

April and September, 21 and 18 nights, Panama Canal, Ft. Lauderdale to Vancouver or reverse, available in 15–21-night segments.

October resumes 10-night Caribbean sailings from Ft. Lauderdale.

Westerdam **Home Ports** Ft. Lauderdale, others vary with itinerary

April–May, August–October, 12 nights, Mediterranean/Western Europe, round trip from Venice; Venice to Rome; Athens to Rome; Lisbon to Rome; Rome to Lisbon; Rome to Venice; Rome to Barcelona; Venice to London; or London to Athens.

June–July, 12 nights, Baltic between Copenhagen and Harwich, via Stockholm, Tallinn, St. Petersburg (2 days), Helsinki, Warnemunde, Visby, Aarhus, Oslo; or, North Cape/Norwegian Fjords, Harwich to Copenhagen.

November, 17 nights, transatlantic, Barcelona to Ft. Lauderdale.

December, 10 nights, Caribbean, round-trip from Ft. Lauderdale, to Aruba, Curacao, Dominica, St. Lucia, Tortola, Half Moon Cay.

Zaandam **Home Ports** Port Canaveral, Vancouver

January–April, October–December, Saturday, 7 nights, round-trip from Port Canaveral to either Tortola, St. Thomas and Half Moon Cay; or to Cozumel, Grand Cayman, Half Moon Cay and either Montego Bay or Ocho Rios,

May–September, 7 nights, Alaska, round-trip from Vancouver to Juneau, Skagway, Glacier Bay, Ketchikan

April and September, 21 nights, Panama Canal, from Port Canaveral to Vancouver or reverse. Available in 16 to 21 nights segments.

Zuiderdam **Home Port** Ft. Lauderdale

Year-round, Saturday, 7 nights, Caribbean round-trip from Ft. Lauderdale to Half Moon Cay, St. Thomas, Tortola, Nassau or Freeport. April to October, alternates with Key West, Cozumel, Grand Cayman, Half Moon Cay.

Kristina Cruises (The Cruise Broker)

Kristina Brahe **Home Port** Helsinki

June–August, 3–5 nights, Finland and Russia, round-trip from Helsinki on visa free cruises to St. Petersburg; or, cruises to the Finnish coast and archipelago.

Kristina Regina **Home Ports** Helsinki, Dakar, Las Palmas, others vary with itinerary

December–February, 7 nights, West Africa/Cape Verde Islands, fly–cruise including air from Helsinki to Dakar, Senegal, calling at Gambia and Cape Verde Islands, air from Cape Verde back to Helsinki.

March–May, September–October, 7–10 nights, Canary Islands, Mediterranean, Western Europe, British Isles as ship positions from Dakar to Helsinki for summer cruises. Reverse route in the fall with additional Mediterranean cruises. Subject to change.

June–August, 3–13 nights, visa free cruises to St. Petersburg, round-trip from Helsinki (3 nights); White Sea (Russia) and Norway; Baltic Sea; Iceland, Faroe Islands and Shetland Islands; Norwegian Fjords and Scandinavia. Subject to change.

MSC Italian Cruises

Lirica (Lyric) **Home Ports** Ft. Lauderdale, Venice
December–June, 11 nights, Eastern Caribbean and Panama Canal, round-trip from Ft. Lauderdale to either San Juan, Antigua, Grenada, Santa Lucia, St. Barts, Tortola; or, Montego Bay, Cartagena, San Blas Islands, Cristobal, Puerto Limon, Key West.

December and June, 17 nights, transatlantic between Genoa and Ft. Lauderdale.

June–November, Sunday, 7 nights, Croatia/Greece/Turkey, round-trip from Venice to Dubrovnik, Bari, Corfù, Kusadasi, Rhodes,

Katakolon. June and October–November, 5 nights, positioning between Genoa and Venice.

Melody **Home Ports** Rio de Janeiro, Genoa, Venice
November–March, Saturday, 7 nights, Brazil, round-trip from Rio de Janeiro to Porto Seguro, Salvador, Arraial Beach, Buzios. November and March, 17 nights, transatlantic between Rio de Janeiro and Genoa.

April–June, Sunday, Western Mediterranean, round-trip from Naples

Palermo, Tunis, Palma de Mallorca, Barcelona, Marseille.

July–November, Monday, 7 nights, round-trip from Venice to Dubrovnik, Bari, Santorini, Mykonos, Piraeus (Athens), Katakolon. June October, 7 and 11 nights, positioning between Genoa and Venice. October 29, 11 nights, Black Sea/Greece/Turkey.

Monterey **Home Port** Genoa
June–November, 11 nights, round-trip from Genoa, to either Greece, Turkey, Cyprus, Egypt, Crete; or Madeira, Canary Islands, Morocco; or Balearic Islands, Spain, Portugal, Morocco, Gibraltar, France; or Greece, Black Sea, Turkey. August, 14 nights, to Crete, Greece, Black Sea, Turkey, Malta.

Opera **Home Port** Genoa
June–November, Sunday, 7 nights, Mediterranean, round-trip from Genoa to Naples, Palermo, Tunis, Palma de Mallorca, Barcelona, Marseille.

November–December, 11 nights, Mediterranean, round-trip from Genoa to either Egypt, Cyprus, Turkey, Greece, Malta; or, Spain, Madeira, Canary Islands, Morocco.

Rhapsody **Home Port** Genoa

April–May and October–November, 11 nights, Canary Islands/Black Sea round-trip from Genoa to either Greece, Black Sea, Turkey; or, Spain, Morocco, Canary Islands, Madeira.

June–October, Monday, 7 nights, round-trip from Genoa, to Naples, Malta, Tunis, Ibiza, St. Tropez.

Norwegian Cruise Line

Norwegian Crown **Home Ports** Buenos Aires, Valparaiso, Philadelphia, New York, Baltimore

January–February 2004 and 2005, 14 nights, Cape Horn between Valparaiso and Buenos Aires Montevideo, Uruguay; Puerto Madryn, Argentina; Port Stanley, Falkland Is.; Cruise Cape Horn; Ushuaia, Argentina; cruise Beagle Channel, Strait of Magellan and Patagonic Channels; Puerto Chacabuco and Puerto Montt, Chile.

March 2004 and 2005, November–December, 2004, 15 and 13 nights, Panama Canal, Caribbean/Bermuda positioning cruises from Valparaiso, Chile to Miami and Miami to Philadelphia (spring); Baltimore to Miami and Miami to Valparaiso (fall).

April–November, 6, 7 nights, Bermuda or 11–14-night Canada/New England, round-trip from Philadelphia (April–May), New York City (June to September) or Baltimore (September–November) on various itineraries.

Norwegian Dawn **Home Port** New York

January–February, November 2004–February 2005, 10 and 11 nights, Southern Caribbean, round-trip from New York to St. Thomas, Antigua, Barbados, St. Maarten and Tortola (10 nights); or, St. Thomas, Antigua, Barbados, Grenada, Dominica and Tortola (11 nights).

March–November, Sunday, 7 nights, round-trip from New York to Port Canaveral (15 hours), Miami, Nassau and Great Stirrup Cay.

Norwegian Dream **Home Ports** New Orleans, Dover

January–March, September 2004–March 2005, 7 nights, Western Caribbean round-trip from New Orleans to Cozumel; Roatan, Honduras; Belize City, Belize and Cancun. March 27, 8 nights, New Orleans to Miami via Cozumel, Mexico; Belize City, Belize and San Andres, Colombia.

March 2004 and 2005, 16 nights, transatlantic, Miami to Rome.

April–May, 2004 and 2005, 12 nights, Western Europe, Rome to Dover or reverse, via Livorno (Florence/Pisa), Genoa, Italy; Cannes, Marseille, France; Barcelona, Cadiz, Spain; Lisbon and Le Havre (Paris).

May–September, 12 nights, Scandinavian Capitals, round-trip from Dover to Kiel Canal, Tallinn, Estonia; St. Petersburg (2 days); Helsinki; Stockholm; Copenhagen; Oslo, Norway.

September, 15 nights, transatlantic, Dover to Miami.

Norwegian Majesty **Home Ports** Charleston, Boston
November–April, 7 nights, Western Caribbean, round-trip from Charleston SC to Grand Cayman, Cozumel and Key West.
May–October, Sunday, 7 nights, Bermuda, round-trip from Boston to St. George with 3 nights in port.
April 2004 and 2005, 15 nights, Caribbean/Colonial America positioning from Charleston SC to Boston.

Norwegian Sea **Home Port** Houston
Year-round, 7 nights, Western Caribbean round-trip from Houston, to Cozumel; Roatan, Honduras; Belize City, Belize and Cancun. (to April 24, 2004); to Cozumel; Roatan, Honduras and Grand Cayman (May 1 2004 to April 30, 2005).

Norwegian Sky **Home Ports** San Juan, Seattle
To April, Sunday, 7 nights, alternating Southern Caribbean round-trip from San Juan to either St. Thomas, Barbados, Dominica, St. Lucia, St. Kitts or St. Thomas, Tortola, St. Maarten, Antigua, Martinique.
April–May, 17 nights, Panama Canal between San Juan and San Francisco and 3 nights, San Francisco to Vancouver.
May–September, 7 nights, Alaska, round-trip from Seattle Juneau, Skagway, Sawyer Glacier, Ketchikan and Prince Rupert, BC. Vancouver to Seattle, seven nights, May 15, 2004, via Ketchikan, Juneau, Skagway, Sawyer Glacier.
October, begins sailing in Hawaii as Pride of Aloha for NCL America.

Norwegian Star **Home Ports** Honolulu, Seattle, Los Angeles
To April, Sunday, 7 nights, round-trip from Honolulu to Hilo, Hawaii; Fanning Island Republic of Kiribati (passport required), Kahului, Maui; and Nawiliwili, Kauai. 8 nights, Honolulu to Vancouver, May 2, 2004.
May to September, 7 nights, round-trip from Seattle, to Juneau, Skagway Glacier Bay, Ketchikan, Victoria. 7 nights, Seattle to Vancouver;– September 12 same ports without Victoria.
September 2004, May 2005, 7 nights, Pacific Coast positioning between Vancouver and Los Angeles.
September 2004–April, 2005, 7 nights, Mexican Riviera, round-trip from Los Angeles to Acapulco (overnight), Zihuatanejo/Ixtapa, Puerto Vallarta, Cabo San Lucas.

Norwegian Sun **Home Ports** Miami, Vancouver
To April, Saturday, 7 nights, Western Caribbean, round-trip from Miami to Cozumel, Costa Maya, Grand Cayman and either Ocho Rios or Montego Bay, Jamaica.

April 2004 and 2005, October, 2004, 16 and 17 nights, Panama Canal, between Miami and Los Angeles; 5 nights, Pacific Coast, between Los Angeles, Vancouver.

May–September, Sunday, 7 nights, Alaska round-trip from Vancouver to Ketchikan, Juneau, Skagway, Wrangell, Sawyer Glacier.

October 2004–April 2005, Saturday, 7 nights, Western Caribbean, round-trip from Miami to Grand Cayman; Roatan, Honduras; Belize City, Belize; Cozumel.

Norwegian Wind   **Home Ports**   Honolulu, Vancouver

To April, Saturday, 7 nights round-trip from Miami to Cozumel, Belize City, Roatan, Grand Cayman.

April–May, 16 nights, Panama Canal, Miami to Los Angeles; 5 nights, Pacific Coast, Los Angeles to Vancouver. 11 nights, Hawaii, Vancouver to Honolulu.

May, begins Hawaii sailing for NCL America.

Norway   Out of service; status to be determined

NCL America

Norwegian Wind   **Home Port**   Honolulu

Year-round from May 19, 2004, 10 and 11 nights, round-trip from Honolulu to Fanning Island (Republic of Kiribati), Hilo, Kona, Nawili-wili, Lahaina (overnight on board on 11-night cruises). May 8, 2004, 11 nights, Vancouver to Honolulu, via Hilo, Kona, Lahaina, Nawiliwili.

Pride of Aloha   **Home Port**   Honolulu

Year-round from October 1, 2004, 3 and 4 nights, round-trip from Honolulu, Friday, 3 nights to Nawiliwili, Kauai and Kahului, Maui; –Monday, 4 nights to Hilo, Hawaii; Kahului, Maui; Nawiliwili, Kauai.

Pride of America   **Home Port**   Honolulu

Year-round from July 4, 2004, 7 nights, round-trip from Honolulu to Nawiliwili, Kauai (overnight); Hilo, Hawaii; Kona, Hawaii; Kahului, Maui (overnight). The ship is in port every day and offers scenic cruising on Tuesday afternoon and evening.

Oceania Cruises

Insignia   **Home Port**   Varies with itinerary

April–May, August–October, 10–14 nights, Mediterranean, either Barcelona to Athens; Athens to Rome; Rome to Barcelona; Barcelona to Venice; Venice to Lisbon; Lisbon to Barcelona; Venice to Istanbul; Istanbul to Barcelona; Istanbul round trip; or, Barcelona to Barbados.

May–July, 12 and 14 nights, Western Europe and British Isles, either Lisbon to Dover; round-trip from Dover; or Copenhagen to Dover.

November, 14 nights, transatlantic, Barcelona–Barbados.

Regatta   **Home Ports**   Miami, Stockholm, Dover, others vary with itinerary

November–March, 10–14 nights, Caribbean, Panama Canal, Mexican Riviera, either round-trip from Miami; between Miami and Puerto Caldera; or, between Puerto Caldera and Los Angeles.

March–May, August–November, transatlantic, Mediterranean and Western Europe, either Miami to Lisbon, Lisbon to Barcelona; Barcelona to Venice; Venice to Barcelona; Barcelona to Lisbon; Lisbon to Rome; Rome to Barcelona; Lisbon to Dover; Dover to Lisbon; or, Lisbon to Miami.

June–August, 12 and 14 nights, Baltic, Norwegian Fjords, Norway and Britain, either between Dover and Stockholm, via Bruges, Amsterdam, Kiel Canal, Berlin, Gdansk, Copenhagen, Helsinki, St. Petersburg (2 nights), Tallinn; or, Dover to Copenhagen via Norwegian Fjords; or, Copenhagen to Dover via Norway and Britain.

Orient Lines

Marco Polo   **Home Port**   Varies with itinerary

December and February, 14–33 nights, South America, Barbados to Santiago (20 nights); Barbados to Ushuaia (33 nights); Santiago to Ushuaia (19 nights); Buenos Aires to Manaus (19 nights); Manaus to Barbados (14 nights); or, Buenos Aires to Barbados (31 nights).

January–February, 12, 16, 31 nights, Antarctica, Cape Horn, Falkland Islands, South Georgia, Chilean Fjords (Only 450 passengers allowed by authorities; ship's normal complement is up to 800). Includes lectures by scientists, wildlife viewing from Zodiacs, and visits to scientific stations. Antarctic ports may vary depending on ice conditions. Cruise-tours include flights from Miami, pre and/or post cruise hotel and tours. Sail round-trip from Ushuaia to Buenos Aires or Ushuaia to Manaus.

March–May, September–November, 11–35 nights, transatlantic, Mediterranean, Western Europe, Grand Europe, from Barbados to Athens and various itineraries from Barcelona, Athens, Venice, Rome, Southampton, Stockholm, or, Dover.

June–August, 11 and 18 nights, Baltic and Norwegian Fjords cruises between Copenhagen and Stockholm, 11 nights, to Tallinn, St. Petersburg (two days), Helsinki and Stockholm; or, round-trip from Copenhagen, 11 nights, to Flam, Gudvangen, Hellesylt, Geiranger, Bergen, Oslo, Aarhus. Combine for 18-night cruise-tour. May and August, 16 nights, between Dover and Copenhagen.

P&O Cruises

Adonia   **Home Ports**   Southampton, Barbados

January–April, 80 nights, World Cruise, round-trip from Southampton via Mediterranean, Suez Canal, India, Southeast Asia, China, circle Australia, Singapore, Indian Ocean, South Africa, Namibia, Senegal, Madeira. Available in segments of 17–63 nights.

April—July and September–October, 3–17 nights, Mediterranean, Canary Islands, Iberia, Atlantic Islands, Holland/France/Ireland, round-trip from Southampton.

May–August, 13–15 nights, Norway or Baltic, round-trip from Southampton.

December, 14–16 nights, Caribbean/Panama Canal, round-trip from Barbados; between Barbados and New Orleans; or, between Barbados and Acapulco.

Aurora   **Home Port**   Southampton

January–April, 80 nights, World Cruise, westbound from Southampton via Madeira, Caribbean, Panama Canal, Acapulco, San Francisco, Hawaii, Samoa, Fiji, New Zealand, Australia, Philippines, China, Thailand, Singapore, India, Egypt, Suez Canal, Greece, Portugal. Available in segments of 14–47 nights.

April–December, 1–18 nights, Canary Islands/Madeira; Iberia; or, Mediterranean, round-trip from Southampton. August, 3 nights, Belgium and Guernsey. September, December, 1- and 2-night party cruises to nowhere.

May and July, 13 and 14 nights, North Cape and Baltic, round-trip from Southampton.

December 18, 22 nights, Holiday Caribbean cruise, round-trip from Southampton.

Oceana   **Home Ports**   Southampton, Barbados

November–April, 14 nights, Caribbean, round-trip from Ft. Barbados on various Circle Caribbean itineraries.

April and October, 14 nights, transatlantic, between Barbados and Southampton.

May–October, 6–17 nights, Canary Islands/Madeira; Iberia; English Channel; or, Mediterranean, round-trip from Southampton.

June–August, 7–13 nights, Norway; Denmark; or, the Baltic, round-trip from Southampton.

November 2004–April 2005, 14 nights, resumes Circle Caribbean cruises from Barbados. April 2005, 13 nights, Barbados–Southampton.

Oriana   **Home Port**   Southampton, others vary with itinerary

January–February, 15–16 nights, Circle South America, Barbados to Valparaiso; Valparaiso to Rio de Janeiro; Rio de Janeiro to Barbados. February, 15 nights, between Barbados and New Orleans.

March, 14 nights, transatlantic, Barbados to Southampton.

April and December, 22 nights, Caribbean, round-trip from Southampton.

May–November, 7–18 nights, Iberia; Adriatic; Mediterranean; Greece/Turkey; Black Sea; Canary Islands; or, Azores and Canaries, round-trip from Southampton.

June, 15 nights, Norway/Iceland, round-trip from Southampton.

December, 11 nights, New Year's cruise, Canary Islands and Madeira for the New Year's fireworks, round-trip from Southampton.

Peter Deilmann Cruises

Deutschland   **Home Port**   Kiel, others vary with itinerary

December 2003–April 2004, 13–27 night World Cruise segments: Barbados to San Diego; Panama to Honolulu;– San Diego to Wellington, New Zealand; Honolulu to Wellington; Wellington, New Zealand to Darwin, Australia; Darwin to Yokohama, Japan; Yokohama to Singapore; Singapore to Mumbai (Bombay), India; Mumbai to Piraeus (Athens).

April–May, 6–10 nights, Greek Isles/Turkey/Italy, round-trip from Piraeus or between Piraeus and Rome. May 15 nights, positions from Barcelona to Kiel.

May–September, 7–17 nights, Baltic, Norwegian Fjords/North Sea, Norwegian Fjords/Arctic Circle, Iceland/Greenland, British Isles, either round-trip from Kiel, Germany; Kiel to Cuxhaven, Germany; Cuxhaven to Reykjavik, Iceland; or, Reykjavik to Kiel.

September–October, 13 and 17 nights, Western Europe/transatlantic, Canada/New England, U.S. East Coast from either Cuxhaven to Halifax; Halifax to Montreal; Montreal to New York; or, New York to Montego Bay, Jamaica.

November–December, 13 and 14 nights, Eastern or Western Caribbean, Montego Bay to Santo Domingo or round-trip from Santo Domingo.

December, 15–18 nights, Panama Canal, Cape Horn, Brazil, transatlantic, from either Santo Domingo to Valparaiso; Valparaiso to Buenos Aires; Buenos Aires to Belem; or, Belem to Lisbon.

Princess Cruises

Caribbean Princess   **Home Port**   Ft. Lauderdale
From April 24, 2004, year-round, round-trip from Ft. Lauderdale, Saturdays, 7 nights, to St. Thomas, St. Maarten, Princess Cay. April to October, alternates with a Western itinerary calling at Grand Cayman, Ocho Rios (or Montego Bay), Cozumel, Princess Cay.

Coral Princess   **Home Ports**, Vancouver, Ft. Lauderdale
October–April, 10 nights, Panama Canal round-trip from Ft. Lauderdale to Cartagena, Colombia; Puerto Limon, Costa Rica; partial transit of the Canal, Grand Cayman, Cozumel. Belize City, Belize, replaces Cartagena, Colombia on October 2004–April 2005 sailings.

April and September, 15 nights, Panama Canal, positions between Ft. Lauderdale and Vancouver, available in segments.

May–September, Saturday, 7 nights, Alaska, between Vancouver and Whittier via Ketchikan, Juneau, Skagway, Glacier Bay, College Fjord.

Dawn Princess   **Home Ports**   San Juan, Vancouver, Ft. Lauderdale—others vary with itinerary
October–April, 7 nights, Southern Caribbean, round-trip from San Juan to either Barbados, St. Lucia, St. Maarten, Tortola, St. Thomas; or, St. Kitts, St. Thomas, Grenada, Caracas (La Guaira), Aruba

April and September, 2–15 nights, Panama Canal, Mexican Riviera and Pacific Coast. San Juan to Acapulco; Los Angeles to Ft. Lauderdale; Ft. Lauderdale to San Francisco. Acapulco to Los Angeles; Los Angeles to Vancouver; San Francisco to Vancouver.

May–September, Monday, 7 nights, Alaska between Vancouver and Whittier, via Ketchikan, Juneau, Skagway, Glacier Bay, College Fjord.

October 2004–April 2005, 10 nights, round-trip from Ft. Lauderdale, alternating Western/Southern Caribbean to either Curacao, Isla Margarita, Barbados, Dominica, St. Thomas, Princess Cay; or, Princess Cay, St. Thomas, St. Maarten, Ocho Rios, Grand Cayman, Cozumel.

Diamond Princess   **Home Ports**   Seattle, Los Angeles (Long Beach)
March–April and September 2004–April 2005, 7 nights, Mexican Riviera, round-trip from Los Angeles (Long Beach terminal) to Puerto Vallarta, Mazatlán, Cabo San Lucas.

May and September, 1–6 nights, Pacific Coast, between Los Angeles and Vancouver, or, Vancouver and Seattle.

May–September, Saturday, 7 nights, Alaska, round-trip from Seattle to Juneau, Skagway, Ketchikan, Tracy Arm, Sawyer Glaciers and Victoria.

Golden Princess   **Home Ports**   Ft. Lauderdale, San Juan
October 2003–May 2004, Saturday, 7 nights, Eastern Caribbean, round-trip from Ft. Lauderdale to St. Maarten, St. Thomas, Princess Cay.

From May 2, 2004, year-round, 7 nights, Southern Caribbean, round-trip from San Juan to either Barbados, St. Lucia, Antigua, St. Maarten, St. Thomas; or, St. Thomas, St. Kitts, Grenada, Caracas, Aruba.

Grand Princess   **Home Ports**   Ft. Lauderdale, Copenhagen, New York, Galveston

To May 2004, Sunday, 7 nights, round-trip from Ft. Lauderdale to Princess Cay, Grand Cayman, Majahual, Costa Maya, Cozumel.

May and August, 16 and 17 nights, transatlantic, Ft. Lauderdale–Copenhagen, or, Copenhagen–New York.

May–August, 10 nights, Baltic, round-trip from Copenhagen to Nynashamn, Helsinki, St Petersburg (two days), Tallinn, Gdansk, and either Oslo and a day at sea or Warnemunde/Berlin and an afternoon and overnight on board in Copenhagen.

September–October, 7 nights, Canada/New England, round-trip from New York City to Halifax (Nova Scotia), Saint John (New Brunswick), Bar Harbor (Maine), Boston, Newport (Rhode Island).

November 2004–April 2005, Saturday, 6 and 7 nights, round-trip from Galveston to Belize, Costa Maya, Grand Cayman, Cozumel.

Island Princess   **Home Port**   Ft. Lauderdale, Vancouver

To April, 2004, 10 nights, Panama Canal, round-trip from Ft. Lauderdale to Grand Cayman, Limon (for a full day Costa Rica), Cozumel and Cartagena, plus partial transit of the Panama Canal.

May and September, 2–14 nights, Panama Canal and Pacific Coast; Ft. Lauderdale to Los Angeles; Los Angeles to Vancouver or reverse.

May–September, Saturday, 7 nights, Alaska, between Vancouver and Whittier via Ketchikan, Juneau, Skagway, Glacier Bay, College Fjord.

September 2004–April 2005, 15 nights, Hawaii, round-trip from Los Angeles to Hilo, Kona, Honolulu, Nawiliwili, Lahaina.

Pacific Princess   **Home Port**   Sydney, others vary with itinerary

November–April, South Pacific cruises from Sydney for PandO Cruises Australia.

April–May and August–September, 12–24 nights, South Pacific, Sydney to Papeete; Papeete to Honolulu; Honolulu to Osaka; Honolulu to Papeete; or, Papeete to Ft. Lauderdale.

June–July, 12 and 16 nights, Asia, Osaka to Bangkok; Bangkok to Beijing; or, Beijing to Osaka.

September–October, 28 nights, transatlantic and trans–Indian Ocean, Ft. Lauderdale to Cape Town via St. Kitts, Dominica, Trinidad, Devil's Island, Fortaleza (Brazil), Dakar (Senegal), Ghana, Togo, Walvis Bay and Luderitz (Namibia); or, Cape Town to Sydney via East London and Durban (South Africa), Madagascar, Mauritius, and Fremantle, Adelaide, Melbourne, Tasmania (Australia).

Regal Princess **Home Ports** Ft. Lauderdale, Los Angeles, San Francisco, New York

November 2003–April 2004, 15 nights, Hawaii or Panama Canal, round-trip from Los Angeles to Hilo, Kona, Honolulu, Kauai, Lahaina; or, between Los Angeles and Ft. Lauderdale via Cabo San Lucas, Acapulco, Puntarenas, Cartagena, Aruba and Ocho Rios.

May–August, 10 nights, Alaska, round-trip from San Francisco to Victoria, Ketchikan or Sitka, Skagway or Haines, Juneau, and the Sawyer Glaciers in Tracy Arm.

August, 18 nights, San Francisco to New York via Cabo San Lucas, Acapulco, Huatulco, Cartagena, Aruba, St. Kitts, St. Thomas.

September–October, 10 nights, Canada/New England between New York and Montreal via Quebec City, Saguenay River, Halifax, St. John, Bar Harbor, Boston, Newport. October 31, 14 nights, Montreal–Ft. Lauderdale.

November 2004–April 2005, 15 nights, Panama Canal, between Ft. Lauderdale and Los Angeles or San Diego via Cabo San Lucas, Acapulco, Puntarenas, Cartagena, Aruba, and Ocho Rios. April 23, 2005, 15 nights, Ft. Lauderdale to San Francisco.

Royal Princess **Home Ports** Buenos Aires, Valparaiso, Southampton, others vary with itinerary

December 2003 and 2004, 24 nights, Antarctica, from Cape Town, South Africa to Santiago, Chile via the South Atlantic Islands and Antarctic Peninsula, Cape Horn and Chilean Inside Passage. January 2004, resumes 14-night Cape Horn cruises between Santiago and Buenos Aires.

January–February 2004 and 2005, 14 nights, Cape Horn/Strait of Magellan, between Buenos Aires and Valparaiso, via Puerto Montt, Seno Eyre Fjord, Punta Arenas, Beagle Channel, Ushuaia, Cape Horn, Falkland Islands, Puerto Madryn and Montevideo.

March 2004 and 2005, 12–17 nights, South America/Amazon, Ft. Lauderdale to Manaus; 12 nights, March 25, 2004 and April 9, 2005. Round-trip from Ft. Lauderdale, 16 nights, March 24, 2005, Orinoco River and Southern Caribbean.

April 2004 and 2005, 21 nights, transatlantic, Manaus, Brazil to Rome.

May–August, 12 nights, Western Europe, Iberia, British Isles, Norwegian Fjords, Iceland, round-trip from Southampton.

September–October, 30 nights, Middle East/Asia, Rome to Bangkok.

October–November, 16 and 30 nights, Asia and Africa, Bangkok to Beijing; Beijing to Bangkok; or, Bangkok to Cape Town.

December, resumes Antarctica and South America cruises.

Sapphire Princess   **Home Ports**   Seattle, San Francisco, others vary with itinerary

May–September, Sundays, 7 nights, Alaska, round-trip from Seattle to Juneau, Skagway, Ketchikan, Tracy Arm, Sawyer Glaciers, Victoria.

September–November, 10 nights, Mexican Riviera, round-trip from San Francisco to Catalina Island, San Diego, Puerto Vallarta, Mazatlán, Cabo San Lucas.

November 2004–March 2005, 12–30 nights, South Pacific, Los Angeles to Sydney; between Sydney and Auckland, via Melbourne, Tasmania, Fjordland (Milford and Dusky Sounds), Dunedin, Christchurch, Wellington plus Tauranga and Bay of Islands on December 23 sailing; Sydney to Bangkok.

March–April, 2005, 12–19 nights, Asia/Alaska, Bangkok to Beijing; Beijing to Osaka; Osaka to Seattle.

Star Princess   **Home Ports**   Ft. Lauderdale, others vary with itinerary

December 2003–February 2004, 12–14 nights, Australia/New Zealand between Sydney and Auckland. February 14, 18 nights, Sydney to Bangkok via Great Barrier Reef.

March 3, 2004, 30 nights, Bangkok to Venice via Southeast Asia, India, Suez and Turkey.

May–September, 12 nights, Mediterranean, between Barcelona and Venice, via Cannes or Monte Carlo, Livorno (for Florence and Pisa), Naples, Athens, Kusadasi and Istanbul with overnight on board in both Barcelona and Venice eastbound, overnight on board in Venice westbound; or, between Venice and Rome; Venice and Barcelona; or, Barcelona to Rome.

October, 16 nights, transatlantic, Venice to Ft. Lauderdale.

October 2004 to April, 2005, Sunday, 7 nights, Eastern/Western Caribbean, round-trip from Ft. Lauderdale to either San Juan, St. Thomas, Tortola Princess Cay; or, Princess Cay, Grand Cayman, Ocho Rios, Cozumel.

Sun Princess   **Home Ports**   Ft. Lauderdale, Vancouver

October 2003–April 2004, 10 nights, Eastern/Southern Caribbean, to either St. Vincent, Antigua, Barbados, St. Maarten, St. Thomas and Princess Cay; or, Curacao, Isla Margarita, Barbados, Dominica, St. Thomas, Princess Cays.

April and September, 15 nights, Panama Canal positioning, Ft. Lauderdale to San Francisco; San Francisco to Ft. Lauderdale; Ft. Lauderdale to Los Angeles.

May–September, Monday, 7 nights, between Vancouver and Whittier via Skagway, Juneau and Ketchikan, plus cruising College Fjord, the Inside Passage and Glacier Bay National Park.

October 2004–April 2005, 10 nights, Eastern/Southern Caribbean, round-trip from Ft. Lauderdale to either St. Vincent, Grenada, St. Lucia, Martinique, St. Thomas and Princess Cay; or, Princess Cay, St. Thomas, St. Maarten, St. Kitts, Barbados and Antigua.

April–May 2005, 15 nights, Panama Canal positioning, Ft. Lauderdale to Los Angeles.

Tahitian Princess **Home Port** Papeete

Year-round, 10 nights, Polynesia, round-trip from Papeete: Polynesia/Cook Islands to Bora Bora (overnight on board), Moorea, Huahine, Raiatea, Rarotonga plus scenic cruising of Tahaa and overnight on board in Papeete; or, Polynesia/Marquesas to Moorea, Nuku Hiva, Hiva Oa, Rangiroa, Raiatea, Bora Bora, plus scenic cruising of Tahaa and the Tuamotu Atolls and overnight on board in Papeete.

April 12, 2005, 12 nights, Papeete to Honolulu, via Moorea; Bora Bora; Christmas Island; Hilo, Hawaii; Lahaina, Maui; Nawiliwili, Kauai.

Radisson Seven Seas Cruises

Paul Gauguin **Home Port** Papeete

Year-round, Saturday, 7 nights, French Polynesia from Papeete, Tahiti to Raiatea, Tahaa (Motu Mahana), Bora Bora and Moorea with an overnight onboard ship in Bora Bora, Moorea and Papeete.

November, 14 nights, Society Islands/Marquesas.

Radisson Diamond **Home Ports** San Juan, others vary with itinerary

January–April, 4–7 nights, Caribbean round-trip from San Juan.

April and November, 9 and 33 nights, transatlantic San Juan to Madeira or reverse; or, Istanbul to San Juan.

May–October, 7 nights, Greek Isles, Eastern or Western Mediterranean, from either Madeira, Barcelona, Monte Carlo, Rome, Venice, Athens or Istanbul. October 4, 2004, 10 nights, Rome to Madeira.

November–December, 3–10 nights, Caribbean, round-trip from Ft. Lauderdale or San Juan; or, from San Juan to Ft. Lauderdale.

Seven Seas Mariner **Home Ports** Vancouver, Seward others vary with itinerary

January–February, 12, 16, 19, 59 nights, Circle South America in segments: Ft. Lauderdale to Lima; Lima to Buenos Aires; Buenos Aires to Manaus; or, Manaus to Ft. Lauderdale.

February–May, November–December, 7, 10 and 14 nights, Panama Canal, Mexican Riviera, between Ft. Lauderdale and Los Angeles or round-trip from Los Angeles.

April and December, 3–7 nights, Caribbean, round-trip from Ft. Lauderdale or San Juan.

May–September, Wednesday, 7 nights, Alaska, between Vancouver and Seward. Positions Los Angeles to Vancouver, seven nights, May 19, 2004 calling at Port Hueneme, San Francisco, Astoria, Seattle, Victoria.

September–October, 11–15 nights, Japan/China, Seward to Tokyo, Tokyo to Hong Kong; Tokyo to Los Angeles.

December, 12 nights, South America, Ft. Lauderdale to Callao.

Seven Seas Navigator   **Home Ports**   New York, Norfolk, Ft. Lauderdale, San Juan others vary with itinerary

January–April, 5–11 nights, Caribbean, round-trip from Ft. Lauderdale; round-trip from San Juan; or, between Ft. Lauderdale and San Juan

April, 5–9 nights, Caribbean, Bermuda, round-trip from Ft. Lauderdale. April 28, 2004, 7 nights, Freeport to New York,

May–September, 7 nights, Bermuda, round-trip from New York or Norfolk.

June, September–October, 7 and 9 nights, Canada/New England, between New York and Montreal. October 24, 2004, 7 nights, New York to San Juan.

October–December, 7–10 nights, Caribbean, from San Juan, Tampa, West Palm Beach or Ft. Lauderdale.

Seven Seas Voyager   **Home Port**   Varies with itinerary

January–April, 94 nights, Circle Pacific, round-trip from Los Angeles, available in segments: Los Angeles to Sydney, 22 nights; Sydney to Perth, 20 nights; Perth to Hong Kong, 18 nights; or, Tokyo to Los Angeles, 16 nights.

April and November, 8, 9, 14 nights, Panama Canal and transatlantic, Los Angles to Ft. Lauderdale; Ft. Lauderdale to Madeira; Tenerife to Ft. Lauderdale.

May, September–November, 7–11 nights, Mediterranean from Monte Carlo, Barcelona, Istanbul.

June and September, 10–11 nights, Western Europe/British Isles, Monte Carlo to Dover; Dover to Copenhagen via British Isles; Rouen to Monte Carlo.

July–August, 7 nights, Baltic, Norwegian Fjords, round-trip from Copenhagen or between Stockholm and Copenhagen. August 27, 2004, 11 nights, Stockholm to Rouen.

December, 5–11 nights, Caribbean, round-trip from Ft. Lauderdale or between Ft. Lauderdale and San Juan.

Royal Caribbean International

Adventure of the Seas   **Home Port**   San Juan

Year-round, Sunday, 7 nights, Southern Caribbean round-trip from San Juan to Aruba, Curaçao, St. Maarten, St. Thomas. May to October, alternate Sundays, cruises to St. Thomas, Antigua, St. Lucia, Barbados.

Brilliance of the Seas   **Home Ports**   Miami, Barcelona

To April, 10 and 11 nights, Southern/Western Caribbean, round-trip from Miami to Grand Cayman, Aruba, Panama Canal and Puerto Limon, Costa Rica (10 nights) and to Key West, Cozumel, Grand Cayman, Ocho Rios, Aruba and Curacao (11 nights).

April and October, transatlantic between Miami and Barcelona.

May–October, 12 nights, round-trip from Barcelona, to either Villefranche (Nice/Monte Carlo); Livorno (Florence/Pisa); Naples; Venice; Dubrovnik; Corfu; Rome; or, Villefranche; Livorno (Florence/Pisa); Rome; Santorini; Kusadasi (Ephesus); Mykonos; Naples.

November 2004–April 2005, 10 and 11 nights, Southern/Eastern Caribbean, round-trip from Miami to Grand Cayman, Aruba, Panama Canal and Puerto Limon, Costa Rica (10 nights) or San Juan, St. Thomas, St. John, St. Lucia, St. Maarten, Labadee (11 nights).

Enchantment of the Seas   **Home Port**   Ft. Lauderdale

Year-round, 4 and 5 nights, Western Caribbean, round-trip from Ft. Lauderdale, 4 nights, alternating Thursdays to Key West, Cozumel; 5 nights, alternating Mondays to Belize City, Cozumel, Key West; 5 nights, alternate Saturdays to Ocho Rios, Grand Cayman.

Explorer of the Seas   **Home Port**   Miami

Year-round, Saturday, 7 nights, alternating Eastern and Western Caribbean from Miami to San Juan, St. Maarten, St. Thomas, Nassau (Eastern); or, Labadee (RCI's private resort), Ocho Rios, Grand Cayman, Cozumel (Western to May 2, 2004); or, Belize City, Costa Maya, Cozumel, Grand Cayman (Western from May 9, 2004).

Grandeur of the Seas   **Home Ports**   New Orleans, Baltimore

To April, Saturday, 7 nights, Western Caribbean, round-trip from New Orleans to Progreso, Cozumel, and either Key West or Grand Cayman.

May, September–October, 10 and 11 nights, round-trip from Baltimore to either Baltimore, Key West, Cozumel, Belize, Coco Cay, Freeport (10 nights); or, Port Canaveral, Coco Cay, St. Thomas, St. Maarten, San Juan, Freeport (11 nights). September 13, October 4, 11 nights, Canada/New England, to Bar Harbor, Halifax, Sydney, Quebec City, Saguenay River, Portland.

June–September, 7 nights, Bahamas, round-trip from Baltimore to Freeport, Key West, Coco Cay, Port Canaveral; or, Port Canaveral, Nassau, Freeport.

November 2004–May 2005, 7 nights, Western Caribbean, round-trip from New Orleans to Cozumel, Grand Cayman and either Costa Maya or Key West.

Jewel of the Seas **Home Ports** Harwich, Boston, Ft. Lauderdale

May–August, 12 nights, Baltic, round-trip from Harwich to Oslo, Copenhagen, Stockholm, Helsinki, Stockholm St. Petersburg (two days), Tallinn. June 21, 2004 to Paris, Plymouth, Cork, Dublin, Glasgow, Norwegian Fjords, Bergen, Flam, Geiranger, Hellesylt, Amsterdam.

September, 10 nights, transatlantic, Harwich to Boston.

September–October, 10 nights, Canada/New England, round-trip from Boston to Bar Harbor, Halifax, Sydney, Quebec City, Saguenay River St. John, Portland. 7-night sailing, September 11, does not call at Quebec City or the Saguenay River.

November 2004–April 2005, 6 and 8 nights, Eastern/Western Caribbean round-trip from Ft. Lauderdale to either San Juan, St. Maarten, Antigua, St. Thomas, Nassau; or, Key West, Cozumel, Costa Maya, Grand Cayman.

Legend of the Seas **Home Ports** San Diego, Miami, Honolulu, Ensenada

January–February, 14 nights, Panama Canal, between San Diego and Miami, via Cabo San Lucas and Acapulco Mexico; Puntarenas/Caldera, Costa Rica; Cristobal Pier or Fuerte Amador, Panama; and Aruba. Alternates with Hawaii itinerary below.

To May, 10 and 11 nights, Hawaii between Honolulu and Ensenada via Hilo and Kailua Kona, Hawaii; Nawiliwili, Kauai; and overnight in Lahaina, Maui. Overnight in Honolulu on 11-night cruises; alternates with Panama Canal itinerary above, January–February.

May–September, Sunday, 7 nights, Mexican Riviera, round-trip from San Diego to Cabo San Lucas, Mazatlán, Puerto Vallarta.

October 2004–April 2005, resumes alternating Panama Canal/Hawaii cruises.

Majesty of the Seas **Home Port** Miami

Year-round, Bahamas from Miami, 3 nights on Fridays to Nassau, and Coco Cay (RCI private Bahamian island); 4 nights on Mondays adds Key West.

Mariner of the Seas **Home Port** Port Canaveral

Year-round, Sunday, 7 nights, Eastern/Western Caribbean, round-trip from Port Canaveral, to either Nassau, St. Thomas, St. Maarten; or, Labadee, Ocho Rios, Grand Cayman, Cozumel.

Monarch of the Seas **Home Port** Los Angeles

Year-round, 3 and 4 nights, Mexican Riviera, round-trip from Los Angeles, 3 nights, Fridays to Ensenada; 4 nights, Mondays, to Ensenada, San Diego, Catalina Island.

Nordic Empress **Home Ports** Tampa, New York, San Juan

To April, 7 nights, Western Caribbean, round-trip from Tampa to Grand Cayman, Belize City, Cozumel.

May–October, Sunday, 6 and 8 nights, Bermuda, round-trip from New York to Bermuda, King's Wharf and Hamilton (6 nights); St. George Island, Kings Wharf, Hamilton (8 nights).

October 2004–April 2005, 3 and 4 nights, Eastern Caribbean, round-trip from San Juan to St. Thomas, St. Maarten (3 nights); or, Santo Domingo and Catalina Island 4 nights).

Navigator of the Seas **Home Port** Miami

Year-round, Saturday, 7 nights, alternating Eastern and Western Caribbean, round-trip from Miami to either Nassau, St. Thomas, San Juan, Labadee (Eastern); or Labadee, Ocho Rios, Grand Cayman, Cozumel (Western to October 31, 2004); or, San Juan, St. Thomas, St. Maarten, Nassau (Western from November 6, 2004).

Radiance of the Seas **Home Ports** Ft. Lauderdale, Vancouver, Miami, others vary with itinerary.

To April, Sunday, 7 nights, round-trip from San Juan to Key West, Cozumel, Costa Maya, Grand Cayman or San Juan, St. Maarten, St. Thomas, Nassau; or, Key West, Cozumel, Costa Maya, Grand Cayman

April and October, 14 and 15 nights, Panama Canal, Ft. Lauderdale to San Diego; or, San Diego–Miami.

May–September, 7 nights, Alaska Inside Passage, round-trip from Vancouver to Juneau, Skagway, Hubbard Glacier, Ketchikan.

October 2004–April 2005, Sunday, 7 nights, round-trip from Miami to either, Coco Cay, St. Thomas, St. Maarten; or, Labadee, Ocho Rios, Grand Cayman, Cozumel.

Rhapsody of the Seas **Home Port** Galveston

Year-round, 7 nights, round-trip Galveston, to Key West, Grand Cayman, Cozumel.

Serenade of the Seas **Home Ports** San Juan, Vancouver

To April and October 2004–April 2005, Sunday, 7 nights, Southern Caribbean, round-trip from San Juan to St. Thomas, St. Maarten, Antigua, St. Lucia, Barbados.

April and October, 14 and 12 nights, Panama Canal, San Juan–San Diego and reverse.

May and September, 10, 11, 12 nights, Hawaii, between Ensenada and Honolulu or between Honolulu and Vancouver via Nawiliwili, Kauai; Lahaina, Maui (overnight); Kailua Kona and Hilo, Hawaii. Overnight in Honolulu on some sailings.

May–September, Sunday, 7 nights, Alaska, round-trip from Vancouver to Juneau, Skagway, Hubbard Glacier (cruising), Ketchikan and Misty Fjords.

Sovereign of the Seas **Home Port** Port Canaveral
Year-round, 3–4 nights, Bahamas from Port Canaveral to Nassau and Coco Cay on Thursdays and Sundays.

Splendour of the Seas **Home Ports** Galveston, Barcelona, Tampa
To April, 10–11 nights, Western Caribbean or Panama Canal round-trip from Galveston to either Progreso, Cozumel, Grand Cayman, Belize, Key West (10 nights); or, Puerto Limon, Panama Canal, Cartagena, Grand Cayman (11 nights).

May and October, 14 nights, transatlantic, Galveston to Barcelona; Barcelona to Tampa.

May–October, 7 nights, Saturday, Mediterranean, round-trip from Barcelona to Villefranche (Monte Carlo/Nice), Livorno (Florence/Pisa), Rome, Naples, Malta.

November 2004–April 2005, Sunday, 7 nights, Western Caribbean, round-trip from Tampa to Grand Cayman, Costa Maya, Belize, Cozumel.

Vision of the Seas **Home Ports** Los Angeles, San Diego, Vancouver, Seward
To April and October 2004–April 2005, 7 nights, Mexico, round-trip from Los Angeles and San Diego (May) to Cabo San Lucas, Mazatlán, Puerto Vallarta.

May–September, Friday, 7 nights, Alaska, between Vancouver and Seward, via Ketchikan, Skagway, Juneau, Icy Strait, Hubbard Glacier plus Misty Fjords on the southbound. 5 nights, San Diego to Vancouver, May 23, 2004 via San Francisco and Victoria.

September–October, 11 and 12 nights, Hawaii, Vancouver to Honolulu or, Honolulu to Ensenada, via Nawiliwili, Kauai; Lahaina, Maui (overnight); Kailua Kona and Hilo, Hawaii.

Voyager of the Seas **Home Ports** Miami, New York
To April, Sunday, 7 nights, Western Caribbean, round-trip from Miami to either Labadee, Ocho Rios, Grand Cayman, Cozumel; or, Costa Maya, Grand Cayman, Cozumel, Belize.

May–October, 9 and 5 nights, Caribbean or Canada, round-trip from New York to either Labadee, Ocho Rios, Grand Cayman and Freeport (9 nights); or, to St. John NB, Halifax NS (5 nights).

November 2004–April 2005, Saturday, 7 nights, Western Caribbean, round-trip from Miami to either Labadee, Ocho Rios, Grand Cayman, Cozumel; or, Nassau, St. Thomas, San Juan, Labadee.

Royal Olympia Cruises

Odysseus **Home Ports** Piraeus, others vary with itinerary

December 2003–March 2004, 10–24 nights, transatlantic, South America, Nice to Buenos Aires; between Buenos Aires and Valparaiso; Buenos Aires to Las Palmas; Las Palmas to Nice.

April–November, Saturday, 7 nights, Mediterranean, round-trip from Genoa to Marseilles, Ibiza, Motril, Malaga, Tangier, Gibraltar, Barcelona.

April and October, 14 nights, Mediterranean, Nice to Genoa or round-trip from Genoa to either Rome, Greece, Turkey; or, Spain, Portugal, Madeira, Morocco; or, Tunisia, Libya, Elba, Corsica, Sicily; or, Egypt, Crete, Lebanon, Greece.

Olympia Countess **Home Ports** Piraeus, Cape Town, Durban

April 2004, 22 nights, Africa/Suez Canal, Durban, South Africa to Athens via Indian Ocean Islands, East Africa, Egypt.

May–November, 3–4 nights, Greek Islands and Ephesus, round-trip from Piraeus, Friday, 3 nights to Mykonos, Rhodes, Patmos, Kusadasi; Monday, 4 nights same ports plus Crete and Santorini.

Olympia Explorer **Home Port** Venice, Los Angeles, others vary with itinerary

January, 14 nights, Hawaii, round-trip from Los Angeles or San Francisco. February–March, 11–20 nights, Circle South America from San Francisco to Los Angeles via Mexico, Costa Rica, Panama, Ecuador, Peru, Patagonia, Cape Horn, South Shetlands, Antarctica, Falkland Islands, Amazon River, Orinoco River with two days in Callao Peru; Ushuaia, Argentina; Rio de Janeiro and three days in Buenos Aires. Available in 11 to 20-day segments from San Francisco, Callao, Peru; Ushuaia, Argentina; Buenos Aires, Argentina.

April, 20 nights, transatlantic, Ft. Lauderdale to Venice.

May–November, Sunday, 7 nights, Adriatic and Aegean, round-trip from Venice to Dubrovnik, Katakolon, Istanbul, Mykonos, Santorini, Athens, Corfu.

Olympia Voyager **Home Ports** Piraeus, Ft. Lauderdale, Genoa, others vary with itinerary

January, 17 nights, Amazon and Orinoco Rivers, round-trip from Ft. Lauderdale.

January–March, 7 nights, Western Caribbean, round-trip from Ft. Lauderdale; 11 nights, transcanal, Ft. Lauderdale to Los Angeles;

16 nights, Panama Canal, San Francisco to Ft. Lauderdale.

February–March, 14 nights, Hawaii, round-trip from Los Angeles or San Francisco.

April, 21 nights, transatlantic, Ft. Lauderdale to Genoa.

May–November, 7 nights, Mediterranean, round-trip from Genoa to Nice, Rome, Messina, Santorini, Mykonos, Kusadasi, Patmos, Athens. Can be taken round-trip from Nice or Rome.

Stella Oceanis **Home Port** Venice

Summer 2004, 14 nights, Mediterranean and Black Sea, round-trip from Venice to either the Black Sea; Greece/Turkey; or, Croatia, Corfu, Greece, Malta, Sicily.

Stella Solaris **Home Port** Varies with itinerary

Summer 2004 t.b.a.

November–May, 12–15 nights, World Cruise segments, Piraeus to Ft. Lauderdale; Ft. Lauderdale to Los Angeles; Los Angeles to Papeete; Papeete to Sydney; Sydney to Yokohama; Yokohama to Singapore; Singapore to Cape Town; Cape Town to Rio de Janeiro; Rio de Janeiro to New York; New York to Amsterdam.

Triton **Home Ports** Piraeus, Amsterdam

May–September, 10–11 nights, Baltic or Norwegian Fjords, round-trip from Amsterdam to either Kiel Canal, Gdansk, St. Petersburg, Helsinki, Stockholm, Copenhagen, Dover; or, Cuxhaven, Bergen, Hellesylt, Geiranger, Trondheim, Olden, Flam, Gudvangen, Stavanger, Dover.

May and September, 10 and 14 nights, Western Europe or British Isles, Nice to Dover; Dover to Amsterdam via British Isles; or, Amsterdam to Piraeus.

October, 7 nights, Aegean, Egypt/Turkey or Black Sea, round-trip from Piraeus.

World Renaissance **Home Port** Piraeus

April–October, Friday, 7 nights, Greek Isles/Turkey round-trip from Piraeus to Istanbul, Mykonos, Patmos, Kusadasi, Rhodes, Heraklion, Santorini.

Seabourn Cruise Line

Seabourn Legend **Home Ports** Ft. Lauderdale, Nice, Rome, Barcelona

January–February 2004 and 2005 14 nights, Panama Canal/Costa Rica from Ft. Lauderdale to Puerto Caldera, Costa Rica or reverse via Belize City, Hunting Caye, Belize; Roatan, Honduras; Puerto Limon, Costa Rica; Panama Canal; Gamboa, Fuerte Amador, Panama; Playa Flamingo and Puerto Quepos, Costa Rica.

March 2004 and 2005, 7 nights, Caribbean, Ft. Lauderdale to St. Thomas; round-trip from St. Thomas; or, round-trip from Ft. Lauderdale.

March and November, 11 nights, Transatlantic, St Thomas to Lisbon; or, Santa Cruz de Tenerife to Ft. Lauderdale.

April and October, 7–14 nights, Iberia, Morocco, Canary Islands, round-trip from Lisbon; Lisbon to Barcelona; Barcelona to Malaga; or, Malaga to Santa Cruz de Tenerife.

April–October, 7 and 14 nights, French and Italian Rivieras between Barcelona and Nice or Nice and Rome.

November, resumes Costa Rica/Panama Canal cruises.

Seabourn Pride **Home Port** London, others vary with itinerary

January–February 2004 and 2005, 7–18 nights, South America/Amazon, Ft. Lauderdale to Valparaiso; Valparaiso to Buenos Aires; Buenos Aires to Rio de Janeiro; Rio de Janeiro to Manaus; or, Manaus to Ft Lauderdale.

February–March, 2004 and 2005, 7 nights, Caribbean, between Ft. Lauderdale and St. Thomas; or, round-trip from St. Thomas.

March and August, 12 and 18 nights, transatlantic, Ft. Lauderdale to Lisbon; or, London to New York.

March–May, 11–16 nights, Iberia/Canary Islands/Mediterranean, round-trip from Lisbon; Lisbon to Barcelona; Lisbon to Barcelona; Barcelona to Istanbul; Barcelona to Athens; Athens to Lisbon; or, Istanbul to Lisbon.

May–August, 11 and 14 nights, Western Europe/British Isles/Baltic/Scandinavia, alternating itineraries round-trip from London.

September–October, 3–18 nights, Canada/New England/Colonial USA, New York to Quebec City; Quebec City to New York; round-trip from New York; or, New York to Nassau.

November–December, 7 and 14 nights, Caribbean and Orinoco River, Ft. Lauderdale to Barbados; round-trip from Barbados; Barbados to Ft. Lauderdale; or, round-trip Ft. Lauderdale.

Seabourn Spirit **Home Port** Varies with itinerary

January–April, 11–24 nights, Southeast Asia/South Pacific/India/Middle East, Singapore to Cairns; Cairns to Lyttelton, New Zealand or reverse; Lyttelton to Lautoka, Fiji or reverse; Cairns to Hong Kong; Hong Kong to Singapore; Singapore to Mumbai; or, Mumbai to Alexandria.

April–November, 7 nights, Eastern Mediterranean/Greek Isles/ Adriatic, from Alexandria, Istanbul, Venice, Rome, or Athens. 12-night cruise Istanbul to Alexandria, November 9.

November–December, 22 nights, Africa, Alexandria to Mombasa with post cruise safari; Mombasa to Singapore with pre–cruise safari.

December, 12 and 14 nights, Southeast Asia, round-trip from Singapore; or, Singapore to Hong Kong.

January–March, 2005, 14 nights, Southeast Asia, round-trip from Singapore; or, between Singapore and Hong Kong.

SeaDream Yacht Club

SeaDream I **Home Ports** San Juan, St. Thomas, others vary with itinerary

December–April, 7 nights, Eastern Caribbean, round-trip from St. Thomas. March, 4–5 nights, round-trip from San Juan. March and April, 7 nights, between San Juan and St. Thomas. April, 13 nights, transatlantic, San Juan to Malaga.

May, 4–7 nights, Mediterranean, Malaga to Monte Carlo; Monte Carlo to Nice; round-trip from Nice or Monte Carlo; or, Monte Carlo to Rome.

June–October, 7 nights, Mediterranean, from Rome, Monte Carlo, Venice, Athens, Istanbul, or Nauplion. October 26, 12 nights, transatlantic, Lisbon to San Juan.

November 2004–January 2005, 5 and 7 nights, Caribbean, from San Juan or St. Thomas.

SeaDream II **Home Ports** St. Thomas, San Juan, Antigua, others vary with itinerary

December–April, 7 nights, Southern/Eastern Caribbean, round-trip from Barbados, St. Thomas, San Juan, Antigua or positioning between these ports.

May–November, 7 nights, French and Italian Rivieras, between Rome and Monte Carlo; or, round-trip from Rome or Monte Carlo. May, 5 nights, round-trip from Nice; or, Nice to Monte Carlo.

December 2004–January 2005, 7 nights, Caribbean from St. Thomas.

Silversea Cruises

Silver Cloud **Home Port** Varies with itinerary

Winter 2003–2004, out of service

April–May and September–October, 6–15 nights, from Monte Carlo, Barcelona, Lisbon, (spring) and Malaga, Barcelona, Monte Carlo, Venice, Rome, Athens (fall).

May and August, 7–15 nights, Western Europe and Great Britain from Honfleur, Monte Carlo, Southampton, or, round-trip from Southampton.

June–July, 7 nights, Baltic between Copenhagen and Stockholm via St. Petersburg, Tallinn and Helsinki. August 15, 2004, 10 nights, Baltic and Holland from Copenhagen–London (Tower Bridge). June 21, 2004, 17 nights, North Cape and Arctic Russia, round-trip from Copenhagen.

October–December, 4–16 nights, Middle East/Asia/Australia from Athens, Port Said, Dubai, Mumbai, Singapore, Hong Kong, Ho Chi Minh City, or, Sydney.

Silver Shadow **Home Port** Varies with itinerary

January–February, 9–16 nights, Australia/New Zealand, from Singapore, Sydney, Auckland, or, Cairns.

March–May, 6–16 nights, Southeast Asia/China/Japan from Bangkok, Singapore, Beijing, Kobe, or, Tokyo.

May–September, 7–12 nights, Alaska from Tokyo, Anchorage, Vancouver, Seattle, or, San Francisco.

September–December, 7–15 nights, Pacific Coast, Mexican Riviera, Peru, or Panama Canal from San Francisco, San Diego, Puerto Caldera, or, Barbados.

Silver Whisper **Home Port** Varies with itinerary

January–March, 7–16 nights, South America, from Colon, Valparaiso, Ushuaia, Buenos Aires, or, Punta Arenas.

January and October–December, 7–14 nights, Caribbean from Ft. Lauderdale, New Orleans, Colon, or, Aruba.

April and September, 8–16 nights, transatlantic crossings, Barbados to Barcelona; London to New York available in segments London to Reykjavik and Reykjavik to New York.

May–August, 6–12 nights, Mediterranean, from Barcelona, Monte Carlo, Rome, Athens, Istanbul, or, Venice.

September–October, 8–12 nights, Canada/New England from Montreal or New York.

October–December, 7–14 nights, Caribbean, from Ft. Lauderdale, Colon, or, Aruba.

Silver Wind **Home Port** Varies with itinerary

January–April, 7–14 nights, Caribbean, Panama Canal, Mexican Riviera from Rio de Janeiro, Barbados, Ft. Lauderdale, Puerto Caldera, San Diego, or, New Orleans.

April and October, 12 and 14 nights, transatlantic, Barbados to Las Palmas and Barcelona to Barbados.

April–October, 6–12 nights, Mediterranean from Barbados, Lisbon, Barcelona, Rome, Monte Carlo, Athens, Venice, Istanbul, or, Nice.

November–December, 7–16 nights, Amazon/Brazil; or, Cape Horn; from Barbados, Manaus, Rio de Janeiro, Buenos Aires Ushuaia, or, Valparaiso.

Star Clippers, Inc.

Note: All ports may not be included on every Star Clipper cruise, as itineraries are subject to weather conditions and alterations by the captain, in search of calm sailing and best anchorage .

Royal Clipper **Home Ports** Barbados, Rome

November–April, Saturday, 7 nights, Southern Caribbean alternating Windward and Grenadine Islands, round-trip from Barbados to either St. Lucia, Iles des Saintes, Antigua, St. Kitts, Dominica, Martinique; or, Grenadines, Grenada, Tobago Cays, St. Vincent; St. Lucia, Martinique.

April, October, 21 nights, transatlantic, between Barbados and Rome available in segments.

May–July, 7 nights, Western Mediterranean, alternating cruises round-trip from Rome to either Sicily; Malta; Panarea and Venotere, Italy; or, Ponza, Sorrento, Lipari and Stromboli, Italy and Sicily.

July–September, 10 and 11 nights, Mediterranean, alternating cruises between Rome and Venice calling at Capri, Lipari, Taormina, Corfu and Dubrovnik, Korcula, Hvar, and Pula, Croatia (11 nights) or Pula, Losinj, Hvar, Korcula, and Dubrovnik, Croatia; Taormina, Lipari, and Sorrento (10 nights).

Star Clipper   **Home Ports**   St. Maarten, Cannes

November–April, Sunday, 7 nights, Caribbean, round-trip from St. Maarten, to either St. Barts, Nevis, Guadeloupe, Dominica, Iles des Saintes, Antigua; or, Anguilla, Virgin Gorda, Norman Island, Jost van Dyke, St. Kitts, St. Barts. April and October, 26 and 29 nights, transatlantic, Antigua to Cannes, Cannes to St. Maarten available in segments.

May–October, Saturday, 7 nights, Western Mediterranean, alternating cruises round-trip from Cannes to either Corsica; Elba; Portovenere and Portofino, Italy; Monte Carlo; or, Porquerolles, France; Sardinia; Corsica; St. Tropez.

Star Flyer   **Home Ports**   Phuket, Athens

November–March, Saturday, 7 nights, Far East, alternating southern and northern routes, round-trip from Phuket or between Phuket and Singapore: Round-trip from Phuket to either Batong Group, Ko Lipe, Ko Khai, Phang Nga/Ko Hong, Similian Islands, Thailand and Penang, Malaysia; or Surin Islands, Similian Islands, Ko Kradan, Phi Phi Islands, Ko Khai Nok Thailand and

Langkawi, Malaysia. Between Singapore and Phuket calling at either Similian Islands, Phang Nga/Ko Dan Hok, Ko Adang, Thailand; Penang and Malacca, Malaysia; or Malacca and Langkawi, Malaysia; Ko Lipe and Ko Khai Nok, Thailand.

March and October, 37 nights, positioning cruises between Athens and Phuket.

May–October, Saturday, 7 nights, Eastern Mediterranean, alternating cruises, round-trip from Athens to either Kusadasi, Turkey; Pythagoria, Samos, Patmos, Delos, Mykonos, Sifnos, Greece; or, Rhodes, Santorini, Hydra, Greece; Bodrum, and Dalyan, Turkey; or, 7 nights, between Athens and Istanbul, May 29, June 5, September 18 and 25, 2004 via Delos, Mykonos, Patmos, Bodrum, Kusadasi, Dikili.

Star Cruises

MegaStar Aries (chartered)

MegaStar Taurus (chartered)

Star Pisces **Home Port** Hong Kong
  Year-round, 1 night to nowhere from Hong Kong catering to gamblers
and first–time cruisers. Subject to change.

SuperStar Aries **Home Port** t.b.a.

SuperStar Capricorn **Home Port** Pyongtaek (Korea)
  Year-round, 2, 5, 7, nights, China/Japan, round-trip from Pyongtaek,
Korea to Kagoshima and Nagasaki, Japan (5 nights Sunday); or, to
Dalian, China (2 nights Friday); or combine for 7-night cruise. Subject
to change

SuperStar Gemini **Home Port** Keelung
  Year-round, 1–3 nights, West Pacific Cruises, round-trip from
Keelung, Taiwan to Yonaguni Island, Japan (1 nights); or, to Miyako,
Japan (2 nights); or, cruising Yonaguni Island (2 nights); or, to Naka-
gusuku and Motobu, Japan (3 nights); or, to Naha, Okinawa (3 nights).
Subject to change.

SuperStar Leo **Home Port** Hong Kong
  Year-round, 2, 3, 5, or 7 nights, China/Vietnam, round-trip from
Hong Kong to Sanya, Hainan Island; Halong Bay, Vietnam (3 nights);
round-trip from Hong Kong to Xiamen (2 nights). Combine for a 5-
night cruise. An exclusive arrangement secured by Star Cruises will
enable Chinese nationals to cruise with only border pass from Hainan
Island to Halong Bay, thereby reducing the need to apply for a visa. Special 7-night sailings with 3 days in Shanghai are offered several times a
year. Subject to change.

SuperStar Virgo **Home Port** Singapore
  Year-round, 2, 3, or 5 nights, Malaysia/Thailand/Myanmar, round-
trip from Singapore to Langkawi Island, Phuket (3 nights); or, to
Malacca, Port Klang (Kuala Lumpur) (2 nights); combine for a 5-night
cruise. Round-trip from Singapore to Port Klang, Penang, Malacca (5
nights); or, Bangkok, Ko Samui (5 nights); or, to Phuket, Yangon (Myanmar), Penang (7 nights). Subject to change.

Swan Hellenic Cruises

Minerva II **Home Port** Varies with itinerary
  January–February, 14, 15, and 20 nights, Panama Canal and Circle
South America, from New Orleans to Panama City or Lima; Panama

City to Valparaiso; Valparaiso to Buenos Aires; Buenos Aires to Manaus; Manaus to Cartagena; or, Cartagena to Nassau.

March–April, 14 and 15 nights, Colonial America and transatlantic, Nassau to New York; or, New York to Cadiz.

May–June, September–October, 8 and 15 nights, Mediterranean and Black Sea, various itineraries from Cadiz, Athens, Istanbul, Venice, or, Naples.

July–September, 10– 15 nights, Western Europe, Britain, Norwegian Fjords, North Cape, Baltic, from Barcelona, London, Dover, or Copenhagen.

October 2004–January 2005, 15–17 nights, Suez Canal, Africa, Indian Ocean, Asia from Athens, Safaga, Mombasa, Mauritius, Cape Town, Seychelles, or, Singapore.

Travel Dynamics International

Callisto **Home Port** Varies with itinerary

March–November, 10 and 11 nights, Eastern Mediterranean on various itineraries including Circumnavigation of Crete; Greek Isles from Athens to Lavrion; Exploration of Turkey from Izmir to Istanbul.

Clelia II **Home Ports** Piraeus, Venice, others vary with itinerary

April–November, 10–11 nights, Mediterranean on various itineraries including Ionian and Adriatic Seas; Voyage Around Italy; Greece/Turkey/Italy, round-trip from, or between, Piraeus and Venice.

Orion **Home Ports** Vary with itinerary

December–February, 14 and 22 nights, Antarctica, round-trip from Ushuaia to Cape Horn and the Antarctic Peninsula. February, 23 nights, Antarctica, from Ushuaia to Port Stanley, Falkland Islands via Cape Horn, Antarctic Peninsula, Elephant Island, South Orkney Islands, South Georgia, Falkland Islands.

March–May, 11–18 nights, South America, Amazon and Orinoco Rivers, between Rio de Janeiro and Belem; Belem to Iquitos, Peru or reverse; or, Belem to Curacao.

May and October, 10 nights, U.S. East Coast, Freeport to Baltimore; or, Halifax to Jacksonville.

June–July and September, 8 nights, Great Lakes, between Montreal and Milwaukee via St. Lawrence Seaway, Thousand Islands, Port Weller, Niagara Falls, Welland Canal, Windsor, Greenfield Village, Port Huron, Prairie Point, Manitoulin Island, Whitefish Bay, Tahquamenon Falls State Park, Mackinac Island.

June–August, 8–11 nights, Canada's Maritime provinces, Canadian Arctic and Greenland, on cruises and fly–cruises between Halifax to

Montreal; Montreal to Greenland; cruising within Greenland and Baffin Island; or, circumnavigation of Newfoundland.

November, 29 nights, Panama Canal to Tierra del Fuego, from Panama City to Ushuaia available in segments from Panama City to Antofagasta (15 nights); Antofagasta to Ushuaia (13 nights).

Windjammer Barefoot Cruises

Amazing Grace   **Home Ports**   Freeport, Trinidad
Year-round, 12 nights, between Freeport and Trinidad, visiting nine to 12 of the following islands: Antigua, Bequia, Conception, Cooper Island, Dominica, Dominican Republic, Grand Bahama, Grand Turk, Great Inagua, Grenada, Iles des Saints, Jost van Dyke, Nevis, Norman Island, St. Barts, St. Kitts, St. Lucia, St. Maarten, Tortola, Trinidad, Virgin Gorda.

Flying Cloud   Out of service indefinitely.

Legacy   **Home Ports**   St. Thomas, Miami, Aruba
September–November, 5 nights, ABC islands, round-trip from Aruba to Bonaire, Curacao, Klein Curacao.

December to May, 5 nights, round-trip from St. Thomas– to Jost van Dyke, Norman Island, St. John, Virgin Gorda, Tortola, St. Thomas.

May–August, 3, 4, 7 nights, round-trip from Miami to Bimini, Gun Cay, Berry Islands, Great Abaco, Freeport, Nassau (7 nights) available in 3 and 4-night segments, one way between Miami and Nassau.

Mandalay   **Home Ports**   Antigua, Grenada, Colon
Winter–Spring, 12 nights, between Antigua and Grenada, calling at Bequia, Carriacou, Dominica, Grenada, Iles des Saints, Martinique, Mayreau, Nevis, St. Lucia, St. Vincent, Tobago Cays.

Summer–Fall, 5 nights, Venezuela, round-trip from Colon, Panama to Panama and the San Blas Islands. Subject to change.

Polynesia   **Home Port**   St. Maarten, St. Lucia
Winter–Spring, Monday, 5 nights, round-trip from St. Maarten to St. Barts, Anguilla, Tintamarre, Saba; or, St. Barts, Eustatius, Nevis and St. Kitts.

Summer–Fall, Monday, 5 nights, round-trip from St. Lucia, to Grenada, St. Lucia, St. Vincent. Subject to change.

Yankee Clipper   **Home Port**   Grenada
Year-round, Monday, 5 nights, round-trip from Grenada to Bequia, Carriacou, Grenada, Mayreau, St. Vincent, Tobago Cays, Union Island.

Windstar Cruises

Wind Spirit   **Home Ports**   St. Thomas, Athens others vary with itinerary
December–April, 7 nights, round-trip from St. Thomas to St. John, St. Martin, St. Barts, Tortola, Jost Van Dyke, or, Virgin Gorda

April, November, 14 nights, transatlantic, between St. Thomas and Lisbon.

April–October, Saturday, 7 nights, between Athens and Istanbul to Mykonos, Santorini, Rhodes, Bodrum and Kusadasi; or, between Rome and Athens; Athens and Rome; Rome and Nice; Rome and Barcelona; or, Barcelona and Lisbon.

December, resumes Caribbean cruises from St. Thomas.

Wind Star   **Home Port**   Papeete

Year-round, Friday, 7 nights, round-trip from Papeete, Tahiti to Raiatea, Huahine, Bora Bora, Moorea. June 18, September 17, 14 nights, visits ports in the neighboring Marquesas Islands, and Rangiroa, Bora Bora, Moorea.

Wind Surf   **Home Ports**   St. Thomas, others vary with itinerary.

December–March, 7 nights, Caribbean, round-trip from St. Thomas, to Isles des Saintes, Nevis, St. Barts, Isla Culebra (Puerto Rico), St. John.

April and November, 14 nights, transatlantic, St. Thomas to Lisbon; or, Lisbon to Ft. Lauderdale.

April–June, September–November, Sunday, 6–8 nights, Mediterranean, between Lisbon and Barcelona; Barcelona and Nice; Nice and Rome; Rome and Malta; or, Malta and Venice.

June–August, 7–13 nights, Western Europe/British Isles/Baltic, Lisbon–London; London–Copenhagen; round-trip from Copenhagen; or, London–Lisbon.

December, resumes 7-night cruises from St. Thomas.

Destination Index

Central America

Europe

Transatlantic Cruises

United States

Subject Index

To find specific ships, consult the Cruise Ship Index; for itineraries, see the Itinerary Index; and to find cruise lines serving particular destinations, consult the Destination Index.

Unofficial Guide to Cruises Reader Survey

If you would like to express an opinion about your cruise or this guidebook, complete the following survey and return to:

Unofficial Guide Reader Survey
P.O. Box 43673
Birmingham, AL 35243

Name of ship: Today's date:
Date, duration, and destination of cruise:
Please circle one of the following:

—*Was this your*   1st   2nd   3rd   4th   5th   6th or
more cruise?
—*Would you take another cruise on this ship?*   Yes   No
—*Recommend it to a friend?*   Yes   No
—*Do you plan to cruise*   within a year   within next 3 years   longer?
—*Your age:*   teens   20s   30s   40s   50s   60s   70s   over 80
—*You are:*   employed   self-employed   retired
—*Line of work:*

Please score items below from 1 to 10 with 10 being the highest or best.
Feel free to add your comments.

Value for money:

Total cruise experience:

Your overall impression of the ship *(appearance, appeal, furnishings and decor, cleanliness, sports and recreation facilities, consistency, comfort, boarding/disembarking procedures):*

Cruise director *(available, helpful, friendly):*

Cruise staff:

Dining room food *(choices, quality, taste, presentation):*

Breakfast and lunch buffet:

Dining room service:

Bar service:

Cabin *(size, layout, soundproofing, cleanliness, appearance, condition):*

Bathroom:

Cabin attendant *(service, attitude):*

Enrichment programs, lectures, games *(variety and quality):*

Entertainment in the main lounge:

Entertainment in other lounges:

Children's programs:

Youth counselors:

Shore excursions *(guides, variety, advanced information, value):*

Some more questions:

—Was the food quality better, worse, or about what you expected?

—Were wine and bar prices low, moderate, or high?

—Was the music level tolerable or too loud, especially by the pool?

—Were you bothered by announcements over the public address system?

—Was the promotion of shipboard shops low key, moderate, or hard sell?

—Was the lifeboat drill well executed?

—Did you choose your cruise for its itinerary?

—Which ports of call did you like best?

—Were port talks poor or helpful?

—Did the speakers plug specific shops?

—Was passenger information available prior to the cruise? in your cabin? during the cruise?

Your hometown:

How did you learn about your cruise?

How did you learn about this book?

Where did you buy your cruise?

When and where did you buy this book?

(Optional) If you are available for a telephone interview, please give us your name, address, telephone number, and a convenient time to call.

THANK YOU!